PRODUCTION AND OPERATIONS MANAGEMENT

Fourth Edition

PRODUCTION AND OPERATIONS MANAGEMENT

Concepts, Models, and Behavior

Everett E. Adam, Jr.

Ronald J. Ebert

Prentice-Hall, Englewood Cliffs, NJ 07632

Library of Congress Cataloging-in-Publication Data

Adam, Everett E.
Production and operations management.

Includes index.
1. Production management. I. Ebert, Ronald J.
II. Title.
TS155.A29514 1989 658.5 88-31766
ISBN 0-13-725029-0

Editorial/production supervision: *Pamela Wilder*
Interior and cover design: *Judith A. Matz-Coniglio*
Cover art: Jack Tworkov, "Alternative II." Oil on canvas, 54 x 54 inches, 1977.
Photograph courtesy of Nancy Hoffman Gallery, New York City.
Manufacturing buyer: *Margaret Rizzi*

A Division of Simon & Schuster
Englewood Cliffs, New Jersey 07632

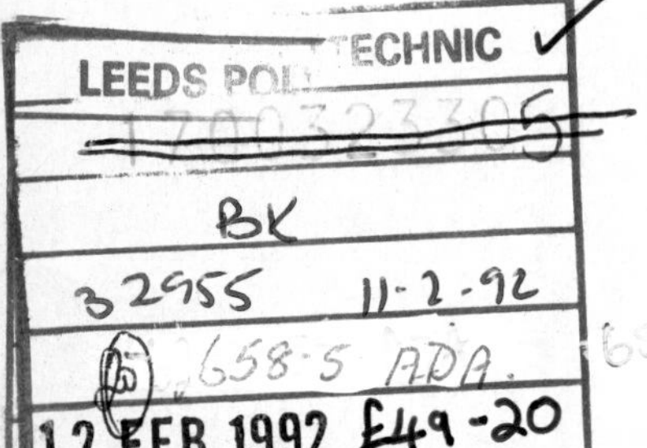

Printed in the United States of America
10 9 8 7 6 5 4 3

ISBN 0-13-725029-0

Prentice-Hall International (UK) Limited, *London*
Prentice-Hall of Australia Pty. Limited, *Sydney*
Prentice-Hall Canada Inc., *Toronto*
Prentice-Hall Hispanoamericana, S.A., *Mexico*
Prentice-Hall of India Private Limited, *New Delhi*
Prentice-Hall of Japan, Inc., *Tokyo*
Simon & Schuster Asia Pte. Ltd., *Singapore*
Editora Prentice-Hall do Brasil, Ltda., *Rio de Janeiro*

TO:
Joy, Scott, and Kevin
Mary, Kristen, and Matt

Contents

Preface

This fourth edition of *Production and Operations Management: Concepts, Models, and Behavior* was developed to retain the core concepts, models, and managerial orientation of previous editions, but to reflect recent changes in production and operations management practice and research. It responds to extensive market research regarding what teachers of operations management believe would be the best content and presentation for student learning.

Although the operations function exists in every organization, it is often misunderstood by practitioners and is sometimes elusive to students of business and management. Part of the problem lies in the changing nature of the field of study. As we enter the 1990s it is apparent that new technologies, competition from emerging industrialized nations outside Europe and North America, and the productivity and quality demands from owners and consumers continue to reshape production and operations management. These pressures have resulted in a mismatch between education and practice for many operations management practitioners.

In the educational setting, students are often left with the feeling that operations is distinctly different and separate from management. In some instances, analysis and quantitative techniques are emphasized at the expense of a basic unifying framework for the overall role of operations management in organizations. We continue our efforts to fill this void with the unifying theme of this book: planning, organizing, and controlling —the classical process school of management. This edition also relies on operations strategy as a guide for topical integration.

For students and teachers alike, our integrative framework serves admirably in lending coherence to the numerous revisions that appear in the fourth edition. We retain design features crucial to the success of previous editions—a book that is readable (clarity, level, explanations of analyses, etc.), comprehensive, integrative, contemporary in content, and uses many examples and summary tables. We make an effort to improve the instructor's ease of teaching by providing a shorter book, with chapters of similar length, and continued use of supplements. Specifically the book is now 17 chapters (from 20), has 7 chapter supplements (from 8), adds a chapter on product and process design choices early in the book (Chapter 4), expands quality from one very long chapter into two chapters (15 and 16), closes the book with one crisp chapter on change and operations (rather than 3 chapters), and at the end of many chapters provides computer exercises that can be solved with software developed by Prentice Hall for this book (QSOM). Collectively, these changes reshape the book to provide the reader with a contemporary treatment of production and operations management.

In the eyes of many practitioners there is a gap between what they must deal with operationally and what they studied in production/operations books. This is particularly true for those who were introduced to production/operations management as a quantitative/systems analysis discipline. Therefore we continue to emphasize a balance between the quantitative aspects and important behavioral applications. When problems are behavioral (quality motivation, for example), we introduce such contemporary techniques as behavior modification, quality circles, and attitude change procedures to deal with them; when they are quantitative (inventory control, for example) we stress appropriate techniques of quantitative analysis.

Other important features that continue to be a major portion of this book are: a use of supplements to present more rigorous quantitative analysis (yet a book that stands alone without the use of supplements); the continued use of service sector applications and examples that reinforce "operations" as a broad term encompassing manufacturing, agriculture, and services; and a book organized so readers understand the flow —moving from managing operations (Part I) through design (Parts II and III) and then operating the facility (Parts IV, V, and VI).

Our intent, as in previous editions, is to provide a student-oriented presentation at an introductory level. The material is presented in a simple, straightforward fashion. To assist student understanding, we provide end-of-chapter materials designed to reinforce the essentials of each chapter: solved problems, revised review questions and problems, a glossary, usually a case, and computer assisted exercises. These computer exercises use the Quantitative Systems for Operations Management (QSOM) micro-computer software package developed by Prentice Hall for this edition. It is user friendly and leaves the student with an appreciation of how the computer can be used in operations management to increase decision-making accuracy for moderately complex situations. The software is available through Prentice Hall.

To sum up, distinguishing features of this book are an integrating framework, featuring management process, resource conversion, and concepts, models, and behavior; behavioral applications within production/operations; inclusion of the service sector via an operations orientation; and a student emphasis, featuring an introductory treatment, continuity among chapters, and learning enhancement within chapters with specially prepared executive comments, numerous examples, chapter summaries, cases, glossaries, review and discussion questions, problems, computer exercises, and the student *Study Guide and Workbook*, featuring an independent study approach.

We wish to thank our many peers nationally who, after thoughtful use of the first three editions, provided constructive suggestions for this edition. We appreciate the time and effort expended by the operations managers and executives who prepared the chapter introductions. They have made a voluntary contribution; we hope students will enjoy and benefit from their comments. We are also indebted to those who reviewed this and previous editions, many of whom are found on the Editorial Review Board. Again, we appreciate the contribution of Marilyn Kippley, our typist, who is professional in every aspect of her work. We also wish to acknowledge the resource support of the University of Missouri-Columbia.

Everett E. Adam, Jr.
Ronald J. Ebert

Editorial Review Board

PART I MANAGING OPERATIONS

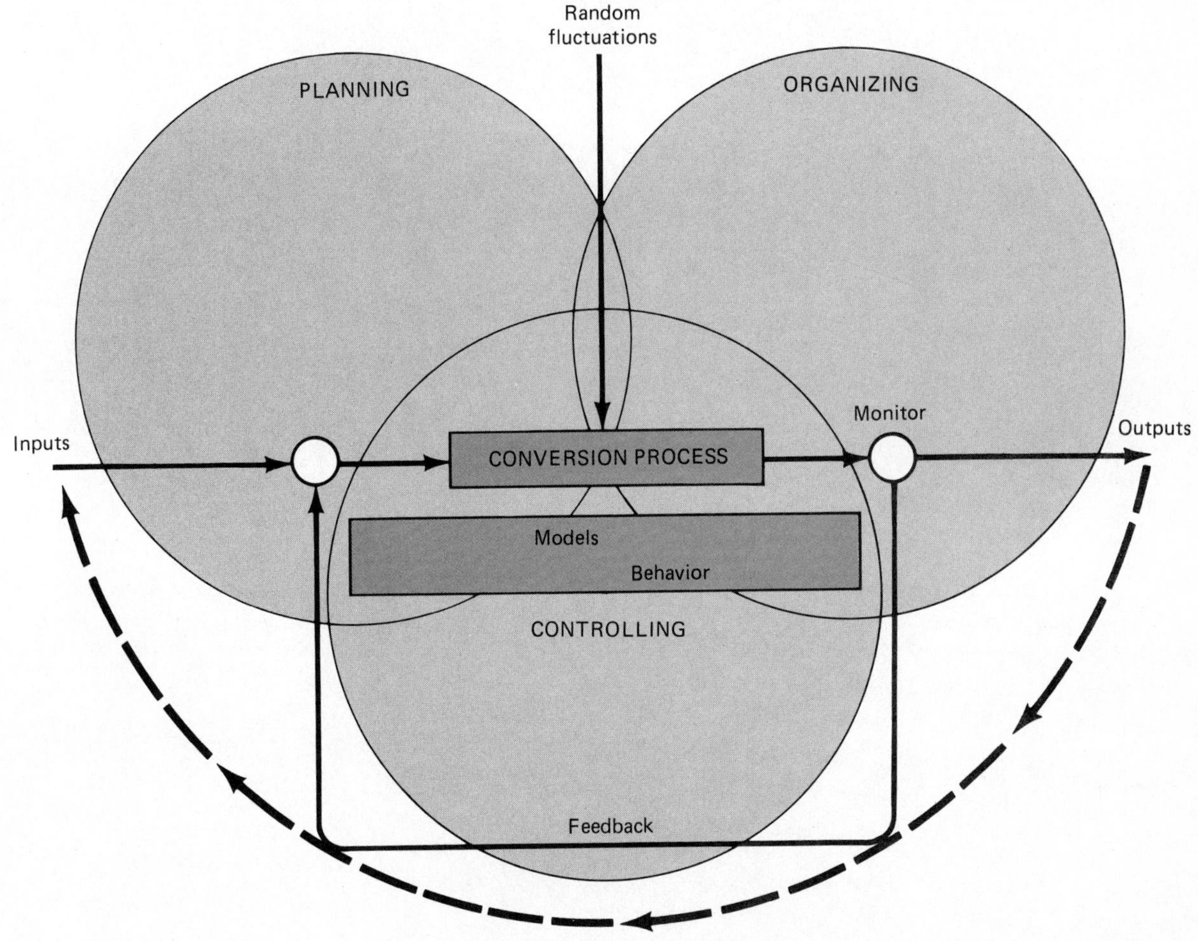

Management variables and the operations conversion system

1

Operations Management

While all managers are involved in planning, organizing, and controlling, operations managers have the direct responsibility for "getting the job done." They must provide the leadership that is needed to produce the product or service demanded by the customer.

In the aerospace industry, our operations organizations grew out of the manufacturing departments of the past, whose responsibilities were generally fabrication and assembly. They were succeeded by the production organizations of the immediate post-World War II period, where functions like manufacturing planning, tooling, plant engineering, and production control were added. Today's operations divisions are additionally responsible for purchasing, material control, quality assurance, and in some cases, engineering and program management.

This evolution has produced broadly capable operations teams, responsible for the quality of the product, as seen by the customer; for the organization's productivity, which determines the product's competitive cost; and for responsiveness to the customer's needs.

With quality and productivity more competitively significant than ever before, operations management has added behavioral and modeling approaches to its historical use of the classical/scientific schools of management techniques.

All of these many elements come into play in the fascinating field of operations management.

William T. Gross
Executive Vice President
Douglas Aircraft Company
Long Beach, California

Mr. Gross's comments exemplify the widely shared experience of managers in many organizations and industries. Operations management is a significant part of all our lives; it is multifaceted, involving diverse activities and skills; and it is an interesting, action-oriented area. Looking beyond Mr. Gross's comments, however, across thousands of organizations nationwide, some serious concerns persist about the well-being of operations management and its role in our nation's economic future.

At the onset of the 1980s, while Japan's productivity continued its healthy surges, the leaders of business and government worldwide were alarmed at the productivity stagnation in the United States. What had happened to the giant of commerce and industry? What led to its lethargy? What have we learned in the ensuing years? What can be done to restore its stately posture? Answers to these questions reside in the ways we manage our organizations and their operations.

While U.S. productivity waned, its society was at the same time unrelenting in its concern over other related issues—maintaining adequate energy sources, preserving the environment, and meeting the demand for its goods and services at home and abroad. These factors continue to impose complex demands on our organizations. Today management faces unparalleled challenges from a more educated, affluent, demanding, and concerned society than ever before, as well as from keener international competition. Never before have management challenges and the costs of failure been greater—and never before have the techniques and knowledge to meet these challenges been more available to operating managers.

The complexities of our contemporary world have heightened our dependence on organizations and the people who manage them; yet often we fail to understand and appreciate the process of management. Moreover, as we've learned from our recent costly experiences, we have seriously neglected the operations of our organizations; we have taken for granted our preeminence as capable producers. No longer can we afford to do so. We need to reexamine the processes by which goods and services are created and to revitalize the ways that we manage the human and material resources for doing so. This book aims to meet these needs. It presents the concepts, terminology, problems, and the opportunities that comprise operations management.

We begin this first chapter by describing what is meant by the "operations function" in organizations. Then, by tracing its history, we observe how operations management has evolved from simple beginnings to achieve its current stature as a major element of competitive strategy in contemporary organizations.

THE OPERATIONS FUNCTION IN ORGANIZATIONS

The *operations function (system) is that part of the organization that exists primarily to generate and produce the organization's products.* In some organizations the product is a physical good (refrigerators, breakfast cereal), while in others it is a service (insurance, health care for the elderly). What do such diverse organizations as manufacturing companies, financial institutions, and health care facilities all have within their operations system? The basic elements they share in common are shown in Figure 1.1. They have a *conversion process*, some resource *inputs* into that process, the outputs resulting from the conversion of the inputs, and *information feedback* about the activities in the operations system. Once they are produced, the goods and services are converted into cash (sold) to acquire more resources to keep the conversion process alive.

Try to recall examples of real organizations as you think about the conversion process shown in Figure 1.1. Perhaps you have worked in a department store, on a farm, for a construction company, or in an automobile assembly plant. What were the inputs? A department store's inputs include the land upon which the building is located; your labor as a stock clerk; capital in the form of the building, equipment, and merchandise; and the management skills of the store managers (see Figure 1.2).

On a farm the operations system is the transformation that occurs when the farmer's inputs (land, equipment, labor, etc.) are converted into such outputs as corn, wheat, or milk. The exact form of the conversion process varies from industry to industry, but it is an economic phenomenon that exists in every industry. Economists refer to this transformation of resources into goods and services as the *production function*. For all operations systems the general goal is to create some kind of *value-added*, so that the outputs are worth more to consumers than just the sum of the individual inputs. To the consumer, the resulting products offer utility due to the form, the time, or the place of their availability from the conversion process.

The random fluctuations indicated in Figures 1.1 and 1.2 consist of unplanned or uncontrollable influences that cause actual output to differ

FIGURE 1.1
The operations system

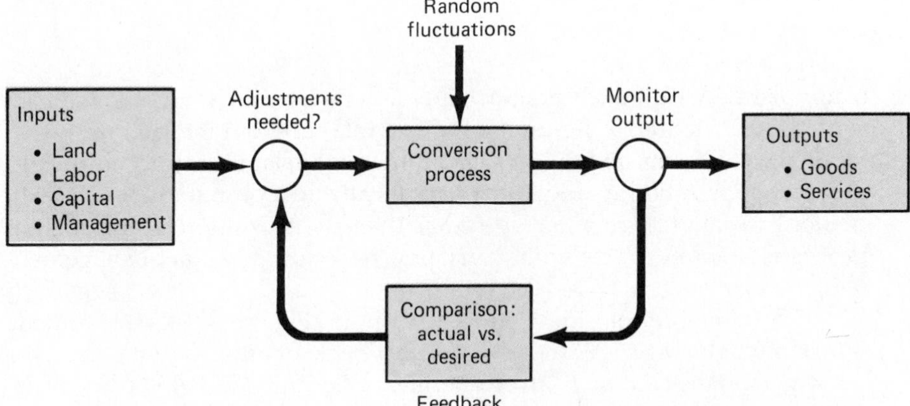

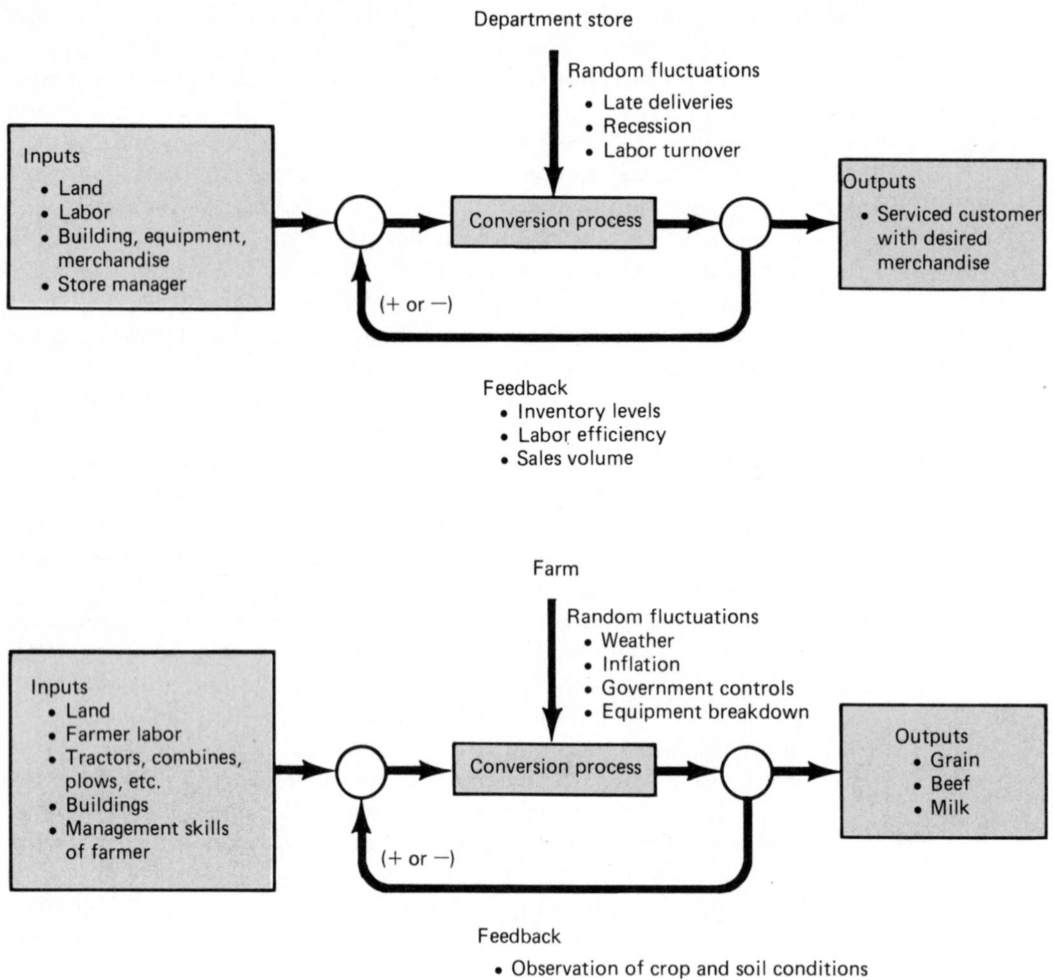

FIGURE 1.2
The operations systems for a department store and a farm

from planned output. Random fluctuations can arise from external sources (fire, floods, or lightning, for example) or from internal problems inherent in the conversion process. Inherent variabilities of equipment, material imperfections, and human errors all affect output quality. In fact, random variations are the rule rather than the exception in production processes; therefore, reducing variation becomes a major management task.

The function of the feedback loop in Figure 1.1 is to provide information linkages. Without some feedback of information, management personnel cannot control operations because they don't know the results of their decisions.

Technologies of Conversion

The transformation of inputs into outputs varies considerably with the technology employed. By *technology,* we mean the types of transformation activities taking place, including the level of scientific sophistication in plant, equipment, skills, and product (or service) in the conversion process. A soft-drink bottling operation, for example, features a highly mechanized, capital-intensive conversion process. A scientific research laboratory utilizes highly trained, professional scientists and specialized equipment. Other industries use low-skilled labor, minimal equipment, and simple processes to provide products and services.

Manufacturing Operations Versus Service Operations

Manufacturing (or production) involves the conversion of resources into a *tangible* output, a product. Services, as contrasted with manufacturing, involve the conversion of resources into an *intangible* output—a deed, a performance, an effort. Consider the introduction to this chapter where Mr. Gross discussed the aerospace industry. Douglas Aircraft Company produces airplanes, clearly a product. Yet, other McDonnell Douglas Corporation components, such as the Information Systems Group (ISG), provide services. ISG, for example, delivers computer services to hospitals, architects, and other businesses—services such as programming, data analysis, and data storage using ISG's computers. Other McDonnell Douglas components launch spacecraft, provide contract research services, assemble missiles, and design and manufacture fighter aircraft. This mixture of service and manufacturing is typical of most aerospace firms.

Distinguishing Between Manufacturing and Service Operations Differing between manufacturing and service technologies can be difficult. Generally, we consider distinguishing characteristics such as

- Tangible/intangible nature of output
- Consumption of output
- Nature of work (jobs)
- Degree of customer contact
- Customer participation in conversion
- Measurement of performance

To oversimplify, manufacturing has tangible outputs (products), customer consumption of outputs over time, jobs that use less labor and more equipment, little customer contact, no customer participation in the conversion process (in production), and sophisticated methods for measuring production activities and resource consumption as products are made. Services, on the other hand, have intangible outputs, immediate consumption, jobs that require a lot of labor but some equipment, direct customer contact, frequent customer participation in the conversion process, and rather elementary methods for measuring conversion activities and resource consumption. Some services are equipment-based—computer programming services, railroad services, and telephone services—whereas other services are people-based—tax accounting services, hair styling, and golf instruction. We'll also come to understand that service capacity is time perishable (capacity and demand must be synchronized) and that service locations are dictated by customer location (requiring multiple sites of a small scale).

Let's look a little closer at the extent that customers are present or involved in the conversion process. In service operations, managers sometimes find it useful to distinguish between *output* and *throughput* types of customer involvement. Outputs are the generated services; throughputs are the items going through the process. In a pediatrics clinic the output is the medical service to the child who, by going through the conversion process, is also the throughput. At a fast-food restaurant, in contrast, the customer does not go through the conversion process. The outputs are hamburgers and french fries in a hurry (both goods and services), while the throughputs are the food items as they are prepared and converted. The customer is neither a throughput nor an output. Both the clinic and the restaurant provide services, even though the outputs and throughputs differ considerably.

In this book we seek a balance between manufacturing and services. As much as possible we'll use the term *operations,* as we have here in discussing the operations function, to include either manufacturing or service-producing functions. Examples are drawn from both manufacturing and service industries.

HISTORICAL EVOLUTION OF PRODUCTION AND OPERATIONS MANAGEMENT

For over two centuries operations management has been recognized as an important factor in our economic well-being.

Progressing through a series of names—*manufacturing management, production management,* and *operations management*—all of which describe the same general discipline, the order of the terms reflects the evolution of modern operations management. The traditional view of manufacturing management began in the eighteenth century with Adam Smith's recognition that the subdivision and specialization of labor can result in economic benefits. He recommended breaking jobs down into subtasks and reassigning workers to specialized tasks in which they would become highly skilled and efficient. In the early twentieth century, Frederick W. Taylor implemented Smith's theories and crusaded for scientific management throughout the vast manufacturing complex of his day. From then until about 1930, the traditional view prevailed, and many techniques we still use today were developed. A brief sketch of these and other contributions to manufacturing management is highlighted in Table 1.1.

Production management became the more widely accepted term from the 1930s through the 1950s. As Frederick Taylor's work became more widely known and other contributors to management adopted the scientific approach, techniques were developed that focused on economic

Table 1.1 Historical summary of operations management

Date (approximate)	Contribution	Contributor
1776	Specialization of labor in manufacturing	Adam Smith
1799	Interchangeable parts, cost accounting	Eli Whitney and others
1832	Division of labor by skill; assignment of jobs by skill; basics of time study	Charles Babbage
1900	Scientific management; time study and work study developed; dividing planning and doing of work	Frederick W. Taylor
1900	Motion study of jobs	Frank B. Gilbreth
1901	Scheduling techniques for employees, machines, jobs in manufacturing	Henry L. Gantt
1915	Economic lot sizes for inventory control	F. W. Harris
1927	Human relations; the Hawthorne studies	Elton Mayo
1931	Statistical inference applied to product quality; quality control charts	Walter A. Shewhart
1935	Statistical sampling applied to quality control; inspection sampling plans	H. F. Dodge and H. G. Romig
1940	Operations research applications in World War II	P. M. S. Blacket and others
1946	Digital computer	John Mauchly and J. P. Eckert
1947	Linear programming	George B. Dantzig, William Orchard-Hays, and others
1950	Mathematical programming, nonlinear and stochastic processes	A. Charnes, W. W. Cooper, H. Raiffa, and others
1951	Commercial digital computer; large-scale computations available	Sperry Univac
1960	Organizational behavior; continued study of people at work	L. Cummings, L. Porter, and others
1970	Integrating operations into overall strategy and policy	W. Skinner
	Computer applications to manufacturing, scheduling, and control, material requirements planning (MRP)	J. Orlicky and O. Wright
1980	Quality and productivity applications from Japan; robotics, computer aided design and manufacturing (CAD/CAM)	W. E. Deming and J. Juran

efficiency at the core of manufacturing organizations. People in their physical environments were "put under a microscope" and studied in great detail to eliminate wasteful efforts and achieve greater efficiency. At this same time, however, management began modifying its views, having discovered that workers have multiple needs, not just economic needs. Psychologists, sociologists, and other social scientists began to study people and human behavior in the work environment. In addition, economists, mathematicians, and computer scientists contributed newer, more sophisticated, analytical approaches.

With the advent of the 1970s, two distinct changes in our views were emerging. The most obvious of these was the new name, *operations management*, that was a reflection of shifts in the service and manufacturing sectors of the economy. As the service sector became more prominent, the change from production to operations emphasized the broadening of our field to service organizations as well as to those that produced physical goods. The second, more subtle change, was the beginning of an emphasis on synthesis, rather than just analysis, in our management practices. Spearheaded most notably by Wickham Skinner, American industry was awakened to its negligence of the operations function as a vital weapon in the organization's overall competitive strategy. Previously preoccupied with an intensive analytical orientation and an emphasis on marketing and finance, we had failed to ensure that our operations activities were integrated coherently into the highest levels of strategy and policy to provide focused, rather than diverse and fragmented, directions for our organizations. Today, as a consequence, the operations function is experiencing a renewed role as a vital strategic element for meeting consumers' needs throughout the world.

A SYSTEMS VIEW OF OPERATIONS: DEFINING THE SUBSYSTEM

Organizations Viewed as Systems

What is a system? In a very general sense, a *system* is a collection of objects united by some form of regular interaction and interdependence. Systems can vary from large physical collections of subcomponents, such as nationwide communications networks, to more minute abstract examples —someone's "system" for processing paperwork in an office, for example. Regardless of the precision of the term, however, models are often developed to represent a system or some aspect of it. These models, which show functional relationships, are used to facilitate communication among people who are mutually interested in whatever system is under consideration. The systems concept, as applied to organizations, can help develop our understanding of operations.

A systems model of the organization itself identifies the subsystems, or subcomponents, that make up the firm. As Figure 1.3 shows, a business firm might well have finance, marketing, accounting, personnel, engineering, purchasing, and physical distribution functions in addition to production/operations. These functions are not independent but are interrelated to one another in many vital ways. We have chosen to show production/operations with major interactions between finance and marketing and lesser interaction with other functions. Decisions made in the production/operations subsystem often affect the behavior and performance of other subsystems. Finally, we should understand that the boundaries separating the various subsystems are not clear and distinct. Where do the responsibilities of production/operations end and those of physical distribution begin? The answers to such questions are often unclear and sometimes never resolved.

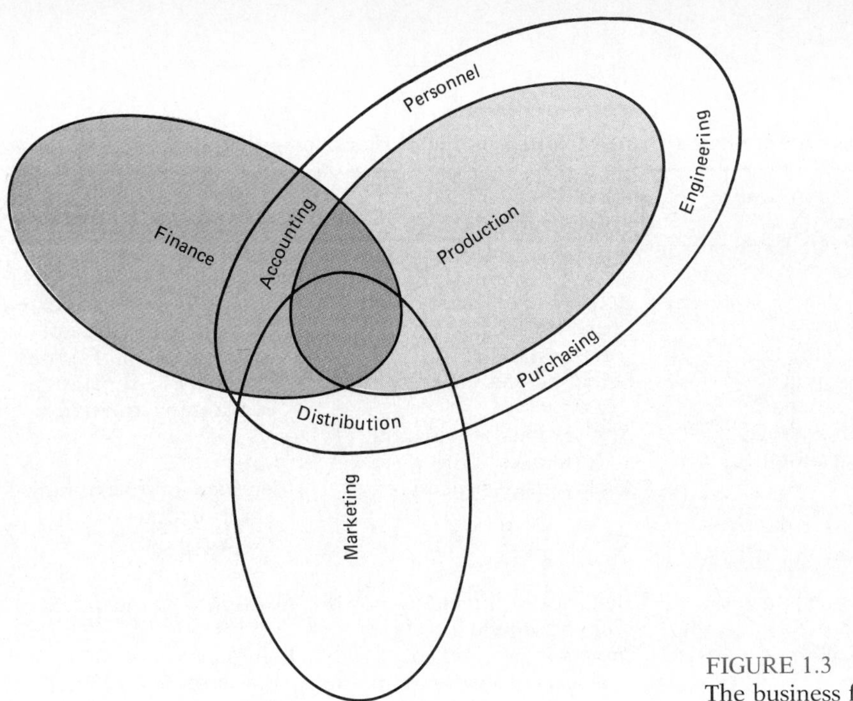

FIGURE 1.3
The business firm: A systems view

MANAGING THE OPERATIONS SUBSYSTEM

We have described the operations subsystem; the real problem, however, is not to identify it but to operate it effectively. The conversion process must be managed by someone, and that someone is the operations manager.

Operations Management Defined

The operations manager's job is to manage the process of converting inputs into desired outputs. Our definition of operations management is, then, the management of the conversion process, which converts land, labor, capital, and management inputs into desired outputs of goods and services. In doing so, the practicing manager uses various approaches from the classical, behavioral, and modeling views of management. As summarized in Table 1.2, our perceptions of management responsibilities and concepts have evolved through the years, and we have gained insights from a variety of sources with different orientations.

Classical

Classical management has contributed the *scientific management* and *process theories* to the operations manager's knowledge. The basis of *scientific management* is a focus on economic efficiency at the production core of the organization. Of central importance is the belief that rationality on the part of management will obtain economic efficiency. *Economic efficiency,* a term that many organizations have retained today, refers to the ratio of outputs to inputs. *Organization efficiency* typically is a ratio of product or service outputs to land, capital, or labor inputs.

$$\text{Efficiency (\%)} = \frac{\text{Output}}{\text{Input}} \times 100\% \qquad (1.1)$$

Table 1.2 Operations management elements from various schools of management thought

School	Some Important Assumptions	Primary Focus	General Contributions to Management
Classical			
Scientific management	People motivated by economics alone Managerial rationality Organization a closed system (certainty)	Economic efficiency Physical aspects of work environment Scientific analysis of work tasks Applications of techniques to work tasks	Demonstration of benefits from specialization of labor, division of labor, job analysis, separation of planning and doing
Process orientation		Management processes	Identification of principles and functions of management
Behavioral			
Human relations	People complex; possess multiple needs	Behavior of individual in work environment	Awareness of individuals
Behavioral science	Human beings social creatues	Interpersonal and social aspects of work environment	Identification of behavioral variables that relate to organizational behavior
Social systems	Organization an open system	Interactive relationships of organization with its environment	Development of theories relating organizational behavior to human characteristics and organizational variables
Modeling			
Decision making	Decision-making processes are the primary managerial behaviors	Information acquisition, utilization, and choice processes	Development of guides for improving decision making
Systems theory	Organization—an open system Organization—a complex of interrelated subcomponents	Identification of organization boundaries, interrelationships among subsystems, and relationships between organization and larger environment	Development of approaches for predicting and explaining system behavior
Mathematical modeling	Main elements of organizations can be abstracted, interrelated, and expressed mathematically	Quantification of decision problems and systems Optimization of small set of situations	Development of explicit rules for management decisions Development of methods for analyzing organization systems or subsystems

EXAMPLE Management is concerned with labor efficiency, especially when labor is costly. To determine how efficient labor is in a given situation, management sets an *individual standard,* a goal reflecting an average worker's normal amount of output per unit of time under normal working conditions. Say that the standard in a cafeteria is the preparation of 200 salads per hour. If labor input produces 150 salads per hour, how efficient is the salad operation?

$$\text{Labor efficiency} = \frac{\text{Labor output}}{\text{Labor input}} \times 100\% = \frac{150 \text{ salads}}{200 \text{ salads}} \times 100\%$$

$$= 75\%$$

Compared with the standard, this operation is 75 percent efficient in the preparation of salads.

The *process school of management* thought, also referred to as the *administrative or functional approach to management*, was developed in the early 1900s. Management was viewed as a continuous process involving the functions of planning, organizing, and controlling by a manager, who influences others through the functions he or she performs. These functions are as follows:

1. *Planning* includes all those activities that result in developing a course of action. These activities guide future decision making.
2. *Organizing* involves all activities that result in some structure of tasks and authority.
3. *Controlling* activities are those that assure that the performance in the organization takes place in accordance with planned performance.

These activities overlap in practice, as shown in Figure 1.4.

Behavioral

The *behavioral school of management* began in the 1920s with a *human relations* movement that emerged quite unexpectedly from some research studies intended to examine the effects of changes in the physical work environment on production output—a typical scientific management study. Some social scientists on the research team, however, observed that changes in output were often due to factors other than just physical changes in the work area. Specifically, workers seemed to respond

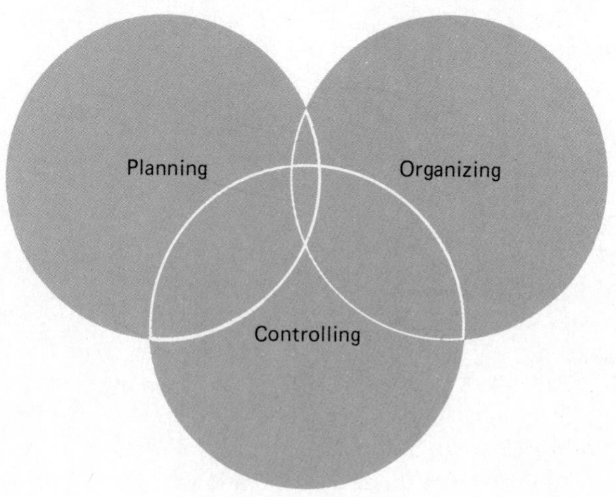

FIGURE 1.4
The management process

favorably to the individual care, attention, and interest that the experimenters had shown toward their work. Productivity increased. The main outgrowth of this research was a new attitude that seriously questioned scientific management's man-as-machine concept.

The answer to the human relations question has been provided by *behavioral science* and *social systems* theories: People in their work environment, as elsewhere, are extremely complex. Applied psychologists have developed *behavioral science* theories of the individual; social psychologists, sociologists, and cultural anthropologists have developed *social systems* theories of people in groups at work.

Modeling

The modeling school of management is concerned with decision making, systems theory, and mathematical modeling of systems and decision-making processes. The *decision-making* orientation considers making decisions to be the central purpose of management. Advocates of *systems theory* stress the importance of studying organizations from a "total systems" point of view. According to this school, identifying subsystem relationships, predicting effects of changes in the system, and properly implementing system change are all part of managing the total organization. With its foundations in operations research and management science, *mathematical modeling* focuses on creating mathematical representations of management problems and organizations. For a particular problem, the variables are expressed mathematically, and the model is used to demonstrate different outcomes that would result from various possible managerial choices.

A FRAMEWORK FOR MANAGING OPERATIONS

In this book, we draw from these various approaches a framework for our study of operations management. Our integration of management will expand upon the management themes in Figure 1.5.

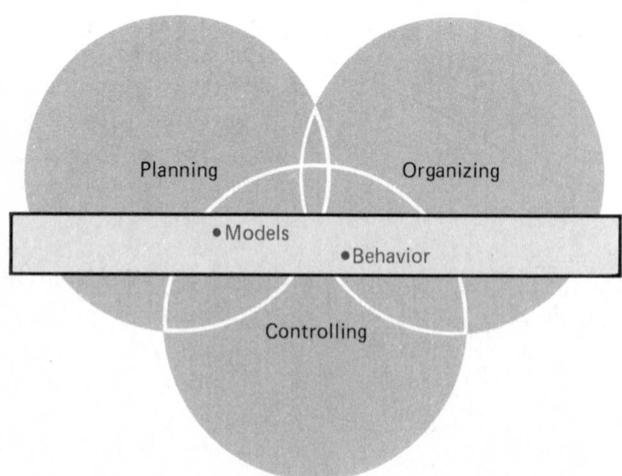

FIGURE 1.5
Management themes in operations

Planning The operations manager selects the objectives for the operations subsystem of the organization and the policies, programs, and procedures for achieving the objectives. This stage includes clarification of the role and focus of operations in the organization's overall strategy. It also involves efforts directed toward product planning, facilities designing, and using the conversion process.

Organizing The operations manager establishes an intentional structure of roles and information flows within the operations subsystem. He or she determines and enumerates the activities required to achieve the operations subsystem's goals and assigns authority and responsibility for carrying them out.

Controlling To ensure that the plans for the operations subsystem are accomplished, the operations manager must also exercise control. Outputs must be measured to see if they conform to what has been planned. Controlling costs, quality, and schedules is at the very heart of operations management.

Behavior In executing planning, organizing, and controlling functions, operations managers are clearly concerned with how their actions affect human behavior. They also want to know how the behavior of subordinates can affect management's planning, organizing, and controlling actions. In operations we are interested in the behavior of subordinates and managers, especially their decision-making behavior.

Models As operations managers plan, organize, and control the transformation process, they encounter many problems and must make many decisions. They can frequently simplify these difficulties by using models. Types of models and examples of their uses are illustrated in some detail as we cover the functional problems of operations management.

Problems of the Operations Manager

Operating managers are concerned with many different problem areas: cost control in brokerage houses, quality of services in hospitals, and rates of production output in furniture factories. Although operations managers occupy positions at several levels of their organizations, and although they work in different kinds of organizations, they all share some kinds of problems. The results of a study, The Manufacturing Futures Project, conducted at Boston University, reveal the kinds of activities 160 executives are concerned with in U.S. and Canadian firms. The respondents, managers or directors of operations, plant managers, divisional general managers, vice presidents, and others with related duties showed that many of their firms' most prominent activities for improving operations had to do with planning, organizing, and controlling the operations system and its conversion process (Table 1.3). You can see that some of their activities are primarily identified with each of the three functions of management. Production planning, defining manufacturing strategy, and product redesign, for example, are *planning-oriented*. Changing the organization, labor/management relations, and developing integrated information systems are examples of *organizing* activities. Inventory control,

Table 1.3 Activities emphasized by organizations to improve operations

%[a]	Activity	%[a]	Activity
90.6	Production planning, scheduling/inventory control systems	44.4	Developing new processes for new products
76.9	Supervisor training	43.1	Vendor relations, procurement procedures
66.3	Capacity expansion	42.5	Focusing factories
63.1	Worker safety programs	41.3	Narrowing product line; standardizing
58.8	Defining a manufacturing strategy	39.4	Making existing systems work better
57.5	Motivating direct labor employees	35.0	Giving workers a broader range of tasks to perform
55.0	Value analysis-product redesign	33.1	CAD (computer-aided design)
54.4	Improved maintenance practices	31.9	Giving workers more responsibility for planning and organizing work
53.1	Changing the manufacturing organization	29.4	CAM (computer-aided manufacture)
51.3	Changing labor/management relationships	26.9	Plant relocation
50.0	Developing integrated information systems	25.0	Group technology
48.1	Lead-time reduction	21.3	Office automation
47.5	Quality circles	20.0	Zero defects programs
46.9	Developing new processes for old products	20.6	Reducing size of manufacturing units
46.3	Automating jobs		

[a]Percentage of respondents whose business unit has placed an emphasis on this activity in the last five years with the objective of improving operations.

Source: The Manufacturing Futures Project: Summary of Survey Responses (Boston University School of Management, 1982), pp. 20–21.

maintenance improvement, and lead-time reduction exemplify *control*-oriented activities. The more recent manufacturing surveys do not collect these data. We doubt there have been major changes in the activities, only in their relative rankings. This is explained somewhat in the next chapter when the 1986 survey is reviewed.

THE STRATEGIC ROLE OF OPERATIONS

As one studies and practices operations management, it is easy to become preoccupied with the detailed economic and engineering aspects of the conversion process and lose sight of its fundamental purpose for existence. This, in fact, has occurred in many U.S. companies, and the results have been costly from an overall organizational viewpoint. Economy and efficiency of conversion operations are secondary goals, not primary goals, of the overall organization. Primary overall goals are related to market opportunities.

A Strategic Perspective

In Figure 1.6 we see the basic downward flow of strategy influence leading to conversion operations and results. The general thrust of the process is guided by competitive and market conditions in the industry, which provide the basis for determining the organization's strategy. Where is the industry now, and where will it be in the future? What are the existing and potential markets? What market gaps exist, and what competencies do we have for filling them? A careful analysis of market segments and the ability of our competitors and ourselves to meet the needs of these segments will determine the most effective direction for focusing an organization's future efforts.

After assessing the potential within an industry, an overall organiza-

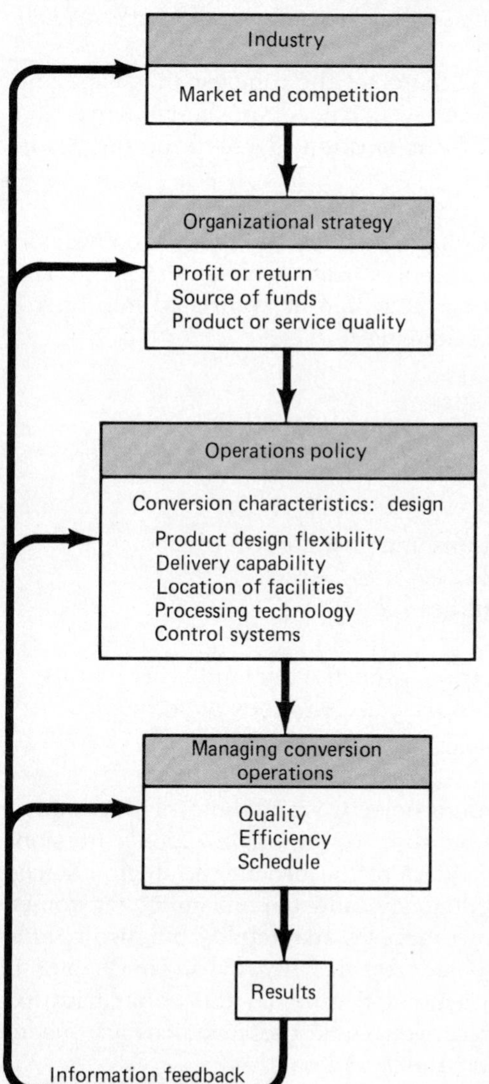

FIGURE 1.6
Operations as a strategic element in accomplishing organizational goals

tional strategy must be developed, including some basic choices of the primary basis for competing. In doing so, priorities are established among the following four characteristics:

- Quality (product performance)
- Cost efficiency (low product price)
- Dependability (reliable, timely delivery of orders to customers)
- Flexibility (responding rapidly with new products or changes in output volume)

In recent years, we've learned that most organizations can't be best on all these dimensions and, by trying to do so, they end up doing nothing well. Furthermore, when a competency exists in one of these areas, an attempt to switch to a different one can lead to a downfall in *effectiveness* (meeting the primary objectives).

These basic strategic choices, then, set the tone for the shape and content of the operations function and what it accomplishes. A conversion process designed for one type of focus is often ill-suited for success in another, alternative, focus.

Operations Objectives

The overall objective of the operations subsystem is to provide conversion capabilities for meeting the organization's basic goals and strategy. The organization's chosen strategic focus can then be translated into operations subgoals, which specify the following:

1. Product (service) characteristics
2. Process characteristics
3. Product (service) quality
4. Efficiency
   (a) Effective employee relations and cost control of labor
   (b) Cost control of material
   (c) Cost control in facility utilization
5. Customer service (schedule)
   (a) Producing quantities to meet expected demand
   (b) Meeting the required delivery date for goods or services
6. Adaptability for future survival

The priorities among these operations objectives and their relative emphases should be direct reflections of the overall organization's mission. Relating these six operations objectives to the broader strategic choices above, it is clear that quality, efficiency, and dependability (customer service) are similar. Flexibility encompasses adaptability but also relates to product (service) and process characteristics. As we'll see in Chapter 4, product and process choices to a great degree set the boundaries for meeting the other operations objectives. Once these choices are made, operations must live them out over time.

Operations Alternatives and Tradeoffs

The operations objectives can be attained through the decisions that are made in the various operations areas. Each decision area involves important tradeoffs. Tradeoffs exist among product and process choices versus the longer-term operating choices regarding quality, efficiency, schedule, and adaptability.

Consider the mid-1980s popularity of frozen yogurt desserts as an alternative to ice cream. Once a product focus is made to sell yogurt in ice cream–type parlors, many choices must be made. Where should facilities be located? How large should they be? What degree of automation should be used? What labor skill mix is required to support this automation level? Where will the frozen yogurt be produced? On site? How do these decisions impact quality, efficiency, schedule (customer service), and adaptability? Are we prepared for product and service change, or do these decisions lock in our operations? These are examples of the tough, crucial tradeoffs that are at the heart of understanding the choices that must be made when planning strategically and tactically.

TRENDS IN OPERATIONS MANAGEMENT

What new demands are being made of operations managers today? How will their jobs change in the future? Answers to such questions are speculative, but we can find some clues by observing recent trends in overall economic activities.

Shifts in Economic Activity

Are people doing the same kinds of work today that they have done in the past? The question is important because operations management will usually be found where economic activity is occurring. Table 1.4 provides

Table 1.4 Distribution of employed workers by major sectors of the economy, 1900–1985

Year	Agriculture and Other Extractive Industries	Industry	Services	Total
1900	38%	34%	28%	100%
1910	34	37	29	100
1920	30	39	31	100
1930	27	35	38	100
1940	25	34	41	100
1950	15	40	45	100
1960	11	39	50	100
1970	5	34	61	100
1980	4	28	68	100
1985	4	26	70	100

Source: Victor Fuchs, *The Service Economy* (New York: Columbia University Press, 1968), p. 207, with permission of the NBER; *Statistical Abstract of the United States 1972,* pp. 227–30; U.S. Department of Labor, Bureau of Labor Statistics, 1975, 1979, 1984, 1986.

us with some answers. We can see that there has been an employment shift from agriculture and other extractive (mining and contract construction) industries to the service sector, agriculture decreasing from 38 percent of the employed workers in 1900 to 4 percent in 1985, and service workers increasing from 28 percent in 1900 to 70 percent in 1985. The percentage of workers employed in industry has dwindled steadily. Will this trend continue? We suspect not. It is quite possible that the percentage of workers in the service sector will gradually continue to grow, but this growth most likely will be relatively slow. The most recent data suggest it will come from workers shifting from industry to the service sector, while the percentage of agricultural workers will remain around 4 percent.

One point is clear. The largest sector of the U.S. economy today is in services. In 1929 of the 47.6 million people employed in the United States, 18.1 million were employed in services. In 1984, 106.8 million people were employed, 75.8 million in services. The fastest growing service sector has been government services, with repair services a close second. In number of actual workers, the total labor force has increased some 59 million workers—57.7 million of whom work in the service sector.[1] Personal consumption expenditures, along with employment, have also shifted toward services. In 1983, 50 percent of consumer expenditures were for services and 50 percent for durable and nondurable goods.

More economic activity in the service sector suggests that many of you may find yourselves employed in service industries in the future. In this book we take the position that operations management concepts, skills, and techniques are transferable *across* the industry/service sectors and *within* industries and services. Our examples and explanations therefore apply to both kinds of operations, even if only one is mentioned.[2]

PRODUCTION AND OPERATIONS MANAGEMENT CAREERS

In 1984 there were 106.8 million workers in the U.S. labor force. Some 7 million of these, we estimate, filled supervisory positions in finance, operations, and marketing. The characteristically high labor intensity in operations means there is a disproportionately high share of managerial jobs in this area. In production and operations, many future managers can find careers.

Entry Positions in Production/Operations Management

If your career objectives are to advance to a top management position, operations is a reasonable avenue to travel. One *Fortune* survey of the 500 largest U.S. individual companies found that chief executive officers had a production/operations career emphasis 18.6 percent of the time.[3] Besides

[1]U.S. Department of Labor, Bureau of Labor Statistics, 1972, 1975, 1979, 1984, and 1986.

[2]The development of operations problem solutions and their transfer to service sector organizations is discussed in V. A. Mabert, "Service Operations Management: Research and Application," *Journal of Operations Management* 2, no. 4 (August 1982), 203–9.

[3]Charles G. Burch, "A Group Profile of the *Fortune* 500 Chief Executives," *Fortune* (May 1976), pp. 173–77, 308–12.

the top position in the organization, there is generally a vice president or similar officer responsible for production/operations. This raises the question of how one might gain such a position. What entry positions allow people to gain experience for promotion within operations?

Two entry tracks are evident—a line and a staff approach. Typical line positions include first-line supervisors, management trainees, and foremen. Staff positions include computer analysts, project analysts, inventory and material planning and control, production planning, logistics, and quality control. Our recent experiences indicate ample opportunities in all these areas, especially in first-line supervision and computer-related and materials management positions. In any of these jobs you will likely obtain *product or service knowledge* about the firm for which you work—a necessity for most top management positions.

FIGURE 1.7
General model for managing operations

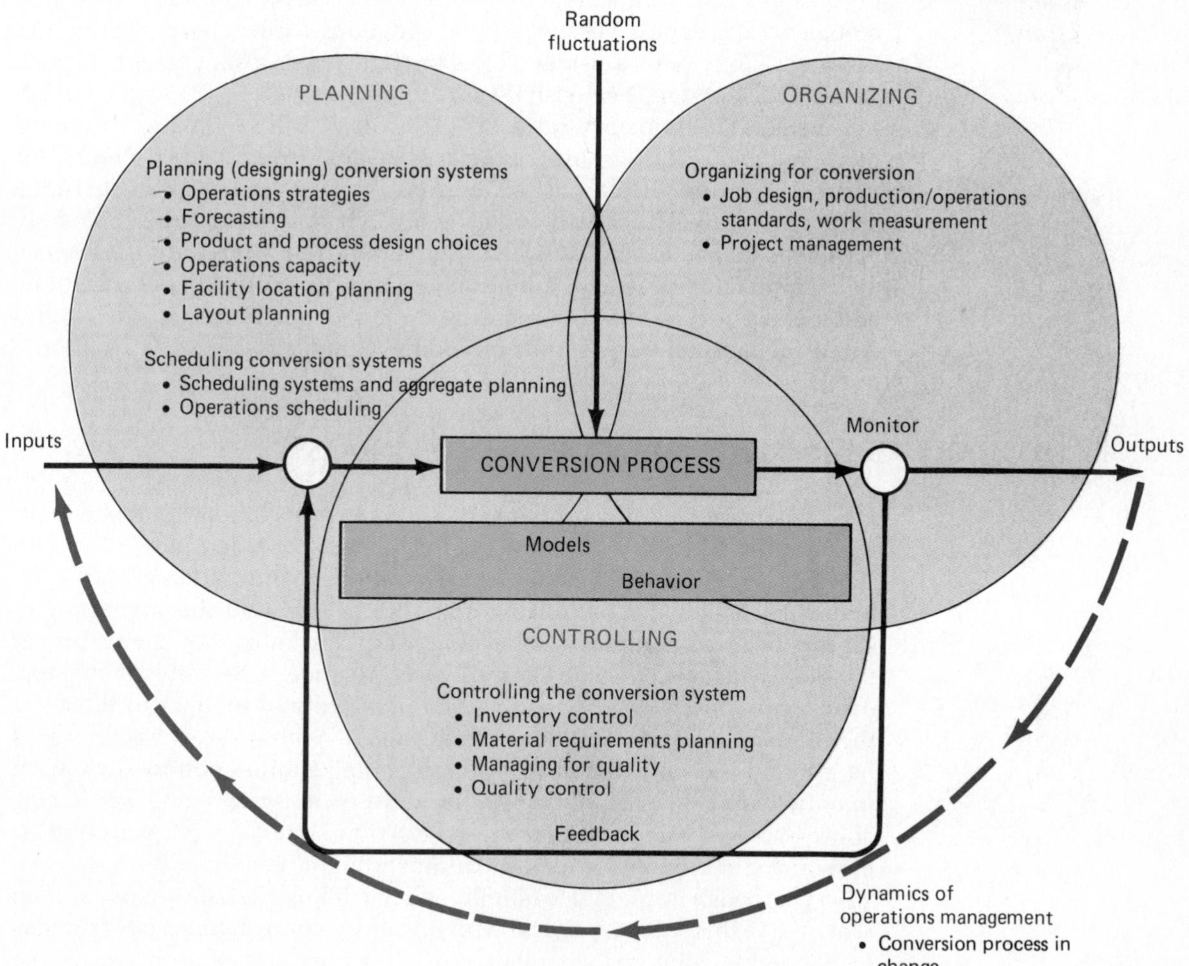

EXAMPLE In a recent semester two different industry guests visited an undergraduate production/operations management class. In response to student questions on careers, one guest, the personnel manager at a new Quaker Oats Company manufacturing facility, stressed an interest in management, production/operations management, and industrial engineering students for entry first-line foreman positions. As she explained them, the jobs were in a clean, modern facility with good opportunity for line or staff advancement. The second guest, the operations vice president at First National Bank of Kansas City, stressed an interest in operations management majors for entry positions in operations analysis, a staff function directly supporting bank operations. After six months to two years, operations analysts typically move to line supervisory positions. In both cases, promotion was available within operations and to other functions (marketing, finance, etc.) as well.

Career Choice in Production/ Operations Management

Because of their importance in our lives, careers deserve reasoned thought and direction. We suggest that in making career choices in production/operations you consider (1) opportunity for advancement, professional development, and visibility in the organization; (2) expected job satisfaction; (3) monetary rewards; (4) quality of life (climate, entertainment, etc.); (5) work group characteristics; and (6) individual needs and desires (location, health considerations, etc.). P/OM career decisions are amenable to change. Although you might have to learn new technology in a major job change, P/OM skills are generally transferable across services and manufacturing and within each sector. Professional organizations and journals occasionally summarize career opportunities in their operations management areas, thus providing a good source of information.

CONTEMPORARY OPERATIONS MANAGEMENT TOPICS

Modern operations management is a complex proposition. To deal with it, we have divided this book into six major parts. In each part, we relate specific operations management considerations to the contemporary issue under discussion. By organizing our coverage around the management subfunctions of planning, organizing, and controlling, we strive for an integrative perspective (see Figure 1.7). By relating each problem area to a common theme, we hope to suggest a continuity of thought to illustrate the fundamentals of operations management. Within this framework, we have found it useful to approach the planning subfunction by dividing it into two major parts: *planning* the conversion system and *scheduling* conversion systems. Planning the conversion system revolves around its design; while scheduling focuses on operating it once it exists.

One major topic, for example, is controlling the conversion system (Part V). In this section we deal with inventory control, materials management, and quality management—all necessary activities of operating managers. As we discuss each of these separately, we develop relevant concepts and terminology, identify problems, and present problem-solving techniques. When problems are behavioral (e.g., quality motivation), we introduce contemporary techniques like quality circles and attitude change procedures to deal with them. When problems are process-oriented (e.g., quality control), we show why models and such methods as sampling theory and control procedures are appropriate.

Before considering specific solutions to operations problems, however, we must first explore the major problems, issues, and challenges that are facing operations managers. These include questions on productivity, technology, competition, and strategies, all of which create the challenges for effective performance today. It is this set of questions that we consider next.

SUMMARY

This chapter has highlighted the role of the operations function in organizations and the importance of managing it effectively. *Operations* was defined in terms of the mission it serves for the organization, the technology it employs, and the human and managerial processes it involves. Using this approach, we were able to see the breadth of issues the operations manager faces, as well as the kinds of problems and decisions that arise in operations management.

To understand and solve operations problems we adopted a framework that draws upon the concepts from three schools of management thought—classical, behavioral, and modeling. Systems concepts can be useful for understanding organizations and the role of the operations function within them. Operations management makes use of these systems, models, and various techniques in directing the conversion process, which converts inputs into desired outputs. Operations managers must become involved in planning, organizing, and controlling operations. As they make decisions and decide among alternatives, they must consider the organization's goals and overall strategy.

Historical shifts in economic activity and predicted changes in the growth of major industries indicate the increasing importance of the service sector. These changes present some new challenges to operations management, and transferring our knowledge of production management into the service sector setting is chief among them.

CASE

Kare-Full Katering, Inc.

Harrison T. Wenk III is a 43-year-old married man with two children, ages 10 and 14. Harrison, who has a masters degree in education, teaches junior high school music in a small town in Ohio. Harrison's father passed away two months ago, leaving his only child with an unusual business opportunity. According to his father's will, Harrison has 12 months to become active in the family food-catering business, Kare-Full Katering, Inc., or it will be sold to two key employees for a reasonable and fair price. If Harrison becomes involved, the two employees have the option to purchase a significant, but less than majority, interest in the firm.

Harrison's only involvement with this business, which his grandfather established, was as an hourly employee during high school and college summers. He is confident that he could learn and perhaps enjoy the marketing side of the business, and that he could retain the long-time head of accounting/finance. But he would never really enjoy day-to-day operations. In fact, he doesn't understand what operations management really involves.

In 1988 Kare-Full Katering, Inc., had $3.75 million in sales in central Ohio. Net profit after taxes was $105,000, the eleventh consecutive year of profitable operations and the seventeenth in the last 20 years. There are 210 employees in this labor-intense business. Institutional contracts account for over 70 percent of sales and include partial food services of three colleges, six captive commercial establishments (primarily manufacturing plants and banks), two long-term care facilities, and five grade schools. Some customer locations employ a permanent operations manager; others are served from the main kitchens of Kare-Full Katering. Harrison believes that if he becomes active in the business, one of the two key employees, the vice president of operations, will leave the firm.

Harrison has decided to complete the final two months of this school year and then spend the summer around Kare-Full Katering—as well as institutions with their own food services—to assess whether he wants to become involved in the business. He is particularly interested in finding out as much as possible about operations. Harrison believes he owes it to his wife and children to fairly evaluate this opportunity.

Case Questions

1. Prepare a worksheet of operations activities that Harrison should inquire about this summer.
2. To manage the firm, how much does Harrison need to know about operations? Why?
3. What problems do you expect Harrison to encounter this summer —both at Kare-Full and at other institutions?
4. If you were Harrison, what would you do? Why?

CASE

Operations Management in a Veterinary Clinic

See if you can identify the inputs, outputs, and conversion processes that exist in a veterinary clinic consisting of three veterinarians, a clerical staff, and two animal control assistants. Identify the primary operations management activities (use Table 1.3 as a guide) that exist in this setting. Lay them out in a framework similar to the one in Figure 1.1. You should consider how the addition of an operations manager to the clinic staff would affect the cost and effectiveness of medical services. Normally in a situation like this, the operations manager would be one of the veterinarians. Could you explain to them why they should hire you to manage operations of the clinic?

REVIEW AND DISCUSSION QUESTIONS

1. Organizations may be viewed as systems. The systems view is important to operations managers since (a) the production/operations system is a part of the firm or organization and (b) within the production/operations function there are subsystems. Explain.
2. Using Figure 1.1, explain the conversion process in a fast-food outlet (McDonald's, for example) and a public swimming pool.
3. (a) What are operations subgoals?
   (b) What is the overall objective of the operations subsystem?
   (c) How do they relate to each other?
4. Energy conservation is an individual, firm, and national concern. If you were a manager of a large department store employing 200 and spending over $10,000 a month on utilities, which approach to (or school of) management might assist you best in reducing energy costs? Why?
5. How does production/operations policy interrelate with accounting and financial policy and marketing policy? What does this interrelationship accomplish?
6. Organization goal accomplishment requires that a strategic element of operations is the consideration of the firm's industry, strategy, operations policy, and conversion process. How do these elements relate to one another? How do they relate to organization goal accomplishment?
7. Relate the conversion diagram in Figure 1.1 to the first fifteen activity areas listed by operations managers in Table 1.3.
8. Compare and contrast the three broad categories of management thought: classical, behavioral, and modeling schools.
9. As an industrialized nation becomes more affluent, people have more leisure time and demand more services than they used to. Many workers enter the labor force later and leave it earlier. How do these changes affect the role of the traditional production/operations manager?
10. A problem with modern assembly line techniques seems to be that workers are apathetic. How could scientific management be used as a basis for solving this problem? How could a human relations philosophy help solve it?
11. Why is there a need for a behavioral school of management thought? Preferably from your own experience or observation, provide a supervisor-subordinate situation that supports your answer.
12. Relate the general model for managing operations (Figure 1.7) to each school of management thought.
13. How do inflation, energy shortages, and a shorter work week each present new challenges to production/operations managers?

PROBLEMS

1. The manager of a cola bottling plant came to work early on Friday, having been out of town on business throughout the week. Before others arrived, he checked the daily labor efficiency report for the bottling plant. Daily efficiency was 102 percent

Monday, 94 percent Tuesday, and 87 percent Wednesday. Going to the assistant manager's desk, he found that actual hours worked on Thursday were 96, cases bottled Thursday were 1,025. The equivalent labor output, the standard, is 12.5 cases per hour. What, if any, questions should the manager ask when employees arrive Friday?

2. An insurance claims office's group labor standard is 150 claims processed per day. So far this week, 160, 125, 140, and 100 claims have been processed daily. The claims backlog is building. Prepare a graph of daily efficiency. What does the graph indicate?

GLOSSARY

Behavioral science Theories of human behavior and how it is affected by such processes as leadership, motivation, communication, interpersonal relationships, and attitude change.

Classical school of management Focuses on efficiency at the production core and on the separation of planning and doing work; emphasizes management principles and functions.

Controlling All those activities assuring that performance in the organization takes place in accordance with planned performance.

Conversion process Changing labor, capital, land, and management inputs into outputs of goods and services.

Efficiency Some measure (ratio) of outputs to inputs.

Feedback Information in the control process that allows management to decide whether adjustments in organizational activities are needed.

Human relations Concept that people are complex and have multiple needs and that the subordinate-supervisor relationship directly affects productivity.

Mathematical modeling The creation of mathematical representations of management problems and organizations in order to determine outcomes of proposed courses of action.

Operations management Management of the conversion process, which converts land, labor, capital, and management inputs into desired outputs of goods and services.

Operations subsystem That part of the organization that exists primarily for generating or producing the organization's physical goods or services.

Organizing All activities that result in some structure of tasks and authority.

Planning All those activities that result in developing a course of action and guide future decision making.

Process management One theory of the classical school; it views management as a continuous process involving the functions of planning, organizing, and controlling so as to influence the actions of others.

Random fluctuations Unplanned or uncontrollable environmental influences (strikes, floods, etc.) that cause planned and actual output to differ.

Scientific management One of several classical theories of management; it emphasizes economic efficiency at the production core through management rationality, assumes the economic motivation of workers, and urges the separation of planning and doing work.

Social system One set of behavioral theories examining group relationships and their effect upon productivity.

Specialization of labor Concept of breaking jobs down into specialized subtasks and reassigning work according to the task involved.

System A collection of objects united by some form of regular interaction and interdependence.

SELECTED READINGS

Andrew, C. G., and G. A. Johnson, "The Crucial Importance of Production and Operations Management," *Academy of Management Review* 7, no. 1 (January 1982), 143–47.

Berry, Stephen E., Hugh J. Watson, and William T. Greenwood, "A Survey as to the Content of the Introductory POM Course," *Academy of Management Journal* 21, no. 4, (December 1978), 699–714.

Britney, Robert R., and E. F. Peter Newson, *The Canadian Production/Operations Management Environment: An Audit.* School of Business Administration Research Monograph. London, Ontario: University of Western Ontario, April 1975.

Mabert, V. A., "Service Operations Management: Research and Application," *Journal of Operations Management* 2, no. 4 (August 1982), 203–9.

Skinner, Wickham, "Manufacturing—Missing Link in Corporate Strategy," *Harvard Business Review* 47, no. 3 (May–June 1969).

———, *Manufacturing in the Corporate Strategy.* New York: John Wiley, 1978.

Sullivan, R. S., "The Service Sector: Challenges and Imperatives for Research in Operations," *Journal of Operations Management* 2, no. 4 (August 1982), 211–14.

Wheelwright, S. C., "Reflecting Corporate Strategy in Manufacturing Decisions," *Business Horizons* 21, no. 1 (1978), 57–66.

SUPPLEMENT TO CHAPTER 1

THE ROLE OF MODELS IN OPERATIONS MANAGEMENT

The context in which we use the term *mathematical modeling* refers to the creation of mathematical representations of management problems and organizations in order to determine outcomes of proposed courses of action. In spite of their utility, we must recognize models for what they are—artificial representations of things that are real. As such, they fall short of fully duplicating their real world counterparts. This incompleteness of models should not be interpreted as a strictly negative feature. In fact, it can be desirable, because it clears away extraneous elements and concentrates on the heart of the problem. The modeling process can give us a simplified version of the situation, a representation in which all the minor considerations have been stripped away so the major factors are clearly visible.

Types of Models in Production and Operations Management

In production and operations management, we use several types of models of varying levels of sophistication.

Verbal Models *Verbal* or *written models* are descriptive. *They express in words the relationships among variables.* Suppose a passing motorist asks you to give directions to the nearest gas station. If you tell him the way, you are giving a verbal model. If you write the directions in words (not pictures), you are giving a descriptive model.

Schematic Models *Schematic models show a pictorial relationship among variables.* If you give the passing motorist a map showing the way to the nearest gas station, you would be giving a schematic model. Charts and diagrams are also schematic; they are very useful for showing relationships among variables, as long as all the legends, symbols, and scales are explained.

Iconic Models *Iconic models are scaled physical replicas of objects or processes.* Architectural models of new buildings and highway engineering replicas of a proposed overpass system are iconic models.

Mathematical Models *Mathematical models show functional relationships among variables by using mathematical symbols and equations.* In any equation, x, y, and similar symbols are abstractions (they represent real variables) used to represent precise functional relationships among the variables.

Mathematical Models in P/OM

Optimization Operations managers often use formal models to help analyze problems and suggest solutions. To assist, they often find it helpful to use an *algorithm,* a prescribed set of steps (a procedure) that attains a goal. In *optimization* models, for example, we want to find the *best* solution (the goal), and an *optimization algorithm* identifies the steps for doing so. In operations management we strive for optimization algorithms as aids in problem solving.

Heuristics In other cases, a *heuristic* approach is used. A heuristic is a way (a strategy) of using rules of thumb or defined decision procedures to attack a problem. In general, when we use heuristics we do not expect to attain the best possible solution to a problem; instead, we hope for a *satisfactory* solution *quickly*. Formally developed heuristic procedures are called *heuristic algorithms*. They are useful for problems for which optimization algorithms have not yet been developed.

Modeling Benefits

The extensive use of models, especially schematic and mathematical models, is sometimes questioned by students and practitioners of P/OM. The application of well-defined models often requires assumptions that are sometimes questionable, costs and other data that are difficult to obtain, and forecasts of future events that are not easily obtained. Even so, using a particular model is frequently justified. The knowledge gained from working with models and attempting to apply them can yield valuable insights into the decision problem. The use of explicitly defined models

1. Forces managers to recognize a problem area and decide what types of decisions are required. Simply recognizing the decision points can be a major step forward in many situations.
2. Makes managers recognize the factors involved in the problem and determine what variables can be controlled to affect performance of the system.
3. Forces managers to recognize *relevant* costs and gain some knowledge of their magnitudes.
4. Enables managers to identify the relationships of costs to the decision variables, recognize important tradeoffs among costs, and gain knowledge of the overall interaction of variables and costs.

CLASSIFYING DECISION PROBLEMS

Since many different kinds of decision problems are encountered by the operations analyst, it's a good idea to have a convenient starting point, or frame of reference, for initiating the analysis effort. Classifying problems into different types makes it easier to select models and criteria to use in the analysis. We'll consider two ways of classifying problems: by the degree of uncertainty of outcomes and by the degree of interdependence among decisions.

Uncertainty of Outcomes

When we know for sure what the outcome for each decision alternative will be, we are dealing with a problem under conditions of *certainty*. When a decision alternative can result in more than one possible outcome and we know the relative chances (probabilities) of each outcome's occurrence, we are facing a decision problem under conditions of *risk*. Finally, when an alternative has more than one possible outcome and we do not know their relative chances of occurrence, we face a decision problem under *uncertainty*. Some examples may clarify the solution procedures under conditions of certainty, risk, and uncertainty.

EXAMPLE: CERTAINTY

A chain of supermarkets is going to open a new store at one of four possible locations. Management wishes to select the location that will maximize profitability over the next ten years. An extensive analysis was performed to determine the costs, revenues, and profits for each alternative. The results are shown below.

Location	Ten-year Annual Profit ($ millions)
1	.70
2	.95
3	.60
4	.84

Management has a high degree of confidence in these figures. The decision criterion (profit) has been explicitly identified and accurately calculated for each alternative. Management's strategy is to select the alternative with the highest criterion value, in this case, location 2.

EXAMPLE: RISK

An extensive analysis of the supermarket chain's problem reveals that the profit associated with each alternative is not known for sure. Management is convinced that the ten-year profitability of each location alternative will depend upon future regional population growth. Therefore, the ultimate outcome is not totally within the control of management; it also depends on external considerations. Three possible levels of population growth have been identified; low, medium, and high. The profitability ($ millions) associated with each alternative under each possible level of population growth has been established below.

	Rate of Population Growth		
Location	Low (5% or less)	Medium (above 5% but below 10%)	High (10% or more)
1	$.3	$.8	$ .9
2	.2	.6	1.1
3	.4	.5	.6
4	.6	.7	.8
Probability (p)	.2	.3	.5

At the bottom of the table, the analyst has recorded the probability of occurrence for each possible rate of population growth. Decision strategy in this situation is more difficult than it is under conditions of certainty.

EXAMPLE: UNCERTAINTY If the supermarket chain's management knows that profitability depends on future population growth, but it doesn't know the probabilities of low, medium, or high growth, it is faced with a decision problem under uncertainty. Obviously, strategy is much harder to come by in this case.

Under conditions of certainty, the best location alternative is easily identified. Location 2 clearly yields the highest profit. Under conditions of risk, however, the choice is not so easy. We do not know which location will be best because the rate of future population growth is unknown. In analyzing this situation, we have to arrange the data differently than we did under certainty conditions. Look at the table in the risk example. (A table arranged like this is called a *matrix*.) The levels of profit for low, medium, and high population growth are listed separately for each location. Which alternative is best? If population growth turns out to be low, location 4 is best ($.6 million). If growth is medium, location 1 is best ($.8 million), and if it is high, location 2 is best ($1.1 million). In the analyst's language, the three rates of population growth are called *states of nature*.

A procedure called *expected value* has been applied to our example (see Table S1.1). Expected value is explained by following the table headings. The expected value criterion is highest for alternative 2, $.77 million. If management faced this situation many times and always chose alternative 2, its average profit would be higher than for any other alternative.[4]

Decision problems under uncertainty can also be structured in matrix form. Since the probabilities are not known, however, rational

Table S1.1 Calculation of expected value ($ million)

Alternative	Outcomes × Chances			Summation	Expected Value (profit)
1	$.3 × .2 = .06	$.8 × .3 = .24	$ .9 × .5 = .45	.06 + .24 + .45	= $.75
2	.2 × .2 = .04	.6 × .3 = .18	1.1 × .5 = .55	.04 + .18 + .55	= .77
3	.4 × .2 = .08	.5 × .3 = .15	.6 × .5 = .30	.08 + .15 + .30	= .53
4	.6 × .2 = .12	.7 × .3 = .21	.8 × .5 = .40	.12 + .21 + .40	= .73

[4]You may have noticed something important about location 3. For every population rate (state of nature), location 4 has a better outcome than location 3. When one alternative is equal to or better than another for every possible state of nature, analysts say that it *dominates* that alternative. In this case, 4 dominates 3. Therefore 3 could be eliminated immediately.

strategies for decision making are not well defined or straightforward. Three approaches from among several that analysts use in these circumstances are discussed here. The first, *maximax,* is an optimistic approach; the analyst considers only the best outcome for each alternative. In the risk example, the table illustrating location by rate of growth (ignoring the probability row), the outcomes considered would be $.9 million for alternative 1, $1.1 million for alternative 2, $.6 million for alternative 3, and $.8 million for alternative 4. Among these, alternative 2 yields the maximum profit, and that is the one that would be chosen.

The second approach under uncertainty is *maximin,* a pessimistic approach. With this approach, the analyst considers only the worst possible outcome for each alternative and chooses the "best of the worst" (maximum among the minimums). In the table in the risk example, the figures would be $.3 million for alternative 1, $.2 million for alternative 2, $.4 million for alternative 3, and $.6 million for alternative 4. The best of these is 4.

The third approach, the *principle of insufficient reason,* assumes that since we know absolutely nothing about the probabilities of any state of nature, we should treat each with equal probability and choose on the expected value basis. Using this approach, we would choose alternative 4.

Interdependence Among Decisions

Another way of classifying decision problems is in relation to the number of decision stages that must be considered. At one extreme are single-stage, or static, problems; at the other are multistage, or sequential, problems. Static problems are essentially "one-time-only" decisions. Decisions concerning inventory, "make versus buy," product mix, and location of new facility are often treated as static problems. Our supermarket chain example was treated this way. To simplify the situation, the decision is treated as if it were independent of other decisions.

Multistage treatments, on the other hand, explicitly consider how several sequential decisions are related to one another. The outcome of the first decision affects the attractiveness of the choices at the next decision stage, and so on down the line at each decision point. With multistage problems, the concern is not how to get the best outcome of any single stage but how to make a *series* of choices that will finally result in the best overall set of outcomes from beginning to end. Sequential decision problems are commonly encountered by the operations manager in project management, capacity planning, and aggregate scheduling.

CASE

Safety Sight Company

Safety Sight Company owns two plants that manufacture bicycle headlights. The Edgewater plant has been fully operational in recent years; the Garland facility has been shut down for the past two years. Management anticipates a large increase in demand for bicycle lights, and future production plans are now being developed. Revenue from the sale of headlights is expected to average $8 per unit over the foreseeable future.

The Edgewater plant has been operating a single shift with fixed costs of $2.5 million and a production capacity of 500,000 units annually. Unit variable costs have been $1.60 for this range of output. Greater output volume could be achieved by starting up a second shift. If that were done, it is estimated that unit variable costs on the new shift would be either $6.3, $5.7, or $5.1 with probabilities of .09, .33, and .58, respectively. Production capacity on the second shift would be 500,000 units annually.

To achieve larger volumes of output, the Garland facility could be reopened. The exact annual fixed cost of operating this facility is unknown. Three recent estimates were: $1.8, $1.65, and $1.55 million with probabilities of .4, .5, and .1, respectively. Unit variable cost for first shift operations is expected to be $1.60, the same as for the Edgewater plant. The first shift capacity of the Garland plant is expected to be 500,000 headlights per year.

Management is considering two alternatives: operate the Edgewater plant on two shifts, keeping the Garland plant shut down; or operate both plants on a single shift. Management is sure either alternative will provide capacity to meet the new expected demand. What should they do?

REVIEW AND DISCUSSION QUESTIONS

1. Discuss the advantages and disadvantages of these models in operations management:
   (a) Verbal
   (b) Schematic
   (c) Iconic
   (d) Mathematical
2. By definition, models are incomplete representations of the things being modeled. Discuss the reasons for this fact and its implications from a managerial point of view.
3. Develop a model of the operations function of a large apartment complex or a dormitory. Discuss the ways in which your model is useful and the ways it is limited.

PROBLEMS

1. A delivery company is considering the purchase of a used truck. Its useful service life is estimated to be 3 years with a probability of .1; 4 years with a probability of .4; 5 years with a probability of .3; and 6 years with probability of .2. What is the expected useful life of the used truck?
2. A cab company is considering three makes of autos, A, B, or C to add to its taxi fleet. The daily operating cost of each make depends on the daily usage rate (demand) as shown on the next page.

Cost per Day of Operation

Make	Daily Usage Rate Low	Moderate	High
A	$100	$200	$300
B	190	200	220
C	150	190	230

Which make is best according to the minimax criterion? According to the insufficient reason criterion? If the probabilities of low, moderate, and high usage are .5, .2, and .3, respectively, what is the best make on an expected cost basis?

3. Four alternative manufacturing methods are being considered for a new product. Profitability, which depends on method of manufacture and level of consumer acceptance, is anticipated as shown here.

Profits ($ thousands) from New Product

Manufacturing Method	Projected Consumer Acceptance Low	Moderate	High	Very High
I	$100	$200	$300	$600
II	175	300	400	500
III	250	300	350	425
IV	100	300	400	450
Probability	.25	.35	.20	.20

(a) What is the best manufacturing method according to each of these criteria:
(1) Expected value
(2) Maximin
(3) Maximax
(4) Insufficient reason

(b) Which manufacturing method should be selected? Why?

2

Operations Strategies for Competitive Advantage

Westlake Hardware is a service company, a retail hardware chain with stores in seven midwestern states. We've grown from an original family store founded in 1905, to 10 outlets in 1975, and 49 outlets by 1988. Our recent expansion rate has forced us to set company objectives to assure that all segments of our business are integrated and striving for the same goals. With 49 stores and 1,000 employees spread over a large geographic area and covering diverse markets, it is essential that our operating managers understand our overall company objectives, strategies, and plans, but yet be allowed discretion in adapting to their local situation. This decentralized planning is necessary if we are to react appropriately to local market conditions. Attracting capable operations managers in retailing is essential for both effective planning and the subsequent implementation of those plans in fluid and unique markets.

Scott Westlake
President
Westlake Hardware Inc.
Lenexa, Kansas

The best way to determine an organization's strategy is to observe what the organization actually accomplishes over time. Westlake Hardware, it would appear, has followed a growth strategy, staying in the service business and market area it knows best. We know, however, that this successful, privately held business has emphasized profitable growth; growth with quality customer service, productive operations, and orderly development of capable operations managers and employees.

In this chapter we introduce strategic planning for production and operations and then identify several competitive pressures that successful managers, like Mr. Westlake, can turn into operating advantages for their firms.

STRATEGIC PLANNING

Strategic planning is the process of thinking through the current mission of the organization and *the current environmental conditions facing it, then setting forth a guide for tomorrow's decisions and results.* Strategic planning is built on fundamental concepts: that current decisions are based on *future* conditions and results, that strategic planning is a *process,* that it embodies a *philosophy,* and that it provides a *linkage* or structure within the organization.

Strategic Planning for Production and Operations

In the production or operations function, strategic planning is the broad, overall planning that precedes the more detailed operational planning. Executives who head the production and operations function are actively involved in strategic planning, developing plans that are consistent with both the firm's overall strategies and such other functions as marketing, finance accounting, and engineering.[1] Once developed, production and operations strategic plans are the basis for (1) operational planning of *facilities* (design) and (2) operational planning for the *use* of these facilities. In this book we emphasize these last two planning efforts, but we must also stress that such operational planning should not be done in a vacuum. It must come under the umbrella of effective strategic planning.

Strategic Planning Approaches for Production/Operations One specialist on strategic planning suggests three contrasting modes of strategic planning: the entrepreneurial, the adaptive, and the planning modes.[2] In the entrepreneurial mode, one strong, bold leader takes planning action on behalf of the production/operations function.[3] In the adaptive mode, a manager's plan is formulated in a series of small, disjointed steps in reaction to a disjointed environment.[4] The planning model uses planning essentials combined with the logical analysis of management science.[5]

---

[1]Skinner makes this point when he argues that manufacturing and corporate strategy must be linked through an integrating mechanism—manufacturing strategy. See Wickham Skinner, *Manufacturing in the Corporate Strategy* (New York: John Wiley & Sons, 1978), pp. 27–29.

[2]Henry Mintzberg, "Strategy-Making in Three Modes," *California Management Review* 16, no. 2 (Winter 1973), 44–53.

[3]See Peter F. Drucker, *Management: Tasks, Responsibilities, Practices* (New York: Harper and Row, 1974), Chapter 10, "Strategic Planning: The Entrepreneurial Skill" 121–29.

[4]See, for example, R. M. Cyert and J. G. March, *A Behavioral Theory of the Firm* (Englewood Cliffs, N.J.: Prentice Hall, 1963).

[5]See, for example, George A. Steiner, *Strategic Planning: What Every Manager Must Know* (New York: The Free Press, 1979). For a survey of corporate simulation model use in 346 companies, see Thomas H. Naylor and Horst Schauland, "A Survey of Users of Corporate Planning Models," *Management Science* 22, no. 9 (May 1976), 927–37.

There are many approaches to strategic planning. The key point we want to make is that operations strategies must be consistent with the overall strategies of the firm. Our observations lead us to the conclusion that operations typically utilize the overall corporate approach to strategic planning, with special modifications and, of course, a focus upon operations issues and opportunities. For that reason we want to introduce one general approach to strategic planning—a forced choice model—and one specific approach especially developed for operations.

A Strategic Planning Forced Choice Model One of many planning models that has been used in strategic planning is a *forced choice model*, shown in Figure 2.1. In group sessions or individually, analysts assess environmental considerations together with the organization's current production/operations position, thus forcing management to develop strategic options for operations. This model is explained in considerable detail, including how to apply it using structured group techniques, elsewhere.[6]

A Strategic Planning Operations Model Professor Chris A. Voss of the University of Warwick, England, has set forth a framework for strategy and policy development in manufacturing, which we have modified for services as well.[7] His concept is that manufacturing strategy tries to link

---

[6]See Charles N. Greene, Everett E. Adam, Jr., and Ronald J. Ebert, *Management for Effective Performance* (Englewood Cliffs, N.J.: Prentice Hall, 1985), Chap. 17.

[7]C. A. Voss, *Managing New Manufacturing Technologies*, Operations Management Association, Monograph No. 1 (1986), Appendix 2, pp. 65–68.

FIGURE 2.1
A forced choice model of strategic planning for operations

Source: Charles N. Greene, Everett E. Adam, Jr., and Ronald J. Ebert, *Management for Effective Performance* (Englewood Cliffs, N.J.: Prentice Hall, 1985), p. 544.

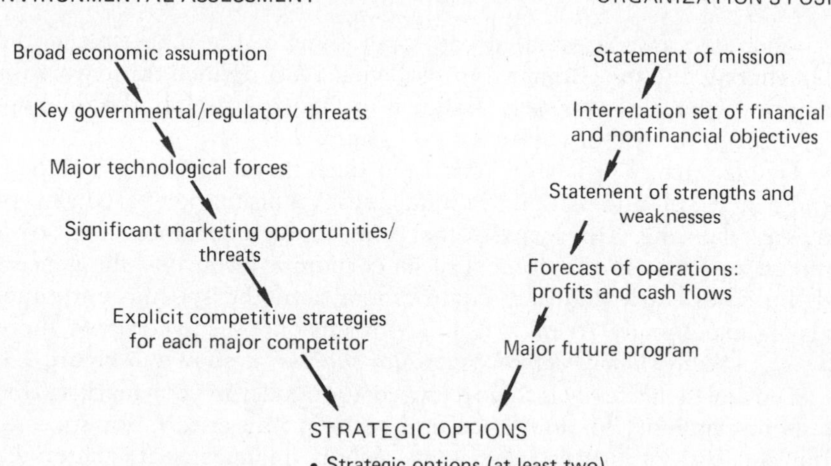
ENVIRONMENTAL ASSESSMENT
Broad economic assumption
Key governmental/regulatory threats
Major technological forces
Significant marketing opportunities/threats
Explicit competitive strategies for each major competitor
ORGANIZATION'S POSITION
Statement of mission
Interrelation set of financial and nonfinancial objectives
Statement of strengths and weaknesses
Forecast of operations: profits and cash flows
Major future program
STRATEGIC OPTIONS
• Strategic options (at least two)
• Requirements for implementing each strategy
• Contingency plans

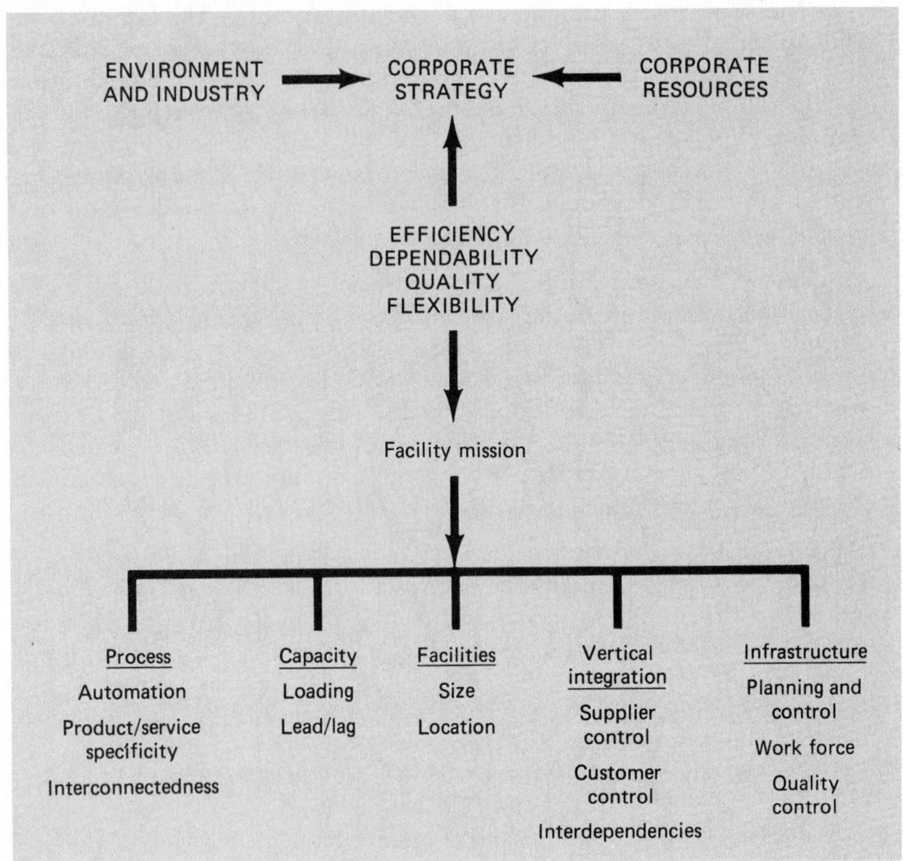

FIGURE 2.2
Operations strategy framework

the policy decisions associated with operations to the marketplace, the environment, and the company's overall goals. A simplified framework for examining operations strategy is shown in Figure 2.2. Note the relationship between the top of Figure 2.2 and Figure 2.1.

One feature of Professor Voss's approach that is crucial to competitiveness (and well understood by the Japanese) is his market-based view of strategic planning. He suggests that any strategic business unit of a company operates in the context of its corporate resources, the general and the competitive industry environment, and the specific corporate goals of the company. In any area the company chooses to compete, there is a set of specific *market-based criteria for success,* as shown in Figure 2.3.

The key to *efficiency* is to be a low-cost producer in your market. This results in capability for low price and is the prime criteria for success. Minimum use of scarce resources—labor, management, materials, equipment/facilities, and energy—while sustaining high outputs is the key

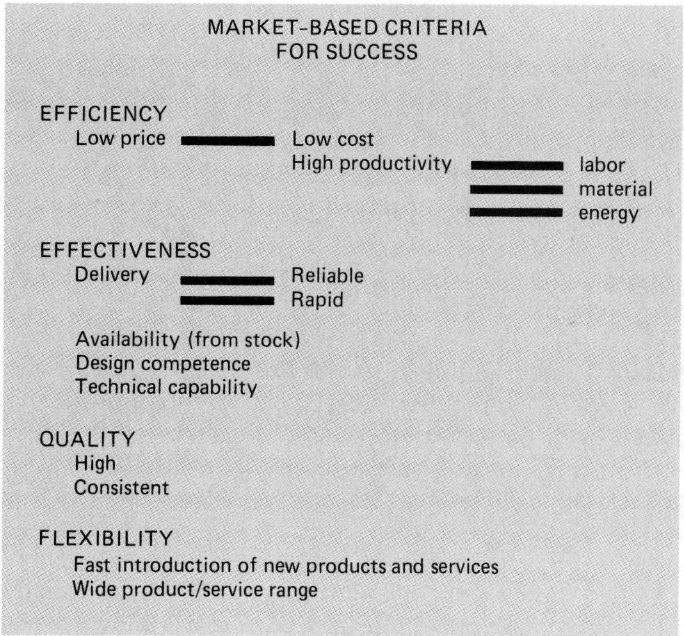

FIGURE 2.3
Market-based criteria for success

to productivity. *Effectiveness* is how well a company is able to meet specific absolute criteria such as delivery and technical capability. *Quality* is the goodness of the product or service—the degree to which it meets customer requirements and internally established specifications. *Flexibility* is adaptability, the capability to change as business conditions change.

How does the planning model of Figure 2.2 work? Given a specific operations mission *established from market-based criteria for success,* operations managers must make choices. The main areas of choices, upon which we elaborate in Chapter 4, are

- *Facilities*—for example, the scale, location, and focus of the facilities
- *Aggregate capacity*—the policies governing the management of aggregate capacity
- *Choice of process*—the type, technology, and degree of product/service specificity
- *Vertical integration*—the degree and nature of vertical integration
- *Operations integration*—the labor policies, payment methods, systems of production and inventory control, which are key elements for management control
- *Operations interface with other functions*—the closeness of and mechanisms for communicating with other functions

The combinations of choices made in all of the areas listed above represent the operations strategy of a particular firm.

Interestingly, Professor Voss explains failure in terms of this framework as well. How does an organization fail? If a company is doing the following, it is liable to fail:

- Focusing on manufacturing performance criteria that do not match the market criteria for success
- Trying to meet incompatible criteria for success within a single market
- Trying to produce goods in a single factory for markets with very differing criteria for success

Although there are many approaches to successful operations strategic planning, the question remains: What, then, is the fundamental relationship between operations and markets?[8] We agree with Professor Voss in that either *the operations strategy must be changed and adapted to maximize the market criteria for success, or the chosen markets should be changed to match more closely operations capability in terms of market criteria for success.*

We have identified three competitive challenges that can restrict the fullest achievement of the firm's operations capability and to those we now turn—productivity and quality, technology and mechanization, and international manufacturing.

PRODUCTIVITY AND QUALITY

Efficiency, productivity, performance—are terms we tend to use interchangeably in discussing behavior and achievement. Efficiency and productivity refer to a ratio of outputs divided by inputs, but performance is a broader term incorporating efficiency and productivity in overall achievement.

Productivity Defined

Productivity can be expressed on a total factor basis or on a partial factor basis. *Total* factor productivity is the ratio of outputs over all inputs:

$$\text{Productivity} = \frac{\text{Outputs}}{\text{Labor} + \text{Capital} + \text{Materials} + \text{Energy}} \qquad (2.1)$$

Outputs relative to one, two, or three of inputs (labor, capital, materials, or energy) are *partial* measures of productivity. Output per labor hour, often called *labor efficiency,* is perhaps the most common partial measure of productivity.

[8]For other guides to successful manufacturing strategic planning and case implementation, see Skinner, *Manufacturing in the Corporate Strategy;* Robert J. Mayer, "Applying Manufacturing Strategy Concepts to Practice," *Strategic Management of Operations: Proceedings of the First Annual Winter Conference of the Operations Management Association* (San Francisco, November 1982), pp. 44–50; Roger W. Schmenner, "Multiplant Manufacturing Strategies Among the *Fortune* 500," *Journal of Operations Management* 2, no. 2 (February 1982), 77–86; and Terry Hill, *Manufacturing Strategy* (London: Macmillan, 1985).

EXAMPLE A small restaurant has averaged 224 customers served during a day over the past year. Hours are 6:00 A.M. to 2:00 P.M., and three employees comprise the total staff. Average labor productivity could be expressed as

$$\text{Labor productivity} = \frac{\text{Output}}{\text{Labor input}}$$
$$= \frac{\text{224 Customers served}}{\text{3 employees} \times \text{8 hours/employee}}$$
$$= \text{8.1 customers served/hour}$$

On Tuesday of this week, 264 customers were served by a full staff. On Wednesday, 232 customers were served, with two employees working full days and one working but two hours. We can find labor productivity for each day as

$$\begin{array}{c}\text{Labor productivity} \\ \text{(Tuesday)}\end{array} = \frac{264}{3 \times 8} = \text{11.0 customers served/hour}$$

$$\begin{array}{c}\text{Labor productivity} \\ \text{(Wednesday)}\end{array} = \frac{232}{(2 \times 8) + 2} = \text{12.9 customers served/hour}$$

For each day, labor productivity was well above this historical average, a level of labor performance that should please the owner (unless it caused customers to wait excessively for service).

Levels of Productivity Productivity can be viewed at two extremes. We can look at the level of an entire nation or at the level of an individual employee. In between these two extremes are industry, organization (firm), division (business unit), and work group levels. Figure 2.4 illustrates total factor productivity—as well as the partial factors, capital and labor—for the U.S. business

FIGURE 2.4
Productivity trends in U.S. private businesses, 1973–1985

Source: Productivity Perspectives (Houston, Tex.: American Productivity Center, 1987), p. 2.

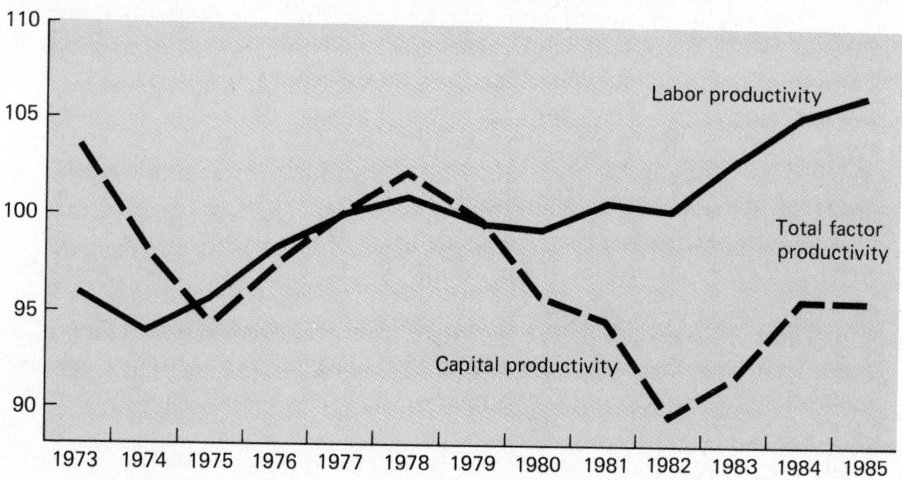

economy over a 12-year span. We can see that although it has been relatively stable, productivity declined in the late 1970s before a recent increase.

Productivity Trends

In Figure 2.4, we saw a rather stagnant U.S. productivity picture for the past decade. From 1960 to 1985, labor productivity growth never exceeded 4 percent in any one year. What about the contribution of capital? This is important to operations managers, as the tradeoff between investment and labor is always under scrutiny. Figure 2.4 illustrates that capital productivity dropped below total factor productivity in 1979 and declined until 1982. Even though capital productivity has been increasing since 1982, it is still a drag on total factor productivity.[9]

What does this mean? It means that capital has not contributed positively, overall, to annual productivity growth during the last few years in the U.S. economy. The prudent operations manager should be aware of this and should seek investments that clearly enhance productivity in his or her operations.

Quality and Productivity

One reason that the competitive position of firms can falter is that the quality of goods and services produced does not meet the customer's expectations. When quality—the appropriateness of design specifications to function and use as well as the degree to which outputs conform to the design specifications—is poor, demand for products and services can diminish quickly. But what does this have to do with productivity?

There is a clear relationship between quality and productivity. Generally, when quality increases, so will productivity. Why? Because waste is eliminated. The amount of resource inputs (the denominator of equation 2.1) required to produce good outputs (the numerator) is reduced. Productivity increases.

If this is so simple, why haven't all U.S. firms figured this out? Many have. Even if one accepts this view, however, achieving high-quality performance is not all that simple. There are also other views of the quality-productivity relationship.

One such view is that quality and productivity move in opposite directions. Think about such processes as typing or data entry at a computer keyboard. As your speed increases, what tends to happen? You tend to make more errors, especially when you go "very fast." Logically, it follows that if you type slowly and carefully, you will make fewer errors. There is a tradeoff between speed and accuracy. As quality increases, speed (and productivity) decrease.

How can these two contrasting positions concerning quality-productivity relationships be resolved? We believe the answer is in the concept of *capability*. We suggest that as long as there is unused capability in the individual (such as the typist) or the productive system (such as a manufacturing facility), increases in speed (and productivity) can be achieved without declines in quality. Or, alternatively, quality can be

[9]*Productivity Perspectives* (Houston, Tex.: American Productivity Center, 1987), p. 2.

improved without changing speed. If one focuses on quality while holding speed constant, quality should increase, waste should be eliminated, and productivity should increase. This can happen as long as the individual, or group of individuals, is willing to exert effort and has the capability to achieve the quality-productivity levels desired. It is the operations manager's task to provide the facilities, tools, and desire (motivation) to do so. This is a very difficult task. Some managers and firms are discovering ways to maintain high quality and increase productivity at the same time. Let's observe some of their techniques.

A Quality-Productivity Strategy Improving quality is one important way to maintain a competitive position in today's markets. Quality can be promoted to customers and employees. Consumers want quality products and services, and employees at all levels in the organization like to be associated with a winner. Most people associate high quality with a winning competitive position. Although employees may balk when they are encouraged to work more productively (because they feel they are being told to work faster), very few, if any, will argue with quality as a goal.

From an economic perspective, when quality is emphasized and subsequently improved, waste is decreased or eliminated. Hours are not wasted reworking products. Material is not thrown away. Operations costs are reduced. At the same time, the customer receives products and services that are "fit" for use. As a result, product prices can be lowered to share this productivity gain with customers, thereby increasing the firm's market share. Or, alternatively, the higher-quality product (as compared with competitors' product offerings) can command a premium price and a more secure market niche. To employees, these results mean increased job security because of a sound competitive position. Stockholders can benefit through higher overall profits and improved asset utilization. In short, high quality can make everyone a winner—a message some firms and managers seem to understand better than others.

Understanding and accepting this quality-productivity strategy is a first step toward its achievement. We encourage you to think seriously about this line of reasoning as you read the balance of this chapter and book.

Quality and Productivity Improvement Efforts

Let's look at a few examples of firms that are seeking productivity and quality gains in order to improve their competitive positions. Westinghouse Electric Company, as a worldwide competitor in a variety of consumer, industrial, defense, and aerospace sectors, has a vital interest in quality and productivity improvement.

EXAMPLE

"At Westinghouse, we are putting top-priority emphasis on productivity and quality improvement, not only because it is necessary for the well-being of our Corporation, but because we believe it is vital for the economic survival of our nation and for our national security.

"About three and one-half years ago, we started this Corporatewide top-priority emphasis on productivity improvement for two basic reasons. First was our need to further improve our Corporate performance, and the second was our concern over increasing international competition. We didn't want this to be a one-shot effort, but rather we wanted productivity improvement to become a way of life throughout the Corporation.

"In early 1979 we formed a Corporate Committee on Productivity, and I was assigned to chair it. Initially, our Committee spent many months studying the situation—first in the United States; then in Europe; and then in the Pacific Basin—particularly in Japan. Significantly, we didn't anticipate, at the outset, that most of our studies would find the Japanese to be so formidable. In my case, I've been visiting Japan for almost 20 years. But—for the first 17 years, as a teacher—and only the past three years, as a student. This "role change" makes an immense difference.

"Significantly also, we didn't realize, at the outset, that quality is as important to productivity—as are people and technology."[10]

As the example illustrates, members of Westinghouse management were profoundly impressed with Japanese manufacturing technology. They were particularly affected by the devotion to quality among their Japanese counterparts. Since then, Westinghouse has undertaken initiatives to adopt quality circles, new technology, and a quality improvement emphasis by concurrently designing both the product and manufacturing process. What has Westinghouse achieved? Setting a goal in constant dollars of 6 percent a year in value added (by Westinghouse) per employee, the Westinghouse Public Systems Company achieved a 7-percent-a-year gain over three years (1979–1982). The Public Systems Company is now seeking a 10 percent improvement per year.

In addition to individual company examples, improvement efforts are being organized into productivity centers and institutes, with more than 300 known centers worldwide.[11] These centers typically have any of four thrusts—training and education, information distribution and promotion, sociotechnical approaches, and industrial engineering and managerial economic emphasis[12]—reflecting the interests of the firms (consumers of center services) they are serving. Forty percent of the centers were estimated to emphasize training and education, with 20 percent primarily emphasizing each of the other three activities. Relative budgets in various parts of the world were aggregated by the authors, with 23.3 percent of

[10]Thomas J. Murrin, President, Public Systems Company, Westinghouse Electric Company, Pittsburgh, Pennsylvania, "Productivity and Quality Improvement," Remarks to Defense Logistics Agency, Bottom Line Conference (Washington, D.C., May 13, 1982).

[11]Robert R. Britney, *1984–85 International Directory of Productivity Centers* (The University of Western Ontario, 1985); Robert R. Britney, Randolph P. Kudar, David A. Johnston, and John Walsh, "A Comparison of International Productivity Centers," *National Productivity Review* (Winter 1986–1987), pp. 71–76.

[12]Robert R. Britney, David A. Johnston, J. M. Legentil, and John Walsh, "Planning for Productivity Gains within the Firm," Working Paper #82–38 (London, Canada: School of Business Administration, The University of Western Ontario, October 1982).

worldwide center expenditures in North America, 32.0 percent in Europe, 21.6 percent in South America, 9.9 percent in Asia, and 11.9 percent throughout the remainder of the world. Perhaps the best known North American facility is the American Productivity Center (APC) located in Houston, Texas.

Services, Quality, and Productivity It should be emphasized that the changes in our thinking apply not just to factories and blue-collar workers but to service industries and offices as well. What promise is there for productivity and quality improvement in services, particularly in white-collar services? Our concluding example provides some insight into TRW's quest for improved white-collar productivity.[13]

EXAMPLE TRW is a multinational, highly diversified corporation with over $5 billion in sales, $3 billion in assets, and 100,000 employees operating in 27 different countries. Products range from car parts to satellite systems. TRW is the second largest computer software producer in the nation, behind only IBM. While 40 percent of TRW's workers are now involved in manufacturing, that number will fall to 5 percent by the year 2000, according to Henry P. Conn, TRW's former vice president for productivity.

TRW has one fundamental objective: TRW seeks to achieve superior performance as an economic unit, with special emphasis on high-quality products and services. This translates into seven goals summarized to reflect financial performance: high quality at competitive prices, market strength, diversification, management and technological innovation, maximum productivity, and effective use of outside-the-company resources (consultants, training, etc.).

Ruch and Werther illustrate by example how TRW organizes to achieve their objectives.[14] The focus is on people. Managers are doing what they should be doing—planning, guiding, communicating, and supporting employees at all levels. Employees are working with a new sense of involvement.

For example, TRW has improved efficiency in computer software –writer jobs. Writers spend less time talking on the telephone, filing, attending meetings, or staring out windows. Instead, they spend as much time as possible actually writing the lines of code that guide missiles or track satellites. They now have individual rather than grouped terminals, computerized mail, and teleconferencing—all with the intent of working more at line activities that add value to the service the company is producing and selling.

---

[13]See "Faced with a Changing Work Force, TRW Pushes to Raise White Collar Productivity," *Wall Street Journal,* August 22, 1983; William A. Ruch, "The Measurement of White-Collar Productivity," *National Productivity Review* (Autumn 1982), pp. 416–26; and William A. Ruch and William B. Werther, Jr., "Productivity Strategies at TRW," *National Productivity Review* (Spring 1983), pp. 109–26.

[14]Ruch and Werther, "Productivity Strategies."

TECHNOLOGY AND MECHANIZATION

In Chapter 1 we referred to the *conversion process* as the central element of the production and operations function. The work of operations management revolves around conversion, where resource inputs are converted or transformed into useful products and services. This conversion process is present in most organizations, but it is distinctly different for a bank, an aerospace firm, or a public utility. The basic technologies of operations differ among industries as well as within various organizations in any one industry. In the public utility, for example, the firm requires engineering skills to design facilities, maintenance abilities for various mechanical and electrical applications, and operating skills for larger pieces of equipment used in operations. *The blending of labor, land, capital, and management —and the scientific expertise needed for this task—are at the very heart of technology* in operations.

In some instances, machinery is substituted for hand labor. *Mechanization is the process of bringing about the use of equipment and machinery* in production and operations. In a bank, for example, some jobs—such as checking account reconciliation and statement preparation—are mechanized. Other tasks, such as the interview in which information is initially gathered by a loan officer to start the loan qualification process, are not mechanized.

Organizations today face decisions regarding which variations in technology to employ and what degree of mechanization is best. Many of the challenges for improved productivity and quality are answered by managers and owners as they adopt more sophisticated technologies and increased mechanization. However, the costs associated with an inappropriate strategy for technology and mechanization are great. On the one hand, competitors who effectively substitute capital and equipment for labor in order to gain lower production and operating costs may increase market share very quickly. For example, highly mechanized companies in Japan and Korea caused a loss in market share for the U.S. steel industry. On the other hand, action to increase mechanization, when it is unnecessary or inappropriate, may be quite costly. A firm may be saddled with high fixed costs relative to other companies in the industry. Management may be unable to reduce variable costs of manufacturing sufficiently to recover the costs of mechanization.

What degree of technological change, mechanization, and automation is strategically best? The judgments required by any one organization to respond correctly to this question are often critical to the long-term survival of the business. It takes experience and wisdom to make such a decision; these qualities cannot be learned in a book. However, we can introduce you to some of the mechanization alternatives being faced by businesses today. In Chapter 4 we discuss process design. Here we simply want to recognize the competitive nature of technology and mechanization choices. Through our discussion of these choices—such as computers, robotics, and computer-aided design—you may gain some insights into the complexity of these decisions and the cost/benefit tradeoffs that are involved.

INTERNATIONAL PRODUCTION AND OPERATIONS MANAGEMENT

The world is shrinking, and worldwide economic competition is intensifying. Transportation and communication improvements make nations seem closer together. As one nation becomes aware of the products and services that are available in the world at large, demand for those items and services tends to increase. And how is that demand met? In some cases it is not met, especially among poor nations. In other cases, products and services are produced by a given country for internal consumption. In still other situations, goods are imported and the services of other countries are consumed at their origin (since most services cannot be stored). Yet another alternative is for the producing nation to transfer its conversion know-how to the consuming nation. This approach is currently being used by companies that provide services; it is also increasingly prevalent among firms that manufacture products (through licensing arrangements). As a result, there is heightened interest in the *international dimension of production and operations.* Although our interest is managerial, that is, an interest in operations management similarities and differences among nations, we really cannot understand the management issues without some understanding of the economics involved.

The International Productivity Challenge in Production and Operations

How does the productivity growth of the United States compare with that of other industrialized countries? Between 1973 and 1982, the average annual increase in manufacturing productivity was 1.4 percent in Canada, 1.5 percent in the United States, 2.5 percent in the United Kingdom, 4.6 percent in France, 5.1 percent in the Netherlands, 6.1 percent in Belgium, and 6.2 percent in Japan. Japan is at the forefront and the United States and Canada bring up the rear.

Rate of growth is important over the long term, but what are the relative bases of each nation? That is, now that we see who is running the fastest (Japan), who is at the head of the pack? As Figure 2.5 illustrates, the United States is first, with most other industrial nations ahead of Japan in terms of gross domestic product (GDP, an output measure) per employee. Two columns are shown in Figure 2.5. One is from the Bureau of Labor Statistics (BLS) and the unit of measure is per employee; the other column is from another source (Maddison) and the unit of measure is per hour worked. The nations most likely to surpass the United States are the Netherlands, Belgium, and France, as they have both high productivity and high productivity growth rates.

Major Manufacturing Differences Among Japan, Europe, and North America

Further insights into differences among nations are revealed in a major study by Professors Arnaud DeMeyer and Kasra Ferdows (INSEAD, France), Jinchiro Nakane (Science Institute, Japan), and Jeffrey G. Miller (Boston University, U.S.A.), who conduct an annual survey of future directions in manufacturing. Their survey report for 1987 contrasted the

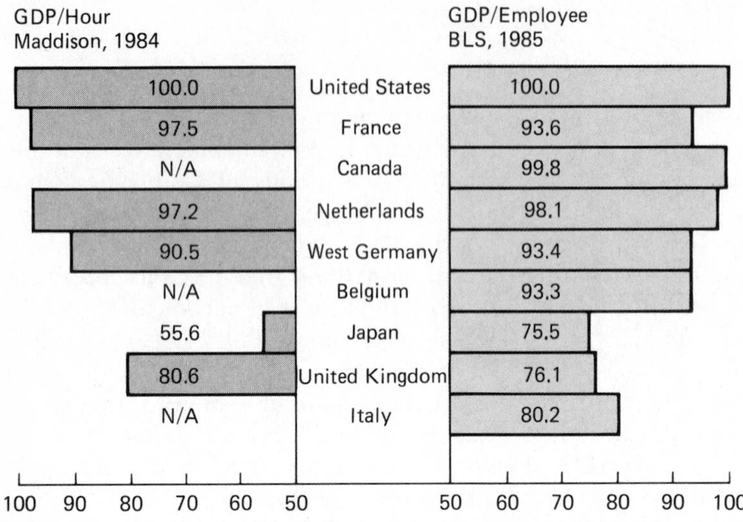

FIGURE 2.5
International productivity levels

Source: Productivity Perspectives (Houston, Tex.: American Productivity Center, December 1987), p. 12.

opinions of 186 U.S., 174 European, and 214 Japanese executives.[15] In 1986, these high-level executives had average sales of $918 million in their business unit.

Competitive Priorities One way to compare manufacturing among industrial centers in the world is to examine the varying competitive priorities listed in Table 2.1.[16] In this table, priorities are presented in decreasing order of importance. The North American executives reflect an emphasis on quality, performance, and service. The Japanese are more concerned with price, speed, and new products. European executives are more like their North American counterparts; they list quality, performance, and service as being most important.

What are the groups doing about these competitive practices? Here we see fewer similarities between North America and Europe (Table 2.2). North American executives are clearly focused on quality improvement, with their top three action items and four of their top six items. The top three action items for European executives are direct labor motivation, production, and inventory control systems, and automating jobs. Japanese executives have action plans focused on flexible manufacturing systems, quality circles, and production and inventory control systems. Reacting to this North American concern for quality, treatment of quality improvement comprises two chapters in this book (Chapters 15 and 16).

[15]Arnaud DeMeyer, Jinchiro Nakane, Jeffrey G. Miller, and Kasra Ferdows, "Flexibility: The Next Competitive Battle," *Manufacturing Roundtable Research Report Series* (Boston University School of Management, February 1987). The authors express their gratitude for a willingness on the part of these scholars to share their study results.

[16]*Ibid.*, p. 9.

Table 2.1 Competitive priorities[a]

Europe	North America	Japan
1. Consistent quality (1) (1) (1)	1. Consistent quality (1) (1) (1)	1. Low prices (1) (1) (1)
2. High-performance products (3) (2) (2)	2. High-performance products (2) (2) (3)	2. Rapid design changes (2) (2) (2)
3. Dependable deliveries (2) (3) (3)	3. Dependable deliveries (3) (3) (2)	2. Consistent quality (3) (3) (2)
4. Fast delivery (6) (6) (5)	4. Low prices (6) (5) (5)	4. Dependable deliveries (4) (4) (5)
5. Low prices (5) (5) (6)	5. Fast deliveries (4) (4) (4)	5. Rapid volume changes (6) (6) (6)
6. Rapid design changes (5) (5) (6)	6. Rapid design changes (7) (5) (7)	6. High-performance products (4) (4) (4)
7. After-sales service (8) (8) (7)	7. After-sales service (5) (7) (6)	7. Fast delivery (8) (7) (7)
8. Rapid volume changes (7) (7) (8)	8. Rapid volume changes (8) (8) (8)	8. After-sales service (7) (8) (8)

[a]The priorities are listed according to their importance as ranked in the 1986 survey. Numbers within brackets indicate the ranking of the competitive priorities in 1983, 1984, and 1985, respectively.

Source: DeMeyer, Nakane, Miller, and Ferdows, "Flexibility."

Understanding the Japanese Challenge for Production and Operations

As in previous sections, it is helpful if we begin by comparing productivity between Japan and the United States. We recall that Japan has experienced a higher growth rate in productivity (6.2 percent) than the United States (1.5 percent) over the last decade. Yet Japan's overall productivity, as measured by gross domestic production per employee, was but 75.5 percent of that of the United States in 1985 (Figure 2.5). Japan is catching up with the United States, but it still needs to make a lot of progress.

Japanese Management North American managers are keenly interested in Japanese management style and in discovering what the Japanese do differently. What is it that leads to success in Japan? Is it culture, environment, management skills, or beliefs about people? Management scholars and consultants are probing these issues and offering suggestions.

A popular view was presented in the early 1980s by William Ouchi; his analysis focused on characteristics of *organizations* as the basis for comparison.[17] Ouchi listed such distinguishing features of Japanese organizations as lifetime employment, slow evaluation and promotion, nonspecialized career paths, implicit control mechanisms, collective decision making, collective responsibility, and holistic concern for employees. In contrast, qualities inherent in American organizations include short-term employment, rapid evaluation and promotion, specialized career paths, explicit control mechanisms, individual decision making, individual responsibility, and a more segmented concern for workers.[18] Ouchi offers a

[17]William C. Ouchi, *Theory Z: How American Business Can Meet the Japanese Challenge* (Reading, Mass.: Addison-Wesley, 1981).

[18]This comparison is drawn from J. Bernard Keys and Thomas R. Miller, "The Japanese Management Theory Jungle," *Academy of Management Review* 9, no. 2 (April 1984), 342–53.

Table 2.2 **The ten most important action plans**[a]

Europe	North America	Japan
Direct labor motivation (3)	Statistical process control (7)	
		Flexible manufacturing systems (1)
Production and inventory control systems (4)	Zero defects ( )	Quality circles (3)
Automating jobs (2)	Vendor quality (2)	Production and inventory control systems (4)
Integrating information systems in manufacturing (1)	Improving new product introduction capability ( )	Automating jobs (2)
Supervisor training (6)	Production and inventory control systems (1)	Lead-time reduction (9)
Manufacturing reorganization (10)	Statistical product control ( )	Introduction of new processes for new products (2)
Integrating information systems across functions (7)	Integration of information systems in manufacturing (1)	Reducing set-up time (10)
Defining a manufacturing strategy (11)	Developing new processes for new products (10)	Direct labor motivation (8)
Lead-time reduction (12)	Direct labor motivation (8)	Worker safety (6)
Vendor quality (5)	Lead-time reduction ( )	Giving workers a broader range of tasks ( )

[a]Numbers between brackets indicate rank order in 1985. If no rank order is indicated, in 1985 the rank order was higher than 12. For previous years, these data were collected somewhat differently, and comparisons of rank orders are difficult to make.

Source: DeMeyer, Nakane, Miller, and Ferdows, "Flexibility."

new American approach, called *Theory Z.* He believes that some features of Japanese organizations could be successfully replicated in American organizations. Theory Z would be a synthesis; it would include the best aspects of both approaches.

Richard Pascale and Anthony Athos, taking a different approach than Ouchi's, have developed a model that analyzes Japanese and American firms based on seven variables: the "hard S's"—structure, strategy, and systems—and the "soft S's"—skills, staff, subordinate goals, and style. Without elaborating on these definitions (or concepts) and the rationale behind them, it is difficult to evaluate the validity of their argument that American firms are best at the "hard S's" and Japanese firms are best at the "soft S's."[19] The "soft S's" involve people. Pascale and Athos, both business school professors, give the Japanese high scores for their behavioral interactions with, and treatment of, employees. Many of the authors' arguments stem from comparisons of the Japanese firm, Matsushita Corporation, and the American firm, ITT. Those interested in comparative management between Japan and the United States will want to read this book. It is highly relevant to the study of management within operations.

Although there are many more studies that define and explain management characteristics, we feel it is essential to mention the work of Cole, who clearly identifies the setting in which Japanese firms are successful in dealing with people at work.[20] For example, he has excellent insights into why quality circles work well in Japan. Professor Cole has been studying and writing about the Japanese worker for over a decade, and he provides useful observations about Japanese behavior and culture. Cole's work provides something of a transition for us as we now turn to a discussion of successful Japanese management techniques we think are quite important to manufacturing.

Japanese Manufacturing Management Japanese manufacturing techniques are having an impact throughout the world. Our approach is to treat these topics where they appear naturally in this book, rather than treat them all here. American manufacturers have been keenly aware of the manufacturing processes and methods of the Japanese, especially their approaches to quality (quality circles and the use of statistical quality control), inventory management, and automation in process and repetitive manufacturing. In Chapters 15 and 16 we take a closer look at the quality picture in Japan. In Chapters 12 to 14, inventory concepts, techniques, and applications are developed, which will include a discussion of Japanese approaches to limiting inventory.[21] We will touch on Japanese manufacturing processes in our discussion of planning and utilizing the conversion system, especially in the areas of facility layout (Chapter 7) and production scheduling (Chapters 10 and 11).[22]

---

[19]Richard T. Pascale and Anthony G. Athos, *The Art of Japanese Management* (Warner Books, 1981).

[20]R. E. Cole, *Work, Mobility, and Participation: A Comparative Study of American and Japanese Industry* (Berkeley, Calif.: University of California Press, 1979).

[21]See Robert W. Hall, *Zero Inventories* (Homewood, Ill.: Dow Jones Irwin, 1983). For a shorter synopsis, see Robert W. Hall, "Driving the Productivity Machine: Production Planning and Control in Japan," A Research Report by the American Production and Inventory Control Society (Falls Church, Va., 1981).

[22]Richard J. Schonberger, "The Transfer of Japanese Manufacturing Management Approaches to U.S. Industry," *The Academy of Management Review* 7, no. 3 (July 1982), 479–87; *idem., Japanese Manufacturing Techniques* (New York: The Free Press, 1982); Thomas E. Vollman, William L. Berry, and D. Clay Whybark, *Manufacturing Planning and Control Systems* (Homewood, Ill.: Richard D. Irwin, 1984); Lee J. Krajewski, Barry E. King, Larry P. Ritzman, and Danny S. Wong, "A Viable U.S. Manufacturing Strategy: Reshaping the Production Environment," *Operations Management Review* 2, no. 3 (Spring 1984), 4–10.

MEETING THE INTERNATIONAL CHALLENGES IN PRODUCTION AND OPERATIONS MANAGEMENT

Any projections of the critical international issues that will face operations managers into the 1990s are speculative indeed. Clearly, however, as you begin your career in operations, you will encounter issues and problems at the grass-roots level within the organization. And, as you progress through your career, you will become more involved with deciding the overall strategies your firm must pursue in its operations. With this broader perspective in mind, the following operations issues are important to assure success in international competition.

1. Other nations are increasing their levels of productivity at a faster rate than the United States. This progress must be monitored both in terms of nations and individual firms. Which countries are moving fastest to catch the leader, the United States?
2. Industry-by-industry productivity analyses within a national economy allow the operations executive to focus broadly on his or her competition.
3. Firm-by-firm comparisons and case situations in other nations can be helpful. What are our strongest foreign competitors doing? How? Why?
4. Quality might well be the strategic variable to make our firm competitive internationally.
5. If developing nations have labor advantages, what should our operations strategy be toward replacing high-cost U.S. workers with (1) mechanization or (2) direct ownership of overseas (foreign) feeder plants in developing countries with low labor costs? What are the economic tradeoffs among mechanization, worldwide labor costs, transportation, and other cost factors in our operations?
6. What can we learn from the Pacific Basin countries, especially Japan, concerning successes in management style and manufacturing practices?[23]

These and other issues specific to a firm or industry seem critical to successful global operations. We hope that you share our excitement about this challenge.

---

[23]We have not touched on activities in China, both the Peoples Republic of China and Taiwan, which are emerging competitors with Korea and other nations. See, for example, Leon S. Lasdon, "Operations Research in China," *Interfaces* 10, no. 1 (February 1980), 23–27, and Paul Gray and Burton V. Dean, "The Chinese–U.S. Symposium on Systems Analysis," *Interfaces* 12, no. 1 (February 1982), 44–49.

MEETING THE COMPETITIVE CHALLENGE IN PRODUCTION AND OPERATIONS MANAGEMENT

Our attention has been focused on strategic planning and three major competitive issues: productivity, mechanization, and international competition. The challenges are before us. It should be exhilarating to manage in operations for the remainder of this century. Businesses, government agencies, academics, and students are taking production and operations management seriously. The function is becoming increasingly significant in our society. In the remainder of this book, we will try to equip you with a knowledge of the concepts, models, and behavioral approaches you will need in order to meet the challenges ahead.

SUMMARY

This chapter illustrated how the broad business strategy of the firm is utilized in developing more specific operations strategies so that market changes can be responded to or, over time, new markets can be found for the organization's operations capacity.

Consumers, owners, citizens, and employees are increasingly aware of the competitive environment in which they live. Within individual organizations, operations challenges are substantial. In this chapter we focused on *productivity, technology and mechanization*, and *international business* as each affects operations management. We discovered that recent U.S. productivity levels have not increased as rapidly as during the post–World War II period. The quality-productivity connection was discussed as a strategic issue for the firm. Our presentation of the international challenge in operations built upon previous productivity discussions; we also examined the accomplishments of Europe and Japan as compared with the United States.

In summary, the competitive challenges presented in this chapter abound in many organizations. The balance of the book focuses on meeting these challenges through a better understanding of operations concepts, models, and behavioral applications.

CASE

Martha's Burger Queen

Martha Thompson, who has worked in restaurants for 20 years, opened her first short-order "Mom-and-Pop" café 12 years ago. She is regarded in her community as an excellent small-business-person. In 1982 she sold her small café and went to work as a professional manager for a fast-food hamburger franchise. In 1984 she resigned and opened Martha's Original Burger Queen. Martha's salary is 25 percent higher than the one she earned as a professional manager. In 1984 her Burger Queen broke even; in 1985 it had a net profit after taxes of $10,000. Martha then opened two more restaurants in the same city. The results of all three restaurants are summarized in the accompanying comprehensive report.

Martha states her strategy: "My restaurant concept is to copy fast-food chains such as McDonald's, Burger King, and Jack-in-the-Box. I've tried parties, soybean burgers, breakfast, and larger sandwiches to increase dollar sales per customer. I believe that I should expand rapidly just as those chains seem to be doing, yet maintain a personable, local operations staff and a 'homey' atmosphere. But I seem to have less efficient operations than we did when I managed for a chain. I think my layout is good, as is my food quality. I can't buy in larger volumes, but I do try to turn over my inventory at least weekly. I believe in women employees, especially in management positions. I hire Caucasians, Blacks, and Mexican-Americans, so no one can say I'm prejudiced."

Martha's response to net income difficulties at the second and third restaurants is, "I need to open more restaurants to spread out my fixed costs. Expansion of operations is my strategy, but I'm finding financing hard to come by now."

Martha's Burger Queen comprehensive report

	Martha's Original Restaurant		MBQ2		MBQ3	
	1986	1987	1986	1987	1986	1987
Sales summary						
Revenues	$330,000	$370,000	$210,000	$200,000	$170,000	$150,000
Number customers	132,000	130,00	91,000	90,000	85,000	85,000
Revenues/customer	$2.50	$2.84	$2.30	$2.22	$2.00	$1.76
Expense summary						
Equipment depreciation	$16,500	$16,500	$10,500	$10,500	$8,500	$8,500
Building lease	33,000	33,000	21,000	21,000	17,000	17,000
Operations: Food	82,500	83,400	52,500	52,500	42,500	51,000
Labor	115,500	129,000	73,500	73,500	68,000	68,000
Supplies	16,000	18,000	10,000	10,000	8,500	8,500
Overhead	17,000	17,000	11,000	11,000	8,500	8,500
Gross margin selling and administrative costs						
Advertising	15,000	15,000	12,000	12,000	9,000	9,000
Administration	18,000	18,000	9,000	9,000	8,000	8,000
Net income (loss) before taxes	$16,500	$40,100	$10,500	$500	—0—	($28,500)

Case Questions

1. Of the various strategic planning modes, which do you believe most typifies Martha's Burger Queen? List characteristics of both the strategy mode and case that support your choice.

2. Examining the comprehensive report, which data (if any) support the idea that Martha needs a change in operations strategy?
3. Set forth what you believe is a good business strategy for Martha. Specify an operations strategy that is consistent with the overall strategy.

REVIEW AND DISCUSSION QUESTIONS

1. Explain total factor productivity. What is partial factor productivity? What partial factor productivity measure is likely to be used in production/operations management most frequently?
2. Explain how the strategies developed from Figure 2.1 are utilized as a basis for developing operations strategies (see Figure 2.2).
3. Explain the relationship between quality and productivity. Discuss the apparent alternative positions that (a) both move in the same direction or (b) each moves in opposing directions. Which do you accept? Why?
4. If a firm accepts quality as the strategic variable for improvement of operations, what might the firm expect as results? How would the firm go about improving its competitive position in that manner?
5. Discuss TRW's white-collar productivity improvement effort.
6. Do operations strategies take into account changing market conditions by adapting capability to the market or by finding new markets to fit existing operations capability? Discuss.
7. Consider beginning a new venture—opening a wine and cheese shop in a shopping mall. Using Figure 2.2 as a guide, develop an operations strategy to guide the overall operations of your new venture.
8. Contrast the major manufacturing differences among Japan, Europe, and North America based on the executive survey conducted by DeMeyer, Nakane, Miller, and Ferdows.
9. Review the Japanese approach to management. What do you believe are the key features that contribute to their successful management style? Why?
10. Near the end of this chapter, the authors speculate on several operations issues important to success in international competition. Select any one of these aspects and explain why you think it is important.
11. Briefly explain how *productivity, technology and mechanization,* and *international business* interrelate as they collectively become a formidable challenge to production and operations managers during the remainder of this century.

PROBLEMS

Reinforcing Fundamentals

1. An insurance company has a group standard in the claims department to process 1,250 claims per day when fully staffed with 52 employees. Consider the following data and compute labor productivity for each of the last four weeks. What does this mean?

Week (5 days)	Average Employees	Claims Processed
35	50	6250
36	51	6200
37	51	5850
38	51	5950

2. In Problem 1, if the group productivity standard is maintained, the contribution to profit for each claim processed is $11.00. To achieve this contribution, $13.75/hour in total labor and fringe benefits is expended, as well as total computer equipment and labor support of $12,000/employee/year. In the most recent month, computer costs average $1,200/employee in the claims department.
   (a) Compute total standard costs per month for claims.
   (b) Determine the total factor productivity (labor and computer) in claims last month.
   (c) What is the net contribution to profit, after productivity gains (or losses), for the month?

GLOSSARY

Mechanization The process of bringing about the use of equipment and machinery in production and operations.

Planning conversion facilities *See* Planning the conversion system.

Planning for operations Establishing a program of action for converting resources into goods or services.

Planning the conversion system Establishing a program of action for acquiring the necessary physical facilities to be used in the conversion process.

Productivity The ratio of outputs over inputs; total factor productivity is outputs over the total of labor, capital, materials, and energy.

Quality The appropriateness of design specifications to function and use, as well as the degree to which outputs (products or services) conform to the design specifications.

Strategic planning A process linking the current mission and environment and then setting forth a guide for tomorrow's decisions and results.

Technology The scientific expertise in blending labor, land, capital, and management into useful outputs.

SELECTED READINGS

American Productivity Center, *Productivity Perspectives.* Houston, Tex., 1987.

Cole, R. E., *Work, Mobility, and Participation: A Comparative Study of American and Japanese Industry.* Berkeley, Calif.: University of California Press, 1979.

DeMeyer, Arnaud, Jinchiro Nakane, Jeffrey G. Miller, and Kasra Ferdows, "Flexibility: The Next Competitive Battle," *Manufacturing Roundtable Research Report Series,* Boston University School of Management, February, 1987.

Hall, Robert W., *Zero Inventories.* Homewood, Ill.: Dow Jones Irwin, 1983.

Hill, Terry, *Manufacturing Strategy.* London, England: Macmillan, 1985.

Keys, Bernard J., and Thomas R. Miller, "The Japanese Management Theory Jungle," *Academy of Management Review* 9, no. 2 (April 1984), 342–53.

King, Barry E., Larry P. Ritzman, and Danny S. Wong, "A Viable U.S. Manufacturing Strategy: Reshaping the Production Environment," *Operations Management Review* 2, no. 3 (Spring 1984), 4–10.

Schmenner, Roger W., "Multiplant Manufacturing Strategies Among the Fortune 500," *Journal of Operations Management* 2, no. 2 (February 1982), 77–86.

Schonberger, Richard J., *Japanese Manufacturing Techniques.* New York: Free Press, 1982.

———, "The Transfer of Japanese Manufacturing Management Approaches to U.S. Industry," *The Academy of Management Review* 7, no. 3 (July 1982), 479–87.

Skinner, Wickham, *Manufacturing in the Corporate Strategy.* New York: John Wiley, 1978.

Voss, C. A., *Managing New Manufacturing Technologies.* Operations Management Association, Monograph No. 1, 1986, Appendix 2, "The Manufacturing Strategy Concept," pp. 65–68.

SUPPLEMENT TO CHAPTER 2

FINANCIAL AND ECONOMIC ANALYSES IN OPERATIONS

The Need for Financial and Economic Analyses

Strategic choices have as a basis a blending of both external and internal analyses. Externally, markets and environments are assessed. Internally, operating and financial capabilities are carefully evaluated. In conducting this internal evaluation, operations managers must have a fundamental understanding of applied financial analysis. In developing this understanding, managers need to understand such simple capital budgeting or economic analysis concepts as the time value of money and cost flows, as well as appropriate analysis models. Operations managers face many facility and process choices—both initial investments and replacements that they must accurately assess. Let's examine some basic financial concepts and models useful to operations managers.

Terminology and Concepts

Although it's not always possible to do so, decision makers try to evaluate alternatives logically and comparably. Toward this end, economic analysis borrows some standard terminology from finance and accounting.

Cost and Revenues When considering existing or prospective equipment and facilities, the manager is interested in the costs associated with their ownership and operation. This information is needed, for example, to decide whether old equipment should be retained or replaced by newer models. For financial analysis of investment proposals, accounting costs play a secondary role. *The costs that are used in economic analysis are current costs, actual costs.* Let's examine a few costs that become important to us in analysis.

Opportunity costs are the returns that are lost or forgone as a result of selecting one alternative instead of another. The amount of the opportunity cost is determined by comparing the benefits or advantages of a choice with those of the best alternative. *Sunk costs* are past expenditures that are irrelevant to current decisions. The salvage value of facilities and equipment is a relevant revenue (a negative cost), since existing assets that are abandoned or replaced may be saleable. The income received from an asset sale is the *salvage value.* Salvage value is a market value, similar to the concept of current, actual costs.

Depreciation is an accounting concept for recovering outlays (expenditures) for assets over their lives. Depreciation, a bookkeeping concept, does not reflect current market values. Since we are interested only in market values, of what value is depreciation to the economics of change (replacement)? Depreciation is important only in that the depreciation schedule affects income tax rates, and income taxes affect actual cash flows. The higher the depreciation in any one period, the lower the taxes paid and the greater the cash flows (revenues less expenses). For our purposes here, we simplify matters by ignoring both depreciation and taxes.

Incremental Cash Flows When we evaluate and compare investment opportunities, we have to consider the alternatives' incremental cash flows. When we do a cost comparison of two alternatives, we are interested only in the cost differences, or increments, between them; obviously, cost elements that are shared in common are irrelevant. Cash flows are of central interest in evaluating any investment proposal. All inflows and outflows that result from adopting an alternative should enter into the analysis, including not only initial outlays but also ongoing outlays expected throughout the asset life. Anticipated costs of owning, operating, and maintaining the asset should therefore be considered. To determine incremental cash flows, we must also consider expected revenue from sales and possible salvage decisions. Also important are the *magnitude* (size) of cash flows, the *direction* (revenue or expense) of cash flows, and the *patterns* (exactly when) cash flows take place over the life of the asset.

Life of the Asset

There are several ways of viewing the life of an asset. Consider the life of a piece of equipment. First, we can determine its *accounting life,* the life used to develop a depreciation schedule. Second, we can consider its *machine life,* the length of time the machine could actually function. At the end of the machine life, there might or might not be some salvage value. Machine life typically is of secondary interest to us in economic analysis. We are primarily interested in *economic life,* the period of time the asset performs its useful economic service to the organization. These three measurements may be widely divergent.

Time Value of Money

When analysts speak of the time value of money, they mean the revenues that may be received for money over time. A sum of money held as cash may either depreciate or appreciate in value over time, but it will not earn any revenues unless it is invested. If the same sum of money is invested over time for a specified amount with a guarantee of repayment of the principal, the original sum of money has value over time. This idea of money having value over time is an important consideration in evaluating proposed changes. An example would be a birthday gift of $100 invested at 8 percent interest, the value being $100 initially, $108 after one year, and $116.64 after two years of simple compounding.

Income and Expense Patterns and Associated Compound Interest Factors

Income and Expense Patterns In operations investment and replacement situations, there are six basic patterns of income and expense flows. Figure S2.1 shows three of these flow patterns, and since each pattern has a reverse flow as well, there are six possible cash flows. The three not shown (given P to find S, given P to find R, and given S to find R) would have the same graphical patterns as their counterparts, except that the cash flows would be reversed.

Compound Interest Factors Which income flow pattern applies to our birthday gift example? Given a present sum of money (P), find a future sum of money (S) after n periods. If we consider the time value of money at interest rate i over the n years, we have the concept of a compound

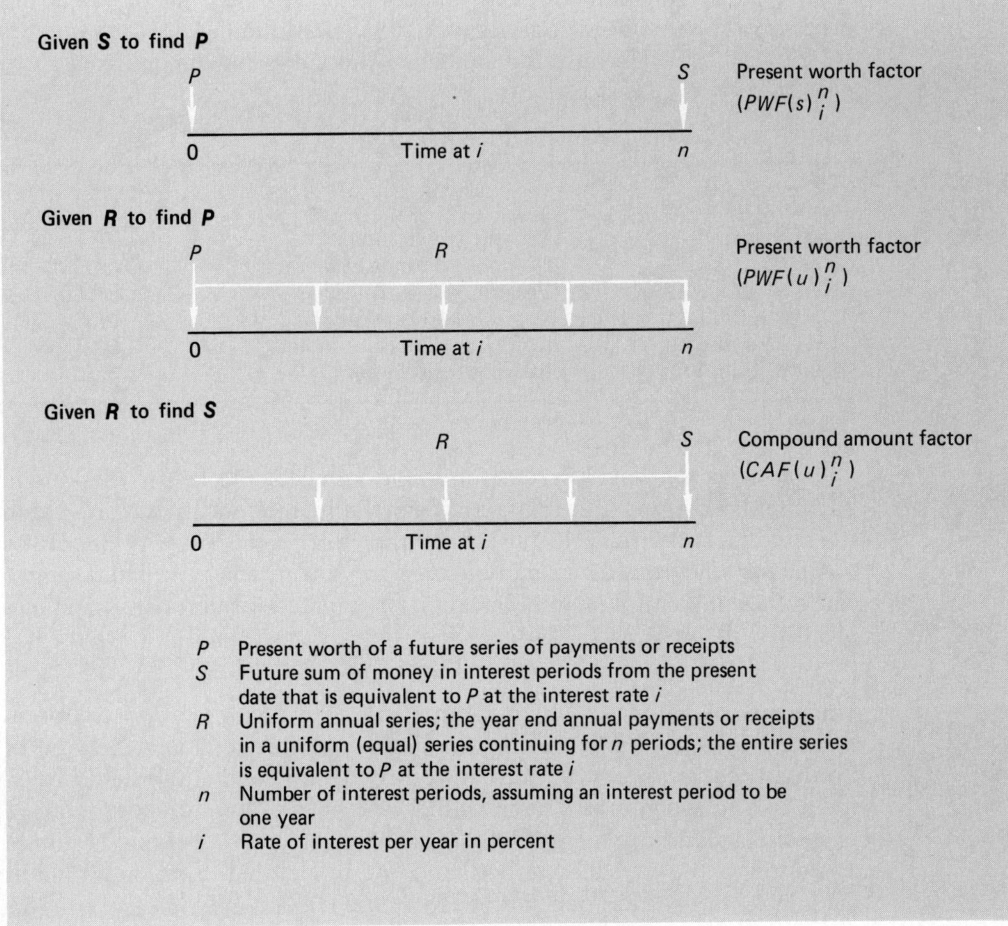
Given S to find P
P
S
Present worth factor
(PWF(s)^n_i)
0
Time at i
n
Given R to find P
P
R
Present worth factor
(PWF(u)^n_i)
0
Time at i
n
Given R to find S
R
S
Compound amount factor
(CAF(u)^n_i)
0
Time at i
n
P Present worth of a future series of payments or receipts
S Future sum of money in interest periods from the present date that is equivalent to P at the interest rate i
R Uniform annual series; the year end annual payments or receipts in a uniform (equal) series continuing for n periods; the entire series is equivalent to P at the interest rate i
n Number of interest periods, assuming an interest period to be one year
i Rate of interest per year in percent

FIGURE S2.1
Income and expense flow patterns and compound interest factors

interest factor. Let's call this particular factor a single payment compound amount factor. It could be defined as $CAF(s)^n_i$ and illustrated:

$$\begin{array}{ccc} P & & S \\ \downarrow & & \downarrow \\ \hline 0 & & n \\ & \text{Time at } i & \end{array} \quad CAF(s)^n_i$$

In terms of our example, the future sum of money, S, is found by looking up the factor in Appendix B (appendices are at the end of the text) and solving for S as follows:

$$\begin{aligned} S &= P[CAF(s)^n_i] \\ &= \$100\ [CAF(s)^2_{.08}] \\ &= 100\ (1.166) \\ &= \$116.60 \end{aligned} \qquad \text{(S2.1)}$$

Note that the answer we get by using equation S2.1 ($116.60) is not precisely the same as the answer we got by computing each year's interest ($116.64). This is because the factor is rounded in the appendix.

Table S2.1 Compound interest factors

Cash Flow	Factor Name	Factor Symbol
Given S to find P	Present worth factor	$PWF(s)_i^n$
Given P to find S	Compound amount factor	$CAF(s)_i^n$
Given R to find P	Present worth factor	$PWF(u)_i^n$
Given P to find R	Capital recovery factor	CRF_i^n
Given R to find S	Compound amount factor	$CAF(u)_i^n$
Given S to find R	Sinking fund factor	SFF_i^n

You do not have to remember the name of the factor (the single payment compound amount factor) nor the interest formula from which the factor was derived $[(1 + i)^n]$ to use the table. *You need only understand the logic of the investment situation, the cash flow patterns given and sought.* The different compound interest factors associated with varying cash flows are listed in Table S2.1.

Methods of Evaluation

There are several formal financial methods of evaluating proposed operations changes, and they vary in the degree of simplicity and the type of information they provide. We focus on the facility and equipment investment or replacement problem, one of several rational operating change problems faced by management. We will choose one model that is simple to calculate, the payback method, and one model that is not as simple to calculate but is often more informative, *net present value.*

Payback One of the most commonly used methods of evaluating investment proposals is to calculate the payback period of the investment as follows:

$$\text{Payback period} = \frac{\text{Net investment}}{\text{Net annual income from investment}}$$

Net investment, in dollars, includes the purchase and installation cost less anticipated future salvage value of the asset under consideration. *Net annual income* is the annual financial benefit (excess of income over expenses) expected from using the asset. The *payback period,* then, measures the length of time required to recover one's investment.

For several reasons, the payback criterion should be used with caution. First, it does not consider the time value of funds. Second, uneven expense and revenue flow patterns cannot be considered. Finally, it ignores all inflows that occur after the payback period. On the other hand, it has the advantages of simplicity and ease of communication. We recommend it not be used as the sole basis of decision but in conjunction with, or as a supplement to, the other methods of analysis.

EXAMPLE Two different orange pickers are being considered by Arizona Orchards, Inc., to assist in harvesting the orange crop at the Chandler, Arizona, farm. Alternative A requires a net investment of $10,000 and is expected to return $2,500/year in net annual income. Investment B is slightly more expensive, $12,000, but is expected to return $2,750/year in income. Calculating the payback period,

$$\text{Payback A} = \frac{\$10{,}000}{\$2{,}500/\text{year}} = 4 \text{ years}$$

$$\text{Payback B} = \frac{\$12{,}000}{\$2{,}750/\text{year}} = 4.36 \text{ years}$$

Alternative A has the shorter payback period.

Net Present Value Net present value considers all cash flows associated with an investment, discounts each unique flow (revenue or expense) back through time to its current equivalent value by using the appropriate compound interest factor, and then sums the net value of all discounted flows at the present time. The result is a *net present value*.

$$\begin{matrix}\text{Net}\\ \text{present}\\ \text{value}\end{matrix} = \sum \left[\begin{pmatrix}\text{Periodic}\\ \text{revenue}\end{pmatrix} - \begin{pmatrix}\text{Periodic}\\ \text{expense}\end{pmatrix} \right] \begin{bmatrix}\text{Compound}\\ \text{interest}\\ \text{factor}\end{bmatrix} - I \qquad \text{(S2.2)}$$

$$NPV = \sum_{1}^{T} (v_t - c_t)\,[PWF(s)_i^t] - I \qquad \text{(S2.3)}$$

where

i = rate of interest per year in percent
I = initial investment made at present time
T = life of investment
v_t = income or receipts occuring in period t, where $t = 1, 2, \ldots, T$
c_t = expenses or disbursements made in period t, where $t = 1, 2, \ldots, T$

The procedure for using net present value is

1. Separate all data by alternatives. Repeat each of the following steps for each alternative.
2. Identify the cash flows. (A diagram of cash flow might be helpful.) On the diagram identify the interest rate and time periods.
3. Write a total net present value equation in words to reflect the situation, the cash flow patterns.
4. Substitute the appropriate dollars and compound amount factors for each flow in the equation.

5. Find the compound amount factors in the appendices and solve, finding the net present value for each alternative.
6. Choose the alternatives with the *greatest* net present value.

Once you have solved a few problems, you'll probably be able to shortcut this procedure considerably. To simplify NPV analysis, we assume that cash flows that occur throughout the year always occur at year-end. Let's take one example through the complete procedure.

EXAMPLE Fireway Company must purchase a piece of replacement equipment and is considering models offered by two competing equipment manufacturers. Both models have a useful life expectancy of six years (no expected salvage value), and Fireway has a cost of capital of 10 percent for its investments. Each model provides an income of $4,000 annually. Alternative A requires an initial outlay of $10,000 and requires maintenance expenditures of $1,000 annually. Alternative B, a deluxe model, requires an initial outlay of $12,000 and annual maintenance costs of $500. Which alternative is less costly? The first step has been completed as the data are already organized according to investment alternative. The cash flows are:

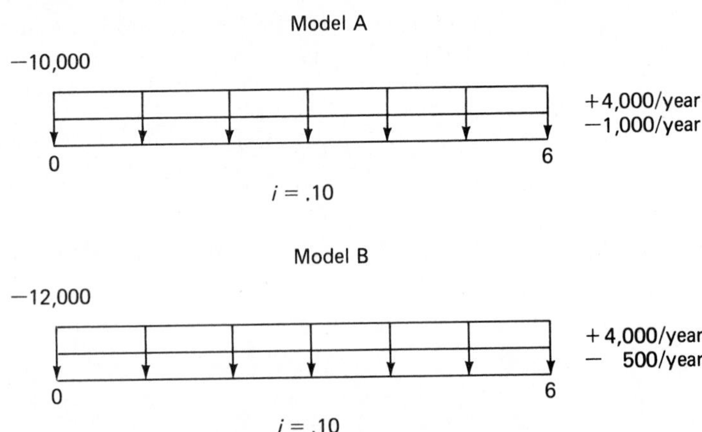

The net present value equation for A would be:

$$
\begin{aligned}
NPV(\text{A}) &= \text{Sum for each of six years (revenue} - \text{expense)(factor)} - I \\
&= (4{,}000 - 1{,}000)(\text{given } R \text{ to find } P) - I \\
&= (4{,}000 - 1{,}000)PWF(u)^{6}_{.10} - 10{,}000 \\
&= 3{,}000(4.355) - 10{,}000 \\
&= 13{,}065 - 10{,}000 \\
NPV(\text{A}) &= +\$3{,}065
\end{aligned}
$$

Similarly, the net present value for B would be:

$$
\begin{aligned}
NPV(\text{B}) &= (4{,}000 - 500)\ (\text{given } R \text{ to find } P) - 12{,}000 \\
&= 3{,}500\ PWF(u)^{6}_{.10} - 12{,}000
\end{aligned}
$$

$$= 3{,}500\ (4.355) - 12{,}000$$
$$= 15{,}242 - 12{,}000$$
$$= +\$3{,}242$$

Choose alternative B over A because \$3,242 >\$3,065.

As you might have figured out, another method of solution could also be used. With this method, use separate present worth factors for each of the six periods and sum the six amounts and the initial investment at the current time, time zero. The answers should be equivalent or nearly so using the rounded table factors with those we calculated above for alternatives *A* and *B*. Let's look at a more complex example.

EXAMPLE Hopi Trucking has just paid \$16,000 cash for a new truck. Hopi management estimates that the useful life of the truck is four years. At the end of four years, the estimated salvage value will be \$2,500. Maintenance and other operating costs are expected to be \$10,000/year for three years and \$12,000 in the fourth year. Assuming we can replace the truck in four years for the same price, how much money must be generated each year from this investment to have at least enough to purchase another truck in four years? Money is worth 8 percent to Hopi, and revenues flow in uniformly to the firm.

First, we must recognize that we are being asked for a dollar amount four years hence, not at the present time. Second we should realize that the \$16,000 truck we now have is a sunk cost. Since we are not considering depreciation and taxes, they will not influence our decision. Let *X* be the dollars of revenue required each year to cover expenses and provide \$16,000 at the end of four years. Our problem then is as follows:

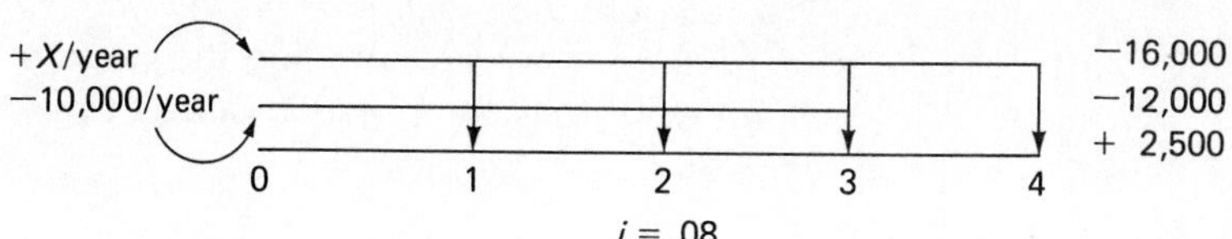

We have −\$10,000 per year occurring for three years and, at the end of the fourth year, −\$12,000 for expenses. We also have \$16,000 for a new truck and +\$2,500 for salvaging our old truck. The cash inflow we are looking for is *X* per year for four years. This can be expressed *at year four:*

$$NPV = -10{,}000\ \underset{\substack{n\,=\,3\\ i\,=\,.08}}{(R \text{ to find } P)}\ \underset{\substack{n\,=\,4\\ i\,=\,.08}}{(P \text{ to find } S)}$$
$$+X\underset{\substack{n\,=\,4\\ i\,=\,.08}}{(R \text{ to find } S)} - 16{,}000 - 12{,}000$$
$$+2{,}500$$

$$
\begin{aligned}
&= -10{,}000[PWF(u)_{.08}^{3}][CAF(s)_{.08}^{4}] \\
&\quad + X[CAF(u)_{.08}^{4}] - 25{,}500 \\
&= -10{,}000\ (2.577)(1.360) + 4.506\ X - 25{,}500 \\
&= 4.506\ X - (35{,}047 + 25{,}500) \\
NPV &= 4.506\ X - 60{,}547
\end{aligned}
$$

Setting $NPV = 0$ (the breakeven for sales and expenses at four years) and solving for X gives:

$$
\begin{aligned}
0 &= 4.506X - 60{,}547 \\
X &= 60{,}547/4.506 \\
X &= \$13{,}437
\end{aligned}
$$

Annual sales revenue will have to be \$13,437 to cover expenses and provide \$16,000 cash at the end of four years.

What should we do if the investment alternatives have *unequal lives?* Clearly, we can't compare them directly. Let's assume that like-for-like replacement can occur at the end of the life of each asset and use the least common multiple of lives over which to compare the investment. If one alternative has a three-year life and one a two-year life, we would make the comparison over six years.

At times, organizations want investments to meet a minimum rate of return. If the net present value at that rate of return is positive, the investment provides greater returns than would the rate used in determining the present value. The investment is made. On the other hand, if the present value is negative, the return is less than that provided by the interest rate used, and the investment is unattractive.

Internal Rate of Return Suppose you have identified the inflows and outflows of an alternative and wish to determine the rate of return it offers. *The internal rate of return is the discount rate i at which net cash flows for the alternative equal zero.* Finding the value of *i* for which the present value of outflows equals the present value of inflows is determined by process of trial and error.

REVIEW AND DISCUSSION QUESTIONS

1. Define the following:
   (a) Opportunity costs
   (b) Sunk costs
   (c) Salvage value
   (d) Depreciation
2. Define accounting life, machine life, and economic life of an asset.
3. Compare the major features of payback, net present value, and internal rate of return methods of evaluation.

PROBLEMS

Reinforcing Fundamentals

1. What is the present value of $1,000 to be invested for seven years at 8 percent interest? At 10 percent interest?
2. What is the present value of a 15-year series of $800 investments if the interest rate is 8 percent? 10 percent?
3. A company is considering two alternative relayout designs. Alternative 1 requires an initial investment of $100,000, will result in $20,000 in annual cost savings for the next ten years, and is expected to have equipment salvage value of $20,000 at the end of ten years. Alternative 2 requires an $80,000 initial investment, will result in $16,000 annual cost savings, and will have no salvage value after ten years. The interest rate is 10 percent.
   (a) Which alternative is best using the payback criterion?
   (b) Which alternative is best using the net present value criterion?
4. An investment alternative requires an initial outlay of $71,500, is expected to have a five-year useful life, and will have a salvage value of $10,600 after five years. Annual incremental revenues will be $20,500, and annual increment operating expenses will be $7,200 during the useful life. What is the internal rate of return for this alternative?
5. A hospital is evaluating two machines to purchase to use in the analysis of blood samples. One unit is more expensive than the other, but because of its high degree of automation it has a lower labor cost. Both machines meet the hospital's needs and are essentially worthless at the end of their economic life. Money is worth 10 percent.

	Unit 1	Unit 2
Purchase cost	$15,000	$22,000
Economic life	3 years	3 years
Labor costs per year	$14,000	$ 9,000
Installation cost	$ 4,000	$ 5,000
Maintenance costs		
First year	$ 500	$ 1,000
Increase per year	$ 100	$ 500
Book value		
End of first year	$15,000	$20,000
End of third year	$ 3,000	$ 3,000

   (a) Using *present worth,* which unit should the hospital purchase?
   (b) Explain to the pathologist (an MD) in charge of the lab how the *present worth* approach can provide useful data for capital budgeting purposes.

Challenging Exercises

6. As purchasing agent for Kansas City Industries, you have the following two equipment replacement alternatives:

	Alternative 1	Alternative 2
Machine life (years)	2	3
Economic life (years)	1	2
Initial investment	Negotiable	$20,000
Annual maintenance cost	-0-	$ 1,000
Salvage value end of machine life	$1,000	$ 2,000
Salvage value end of economic life	$4,000	$ 5,000
Value of money	10%	10%

Your problem is to find the upper bound (or maximum amount) of the initial investment you are willing to negotiate in alternative 1 (i.e., any amount greater than the upper bound would make alternative 2 the most economical). Use present worth to determine the upper bound.

7. The vice president of operations for a telephone company has decided to replace a central dispatching office. In one of the design details, two alternatives are proposed. The more costly of the two alternatives will require an additional investment (over and above the other alternative) of $35,000 in construction costs. However, under this alternative it will be easier to bring in additional cables, since service expansion is required later. The estimated savings are $6,000/year for the fifth to ninth year. What must the minimum savings be from the tenth to twentieth years in order to make the additional investment attractive, if the rate of interest is 10 percent and the estimated life of the structure is 20 years? No savings are expected for the first 4 years.

GLOSSARY

Accounting life Length of an asset's life determined for the purpose of developing a depreciation schedule.

Economic life Useful life of an asset.

Internal rate of return Interest rate at which the present value of inflows equals the present value of outflows.

Machine life Length of time an asset (machine) is capable of functioning.

Net present value Technique of discounting all cash flows of an investment back to their present values and netting out the inflows against the outflows.

Opportunity costs Returns that are lost or forgone as a result of selecting one alternative over another.

Payback period Period of time required for investment net income to equal net outlays.

Present value of a future sum Future sum divided by the growth rate of funds over the relevant time period.

Salvage value Income received from sale of an asset.

Sunk costs Past expenditures that are irrelevant to current decisions.

Time value of money Concept that recognizes that a sum of money has the potential for generating returns (revenues) over time.

PART II PLANNING (DESIGNING) THE CONVERSION SYSTEM

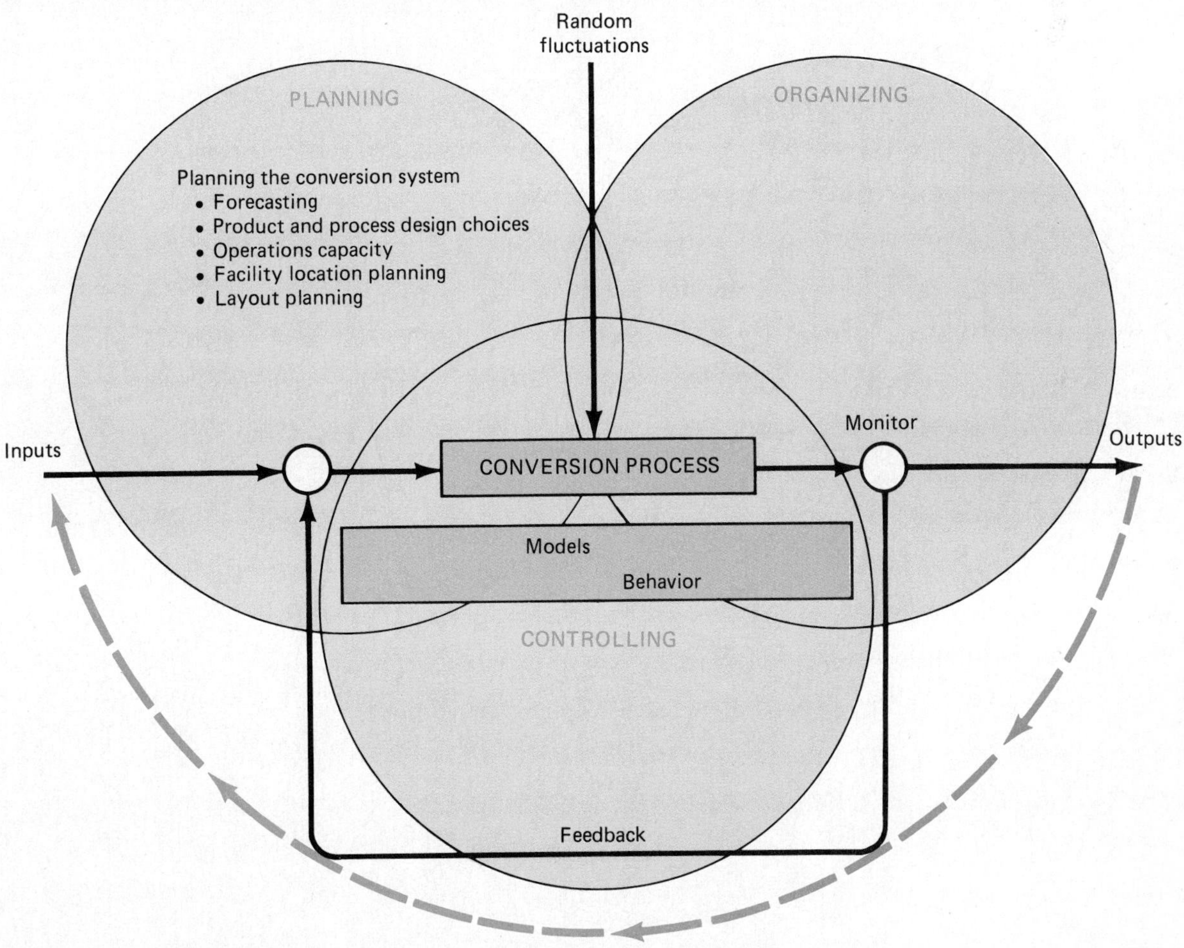

Production and operations management activities

3

Forecasting

While all elements of operations management are important, I view forecasting as one of the key critical elements in the operations structure. As you study this chapter, which provides an excellent overview of forecasting techniques and models, it will be important to recognize the different models and when to use them based upon your needs.

At Donaldson Company, Inc., we serve a multitude of customers with a wide variety of products ranging from the size of a house to the size of a filter for 3½-inch disc drives. We serve our customers through our plants in the United States and throughout the world. The needs of the market are changing for us, and we have to respond more quickly than ever before with product delivery. To do this, we have placed a higher emphasis on forecasting. As this chapter summary says, "Forecasting is the the use of past data to determine future events." At Donaldson Company, forecasting is essential to improving our competitive edge.

Richard M. Negri
Vice President and General Manager
Manufacturing Division
Donaldson Company, Inc.
Minneapolis, Minnesota

From this comment by the vice president responsible for manufacturing at Donaldson Company, Inc., we see how the company must respond quickly to market changes in order to improve its competitive edge. Mr. Negri believes that forecasting enables the company to respond more quickly and accurately than would otherwise be possible.

We know that in the management process, planning, organizing, and controlling are not independent processes; they interrelate and overlap. If operations have been properly planned and organized, control is easier and smoother. This is where forecasting comes in. It can reduce the costs of readjusting operations in response to unexpected deviations by specifying future demand. Clearly, if future demand for goods and services is accurately estimated, operating efficiency increases. Let's see how successful firms such as Donaldson might use forecasting in operations.

FORECASTING IN OPERATIONS

In a broad sense, forecasting presents an unresolved philosophical dilemma. "You can never plan the future by the past," said Edmund Burke; but Patrick Henry disagreed: "I know of no way of judging the future but by the past." In operations management, we try to forecast a wide range of future events that could potentially affect success. Most often the basic concern is with forecasting customer demand for our products or services. We may want long-run estimates of overall demand or shorter-run estimates of demand for each individual product. Even more detailed estimates are needed for specific items or subcomponents that go into each product.

We can distinguish among these different kinds of forecasting needs by considering how far into the future they focus. Detailed forecasts for individual items are used to plan the short-run use *of* the conversion system. At the other extreme, overall product demand forecasts are needed for strategies and planning capacity, location, and layout on a much longer time horizon. Different forecasting time horizons must be used to obtain information needed for various types of planning decisions, as Figure 3.1 shows.

Forecasting Defined

In business, economic, and political communities *forecasting* has various meanings. In operations management, we adopt a rather specific definition of *forecasting,* and we distinguish it from the broader concept of *prediction.*

> Forecasting is a process of estimating a future event by casting forward past data. The past data are systematically combined in a predetermined way to obtain the estimate of the future.
>
> Prediction is a process of estimating a future event based on subjective considerations other than just past data; these subjective considerations need not be combined in a predetermined way.[1]

As these definitions make clear, forecasts can only be made when a history of past data exists. An established TV manufacturer, for example,

[1]R. G. Brown, *Smoothing Forecasting and Prediction of Direct Time Series* (Englewood Cliffs, N.J.: Prentice Hall, 1963), p. 2.

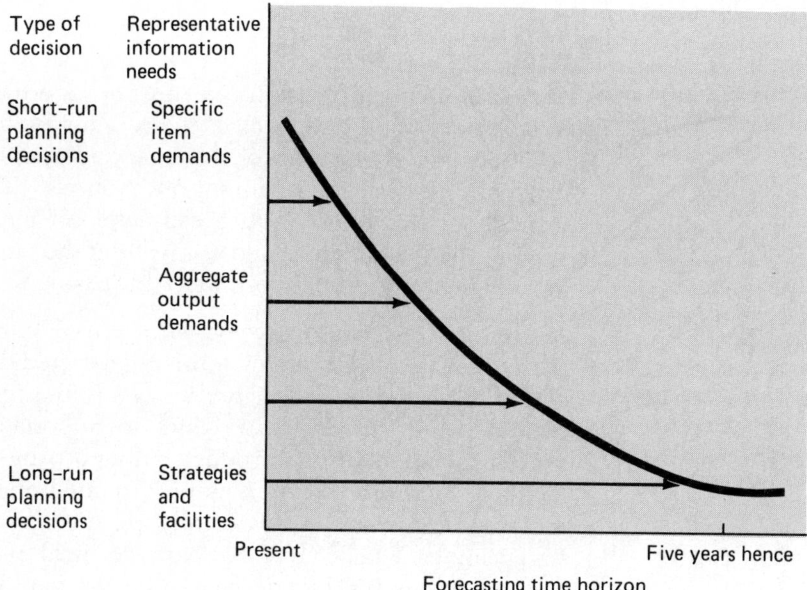

FIGURE 3.1
Forecasting requirements in production/operations

can use past data to forecast the number of coasters required for next week's TV assembly schedule. A fast-food restaurant can use past data to forecast the number of hamburger buns required for this weekend's operations. But suppose the manufacturer offers a new TV model or the restaurant decides to offer a new food service. Since no past data exist to estimate first year sales of the new products, prediction, not forecasting, is required. For predicting, good subjective estimates can be based on the manager's skill, experience, and judgment; but forecasting requires statistical and management science techniques.

In business in general, when people speak of forecasts, they usually mean some combination of both forecasting and prediction. Commonly, forecasting is substituted freely for *economic forecasting,* which implies some combination of objective calculations and subjective judgments. We caution students and operations managers to avoid misunderstandings by clarifying what they mean by "forecasting" when they are discussing perceived problems, solution methods, and subsequent actions based on forecasts.

Forecasting and Operations Subsystems

The aggregate demand forecast is normally obtained by estimating expected volumes of sales, expressed in dollars, and then converting these estimates from sales dollars into homogeneous production units. Production units, such items as the number of televisions in a plant, number of patients fed in a hospital, number of books circulated in a library, or number of lots of common stock sold in a brokerage house, can then be subdivided into component parts and converted into estimates of direct labor hours or material requirements. The resulting product forecasts are used as a basis for planning and controlling production subsystems, as shown in Figure 3.2.

In studying forecasting, we must be careful not to immerse ourselves in techniques and lose track of the reasons for forecasting. Forecasting is an important component of strategic and operational planning. It establishes the linkage for planning and control systems discussed in detail throughout this book. Future estimates are necessary for planning the system, then scheduling and controlling the system to facilitate effective and efficient output of goods and services.

Planning (Designing) the System As Figure 3.2 shows, in planning the system we need to know future aggregated demands so that processes can be designed or redesigned to create the product flows necessary to meet demand. The degree to which we automate, for example, depends a great deal upon future product demand. Automated, continuous flows facilitate high production volumes; manual or semiautomated, intermittent flows (batching) are generally more economical for smaller production volumes. The demand estimate is critical to this design decision. Once process design, product design, and equipment investment decisions have been made for an anticipated volume, we are locked into a facility of specified capacity. Thereafter wide variations between anticipated de-

FIGURE 3.2
Demand forecasting and production/operations subsystems

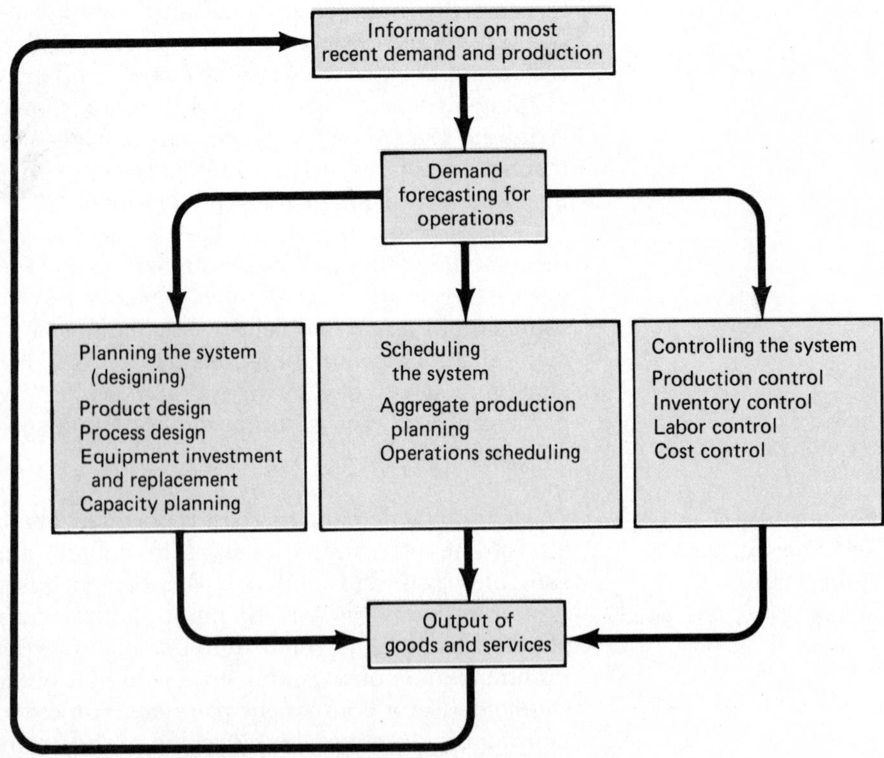

mand and actual demand can result in excessive production and operating costs.

Capacity planning, which makes use of long-run estimation, is one of the areas in production/operations that is both critical and not well understood or developed. In steel, power generation, and other basic industries, if capacity is not expanded fast enough, both individual firms and the national economy suffer. On the other hand, too much capacity is a burdensome demand. Jet aircraft, at $20 million each, cannot just be purchased and stocked for occasional demand, since the cost of excess capacity is considerable.

Scheduling the System For deciding how best to use the existing conversion system, accurate demand forecasts are very important. Management needs intermediate-run capacity forecasts—demand forecasts for three months, six months, and a year into the future. Both current and future work force levels and production rates must be established from these forecasts. Job scheduling in intermittent and continuous operations is more stable if future demand is accurately specified.

Controlling the System Managers need forecasts of demand for operating decisions in inventory control, production control, labor control, and overall cost control. Accurate forecasts are needed for the immediate future—hours, days, and weeks ahead. No longer acceptable is an earlier generations' assumption that "all that is produced can be sold" or that "any service that is offered will be purchased."

Characteristics of Demand Over Time

For the systematic analysis of historical data that forecasting problems require, managers commonly use a time series analysis. Analysts plot demand data on a time scale, study the plots, and often discover consistent shapes or patterns. A time series of demand might have, for example, a constant, trend, or seasonal *pattern* (Figure 3.3) or some combination of these patterns (Figure 3.4). A pattern is the general shape of the time series, the general form of its central tendency. Although some individual data points do not fall in the pattern, they tend to cluster around it. To

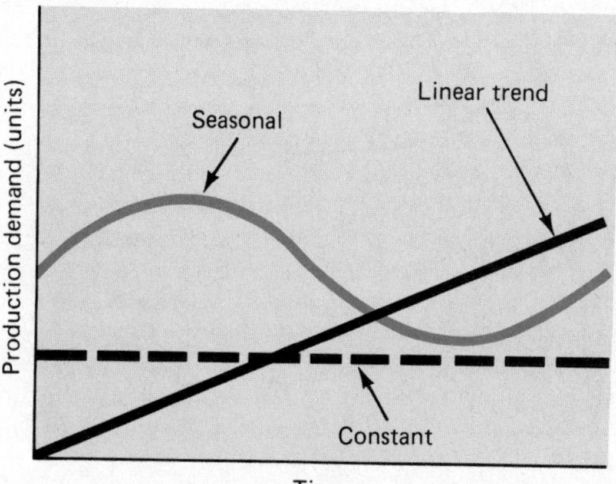

FIGURE 3.3
Demand patterns

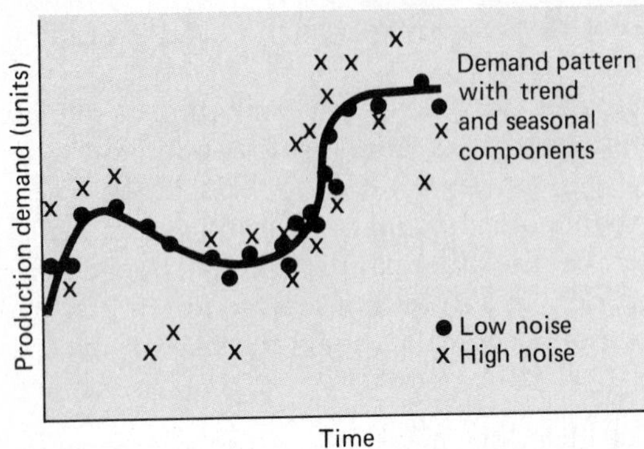

FIGURE 3.4
Noise in demand

describe the dispersion of individual demands about a pattern, we use the term *noise*. A condition of low noise exists when the points are tightly clustered around the pattern. High noise means the points are highly dispersed. Figure 3.4 shows both high and low noise levels. If you tried to envision the data in Figure 3.4 without the solid line showing the pattern, you might find it difficult to identify the general pattern. Because noise in the demand can effectively disguise the pattern, manual forecasting, and computer modeling as well, can be very difficult; the result can be high forecast errors.

Analysts use the term *stability* to describe a time series' tendency to retain the same general shape over time. The shapes of demand patterns for some products or services change over a period of time, and the shapes for others do not. Future demands are easier to forecast when the pattern is *stationary* (stable) than when it is *dynamic* (unstable). Figure 3.5, taken from a study of demand for frosted microscope slides in a large medical center, shows an example of shifting demand. Examination of the actual demand reveals noticeable upward shifts beginning at about period (week)

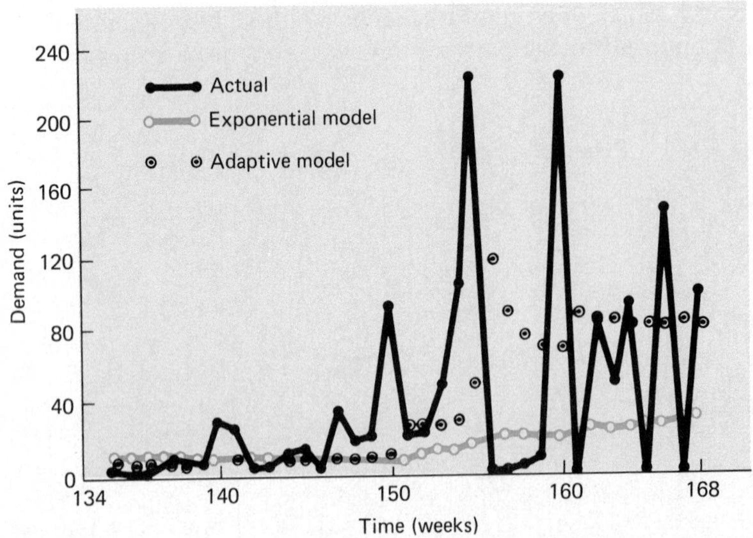

FIGURE 3.5
Frosted microscope slide demand

Source: Everett E. Adam, Jr., William L. Berry, and D. Clay Whybark, "The Hospital Administrator and Management Science," *Hospital & Health Services Administration* 19, no. 1 (Winter 1974), 38.

150. Later, these shifts become more pronounced. In the study, two forecasting models—simple exponential smoothing and adaptive exponential smoothing—were used to forecast actual demand. These models are discussed later in this chapter; here we just observe that one model, the adaptive, responds more quickly to the demand shifts than the other model.

Dependent Versus Independent Demand

Demand for a product or service is *independent* when it is unrelated to demand for any other product or service. Conversely, *dependent* demand for a product or service occurs when the demand for two or more items interrelates. The dependency may occur when one item demand is derived from a second item (vertical dependency) or when one item relates in another manner to the second item (horizontal dependency). In a movie theater, for example, demand for film postage is independent of demand for popcorn. Vertical dependency might be the relationship between popcorn and theater ticket (patron) demand. Horizontal dependency might be the relationship between popcorn demand and popcorn box demand.

When dependent demand exists in operations management, only the parent item need be forecast; all dependent items can be related to that forecast. If items are independent, there needs to be a forecast for each item. Our discussion in Chapter 14 on material requirements planning (MRP) will further develop this concept.

Forecast Error

Later, when we evaluate different forecasting methods, we'll need a measure of effectiveness. Forecast error is the scorekeeping mechanism most commonly used. *Forecast error is the numeric difference between forecasted and actual demand.* Obviously, a method that results in large forecast errors is less desirable than one yielding fewer errors.

MAD Equation 3.1 defines a most important error measure, mean absolute deviation (MAD):

$$\text{MAD} = \frac{\text{Sum of absolute deviations for all periods}}{\text{Total number of periods evaluated}} \qquad (3.1)$$

$$= \frac{\sum_{i=1}^{n} |\text{Forecasted demand—Actual demand}|_i}{n}$$

In each period *(i)*, you compare the actual demand to the amount you forecasted. If your forecast was perfect, actual equals the forecasted amount, and there is zero error. As forecasting continues, the degree of error is accumulated and recorded, period by period. After any number of periods *(n)* has elapsed, you may use equation 3.1 to calculate the average (mean) size of the forecasting error to date. Notice that MAD is an average of several *absolute deviations;* errors are measured without regard to sign. MAD expresses the extent but *not the direction* of error.

There is a relationship between mean absolute deviation and the classical measure of dispersion for forecast error, the standard deviation (σ_e). If the forecast is working properly, forecast errors are normally distributed. When this is so, the *smoothed mean absolute deviation* (SMAD) is used to estimate the standard deviation. The relationship is

$$\sigma_e \cong 1.25 \text{ SMAD}$$

Exponential smoothing will be explained later in this chapter; for now you may think of exponentially smoothed MAD as an average MAD over time.

Bias Equation 3.2 is a less commonly used error measure called *Bias*:

$$\text{Bias} = \frac{\text{Sum of algebraic errors for all periods}}{\text{Total number of periods evaluated}} \tag{3.2}$$

$$= \frac{\sum_{i=1}^{n} (\text{Forecasted demand—Actual demand})_i}{n}$$

Unlike MAD, *Bias* indicates the *directional* tendency of forecast errors. If the forecasting procedure repeatedly overestimates actual demand, Bias will have a positive value; consistent underestimation tendencies will be indicated by a negative value.

EXAMPLE An aluminum extruder estimates demand for a shower stall extrusion to be 500/month for each of three future months. Later the actual demands turned out to be 400, 560, and 700. His forecast errors, MAD and Bias, are calculated here.

$$MAD = \frac{|500 - 400| + |500 - 560| + |500 - 700|}{3}$$

$$= \frac{100 + 60 + 200}{3}$$

$$= 120 \text{ units}$$

$$Bias = \frac{(500 - 400) + (500 - 560) + (500 - 700)}{3}$$

$$= \frac{100 - 60 - 200}{3}$$

$$= -\ 53 \text{ units}$$

As you can see, MAD is 120 units, and bias is −53 units. Since MAD measures the overall accuracy of the forecasting method, we would conclude that this aluminum extruder does not have a very accurate model. He has a high average absolute error, 24 percent of the forecasted number of shower stall extrusions. Bias measures the *tendency consistently to over- or underforecast.* In this example, the extrusion forecaster has a tendency to underestimate by 53 units; since actual demand averages 553 units, Bias is, on the average, a 9.6 percent underforecast.

An ideal forecast would have zero MAD and Bias. We find in practice, however, that there is usually a tradeoff between MAD and Bias; in some situations, one must be held low at the expense of the other. If you must stress one at the expense of the other, perhaps MAD should be the focus. Lowering MAD to or near zero will automatically hold Bias low also.

Costs of Errors How important is forecast accuracy? It depends on the situation. Often important decisions are based on forecasted information, and large errors can result in very costly mistakes. Some kinds of estimation errors are more costly than others. In some settings the *direction* of error is critical; in other cases the *magnitude* of error is most important. Although the exact costs of errors are often difficult to determine, forecast errors can and should be converted into costs, even though such a conversion may have to be approximated intuitively. We now are finding studies directed at investigating the impact of forecast error on production-inventory cost. Materials requirements planning (MRP)-based, production-inventory system studies illustrate how forecast error reduction can result in lower overall manufacturing costs.[2]

Forecasting in the Service Sector

Traditional production applications are beginning to appear in service sector operations. The Production/Operations Management (P/OM) Division of the Academy of Management commissioned a study of service sector operations where a questionnaire was distributed to 251 P/OM Division members, primarily to management professors.[3] Responses indicated that of all the traditional P/OM techniques, forecasting is the most frequently applied technique in the service sector. It ranked ahead of the other important techniques—systems theory and modeling, job design and work measurement, inventory models, and human behavior models. These results, paired with increased economic activity in the service sector, suggest that the importance of forecasting will continue to increase in the future.

Intuitive or Formal Approaches?

In the practice of operations management today, two fundamental approaches to forecasting are dominant—intuitive estimates of the future and formal statistical modeling. The *intuitive approach,* which is based on experience, is essentially a summary of a manager's guesses, hunches, and judgments concerning future events. This approach is as much prediction as it is forecasting. The *statistical modeling approach* systematically combines specific numerical data into a summary value that is then used as a forecast. Within the statistical approach are two basic types of models, which are distinguished by the type of data they use. *Demand-based* models

---

[2]Joseph R. Biggs and William M. Campion, "The Effect and Cost of Forecast Error Bias for Multi-Stage Production-Inventory Systems," *Decision Sciences* 13, no. 4 (October 1982), 570–84; T. S. Lee and Everett E. Adam, Jr., "Forecasting Error Evaluation in Material Requirements Planning (MRP) Production-Inventory Systems," *Management Science* 32, no. 9 (September 1986), 1186–1205.

[3]Everett E. Adam, Jr. et al., "P/OM Service Sector Study Group Report" (Paper presented at the Academy of Management Conference, New Orleans, August 1975).

rely solely on historical data about the item that is being forecasted. If we desire a forecast of monthly demand data for a lounge chair, for example, our model requires historic monthly demand data for lounge chairs. *Causal* models, on the other hand, may use additional types of data as well. These models might formally relate lounge chair demand to other variables believed to influence demand, such as the number of new housing starts.

Costs and Accuracy There is clearly a cost/accuracy tradeoff in selecting a forecasting approach. The more sophisticated approaches tend to have relatively high costs of implementation and maintanance, but they often provide more accurate forecasts with resulting lower operating costs. Figure 3.6 illustrates one hypothetical cost situation. Note that for any forecasting situation there is an optimal cost region where reasonable accuracy is obtained. Our goal in forecasting for operations is to operate somewhere in this optimal region.

FIGURE 3.6
Cost/accuracy tradeoffs in forecasting

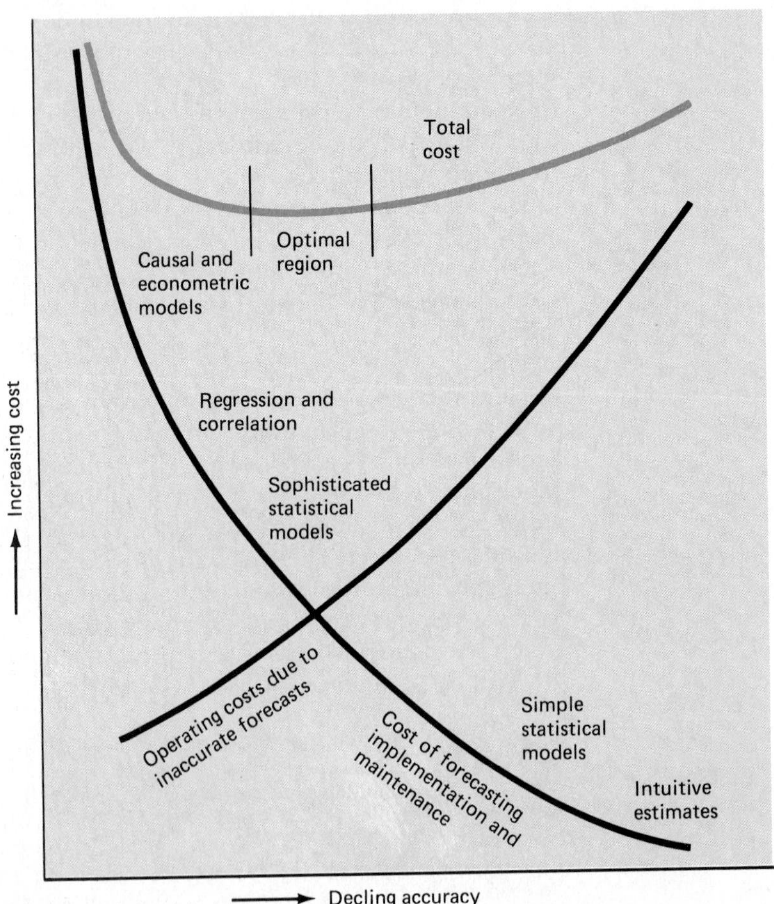

Table 3.1 Representative forecasting techniques summarized

Model Type	Description
Qualitative Models	
Delphi method	Questions panel of experts for opinions
Historical data	Makes analogies to the past in a judgmental manner
Nominal group technique	Group process allowing participation with forced voting
Naive (Time Series) *Quantitative Models*	
Simple moving average	Averages past data to predict the future based on that average
Exponential smoothing	Weights old forecasts and most recent demand
Causal Quantitative Models	
Regression analysis	Depicts a functional relationship among variables
Economic modeling	Provides an overall forecast for a variable such as gross national product (GNP)

An Overview of Specific Forecasting Methods

We have emphasized that forecasting is a critical part of strategic and operational planning. Rather than get too deeply into specifying types of forecasts for varying situations, we shall summarize: The less analytical, qualitative forecasting methods are frequently used for longer-range strategic planning and facilities decisions; the more analytical, time series analysis models are frequently used for operational planning, such as in production and inventory control. Causal forecasting techniques, which are used for a variety of planning situations, are especially helpful in intermediate-term aggregate planning. Let's now look more closely at some of these techniques.

Table 3.1 summarizes modern forecasting techniques. The techniques have been grouped into qualitative methods, naive (time series) analysis, and causal models. The most frequently used techniques for operations management situations are the qualitative and naive (time series) models. The causal models are often more costly to implement and do not offer increased accuracy for short-term item forecasting problems typically faced by the production/operations manager. Even though the qualitative techniques are very popular, they have definite accuracy limitations. We'll limit ourselves to a brief discussion of two qualitative methods and then proceed to some useful naive (time-series) models.

Qualitative Techniques

Delphi The *Delphi technique* is a group process intended to achieve a consensus forecast, often a technological forecast. The process asks a panel of experts from either within or without the organization to provide written comments on the point in question.

The procedure works as follows:

1. A question, the situation needing a forecast, is provided in writing to each expert in a general form. Each expert makes a brief prediction.
2. The coordinator who provides the original question brings the statements together, clarifies them, and edits them.

3. The summaries of the experts provide the basis for a set of questions the coordinator now gives to the experts. These are answered.
4. The written responses are brought together by the coordinator, and the process is repeated until the coordinator is satisfied with the overall prediction that can be synthesized from the experts.

The key to the Delphi technique lies in the personnel involved. The panel members frequently have diverse backgrounds: Two physicists, a chemist, an electrical engineer, and an economist might make up a panel. The coordinator must be talented enough to synthesize diverse and wide-ranging statements and arrive at both a structured set of questions and a forecast.

An advantage of this method is that since direct interpersonal relations are avoided, there are no personality conflicts or dominance by one strong-willed member of the group. The Delphi method has worked successfully for those involved with technological forecasting, for example, to forecast solar electric energy market penetration by the year 2000.[4]

EXAMPLE During the 1970s at American Hoist and Derrick Company, management felt a need for incorporating its judgments into sales forecasting. Starting with 1975 sales forecasts, management wanted to increase forecasting accuracy to determine just how fast production capacity should be expanded. The Delphi technique was selected to temper historical data with informed judgment. Three rounds of questionnaires were necessary to synthesize judgments of 23 key corporate individuals. Previous forecast errors ranged between ± 20 percent. In 1975 the Delphi forecast was $359.1 million and actual sales $360.2 million, an error of +0.3 percent. The 1976 forecast was $410 million and actual sales $397 million, an error of −3.3 percent. The previous forecasting errors were reduced significantly, from 20 percent to less than 4 percent.[5]

Nominal Group Technique The basic assumption behind the nominal group technique is that a structured group of knowledgeable people will be able to arrive at a consensus forecast. The process works like this. Seven to ten people are asked to come to a meeting room and sit around a table in full view of one another, but they are asked not to speak to one another. The group facilitator hands out copies of or writes on a blackboard the question needing a forecast. Each group member is asked to write down ideas about the question. After a few minutes, the group facilitator asks each individual in turn to present to the group one idea from his or her

[4]Rakesh K. Sarin, "An Approach for Long-Term Forecasting with an Application to Solar Energy," *Management Science* 25, no. 6 (June 1979), 543–54.

[5]Shankar Basu and Roger G. Schroeder, "Incorporating Judgments in Sales Forecasts: Application of the Delphi Method at American Hoist and Derrick," *Interfaces* 7, no. 3 (May 1977), 18–27.

list. A recorder writes each idea on a flip chart so that everyone can see it. No discussion takes place in this phase of the meeting; members continue to give their ideas in a round robin manner until all the ideas have been written on the flip chart.

Usually somewhere between 15 and 25 propositional statements result from the round robin, depending upon the question and group composition. During the next phase of the meeting, the members of the group discuss the ideas that have been presented. The facilitator makes sure that all the ideas are discussed; members may ask for clarification of the ideas on the chart. Often similar ideas are combined, and the total number of propositions is reduced. When all discussion has ended, members are asked to vote independently by ranking the ideas, in writing, according to priority. The group decision is the mathematically pooled outcome of the individual votes.

The objectives of the process are:

1. To assure different processes for each phase of creativity
2. To balance participation among members
3. To incorporate mathematical voting techniques in the aggregation of group judgment

The nominal group technique arrives at a forecast, which is the alternative receiving the most votes from the group. Sometimes after the group has been dismissed, several of the high-ranking forecasts can be combined into a broader consensus forecast. The keys to the nominal group process are clearly identifing the question to be addressed; allowing creativity; encouraging limited, directed discussion; and ultimately voting.

USEFUL FORECASTING MODELS FOR OPERATIONS

Basic Averaging Models

Many models use historical data to calculate an average of past demand. This average is then used as a forecast. There are several ways of calculating an average; here are a few.

Simple Average A *simple average* (SA) is an average of past data in which the demands of all previous periods are equally weighted. It is calculated as follows:

$$SA = \frac{\text{Sum of demands for all past periods}}{\text{Number of demand periods}} \tag{3.3}$$

$$SA = \frac{D_1 + D_2 + \dots + D_k}{k}$$

where

D_1 = the demand in the most recent period
D_2 = the demand that occurred two periods ago
D_k = the demand that occurred k periods ago

When simple averaging is used to create a forecast, the demands from all previous periods are equally influenced (equally weighted) in determining the average. In fact, a weighting of $1/k$ is applied to each past demand:

$$SA = \frac{D_1 + D_2 + \ . \ . \ . \ + D_k}{k} = \frac{1}{k}D_1 + \frac{1}{k}D_2 + \ . \ . \ . \ + \frac{1}{k}D_k$$

Before proceeding further, perhaps we should consider why we are averaging at all. As you may remember from our earlier discussion of "noise" in the demand data, we are trying to detect the underlying general pattern or central tendency of demand. The demand for any one period will probably be above or below the underlying pattern, and the demands for several periods will be dispersed or scattered around the underlying pattern. Therefore, if we average all past demands, the high demands that occurred in several periods will tend to be offset by the low demands in the other periods. The results will be an average that is representative of the true underlying pattern, particularly as the number of periods used in the average increases. Averaging reduces the chances of being misled by a random fluctuation occurring in any single period. Yet, if the underlying pattern changes over time, simple averaging will not detect this change.

EXAMPLE At Welds Supplies, total demand for a new welding rod has been 50, 60, and 40 dozen each of the last quarters. The average demand has been:

$$SA = \frac{D_1 + D_2 + D_3}{3}$$
$$= \frac{50 + 60 + 40}{3}$$
$$= 50$$

A forecast for all future periods could be based on this simple average and would be 50 dozen welding rods per quarter.

Simple Moving Average A *simple moving average* (MA) combines the demand data from several of the most recent periods, their average being the forecast for the next period. Once the number of past periods to be used in the calculations has been selected, it is held constant. We may use a 3-period moving average or a 20-period moving average, but once we decide, we must continue to use the same number of periods. After selecting the number of periods to be used, we weight the demands for each equally to determine the average. The average "moves" over time in that after each period elapses, the demand for the oldest period is discarded, and the demand for the newest period is added for the next calculation, overcoming the major shortcoming of the simple averaging model.

A simple n-period moving average is:

$$MA = \frac{\text{Sum of old demands for last } n \text{ periods}}{\text{Number of periods used in the moving average}} \quad (3.4)$$

$$MA = \frac{\sum_{t=1}^{n} D_t}{n} = \frac{1}{n}D_1 + \frac{1}{n}D_2 + \ldots + \frac{1}{n}D_n$$

where

$t = 1$ is the oldest period in the n-period average
$t = n$ is the most recent period

EXAMPLE Frigerware has experienced the following product demand for ice coolers the past six months:

Time	Number of Ice Coolers Demanded
January	200
February	300
March	200
April	400
May	500
June	600

The plant manager has requested that you prepare a forecast using a six-period moving average to forecast July sales. It is now July 2, and we are to begin our production run on ice coolers July 6.

$$MA = \frac{\sum_{t=1}^{6} D_t}{6} = \frac{200 + 300 + 200 + 400 + 500 + 600}{6}$$
$$= 367$$

Using a six-month moving average, July forecast is 367. Now examine the data. Perhaps a three-month moving average might be better than a six-month. If we use three months

$$MA = \frac{\sum_{t=1}^{3} D_t}{3} = \frac{400 + 500 + 600}{3}$$
$$= 500$$

If we used a one-month moving average, next month's sales is last month's actual demand, and the July forecast is 600.

We must make some recommendation to the plant manager for Frigerware. For now, let's recommend using a three-month moving average of 500 ice coolers for July, since that number looks more representative of the time series than a six-month moving average, and it is based on more data than is the case with a one-month moving average.

Weighted Moving Average Sometimes the forecaster wishes to use a moving average but does not want all n periods equally weighted. A *weighted moving average (WMA)* model is a moving average model that incorporates some weighting of old demand other than an equal weight for all past periods under consideration. The model is simply

$$WMA = \text{Each periods' demand times a weight, summed over all periods in the moving average} \quad (3.5)$$

$$WMA = \sum_{t=1}^{n} C_t D_t$$

where

$$0 \leq C_t \leq 1.0$$

$$\sum_{t=1}^{n} C_t = 1.0$$

This model allows uneven weighting of demand. If n is three periods, for example, we could weight the most recent period twice as heavily as the other periods by setting $C_1 = .25$, $C_2 = .25$, and $C_3 = .50$.

EXAMPLE For Frigerware, a forecast of demand for July using a three-period model with the most recent period's demand weighted twice as heavily as each of the previous two periods' demand is:

$$WMA = \sum_{t=1}^{3} C_t D_t = .25(400) + .25(500) + .50(600)$$

$$WMA = 525$$

An advantage of this model is that it allows you to compensate for some trend or for some seasonality by carefully fitting the coefficients, C_t. If you want to, you can weight recent months most heavily and still dampen somewhat the effects of noise by placing small weightings on older demands. Of course, the modeler or manager still has to choose the coefficients, and this choice will be critical to model success or failure.

Exponential Smoothing

Exponential smoothing models are well known and often used in operations management. The reasons for their popularity are two: They are readily available in standard computer software packages, and the models require relatively little data storage and computation, an important consideration when forecasts are needed for each of many individual items. Many computer companies have spent considerable time developing and marketing forecasting software and educating managers in how to use it. In addition, some major professional and trade associations, among them the American Production and Inventory Control Society (APICS), have introduced their members to these techniques.

Exponential smoothing is distinguishable by the special way it weights each of the past demands in calculating an average. The pattern of weights is *exponential* in form. Demand for the most recent periods is weighted most heavily; the weights placed on successively older periods decay exponentially. In other words, the weights decrease in magnitude the further back in time the data are weighted; the decrease is nonlinear (exponential).

First Order Exponential Smoothing To begin, let's examine the computational aspect of first order exponential smoothing. The equation for creating a new or updated forecast uses two pieces of information: actual demand for the most recent period and the previous (most recent) forecast. As each time period expires, a new forecast is made:

$$\text{Forecast of next period's demand} = \alpha \begin{pmatrix} \text{Most} \\ \text{recent} \\ \text{demand} \end{pmatrix} + (1 - \alpha) \begin{pmatrix} \text{Most} \\ \text{recent} \\ \text{forecast} \end{pmatrix} \quad (3.6)$$

$$F_t = \alpha\, D_{t-1} + (1 - \alpha)F_{t-1}$$

where

$$0 \le \alpha \le 1.0, \text{ and } t \text{ is the time period}$$

After time period $t - 1$ ends, you know the actual demand that occurs (D_{t-1}). At the *beginning* of period $t - 1$, you made a forecast (F_{t-1}) of the demand during $t - 1$. Therefore, at the *end* of $t - 1$, you have both pieces of information needed for calculating a forecast of demand for the upcoming time period, F_t.

Why is this model called *exponential smoothing?* An expansion of equation 3.6 shows

Since

$$F_t = \alpha\, D_{t-1} + (1 - \alpha)F_{t-1} \quad (3.7)$$

then

$$F_{t-1} = \alpha\, D_{t-2} + (1 - \alpha)F_{t-2} \quad (3.8)$$

and similarly

$$F_{t-2} = \alpha\, D_{t-3} + (1 - \alpha)F_{t-3} \quad (3.9)$$

We begin expanding by replacing F_{t-1} in equation 3.7 with its equivalent, the right side of equation 3.8.

$$F_t = \alpha\, D_{t-1} + (1 - \alpha)\,[\alpha\, D_{t-2} + (1 - \alpha)F_{t-2}] \quad (3.10)$$
$$F_t = \alpha\, D_{t-1} + \alpha(1 - \alpha)D_{t-2} + (1 - \alpha)^2F_{t-2}$$

We continue expanding by replacing F_{t-2} in equation 3.10 with its equivalent, the right side of equation 3.9:

$$F_t = \alpha\, D_{t-1} + \alpha(1 - \alpha)D_{t-2} + (1 - \alpha)^2\,[\alpha\, D_{t-3} + (1 - \alpha)F_{t-3}] \quad (3.11)$$
$$F_t = \alpha\, D_{t-1} + \alpha(1 - \alpha)D_{t-2} + \alpha(1 - \alpha)^2\, D_{t-3} + (1 - \alpha)^3\, F_{t-3}$$

Equation 3.11 can be rewritten as follows:

$$F_t = \alpha(1 - \alpha)^0 D_{t-1} + \alpha(1 - \alpha)^1 D_{t-2} + \alpha(1 - \alpha)^2 D_{t-3} + (1 - \alpha)^3 F_{t-3} \quad (3.12)$$

We have expanded equation 3.7 to obtain equation 3.12. The expansion could be continued further, but it is not necessary for illustrating our point; equation 3.12 shows the relative weight that is placed on each past period's demand in arriving at a new forecast.

Since $0 \leq \alpha \leq 1.0$, the terms $\alpha(1 - \alpha)^0$, $\alpha(1 - \alpha)^1$, $\alpha(1 - \alpha)^2$, and so forth are successively smaller in equation 3.12. More specifically, these weights decay exponentially, that is, they decrease by a constant percentage each period back into the past. The most recent demand, D_{t-1}, is given the most weight, while the older data are weighted less and less heavily. Suppose, for example, that we are using $\alpha = .2$. Then $\alpha(1 - \alpha)^0 = .2$, $\alpha(1 - \alpha)^1 = .16$, $\alpha(1 - \alpha)^2 = .128$, and so forth, and these are the relative weightings being placed on D_{t-1}, D_{t-2}, D_{t-3}, and so forth, respectively. Remember, all of this is being accomplished automatically when you use equation 3.7, the simple forecasting equation.

EXAMPLE Phoenix General Hospital has experienced irregular, and usually increasing, demand for disposable kits throughout the hospital. The demand for a disposable plastic tubing in pediatrics for the last two months has been: September, 300 units and October, 350 units. The old forecast procedure was to use last year's average monthly demand as the forecast for each month this year. Last year's monthly demand was 200 units. Using 200 units as the September forecast and a smoothing coefficient of .7 to weight recent demand most heavily, the forecast for *this* month, October, would have been (t = October):

$$\begin{aligned} F_t &= \alpha D_{t-1} + (1 - \alpha)F_{t-1} \\ &= .7(300) + (1 - .7)200 \\ &= 210 + 60 \\ &= 270 \end{aligned}$$

The forecast for November would be (t = November):

$$\begin{aligned} F_t &= \alpha D_{t-1} + (1 - \alpha)F_{t-1} \\ &= .7(350) + (1 - .7)270 \\ &= 245 + 81 \\ &= 326 \end{aligned}$$

Instead of last year's monthly demand for 200 units, November's forecast is for 326 units. The old forecasting method, the heuristic based on a simple average, provided a considerably different forecast from the exponential smoothing model.

Smoothing Coefficient Selection As with other statistical forecasting models, in exponential smoothing we have the problem of parameter selection; that is, we must fit the model to the data. To begin forecasting, some reasonable estimate for an old beginning forecast is necessary.

Likewise, a smoothing coefficient, α, must be selected. This choice is critical. As equation 3.6 shows, a high α places heavy weight on the most recent demand, and a low α weights recent demand less heavily. A high smoothing coefficient could be more appropriate for new products or items for which the underlying demand is shifting about (dynamic or unstable). An α of .7, .8, or .9 might be best for these conditions, although we question the use of exponential smoothing at all if unstable conditions are known to exist. If demand is very stable and believed to be representative of the future, the forecaster wants to select a low α value to smooth out any sudden noise that might have occurred. The forecasting procedure, then, does not overreact to the most recent demand. Under these stable conditions, an appropriate smoothing coefficient might be .1, .2, or .3. When demand is slightly unstable, smoothing coefficients of .4, .5, or .6 might provide the most accurate forecasts.

Figure 3.7 illustrates forecasting performance for two different smoothing coefficients for an unstable demand series. The exponential smoothing model with the higher α volume performs best; it adapts more quickly to the shift in demand in period 6 than did the lower α value.

Advantages Simple exponential smoothing and the other exponential smoothing models share the advantages of requiring that very few data points be stored. To update the forecast from period to period, you need only α, last period's demand, and last period's forecast. Remember, this model incorporates in the new forecast *all past demands*. The model is easy to understand and easily computerized for thousands of part numbers, supply items, or inventory items. The smoothing coefficient can be set for classes or families of items to minimize the cost of parameter selection. We have observed use of the model in both the manufacturing

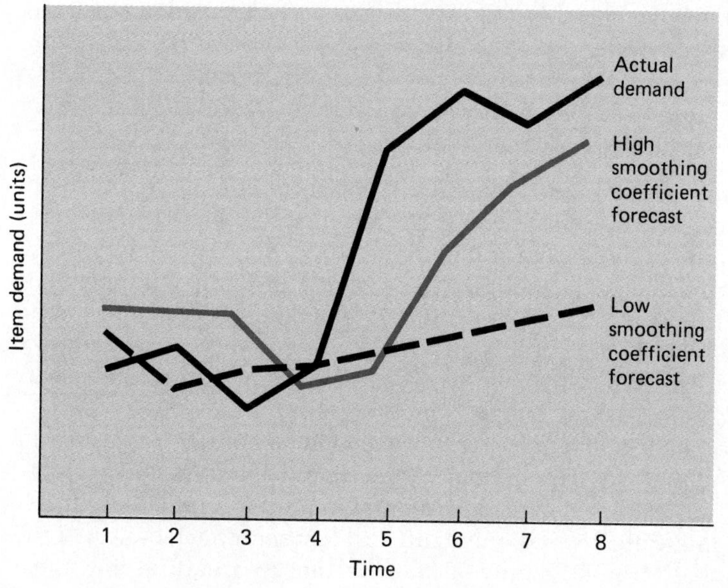

FIGURE 3.7
Selection of smoothing coefficients

and service sectors. The model's operating simplicity and efficiency for economically obtaining "quick and easy" forecasts are its main advantages.

Selecting Forecasting Parameters and Comparing Models The procedure for selecting forecasting parameters is given in the first four steps that follow; the fifth step is used for comparing and selecting models:

1. Partition the available data into two subsets, one for fitting parameters (the "test" set) and the other for forecasting.
2. Select an error measure to evaluate forecast accuracy of the parameters to be tried. MAD and/or Bias are useful error measures.
3. Select a range of α values to be evaluated. Using one of the α values, apply the forecasting model to the test set of data, recording the resulting forecast errors. Then, selecting a new value for α, repeat the process. Continue this process until representative α values in the selected range have been tested.
4. Select the α value that resulted in the lowest forecast error when applied to the test data. Your model is now fit to the demand data.
5. Forecast with the exponential (or moving average) model that you have fit to test data on the balance of the data. You can also use these data to compare alternative models that have previously been fit to representative demand data.

If you do not intend to compare models, there is no need to partition the data; *all* the data can be used as the test data in steps 1 through 4. Those familiar with computer programming can visualize how using computers can speed computations when this procedure is followed.

Adaptive Exponential Smoothing If the modeler or manager is unsure about the stability or form of the underlying demand pattern, adaptive exponential smoothing provides a good forecasting alternative. In adaptive exponential smoothing, the smoothing coefficient, α, is not fixed; it is set initially and then allowed to fluctuate over time based upon changes in the underlying demand pattern.

Incorporating Trend and Seasonal Components Exponential smoothing models, as well as moving average models, can be modified to incorporate trend and seasonal components. Above we have been forecasting the entire time series as though it had only a constant component (see Figure 3.3). If there is a trend, we could exponentially forecast the trend component. Similarly, we could exponentially forecast a seasonal component, should one exist. Then we would build a composite forecast by putting the constant, trend, and seasonal together.

For example, a constant forecast of 1,050 units could be adjusted for a positive trend that was exponentially forecast to be 100 units. This total, when added as next period's forecast (1,150 units), could be further adjusted by a multiplicative exponentially forecast seasonal factor. Assume that the seasonal forecast is only 90 percent due to a natural downturn (seasonality). The resulting composite forecast is 1,035 units (90 percent of 1,150). Formulas are readily available for models such as this exponential smoothing model with additive trend and multiplicative seasonal factors.

Double Exponential Smoothing Double exponential smoothing tends to smooth out noise in stable demand series. We are aware of one large pharmaceutical manufacturer who uses this model to forecast item demand for the thousands of drugs produced.

The model is straightforward; it smooths the first order exponential smoothing forecast and the old double exponential smoothing forecast.

$$\text{Forecast next period} = (\alpha)\begin{array}{l}\text{First order}\\ \text{exponential}\\ \text{smoothing}\\ \text{forecast next}\\ \text{period}\end{array} + (1-\alpha)\begin{array}{l}\text{Most recent}\\ \text{double}\\ \text{exponential}\\ \text{smoothing}\\ \text{forecast}\end{array} \qquad (3.13)$$

$$FD_t = \alpha F_t + (1 - \alpha)FD_{t-1}$$

where

$$0 \leq \alpha \leq 1.0$$

Notice that F_t is the first order exponential smoothing model set forth as equation 3.6 and must be calculated *before* FD_t can be found.

EXAMPLE

Milo, Inc., has a first order exponential smoothing model that has provided a forecast of 103,500 bushels for #3 grade wheat in Boone County in July. Last year's June production of #3 grade wheat was 70,500 bushels. We will use that figure as an estimate of the most recent double exponential smoothing forecast. Given that $\alpha = .20$ appears to be a good smoothing coefficient for Milo, Inc., calculate a double exponential smoothed forecast for July.

Let t = July

Then,

$$\begin{aligned} FD_t &= \alpha F_t + (1 - \alpha)FD_{t-1} \\ &= .2\ (103{,}500) + (1 - .2)(70{,}500) \\ &= 20{,}700 + 56{,}400 \\ &= 77{,}100 \end{aligned}$$

Our forecast for July is 77,100 bushels.

Regression

Linear Regression *Regression analysis* is a forecasting technique that establishes a relationship between variables. One variable is known and used to forecast the value of an unknown random variable. From past data a functional relationship is established between the two variables. We consider the most simple regression situation here, for only two variables and for a linear functional relationship between them.

Our forecast of next period's demand, F_t, is expressed by

$$F_t = a + bX_t \qquad (3.14)$$

where F_t is the forecast for period t, given the value of the variable X in period t. The coefficients a and b are constants; a is the intercept value for the verticle (F) axis and b is the slope of the line. Often this equation is expressed in the more familiar form

$$Y = a + bX \qquad (3.15)$$

We have substituted F for Y, to indicate F is the forecasted value. In equation 3.14, forecasted demand, F_t, reflects the future. However, to actually find coefficients a and b, old demand is utilized rather than the old forecast. We use D_t to reflect old demand and to find coefficients a and b. Then, once we want to forecast new demand, we use F_t to represent forecasted demand. The coefficients a and b are computed by the following two equations:

$$b = \frac{n\,(\Sigma X_t D_t) - (\Sigma X_t)\,(\Sigma D_t)}{n\,(\Sigma X_t^2) - (\Sigma X_t)^2} \qquad (3.16)$$

$$a = \frac{\Sigma D_t - b\Sigma X_t}{n} \qquad (3.17)$$

where

$$D = a + bX \qquad (3.18)$$

EXAMPLE A paper box company makes carryout pizza boxes. The operations planning department knows that an accurate forecast of pizza boxes for a major customer depends upon the customer's advertising expenditures, which they can receive in advance of the expenditure. Operations planning is interested in establishing the relationship between the pizza company's advertising and sales. Once that is established, the pizza boxes ordered, in dollar volume, is known to be a fixed percent of sales.

Quarterly advertising and sales

Quarter	Advertising ($100,000)	Sales ($ million)
1	4	1
2	10	4
3	15	5
4	12	4
5	8	3
6	16	4
7	5	2
8	7	1
9	9	4
10	10	2

Computing b and then a, where advertising is X_t for quarter t, sales is D_t for quarter t, and forecast is F_t for future period t.

Quarter	X Advertising	D Sales	X^2	D^2	XD
1	4	1	16	1	4
2	10	4	100	16	40
3	15	5	225	25	75
4	12	4	144	16	48
5	8	3	64	9	24
6	16	4	256	16	64
7	5	2	25	4	10
8	7	1	49	1	7
9	9	4	81	16	36
10	10	2	100	4	20
Σ	96	30	1060	108	328

$$b = \frac{10(328) - (96)30}{10(1060) - (96)^2} = .29$$

$$a = \frac{30 - .29(96)}{10} = .22$$

Thus, the estimated regression line, the relationship between future sales (F_t) and advertising (X_t) is

$$F_t = .22 + .29\ X_t$$

In the example above, the operations planner can now ask for planned advertising expenditures, and from that sales can be forecast. Say, for example, next quarter advertising is expected to be \$1,100,000. Substituting 11 for X_t into the equation above gives

$$F_t = .22 + .29(11) = 3.41$$

Sales are forecast as \$3,410,000. If box orders are 5 percent of sales, the operations planner could expect the total dollar orders to be \$170,500 for the quarter (.05 × \$3,410,000). Such an estimate can be very helpful in overall operations planning.

Although linear regression methods are computationally more complex than the others we've discussed, they have been found useful in some situations. They may be applied, for example, when a plot of the data suggests that the underlying pattern is a straight line, or nearly so. When data are linear and stable, linear regression can sometimes be used. It requires much data, however, and they can be cumbersome and costly to store. It's also costly to perform the required calculations period by period, often weekly, for thousands of production or operations supply items.

SELECTION OF THE FORECASTING MODEL

We've discussed several statistical forecasting models for demand estimation in planning and control. As a manager, you now have the task of selecting the best model for your needs. Which one should you choose, and what criteria should you use to make the decision?

As we've said before, criteria that influence model selection are *cost* and *accuracy*. Accuracy (forecast error), as measured by MAD and Bias, can be converted into cost (dollars). *Costs to be considered in model selection are implementation costs, systemic costs, and forecast error costs.* Of the three, forecast error costs are perhaps the most complex to evaluate. They depend upon the noise in the time series, form of the demand pattern, length of the forecasting time horizon, and measure of forecast error. There is no substitute for careful analysis of typical item demands, including plots, when a model is being selected.

Several studies have evaluated and compared the performance of different models. In general, different models are best, depending on the type of demand pattern, noise level, and length of forecast period. It is typical in forecasting to have a choice of several good models for any one demand pattern when the choice is based only on forecast error. Double exponential smoothing is the best model in many studies.

Combining Naive Forecasting Models

In comprehensive studies it has been found that simple average and weighted average of forecasts from different forecasting methods outperformed most or perhaps even all of the individual methods.[6] From these studies we can conclude that the forecasting accuracy improves, and that the variability of accuracy among different combinations decreases, as the number of methods in the average increases. Combining forecasting models holds considerable promise for operations. As Makridakis and Winkler state, "Combining forecasts seem to be a reasonable practical alternative when, as is often the case, a true model of the data generating process or a single best forecasting method cannot or is not, for whatever reasons, identified."[7]

---

[6]Spyros Makridakis, et al., "The Accuracy of Extrapolation (Time Series) Methods: Results of a Forecasting Competition," *Journal of Forecasting* 1 (1982), 111–153; Spyros Makridakis and Robert L. Winkler, "Averages of Forecasts: Some Empirical Results," *Management Science* 29, no. 9 (September 1983), 987–996; Spyros Makridakis, "The Art and Science of Forecasting: An Assessment and Future Directions," *International Journal of Forecasting* 2 (1986), 15–39; Michael J. Lawrence, et al., "The Accuracy of Combining Judgmental and Statistical Forecasts," *Management Science* 32 (1986), 1521–32; and Thomas D. Russell and Everett E. Adam, Jr., "An Empirical Evaluation of Alternative Forecasting Combinations," *Management Science* 33 (1987), 1267–76.

[7]Makridakis and Winkler, "Averages of Forecasts," p. 987.

BEHAVIORAL DIMENSIONS OF FORECASTING

To understand some of the dimensions of forecasting you have to consider human behaviors, because forecasts are not always made with statistical models. Individuals can and do forecast by intuitively casting forth past data, and they often intervene in other ways in the statistical forecasting procedure as well. A manager may feel that item forecasts generated by models must be checked for reasonableness by qualified operating decision makers. Forecasts generated by models should not be followed blindly; potential cost consequences must be carefully considered. When intervening, decision makers can take into account qualitative data that are not in the model. Decision makers should use the forecasting model as an *aid* in decision making; they should not rely totally on the forecasting model for all decisions.

Individual Versus Model Forecasting

Many, perhaps most, forecasts for production/operations are individual intuitive forecasts. We have observed intuitive forecasts, for example, in large firebrick manufacturing facilities and in hospitals. One of the problems for implementing item forecasting models lies in convincing the intuitive forecaster that he or she is not doing as good a job as could be done by a model.

Intuitive Forecasting as a Judgmental Process

Currently, little is known about the relative effectiveness of intuitive forecasting. We can, however, provide a structured approach for examining this area of human behavior by analyzing some of the mental processes involved. A forecast may be regarded as the culmination of a process consisting of several stages, including information search and information processing. It results in human inferences about the future that are based on particular patterns of historical data presented to the forecaster. We can speculate about a number of environmental factors that may affect these mental processes and thereby affect intuitive forecasting performance.

Meaningfulness The forecasting task itself requires the consideration of a restricted set of information cues about historical demand. When we discuss job enrichment and job design (Chapter 8), we find that if repetitious tasks can be made meaningful to the person performing them, positive effects usually result. Imparting meaningfulness, then, may be expected to affect intuitive forecasting performance; the more meaningful the forecasting task, the more accurate the intuitive forecast.

Pattern Complexity *Pattern complexity,* the shape of the demand function, is a critical variable in intuitive forecasting, just as it is in model forecasting. Some behavioral studies lead us to suggest that intuitive forecasters may perform better on linear than on nonlinear demand patterns. In addition, people apparently try to use nonlinear data in a linear manner.

Degree of Noise Given sufficient historical data, the forecasting problems are trivial for most cases without noise. Introducing random variations, however, often brings about a condition called *cue uncertainty*. Very large noise levels obscure the basis for accurate forecasting, and often the result is lower forecast accuracy.

Individual Variability Another finding in intuitive forecasting studies is the wide variability of performance among the forecasters. When comparing forecasters with models, there are typically a few very good forecasters, but there are even more very poor forecasters. If planning and directing production and operations are based on poor intuitive forecasts, these variations in performance can be very expensive.

Individual Versus Model Performance How do individuals compare to naive forecasting models? In studies, exponential smoothing models, when fit to the historical demands given to intuitive forecasters, significantly outperformed group average performance. Only a very few good intuitive forecasters outperformed the models. The operations manager would be wise to consider models as an alternative to individuals. Models generally are more accurate, and if a large number of items must be forecast, the models are more economical.

Forecasting, Planning, and Behavior An excellent literature review and evaluation compares many modeling and psychological dimensions of forecasting, planning, and decision making.[8] Many information processing limitations and biases involving human judgment apply to forecasting and planning as well. Errors found to exist in forecasting procedures include accumulation of redundant information, failure to seek possible disconfirming evidence, and overconfidence in judgment. In addition, insufficient attention has been given to the implications of numerous studies that show that the predictive judgment of humans is frequently less reliable than that of simple quantitative models. Those interested in the behavioral aspects of forecasting or the forecasting and planning interactions will want to examine this comparative analysis more closely.

SUMMARY

This chapter illustrated that in operations management, we deviate from the general business concept of business forecasting and define forecasting as the use of past data to determine future events. Prediction, on the other hand, refers to subjective estimates of the future. The skill, experience, and sound judgment of a manager are required for good predictions; often statistical and management science techniques must be used to make reasonable forecasts.

[8]Robin M. Hogarth and Spyros Makridakis, "Forecasting and Planning: An Evaluation," *Management Science* 27, no. 2 (February 1981), 115–38.

We saw that there is a cost/accuracy tradeoff in selecting a forecasting approach. Generally, the less expensive the forecasting procedure, the less accurate the results. We discussed three basic groupings of forecasting techniques: qualitative models, naive (time series) analyses, and causal models. The individual item forecasting situation most frequently encountered in production/operations is best approached with naive (time series) models.

Research results illustrated that the best forecasting model to use depends upon the forecast time horizon; noise; the measure of forecast error; and, most important, the demand pattern. We noted that there appears to be no one forecasting model that is best for all demand patterns, although double exponential smoothing does as well as any other.

Often, forecasts are not made with statistical models; individuals can and do intuitively use past data to forecast future events. Our discussion showed, however, that generally, individual forecasting performance *decreases* with lack of meaningfulness, increased pattern complexity, and increased cue uncertainty. Nevertheless, although, generally, forecasting models tend to outperform most intuitive forecasts, there are, however, a few individuals who seem consistently to outperform the models.

CASE

Northwestern Hospital Supply, Inc.

Suzi Trotter was hired by a hospital supply company, Northwestern Hospital Supply, Inc., as a salesperson two years ago. Having been successful in developing sales in western Oregon, Suzi has been shifted to operations and is now an operations analyst. She knows that if she can perform well in this job, she will likely be a regional operations manager or an area sales manager in 12 to 36 months.

Suzi's first assignment is to recommend an item forecasting procedure for a family of parts that includes orthopedic supplies. The demand for one representative item, burn dressing rolls, is shown in the table below. The current forecasting procedure for this item is an intuitive estimate by an experienced supply clerk. After reviewing class notes from an operations course she took three years ago at Oregon State, Suzi has decided to test a forecasting model, first-order exponential smoothing. Her supervisor thinks the data are seasonal and would like a model that reflects seasonality. Suzi would like to use the company's computer to test differing values of the smoothing coefficient, but she is unsure of her programming skills.

After thinking about a forecasting model and selecting parameters (such as starting values and smoothing coefficients), Suzi has decided to use MAD as her primary evaluation mechanism. She has heard of Bias, but remembers nothing of significance that would suggest she should use it.

Burn dressing roll demand

Time Period (week)	Sales	Time Period (week)	Sales
1	1084	25	964
2	1056	26	936
3	1090	27	970
4	953	28	833
5	868	29	748
6	868	30	847
7	1034	31	905
8	1088	32	968
9	1069	33	861
10	856	34	736
11	876	35	757
12	796	36	752
13	1023	37	903
14	1003	38	883
15	1036	39	916
16	835	40	715
17	747	41	691
18	856	42	736
19	1008	43	888
20	1036	44	908
21	920	45	909
22	805	46	685
23	816	47	696
24	776	48	692

Case Questions

1. Plot the data and identify any patterns you observe from the plot.
2. Design an analysis procedure for Suzi Trotter. Include forecasting model(s), evaluation measure(s), and the procedure for setting starting values and model parameters for any model to be tested.
3. How could simple moving average and first order exponential models be modified to include adjustments for trend and seasonal data?
4. Carry out the recommended analysis in Question 2. Using a computer with software such as the QSOM package or programmable calculator might be beneficial but is not necessary.
5. Discuss the implementation problems Suzi might encounter once her analysis is complete.

CASE

Spradling Enterprises

Spradling Enterprises manufactures household cleaning products. One product, Stain-ReMover, product number SRM-10, has been difficult to produce in enough volume to sustain inventory between production batches. The table illustrates monthly demand in 24-case lots for the last 15 months, essentially the total life of SRM-10.

Monthly demand for SRM-10 in 24 case lots

Month	Demand	Month	Demand
December 1987	22	August	57
January 1988	40	September	55
February	32	October	65
March	55	November	73
April	67	December	90
May	53	January 1989	81
June	90	February	93
July	62		

The production manager has asked production control to reexamine the item forecasting procedure for this product. In production control, the initial 12 month forecast from marketing is always used for a new product. In the absence of other instructions, their forecast of 50 lots per month has been used to date for SRM-10.

Spradling Enterprises uses first order exponential smoothing for forecasting item demand for all items after one year of product experience has occurred. Either a slow smoothing (smoothing coefficient of .2) or a fast smoothing (smoothing coefficient of .7) model is used for each product. The choice of fast or slow smoothing is based primarily on mean absolute deviation (MAD) over the last six periods of data, with some consideration given secondarily to Bias. The initial forecast needed to evaluate fast or slow smoothing for a new product is always the marketing forecast.

The production control manager is concerned about the specific problem of changing the SRM-10 forecast to correspond with current procedures and the more general problem of developing a checklist for reviewing the existing forecasting procedure for possible improvement.

REVIEW AND DISCUSSION QUESTIONS

1. Contrast forecasting and prediction and given an example of each.
2. Forecasting is an important information input for operations subsystem decisions. Explain what might be forecast for a supermarket operation and relate that information to Figure 3.2.
3. Explain what demand noise, pattern, and stability are in time series analyses.
4. Which would you use in evaluating a forecast, MAD or Bias? Why?
5. Present any evidence that suggests forecasting is an important problem in the service sector.
6. Examine Table 3.1, which summarizes modern forecasting techniques. Is there any one best technique? What can be concluded from this table?
7. Contrast the cost/accuracy tradeoffs in forecasting model selection between sophisticated statistical models and intuitive estimates.
8. Explain how the nominal group technique would arrive at a consensus forecast.
9. Explain how the Delphi technique would arrive at a consensus forecast.

10. Individuals forecast intuitively. What are some of the variables that affect the relative effectiveness of those intuitive forecasts?
11. Compare intuitive forecasting to naive statistical forecasting models. As an operations manager, how would you forecast—intuitive or by model? Why?

PROBLEMS

Solved Problems

1. Demand for part number 2710 has been as shown below. Our forecast for April was 100 units. With a smoothing constant of .20 and using first order exponential smoothing, what is the July forecast? What do you think about a .20 smoothing constant?

Time	Actual Demand
April	200
May	50
June	150

$$F_t = \alpha D_{t-1} + (1 - \alpha)F_{t-1}$$

$$F_{\text{MAY}} = .20(200) + (1 - .2)100$$
$$120$$

$$F_{\text{JUNE}} = .2(50) + (1 - .2)120$$
$$106$$

$$F_{\text{JULY}} = .2(150) + (1 - .2)106$$
$$= 114.8 \cong 115$$

The July forecast is 115 units (fractional units should be rounded to be realistic). The .20 smoothing constant implies that recent demand should not be weighted heavily. This seems appropriate for this data. If demand is unstable, a higher constant should be used. The forecast should react quickly to changes in demand. However, if over a long period demand smooths out, the .20 constant may be satisfactory, since it helps to remove noise. It is almost impossible to select a smoothing coefficient with only three periods of data.

2. An ice cream parlor experienced the following demand for ice cream last month. The current forecasting procedure is to use last year's corresponding weekly sales as this year's forecast.

Week	Forecasted Demand (gallons)	Actual Demand (gallons)
June 1	210	200
June 8	235	225
June 15	225	200
June 22	270	260

Calculate MAD and BIAS and interpret each.

$$\text{MAD} = |210 - 200| + |235 - 225| + |225 - 200| + |270 - 260|$$
$$= \frac{55}{4}$$
$$= 13.75$$

$$\text{Bias} = (210 - 200) + (235 - 225) + (225 - 200) + (270 - 260)$$
$$= \frac{55}{4}$$
$$= +13.75$$

Since all monthly errors are positive, each error measure gives the same results: The forecasts are consistently high, an average of 13.75 gallons /week.

Reinforcing Fundamentals

3. A mole and gopher poison manufacturer has experienced the following monthly demand for an environmentally improved pesticide poison.

Month	Demand Item #Corn-201 (cases)
February	620
March	840
April	770
May	950
June	1000

(a) Using a simple average, what would the forecast have been for May and June?
(b) What would the three-month simple moving average have been for May and June?
(c) Which forecasting method would you recommend? Why?

4. The monthly cost of overstocking crates of bananas in a grocery chain is estimated to be $5.50 times the absolute value of average daily Bias for any one month.
(a) Express this relationship as a cost function.
(b) If daily Bias was a positive 137 crates last month, what was the total cost for that error?
(c) How much should managment be willing to spend for a perfect forecast?

5. A hardware chain, Max's, experienced the following demand for paint last month. The current forecasting procedure is to use last year's corresponding weekly sales as this year's forecast. Calculate MAD and Bias and interpret each.

Week	Forecasted Demand (gallons)	Actual Demand (gallons)
June 1	1,320	1,310
June 8	1,335	1,325
June 15	1,350	1,325
June 22	1,370	1,360

6. A department store analyst is interested in using the *change in price* of sugar in any given month to predict the change in price of candy the following month. She chooses a widely watched exchange and observes the following monthly sequence of *prices* (not price changes);

80, 82, 85, 81, 80, 80, 80, 84, 88, 89, 90, 88, 84

Candy prices in the same months are:

105, 100, 105, 114, 107, 105, 104, 105, 110, 117, 120, 121, 118

(a) Construct the appropriate scatter diagram and plot the data.
(b) Find the estimated regression line.
(c) What do you conclude about the relationship the analyst is interested in? Might this lead to improved forecasts? How can that help store operations?

7. In finished goods, Blakeman's Supply stocks three horsepower motors. Weekly demand for 12 typical weeks is:

Week	Demand for 3-hp Motor	Week	Demand for 3-hp Motor
42	20	48	9
43	17	49	4
44	12	50	6
45	14	51	5
46	8	52	4
47	10	53	3

(a) Calculate a weighted moving average forecast for weeks 54 and 55 using a three-period model with the most recent period's demand weighted three times as heavily as each of the previous two period's demands. After forecasting period 54, actual demand was 6 motors for the period.
(b) Examining the data visually, what would you suggest as a possible alternative weighted moving average model? Why?

8. A lumber company forecasts demand based on the last two months simple moving average. What would the forecast be for the following items for May? Specify any assumptions you make.

	Exterior Plywood Sheets		B & D Saws		Craft Paper Rolls	
Month	Demand	Forecast	Demand	Forecast	Demand	Forecast
January	20	25	10	15	2	0
February	missing data	20	10	10	0	1
March	50	—	10	10	1	1
April	60	—	12	10	missing data	1

Does the company need to continue to carry four months of past data for this forecasting model?

9. A small electronics company produces pocket calculators and keeps item demand monthly. The following demand data are for a representative calculator: November, 45; December, 57; January, 60. Using 50 as the first order exponential smoothing forecast for November, forecast February sales.

10. New Cap, a local manufacturing firm, is introducing a new line of men's hunting caps. New Cap wants to forecast component items for these hats with its existing simple exponential smoothing forecasting model. Management has no historical data for these hunting caps.
(a) What can you recommend to New Cap concerning initialization of parameters and a smoothing coefficient for monthly forecasts for the next six months? Why?
(b) After four months you have the following data on *actual* demand. Would you agree with New Cap's choice of a smoothing coefficient of .3, or would you

choose .9 the *only* other value it wants to consider for now? Assume that June's forecast was 100.

Month	Caps Shipped (doz.)
June	50
July	175
August	225
September	400

11. A company statistician is interested in the relationship between the length (in inches) and the weight (in pounds) of extrusions. Extrusions come in all sizes, shapes, and thicknesses. A random sample of extrusions is taken, with the following results (X = length in inches, F = weight in pounds):

X: 70 75 64 67 71 70 68 76 68 69 70
F: 175 198 156 180 178 182 160 204 167 169 162

(a) Construct a scatter diagram.
(b) Find a and b, and draw the estimated regression line of F on X.
(c) Does the use of a linear regression model improve our ability to predict F, given X?
(d) If an extrusion is chosen at random and is 70 inches long, use the estimated regression line to predict weight. Such a "prediction" is different from "demand forecasting," but is an important use of regression in operations.

12. A university central store experiences demand for staplers, which appears to follow the following distribution:

Time Period	Staplers Demanded	Time Period	Staplers Demanded
10	92	15	138
11	117	16	"182"
12	105	17	"187"
13	135	18	"185"
14	143	18	"210"

We have a forecast of 150 units for period 16. The quotes (" ") mean actual demand is known at the end of that period. Using first order exponential smoothing with a moderately responsive smoothing coefficient of .3, forecast demand for periods 17 through 20. Now plot the actual and forecasted values for all periods for which you have data. Recommend to management an improved forecasting method and support your recommendation.

13. Smithton Corporation uses a first order exponential smoothing model. For one item, the model provided a demand forecast of 75,500 units. This was used as November's production requirement. Although demand was actually 72,700 units during November, 75,500 units were produced. Calculate a double exponential smoothed forecast for December using 70,000 units as November's double exponential smoothed forecast. All smoothing coefficients are .3.

Challenging Exercises

14. For the last three years, Professor Gregopolus has been intuitively forecasting the number of students who will enroll in her classes. She really believes that no one knows as much about the value of her classes as she does. Therefore, how could others possibly forecast enrollments better than she? Her forecasts and actual enrollments are given below (rounded to multiples of ten).

(a) What has Professor Gregopolus's accuracy been, based on MAD and Bias? Explain what this means to Professor Gregopolus.
(b) Use 60 students as the forecast for Spring 1982, a smoothing coefficient of .2, and MAD to evaluate the model forecast with first order exponential smoothing.
(c) What can you tell Professor Gregopolus about individual intuitive versus modeling as approaches to forecasting?
(d) Based on all of the above, what do you recommend to Professor Gregopolus as a forecasting approach?

Semester	Forecast	Actual	Semester	Forecast	Actual
Fall 1981	—	70	Fall 1983	80	120
Spring 1982	90	60	Spring 1984	120	80
Fall 1982	90	70	Fall 1984	150	60
Spring 1983	100	60			

15. An operations manager is interested in forecasting how training will affect efficiency for production workers assigned to a new job. He gave five different amounts of training, varying from one-half a day to 4 days. Ten workers took each of the training levels, 50 workers in all. The table below shows each worker's labor efficiency for the first week's work, 100 being the standard or expected output.

	X, training in days				
	0.50	1	2	3	4
Y, efficiency	117	106	76	125	85
	85	81	88	113	129
	112	74	115	93	90
	81	79	113	89	124
	105	118	108	117	117
	109	110	84	118	121
	80	82	83	81	97
	73	86	81	86	93
	110	111	112	88	122
	78	113	120	120	92

(a) Find the linear regression equation for predicting *Y* from *X*.
(b) Plot the linear regression equation, along with the data, on a scatter diagram. What does this mean to the manager?
(c) Calculate the mean and variance for each training group. What can you conclude from comparing groups?

16. You are given the following demand for Zeaker's streaker sneakers:

Date	Demand
March 1	20
8	120
15	150
22	75
April 1	50

As a buyer for Bowling Green's largest sneaker outlet, you have been told to forecast streaker sneaker demand weekly in April using first order exponential smoothing.
(a) What smoothing coefficient would you choose? Why?

(b) If the manager's forecast for April 1 is 75, using that as your starting value, what is your forecast for April 8?

17. Recently, demand for a new carburetor filter stocked by a regional supply house has increased drastically (mechanics and the general public are becoming aware of the filter's fuel economy). Weekly demand is given below.

Week	Actual Demand	Week	Actual Demand	Week	Actual Demand
23	100	31	450	39	927
24	75	32	510	40	950
25	210	33	600	41	945
26	250	34	550	42	1,050
27	350	35	725	43	1,150
28	365	36	775	44	1,200
29	400	37	750	45	1,210
30	425	38	825	46	1,295

(a) Fit a first order exponential smoothing model that minimizes MAD to these data.

(b) Attempt to reduce the overall MAD (for the 24 periods of data) by using another model. Feel free to develop a model or to choose a model from a source other than this text. Explain *why* you proceeded as you did.

18. Barfy Burgers, Inc., is a large northeastern hamburger chain that has just completed its fifth year of operation. Every month Barfy must make its meat purchases for the succeeding month. Due to historical demand fluctations, Buster Barfy, vice president of operations, has difficulty knowing what future sales to expect. Shown below are the number of pounds of meat demanded during each month of the firm's first five years of operation.

	Jan	Feb	Mar	Apr	May	June	July	Aug	Sept	Oct	Nov	Dec
1981	695	693	714	733	740	684	723	750	790	734	718	730
1982	768	772	765	722	719	777	753	762	732	780	750	705
1983	828	776	823	859	778	776	763	810	759	834	837	786
1984	814	790	841	817	849	769	904	808	809	828	885	849
1985	866	850	869	818	802	754	844	811	811	817	801	810

Based on Barfy's past demand, determine the monthly demand for January 1986.

19. Compare first order exponential smoothing and double exponential smoothing over March and April. Minimize the tracking signal *(TS)*

$$TS = \frac{Bias}{MAD}$$

for your recommendation of a model.

Time Period	Parts Demanded	First Order Exponential Smoothing (smoothing coefficient = .4)	Double Exponential Smoothing (all smoothing coefficients = .4)
January	100	120	110
February	"200"[a]		
March	"150"		
April	"120"		

[a]" " denotes demand at that month's end, after that month's forecast.

20. E-Z Photocopying Service (EZPS) has experienced weekly demand for photocopying at the university copying center as shown below. Currently, the forecasting procedure is to use the previous week's average daily demand as the next week's daily forecast. Staffing decisions for the next week are based on this forecast.

Week	Average Daily Demand (thousands)	Week	Average Daily Demand (thousands)
Feb. 7	27	March 6	32
Feb. 14	20	March 13	30
Feb. 21	22	March 21	38
Feb. 28	30	March 28	

(a) Find the forecasted demand for the week of March 28 using double exponential smoothing as the forecasting model. Use smoothing constants of .2, and February 28 actual demand as the estimate for March 6 forecasted demand required. Forecast for March 28 based on experience in March (i.e., do not forecast February at all).
(b) Using MAD as your criterion for evaluation, do you recommend double exponential smoothing or the current forecasting procedure?
(c) What might EZPS management do to further improve forecasting accuracy?

Utilizing the QSOM Computer Software[9]

21. Reconsider the data in Problem 17, which starts with week 23 and output demand of 100.
(a) Using the data and the QSOM time series forecasting option, fit a first order experimental smoothing model that minimizes MAD to this data.
(b) Plot and print your results for best fitting model.

22. Consider the quarterly houseboat demand below for URboat, a regional manufacturer.

Year and Quarter		Demand (units)	Year and Quarter		Demand (units)
1983	QI	50	1986	QI	62
	QII	45		QII	56
	QIII	52		QIII	65
	QIV	56		QIV	71
1984	QI	53	1987	QI	65
	QII	48		QII	60
	QIII	57		QIII	70
	QIV	62		QIV	77
1985	QI	56	1988	QI	73
	QII	50		QII	66
	QIII	60		QIII	75
	QIV	67		QIV	85

(a) Plot the data and examine for trends and seasonality. Read the data into QSOM.
(b) Using smoothing coefficients of .2, .4, .6, and .8, along with first order exponential smoothing, select the best coefficient (lowest MAD and Bias

[9]QSOM is a software package developed by Prentice Hall as an operations management text supplement. QSOM utilizes microcomputers. See the Preface, and contact Prentice Hall regarding availability. Instructors should see the *Instructor's Manual.*

values, equally weighted). Plot and print out results for your best fitting model.

(c) If your examination of the data shows *no* trend and/or seasonality, use the double exponential smoothing model. If there is trend in the data, try exponential smoothing with linear trend utilizing a smoothing coefficient of .2. Record the MAD value.

(d) If there is trend and seasonality, try the Winter's model presented in QSOM. For this model, you must enter three coefficients for each run (coefficient 1 = constant component, coefficient 2 = trend component, coefficient 3 = seasonal component). All coefficients may be the same. Use a smoothing coefficient of .2 for all three components and record the MAD value.

(e) Select one of these three models in Parts c and d and do an analysis similar to your first order exponential smoothing analysis in Part b for the best fitting model. Print results with lowest MAD value of best fitting model. Note: If Winter's model is the best fitting, use all combinations of .3 and .7 for each of the three coefficients to determine lowest MAD and for printout.

GLOSSARY

Adaptive exponential smoothing Models in which smoothing coefficient is not fixed but is set initially and then allowed to fluctuate over time based upon changes in the underlying demand pattern.

Bias Forecast error measure that is the sum of actual errors for all periods divided by the total number of periods evaluated; gives the average of the forecast errors with regard to direction; shows any tendency consistently to over-/or underforecast.

Causal forecasting models In a formal manner these relate demand to variables that are believed to influence demand.

Demand pattern General shape of the time series; usually constant, trend, seasonal, or some combination of these shapes.

Demand stability Tendency for a time series to retain the same general shape over time.

Exponential smoothing models An averaging method that exponentially decays the weight of an old demand on the current forecast.

Forecast Use of past data to determine future events; an objective computation.

Forecast error The difference between forecasted demand and actual demand.

Intuitive forecasts General approach to forecasting that is essentially the manager's guesses and judgment concerning future events; qualitative forecasting methods.

Mean absolute deviation (MAD) Forecast error measure that is the sum of the absolute deviation of actual demand and forecast for all periods divided by the total number of periods evaluated; gives the average of forecast errors without regard to direction.

Noise Dispersion of individual demands about a demand pattern.

Prediction Subjective estimates of the future.

Simple average Average of past data in which the demands of all previous periods are equally weighted.

Simple moving average Average of several of the most recent periods' demand; most recent time periods are added and oldest ones dropped to keep calculations current.

Statistical forecasting models Casting forward past data in some systematic method; used in time series analysis and projection.

Time series analysis In forecasting problems, demand data are plotted on a time scale to reveal patterns of demand.

Weighted moving average Moving average model that incorporates some weighting of old demands other than an equal weight for all past periods under consideration.

SELECTED READINGS

Ahlers, David, and Josef Lakonishok, "A Study of Economists' Consensus Forecasts," *Management Science* 29, no. 10 (October 1983), 1113–25.

Biggs, Joseph R., and William M. Campion, "The Effect and Cost of Forecast Error Bias for Multi-Stage Production-Inventory Systems," *Decision Sciences* 12, no. 4 (October 1982), 570–84.

Box, G. E. P., and G. M. Jenkins, *Time Series Analysis,*

Forecasting, and Control. San Francisco: Holden-Day, 1970.

Brown, R. G., *Smoothing, Forecasting and Prediction of Discrete Time Series.* Englewood Cliffs, N.J.: Prentice Hall, 1963.

Delbecq, Andre, Andrew Van deVen, and David Gustafson, *Group Techniques for Program Planning.* Glenview Ill.: Scott, Foresman, 1975.

Hogarth, Robin M., and Spyros Makridakis, "Forecasting and Planning: An Evaluation," *Management Science* 27, no. 2 (February 1981) 115–38.

Lawrence, Michael J., et al., "The Accuracy of Combining Judgmental and Statistical Forecasts," *Management Science* 32 (1986), 1521–32.

Lee, T.S., and Everett E. Adam, Jr., "Forecasting Error Evaluation in Material Requirements Planning (MRP) Production-Inventory Systems," *Management Science* 32, no. 9 (September 1986), 1186–1205.

Makridakis, Spyros, et al., "The Accuracy of Extrapolation (Time Series) Methods: Results of a Forecasting Competition," *Journal of Forecasting* 1 (1982), 111–153.

Makridakis, Spyros and S. C. Wheelwright, *Forecasting Methods and Applications.* New York: John Wiley, 1978.

Makridakis, Spyros, and Robert L. Winkler, "Averages of Forecasts: Some Empirical Results," *Management Science* 29, no. 9 (September 1983), 987–96.

Muth, J. F., "Optimal Properties of Exponentially Weighted Forecasts," *Journal of the American Statistical Association* 55, no. 290 (June 1960), 297-306.

Thomopoulos, Nick T., *Applied Forecasting Methods.* Englewood Cliffs, N.J.: Prentice Hall, 1980.

4

Product and Process Design Choices

Development of a turbofan engine to power a modern commercial passenger transport requires an investment of $1 billion and takes approximately four years of design and testing.

The investment must commence, along with the engineering effort, before the actual market is developed. As the market unfolds, the aircraft and the engine are modified to insure acceptability and profitability at the time of introduction.

It is imperative during the initial design period that dialogue is firmly established between the engineering teams and the manufacturing teams. This dialogue and the resultant team-building not only assures a "design to cost" philosophy but aids the development process when a component must be redesigned for cost, market, or reliability reasons.

In the entire design and development phase, a "real time" data bank must be established so that the entire team can know the status of drawing releases, hardware promises, required dates, and problem areas. It is only with this knowledge that program management can make the decisions and implement the actions needed for an on-time, on-budget engine development program.

Because of their complexities, the core of engine development programs is the team effort where specialists (manufacturing, engineering, test, and marketing) join together using a common "real time" data base to identify and provide solutions to those problems which will occur during the program. This insures a product which will be accepted in the market and provides an acceptable return on investment.

James W. Tucker, General Manager
Evendale Product Engineering Operation
Aircraft Engine Engineering Division
General Electric Company
Cincinnati, Ohio

In planning the conversion system, major decisions are made concerning the design of the product or service as well as the design of conversion processes to produce the product or service. We address these decisions by first presenting the design of new products, followed by the design of manufacturing processes. After presenting each separately for manufacturing, we consider service product and process design choices together.

NEW PRODUCT DESIGN (PRODUCT DEVELOPMENT)

The Origin of New Products

Entrepreneurs frequently form new businesses on the basis of a unique product idea or needed service. As competitors infringe and replicate products and services or as the useful product life (to consumers) diminishes, firms ordinarily prepare to bring new products or services on stream. These new product and service ideas come from various sources, including customers, marketing staff, research and development, top management, production staff, engineering, and employees throughout the firm. Once launched, even good products have limited lives and, to remain viable, the organization seeks a flow of new product possibilities. Let's examine the product's birth-to-mortality pattern.

Product Life Cycle

The demand for a product, its market acceptance, generally tends to follow a predictable pattern called the *product life cycle*.[1] From the standpoint of marketing strategy, the pattern suggests that rather than having indefinite lives, products go through a series of stages, beginning with low demand during market development, and proceding through growth, maturity, high-volume saturation, and finally decline. The time spans of the stages vary considerably across industries. For novelty products, the time from birth to death may be as short as a few weeks or months. For other products the life cycle may span many years or even decades. In any case the very nature of this pattern raises significant questions for operations management. When will the various stages occur, and how must operations accommodate them? What facilities, materials, labor, and management systems are optimal for meeting anticipated demand? What should be done with existing facilities and conversion processes as products procede through their various stages? Let's look at some major operations issues arising from the product life cycle.

Operations Issues in the Product Life Cycle From an operations management, rather than a marketing, viewpoint, the life cycle can be reconstructed into four stages, as shown in Figure 4.1, to reveal four important issue areas. As you can see, the operations strategy and

[1]For an empirical approach to evaluating product life cycles, see Cornelis A. deKluyver, "Innovation and Industrial Product Life Cycles," *California Management Review* 20, no. 1 (Fall 1977), 21–23. Process and facility life cycles are discussed in Roger W. Schmenner, "Every Factory Has a Cycle," *Harvard Business Review* 61, no. 2 (March–April 1983), 121–29.

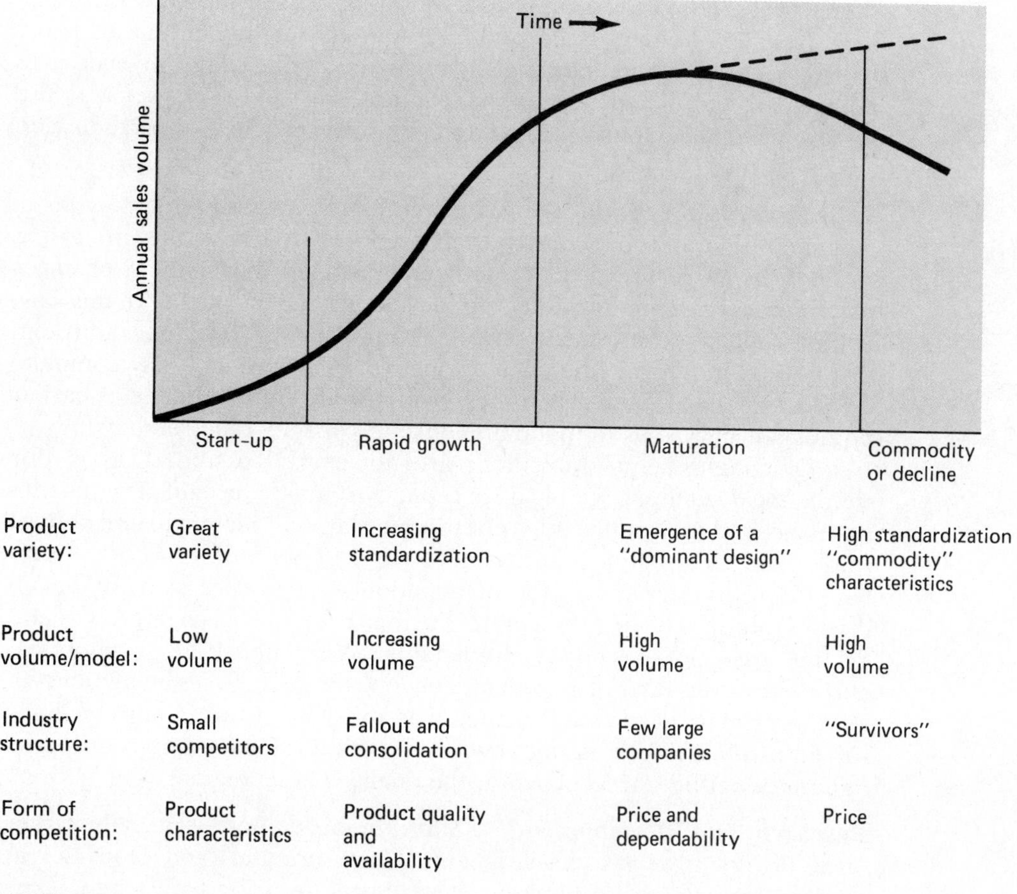

Time
Annual sales volume
Start-up
Rapid growth
Maturation
Commodity or decline
Product variety:
Great variety
Increasing standardization
Emergence of a "dominant design"
High standardization "commodity" characteristics
Product volume/model:
Low volume
Increasing volume
High volume
High volume
Industry structure:
Small competitors
Fallout and consolidation
Few large companies
"Survivors"
Form of competition:
Product characteristics
Product quality and availability
Price and dependability
Price

FIGURE 4.1
Characteristics of the product life cycle important to manufacturing process technology

Source: R. H. Hayes and S. C. Wheelwright, *Restoring Our Competitive Edge* (New York: John Wiley & Sons, 1984), p. 203.

conversion technology have to be adaptive throughout the life cycle because product variety, volume, industry structure, and form of competition all are changing. Consider, for example, differences in the demands on product design and production expertise in the start-up phase, where the product design is unstable and many engineering changes are adopted, versus the final stage where there is high standardization of the product and, consequently, a very stable and refined conversion process.

As fewer but larger competitors emerge, the form of competition shifts dramatically, requiring commensurate changes in the manufacturing competence. Whereas the early life-cycle stages exploit the product's unique characteristics and quality, later success depends more on price competition and delivery capabilities. Survival depends on developing competence in producing a stable product with high volume in contrast to the earlier competence with a high product variety, low-volume conversion process. The conversion process has changed substantially, including new types of human skills and orientations, equipment and facility revisions, and different planning and control systems. What can be done to prepare for and influence these adaptations? Part of the answer is to use research and development (R&D) to create new products and production processes.

Phasing Multiple Products A general strategy of phasing new products in and old products out is often used to sustain existing processing technology. As existing products are demanded less during the later stages of their life cycles, new products are developed and produced. In this way, output capacity can remain stable. While one product goes through maturation and begins the decline stage, another product may complete the start-up stage. Similarly, other products are initiated later as earlier products decay, so as to maintain constant capacity requirements.

Of course, actual transitions are not nearly so smooth as in our simple ideal example. Rarely does capacity remain constant. The technologies needed to produce different products are not identical, and at least some changes are almost always necessary. Organizations do not always have a new product waiting for introduction at the precise moment that an existing product begins to decline. Furthermore, the rates of growth and decline may not be highly predictable. With marketing promotional efforts, however, rates of growth and decline can sometimes be influenced. IBM, an expert at planned change, has introduced new computer lines since the late 1950s. Phasing new computers into and old ones out of its basic product line, IBM plans for the changes in its market.

Research and Development Many organizations, especially larger ones, do not leave the development of new products and processes to chance. They direct formal concerted efforts toward creating new products, finding new uses for existing products, and developing new processes that will reduce capital or manufacturing costs. These are the objectives of research and development.[2]

A new successful product or process does not happen overnight. Most often it occurs over a succession of steps and involves the talents and expertise of many people. As new product ideas are created, they go through stages of evaluation for economic feasibility, market potential, functional testing, and so on. As shown in Figure 4.2, only a small percentage of the new product ideas become commercial realities, illustrating why R&D is so expensive. Some new product ideas survive several stages of costly development before dying because of technological infeasibility; their R&D costs are never recovered. These risks are offset, however, by those few commercially successful products that generate sufficient revenues to make R&D a worthwhile long-term venture. Consider, for example, a relatively new process for tagging salmon used in wildlife management. Historically the process involved catching the fish, physical-

[2]The role of R&D in organizational change is discussed by Neil V. Hakala, "Administration of Industrial Technology," *Business Horizons* 20, no. 5 (October 1977), 4–10.

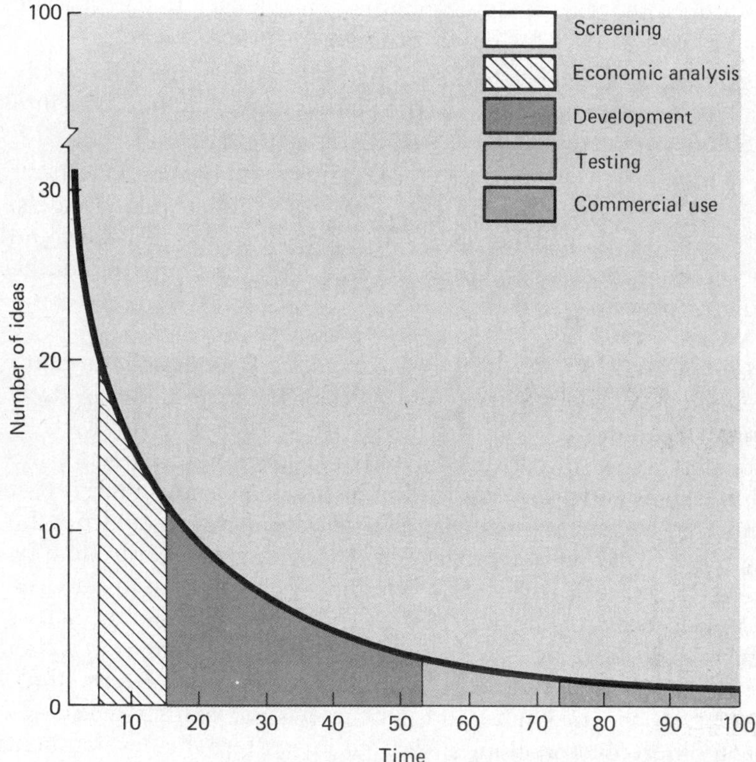

FIGURE 4.2
Decay curve of new product ideas

Source: R.A. Johnson, W. T. Newell, and R. C. Vergin, *Production and Operations Management: A Systems Concept* (Boston: Houghton Mifflin Company, 1974), p. 144.

ly handling it, tagging, and physically releasing the fish. The new process consists essentially of "tagging" by remote laser beam, thus eliminating the need for physically catching, tagging, and releasing. Now think of the research and development efforts that were required to bring about this new process. Many years ago the theories of physics underlying the laser were conceptualized. Later, developmental research in physics and electronics resulted in a working laser beam. Since then many scientists and engineers have developed applications of laser beams in space explorations, health, science, industry, and other settings. Only recently, with the help of fish biologists, has this new tagging process been brought into use. Overall we can identify fundamentally different components of innovation.

Components of Innovation There are four generic components of technological innovation: basic research, applied research, development, and implementation.

- *Basic research:* Research activities that represent original investigation for the advancement of scientific knowledge and that do not have specific commercial objectives. They may, however, be in the field of present or potential interest of the company.
- *Applied research:* Research that represents investigation directed

toward the discovery of new scientific knowledge. It has specific commercial objectives for either products or processes.

- *Development:* Technical activities concerned with nonroutine problems that are encountered in translating research findings into products or processes.
- *Implementation:* Once the other components of innovation have been completed, the remaining process involves building pilot models, designing and building the necessary equipment and facilities, and initiating the marketing channels necessary for dissemination of the product or process.

Organization of R&D In most companies R&D is a staff function located at either the corporate or divisional level. Three examples of R&D organizational structure are shown in Figure 4.3. In part a, R&D is centrally located. From this location, R&D can economically serve the needs of all divisions and avoid duplication of effort. A disadvantage is that the R&D unit may be geographically and organizationally remote from the immediate needs of the various divisions. This difficulty is overcome by decentralized R&D (part b). This structure, however, can tend to raise the overall corporate costs of the R&D effort insofar as duplication across divisions may result. Decentralization is well suited to companies in which applied research and development dominate the overall R&D effort, particularly when the products and processes have a high degree of technological differentiation along divisional lines. Here the development efforts are specialized, tailored to the nature of each specific division.

FIGURE 4.3
R&D location in organization structure

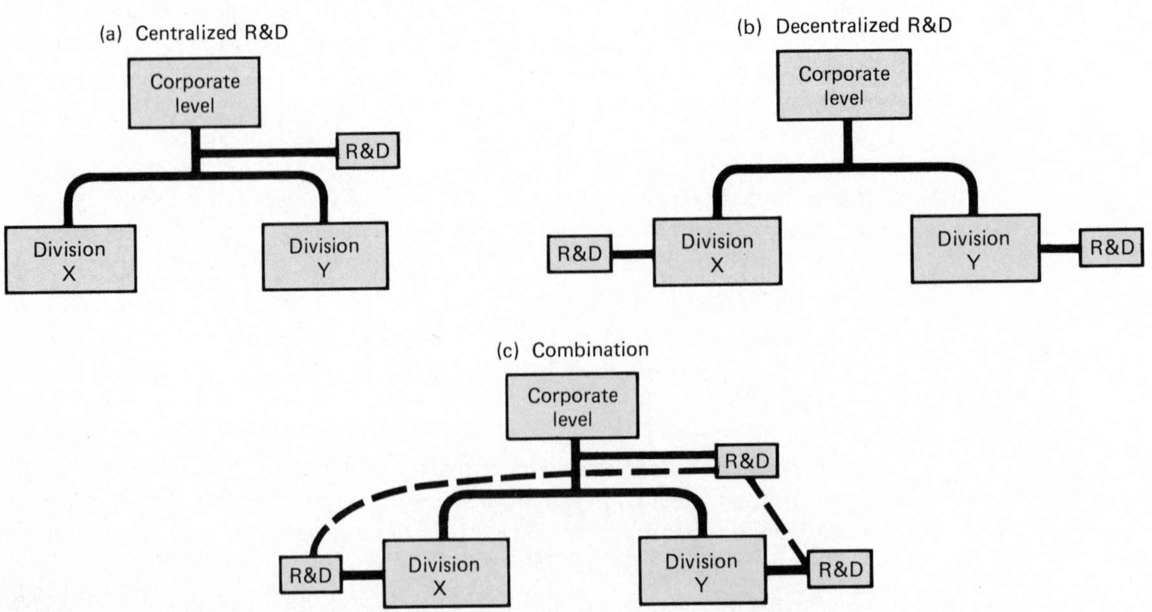

The combination structure (part c) attempts to reap the best of the benefits offered by both centralization and decentralization. R&D units at divisional levels can be specialized toward the special needs at that level, especially in the developmental and applied areas. Some of the applied research and perhaps all of the basic research may be centralized at the corporate level. Development and innovation frequently occur at the divisional level. The dotted lines among the three R&D units reflect subsidiary relationships among them; relevant results of basic or applied research at one level are transferred to the others. On occasion, the progress of development efforts at a divisional level may be impeded because further applied research is needed. If the corporate R&D unit, for example, is the only one prepared to work in the necessary applied area, the problem must then be referred to it until a solution is reached.

The Product Development Process

The development of a new product is a major undertaking that has identifiable stages as shown in Figure 4.4. As the development project progresses through each phase, its risks and potential are scrutinized, both technically and businesswise, so that any new product proposal may die or be delayed at any stage in the process.

Needs Identification Once a product idea surfaces, it has to be validated to ensure that it fulfills some consumer need. The need is justified by demonstrating that the proposed product characteristics constitute fitness for use by the consumer, and, through evaluation of competitive products, by demonstrating that existing products do not fulfill the need.

Advance Product Planning (Feasibility Study) Following needs identification, the second aspect of product development is advance product planning. It includes a variety of activities such as preliminary market analyses; creating a number of alternative concepts for the product; clarifying its operational requirements; establishing design criteria and their priorities; and estimating logistics requirements for producing, distributing, and maintaining the product in the field during use by the customer.

An important result from this stage of development is the conceptual design of the product. The concept for a new kind of fishing rod, for example, would involve articulation of its weight, strength, shape, bending characteristics, retail price, and so on. These basic properties are called the *product concept* or *design concept*. Although concept determination has traditionally been the bailiwick of marketing and engineering, many industries have learned that excluding production and operations personnel can be fatal for the firm and its production processes. The ultimate goal of production, after all, is the efficient delivery of useful products, including timely development and availability in the market, and this cannot occur unless appropriate conversion processes have been initiated early in the development process.

Advance planning poses a point of friction between business and technical personnel when solid technical ideas are adjudged to have

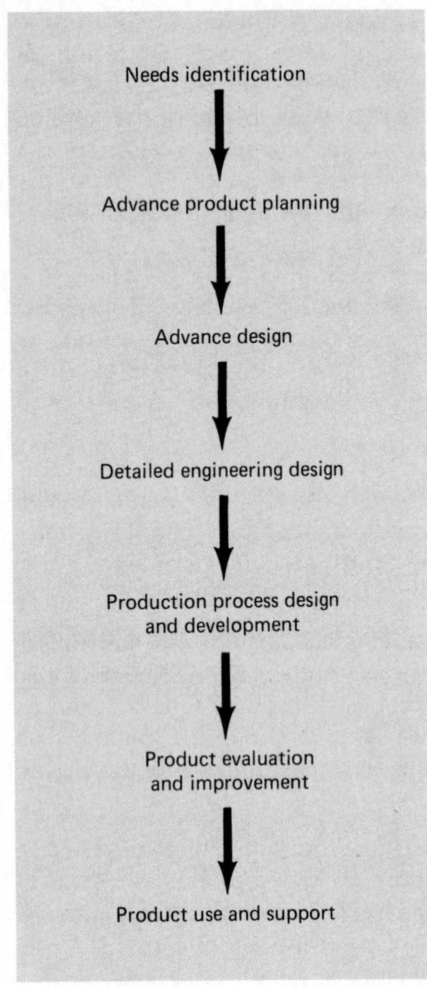

FIGURE 4.4
Product development process

insufficient business merit and, hence, fall by the wayside. Preliminary market analysis including sales projections, and economic analysis including estimates of production operating costs, overhead, and profitability may require abandonment of a technically attractive new idea. In selecting products and services, management must balance markets, economic factors, available technology, and the firm's overall resource picture—all within the framework of the organization's strategic mission.

Advance Design Basic and applied research are undertaken to investigate technical feasibility and to identify product design tradeoffs in greater depth. Promising design alternatives are evaluated to identify critical performance parameters and to determine likely areas that will require design support such as analytical testing, experimentation, physical modeling, and prototype testing.

Detailed Engineering Design This stage is a series of engineering activities to develop a detailed definition of the product, including its subsystems and components, materials, sizes, shapes, and so on. The engineering process typically involves analysis, experimentation, and data collection to find designs that meet several *design objectives:* (1) design for *function* (functional design) to ensure the product can perform as intended; (2) design for *reliability* so that the product is available for use with minimal prospects for failure; (3) design for *maintainability* to provide accessibility for economical maintenance of the product; (4) design for *safety* to ensure minimal operating hazards to the user and the environment; and (5) design for *producibility* to assure that the product can be produced at the intended cost and volumes. Data from computer analyses, simulations, and physical prototypes (mockups) provide tests of the design alternatives and validation that the final design meets the various design objectives. Since some of the objectives can conflict with one another, design tradeoffs are necessary in arriving at an optimal product design. Typically, the final design includes drawings and other documentation as well as a working *prototype* of the product.[3]

Production Process Design and Development Downstream from detailed product design, process engineering and manufacturing planning translate the product design into facility and equipment requirements for materials acquisitions, production, warehousing, transportation, and distribution associated with manufacturing the product and getting it into the hands of the consumer. Activities here, however, go beyond just hardware considerations: They also include the design of production planning and control systems, computer information systems, and human resource systems.

Product Evaluation and Improvement Product reevaluation and improvement occur continuously throughout the lives of most products. Improvement possibilities are gained from product life tests, field performance and failure data, and from technical breakthroughs in materials and equipment. Formal research and evaluation programs are used to monitor, analyze, report, and redesign the product.

Product Use and Support An important stage of product development considers support for the product after it is in the hands of the consumer. Assistance with support systems might be needed in the field to (1) educate users on specific applications of the product; (2) provide warranty and repair service; (3) distribute replacement parts; and (4) upgrade the product with design improvements.

Competitive Losses from Disintegrated Design Processes

United States industry is suffering extensive losses to its competitors, most notably to the Japanese, by adopting a disintegrated and sequential approach to new product development. The Western approach subdivides the overall development effort into specialized subtasks for technical specialists in diverse departments. These specialists, often isolated, tend to

---

[3]For details of the engineering design activities, see B. S. Blanchard, *Engineering Organization and Management* (Englewood Cliffs, N.J.: Prentice Hall, 1976), chap. 5.

focus on their own specialty expertise without much concern for integrating their efforts with others. Consequently, the development process is executed sequentially in isolated stages. In many companies, for example, process engineers are not brought into the development project until after the detailed product design is finished. Consequently, months or even years are lost in launching the design and development of the manufacturing equipment. The result is a slow, nonintegrated, and expensive development process. Competitors are experiencing major advantages by getting new products into the marketplace with two-year lead times as compared with four-year lead times with the slower segmented approach. Their greater product development productivity stems from having less organizational compartmentalization of the design activities, using more technical generalists rather than emphasizing task specialization, and being willing to clarify design objectives at the outset of each product development project.[4]

Product Reliability

A top executive at a major automotive manufacturer recently reviewed what North American consumers want most in their products. Of the five to ten top attributes, reliability was first, ahead of comfort, price, style, and many other important product features. *The product's reliability is the probability that it will perform as intended for a prescribed duration or lifetime under specified operating conditions.* Unreliability is reflected in the product's failure rate. Figure 4.5 shows the shape of the failure rate experience for a typical product. The highest rates of failure occur (a) during initial use due to previously undetected faulty subcomponents or shipping damage, and (b) in the wear-out phase following its useful performance life. New product design is especially concerned with the failure rate during the useful performance life (the shallow portion of the "bathtub" curve). Reliability engineering determines the best height

[4]See R. J. Ebert, E. A. Slusher, and K. M. Ragsdell, "Information Flows in Product Engineering Design Productivity," in *Engineering Management: Theory and Applications* eds. D. J. Leech, J. Middleton, and G. N. Pande (Redruth, Cornwall, England: M. Jackson & Son Publishing Ltd., 1986), 329–36.

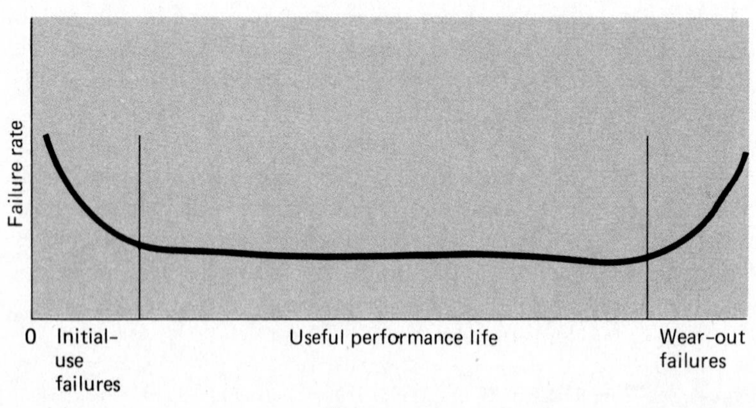

FIGURE 4.5
Product failure curve

(failure rate) and the best time duration (useful performance life) for each new product, based on financial, technical, and consumer considerations. Products such as bandages, newspapers, and food are expected to have short lives or to be used only once. Other products, refrigerators, for instance, consist of many subcomponents expected to function in concert over extended time periods. Once we have determined the desired product reliability, two basic design questions arise: What reliability is required of each of its subcomponents if we wish to achieve the reliability goal for the final product? Which subcomponents should then be selected (used) to most economically meet this desired reliability?

Often a final product does not perform properly unless *all* of its subcomponents function correctly. In cases such as these the reliabilities of individual subcomponents must be greater than the reliability desired for the final product. This situation exists whenever the chances of failure for each subcomponent are independent of one another.

Product reliability is usually expressed in terms of a probability. The probability of the system functioning successfully equals the product of the probabilities of all its subcomponents. Once reliability has been met, we can base subcomponent selection on economic considerations.

EXAMPLE Suppose we wish to produce a product consisting of two subcomponents. We want the product to have a useful life expectancy of one year with .90 probability. The product functions successfully only as long as *both* subcomponents function. Upon failure of one (or both) subcomponents, the product ceases to function. How reliable must each subcomponent be? The table below shows the prices we must pay vendors to supply the two subcomponents for increasing levels of reliability.

Subcomponent	Reliability of Subcomponent		
	.90	.95	.98
A	$50	$90	$140
B	70	90	110

Since we want a product reliability of .90, we could select subcomponents each having .90 reliability. The resulting product will meet our reliability standard if both subcomponents A and B operate successfully for one year. The probability of *both* events occurring is $.90 \times .90 = .81$, which is the reliability of the final product. We see, then, that subcomponent reliability must be greater than the desired reliability of the final product.

The result of using subcomponents A and B when each has .98 reliability would be $P = .9604$ or $.98 \times .98$.

Similarly, for A and B having .95 reliabilities, $P = .9025$. Both of these options would meet or exceed the desired product reliability.

Which versions of subcomponents A and B should be used in our product? We answer the question by first identifying all combinations of A and B that satisfy our overall reliability goal. Then we pick the combination of A and B that is least costly. Four alternative combinations of A and B meet or exceed the product reliability goal; five combinations, 5 through 9, are unsatisfactory.

Overall Reliabilities and Costs

Alternative	Subcomponents		Overall Reliability	Cost
	A	B		
1	.95	.95	.9025	\$ 90 + 90 = \$180
2	.98	.98	.9604	140 + 110 = 250
3	.95	.98	.9310	90 + 110 = 200
4	.98	.95	.9310	140 + 90 = 230
5	.90	.90	.8100	
6	.90	.95	.8550	
7	.90	.98	.8820	
8	.95	.90	.8550	
9	.98	.90	.8820	

We would select alternative 1 on the basis of economic criteria.

As you can see, reliability analysis requires probabilities of successful operation of subcomponents. This information, called *failure-rate data,* is obtained from test results and field use experience. An evaluation of how subcomponent failures can affect overall system reliability helps in evaluating alternative changes in product design.

Modular Design and Standardization

Modular design and component standardization are two aspects of product design with special significance to operations management because they directly affect the conversion process, either by simplifying it or adding to its complexity and operating costs.

Modular Design *Modular design* is the creation of products from some combination of basic, preexisting subsystems. If, in selecting a personal computer system, for example, you are offered your choices from among three video monitors, two styles of keyboards, two computers, and three printers, all of which are compatible, you would have a total of 36 (3 × 2 × 2 × 3) different computer systems from which to choose. The modular design concept gives consumers a range of product options and, at the same time, offers considerable advantages in manufacturing and product design. By stabilizing the designs of the modules, they are easier to build. During field usage, problems are easier to diagnose and the modules are easier to service. Production proficiency increases as personnel make refinements to and gain experience with the manufacturing processes for standardized sets of modules. Similarly, materials planning and inventory control can be simplified, especially in finished goods inventories. Now, rather than storing inventories of all 36 finished computer systems, some of which will be needed but many of which will not, we instead store just the subsystems or modules. Then, when a particular computer system is demanded, the producer can focus on quickly retrieving and assembling the appropriate modules into the desired configurations and avoid the high costs of idle finished goods inventories.

Standardization Product standardization offers benefits to consumers and producers alike. Customers can count on simplicity and convenience in purchasing standardized products like household doors, screws and other fasteners, spark plugs, and so on. Similarly, the adoption of uniform (standardized) pricing code labels on merchandise containers has enhanced productivity in the retailing sector. In designing new products, too, standardization can bolster productivity by (1) avoiding unnecessary engineering design when a suitable component part already exists; (2) simplifying materials planning and control during production because fewer different components are in the system; (3) reducing components production (if the component parts are produced in-house); and (4) reducing purchasing requirements and vendor relationship coordination (if components are purchased). The risky side of standardization relates to the stagnation of innovation; while you rely on standardized designs, your competitor may upstage you with a new product feature that you cannot match because your creative design capabilities are dormant.

MANUFACTURING PROCESS TECHNOLOGY

New products are not physical realities until they are produced in a manufacturing process. *Process technology* refers to the collection of equipment, people, and procedures (systems) used to produce the firm's products and services.[5] Key POM process decisions relate to organizing the process flows, choosing the appropriate product-process mix, adapting the process to meet strategic requirements, and evaluating automation and high-technology processes.

Ways to Organize Process Flows

Five generic types of process flows are project, job shop, batch, assembly line, and continuous flow. Each is more or less suited to different product-market situations, and each has its unique operating characteristics, problems, and challenges. Selected characteristics of these five technologies are summarized in Table 4.1.

Project Project organizations deal with one-of-a-kind products that are custom tailored to the unique requirements of each customer. A general construction company, with its many kinds and sizes of projects, is an example. Since the product specifications cannot be standardized and a variety of products is typical, the conversion process must feature flexibility in its equipment capabilities, human skills, and procedures. The

[5]Hayes and Wheelwright, "Restoring," p. 165. See also Terry Hill, *Manufacturing Strategy* (Houndmills, Basingstoke, Hampshire, England: Macmillan Education LTD, 1985).

Table 4.1 Selected characteristics of different process technologies

Characteristic	Project	Job Shop	Batch	Line	Continuous
		Equipment and Physical Layout Characteristics			
Typical size of facility	Varies	Usually small	Moderate	Often large	Large
Process flow	No pattern	A few dominant flow patterns	One or two single dominant patterns	A rigid flow pattern	Clear and inflexible
Speed of process	Varies	Slow	Moderate	Fast	Very fast
Run lengths	Very short	Short	Moderate	Long	Very long
Rate of change in process technology	Slow	Slow	Moderate	Moderate to high	Moderate to high
		Direct Labor and Work Force Characteristics			
Labor content	High	Very high	Varies	Low	Very low
Worker skill level	High	High	Mixed	Low	Varies
Worker training requirements	Very high	High	Moderate	Low	Varies
		Material and Information Control Characteristics			
Material requirements	Varies	Difficult to predict	More predictable	Predictable	Very predictable
Production information requirements	Very high	High	Varies	Moderate	Low
Scheduling	Uncertain, frequent changes	Uncertain, frequent changes	Varies, frequent expediting	Process designed around fixed schedule	Inflexible, sequence often dictated by technology
		Primary Operating Management Characteristics			
Challenges	Estimating, sequencing tasks, pacing	Estimating, labor utilization, fast response, debottlenecking	Designing procedures, balancing stages, responding to diverse needs	Productivity improvement, adjusting staffing levels, rebalancing when needed	Avoiding downtime, timing expansions, cost minimization

Source: Adapted from Hayes and Wheelwright, "Restoring," pp. 180–82.

conversion technology features adaptive problem solving, teamwork, and project management for the coordinated design and production of unique products.

Job Shop A job-shop process flow occurs in facilities that manufacture small batches of many different products, each of which is custom designed and, consequently, requires its own unique set of processing steps, or routing, through the production process. Consider, for example, the jobs done by a local printing shop. Each product uses only a small portion of the shop's human resources and general purpose equipment. With large numbers of diverse jobs, elaborate job-tracking and control systems are used, much time is spent waiting for access into the next machine center, and some machine centers are overloaded while others are idle, depending upon the current mix of jobs in the system.

Batch Batch process flows are a step up from job shops in terms of product standardization, but they are not as standardized as the products in assembly line flows. Within the wide range of products in the batch facility, several emerge as repeat products that are demanded in larger volumes. These few dominant products differentiate batch facilities from job shops; however, there is still not enough product dominance to warrant dedicated equipment and processes. Consequently, batch shops produce wide varieties of products and a wide variety of volumes as well. The system must be general purpose and flexible for the low-volume/high-variety products, but the higher volume batches of standardized products can be processed differently, for example, by producing some batches to stock rather than to customer order.

Assembly Line Line (assembly line) processes, as contrasted to job-shop flow patterns, are encountered in facilities that produce a narrower range of standardized products. Laundry appliances are a representative example. Since the product designs are known in advance and are relatively stable, specialized equipment, human skills, and management systems can be developed and dedicated to the limited range of products and volumes. Beyond this range, the system is inflexible.

Continuous Continuous processes occupy one extreme on the continuum of process flows. Chemical plants and oil refineries exemplify continuous processes. Materials and products are produced in continuous endless flows, rather than in batches or discrete units. The product is highly standardized, as are all of the manufacturing procedures, the sequence of product buildup, materials, and equipment. Continuous flow processes are high-volume, around-the-clock operations with capital-intensive, specialized automation.

Technology Life Cycle

Process technologies have life cycles that are generally related to the product life-cycle stages as shown in Figure 4.6. Over time, unit manufacturing costs diminish for mature products. From product start-up through to the decline stage, manufacturing processes experience changes in their organization, throughput volumes, rates of process innovation, and automation. To illustrate, the process organization is typically job shop at

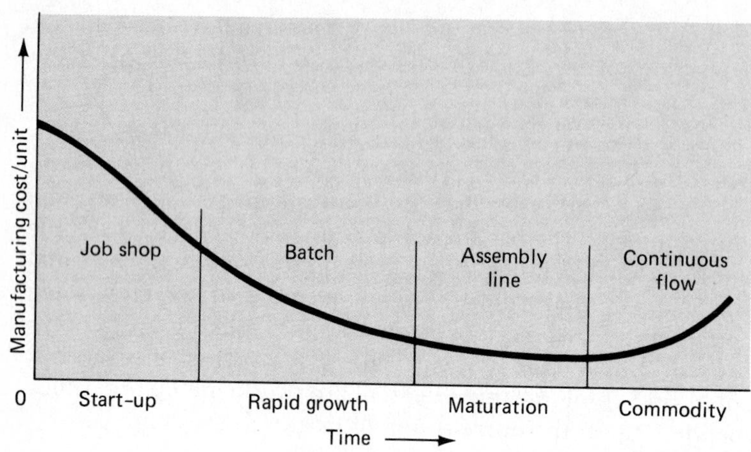

FIGURE 4.6
The process life cycle

start-up and moves toward a continuous flow organization if the product survives to become a commodity. Throughput volumes and automation are low at start-up and high during maturation and decline. The changes occur with the passage of time, and they require some matchups between the manufacturer's product and process structures, as we see in the next section.[6]

Product-Process Mix

Typical combinations of product-process structures are illustrated in Figure 4.7. Representative industries are listed on the diagonal of the matrix, and the two "voided" corners indicate product-process combinations that are incompatible and infeasible. Most companies, divisions, or plants can be located on the matrix, depending upon the current life-cycle stage of their dominant product line. As the product shifts to a different stage, the manufacturing process structure also shifts, and new manufacturing priorities emerge. Whereas manufacturing flexibility and quality are dominant bases for competing in earlier stages, competitive priorities shift toward delivery dependability and product cost during the later life-cycle stages.

This product-process matrix helps us understand why and how companies change their production operations. The products, market requirements, and competition change with the passage of time and induce changes in our equipment, procedures, and human resources. If process changes are not made to accommodate product life cycles and their associated competitive priorities, we create product-process incompatibilities. The result is competitive disadvantage.

The Growth of Automation in Manufacturing Processes

Manufacturing specialists refer to both current and anticipated changes in technology and automation as the "factory of the future." The driving force behind this factory will be a series of digital computers. Some refer to this concept as *flexible manufacturing systems* (FMS), systems where workstations, automated material handling and transport, and com-

[6]For a discussion of product and process life-cycle relationships, see Hayes and Wheelwright, "Restoring." See also Hill, *Manufacturing Strategy*.

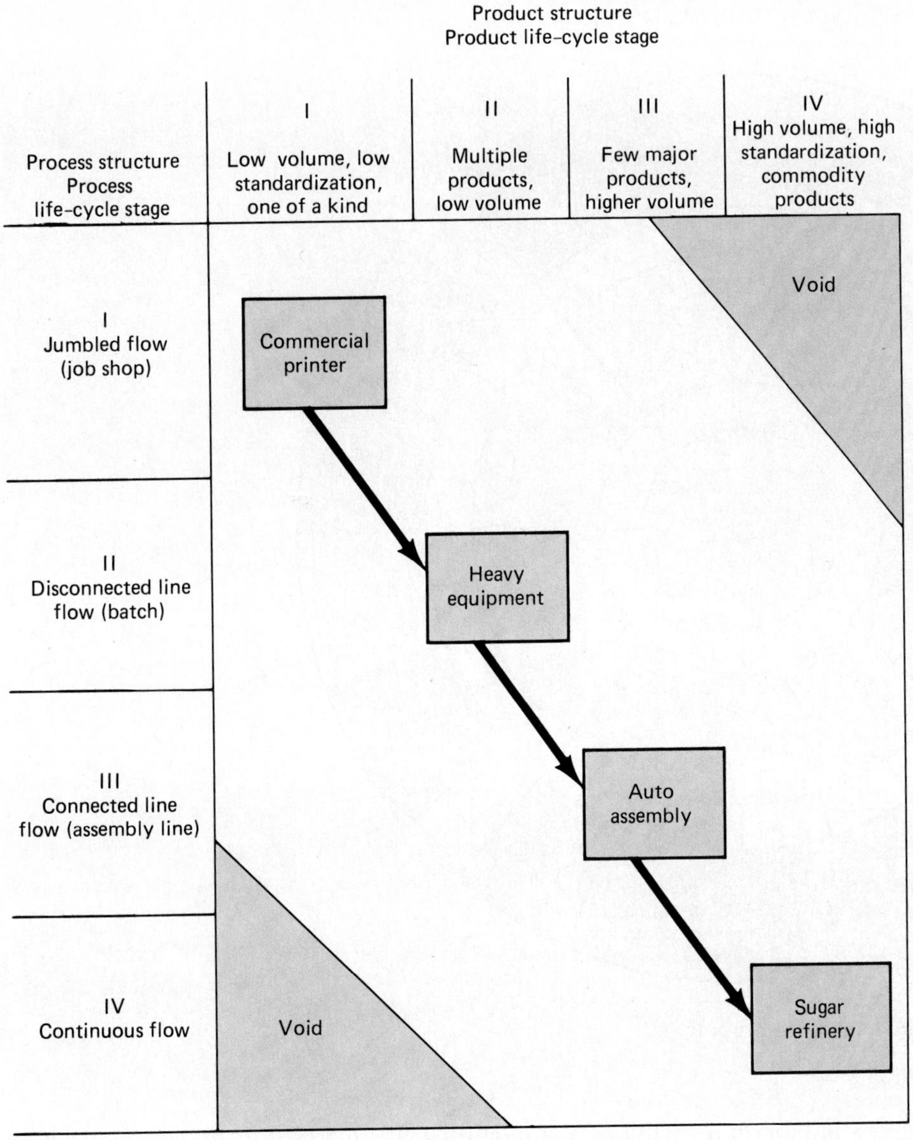

FIGURE 4.7
Matching major stages of product and process life cycles—the product-process matrix

Source: Hayes and Wheelwright, "Restoring," p. 209.

puter control are integrated. Still others refer to this futuristic manufacturing concept as *computer-integrated manufacturing* (CIM).[7] Computer-integrated manufacturing centers around a manufacturing database con-

[7]Basic reference material utilized in this section includes Thomas G. Gunn, "Computer Integrated Manufacturing," *Proceedings of the 1982 Academic-Practitioners Liaison Operations Management Workshop* (Michigan State University, July 1982), pp. 1–22; Thomas G. Gunn, "The Mechanization of Design and Manufacturing," *Scientific American* 247, no. 3 (September 1982), pp. 114–31; and promotional materials provided by McAuto, a subsidiary of McDonnell Douglas Corporation, St. Louis, Mo.

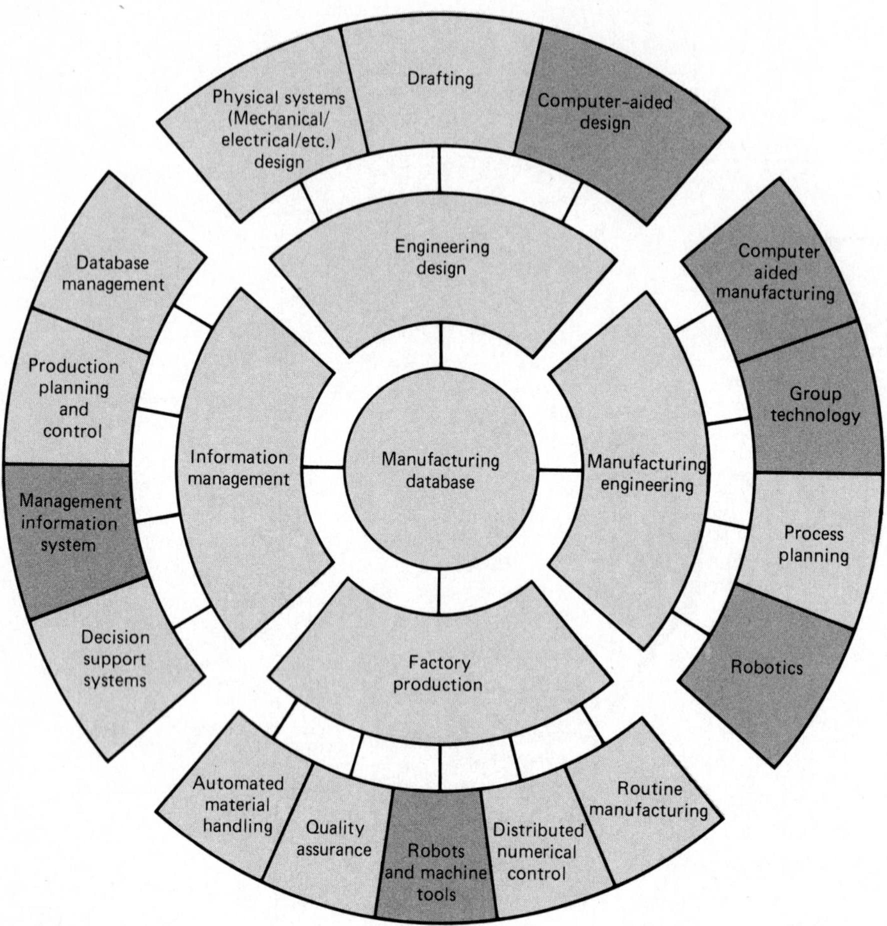

FIGURE 4.8
Computer-integrated manufacturing subfunctions

sisting of four primary manufacturing functions: engineering design, manufacturing engineering, factory production, and information management, as shown in Figure 4.8. The shared database is the glue that synchronizes the four activity areas into a unified whole and, thereby, offers potential productivity gains. The database stores all product-related and process-related information required to produce that part or product. It contains information about the machines and tools required, the materials necessary to make the product and all intermediate parts, the sequence of manufacturing steps, and various information items such as quantities demanded, due dates, and vendors for purchased parts.

EXAMPLE One of the more complex assemblies currently manufactured is that of large airplanes such as the Boeing 727 and 747 and the Douglas DC10 and MD80. In observing the assembly and test flight procedures of one of these large commercial passenger planes, we were told that over 200,000 parts must be assembled to produce a complete airplane. Data are centrally stored in a manufacturing database. It may be retrieved—and sometimes reentered in the database in a different form—by members of engineering design, manufacturing engineering, factory production, and information management. The production and support staffs are very large—typically 15,000 or more employees—to design and manufacture one airplane model. Several airplanes a month may be produced, with an approximate sales value of $20 million each. The technological and mechanization challenges associated with such production are great. At present, no nation in the world approaches the sophistication, reliability, and performance of U.S. commercial and military aerospace manufacturers.

Computer-integrated manufacturing, while not yet a reality, is a vision of things to come.[8] Some elements of the CIM concept are operational in many companies today, and the impetus is toward a computer-based system that more fully integrates the entire product development process from concept to market. In a sense, then, the "manufacturing" label (in CIM) is a misnomer because the system involves engineering (of products and processes) as well as production.

Computer-Aided Design (CAD) New products and components begin with a design concept that, eventually, is translated into specifications to provide the desired functional and aesthetic characteristics. The design process traditionally has been an iterative one in which product specifications are refined in successive stages based upon the designer's experience, computations, sketches, and drawings. CAD, using computational and graphics software, has substantially enhanced design productivity. The geometry of the component can be graphically displayed and manipulated easily on video monitors. Alternative designs can be evaluated more quickly and some of the time and expense of physical mock-ups, models, and prototypes are eliminated. Furthermore, by accessing the database, an already-existing design may be found and, thereby, duplicative design efforts are eliminated. These reductions in design costs and lead times are supplemented by savings in other operational areas as well. Once a satisfactory design is determined, for example, it is stored in the database and can be transmitted electronically; it is rapidly accessible to manufacturing engineering, production, and purchasing. And, as the component is redesigned, the new design is transmitted in a timely and accurate manner that eliminates erroneous use of obsolete designs.

What does CAD accomplish? Generally, drafting productivity improves by a factor of three or more, and there are several additional overall benefits to manufacturers. At General Motors, for example, the design time for a new automobile has been reduced from 24 to 14 months. A

[8]See W. H. Slautterback and W. B. Werther, Jr., "The Third Revolution: Computer-Integrated Manufacturing," *National Productivity Review* 3, no. 4 (Autumn 1984), 367–74.

manufacturer of molds for plastic parts was able to increase output from 30 mold cavities per year to 140, solely because of the increased efficiency afforded by a computerized design system.[9] Similar savings in time, along with increased productivity, are common in other manufacturing applications.

Computer-Aided Manufacturing (CAM) *Computer-aided manufacturing systems* control the operations of machine tools on the shop floor. The machines typically can perform a variety of operations, not just one, and the machine memory receives instructions from a computer on the sequence and specifications of its operations. CAM offers several production benefits: The machine operations are usually more reliable than those by skilled operators; product quality is more consistent from unit to unit; closer tolerances can be obtained; and labor costs are lower because less operator time is needed. These benefits, of course, don't come free of costs. Manufacturing engineering must create the equipment and software that governs machine operation. They work closely with engineering design to ensure a workable, affordable matchup of the manufacturing processes and the design of the products and components. Further, from production's standpoint, the equipment and software must provide changeover capabilities for flexible production runs and reliable performance to meet production schedules for various components and products. The computer programs can be stored in the manufacturing database, retrieved, updated, and revised as components are added or redesigned, accessed as needed by production, and transmitted electronically in-house or externally by satellite to other divisions and facilities.

One major aerospace manufacturer, however, advises that too much CAM can be costly. A wrong computer program, without visual inspection and some flexibility on the part of the machine operator, may result in many erroneous parts being produced, even though they are produced quite efficiently. These comments suggest that human involvement is not being eliminated by the CAD/CAM technology but, rather, that it is being deployed in new ways.

The objective in computer-integrated manufacturing is to take the "/" out of CAD/CAM. Conceptually, it is desirable to have the final engineering design determine the machine settings on the factory floor. McAuto's UNIGRAPHICS is a system that attempts to do just that.

EXAMPLE One user, the Business Forms Division of Harris Corporation, in Dayton, Ohio, uses CAD/CAM to facilitate the production of quality presses.[10] The first five-terminal network was installed in 1976 and paid for itself through increased productivity in just 2.6 years. A second five-terminal network was installed in 1978 with a payback in 1.9 years. Mike Kuntz, manager of

[9] Gunn, "Mechanization," 121.

[10] "Harris Uses McAuto UNIGRAPHICS for Quality Presses," A McAuto Client Profile (St. Louis, Mo.: McAuto, A Division of McDonnell Douglas Corporation, 1984).

the CAD/CAM group at Harris, reflects on the CAD/CAM installations: "In engineering work, our overall productivity increase due to UNIGRAPHICS is 3.5 to 1, although some applications show as much as 24-to-1 savings," Kuntz says.

Robotics and Robots A *robot* is a mechanical machine that is programmable, which means that a sequence of moves can be preset to be repeated time after time, then reset again to perform another set of moves. Robots replace humans for some very heavy, dirty, dangerous, or unpleasant tasks where the job is very routine (monotonous) in nature. The art of selecting robots for various applications—and knowing when *not* to use them—is called *robotics.*

Among the more common applications of robots in the United States are loading and unloading machine tools, painting, and spot welding—especially in the automotive and appliance industries. The primary advantage of robots over human workers is that their performance never varies. Quality levels are maintained without distraction or fatigue. Reliability is often greater—the robot shows for work each day and is just as consistent Monday morning and Friday evening as every other hour of the week. Reprogrammable robots can perform a variety of specialized tasks and task sequences to precise specifications, and they require less plant space than do alternative production processes.

Economically, a robot in the United States costs from $50,000 to $100,000 installed. The following example shows how a robot can be economically justified for the tasks that it can perform.[11]

EXAMPLE A robot, installed, will cost $76,500 for an unpleasant job involving stacking full cans of paint in a paint factory. The robot can be used 20 hours/day, on the average, seven days/week. The robot should last five to ten years under such usage with but a few major repairs. An employee is paid $10/hour and $7/hour in fringe benefits, including social security payments by the company. To recover only the initial investment, the robot need work:

$$\text{Hours to work} = \frac{\$76{,}500}{\$17.00/\text{hour}} = 4{,}500 \text{ hours}$$

The plant operates only two shifts, a total of 16 hours/day, for 5 days/week and 50 weeks/year. The total hours a robot would be used per year would be:

[11]In 1983 the average price of spot-welding robots was $78,000. In 1965 the average hourly cost of an autoworker was $5 per hour, as was the hourly cost of a robot. By 1980 costs were $16 and $5 per hour, respectively. From Emilia Askari, "The Robots of '1984'," *Miami Herald,* March 19, 1984, p. 9. Also see Kenneth M. Jenkins and Alan R. Raedels, "The Robot Revolution: Strategic Considerations for Managers," *Operations Management Review* 7, no. 2 (Winter 1983), 41–44.

$$\text{Hours/year plant open} = 16 \text{ hours/day} \times 5 \text{ days/week} \times 50 \text{ weeks/year}$$
$$= 4{,}000 \text{ hours/year}$$

In a little over a year, the robot would recover its initial outlay. The payback period would be:

$$\frac{\text{Payback}}{\text{(years)}} = \frac{4{,}500 \text{ hours}}{4{,}000 \text{ hours/year}}$$
$$= 1.125 \text{ years}$$

The rapid recovery of the initial investment is indeed very attractive.

Although the operating costs for the robot were ignored in the simplified example, we see that a robot can offer attractive financial returns to the firm.[12]

How many robots will we need by the year 2000? In 1979 less than ten U.S. companies turned out \$28 million worth of robots. By early 1984, American industry was buying \$169 million a year worth of robots from more than 60 manufacturers. Giants such as General Motors, the Westinghouse Corporation, IBM, and General Electric incorporated robots into their operations.[13]

As our experience with robots increases, we're finding out that they affect other functional areas in some unanticipated ways. In spot-welding metal components, for example, engineers traditionally have overdesigned manufacturing specifications by calling for more welds than were really needed, anticipating that the human welder would miss one or two welds with the onset of fatigue or distractions on the job. Robots, in contrast, never miss a weld and consequently, engineers are rethinking their traditional overdesign practices. While the robot's computer programs and operational specifications do not reside in the manufacturing database of most organizations today, the computer-integrated manufacturing concept is aimed toward doing so in the future.

Group Technology (GT) *Group technology* is a way of organizing and using data for parts with similar properties; it is a tool for standardization. Characteristics of parts, such as their length, diameter, type of material, and density, are recorded for each item in the manufacturing system. The computer can then sort for all similar parts—for example, all titanium screws less than 1½ inches long and of ½ inch maximum diameter. A designer—in engineering or manufacturing—might well find an existing useful titanium screw and avoid the cost of designing a new one. By identifying design attributes and grouping families of items, the computer can aid in tasks too large for the most experienced designer to accomplish manually or mentally.[14]

---

[12]For insight into managing installations, see Fred K. Foulkes and Jeffrey L. Hirsch, "People Make Robots Work," *Harvard Business Review* (January–February 1984).

[13]Askari, "The Robots of '1984'," 1, 7–11.

[14]See a user survey in Nancy Lea Hyer, "Management's Guide to Group Technology," *Operations Management Review* 2, no. 2 (Winter 1984), 36–42.

EXAMPLE At Otis Engineering, an engineering and manufacturing company with over $5 billion in sales in 1978, group technology was applied in an environment with over 200,000 drawings to search. Historically, Otis employees had found that it was usually faster to design a new part than to search for a similar part already in existence. In addition to engineering design savings, substantial operations savings occurred as well. After only 10 months of operation, approximately 580 hours of setup time was saved, averaging 12 minutes/part produced. A 55 percent capacity savings was experienced in some work centers. The program was expanded, resulting in approximately 8,500 machine hours saved, a 45 percent capacity savings, and a 9-month payback for training and coding. The scheduling department experienced similar positive results. Parts that workers had previously produced in 80 days now cleared manufacturing in only 38 days.[15]

How did Otis Engineering achieve all of this? Parts were not only grouped (classed) by GT and manufactured in existing layouts, but also by families of parts where efficiency could be realized in setups, run-times, and in-process inventory.

Trends in Mechanization and Automation As our manufacturing becomes more mechanized we can learn from the experiences of those who have participated in changeovers of process technologies. A survey of users, vendors, and "experts" revealed three key responses about the adoption of factory automation: (1) Leading-edge automation users believe in learning by doing—they have developed, incrementally, an internal base of experience with automation technologies; (2) suppliers claim that most manufacturers are not sophisticated customers—they lack either the technical or strategic perspectives to make correct decisions on automation; and (3) the most difficult problems in achieving computer-integrated manufacturing are managerial rather than technical.[16] Implementation requires technical resources, reward structures, and new interdepartmental communications for success.

A final and obvious issue related to automation is unemployment in the work force. Emilia Askari estimates that by 1990 U.S. job displacement due to robots will be between 17,400 to 28,200 employees in welding and 18,400 to 47,600 employees in assembly.[17] What will these workers do? Individually, this is a serious problem because they are typically lower-skilled persons. Retraining, reassignment, and changing occupations are all better alternatives than unemployment. New jobs might be created from economic growth, resulting in some relief.

---

[15]Bob Alton, "Group Technology," *Proceedings of the 1982 Academic-Practitioners Liaison Operations Management Workshop* (Michigan State University, July 1982), 38–42.

[16]Stephen R. Rosenthal, "A Survey of Factory Automation in the U.S.," *Operations Management Review* 2, no. 2 (Winter 1984), 3–13.

[17]Askari, "The Robots of '1984'," 1, 7–11.

In the robotics industry alone, between 32,000 and 64,100 new jobs are expected—but these will not necessarily be appropriate for individuals replaced by the robot. In fact, that is quite unlikely; workers will need technological skill to plan, design, and produce robots. It is clear that mechanization provides opportunities as well as problems and challenges.

DESIGN OF SERVICES AND SERVICE PROCESSES

Although services, as opposed to products, constitute the largest sector of the U.S. economy in terms of both workers and gross national product, it is interesting that there is no clear agreement on the demarcation between a "product" and a "service." While many people think of IBM as a producer of computers, for example, others contend their primary business is services in the form of applications consulting and customer assistance in using, maintaining, upgrading, and servicing computer systems. The fact is that in today's competitive world, most market offerings are some combination of both product and service as shown in Figure 4.9. The idea is that every consumer purchase falls somewhere on the scale of relative dominance between its service and product elements. The offering of a standard necktie is clearly product-dominant and, in contrast, a tailored suit contains a significant service element in addition to the physical apparel. To be competitive, organizations have to recognize differences in the product/service elements of their market offerings, and they have to develop and operate their process technologies accordingly.

Design of Services

The design of services involves the same generic stages as the design and development of products (Figure 4.4). It begins with the identification of a consumer need and the development of a service concept that fulfills the need. When Federal Express saw the need for fast, dependable shipping services, they developed a new "delivery system" concept that features private ownership, a limited range of services, and a complete pickup-process-delivery cycle that emphasizes convenience and nationwide accessibility. The concept identification led to detailed design of the services and the unique processing technologies (including equipment, human resources, and procedures), and continues today with refinement and redesign of the services in the field.

Although the generic steps may be the same, there are some big differences between product and service development. For those services that do not contain a physical or tangible component, the detailed design stage obviously does not involve the engineering, testing, components analyses, and prototype building found in product development. Further downstream in service development, the design of the processing technology involves different issues and considerations than those in product

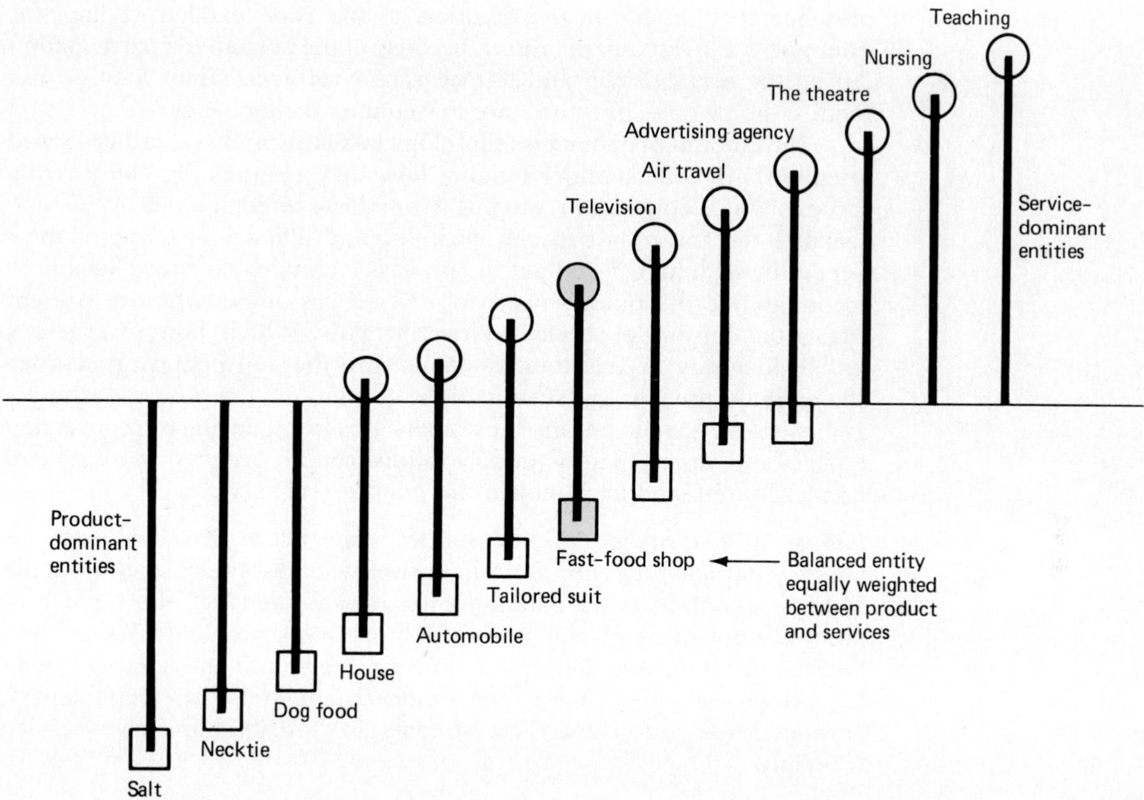

FIGURE 4.9
Scale of service versus product dominance

Source: G. Lynn Shostack, "How to Design a Service," *European Journal of Marketing* 16, no. 1 (1982), 52.

technologies because of the client or customer's presence in the conversion process, as we see next.

Service Process Technologies

Process technologies for services are at least as diverse, and perhaps more so, than product conversion processes. Services experience wide variations in the amount of customer contact and in the labor versus capital intensiveness of their operations. Consequently, there are different types of problems, issues, and essential competencies for success across the various service technologies.

Customer Contact *Customer contact* refers to the customer's presence in creating the service, and it occurs in two ways. First is the customer's involvement in *designing or customizing* the service. In buying a new home, for example, the customer can be intensively active in the design, working closely with an architect. Or the buyer can opt for a standard design without any customizing. A second type of contact is the customer's presence *in and during* the creation of the service. Hair styling, for example, is a high-contact process because of the customer's participation during the service. Wig and toupee repair services, when they do not require the owner's presence, are low-contact technologies.

The amount of contact is helpful in classifying and evaluating service organizations and in understanding how they operate. By categorizing services on a continuum ranging from low- to high-contact, we can visualize the tradeoffs between flexibility and efficiency of operations.[18] Generally, with higher contact the process technology is more flexible to accommodate the unique needs of diverse customers who are present during the delivery of services. When flexibility is high, however, there is less opportunity or freedom to standardize the conversion process for efficiency. At the low-contact end of the continuum, the process technology can be less flexible because customers are absent during the conversion process and, consequently, the operations can be oriented more toward standardization and efficiency in their delivery of services.

Labor Intensiveness Some service conversion processes, such as nursing and teaching, are labor-intensive; whereas others, including the 24-hour automatic teller machines, are capital-intensive. These different processes obviously present contrasting operating problems. While work force scheduling and employee training are dominant concerns in a labor-intensive environment, the emphasis might be on technological advancements and capital investments in a capital-intensive service company.

Service Process Matrix By combining the two dimensions—customer contact and labor intensiveness—four distinctive types of service processes are evident (Figure 4.10). Many service organizations fit clearly into each cell of the matrix, and they have differing operations challenges and problems.

Quasi-manufacturing (e.g., Federal Express), with low labor intensity and low customer contact, offers rigidly standardized services, is very concerned with developing reliable delivery schedules, and makes major capital equipment decisions in a bureaucratized setting. *Mass services* (e.g., the city school system), while still in a bureaucratic system with standardized service offerings, are much more involved with training, development, and scheduling of the human resources that are so critical for successful service delivery in this labor-intensive conversion process. *Custom-shop services* (e.g., a hospital) must be capable of providing customized patient services with a professional staff in a relatively capital-intensive conversion technology that emphasizes cost containment and large capital investment decisions. The hallmark of the *professional service* (e.g., tutoring) is customized service through intensive interaction be-

[18]See R. Chase, "Where Does the Customer Fit in a Service Operation?" *Harvard Business Review* 56, no. 6 (November–December 1978), 137–42.

	Low Customer Contact	High Customer Contact
Capital Intensive	Quasi-manufacturing Postal services, check processing, automated warehousing	Custom-shop Services Charter travel services, long-distance telephone services, medical treatment
Labor Intensive	Mass Services Teaching, live entertainment, cafeteria	Professional Services Legal counseling, medical diagnosis, tutoring
	(rigid process technology)	(flexible process technology)

FIGURE 4.10
A matrix of service processes

tween the customer and professional personnel. Since the professional is governed as much or more by professional norms than by organizational rules, superior-subordinate relationships are looser, and the professional's skills in relating to the customer are essential.

Trends in Service Automation

As we have seen, mechanization and technology issues are as important to services as they are to manufacturing. In fact, service mechanization is probably easier for most of us to relate to through our personal experiences with automated banking, electronic grocery scanners, and the like. The vast numbers of people employed in services indicate that substantial productivity potential exists in our office operations. In many service industries, such as commercial banking and insurance, productivity gains are associated with how information is managed. Since information is perhaps the key resource in the white-collar environment, there is a growing emphasis on managing it just as we do other resources.

Office automation (OA) is a computer-based system for managing information resources including word processing; report generation; and data handling of clerical, professional, and management personnel. It seeks to maximize the productivity of office resources.[19]

OA's most distinctive feature is the emphasis on *integrated* automation:

> The goal of the integrated electronic office is to connect every piece of office equipment—mainframes, personal computers, photocopiers, and other devices—to every other, not only in one location but

[19]J. C. Crawford, "Successfully Evaluating and Implementing Office Automation," *CA Magazine*, August 1984, 106.

in company branches and in suppliers' and customers' offices throughout the world. . . .[20]

Highly integrated systems are feasible today due to the abundance of affordable, advanced telecommunications and electronics technologies. These devices have changed white-collar job content and capabilities, streamlining the flows of communications among work stations and people. Information is created and transmitted more rapidly and directly than in pre-OA systems. Desktop terminals provide easy data entry, either by voice or keyboard, for messages to be transmitted directly to the recipient's terminal. Photocopies or facsimilies of the message can be produced quickly on equipment that is directly integrated with the sender's or receiver's terminal. Teleconferencing through terminals provides direct communications among executives in remote locations, thus avoiding mail delays or traveling costs for meeting together at one location. User-friendly word processing systems provide a faster, more accurate means of producing letters, reports, and other documents than do earlier types of equipment. Electronic spreadsheets, database software, and graphics software enable professionals and executives to retrieve and manipulate data for problem analysis, decision making, and reporting.

SUMMARY

In planning conversion systems, we discussed three major decision areas—the design of new products, the design of conversion processes, and the design of services to be offered. We illustrated how the product life cycle enables us to understand how and why the conversion process and its operations change throughout the product's life. As products mature and decline, we saw the need for new products from research and development. The product development process, beginning with needs identification and continuing on through product support in the field, was shown to involve technical, organizational, and behavioral elements that collectively determine new product lead times and costs. Closely associated with product development was the design of production processes that also have life cycles. An examination of five different ways to organize production technologies disclosed differences in their equipment, human resource requirements, procedures, and operating characteristics. In shifting from products to services, we found that although the design of services entails the same basic steps as product design, the details of executing those steps are quite different. The basis for the differences was shown to stem from the nature of service process technologies which encompass differing amounts of customer contact and labor intensiveness. The implications of these differences for operations management were summarized in a service process matrix.

[20]M. Hart, "How the Office of the Future Is Shaping Up," *CA Magazine*, August 1984, 72.

CASE

Melanie Elizabeth's Dilemma

An established transformer manufacturer supplies high-voltage transformers to utilities throughout the world. Located in southern Indiana, sales the last three years have averaged 60 percent in North America, 20 percent to South America, and 20 percent to the Pacific Basin. The table shows some selected company data for this manufacturing plant, which does all the manufacturing for this division.

Chris, the plant manager, and his brother Nat, the director of engineering, are at odds about purchasing several state-of-the-art robots for welding a continuous seam on the transformers. Transformers manufactured by this company are designed to hang on telephone poles near residences or commercial buildings. Since they are used outdoors, they must be totally airtight. This welding operation is critical to an airtight, high-quality transformer. Chris insists that the robots are not cost justified; he also fears they will cause problems with the direct labor employees now doing the welding. Chris is concerned that the use of robots may jeopardize upcoming labor negotiations and that it will force manufacturing to use equipment they don't know how to operate. Nat argues that the use of robots will reduce manufacturing expenses and improve the overall quality of the welding department. Another potential advantage is that the engineering group will develop robotics skills for future use.

Chris and Melanie Elizabeth work for the same group vice president. Melanie Elizabeth works with the vice president at corporate headquarters in Chicago. As the vice president's staff assistant, Melanie

Indiana plant data

Last year (1985) sales	$13,750,000
Cost of goods sold (1985)	$11,500,000
Labor	$ 4,750,000
Material	$ 6,000,000
Overhead	$ 750,000
Invested capital (1985)	$ 3,500,000
Number of employees	1,150
Direct labor	750
Direct labor, welding	121
Nondirect labor	400
Average direct labor wages and fringes	$18.75/hour
Welding labor productivity (current month)	93.7%
Welding material usage variance (positive usage is more than standard; current month)	+16%
Cost one robot, installed	$103,000
Robot characteristics	
Direct workers replaced (two shifts)	3
Total cost operation annually	$ 10,300
Estimated useful life	5 years
Plant operations	2 shifts, 50 weeks/year

Elizabeth has been asked to gather facts concerning the Indiana plant's intended robotics application. She is to make a recommendation to Chris, Nat, and the group vice president at a meeting at the plant in three weeks. Melanie Elizabeth is also aware of the possibility that the entire plant will be moved to the Philippine Islands in the next two years. Average labor rates and fringe benefits in the Phillippines are expected to be $4.75/hour. The decision to move will be based in part upon upcoming union negotiation results and union leader/member willingness to participate in the change. Melanie Elizabeth's assignment is to get all the economics and judgmental issues on the table, not to make a final choice for the company.

Case Questions

1. In the role of Melanie Elizabeth
   (a) Prepare the best case to support Chris's position.
   (b) Prepare the best case to support Nat's position.
2. With three weeks remaining, what would you like to gather in terms of additional information? Why?
3. If you were Melanie Elizabeth and were asked for a recommendation without additional information, what would you suggest? Why?

REVIEW AND DISCUSSION QUESTIONS

1. Explain the relationships between technology, mechanization, and the work force by (a) defining each and (b) explaining how technology and mechanization are affecting the work force.
2. Explain computer-integrated manufacturing. Figure 4.8 should be useful in your discussion.
3. Robots, CAD, CAM, numerical control, manufacturing database, and group technology are terms used in manufacturing but are difficult to grasp. After studying each, prepare a short essay that explains these terms in nontechnical language a high school senior could be expected to understand.
4. What do you think are the significant issues about robots and robotics?
5. Identify and discuss difficulties and problems that can arise in implementing an integrated information system for new product development.
6. The concept of product and process life cycles has implications for technological changes, employee behavior, and organizational structure. Discuss these implications.
7. Select four products or services that can be brought into the classroom for demonstration. Analyze the characteristics of each of them and show where they are located on Figure 4.9.
8. Identify two services that clearly fit in the cells of Figure 4.10. Identify two other services that are not reasonably identifiable with any cell in the matrix.
9. Demonstrate how the growth of automation can affect the product/service development process. Use specific products and services for examples.

10. Identify examples of operations that fall on the major diagonal of the product-process matrix (Figure 4.7).
11. Select a simple product (e.g., dog house, barbeque grill, spoon) and show what would be involved in a major redesign of the product. Address each stage of the product development process, including its major operations issues and problems.
12. Identify a consumer service need (keep it simple) and outline what would have to be done in each stage of the development process to create a service that fulfills the need.
13. As an operations manager what steps would you take to improve your company's performance on lead time for new product development? Suppose your product line is small photocopy machines and you wish to reduce development lead time from 3 years down to 18 months.
14. If you were beginning a new venture opening a wine and cheese shop in a shopping mall, what would your short-term production/operations objectives be?

PROBLEMS

Solved Problems

1. A commercial airplane manufacturer is concerned over the reliability of the radar subsystem placed in the cockpit of the aircraft. This purchased radar system is used for instrument (automatic) landings. Given the data below, we want to analyze the reliability of a specific purchased radar system currently in use.

   Ten radar systems were operated in the airplane manufacturer's laboratory for 500 flights each. Each simulated flight required use of the radar, and the flight landings averaged 20 minutes. Two radar systems failed, one after 121 flights and the second after 273 flights.

   To compute the percentage of radar systems failing,

$$\begin{aligned}\text{Failures (\%)} &= \frac{\text{Number of failures}}{\text{Number tested}} \times 100\% \\ &= 2/10 \times 100\% = 20\%\end{aligned}$$

   Next, we compute the number of failures per operating hour,

$$\begin{aligned}\text{Failures/unit-hour} &= \frac{\text{Number of failures}}{\text{Operating time}} \\ \text{Total time} &= (10 \times 500 \times .33 \text{ hour}) = 1{,}650 \text{ hours} \\ \text{Nonoperating time} &= (1 \times 379 \times .33) + (1 \times 227 \times .33) \\ &= 200 \text{ hours} \\ \text{Operating time} &= (1650 - 200) = 1450 \text{ hours} \\ \text{Failures/unit-hour} &= \frac{2}{1450} = .000138\end{aligned}$$

   Examining failures/unit-hour operating, the failure rate of .000138 seems low. However, it is very likely this is too high for the airplane and airline to have but one radar system in the airplane. The analysis assumes the airline would not repair or replace the radar system when it fails, which is also quite unlikely. The analysis assumes the 200 down hours were in some 600 flights, flights being flown with a defective radar system. That isn't likely to happen under most airplane maintenance systems. It is likely, however, that the manufacturer would look to another supplier for a more reliable radar system.

Reinforcing Fundamentals

2. A product has two subcomponents, A and B. Failure of either A or B results in failure of the product. The probabilities of A and B performing successfully for 1,500 times are .96 and .92, respectively, and are independent.
   (a) What is the probability that the product will operate properly 1,500 or more times?
   (b) What is your answer to Part a if the probabilities for A and B are .85 and .75, respectively?
3. A product has three subcomponents, A, B, and C. Failure of A can cause the failure of the product. Failure of either only B or C would not cause the failure of the product. However, the product fails if both B and C fail simultaneously. The probabilities of A, B, and C performing successfully are .95, .85, .80, respectively.
   (a) Draw a system diagram for this reliability situation.
   (b) What is the probability that the product works successfully?
4. A robot, installed, is estimated to cost $68,000. This robotics application is directed at replacing one employee per shift on a routine, repetitive task that the employee and robot can do equally well. The plant works three shifts a day, five days a week, 47 weeks a year. Total labor wages and fringes average $9.25/hour in this facility. Absenteeism has averaged 11 percent the last year in this job. Every hour the equipment is idle from absenteeism, the company loses a $5 contribution to profit, which cannot be recovered. The robot is expected to be "down" (not available) 1 percent of the time and is expected to have a three-year useful life. Should the company make the investment based on this economic analysis?
5. Consider the impact of the robot installation on the three employees in Problem 4. If you could get absenteeism reduced to 1 percent by showing this analysis to employees, could they keep their jobs? If not, what alternatives typically exist for retaining the employees?
6. In Problem 4, what wage rate would be necessary for the employees to be economically equivalent to the robot, if all other factors remained constant? Would employees be likely to accept this rate? Why?

Challenging Exercises

7. Relectro Corporation produces a miniature electric motor consisting of four basic subcomponents: coil, prime circuit, switch, and simo-wire. Relectro promises its customers a two-year motor life with a probability of .95. Failure of any of the basic components renders the motor useless. Consideration is being given to redesigning the product for purposes of cost reduction. Engineers have gathered the following reliability and cost data for components that could be purchased from new vendors.

Data for existing components

Component	Unit Cost	Two-year Failure Probability
Coil	$17.00	.01
Prime circuit	8.50	.03
Switch	1.50	.05
Simo-wire	4.00	.01

Data for new vendors

	Vendor X		Vendor Y	
Component	Unit Cost	Two-year Failure Probability	Unit Cost	Two-year Failure Probability
Coil	$16.25	0.010	$21.00	0.005
Prime circuit	12.00	0.020	15.00	0.001
Switch	2.50	0.030	4.00	0.025
Simo-wire	4.00	0.010	4.50	0.010

Perform a reliability and cost analysis to support your recommendations for redesign of the motor.

GLOSSARY

Applied research Investigation directed to discovery of new scientific knowledge with specific commercial objectives toward products or processes.

Basic research Original investigation for the advancement of scientific knowledge.

Computer-aided design (CAD) Computer software programs allowing the designer to carry out geometric transformations rapidly.

Computer-aided manufacturing (CAM) Computer software programs that control the actual machine on the shop floor.

Computer-integrated manufacturing Digital computers utilizing a manufacturing database that encompasses engineering design, manufacturing engineering, factory production, and information management.

Development Technical activities encountered in translating research findings into products or processes.

Group technology A way of organizing and using data for parts with similarities; it is a tool for standardization.

Life cycle Pattern of demand throughout the product's life; similar patterns and stages can be identified for the useful life of a process.

Mechanization The process of bringing about the use of equipment and machinery in production and operations.

Research and development Organizational efforts directed toward product and process innovation; includes stages of basic research, applied research, development, and implementation.

Robot A programmable mechanical machine capable of moving materials and performing routine, repetitive tasks.

Robotics The art of selecting robots for various applications.

Technology The scientific expertise in blending labor, land, capital, and management into useful outputs.

SELECTED READINGS

Abernathy, W. J., "Production Process Structure and Technological Change," *Decision Sciences* 7, no. 4 (October 1976), 607–19.

Blanchard, B. S., *Logistics Engineering and Management* (2nd ed.). Englewood Cliffs, N.J.: Prentice Hall, 1981.

deKluyver, C. A., "Innovation and Industrial Product Life Cycles," *California Management Review* 20, no. 1 (Fall 1977), 21–33.

Grant, E. L., W. G. Ireson, and R. S. Leavenworth, *Principles of Engineering Economy* (6th ed.). New York: Ronald Press, 1976.

Gunn, Thomas G., "The Mechanization of Design and Manufacturing," *Scientific American* 247, no. 3 (September 1982), 116.

Hakala, N. V., "Administration of Industrial Technology," *Business Horizons* 20, no. 5 (October 1977), 4–10.

Hayes, R. H., and S. C. Wheelwright, "Link Manufacturing Process and Product Life Cycles," *Harvard*

Business Review 57, no. 1 (January–February, 1979), 133–40.

———, *Restoring Our Competitive Edge: Competing Through Manufacturing*. New York: John Wiley, 1984.

Hetzner, William A., Louis G. Tornatzky, and Katherine J. Klein, "Manufacturing Technology in the 1980's: A Survey of Federal Programs and Practices," *Management Science* 29, no. 8 (August 1983), 951–61.

Hill, Terry, *Manufacturing Strategy* (Houndmills, Basingstoke, Hampshire England: Macmillan Education LTD, 1985).

Hyer, Nancy Lea, "Management's Guide to Group Technology," *Operations Management Review* 2, no. 2 (Winter 1984), 36–42.

Liao, W. M., "Effects of Learning on Resource Allocation Decisions," *Decision Sciences* 10, no. 1 (January 1979), 116–25.

Schmenner, Roger W., "Every Factory Has a Cycle," *Harvard Business Review* 61, no. 2 (March–April 1983), 121–29.

Shostack, G. Lynn, "How to Design a Service," *European Journal of Marketing* 16, no. 1 (1982), 49–63.

Stobaugh, Robert, and Piero Telesio, "Match Manufacturing Policies and Product Strategies," *Harvard Business Review* 61, no. 2 (March–April 1983), 113–20.

SUPPLEMENT TO CHAPTER 4

LEARNING CURVES

In our discussion of product and process design choices, we considered the future impact of the choice, that is, how operations managers have to live out the life of the product and process. We also discussed how the manufacturing or service process *changes* over time. Learning curve analysis is one way of evaluating the effects of changes in tasks; it is based on traditional industrial engineering techniques. The learning curve methodology is helpful for identifying and evaluating change alternatives, and it can play an important role in the scientific approach to problem solving.

Learning Curve Analysis

When a new model of an existing product is introduced, especially if the work content is similar, learning curve analysis can be helpful in its manufacture.[21] As an organization gains experience in manufacturing a product, the resource inputs required per unit of output diminish over the life of the product. The hours of labor that go into manufacturing the first unit of a new commercial aircraft are typically much higher than those needed for the one-hundredth unit, for example. As the cumulative output of the model grows, the labor inputs continue to decline. As you know, if you repeat a new task continually, your performance improves. The performance time drops off rather dramatically at first, and it continues to fall at some slower rate until a performance plateau, a leveling off, is reached. This learning phenomenon occurs for groups and organizations as well as for individuals. Furthermore, performance data from many companies show that this learning pattern is often regular and predictable. The general form of this pattern, called the *learning curve,* is shown on arithmetic coordinates in Figure S4.1. In it, the initial unit output requires 60 labor hours to manufacture. As output and experience continue, labor hours per unit diminish to about 23 for the twentieth unit. The general equation for this curve is:

$$Y_i = ki^b \qquad \text{(S4.1)}$$

where

Y_i = labor hours required to produce the ith cumulative unit of output
k = labor hours required to produce the first unit of output (initial productivity)
b = index of learning

This exponential curve becomes a straight line when plotted on logarithmic coordinates.

[21]For a review of learning curve development, see Louis E. Yelle, "The Learning Curve: Historical Review and Comprehensive Survey," *Decision Sciences* 10, no. 2 (April 1979), 302–28.

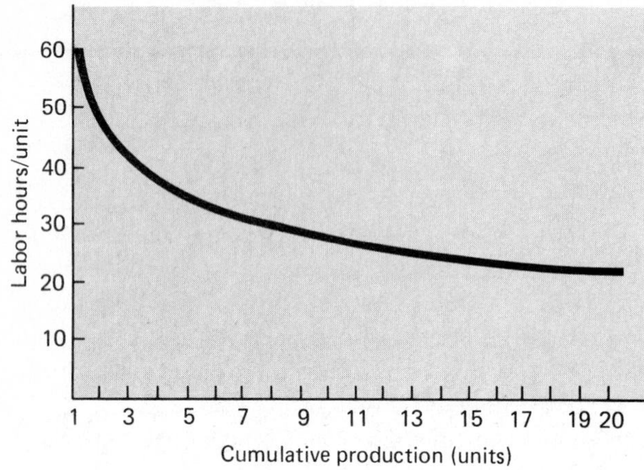

FIGURE S4.1
An 80 percent learning curve plotted on arithmetic coordinates; the first unit requires 60 labor hours

Rate of Learning The rate of learning is not the same in all manufacturing applications. Learning occurs at a higher rate in some applications than others and is reflected by a more rapid descent of the curve. By convention the learning rate is specified as a percentage. A 90 percent curve, for example, means that each time cumulative output doubles, the newest unit of output requires 90 percent of the labor input of the reference unit; if unit 1 requires 100 labor hours, unit 2 will require 90 percent of 100, or 90 hours; unit 4 will require 90 percent of 90 hours, or 81 hours, and so on. Labor hours required for 70, 80, and 90 percent curves are shown here for various levels of cumulative output, assuming 100 labor hours are required for the first unit.

Cumulative Output i (units)	Labor Hours Required for ith Cumulative Unit: 70% Curve	80% Curve	90% Curve
1	100.0	100.0	100.0
2	70.0	80.0	90.0
4	49.0	64.0	81.0
8	34.3	51.2	72.9
16	24.0	41.0	65.6

We have plotted three curves on arithmetic and logarithmic coordinates (Figure S4.2) for 16 cumulative units of output. Arithmetically, the rate of learning is reflected by b, the index of learning. In Figure S4.1, the index of learning for the 90 percent learning curve is $-.1520$. Table S4.1 shows computed values of i^b for 80 and 90 percent curves. By using equation S4.1, you can extend these calculations to cover any desired level of cumulative output beyond those given in the table.

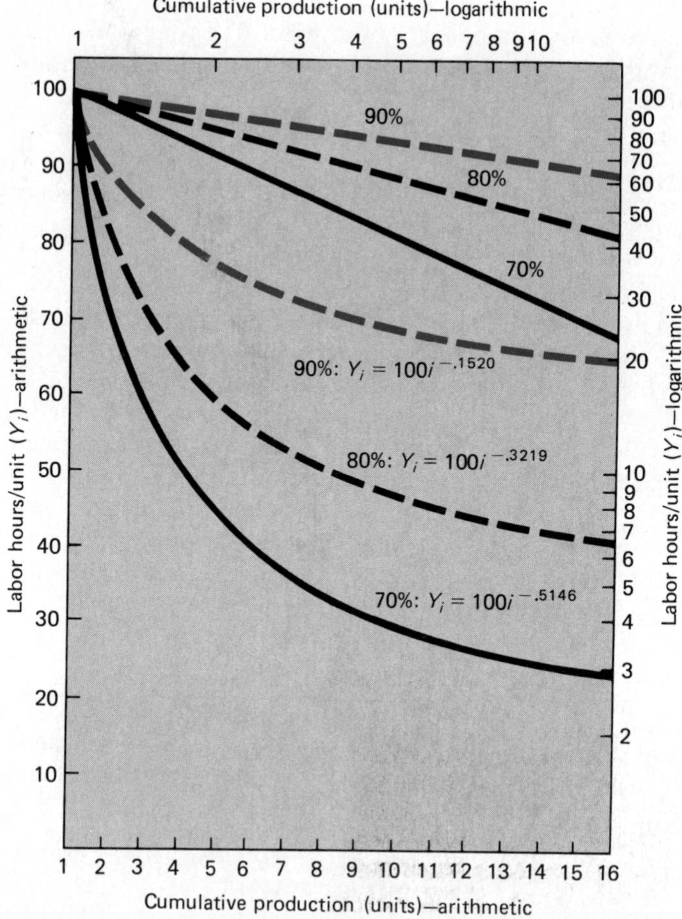

FIGURE S4.2
Arithmetic and logarithmic coordinates for 70, 80, and 90 percent learning curves; first unit requires 100 labor hours

---

EXAMPLE Surefloat Boat Builders has been receiving customer orders for a new model yacht. Based on previous experience at introducing new models, Surefloat engineers estimate that an 80 percent improvement curve is applicable and that the first unit of the new model will require 500 hours of labor. Surefloat has received customer orders for delivery in the next five months as follows:

Month	Number of Yachts Ordered
1	2
2	6
3	10
4	10
5	15
Total	43

The manufacturing manager is concerned about the manpower requirements for meeting these commitments to customers. The manufacturing engineer was asked to provide some information that could be used for manpower planning.

Equation S4.1 applied to the Surefloat situation becomes

$$Y_i = (500)i^{-.3219} \qquad \text{(S4.2)}$$

Using equation S4.2 (or tabled values) for the 80 percent curve, the engineer generated the data in Table S4.2. Surefloat management can use these data to decide how many yachts to produce each month so that the manpower requirements are smoothed across months. The data also enable determination of work force size. Notice the effects of learning in the data. Commitments to customers in month 2 are 200 percent greater than in month 1; yet the manpower to accomplish this increases by only 98 percent over the previous month. As the second column shows, labor hours are reduced rather dramatically initially and then taper off to relatively small increments as the effects of learning diminish with experience.

Table S4.1 Computed values of i^b for 80% and 90% curves: 50 units

i (unit number)	80% Curve ($b = -.3219$)	90% Curve ($b = -.1520$)	i (unit number)	80% Curve ($b = -.3219$)	90% Curve ($b = -.1520$)
1	1.0000	1.0000	26	.3504	.6094
2	.7999	.9000	27	.3461	.6059
3	.7021	.8462	28	.3421	.6026
4	.6400	.8100	29	.3379	.5994
5	.5957	.7830	30	.3346	.5963
6	.5617	.7616	31	.3311	.5934
7	.5345	.7440	32	.3277	.5905
8	.5120	.7290	33	.3245	.5878
9	.4930	.7161	34	.3214	.5851
10	.4766	.7047	35	.3184	.5825
11	.4621	.6946	36	.3155	.5800
12	.4494	.6854	37	.3128	.5776
13	.4380	.6771	38	.3101	.5753
14	.4276	.6696	39	.3075	.5730
15	.4182	.6626	40	.3050	.5708
16	.4096	.6561	41	.3026	.5687
17	.4017	.6501	42	.3002	.5666
18	.3944	.6445	43	.2980	.5646
19	.3876	.6392	44	.2958	.5626
20	.3819	.6342	45	.2937	.5607
21	.3753	.6295	46	.2916	.5588
22	.3697	.6251	47	.2896	.5570
23	.3645	.6209	48	.2876	.5552
24	.3595	.6169	49	.2857	.5535
25	.3548	.6131	50	.2839	.5518

Table S4.2 Engineering data for use in manpower planning

Yacht (cumulative)	Labor Hours per Yacht (rounded)[a]	Month	Number of Yachts Promised	Labor Hours Needed for Monthly Commitments	Change in Labor Hours from Previous Month	Change in Output from Previous Month	Monthly Manpower Equivalents (number of people)[b]
1	500	1	2	900			5.62
2	400						
3	351	2	6	1,773	+98.1%	+200.0%	11.08
4	320						
5	298						
6	281						
7	267						
8	256						
9	246	3	10	2,185	+23.2	+ 67.7	13.65
10	238						
19	194	4	10	1,816	−16.8	—0—	11.35
28	171						
29	169	5	15	2,373	+31.0	+ 50.0	14.83
42	150						
43	149						
				Total labor hours = 9,047	Total yachts = 43		

[a]Obtained from Table S4.1 and equation S4.1, labor hours for yacht one = Y_1 = (500)(1.000) = 500.

[b]A person is assumed to work 20 days/month, 8 hours/day. Thus, a "manpower equivalent" is 20 × 8 = 160 labor hours/month. For each month the manpower equivalent is found by dividing the monthly labor hours by 160. Hence, for month 1, 900 ÷ 160 = 5.62.

EXAMPLE Surefloat management has decided on a selling price of $12,000 a yacht. It expects to receive payment the month following delivery. Each yacht will be produced and delivered during the month in which it was promised previously. Work force size will equal the monthly manpower equivalents shown in the table. Standard wages are $1,000/month/employee. Costs of direct materials, variable materials, overhead, and fixed administrative and marketing overhead are also shown in the table. All these costs are incurred during the month of production.

Table S4.3 Cash flow for six months: Surefloat Boat Builders

	Month					
	1	2	3	4	5	6
Units produced and delivered	2	6	10	10	15	15
Cash inflow from sales	—0—	$24,000	$72,000	$120,000	$120,000	$180,000
Outflows						
Wages	$ 5,620	$11,080	$13,650	$ 11,350	$ 14,830	$ 13,500
Direct materials ($6,000 per yacht)	12,000	36,000	60,000	60,000	90,000	90,000
Variable materials overhead (10% of direct materials)	1,200	3,600	6,000	6,000	9,000	9,000
Fixed administrative and marketing overhead	10,000	10,000	10,000	10,000	10,000	10,000
Monthly outflow	$28,820	$60,680	$89,650	$187,350	$123,830	$122,500
Net monthly cash flow (inflow-outflow)	(28,820)[a]	(36,680)	(17,650)	32,650	(3,830)	57,500
Cumulative cash flow position (month-end)	(28,820)	(65,500)	(83,150)	(50,500)	(54,330)	3,170

[a]Parentheses denote negative cash flow.

Uses of Learning Curves Just as learning curve analysis can be used for manpower planning, it can also be helpful in cash flow planning.[22] Cash flow planning involves identifying the timing of cash outlays and inflows associated with a new product. Notice in the last example that monthly inflows are less than outlays for each of the first three months. Cumulative cash flows are negative through month 5, and Surefloat will have to borrow funds or divert them from other projects to finance operations on the new model yacht during these months.

Parameter Estimation Two parameters, k and b, must be estimated for learning curve analysis. If these parameters are seriously in error, results can be very misleading. Estimates of labor hours for the initial unit

[22]Use of the learning curve in decision making is discussed in Woody M. Liao, "Effects of Learning on Resource Allocation Decisions," *Decision Sciences* 10, no. 1 (January 1979), 116–25.

are based primarily on staff experience and familiarity with the history of the conversion process. Estimation accuracy is closely related to the degree of conversion similarity between the new and previous products. Estimation of the appropriate learning rate is typically accomplished by regression analysis on data from experiences with similar past products.

Sources of Improvement While the learning curve depicts productivity improvement over time, improvement does not take place solely because workers are learning. The sources of productivity changes are numerous, but they include changes in work methods, product engineering modifications, facilities layout improvements, equipment redesign, employee training, and others. We intend the term *learning curve* to subsume the effects of all these sources of productivity progress in summary measure. Learning curve analysis is generally of greatest benefit in labor-intensive conversion processes.

CASE

Cleanair Corporation

Cleanair Corporation designs and manufactures small contaminant filtration units. These units are used in various industrial facilities to reduce emissions contributing to air pollution. Cleanair's research and development department has developed and tested a new model, the Minigasp III, which it believes is now suitable for full-scale marketing. Minigasp I has been successfully marketed for eight years and Minigasp II for four, and Cleanair management believes that Minigasp III faces even brighter marketing prospects. Although similar in many ways to its predecessors, Minigasp III contains an innovative chemical processing system that should give Cleanair a competitive edge in the industry. Management must now decide whether to add Minigasp III to its product line.

The marketing manager says that a $3,000/unit selling price would be very competitive and anticipates sales of one unit in each of months 1 and 2, two units in month 3, three units in month 4, and four units per month thereafter. Payment by the customer is expected during the month of purchase. The operations manager believes he can meet these market demands if the changeover of facilities is started immediately. An initial outlay of $30,000 is necessary to renovate part of the plant and equipment. Costs of manufacture have been estimated as follows:

Direct materials	=	$700/unit
Indirect materials	=	10 percent of direct materials cost
Direct labor	=	$7/labor hour
Indirect labor	=	20 percent of direct labor cost
Additional administrative and marketing costs	=	$3,000/month

In addition, maintenance expenses will be $1,000 in month 1; $750 in month 2; and $500 per month thereafter. Production engineers estimate the initial unit of Minigasp III will require 200 hours of labor to manufacture. Thereafter, they believe an 80 percent learning curve is applicable.

The finance manager questions the advisability of adopting the new product because of the risks involved. If new government regulations were to be created, always a major factor in this industry, the marketability of Minigasp III could be prematurely damaged. Consequently, he suggests the project not be undertaken unless the funds from sales can fully recover the initial $30,000 outlay during the first year of production. As operations manager you are expected to respond to the finance manager.

REVIEW AND DISCUSSION QUESTIONS

1. Under what circumstances is learning curve analysis most applicable?
2. What are the sources of productivity improvement that cause the learning phenomenon?
3. For what kinds of operating decisions can learning curve analysis provide data?

PROBLEMS

1. In response to a consumer inquiry, a manufacturing company is estimating the costs of 25 units of a new product, which is similar to an existing one. Estimates indicate that 400 labor hours are required to produce the first unit. Draw graphs of labor requirements for units 1 through 25 for 80 percent and 90 percent learning curves.
2. Reconsider Problem 1 using the 80 percent improvement curve. Direct labor and variable overhead are estimated at $9/labor hour. Direct materials will cost $600 for each unit produced. Initial tooling for the product costs $15,000. Monthly overhead will cost $6,000/month during the life of the project. The available work force consists of ten operators, each available for 160 hours/month. If a profit of 10 percent on selling price is desired, what should be the selling price?

Utilizing the QSOM Computer Software

3. A manufacturer of industrial transformers is introducing a new product line. The first of a series of similar new transformers was recently completed in 1,600 hours. Assuming a learning rate of 75 percent, use QSOM to develop the learning curve for this situation and the production times for the first 25 units. Now compare your solution to a learning rate of 85 percent. Compare production times for units 10, 20, and 25 for the 75 percent and 85 percent rates, and interpret the differences for management.

5

Operations Capacity

At first glance, the question of capacity planning may seem to have little relevance to a service business like trucking. Actually, it is of the greatest importance. The key point to remember is that the volume of freight will fluctuate significantly, not only from year to year, but from day to day. And any freight not handled today is probably lost forever. You can't stockpile or back order freight; fast service is essential.

Our principal trucking subsidiary, Consolidated Freightways Motor Freight, has 550 freight terminals and has been adding more than one per week for the past five years. We expect this pace to continue for several years.

Some years ago it became obvious that we could not achieve our ultimate goal of serving the entire United States by simply adding terminals to our existing system, in which we moved freight directly from the origin point to the destination. We concluded we would have to devise a system of connected "hubs" or distribution centers, each serving 20 or more "spokes," or satellite terminals. We determined that we would eventually need approximately 32 strategically located hubs and 700 or more satellites. We began in 1975 and today most of that system is in place, operating even more efficiently than we had hoped.

Raymond F. O'Brien
Chairman and Chief Executive Officer
Consolidated Freightways, Inc.
Palo Alto, California

In strategic planning for operations, we see that organizational strategy helps managers define the operations function: It specifies what we want to accomplish in operations. Having specified this mission, we develop policies that guide our planning for operations capacity, location, and layout in the long run, and they guide the ways we use our resources and facilities in the shorter run. It is apparent from Mr. O'Brien's comment that Consolidated Freightways Motor Freight has been considering capacity and location interactions since 1975, and that the results have been very satisfactory.

In this chapter we investigate the capacity decision and how capacity alternatives affect our ability to meet our operations mission. We consider how capacity decisions affect operations costs and break-even relationships, service levels, required investment, and risk to the organization.

CAPACITY PLANNING ENVIRONMENT

The *capacity* of operations refers to the productive capability of a facility; it is usually expressed as volume of output per time period. Operations managers are concerned with capacity for several reasons. First, they want sufficient capacity to provide the timing and quantity of output needed for meeting current and future customer demand. Further, the available capacity affects the efficiency of operations, including the ease or difficulty of scheduling output and the costs of maintaining the facility. Finally, the acquisition of capacity is an investment by the organization. Since we seek a good return on investment, both the costs and the revenues of a capacity decision must be carefully evaluated.

The Need for Capacity Planning

When an organization chooses to "make" more of a product (or service) or decides to "make" a new product (or service), capacity planning is the first operations management activity that occurs. Once capacity is evaluated and a need for new or expanded facilities is determined, location and process technology activities occur. If too much capacity exists, alternatives to reduce capacity must be explored, such as temporarily closing or even selling facilities. In such a situation, there might be a consolidation that requires activities such as relocation, combining technologies, and rearrangement of equipment and process (layout).

Relationship of Capacity and Location Decisions

Often the capacity decision is inseparable from the facility location decision. This condition exists because demand for many services depends on system location and, of course, desired capacity depends upon demand; therefore, we have a circular relationship. Commercial banks, for example, simultaneously expand capacity and future demand for services by using branching strategies. Branch location and size decisions are made after management has considered neighborhood population densities and growth projections, geographic locations of market segments, transportation (traffic) flows, and the locations of competitors. The addition of a new branch offers greater convenience to some existing customers and, management hopes, attracts new ones as well. Obviously this decision affects the revenues, operating costs, and capital costs of the organization.

In the public sector, the capacity decision involves similar considerations. Municipalities face ever-increasing demands for public services, strong public sentiment for tightening budgets, and greater performance accountability. Consequently, officials have increased their efforts to rearrange public resources so they can increase service capacity without increasing costs of operation. Municipal emergency services, for example, are periodically expanded by adding new emergency stations. First, an analysis of the geographic dispersion of demand for services is undertaken to show population growth and shifts. Next, municipal officials plan where to locate new emergency stations, taking into consideration both areas of greatest need and costs of operation and facilities. Although the capacity decision may not involve direct revenues, cost savings for citizens can be considered a form of indirect revenues. These cost savings can result in reduced tax burdens or lower insurance rates in areas with high levels of emergency services.

Modeling techniques, which we will illustrate later in this chapter, are playing a central role in these planning processes. One study, for example, explains how mathematical programming is used for greater ambulance effectiveness considering time-to-scene, time-to-hospital, and distance-to-hospital factors, thereby increasing effective service system capacity.[1] Another study shows how mathematical modeling can determine optimal fleet sizes and vehicle routes for a commercial common carrier.[2] Yet another study demonstrates the value of queuing models in a computer-based information system for the St. Louis County Police Department.[3] The system gives a reliable and valid way to allocate police patrols, thereby using existing capacity more efficiently or reducing the size of operations without diminishing existing service levels. All these examples show how systematic analysis and planning can lead to effective capacity improvement and utilization.

Capacity Planning Decisions

Capacity planning decisions normally involve the following activities:

1. Assessment of existing capacity
2. Forecast estimates of future capacity needs over a selected planning horizon
3. Identification of alternative ways to modify capacity
4. Financial, economical, and technological evaluation of capacity alternatives
5. Selection or choice of a capacity alternative most suited to achieving strategic mission

Measuring Capacity

For some organizations capacity seems simple to measure. Kraft, Inc. can refer to tons of cheese output per year. General Motors Corporation can speak of number of automobiles per year. But what about organizations

[1]C. Saydam and M. McKnew, "A Separable Programming Approach to Expected Coverage: An Application to Ambulance Location," *Decision Sciences* 16, no. 4 (Fall 1985), 381–98.

[2]M. O. Ball, B. L. Golden, A. A. Assad, and L. D. Bodin, "Planning for Truck Fleet Size in the Presence of a Common-Carrier Option," *Decision Sciences* 14, no. 1 (January 1983), 103–20.

[3]N. K. Kwak and M. B. Leavitt, "Police Patrol Beat Design: Allocation of Effort and Evaluation of Expected Performance," *Decision Sciences* 15, no. 3 (Summer 1984), 421–33.

Table 5.1 Measures of operating capacity

Organization	Measure
	Output
Automobile manufacturer	Number of autos
Brewery	Barrels of beer
Cannery	Tons of food
Steel producer	Tons of steel
Power company	Megawatts of electricity
	Input
Airline	Number of seats
Hospital	Number of beds
Job shop	Labor and/or machine hours
Merchandising	Square feet of display or sales area
Movie theater	Number of seats
Restaurant	Number of seats or tables
Tax office	Number of accountants
University	Number of students and/or faculty
Warehouse	Square or cubic feet of storage space

with more diverse product lines? How do you measure the capacity of a law firm or a veterinary clinic? In part, the answers depend on the diversity of the product mix. Even within General Motors, output consists of automobiles, trucks, and locomotives. When the units of output are identical, or nearly so, a common unit of measure may be selected: megawatts of electricity, tons of gravel, number of autos, or barrels of beer. In these cases, capacity is measured in units of *output*.

On the other hand, when product mix is diverse, it is hard to find a common unit of output measure that makes sense. As a substitute, capacity can be expressed in terms of *input* measures. A legal office may express capacity in terms of the number of attorneys employed. A custom job shop or an auto repair shop may indicate capacity by available labor hours and/or machine hours per week, month, or year.

An estimate of capacity, then, may be measured in terms of the inputs or the outputs of the conversion process. Some common examples of capacity measures used by different organizations are shown in Table 5.1.

Capacity Defined *Capacity* is the maximum theoretical rate of productive or conversion capability for the existing product mix of an organization's operations. Capacity incorporates the concept of rate of conversion within an operations setting. A change in product mix can change unit output capacity.

It's often difficult to get a realistic measure of capacity because of day-to-day variations. Employees are sometimes absent or late, equipment breakdowns occur, facility downtime is needed for maintenance and repair, machine setups are required for product changeovers, and vacations must be scheduled. Since all these variations occur from time to time, you can see, then, that the capacity of a facility can rarely be measured in precise terms. Such measures as are used must be interpreted cautiously.

Estimating Future Capacity Needs

Capacity requirements can be evaluated from two extreme perspectives—short-term and long-term.

Short-term Requirements Managers often use forecasts of product demand to estimate the near-term work load the facility must handle. These estimates are obtained from the forecasting techniques presented in Chapter 3. By looking ahead up to 12 months, we can anticipate output requirements for our different products or services. Then we can compare requirements with existing capacity and detect when capacity adjustments are needed.

Long-term Requirements Longer-term capacity requirements are more difficult to determine because of uncertainties in future market demand and technologies. Forecasting five or ten years into the future is a risky and difficult task. What products or services will we be producing then? Today's product may not even exist in the future. Obviously, long-range capacity requirements are dependent on marketing plans, product development, and the life cycles of the products.

Changes in processing technology must also be anticipated. Even if our products remain unchanged, the methods for generating them may change dramatically. Just as capacity requirements depend upon market plans and forecasts, capacity planning depends upon technology plans and forecasts.

Strategies for Modifying Capacity

After existing capacity has been measured and future capacity requirements assessed, alternative ways of modifying capacity must be identified.

Short-run Responses For short-run periods of up to one year, the fundamental capacity of the conversion process is of fixed size. Major facilities are seldom opened or closed as a regular monthly or yearly practice. Many short-run adjustments for increasing or decreasing capacity are possible, however. Which adjustments to make depend on whether the conversion process is primarily labor- or capital-intensive and whether the product is one that can be stored in inventory.

Capital-intensive processes rely heavily on physical facilities, plant, and equipment for performing the conversion operations. Short-run capacity can be modified by operating these facilities more or less intensively than normal. The costs of facility setup, changeover, maintenance, procurement of raw materials, manpower procurement, scheduling, and inventory management can all be increased by such capacity changes.

In labor-intensive processes, short-run capacity can be changed by laying off or hiring people or by having employees work overtime or be idle. These alternatives are also expensive, though, since hiring costs and

Table 5.2 Temporary capacity changes

Capacity Change	Operations Manager's Activity
Inventories	Finished goods may be stockpiled during slack periods to meet later demand.
Backlogs	During peak demand periods, customers may be willing to wait some time before receiving their product. Their order request is filed, and they receive their product after the peak demand period.
Employment levels	Additional employees are hired and employees are laid off as demand for output increases and decreases.
Work force utilization	Employees work overtime during peaks and are idle or work fewer hours during slack demand periods.
Employee training	Instead of each employee specializing in one task, each is trained in several tasks. Then, as skill requirements change, employees can be rotated among different tasks. This is an alternative to hiring and layoffs for getting needed skills of specific types.
Process design	Sometimes job content at each workstation can be changed to allow productivity increases. Work methods analysis can be used to examine and redesign jobs.
Subcontracting	During peak periods, other firms may be hired temporarily to make the product or some of its subcomponents.
Maintenance deferral	Under normal conditions the facility may be shut down at regular intervals to perform preventive maintenance on facilities and equipment. During peak periods, such maintenance programs are temporarily discontinued. Thus the facility can be operated when it would, without preventive maintenance, have had to be idle.

severance pay may be necessary, premium wages may have to be paid, and the risk of losing scarce human skills may increase.

Present strategies for changing capacity also depend upon the extent to which the product can be stored in inventory. For products that are perishable (raw foods) or subject to radical style changes, finished goods inventories may not be feasible. This is also true for many service organizations offering such products as insurance protection, emergency operations (fire, police, etc.), and taxi and barber services. Instead of storing inventories, input resources can be expanded or shrunk temporarily in anticipation of demand. Several of the most common strategies are summarized in Table 5.2.

Long-run Responses: Expansion From World War II through the 1960s, the U.S. economy was one of abundance and growth. Since the decade of the 1970s, the United States has encountered problems of resource scarcity and economic shrinkage. While some sectors of the economy grow, others diminish. Organizations today cannot be locked into thinking only about *expanding* the resource base; they must also consider optimal approaches to *contracting* it. Let's consider the first of these long-run responses, expansion.

EXAMPLE A warehousing operation foresees the need for an additional 100,000 square feet of space by the end of the next five years. One option is to add an additional 50,000 square feet now and another 50,000 square feet two years from now. Another option is to add the entire 100,000 square feet now.

Estimated costs for building the entire addition now are $50/square foot. If expanded incrementally, the initial 50,000 square feet will cost $60 each. The 50,000 square feet to be added later are estimated at $80 each. Which alternative is better? At a minimum, the lower construction costs plus excess capacity costs of total construction now must be compared with higher costs of deferred construction. The operations manager must consider the costs, benefits, and risks of each option.

The costs, benefits, and risks of the expansion alternatives pose an interesting decision problem. By building the entire addition now, we avoid higher building costs, the risk of accelerated inflation (and even higher future construction costs), and the risk of losing additional future business because of inadequate capacity. But there may also be disadvantages to this alternative. First, the organization may not be able to muster the large financial investment initially needed. Second, if we expand now, we may find later that our demand forecasts were incorrect; if ultimate demand is lower than expected, we have overbuilt. Finally, even if forecasted demand is ultimately realized, it may not fully materialize until the end of the five-year planning horizon. If so, we will have invested in an excess capacity facility on which no return is realized for several years. Since our funds could have been invested in some other ways during this time, we have forgone the opportunity of earning returns elsewhere on our investment.

EXAMPLE Extol Corporation's competitive strategy capitalizes on not being a product innovator. Hence, it avoids the major costs of extensive product research and development activities. Instead, Extol rapidly adopts new product developments by competitors and quickly adapts its production capabilities. Handsome financial returns can be realized with this strategy, but everything depends on the timing of product introduction and availability in the marketplace. Accordingly, Extol intentionally overbuilds its physical facilities by 20 percent of expected capacity to avoid lost sales, which are likely to be far more costly than the incremental cost of the additional 20 percent of capacity.

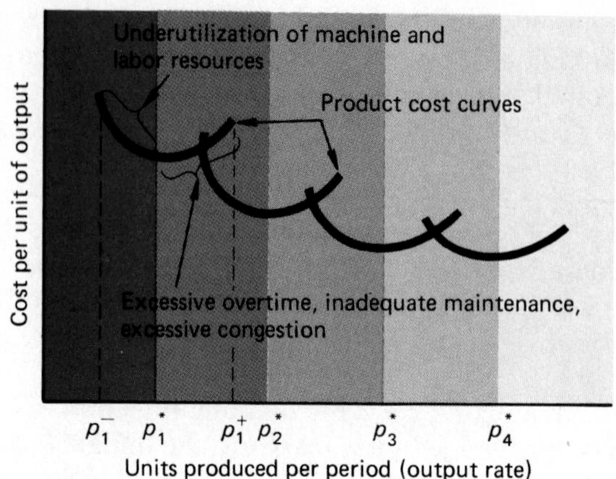

FIGURE 5.1
Product costs related to facility capacity

The general patterns of capacity utilization costs and incremental expansion can be seen in Figure 5.1. The first curve shows the minimum cost output rate, $p_1{}^*$, for an existing productive facility at time 1. Production can fall temporarily to a lower level, $p_1{}^-$, but if it does, machine and labor resources will be underutilized and unit costs will therefore increase. Output could be increased to higher levels, such as $p_1{}^+$, but unit costs would increase because of excessive overtime, inadequate preventive maintenance, and higher congestion in existing facilities.

If we anticipate that demand will be permanently higher, the facility could be expanded to reap the benefits of economies of scale offered by a larger facility. Typically, expansion occurs in increments over time rather than in a single lump. The series of curves in Figure 5.1 shows optimum output rates for each stage of expansion as permanent demand increases. Capacity could be expanded in one step, from $p_1{}^*$ to $p_4{}^*$, but the risk of overexpanding is increased.

Long-run Responses: Contraction and Constant Capacity Capacity contraction most often involves selling off existing facilities, equipment, and inventories and firing employees. As serious declines in demand occur, we may gradually terminate operations. Permanent capacity reduction or shutdown occurs only as a last resort. Instead, new ways are sought to maintain and use existing capacity. Why? Because a great deal of effort, capital, and human skills have gone into building up a technology. Often this technology and skill base are transferable to other products or services. As one product reaches the decline phase of its life cycle, it can be replaced with others without increasing capacity (see Figure 5.2). This phasing in and out of new and old products does not occur accidentally. Research and development departments and market research groups engage in long-range planning to determine how existing capacity can be used and adapted to meet future product demand.

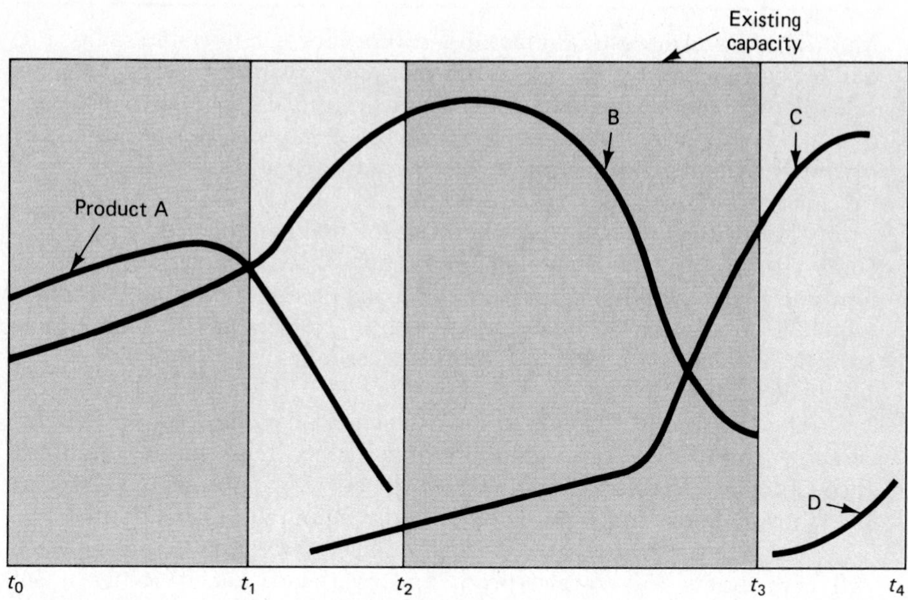

FIGURE 5.2
Ideal use of existing capacity by time-phasing products

CAPACITY PLANNING MODELING

Modeling Alternatives

What models are available to assist in capacity planning? *Present value analysis* is helpful whenever the time value of capital investments and funds flows must be considered. (This is covered in the Supplement to Chapter 2). *Aggregate planning models* are useful for examining how best to use existing capacity in the short run. (These models are presented in Chapter 10). *Breakeven analysis,* discussed in Chapter 6, can provide the breakeven volumes required as a minimum when various expansion alternatives are being costed against projected revenues. In the following pages we present two useful models for evaluating short-run capacity utilization: *linear programming* and *computer simulation.* Then we apply a *decision tree analysis* to the long-run capacity problem of facility expansion. Although we could discuss even more models, these last three serve to illustrate the diversity of capacity-related problems confronting the operations manager.

Linear Programming Applied to Product Mix and Capacity

Our first example of model applications illustrates the difficulties of measuring capacity in a multiproduct firm. As we discuss MultiBand's situation, we'll show you a way of finding the best use of capacity during a short-run planning horizon.

EXAMPLE MultiBand Enterprises manufactures two products, a portable radio (PR) and a citizens' band (CB) radio. The marketing manager states, "We can sell all that can be produced in the near future." She then asks the operations manager, "What is your production capacity per month?" The operations manager replies that his output capacity depends on which product is produced.

"Three kinds of labor are required for making our products: subassembly, assembly, and inspection labor. The two products require different amounts of each kind of labor, so our capacity for next month depends on which products we produce. Next month we will have 316 hours of subassembly labor available, 354 hours of assembly labor, and 62 hours of inspection labor."

The operations manager knows that each CB radio requires .4 hours of subassembly labor time, .5 hours of assembly labor, and .05 hours of inspection. A portable radio can be produced using .5 hours of subassembly labor, .3 hours of assembly labor and .10 hours of inspection labor.

The vice president says, "We know that each CB that we produce and sell contributes $50 toward profit and overhead. Each PR has a $40 contribution margin."

What is MultiBand's output capacity, and what mix of CBs and PRs should be manufactured next month?

The *product mix problem* is faced whenever a firm has limited resources that can be used to produce any of several combinations of products. MultiBand's product mix problem is summarized in Table 5.3.

Table 5.3 Available resources and possible uses by MultiBand

Resource	Amount of Resource Needed to Produce One Unit of Product (hours)		Total Amount of Resource Available (hours)
	CB	PR	
Subassembly labor	.40	.50	316
Assembly labor	.50	.30	354
Inspection labor	.05	.10	62

What is MultiBand's output capacity? It depends on the product mix. If all resources next month are devoted to producing CBs, there will be enough subassembly time to produce 316 hours ÷ .40 hours/unit = 790 units; enough assembly time to produce 354 ÷ .50 = 708 units; and enough inspection time for 62 ÷ .05 = 1,240 CBs. Since a salable CB requires all three kinds of labor, the maximum number of CBs possible is the smallest of these quantities, 708 units. On the other hand, we could produce only PRs. If each resource is devoted totally to PRs, there will be enough subassembly, assembly, and inspection time for producing 632; 1,180; and 620 PRs; the maximum number of completed PRs is thus 620.

MultiBand's capacity utilization alternatives are (1) 708 CBs can be produced by using all available assembly time; (2) 620 PRs can be produced by consuming all available inspection time; or (3) some combination of PRs and CBs can be produced during the month. What is the *best mix* of CBs and PRs to produce? In other words, what is the best way to use existing capacity in the short run? This question can be answered by using a linear programming model, which is described and applied to the MultiBand problem in the supplement to this chapter. Several steps must be taken before this method can be applied.

First, the decision variables must be identified. For MultiBand there are two decision variables—the number of CBs and the number of PRs to be produced next month.

Second, some criterion for choice must be specified to indicate (and measure) the "goodness" or "badness" of each decision alternative. MultiBand's criterion is the total contribution margin (TCM) as shown in equation 5.1.

$$TCM = \begin{array}{l}\text{Contribution} \\ \text{margin from} \\ \text{all CBs} \\ \text{produced}\end{array} + \begin{array}{l}\text{Contribution} \\ \text{margin from} \\ \text{all PRs} \\ \text{produced}\end{array} \tag{5.1}$$

$$TCM = \$50\ CM \quad + \$40\ PR$$

The value of the criterion, TCM, depends on how many CBs and PRs we decide to produce. We wish to select values for CB and PR so that TCM is as large as possible; that is, we wish to maximize *TCM*.

Third, the restrictions limiting the number of products that can be produced must be identified. The restrictions for CBs and PRs are as follows:

Resource (labor)	Amount of Resource Used (hours)		Amount of Resource Available (hours) (resource restriction)	
Subassembly	.40 CB + .50 PR	≤	316	(5.2)
Assembly	.50 CB + .30 PR	≤	354	(5.3)
Inspection	.05 CB + .10 PR	≤	62	(5.4)

Fourth, a systematic procedure to evaluate possible combinations of products must be applied. The combination that results in the highest value of TCM is the one that's selected. By applying a linear programming procedure, we find that the optimal solution for MultiBand is to produce 632 CBs and 126 PRs (approximately) next month. This results in a contribution margin of:

$$\begin{aligned} TCM &= \$50(632) + \$40(126) \\ &= 31{,}600 + 5{,}040 \\ &= 36{,}640 \end{aligned}$$

This product mix will consume all available subassembly and assembly hours, will result in about 18 hours of unused or idle inspection time, and will provide a higher total contribution margin than any other combination of CBs and PRs. It represents the optimal use of existing capacity.

Computer Simulation Used to Evaluate Capacity

In many systems, proper scheduling of the conversion facilities can lead to better utilization of existing capacity. Sometimes a careful analysis reveals that a greater output rate exists than was thought possible. Such an analysis was performed at the University of Massachusetts Health-Service Outpatient Clinic.[4] The facility experienced overcrowding and confusion in waiting rooms, and the professional staff felt overworked and harassed. During the day, when few walk-in patients came and when appointment patients failed to appear, physicians were sometimes idle. Often, physicians were still seeing patients up to an hour past closing time.

A team of analysts set out to find better ways to use the existing capacity and resources of the clinic. Their strategy was to build a Monte Carlo simulation model (Chapter 10) of the clinic and to use the model experimentally to improve the clinic operations. First they examined clinic records to estimate the demand on the system—the number of patient visits per week during regular clinic hours. The historical pattern of patient arrivals was examined by day of week and by time of day. Existing demand patterns resulted in both occasional slack periods and periods of very high patient loads. The analysts used the simulation model to test experimentally the effects of various patient scheduling policies.

The recommendations of the simulation experiment were actually implemented at the clinic during the following year, and several improvements in its operation resulted. Customer (patient) service was improved —patient waiting time was reduced; the number of patients seen by physicians increased more than 13 percent; and the average time that a patient spent with a physician went up by 5 percent. The total number of physician hours allocated to patients decreased by 5 percent; less overtime was required; and the morale of the doctors improved. Clearly, the clinic's existing capacity was increased because resources were scheduled and used more wisely.

Decision Tree Analysis Applied to Capacity Expansion

The linear programming and computer simulation models focus on the short-run question of how to use existing capacity; but the planner also faces long-run decisions. One such decision has to do with capacity expansion. One technique for analyzing this as well as other sequential decisions is decision tree analysis.[5]

Decision tree analysis consists of the following steps:

[4]This case history is based on the study by E. J. Rising, R. Baron, and B. Averill, "A Systems Analysis of a University-Health-Service Outpatient Clinic," *Operations Research* 21, no. 5 (September–October 1973), 1030–47.

[5]An example of extensive use of decision trees yielding substantial economic benefits is presented in T. J. Madden, M. S. Hyrnick, and J. A. Hodde, "Decision Analysis Used to Evaluate Air Quality Control Equipment for Ohio Edison Company," *Interfaces* 13, no. 1 (February 1983), 66–75.

1. Tree diagramming
   (a) Identify all decisions (and their alternatives) to be made and the order (sequence) in which they must be made
   (b) Identify the chance events that can occur after each decision
   (c) Develop a tree diagram showing the sequence of decisions and chance events
2. Estimation
   (a) Obtain a probability estimate of the chances of occurrence for each chance event outcome
   (b) Obtain estimates of the financial (criterion) consequences of all possible outcomes and actions
3. Evaluation and selection
   (a) Calculate the expected value of all possible actions
   (b) Select the action offering the most attractive expected value

Let's use an example to help make a risky, long-run decision about expanding the capacity of an existing facility.

EXAMPLE The city transit system in Smalltown operates its bus system at a $400,000 deficit annually. The city council has decided to raise bus fares to help offset the operating deficit. The director of City Transit believes the fare increase will decrease ridership unless transit system capacity is expanded. The director suggests that expanded services be offered simultaneously with the fare increase to offset negative community reaction. He believes this action will result in one of three levels of ridership: increased, sustained, or reduced.

An influential council member suggests an alternative plan. He would increase the fare now but delay the capacity expansion decision for two years. If this is done, the director is sure, ridership will not increase during the next two years; it will either decrease or be sustained at current levels. If service is expanded two years after the fare increase, ridership may be increased, sustained, or reduced. If service is not expanded in two years, however, the most optimistic estimates are that ridership will either be sustained or reduced, not increased. The director has decided to use a decision tree analysis to evaluate this problem for an eight-year time horizon (the desired length of the planning period).

Tree Diagramming Figure 5.3 shows the initial tree diagram developed by the director. The sequence of decisions and chance events flows from left to right. At the left side of the diagram, we see the first decision (represented by a square) and its two alternatives, each represented by a branch emanating from the square. If service is expanded now (alternative *B*), the decision will be followed by a chance event (circle), which can lead to any of three outcomes: annual ridership during each of the next eight years will either increase, remain unchanged, or decrease. If service is not expanded now (alternative *A*), annual ridership during the next two years is

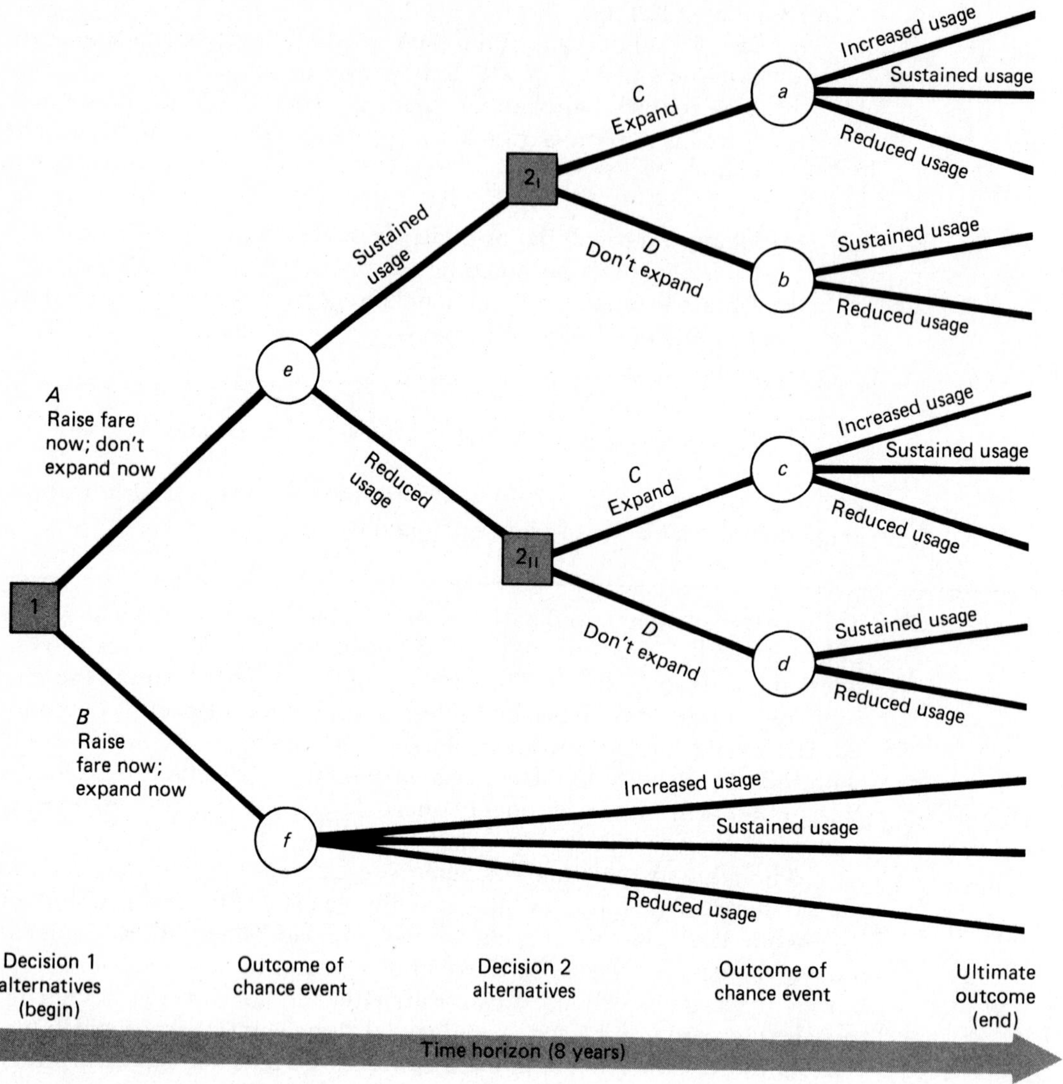

FIGURE 5.3
Decision tree diagram for a city transit system

expected to be either reduced or sustained at the current level. After two years, a second decision must be made. Service will either be expanded or not be expanded (alternatives *C* and *D*). If service is not expanded (*D*), ridership during the next six years will either be sustained or reduced. If service is expanded (*C*), it is also possible that ridership might increase above the current level.

Estimating The next stage of the decision tree analysis involves estimating the outcomes and probabilities of chance events. Probability estimates are needed *wherever a chance event appears* in the diagram. Notice that probabilities for the chance event *f* (Figure 5.4) sum to 1.0. This is because one and only one of these three outcomes must occur. The one-time cost of expanding service is $300,000 if done now (branch *B*) and $450,000 if done two years from now (branch *C*).

For the chance node following decision alternative *B*, the director believes that by expanding services now, the chances for increased ridership are .2, for sustained ridership .5, and for reduced ridership .3 for each of the next eight years. Similarly, probabilities have been estimated for each possible outcome for the chance events that follow alternatives *A*, *C*, and *D*. These various probability estimates for all chance events are shown in Figure 5.4, as are the cost consequences of all outcomes and actions.

Evaluating and Selecting The final phase of the analysis is to calculate expected values of all possible actions. We begin by calculating expected cost of nodes at the right side of the diagram, at the last stage of the problem, and then work backward.

Look at Figure 5.4 again. Suppose the city had taken a course of action that resulted in its being located at node *a*. What will happen to

FIGURE 5.4
Tree diagram with probabilities, outcomes, and costs (cost figures in $ thousands)

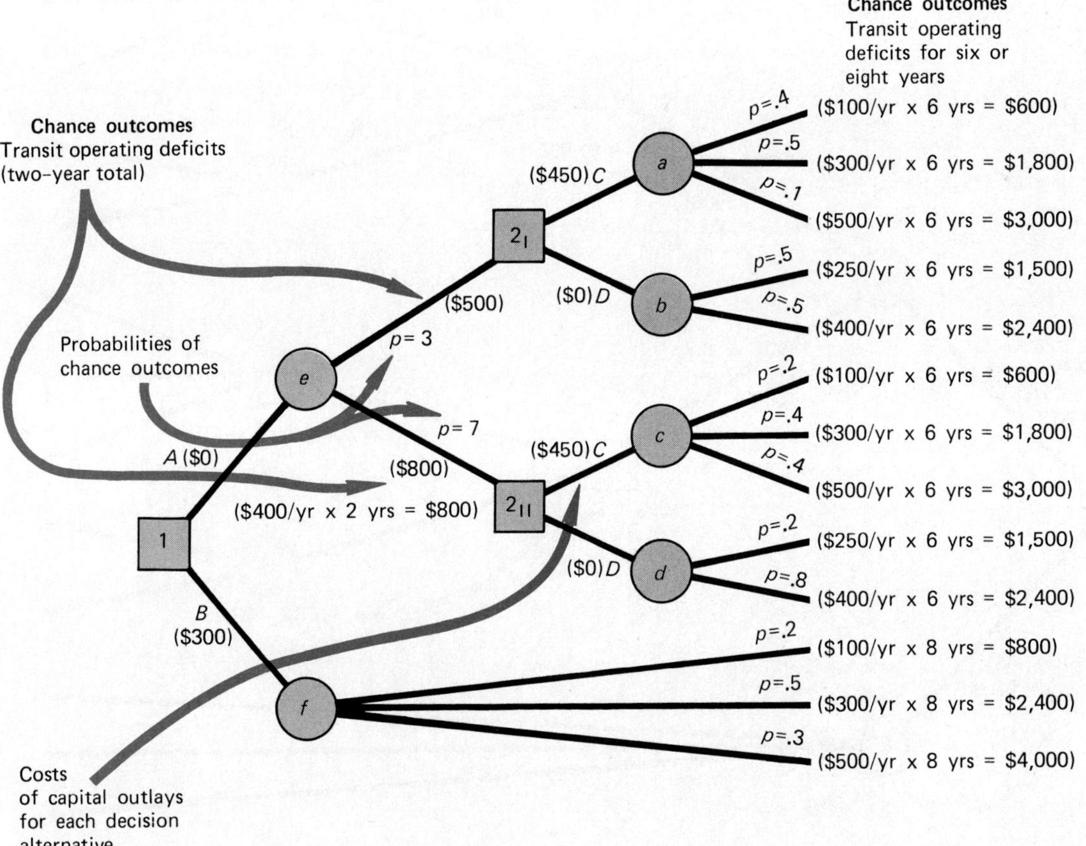

ridership in years 3 through 8? We don't know for sure: This is a chance event. We can, however, calculate the *expected cost (EC)* of the outcomes that follow node *a* (cost figures in \$ thousands):

$$\begin{aligned} EC_a &= (.4)(\$600) + (.5)(\$1{,}800) + (.1)(\$3{,}000) \\ &= 240 + 900 + 300 \\ &= \$1{,}440 \end{aligned}$$

This tells us that if we ever do reach node *a*, the expected cost of all possible outcomes thereafter is \$1,440. We can similarly calculate the expected costs associated with nodes *b*, *c*, and *d* and record these costs for each node on Figure 5.5.

Now compare the expected costs of nodes *a* and *b* in Figure 5.5. Node *a* is more desirable because its expected cost is lower than that of *b*. We now move to the left in the diagram to determine what decisions have to be made to reach nodes *a* and *b*. At decision square 2_I, decision *C* (costing

FIGURE 5.5
Decision tree showing expected costs and best decision strategy (cost figures in \$ thousands)

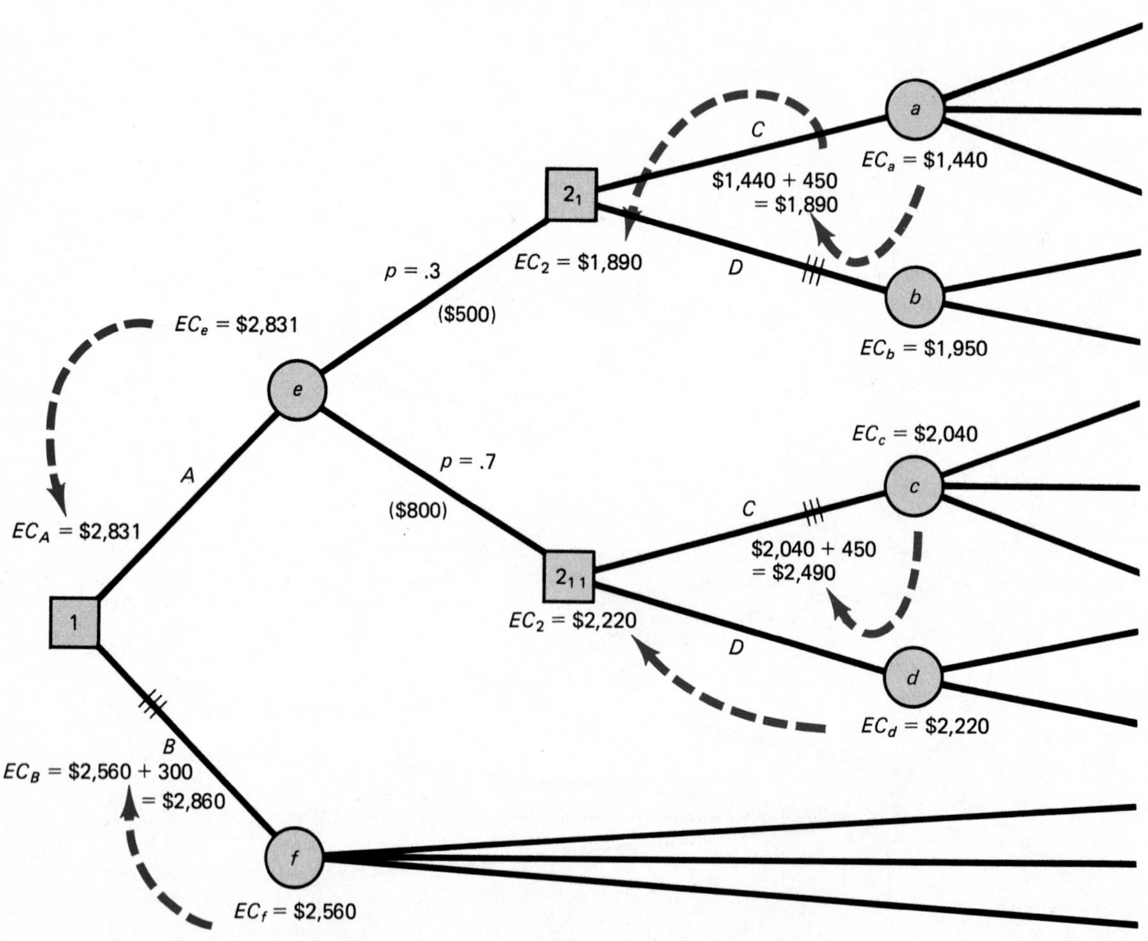

\$450) leads to node *a* with expected cost of \$1,440 thereafter. The overall expected cost, then, of *C* and *a* is \$1,890. Similarly, the overall expected cost of *D* and *b* is \$1,950. Using the expected value criterion, you should pick alternative *C* (expand service) rather than *D*, at square 2_{I}. The expected cost of this best course of action is recorded under decision square 2_{I} in Figure 5.5. Alternative *D* has been crossed out, indicating it is less desirable than alternative *C*.

Let us now repeat this analysis for decision square 2_{II}, which involves nodes *c* and *d*. Given the choice of nodes *c* and *d*, we would prefer *d*. If we find ourselves located at decision node 2_{II}, the desired course of action thereafter would be alternative *D*, which has an expected cost of \$2,220.

Now consider the consequences of being located at node *e*. There is a .3 chance of sustained ridership for two years with a two-year operating deficit (cost) of \$500, followed by the decision to expand service at an expected cost of \$1,890. There is also a .7 chance of reduced usage costing \$800, after which a "no expansion" decision would be made with an expected cost of \$2,200. The expected cost of node *e* is calculated as follows:

$$\begin{aligned} EC_e &= (.3)(\$500 + \$1,890) + (.7)(\$800 + \$2,220) \\ &= 717 + 2,114 \\ &= \$2,831 \end{aligned}$$

The expected cost for node *f* is \$2,560. In order to reach node *f*, decision *B* must be made initially at an additional cost of \$300. The expected cost of reaching node *f* is therefore \$300 plus \$2,560, or \$2,860. We have now determined the best course of action for the entire problem. First, the decision should be made not to expand the transit services initially. If the ridership is sustained during the ensuing two years, the system should be expanded. If ridership is reduced during years 1 and 2, service should not be expanded for years 3 through 8. The expected cost of this course of action is \$2,831 thousands, as shown in Figure 5.5.

MANAGING CAPACITY CHANGE

It is important to emphasize that managing capacity requires a good understanding of the environment within which the organization is operating.[6] This requires an understanding of current demands of existing operations and a vision regarding future business conditions. Based on these factors, effective managers selectively apply the following general guidelines when planning capacity changes:

1. *Stretching output.* Output can be "stretched" to provide rather quick increases in capacity. It is useful to keep in mind the benefits and

[6]For further discussion of capacity change, see David A. Schilling, "Strategic Facility Planning: The Analysis of Options," *Decision Sciences* 13, no. 1 (Jan. 1982), 1–14.

costs of overtime, extra shifts, part-time help, subcontracting, and using inventory intended to buffer against unusual demands.

2. *Shrinking output.* Some alternatives exist for reducing output to reduce capacity quickly. Hiring freezes, employee layoffs, dismissals, terminating rent agreements and leases, and selling pieces of equipment and properties all tend to reduce capacity.
3. *Product mix.* Product mix is a key *management variable,* one that can be controlled somewhat in the short run and one that certainly must be understood when managing capacity. A management audit of how various product mixes have historically affected shipments (or customers served), percent utilization of facilities, labor utilization, and costs can be extremely beneficial in understanding the impact of product mix on capacity.
4. *Permanent capacity change.* There are obvious permanent changes that can be made. These often have far-reaching implications and should be considered carefully in relation to markets, the financial position of the firm and technology alternatives. Equipment investment, new plants or service centers, product redesign, process modifications, management innovations—all interact with and determine the *technology* the organization possesses. In turn, individually and collectively, these changes do affect capacity.

SUMMARY

In this chapter we focused on *capacity* as the maximum rate of productive or conversion capability of an organization's operations. Capacity planning decisions involve assessing existing facilities, estimating future needs, identifying alternatives (strategies), evaluating alternatives, and selecting a capacity alternative.

We noted that capacity is usually measured in terms of an output rate. For some companies with diverse products and for service organizations, however, we saw that about the only measure of capacity is the maximum inputs rather than outputs.

In estimating future capacity needs and evaluating strategies for modifying capacity, our discussion illustrated how short-term and long-term time horizons must be considered. To assist in reaching an acceptable capacity decision, such modeling approaches as linear programming, computer simulation, and decision tree analysis were helpful. Although modeling should not totally overshadow the behavioral implications of reaching a capacity decision, we saw that capacity planning benefits most significantly from the logical analysis in modeling. Product characteristics, economic factors, and processing technology were shown to be paramount in the capacity planning process.

CASE

Paradise Land Management Company

Paradise Land Management owns and operates hotels and apartment complexes near a major metropolitan area. They wish to expand operations in the near future, the goal being to increase net earnings before taxes. Two alternative expansion opportunities are under consideration, the Densmore complex and the Highgate project. Both projects involve the purchase of land on which apartment buildings would be constructed and operated.

The site for the Densmore complex is situated in a respected, quiet, sparsely populated residential neighborhood. The building site for the 70-unit complex can be purchased for $60,000. Building costs are estimated at $1,680,000. Annual maintenance costs would amount to $30,000. Apartment units would rent for $410 per month. Nearby, Paradise plans to construct a recreation facility. It would cost $100,000 and would service both Densmore residents and the residents of Paradise West, the only existing apartment complex in the neighborhood. Paradise West, with 120 units renting for $290 per month, has had an average occupancy rate of 84 percent for the past three years. The addition of Densmore and the recreation facility are expected to increase Paradise West's occupancy rate to 90 percent with probability of .6, or to 95 percent with a probability of .4. Densmore's occupancy rate is expected to be 90 percent (probability of .5), 85 percent (probability of .3), or 80 percent (probability of .2).

The Highgate project calls for 400 units to be constructed on a site costing $220,000 in a high-density population neighborhood with many competing apartments. Building costs would be $4,200,000. Rental revenue per unit would be $240 per month; annual operating costs would be $150,000. The probability of a 90 percent occupancy rate is .2, of an 80 percent rate .5, and of a 70 percent rate .3.

What factors should be analyzed in making this capacity decision?

REVIEW AND DISCUSSION QUESTIONS

1. Define and give examples of normal and maximum measures of capacity.
2. Define and describe the operating capacity of a college of business administration. How should its capacity be measured?
3. Discuss the fundamental differences in short-run versus long-run capacity decisions. What are the major considerations in each?
4. Outline the merits and drawbacks of incremental capacity changes and large lump changes.
5. What are the problems of data and information availability you might have in conducting a decision tree analysis?
6. How is product mix related to the capacity utilization decision?
7. What costs would be affected if you closed one of several warehouses (capacity contraction) in a distribution system? How might revenues be affected?

8. What analytical approaches and models are useful in aiding capacity decisions? Under what circumstances would each model be most beneficial relative to the others?
9. Capacity will be modified in response to demand. Demand will be modified in response to capacity. Which of these two statements is correct? Why?
10. Suppose you were considering expansion of your local fire fighting system. Show what factors should be considered and how you would relate them to one another in your analysis.
11. Explain the relationship between capacity planning and location planning. To illustrate, select a service business and explain the relationship for that business.
12. How would the results of a decision tree analysis be affected if people made erroneous probability estimates? Demonstrate with an example.
13. Briefly describe a practical approach toward managing capacity change. Would it be important for a person wanting to be a general manager, not an operations manager, to understand this process? Why or why not?

PROBLEMS

Solved Problems

1. Annual demand for a manufacturing company is expected to be as follows:

Units demanded:	8,000	10,000	15,000	20,000
Probability:	.5	.2	.2	.1

Revenues are \$35/unit. The existing manufacturing facility has annual fixed operating costs of \$200,000. Variable manufacturing costs are \$7.75/unit at the 8,000 unit output level; \$5.00 at the 10,000 unit level; \$5.33 at the 15,000 unit level; and \$7.42 at 20,000 units of output.

An expanded facility under consideration would require \$250,000 fixed operating costs annually. Variable costs would average \$9.40 at the 8,000 unit level; \$5.20 at the 10,000 unit level; \$3.80 at the 15,000 unit level; and \$4.90 for the 20,000 level.

If we wish to maximize net earnings, which size facility should we select?

Expected net revenue of existing facility

$$\begin{aligned}\text{Expected variable cost} &= [(\$7.75)(8{,}000)(.5) + (\$5.00)(10{,}000)(.2) \\ &\quad +(\$5.33)(15{,}000)(.2) + (\$7.42)(20{,}000)(.1)] \\ &= \$71{,}830\end{aligned}$$

$$\begin{aligned}\text{Expected total cost} &= \text{fixed cost} + \text{variable cost} \\ &= \$200{,}000 + \$71{,}830 \\ &= \$271{,}830\end{aligned}$$

$$\begin{aligned}\text{Expected revenue} &= \$35\ [(8{,}000)(.5) + (10{,}000)(.2) \\ &\quad + (15{,}000)(.2) + (20{,}000)(.1)] \\ &= \$385{,}000\end{aligned}$$

$$\begin{aligned}\text{Expected net revenue} &= \$385{,}000 - \$271{,}830 \\ &= \$113{,}170\end{aligned}$$

Expected net revenue of expanded facility

$$\begin{aligned}\text{Expected variable cost} &= [(\$9.40)(8{,}000)(.5) + (\$5.20)(10{,}000)(.2) \\ &\quad + (\$3.80)(15{,}000)(.2) + (\$4.90)(20{,}000)(.1)] \\ &= \$69{,}200\end{aligned}$$

$$\text{Expected total cost} = \$250{,}000 + \$69{,}200 = \$319{,}200$$
$$\text{Expected net revenue} = \$385{,}000 - \$319{,}200 = \$65{,}800$$

The existing facility maximizes expected net earnings.

2. Solve the decision tree shown in Figure 5.6, in which costs are shown at the ends of the branches.

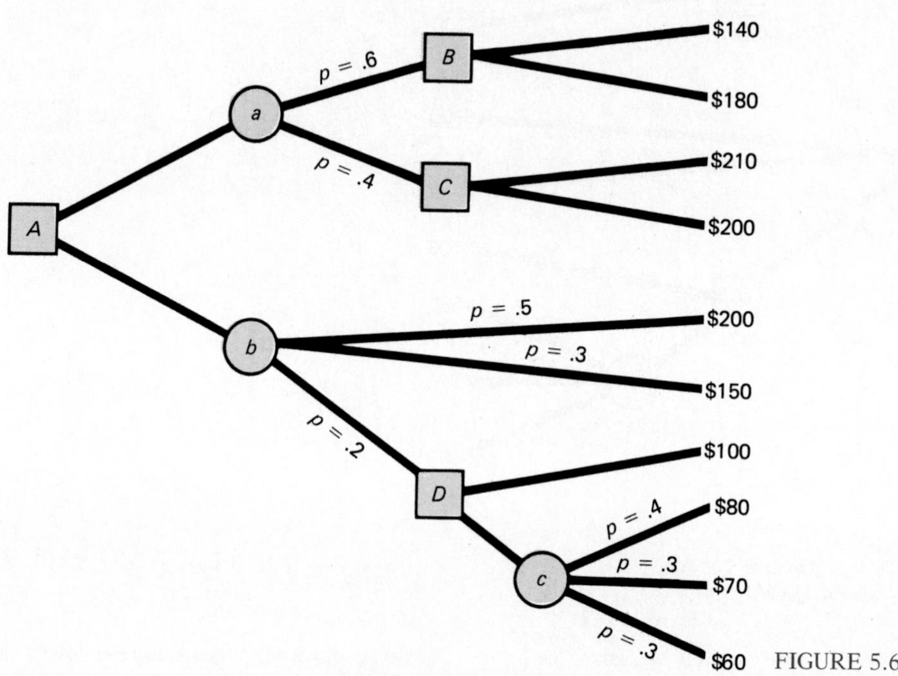

FIGURE 5.6

The solution, shown in Figure 5.7, is found by first eliminating the undesirable alternatives (branches) for decision nodes *B* and *C*. Next, the expected costs of chance event nodes *a* and *c* are calculated (the resulting expected cost is recorded above each node in the solution diagram). Now the most undesirable alternative for decision node *D* is eliminated, and the expected cost of chance event node *b* can be calculated. Finally, the most desirable alternative at decision node *A* is revealed.

Reinforcing Fundamentals

3. A manufacturer of dishware is considering three alternative plant sizes. Demand depends upon the selling price of the product; costs of manufacture also depend on the size of the plant selected. Demand is expected to be:

Demand probabilities

	Selling Price/Set of Dishware		
Annual Demand (sets of dishware)	$60	$42	$40
10,000	.2	.1	.05
20,000	.4	.4	.25
30,000	.3	.4	.40
40,000	.1	.1	.30

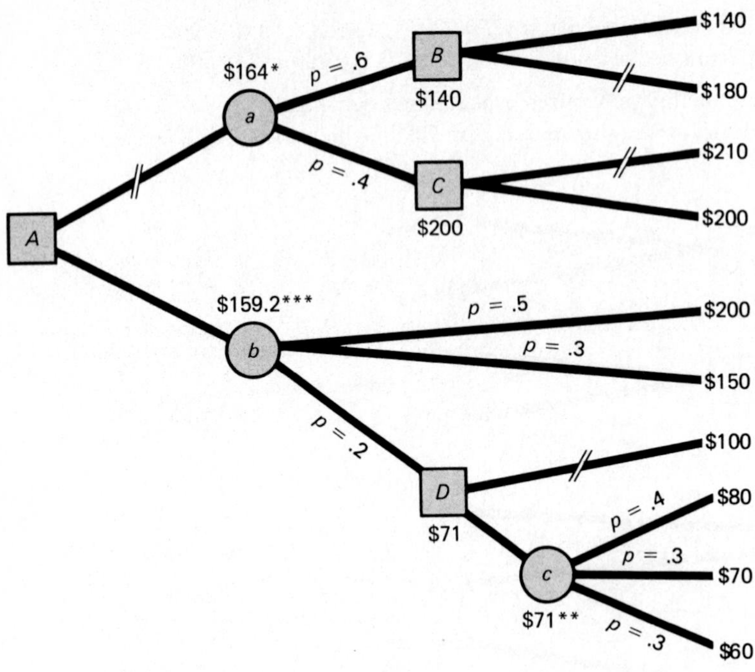

$*EC_a = (.6)(\$140) + (.4)(\$200) = \$164$

$**EC_c = (.4)(\$80) + (.3)(\$70) + (.3)(\$60) = \$71$

$***EC_b = (.5)(\$200) + (.3)(\$150) + (.2)(\$71) = \$159.2$

FIGURE 5.7

Anticipated operating costs for the three plant sizes for different levels of operation are:

Variable manufacturing cost/unit

Level of Plant Operation (units of output)	Plant Size		
	Small	Medium	Large
10,000	$ 21	$ 25	$ 32
20,000	16	14	18
30,000	19	13	12
40,000	26	18	14
Annual fixed cost of operation	$400,000	$420,000	$500,000

Which alternative is most attractive on the basis of annual net earnings?

4. How would your answer to Problem 3 change if variable manufacturing costs were changed to those shown next?

Variable manufacturing costs/unit

Level of Plant Operation (units of output)	Plant Size		
	Small	Medium	Large
10,000	$21	$20	$25
20,000	19	16	18
30,000	19	15	10
40,000	23	18	12

5. Evaluate the decision tree shown in Figure 5.8 for which costs are shown at the branch ends.

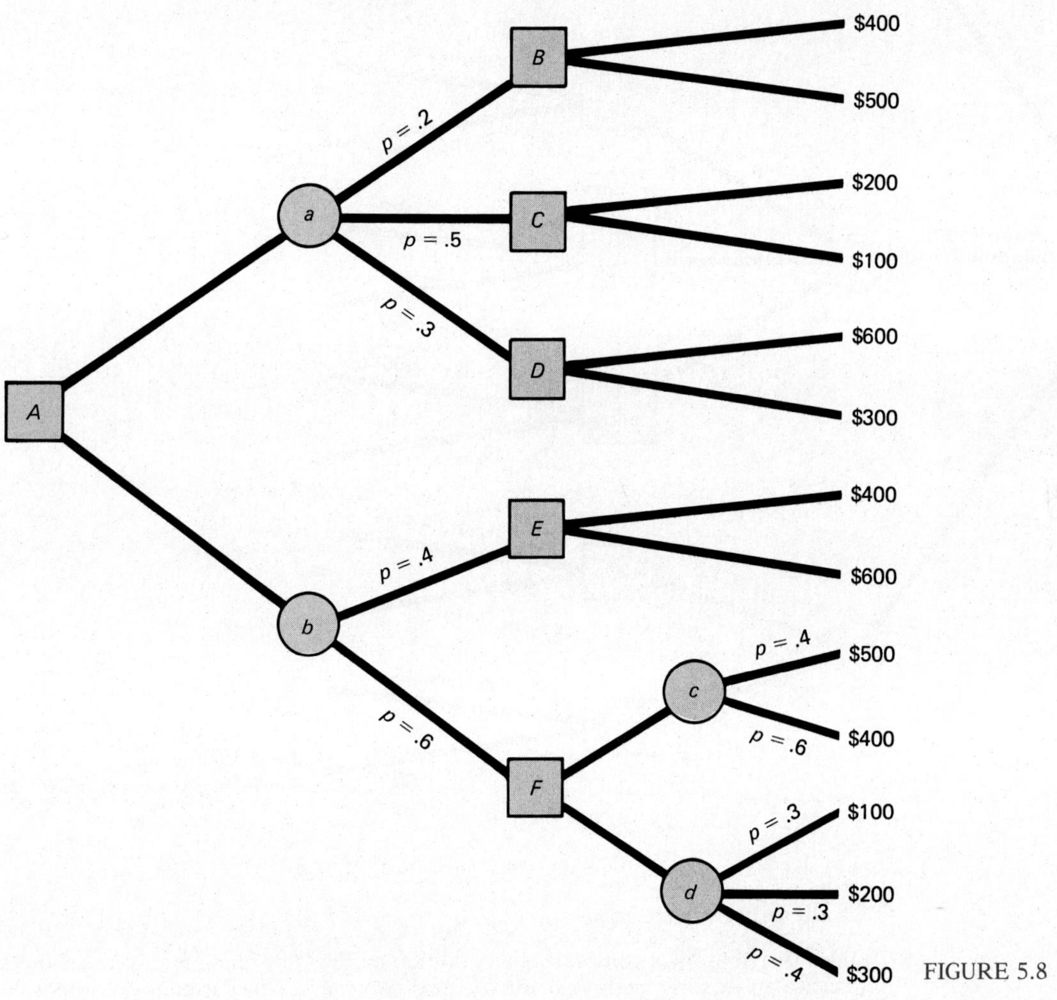

FIGURE 5.8

6. Management, facing a two-stage decision problem (see Figure 5.9), wants to pick a sequence of actions to maximize profits. The first decision (1) has three alternatives: *A*, with a profit of $20; *B*, with a profit of $30; and *C*, with a profit of $40. The chance event following the initial decision has either two or three states of nature,

depending on the initial decision. The probability of each state is shown in Figure 5.9. Thereafter, a second decision, resulting in further profits, must be made. What is the best decision sequence?

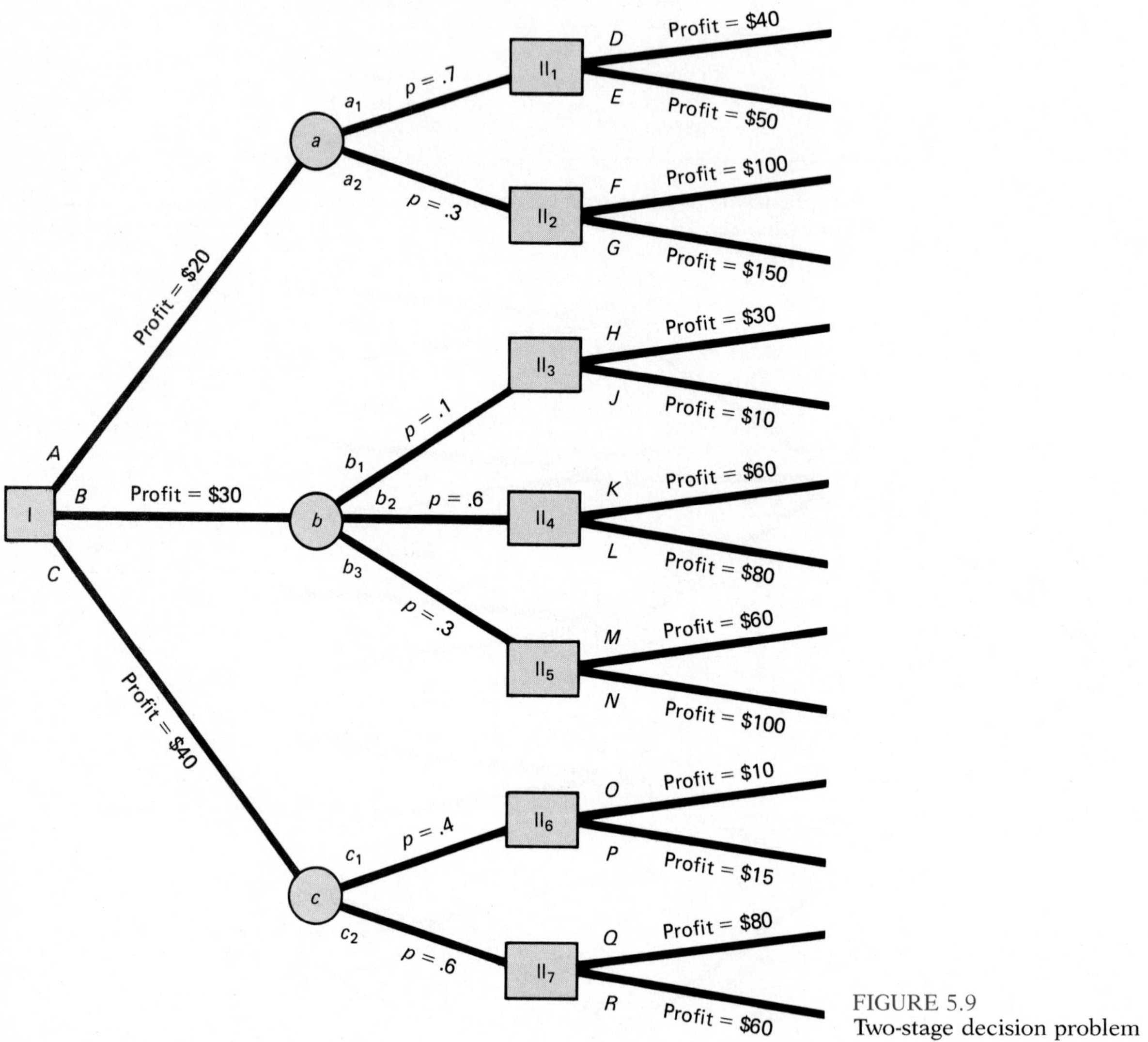

FIGURE 5.9
Two-stage decision problem

Challenging Exercises

7. Micro Distributors is considering an addition of 500,000 square feet of warehouse space to an existing facility during the next two years. Three expansion proposals are being considered: (1) add 100,000 square feet now and 400,000 square feet two years from now; (2) add 200,000 square feet now plus 300,000 square feet in two years; or (3) do the entire addition now. Construction estimates show considerable cost savings for making the additions as soon as possible.

Construction estimates

Alternative	Now: Amount of Expansion (thousands of square feet)	Now: Cost ($ millions)	Two Years from Now: Amount of Expansion (thousands of square feet)	Two Years from Now: Cost ($ millions)
1	100	1.00	400	3.2
2	200	1.75	300	2.6
3	500	3.30	—	—

Micro's marketing personnel suggest a wait-and-see approach with incremental expansion; they favor alternatives 1 and 2. Although expansion is expected to create additional demand, other forces outside Micro's control may result in lower demand, in which case Micro would be left with excessive, unproductive warehousing capacity. A mild expansion now would permit a two-year observation of demand before deciding on additional expansion.

A ten-year planning horizon was chosen. These estimates of demand and net operating revenues were obtained:

Estimates for first two years

	Alternative 1		Alternative 2	
Level of demand	Low	High	Low	High
Total net operating revenue ($ millions)	1.0	1.3	.8	1.4
Probability	.4	.6	.3	.7

Estimates for years 3–10

	Alternative 1				Alternative 2			
	If Expanded After 2 Years		If Not Expanded After 2 Years		If Expanded After 2 Years		If Not Expanded After 2 Years	
Level of demand	Low	High	Low	High	Low	High	Low	High
Total net operating revenue ($ millions)	2.4	7.2	3.8	5.8	2.4	7.2	3.2	6.4
Probability (if demand was high in years 1 and 2)	.2	.8	.3	.7	.2	.8	.3	.7
Probability (if demand was low in years 1 and 2)	.3	.7	.8	.2	.4	.6	.7	.3

For alternative 3, ten-year operating revenue is estimated at $9 million with probability of .5; $6 million with probability of .3, and $2 million with probability of 0.2. Which alternative is best? Justify your recommendation. For simplicity, ignore the time value of money.

8. The Reliable Storage Company has a large warehousing operation. In developing long-range plans, they are considering expansion of storage capacity. Estimates of future storage demand, increased revenues, and costs of expansion have been obtained for the ten-year planning horizon. Management has narrowed the expansion alternatives to three choices: (1) expand now by adding 100,000 square feet of storage space, (2) add 40,000 square feet now and 60,000 square feet three years later, (3) add 40,000 square feet now and nothing later.

   If the entire expansion is done now, construction costs will be lower than they will be later. Further, there will be a greater chance for higher business revenues since enough space will be added to take in new business. There is a chance, however, of overexpanding; if the entire expanded facility is not needed, idle capacity will result. The more conservative alternatives are to expand modestly now, wait and see if demand continues to increase as expected, and expand or do not expand accordingly. This approach reduces the risk of investing funds in an idle, overexpanded facility. However, the wait-and-see alternatives have two disadvantages. First, limited storage capacity in the first three years may result in lost opportunities for more business. Second, future construction costs are expected to be considerably higher than those at present levels. Estimates of relevant factors for this decision are shown in Table 5.4.

Table 5.4 Data for expansion decision of Reliable Storage Company

	Cash Outlays for Expansion		Expected After-tax Cash Flow/Year			
			Years 1–3		Years 4–10	
Decision Alternative	Expansion Cost Now	Expansion Cost 3 Years From Now	If Demand Is High	If Demand Is Low	If Demand Is High	If Demand Is Low
Full expansion now	100,000 sq ft × $16/sq ft = $1,600,000	—0—	$180,000	$90,000	$240,000	$120,000
Expand 40,000 feet now and 60,000 feet in 3 years	40,000 sq ft × $18/sq ft = $720,000	60,000 sq ft × $24/sq ft = $1,440,000	75,000	36,000	210,000	120,000
Expand 40,000 feet now; no further expansion	40,000 sq ft × $18/sq ft = $720,000	—0—	75,000	36,000	75,000	36,000

   For years 1–3, it is estimated that the probability of high annual demand is .7; the probability of low demand is .3. For years 4–10, the probability of high demand is .6, and the probability of low demand is .4. Which decision is best? For simplicity, ignore the time value of money.

9. Watersight Tours, Inc., is deciding whether to hire an additional boat mechanic or to just keep their one current mechanic. Their two tourist boats have daily failure probabilities of .04 and .08, respectively. With one boat out of commission, the company loses $300/hour; the operating loss is $800/hour when both boats are inoperable. The time for a mechanic to repair one boat is four hours. Two mechanics working together can repair a boat in three hours. The second mechanic can be employed at a daily wage of $150. Should Watersight hire the second mechanic? If so, how should the mechanics be used if both boats fail simultaneously?

GLOSSARY

Capacity Productive capability of a facility, usually expressed as volume of output per time period; maximum rate of productive or conversion capability of an organization's operations.

Chance event A happening with several possible outcomes, one of which will occur; the decision maker has no knowledge of or control over which outcome will occur.

Decision tree Device used to structure and analyze a decision problem; used to lay out systematically the sequence of decision points, alternatives, and chance outcomes in diagram form.

Linear programming Mathematical technique that guarantees the optimal allocation of resources to maximize profits or minimize costs.

Present value analysis Method for measuring the worth of an investment in which future cash inflows (and outlays) are converted into an equivalent present value.

Product mix problem Decision situation involving limited resources that can be used to produce any of several combinations of products.

Technology of operations Physical, human, and/or mental processes that are required by the organization to convert input resources into products or outputs.

Throughput Capacity measurement in terms of rate of output or input per time unit.

SELECTED READINGS

Buffa, E. S., *Meeting the Competitive Challenge*. Homewood, Ill.: Richard D. Irwin, 1984, 65–82.

Goldhar, Joel D., and Mariann Jelinek, "Plan for Economies of Scope," *Harvard Business Review* 61, no. 6 (November–December 1983), 141–48.

McLeavey, D. W., and S. L. Narasimhan, *Production Planning and Inventory Control.* Boston: Allyn & Bacon, 1985, 360–69.

Schilling, David A., "Strategic Facility Planning: The Analysis of Options," *Decision Sciences* 13, no. 1, (Jan. 1982), 1–14.

Schmenner, Roger W., *Production/Operations Management: Concepts and Situations.* Chicago: Science Research Associates, 1981, 297–332.

Schroeder, Roger W., *Operations Management: Decision Making in the Operating Function.* New York: McGraw-Hill, 1981, 239–40.

Skinner, Wickham, *Manufacturing in the Corporate Strategy,* New York: John Wiley, 1978, 111–13 and 121–22.

SUPPLEMENT TO CHAPTER 5

LINEAR PROGRAMMING: THE GRAPHICAL AND SIMPLEX METHODS

The purpose of this section is to present the mathematical optimization technique called linear programming. We'll consider three linear programming (LP) methods: graphical, simplex, and transportation. The graphical method is of limited practical value but is helpful for visualizing the underlying concepts of LP. The simplex method can be used to solve any LP problem. The transportation (or distribution) method can be used only on a special type of problem with particular characteristics; it is presented as a supplement to Chapter 6. When such a problem is identified, the transportation method is computationally more convenient to use than the simplex method.

In general, linear programming can be applied to decision problems with these characteristics.

1. *Decision variables.* The numeric values of two or more decision variables are to be determined. (Decision variables are factors under the decision maker's control that, if modified, result in outcomes different from each other.)
2. *Goal.* The goal is to find the best decision values, those that will maximize (or minimize) the objective function.
3. *Objective function.* The objective (criterion) function is a mathematical equation that measures the outcome of any proposed alternative. In LP, the objective function must be linear, as you will see below.
4. *Restrictions.* The values that can be chosen for decision variables are restricted (constrained); complete freedom of choice does not exist. Allowable (feasible) values of decision variables are defined by linear constraint equations.

The General Linear Programming Problem

The following two forms are equivalent statements of the general linear programming problem:

1. *Maximize*

$$Z = C_1X_1 + C_2X_2 + \ldots + C_nX_n$$

where the $X_1, X_2, \ldots, X_n$ is a set of variables whose values are to be determined. The $C_1, C_2, \ldots, C_n$ are value coefficients reflecting the contribution each unit of the corresponding variables makes to the objective function. Notice that Z is a linear function of the variables X_i. When X_i increases by one unit, the value of Z increases by an amount C_i.

Subject to constraints

$$
\begin{array}{l}
A_{11}X_1 + A_{12}X_2 + \ldots A_{1n}X_n \leq B_1 \\
A_{21}X_1 + A_{22}X_2 + \ldots A_{2n}X_n \leq B_2 \\
\vdots \\
A_{m1}X_1 + A_{m2}X_2 + \ldots A_{mn}X_n \leq B_m \\
X_1X_2, \ldots, X_n \geq 0
\end{array}
$$

Where each equation is a constraint imposed on the value of the variables, the $A_{11}, A_{12}, \ldots, A_{mn}$ are coefficients, and the $B_1, B_2, \ldots, B_m$ are initial amounts of resources available. Notice that each constraint is a linear function; when X_j increases by one unit, A_{ij} units of resource B_i are consumed.

2. *Maximize*

$$\sum_{j=1}^{n} C_jX_j$$

Subject to constraints

$$\sum_{j=1}^{n} A_{ij}X_j \leq B_i$$
$$X_j \geq 0$$

where

$$i = 1, 2, \ldots, m$$
$$j = 1, 2, \ldots, n$$

Graphical Method

The purpose of the graphical method is to provide a grasp of the basic concepts that are used in the simplex technique. To use the graphical method:

1. Identify the decision variables
2. Identify the objective (or criterion) function
3. Identify resource restrictions (constraints)
4. Draw a graph that includes all restrictions
5. Identify the feasible decision area on the graph
6. Draw a graph of the objective function, and select the point on the feasible area that optimizes the objective function
7. Interpret the solution

In explaining these steps, we repeat the case of MultiBand Enterprises that is used in Chapter 5.

EXAMPLE MultiBand Enterprises manufactures two products, a portable radio (PR) and a citizens band (CB) radio. The marketing manager states, "We can sell all that can be produced in the near future." She then asks the operations manager, "What is your production capacity per month?" The operations manager replies that his output capacity depends on which product is produced.

"Three kinds of labor are required for making our products: subassembly, assembly, and inspection labor. The two products require different amounts of each kind of labor, so our capacity for next month depends on which products we produce. Next month we will have 316 hours of subassembly labor available, 354 hours of assembly labor, and 62 hours of inspection labor."

The operations manager knows that each CB radio requires .4 hours of subassembly labor time, .5 hours of assembly labor, and .05 hours of inspection labor. A portable radio can be produced using .5 hours of subassembly labor, .3 hours of assembly labor, and .10 hours of inspection labor.

The vice president says, "We know that each CB that we produce and sell contributes $50 toward profit and overhead. Each PR has a $40 contribution margin."

What is MultiBand's output capacity, and what mix of CBs and PRs should be manufactured next month?

Step 1: Identify Decision Variables Citizens band (CB) radios and/or portable radios (PR) can be manufactured by MultiBand. *These are the two decision variables.* The problem is to decide how many CBs and PRs to produce.

Step 2: Identify Objective Function Each CB provides $50 contribution to profit and overhead, and each PR contributes $40. MultiBand's total contribution gain is:

$$TC = (\$50)(\text{CB}) + (\$40)(\text{PR}) \qquad \text{(S5.1)}$$

This *linear objective function* states that total gain (or total contribution, TC) depends on the decision as to how many CBs and PRs to produce. MultiBand would like total contribution to be as large as possible; it wishes to *maximize* TC.

Step 3: Identify Resource Restrictions To produce radios, MultiBand needs three types of labor: subassembly, assembly, and inspection. The available quantities of these three resources are 316 employee hours of subassembly labor, 354 hours of assembly labor, and 62 hours of inspection labor. A CB radio requires .4 hours of subassembly labor, .5 hours of assembly time, and .05 hours of inspection. The manufacture of a PR requires .5 hours of subassembly labor, .3 hours assembly time, and .1 hours of inspection. Thus we have three restrictions, one for each labor resource. The restrictions on the use of these three resources are expressed as linear inequalities.

Resource (labor)	Resource Consumption		Resource Availability (hours)
Subassembly	.4 CB + .5 PR	≤	316
Assembly	.5 CB + .3 PR	≤	354
Inspection	.05 CB + .1 PR	≤	62

Step 4: Draw a Graph of All Restrictions Look at Figure S5.1. The horizontal axis of the graph shows various quantities of CBs that could be produced. The vertical axis shows quantities of PRs. The *solution space* (the part of the graph where the answer to the problem can be found) consists of all points on or to the right of the vertical axis and on or above the horizontal axis, since negative values of CBs or PRs have no meaning. Each point in this space represents some combination of PRs and CBs.

Let's draw the line for the subassembly labor restriction. If the entire 316 subassembly hours are devoted to producing CBs, how many could be produced? Since each CB requires .4 hours, 316 hours ÷ .4 subassembly hours per CB = 790 CBs. This combination of producing zero PRs and 790 CBs is plotted as point *a* on the graph. Another alternative is to produce no CBs. In that case, we have enough subassembly labor to produce 316 hours ÷ .5 subassembly hours per PR = 632 PRs. This combination of products (zero CBs and 632 PRs) is represented by point *b* on the graph. Now, since all restrictions are linear, the line can be drawn connecting points *a* and *b*. Each point on this restriction line represents some combination of CBs and PRs that totally consumes all subassembly labor time. Points falling above or to the right of line *ab* are *infeasible combinations* of CBs and PRs, since they require more than 316 hours of subassembly.

In a similar manner, line *cd* is the assembly labor restriction line, and line *ef* is the restriction line for inspection labor.

Step 5: Identify Feasible Decision Area When management decides how many PRs and CBs to produce, they must adhere simultaneously to all three relevant restrictions. The feasible points lie within the white area (Figure S5.2) bounded by the corner points 0, *f*, *g*, *h*, and *c*.

Step 6: Draw Objective Function and Select the Optimum Point Although all points in the bounded area are *feasible* decision alternatives, some provide a greater total contribution than others. At point *c* (708 CBs, zero PRs), for example, total contribution is (\$50)(708) + (\$40)(0) = \$35,400. But 300 CBs and 300 PRs would only give a total contribution of (\$50)(300) + (\$40)(300) = \$27,000. We must now pick out the *best* point from among the infinite number of points in the feasible area. Our task is simplified, however, because the *best point will lie at one of the corner (extreme) points of the feasible area.* Therefore, one of points 0, *f*, *g*, *h*, or *c* is

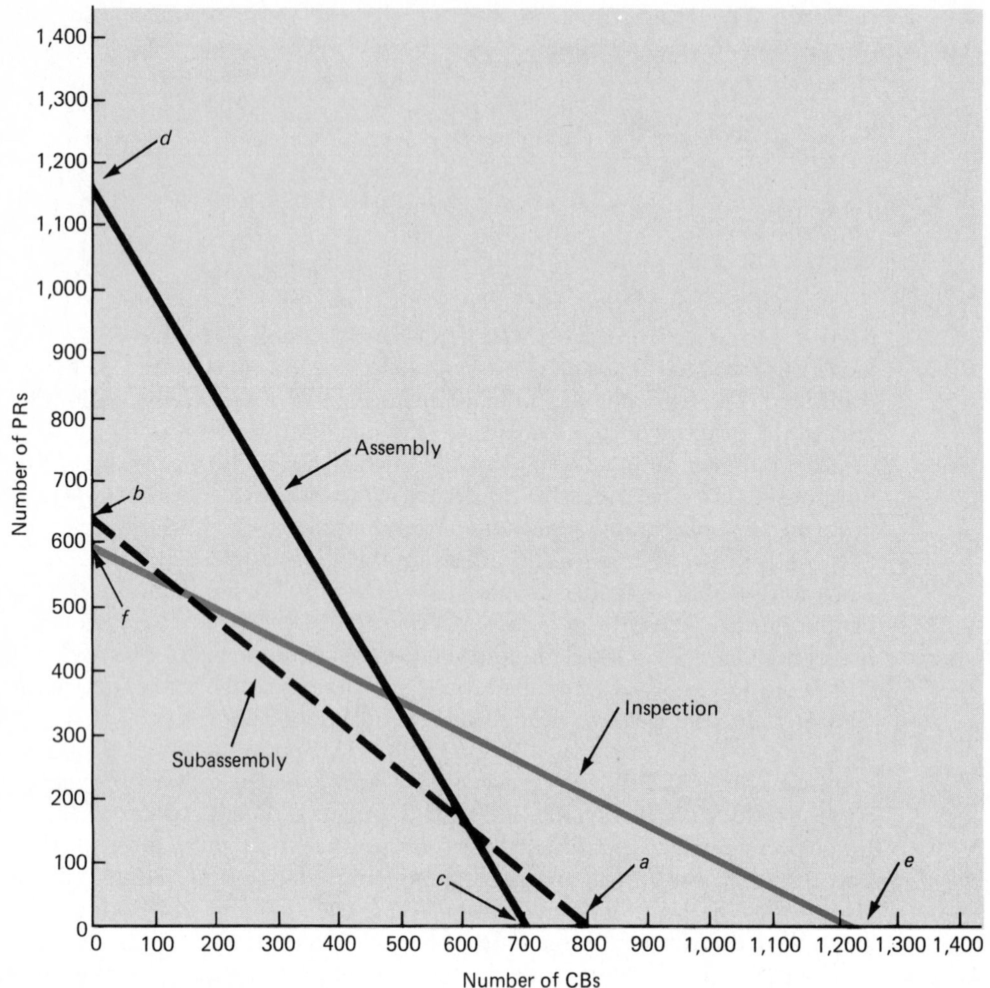

FIGURE S5.1
Restrictions for MultiBand Enterprises

optimal. We could calculate the total contribution for each of these five points and select the one that has the highest value.

A graphical procedure also exists for finding the best point. It requires adding one more line to the graph, an *iso-profit,* or *constant-profit,* line. On an iso-profit line, all the points give the same profit. Suppose we want to find the iso-profit line representing a \$20,000 contribution. Using equation S5.1, we find:

$$\$20,000 = (\$50)(CB) + (\$40)(PR)$$

On Figure S5.2, we have drawn a dotted line connecting all the points at which a \$20,000 profit would be contributed. You can see, for example, that a combination of zero CBs and 500 PRs would contribute \$20,000. In fact, even greater profits can be achieved. Look at the \$30,000 iso-profit line. Some of the points on this line fall outside the feasible area and thus are not legitimate alternatives. Other parts of the line, however, fall in the white area. A $30,000 contribution is therefore attainable.

Two features of these iso-profit lines are particularly noteworthy. First, they are parallel to each other. Second, the farther the lines are removed from the origin of the graph, the greater their contribution. Since all the lines have the same slope, our final step is to continue constructing iso-profit lines that are successively farther away from the origin. This procedure stops when any further movement away from the origin would cause the iso-profit line to lie entirely outside the feasible area. In our example, such a line would pass through point *h*. This point gives the *maximum* contribution; it is the *optimal* decision. When the problem is to maximize the objective function, the iso-profit curve should be the furthest from the origin; when the problem is to minimize, the iso-cost curve should be the closest one to the origin.

The optimal decision at point *h*, interpolated from the graph, calls for

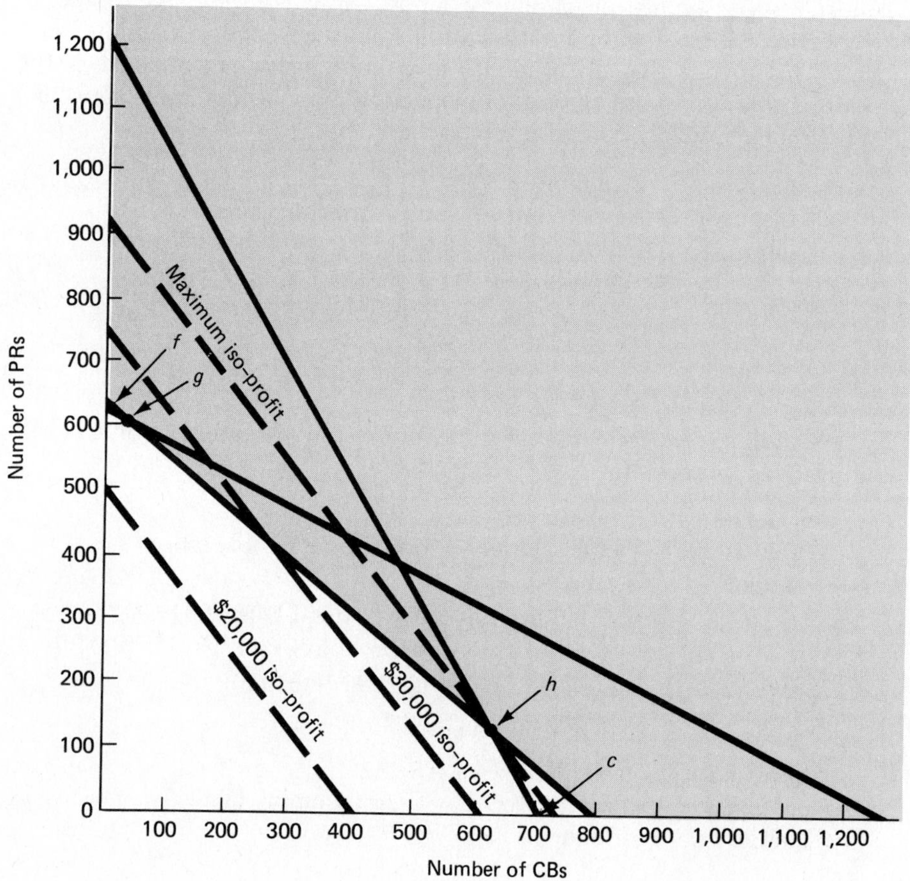

FIGURE S5.2
Area of feasible solutions for MultiBand Enterprises

the production of about 630 CBs and 125 PRs. The approximate value of this decision is

$$TC = (\$50)(630) + (\$40)(125) = \$36{,}000$$

A more precise evaluation of the solution is obtained by noting the characteristic of the optimal point h. This point lies simultaneously on two restriction lines, the subassembly labor line and the assembly labor line. By using simultaneous linear equations, we find the values for PR and CB that satisfy both equations. This occurs when PR = 126.15 and CB = 632.31. The value of this decision is:

$$TC = (\$50)(632.31) + (\$40)(126.15) = \$36{,}661.06$$

Step 7: Interpret the Solution The optimal number of PRs and CBs is now known. How much of our three resources will be used for this product mix? Will any of the resources be unused? We can answer these questions both graphically and algebraically. Observation of the graph shows that the optimal point (h) lies on the subassembly and assembly labor restriction lines, which represent the *maximum* amounts of these resources that are available for use. Therefore, the maximum amounts of these two resources are being used in the optimal solution. There is no unused subassembly or assembly labor. Now consider the usage of inspection labor. The optimal solution falls below the inspection labor line. This means that all available inspection labor is not used in the optimal solution; some amount of inspection labor will be unused or idle. We can algebraically compute the unused labor:

$$\begin{aligned}
\text{Unused inspection labor} &= \text{Available inspection labor} - \text{Used inspection labor} \\
&= 62.0 \text{ hours} - [(.05 \text{ hours/CB})(632.31 \text{ CBs}) \\
&\qquad + (.10 \text{ hours/PR})(126.15 \text{ PRs})] \\
&= 62.0 - (31.62 + 12.62) \\
&= 17.76 \text{ hours}
\end{aligned}$$

Similarly, we confirm that subassembly and assembly labor are fully utilized, as follows:

$$\begin{aligned}
\text{Unused subassembly labor} &= \text{Available subassembly labor} - \text{Used subassembly labor} \\
&= 316.0 \text{ hours} - [(.4 \text{ hours/CB})(632.31 \text{ CBs}) \\
&\qquad + (.5 \text{ hours/PR})(126.15 \text{ PRs})] \\
&= 316.0 - (252.92 + 63.08) \\
&= 0.0 \text{ hours}
\end{aligned}$$

$$\text{Unused assembly labor} = \text{Available assembly labor} - \text{Used assembly labor}$$

$$= 354.0 \text{ hours} \; - [(.5 \text{ hours/CB})(632.31 \text{ CBs}) + (.3 \text{ hours/PR})(126.15 \text{ PRs})]$$
$$= 354.0 \; - (316.16 + 37.84)$$
$$= 0.0 \text{ hours}$$

The graphical method can be used for problems with two or three decision variables. Since most operations management applications involve larger problems, the graphical method is of limited utility. It is useful, however, for visualizing the basics of linear programming.

Simplex Method

The simplex algorithm is a mathematical procedure for finding the optimal solution to a linear programming problem. It begins with an initial solution, which is progressively improved in a series of stages. To use this procedure, the analyst should:

1. Set up the problem in a linear programming framework
2. Create an initial solution
3. Evaluate the existing solution
4. Evaluate variables that could be introduced to improve the solution
5. Select the most advantageous variable to introduce
6. Determine which variable is to leave the solution
7. Revise the solution matrix
8. Repeat steps 3–7 until no further improvement is possible

Step 1: Setting Up the Problem A standard format, a statement of the objective function and constraints, is used to set up the problem. In general form, the LP model is a maximization problem of n variables and m restrictions set up as follows:

Maximize

$$Z = C_1X_1 + C_2X_2 + \ldots + C_nX_n$$

Subject to constraints

$$\begin{aligned}
A_{11}X_1 + A_{12}X_2 + \ldots + A_{1n}X_n &\leq B_1 \\
A_{21}X_1 + A_{22}X_2 + \ldots + A_{2n}X_n &\leq B_2 \\
\vdots \qquad \vdots \qquad\qquad \vdots \quad &\quad \vdots \\
A_{m1}X_1 + A_{m2}X_2 + \ldots + A_{mn}X_n &\leq B_m
\end{aligned}$$

The restrictions above are stated as *inequalities*. The simplex procedure requires that each restriction be converted into an *equality*. This is accomplished by adding a *slack* variable (S_i) to each restriction.

$$\begin{aligned}
A_{11}X_1 + A_{12}X_2 + \ldots + A_{1n}X_n + S_1 &= B_1 \\
A_{21}X_1 + A_{22}X_2 + \ldots + A_{2n}X_n + S_2 &= B_2 \\
\vdots \qquad \vdots \qquad\qquad \vdots \qquad \vdots \quad &\quad \vdots \\
A_{m1}X_1 + A_{m2}X_2 + \ldots + A_{mn}X_n + S_m &= B_m
\end{aligned}$$

S_1 is the slack variable representing the unused or idle quantity of the first resource. It is that portion of B_1 which is not devoted to real products $X_1, \ldots, X_n$. Similarly, S_2 is the amount of resource 2 that is not used. One slack variable is uniquely associated with each resource that is converted from an inequality to an equality. In the simplex procedure, each slack variable has a zero coefficient in the objective function. In the formulation above, therefore, the problem has a total of $n + m$ variables.

In formulating the problem, the conventional practice is to restate the objective function and restrictions so that each includes all of the slack variables. Let's express the MultiBand Enterprise example in the format described below, so that every variable (real and slack) appears in all the equations.

Maximize

$$Z = (\$50)\text{CB} + (\$40)\text{PR} + \$0S_1 + \$0S_2 + \$0S_3$$

Subject to constraints

$$\begin{aligned} &\text{Subassembly labor } (.4)\text{CB} + (.5)\text{PR} + 1S_1 + 0S_2 + 0S_3 = 316 \\ &\text{Assembly labor } (.5)\text{CB} + (.3)\text{PR} + 0S_1 + 1S_2 + 0S_3 = 354 \\ &\text{Inspection labor } (.05)\text{CB} + (.1)\text{PR} + 0S_1 + 0S_2 + 1S_3 = 62 \end{aligned}$$

Step 2: Creating an Initial Solution An initial solution is created by forming the matrix (table) shown in Table S5.1. We begin at the origin, with no real variables and only the slack variables in solution.

Within the dotted rectangle are the coefficients, A_{ij}, of the variables in the restriction equations, i referring to a row and j to a column. At the top of each column is the decision variable, X_j or S_j, depending upon the column to which the coefficients in that column apply. For example, the variable CB has coefficients .4, .5, and .05 in restriction equations 1, 2, and 3, respectively, in step 2. In the first row of the dotted rectangle are the coefficients of the five variables in the first restriction equation. Notice the

Table S5.1 Initial solution matrix for MultiBand Enterprises

C_j ↓	In Solution (basis)	\$50 CB	\$40 PR	\$0 S_1	\$0 S_2	\$0 S_3	(B_i) Production
\$0	S_1	.4	.5	1.0	0.0	0.0	316
0	S_2	.5	.3	0.0	1.0	0.0	354
0	S_3	.05	.1	0.0	0.0	1.0	62
	Z_j	\$0	\$0	\$0	\$0	\$0	\$0
	$C_j - Z_j$	\$50	\$40	\$0	\$0	\$0	

zero coefficients for S_2 and S_3 in the first row. These mean that S_2 and S_3 do not consume any subassembly labor, since they are slack variables for assembly and inspection.

Around the outer perimeter of the dotted rectangle we find some additional notation. The column headed In Solution (basis) lists the *variables that are in the initial or first-stage solution. The number of variables in solution (in the basis) is equal to the number of restrictions.* This is also true for each succeeding stage of the problem. The production column shows the quantity of each variable that is in solution. Thus, the initial solution shows 316 units of S_1, 354 units of S_2, and 62 units of S_3 being produced. Since those are fictitious variables, nothing is really being produced. The next step clarifies this point.

Step 3: Evaluating the Existing Solution Refer again to Table S5.1 and find the C_j values representing the objective function coefficients of each variable. These are used to evaluate the existing solution. The value of the objective function for the existing solution is:

$$Z = (\$50)(0) + (\$40)(0) + (\$0)(316) + (\$0)(354) + (\$0)(62)$$
$$= \$0$$

This initial solution leaves all three resources idle, since none of the resources is used for real products. The economic value of this solution is recorded at the bottom of the production column.

Step 4: Evaluating the Effects of Introducing Other Variables into Solution Is it possible to improve upon the initial solution? It might be if a new variable is introduced into the solution. Before introducing a new variable, however, we need a procedure for evaluating the economic effects of each variable that could be introduced. This is the purpose of the Z_j and $(C_j - Z_j)$ rows of Table S5.1. C_j represents the amount of *increase* in the objective function if one unit of variable j is added into solution. Z_j represents the amount of *decrease* in the objective function if variable j is introduced. $(C_j - Z_j)$ is the net increase. At the bottom of Table S5.1, beneath each variable, the $(C_j - Z_j)$ for each variable is recorded. The C_j values are obtained readily from the objective function, but determination of the Z_j values requires some explanation.

Z_j is obtained by considering the *substitution* rates between variable j and the variables that are currently in solution. These substitution rates are given by the coefficients under variable j in Table S5.1. Consider the CB radio column. If one CB is introduced, .4 subassembly hours, .5 assembly hours, and .05 inspection hours can no longer be idle. Each unit of CB that is added requires "giving up" .4 of an S_1, .5 of an S_2, and .05 of an S_3 that is currently being produced. If we give up the production of S_1, S_2, or S_3, how would the value of the objective function be changed? Since \$0 is contributed by each unit of S_1, S_2, and S_3, the amount of decrease in the objective function is:

$$Z_{CB} = (\$0)(.4) + (\$0)(.5) + (\$0)(.05) = \$0$$

In a similar manner, the Z_j and $(C_j - Z_j)$ values for all variables in the MultiBand problem are recorded at the bottom of Table S5.1.

Steps 5–8: Finding the Best Variables The remaining steps of the simplex method, while cumbersome manually, can be executed quickly and accurately with readily available computer software packages. The remainder of our discussion uses QSB (Quantitative Systems for Business), a user-friendly system that includes several linear programming options, to illustrate the completion of the simplex method.[7]

Steps 5 and 6, selection of entering and leaving variables, are shown in Figure S5.3. Why did QSB select CB as the entering variable? By examining the $(C_j - Z_j)$ row of the initial solution, we see that further improvement is possible. If we add a unit of CB into the solution, the objective function is increased by \$50. Or, if we add a unit of PR, the solution is improved by \$40. Additional units of S_1, S_2, or S_3 have no effect on the objective function, since each has a $(C_j - Z_j)$ value of zero. At each stage of the problem, we can introduce only one new variable. Each new variable must be evaluated so that the most attractive one can be chosen. In this case, CB is the most advantageous variable on a per-unit basis, so it is the one that should be selected.

Why was variable S_2 chosen to leave the solution? In this problem we can have only three variables in the solution at one time, one per constraint equation. If a new variable is introduced, an existing variable must leave

[7]See Y. Chang and R. S. Sullivan. *QSB: Quantitative Systems for Business* (Englewood Cliffs, N.J.: Prentice Hall, 1987). Readers who are interested in the manual procedure for the simplex method are referred to the management science selected readings at the end of this supplement.

FIGURE S5.3
QSB printout: Selection of incoming and outgoing variables (iteration 1)

Iteration 1

		CB	PR	S1	S2	S3		B (i) / A (i, j)
Basis	C (j)	50.00	40.00	0	0	0	B (i)	A (i, j)
S1	0	0.400	0.500	1.000	0	0	316.0	790.0
S2	0	0.500	0.300	0	1.000	0	354.0	708.0
S3	0	0.050	0.100	0	0	1.000	62.00	1240
C (j) − Z (j)		50.00	40.00	0	0	0	0	
* Big M		0	0	0	0	0	0	

Current objective function value (Max.) = 0
(Highlighted variable is the entering or leaving variable)
Entering: CB Leaving: S2

the solution. Since we wish to introduce CB, either S_1, S_2, or S_3 must leave. To find the variable that should leave the solution, QSB focuses on the substitution rates between CB and S_1, S_2, and S_3 (the variables in solution). Each CB requires giving up .4 S_1. There are 316 S_1's available to give up. If we consider only subassembly labor, a maximum of 790 CBs can be introduced, as shown in the right column of Figure S5.3. If we consider assembly labor, a maximum of 354 ÷ .5 = 708 CBs can be put into solution. There are enough idle inspection hours (S_3) to allow 1,240 CBs to be introduced. Since *all* restrictions must be met, we can see that available resources are adequate for adding 708 units of CB into solution. If we do this, all assembly labor is used for producing CBs; none is idle. Thus, assembly labor is the resource that keeps us from introducing more than 708 CBs; it is the *limiting resource* at this stage.

Let's summarize. QSB adds 708 units of CB into solution. To do this, we must give up all 354 units of S_2; that is, we give up all the S_2's that were formerly in solution, and S_2 is the variable that leaves solution. In the revised solution, we are producing 708 CBs and no PRs. Graphically, this is shown as point *c* in Figure S5.2.

After introducing the new variable CB into solution, QSB revises each row of the solution matrix to reflect the changes. The column headings are the same, but the row headings, restriction coefficients, and production quantities must be changed.[8] In terms of the graphical procedure, we are now moving *from the origin to an adjacent extreme point.* The resulting simplex tableau is shown in Figure S5.4.

[8]The detailed procedures for making these changes are available in the reference books cited at the end of this supplement.

FIGURE S5.4
QSB printout: Selection of incoming and outgoing variables (iteration 2)

Iteration 2

		CB	PR	S1	S2	S3		B (i)
Basis	C (j)	50.00	40.00	0	0	0	B (i)	A (i, j)
S1	0	0	0.260	1.000	–.800	0	32.80	126.2
CB	50.00	1.000	0.600	0	2.000	0	708.0	1180
S3	0	0	0.070	0	–.100	1.000	26.60	380.0
C (j) – Z (j)		0	10.00	0	–100	0	35400	
* Big M		0	0	0	0	0	0	

Current objective function value (Max.) = 35400
(Highlighted variable is the entering or leaving variable)
Entering: PR Leaving: S1

After completing the first iteration of the simplex method, the entire procedure is repeated using Figure S5.4 as the new starting point. Accordingly, QSB has identified PR as the next entering variable, to replace S_1. Each entering PR will add \$10 marginal contribution to profit, as noted in the $C(j) - Z(j)$ row, and there are sufficient resources to add 126.2 PRs, which consumes the 32.80 idle hours of subassembly labor. After bringing variable PR into solution, QSB again revises each row of the solution matrix to reflect the changes in the row headings, the production quantities, and the coefficients in the solution matrix. Graphically, QSB has moved us to point h in Figure S5.2.

After completing the second iteration by bringing PRs into solution, the revised solution matrix (Figure S5.5) indicates that no further improvement is possible; all of the values in the $C(j) - Z(j)$ row are zero or negative. The optimal solution has been reached.

The summarized results are shown in Figure S5.6—632.3 CBs and 126.2 PRs will be produced to give \$36,661.54 profit. All of the subassembly and assembly labor is fully consumed, but nearly 18 hours of inspection labor are unused. Consequently, some inspection workers might be moved to other operations where they can be productive. The opportunity cost for subassembly labor (S_1) shows the foregone profit of not having one more hour of that resource; that is, if MultiBand had an additional hour of subassembly labor and used it properly, the resulting marginal contribution to profit would be \$38.46. If, instead, we had an additional hour of assembly labor, the marginal contribution to profit would be \$69.23.

Sensitivity analysis provides useful information for operations management. In the top half of Figure S5.7 you can see the original objective function coefficients for CBs (\$50) and PRs (\$40). We also see their

FIGURE S5.5
QSB printout: Optimal solution for MultiBand

Final tableau (Total iteration = 2)

		CB	PR	S1	S2	S3		B (i)
Basis	C (j)	50.00	40.00	0	0	0	B (i)	A (i, j)
PR	40.00	0	1.000	3.846	–3.08	0	126.2	0
CB	50.00	1.000	0	–2.31	3.846	0	632.3	0
S3	0	0	0	–.269	0.115	1.000	17.77	0
C (j) – Z (j)		0	0	–38.5	–69.2	0	36662	
* Big M		0	0	0	0	0	0	

(Max.) Optimal OBJ value = 36661.54

Summarized Results for MultiB			Page : 1		
Variables No. Names	Solution	Opportunity Cost	Variables No. Names	Solution	Opportunity Cost
1 CB	+632.30768	0	4 S2	0	+69.230774
2 PR	+126.15384	0	5 S3	+17.769232	0
3 S1	0	+38.461536			
Maximum value of the OBJ = 36661.54 Iters. = 2					

FIGURE S5.6
QSB printout: Summarized results for MultiBand

minimum and maximum values within which the optimal solution mix remains the same. CBs, in other words, can have a contribution margin from \$32.00 to \$66.66 without changing the optimal solution mix (the solution remains at the same corner point, *h*, in Figure S5.2). The optimal quantities of CBs and PRs will remain unchanged, but total profit (Z), of course, will change. If the CB coefficient goes outside the stated range, the optimal solution mix will change and, to find it, the problem must be re-solved.

The lower half of Figure S5.7 shows the sensitivity of the right-hand side (RHS) for each restriction. In other words, how would the solution be affected if MultiBand had more or less of a resource than the original amount? Within the indicated range, the same variables remain in the optimal solution, but the optimal *quantities* of them change. If, for example, there were only 283.2 hours of subassembly labor (rather than the original 316 hours), the resulting optimal solution would still contain the same variables (CB, PR, and S_3). Outside the range, however, a different

FIGURE S5.7
QSB printout: Sensitivity analysis for MultiBand

Sensitivity Analysis for OBJ Coefficients						Page : 1	
C (j)	Min. C (j)	Original	Max. C (j)	C (j)	Min. C (j)	Original	Max. C (j)
C (1)	+32.000000	+50.000000	+66.666664	C (2)	+30.000000	+40.000000	+62.500000

Sensitivity Analysis for RHS						Page : 1	
B (i)	Min. B (i)	Original	Max. B (i)	B (i)	Min. B (i)	Original	Max. B (i)
B (1)	+283.20001	+316.00000	+382.00000	B (3)	+44.230766	+62.000000	+ Infinity
B (2)	+200.00002	+354.00000	+395.00000				

mix of variables would be optimal. An alternative interpretation is that within the indicated ranges, the opportunity costs of the solution variables remain as stated in Figure S5.6; otherwise, the opportunity costs change.

Some Additional Considerations

Minimization For purposes of illustration, we have used a maximization problem to present the simplex method. *Minimization* problems are also frequently encountered, and the same basic procedure is applied. The $(C_j - Z_j)$ values in step 4, however, have the reverse meaning in minimization problems; that is, as long as a negative $(C_j - Z_j)$ exists, further improvement is possible. The variable having the largest negative value is selected for introduction into solution. When all $(C_j - Z_j)$ are zero or positive, no further minimization is possible.

Artificial Variables Another circumstance arises when the problem restrictions are not of the less-than-or-equal-to variety used in our example. Two other types of restrictions are commonly encountered. First is the equality of the form:

$$A_1X_1 + A_2X_2 = B_1$$

In this case, a slack variable is not added since an equality already exists. However, a different kind of variable, an artificial variable, is added by QSB to the left side:

$$A_1X_1 + A_2X_2 + A = B_1$$

The artificial variable serves computational purposes in the initial tableau. It is undesirable to have the artificial variable appear in the final solution. Therefore, the coefficient of A (called *Big M* at the bottom of the simplex tableaus in Figures S5.3, S5.4, and S5.5) in the objective function is made to be an arbitrarily large positive value in a minimization problem or an arbitrarily large negative number in a maximization problem. This assures that A will be driven out of solution by the simplex procedure.

Surplus Variables Another type of restriction is the greater-than-or-equal-to restriction:

$$A_1X_1 + A_2X_2 \geq B_1$$

Both a surplus (negative slack) and an artificial variable are added by QSB. The surplus variable converts the expression into an equality:

$$A_1X_1 + A_2X_2 - S = B_1$$

Then, since S has a coefficient of -1, an artificial variable must be added to the left side to create an identity matrix:

$$A_1X_1 + A_2X_2 - S + A = B_1$$

Once QSB converts all the restrictions by adding the necessary artificial and slack variables, the previously described simplex procedure is executed.

REVIEW AND DISCUSSION QUESTIONS

1. Of what value is the graphic method of LP?
2. Define and illustrate the following:
   (a) Linear objective function
   (b) Linear constraint
   (c) Nonlinear objective function
   (d) Nonlinear constraint
3. What is meant by the term *feasibility area* (region of feasibility) in a linear programming model? What is the significance of the corner points?
4. In the simplex method, what is the standard format of problem formulation? Give an example.
5. What is a *slack variable?* Why is it used? How many will there be in an LP problem?
6. How many variables will be in solution at any stage of an LP problem?
7. What is the significance of the $C_j - Z_j$ row of the LP solution matrix?
8. After determining which variable to introduce next into solution, how do you determine how many units of that variable to introduce?
9. In the simplex method, what indicates that an optimal solution has been reached?
10. Define and illustrate
    (a) Artificial variable
    (b) Surplus variable
11. Under what conditions would an LP problem use artificial, surplus, and slack variables? Give examples of each.

PROBLEMS

1. Consider the following LP problem:
   Minimize $C = 16x + 10y$
   Subject to: $12x + 4y \geq 24$
   $6x + 12y \geq 36$
   (a) Using the graphic method, find the optimal solution.
   (b) If the objective function is changed to $C = 16x + 4y$, what is the optimal solution?
2. Solve the following problem using the graphic method of LP:
   Maximize $P = 2A + 2B$
   Subject to: $2A + 3B \leq 16$
   $2A + B \leq 8$
   If the objective function is changed to $P = 2A + 5B$, what is the optimal solution?
3. Product A offers a profit of $4/unit; product B yields $2.50 profit/unit. To manufacture the products, leather, wood, and glue are required in the amounts shown below.

Resources required for one unit

	Product	
Resource	A	B
Leather (pounds)	½	¼
Wood (board feet)	4	7
Glue (ounces)	2	2

The resources on hand include 2,000 pounds of leather, 28,000 board feet of wood, and 10,000 ounces of glue.

(a) State the objective function and constraints in mathematical form.
(b) Find the optimal solution graphically.
(c) Which resources are fully consumed by the optimal solution?
(d) How much of each resource remains unused in the optimal solution?

4. Fatten Fast Feed Company produces a hog feed made from two basic ingredients, X and Y. A ton of Y can be purchased for $120; a ton of X costs $80. Each ingredient contains three types of nutrients, A, B, and C.

Nutrient content (units per ton)

	Nutrient		
Ingredient	A	B	C
X	450	73	69
Y	257	61	208

A ton of hog feed must contain at least 3,600 units of nutrient A, 730 units of nutrient B, and 1,250 units of nutrient C. What proportions of X and Y should be selected to minimize the cost of hog feed?

5. Quick Copy Service has a large backlog of printing jobs to be done. There are 10,000 standard lots of class A jobs and 18,000 standard lots of class B jobs. The cost of processing a standard class A job is $.72, of a class B job, $.33. The manager wishes to minimize processing costs for the coming month; however, some constraints must be met. First, the marketing department has requested that a minimum of 80 percent of the class A jobs and 60 percent of the class B jobs be completed this month. Second, wage payments are already committed for 4,200 direct labor hours for next month in the processing center. A class A job consumes .16 labor hours, and a class B job requires .23 labor hours. The manager wishes to fully utilize the direct labor during the month. How many jobs of each class should be processed?

6. Real Deal Distributors packages and distributes merchandise to retail outlets. A standard shipment can be packaged in small, medium, or large containers. A standard shipment of small containers yields a profit of $4; medium containers, $12; and large containers, $16. Each shipment is prepared manually, requiring packing materials and time. Each shipment must also be inspected.

Resource requirements per standard shipment

Container Size	Packing Time (hours)	Packing Material (pounds)	Inspection Time (minutes)
Small	1.0	2.0	1.5
Medium	2.0	4.0	3.0
Large	4.0	7.0	3.0
Total amount of resource available	1,200	2,400	1,200

(a) Formulate this problem in a simplex format.
(b) What is the optimal number of each container size to produce?

7. Maxim, Inc., sends sales representatives to call on three types of clients: retail, industrial, and professional. Sales revenues of $2,000 result from calling on a retail

client, \$5,000 from an industrial contact, and \$20,000 from each professional client. This month a total of 3,200 hours of sales representative time is available for calling on customers, and \$10,000 is available for travel expenses. Management will not allow more than 20 percent of total sales force time to be devoted to retail clients, and they will not allow more than 30 percent of the travel expense budget to be used for calling on professional clients. Six hours of travel and selling time are required to call on a retail client, 11 hours for an industrial client, and 25 hours for a professional client. Travel expenses are \$10 for each retail contract, \$14 for each industrial client, and \$35 for each professional call. What is the optimal client mix for the coming month?

8. The Farmers Cooperative Oil Company produces two lines of motor oil and a special engine additive called New Motor. All three products are produced by blending two components. These components contribute various properties, including viscosity. (*Viscosity* is the thickness or tendency to flow.) The viscosity in the product is proportional to the viscosities of the blending components. The pertinent data appear in the table. Assume no limitation on demand. Set this up as a linear programming problem to determine how many barrels of each oil product Farmers should produce each week. Clearly define all variables. (Do not solve for the optimal solution.)

Blending Component	Viscosity	Cost Per Barrel (\$)	Availability/Week
1	20	8.50	8,000
2	60	13.00	3,000

Product	Viscosity Required	Profit Contribution Per Barrel
30W oil	30	\$14
40W oil	40	17
New Motor	50	22

9. Greenthumb Landscape Company employs senior and junior tree specialists who are assigned to various landscaping jobs. Daily wages are \$70 for each senior specialist and \$45 for each junior specialist. Working alone, a senior specialist processes an acre of work in four days. A junior specialist requires seven days to process one acre. However, if both types of workers are assigned to a project, two days of senior work and three days of junior work will complete one acre. Greenthumb receives \$600 revenue for each acre it processes. Supervisory requirements depend on the type of tree specialist assigned to a project; .8 days of supervisor time is required for each acre processed by a senior specialist; 1.0 days of supervision is needed for an acre processed by a junior specialist; and 2.0 supervisor days/acre are needed for projects using both junior and senior specialists. In total, 450 days of supervision, 1,200 days of junior specialist labor, and 1,000 days of senior specialist skills are available. How should the work force be utilized to maximize the profit?

10. Given the following simplex tableau:

C_j	In Solution	P_1	P_2	P_3	P_4	P_5	Production
		1	0	1	0	0	4
		0	1	0	1	0	6
		3	0	0	−2	1	6
	Z_j	0	5	0	5	0	30
	$C_j - Z_j$	3	0	0	−5	0	−30

(a) What variables form the basis solution? That is, what variables are in solution?
(b) What are the values of $C_1, C_2, \ldots, C_j$?
(c) Is this the optimal solution? Explain.
(d) Regardless of your answer in Part c, *assume* this is the optimal solution. Your supervisor says we *must* produce 2 units of P_1. What effect would this have on the objective function value of 30 units above?

11. Betherton Furniture Manufacturing has always used an outside carrier to make its deliveries. It is now investigating purchasing trucks and making its own deliveries. Betherton has available 220 workdays which it can use for the trucking operation and $800,000 to invest in trucks. Due to loading restrictions and an unwillingness to become a totally owned private carrier, Betherton will purchase a maximum of 40 trucks; outside carriers will still be used a great deal. The three types of trucks under consideration have characteristics as shown in the table. Formulate, but do not solve, Betherton's situation as a linear programming problem.

Truck Type	Delivery Capacity (ton-miles/day)	Operator Requirements to Meet Delivery Capacity (workdays/vehicle)	Purchase Cost
A	7,300	3	$16,000
B	9,000	6	26,000
C	13,010	6	30,000

Operations Analysis Using QSB

12. What if another department in MultiBand Enterprises (see Chapter 5 and the Supplement to Chapter 5) announces it will transfer 80 "free" labor hours next month to the department that produces CBs and PRs? These hours are in addition to those previously stated in the MultiBand example. How should the labor hours be used (due to worker training, the three types of labor are interchangable)? Prepare your recommendation with supporting data.

SELECTED READINGS

Anderson, D. R., D. J. Sweeney, and T. A. Williams, *An Introduction to Management Science* (3rd ed.). St. Paul, Minn.: West Publishing Co., 1982.

Bierman, H., Jr., C. P. Bonini, and W. H. Hausman, *Quantitative Analysis for Business Decisions* (6th ed.). Homewood, Ill.: Richard D. Irwin, 1981.

Chang, Y., and R. S. Sullivan, *QSB: Quantitative Systems for Business*. Englewood Cliffs, N.J.: Prentice Hall, 1987.

6

Facility Location Planning

In the truckload transportation business, profit margins are relatively thin. We must therefore manage capital very efficiently in order to earn an adequate return on investment. Since physical facilities require significant expenditures of capital, we like to keep the number of facilities to a minimum. However, carriers generally will have a substantially higher market share in territories near their physical facilities, and certain expenses increase as the distance between customers, drivers, and our physical facilities increase. Therefore, the strategic location of an optimal number of physical facilities is vital to success in our business.

Michael L. Lawrence
President and Chief Executive Officer
Burlington Northern Motor Carriers, Inc.
Fort Worth, Texas

Mr. Lawrence has identified a key strategic problem in the motor carrier industry—how many facilities should we have and where should they be located? This problem is encountered by service and goods-producing organizations in both the public and private sectors. Banks, restaurants, recreation agencies, and manufacturing companies are all concerned with selecting locational sites that will best enable them to meet their long-term goals.

The success of location planning both affects and is affected by organizing and control activities. Since the operations manager fixes many costs with the location decision, both the efficiency and effectiveness of the conversion process are dependent upon location. Leading to this decision are analyses with both modeling and behavioral dimensions. Let's examine the facilities location activity in more detail.

NEED FOR FACILITY LOCATION PLANNING

Public and private organizations are concerned with revenue and cost behavior, both of which can be affected by location. We need to understand how each of these profitability components depends on where the facility is situated. First we examine the technique called *break-even analysis.* Then we see how break-even analysis is useful for facility location planning.

Break-even Analysis

Break-even analysis is a graphical or algebraic representation of the relationships among volume, cost, and revenues in an organization. As the volume of output from a productive facility increases, costs and revenues also increase. Costs can generally be divided into two categories—fixed and variable. Fixed costs are those incurred regardless of output volume. They include heating, lighting, and administrative expenses that are the same whether one or one thousand units of output are produced. Variable costs are those that fluctuate directly with volume of output; higher output results in higher total variable costs. Typically, they are the costs of direct labor and material. In Figure 6.1, total revenues and total costs are shown as linear functions of output volume. Costs exceed revenues over the initial range of volume up to point V_{BE}. Point V_{BE} is the *break-even point*—that level of operating volume at which total cost equals total revenues from operations. Thereafter, revenues exceed costs of operation.

Break-even analysis identifies the level of operations (output) that must be reached in order to recover all the costs of operation from revenues. The break-even point depends on the selling price of the product and the operating cost structure. Some conversion processes require large capital outlays and high overhead expenses but low unit variable costs.

FIGURE 6.1
Cost structures and break-even charts for operations in two contrasting locations

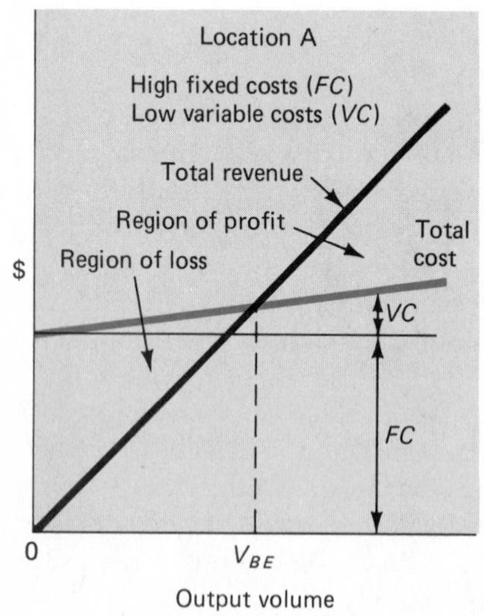

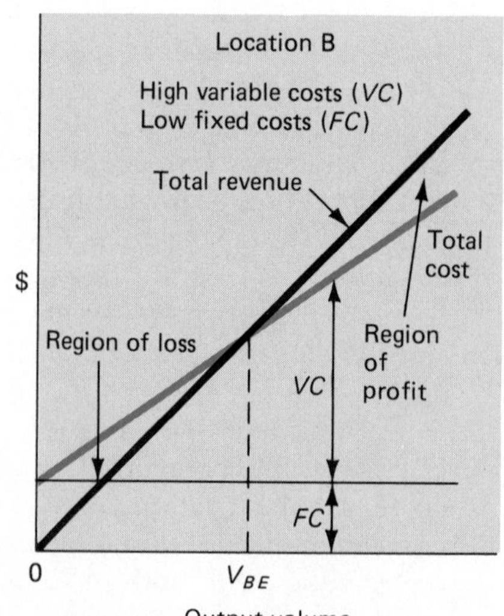

They require a large volume of output to reach break-even, but once they have attained it, profitability increases rapidly. Other conversion processes have low fixed costs and high unit variable costs. Figure 6.1 shows both kinds of cost structures.

Break-even with Discontinuous Revenues and Costs Revenues and/or costs may be curvilinear rather than linear functions (with constant slope) over some ranges of output volume, and the functions may not be continuous with increasing volume. Indeed, a major purpose of break-even analysis is to reveal how the organization's costs and revenues change with volume of output.

Consider the situation in Figure 6.2. The organization has two facilities, A and B, which may be operated during the coming year. Facility A, working a single shift, has a break-even volume of BE_1 units. Thereafter, profitability increases up to the output V_A. If greater profit is desired, facility B must be opened and additional fixed costs incurred. The overall operation (facilities A and B) will not be profitable until a volume of BE_2 units is achieved. Output volumes above BE_2 result in higher profit rates until volume V_B is reached. To achieve outputs above V_B, second shift

FIGURE 6.2
Break-even chart for operating one facility, two facilities, and two facilities on double shifts

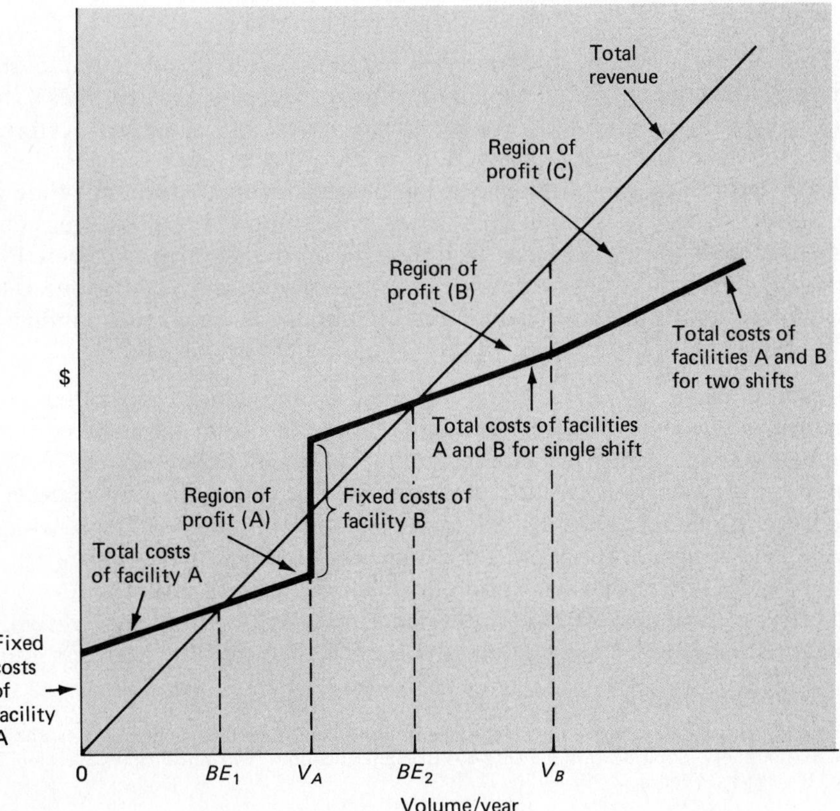

operations are necessary, and variable costs increase accordingly. Beyond V_B, profits continue to increase, but at a slower rate as shown in profit region C.

Information from the break-even chart can now be used for aiding managerial decisions. Once the desired level of profitability for the year has been stated, we can show the volume of output necessary for achieving it. We can also identify how many facilities and shifts will be needed, and we can estimate operating costs and working capital requirements.

Location Effects on Costs and Revenues

Revenues In some industries, revenues depend on having the facility near potential customers. For manufacturing firms that supply customers (who are often themselves manufacturers and assemblers), delivery time can be a crucial component of the strategic mission.[1]

In service industries, the situation is somewhat different. For *stored services,* those not directly consumed, location is not so important. Federal Reserve banks, automotive repair shops, and manufacturers who repair appliances are often quasi-manufacturers in the conversion process, and they don't necessarily have to be located near consumers. On the other hand, for firms that offer *directly consumed services,* location can be critical. Movie theaters, restaurants, banks, apartments, dry cleaning stores, and even public recreation areas obviously must be located at sites that are convenient to the public. If they aren't, consumers will go somewhere else, and revenues will decline.

Fixed Costs New or additional facilities entail fixed initial costs, usually incurred only once, which must be recovered out of revenues if the investment is to be profitable. Acquisition of new and additional facilities involves costs for new construction, addition to existing facilities, purchase and renovation of other existing plants, or rental. And once they're acquired, more money must be spent on equipment and fixtures. The magnitude of these costs may well depend on the site that is selected. A choice merchandising corner location in downtown Washington, D.C. requires a totally different capital outlay from one in Greencastle, Indiana. Construction costs also vary greatly from one place to another.

Variable Costs Once built, the new facility must be staffed and operated, and these costs depend on location. For labor-intensive conversion processes, labor availability and local wage structures are major concerns. Management must also consider proximity to raw materials sources (inputs) and to finished goods markets (outputs), either of which can cause transportation and shipping costs to go up or down.

Seldom does an organization find a single site that is best in terms of all revenue and cost variables. The location offering the highest revenue potential may also incur higher variable costs of operation. Tradeoffs must

---

[1]For a discussion of locational considerations in multiplant manufacturing strategies, see R. W. Schmenner, "Look Beyond the Obvious in Plant Location," *Harvard Business Review* 57, no. 1 (January–February 1979), 126–32.

be made among fixed costs, variable costs, and revenue potential; the final locational choice should be the one that offers the best overall balance toward achieving the organization's mission.

In evaluating any potential site, then, we might consider all these principal revenue and cost factors using a break-even analysis (as in Figure 6.1). For location A, fixed costs are high and variable operating costs are low. The lower fixed costs of location B are offset by its higher variable costs at that facility's location.

Reasons for Locational Changes

In addition to the need for greater capacity, there are other reasons for relocating old facilities or locating new ones:

1. Changes in input resources may occur. The cost or location of labor, raw materials, and supporting resources (such as subcontractors) may change.
2. Shifts in geographical demand may occur. As product markets change, it may be desirable to change facility locations to provide better service to customers.
3. Mergers of companies may result in redundant facilities, some of which must be phased out.
4. The introduction of new products may necessitate locational changes, so that new input resources and product markets can be reached more economically.

GENERAL PROCEDURES FOR FACILITY LOCATION PLANNING

The Preliminary Study

A screening study is usually initiated early in the planning process to identify feasible sites. For some kinds of facilities, particular environmental or labor considerations are crucial. Breweries, for example, require an adequate supply of clean water. Aircraft manufacturers must be located near a variety of types of subcontractors; primary aluminum producers need substantial amounts of electrical power. Some main resources and local factors that must be considered are listed here.

Resources	Local Conditions
Labor skills and productivity	Community receptivity to business
Land availability and cost	Construction costs
Raw materials	Organized industrial complexes
Subcontractors	Quality of life: climate, housing, recreation, schools
Transportation facilities (highways, rail, air, water)	Taxes
Utility availability and rates	

Sources of Information After identifying several key factors, management undertakes a search to find alternative geographic locations that seem consistent with general requirements. Obviously inappropriate alternatives are eliminated from further consideration. Where does all this information come from? Local chambers of commerce provide literature promoting expansion possibilities in various state and local communities. The *Wall Street Journal* and numerous trade publications contain advertisements placed by cities and communities wishing to attract new commerce. The National Industrial Conference Board, federal Departments of Commerce, the Small Business Administration, and the U.S. Census of Manufacturers are among the many sources that provide both general and detailed information for location of facilities. These data include geographic breakdowns of labor availability, population, transportation facilities, profiles of existing types of commerce, and similar information.

Detailed Analysis

Preliminary screening usually narrows serious alternative sites to just a few. At this stage a more detailed analysis ensues. At each potential site a labor survey may be conducted to assess the availability of local skills. Where community reaction remains a serious uncertainty, or where the strength of local consumer response is questionable, pilot studies or systematic surveys may be undertaken. Community response is important, for example, in deciding where to locate a nuclear reactor, a recreation area, a commercial bank, a state prison, or a restaurant. For assessing existing attitudes and for developing strategies to gain favorable acceptance in the community, survey research techniques can be very helpful.

Factor-Rating Systems Factor ratings are frequently used for overall evaluations of location alternatives because (1) their simplicity facilitates communications about why one site is favored over another; (2) they enable managers to bring diverse locational considerations (factors) into the evaluation process; and (3) they foster consistency of judgment when evaluating the relative merits of the alternatives prior to final site selection. Typically, the first step is to list the site characteristics (factors) that are most relevant in the location decision (column 1 in Table 6.1). Next, each characteristic is assigned a numeric weighting, say from 1 (very low) to 5 (very high), reflecting its relative importance in the current site location decision (column 2 in Table 6.1). Then, each location under consideration is rated, say on a scale from 1 (very low) to 10 (very high), for its merits on every characteristic (column 3 in Table 6.1). Finally, the importance weighting is multiplied times the merit rating for each characteristic (column 4 in Table 6.1), and the sum of the resulting numbers yields the total evaluation score for that location. The total scores, comparatively, indicate which alternative locations, on balance, are most promising in consideration of all the various locational characteristics.

Table 6.1 Factor ratings for location alternative A

Characteristic (factor)	Factor Weighting (importance)	Ratings for Location A	Evaluation for Location A
Tax advantages of state and community	4	8	32
Suitability of labor skills	3	2	6
Proximity to customers	3	6	18
Proximity to suppliers	5	2	10
Adequacy of water	1	3	3
Community receptivity	5	4	20
Quality of educational system	4	1	4
Access to rail and air transportation	3	10	30
Climate	2	7	14
Availability of power	2	6	12
			Total Score = 149

FACILITY LOCATION MODELS

Various quantitative models are used to help determine the best locations of facilities. Sometimes, models are tailor-made to meet the specific circumstances of a unique problem. In New York City, for example, a mathematical model was developed for use as a policy tool for determining the best locations of fire companies.[2] Public officials wish to balance available fire fighting service to reduce risks of property damage and fatalities. Among the regions of the city are different compositions of residential and commercial structures, alarm rates, hazard ratings, and street configurations. Furthermore, since many of these characteristics change with time, the problem is dynamic; a good location pattern now may not be so good in future years. The mathematical model for evaluating fire company locations takes into account many of these factors. The expected travel times (to be minimized) of fire companies are related mathematically to all these characteristics of regions in which they might be located: size of the area to be serviced, number of fire companies in the region, average alarm density in the region, street configuration, and travel characteristics of the fire company. This specialized model may be highly effective for locating emergency services in an urban setting.

There are some widely known, general models that can be adapted to the needs of a variety of systems. In the sections below we briefly introduce three types of models that have had application to the location

[2]This model is reported by K. L. Rider, "A Parametric Model for the Allocation of Fire Companies in New York City," *Management Science* 23, no. 2 (October 1976), 146–58.

problem: the simple median model, linear programming, and simulation. All these models focus on transportation costs, although each considers a different version of the basic problem.

Simple Median Model

Suppose we wish to locate a new manufacturing plant that will annually receive shipments of raw materials from each of two existing sources, RM_1 and RM_2. The plant will create finished goods that must be shipped to each of two existing distribution warehouses, DW_1 and DW_2. Given these four existing facilities, shown in Figure 6.3, where should we locate the new plant to minimize annual transportation costs of the entire network of facilities?

The simple median model can help answer this question. This model considers the volume of loads transported on *rectangular* paths.[3] All movements are made in east-west and/or north-south directions; diagonal moves are not considered. The simple median model provides an optimal solution.[4]

Table 6.2 shows the number of loads, L_i, to be shipped annually between each existing facility and the new plant; it also shows the x and y coordinates (location) of each existing facility.

The Model Let's assume that the transportation cost to move a standard load a unit-distance is represented by C_i. Then overall transit cost

[3]See. R. C. Vergin and J. D. Rogers, "An Algorithm and Computational Procedure for Locating Economic Facilities," *Management Science* 13, no. 6 (February 1967), 240–54.

[4]An alternative procedure, the center of gravity method, provides an approximate (but not necessarily optimal) solution and can be found in J. J. Coyle and E. J. Bardi, *The Management of Logistics*, 2nd ed. (St. Paul, Minn.: The West Publishing Co., 1980).

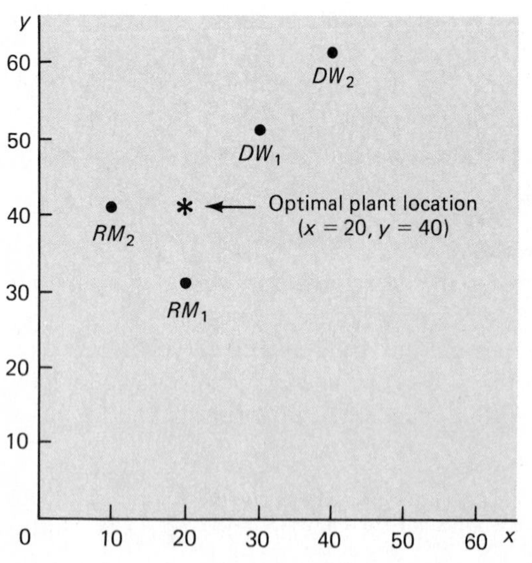

FIGURE 6.3
Existing raw materials sources and distribution warehouses (locations shown on a coordinate system with arbitrary origin)

is measured by adding the number of loads times the distance each is moved times the unit distance cost per load:

$$\text{Transportation cost} = \sum_{i=1}^{n} C_i L_i D_i \tag{6.1}$$

Table 6.2 Locations of existing facilities and number of loads to be moved

Existing Facility (i)	L_i Annual Number of Loads Moved Between Facility i and New Plant	C_i Cost to Move a Standard Load One Unit-Distance	Coordinate Location of Existing Facility i	
			X_i	Y_i
1. RM_1	700	\$1	20	30
2. RM_2	900	1	10	40
3. DW_1	400	1	30	50
4. DW_2	500	1	40	60
	2,500			

In equation 6.1, L_i is the number of loads to be moved between the new plant and existing facility i. In our example there are $i = 4$ existing facilities. D_i represents the distance between the new plant and facility i. The distance each load is to be moved depends on our location choice. We then add together the number of loads times the distance they are moved times the cost of moving such a load from each existing site. The answer represents the cost of all movements in the system.

Since all loads must be on rectangular paths, total distance of a load is measured by its length of movement in the x direction and in the y direction:

$$D_i = |x - x_i| + |y - y_i| \tag{6.2}$$

The variables x and y in equation 6.2 represent the coordinates of any proposed location for the new plant. Once a location is specified, the distance for all load movements (D_i) can be calculated. What we wish to do is find the values for x and y (new plant) that result in minimum transportation cost. We use the following three steps:

1. Identify the median value of the total number of loads moved.
2. Find the x-coordinate value of the existing facility that sends (or receives) the median load.
3. Find the y-coordinate value of the existing facility that sends (or receives) the median load.

The x and y values found in steps 2 and 3 define the desired location for the new facility.

Application of the Model Let us apply the three steps to the data in Table 6.2.

1. *Identify the median load.* Total number of loads moved to and from the new plant will be 2,500. The *median* number of loads is that value above which half the number of loads lie and below which the other half lie. If the total number of loads is odd, the median load will be the middle load. If the total number of loads is even (e.g., 2,500), the median loads will be the two middle loads. For 2,500 loads, the median loads are the 1,250th and 1,251st loads, since 1,249 loads lie above and below these amounts.

2. *Find x-coordinate of the median load.* First we consider movement of loads in the x-direction. Beginning at the origin of Figure 6.3 and moving to the right along the x-axis, observe the number of loads moved to or from existing facilities. Loads 1–900 are shipped by RM_2 from location $x = 10$. Loads 901–1,600 are shipped by RM_1 from location $x = 20$. Since the median loads (1,250, 1,251) fall in the interval 901–1,600, $x = 20$ is the desired x-coordinate location for the new plant.

3. *Find y-coordinate of the median load.* Now consider the y-direction of load movements. Begin at the origin of Figure 6.3 and move upward along the y-axis. Movements in the y direction begin with loads 1–700 being shipped by RM_1 from location $y = 30$. Loads 701–1,600 are shipped by RM_2 from location $y = 40$. Since the median loads (1,250, 1,251) fall in the interval 701–1,600, $y = 40$ is the desired y-coordinate for the new plant.

The optimal plant location, $x = 20$ and $y = 40$, results in minimizing annual transportation costs for this network of facilities. To calculate the resulting cost, we substitute equation 6.2 into equation 6.1.

$$TC = \sum_{i=1}^{n} C_i\, L_i\, (|x - x_i| + |y - y_i|) \tag{6.3}$$

Total cost, \$44,000, is shown in Table 6.3.

Some concluding remarks are in order. First, we have considered the case in which only one new facility is to be added.[5] Second, you should note an important assumption of this model: Any point in the $x - y$ coordinate system is an eligible point for locating the new facility. The model does not consider road availability, physical terrain, population densities, or any other of the many important locational considerations. The task of blending model results with other major considerations to arrive at a reasonable locational choice is a major managerial responsibility.[6]

---

[5]For adding multiple facilities, see R. A. Johnson, W. T. Newell, and R. C. Vergin, *Operations Management: A Systems Concept* (Boston: Houghton Mifflin Co., 1972).

[6]For a successful application that blends model results with other qualitative factors, see A. A. Aly and D. W. Litwhiler, Jr., "Police Briefing Stations: A Location Problem," *AIIE Transactions* 11, no. 1 (March 1979), 12–22.

Table 6.3 Calculation of total cost for optimal plant location (x = 20, y = 40)

(1) Existing Facility i	(2) x_i for Existing Facility	(3) x for New Plant	(4) Distance Loads Move in x-Direction $\lvert x - x_i \rvert$	(5) y_i for Existing Facility	(6) y for New Plant	(7) Distance Loads Move in y-Direction $\lvert y - y_i \rvert$	(8) Total Distance x Cost (C_iD_i) Loads Move (4) + (7) $(\$1)(\lvert x - x_i \rvert = \lvert y - y_i \rvert)$	(9) Number of Loads L_i	(10) Number of Loads Times Distance x Cost Moved (8) × (9) $C_i \times D_i \times L_i$
1	20	20	0	30	40	10	$10	700	$ 7,000
2	10	20	10	40	40	0	10	900	9,000
3	30	20	10	50	40	10	20	400	8,000
4	40	20	20	60	40	20	40	500	20,000
							Total cost = $\sum_{i=1}^{4} C_iL_iD_i$ =		$44,000

Linear Programming

Linear programming may be helpful after the initial screening phase has narrowed the feasible alternative sites to a finite number. The remaining candidates can then be evaluated, one at a time, to determine how well each would fit in with existing facilities, and the alternative that leads to the best overall system (network) performance can be identified. Most often, overall transportation cost is the criterion used for performance evaluation. A special type of linear programming called the *distribution* or *transportation* method, has been found to be of particular usefulness in location planning.[7] It has been applied in the simplified example that follows. The mechanics of this technique are omitted in the example but are demonstrated in the supplement to this chapter.

EXAMPLE

Alpha Processing Company has three midwestern production plants located at Evansville, Indiana; Lexington, Kentucky; and Fort Wayne, Indiana. Plans being developed for operations five years hence will require that 200 shipments of raw materials be delivered annually to the Evansville plant, 300 shipments to Lexington, and 400 shipments to Fort Wayne. Currently, Alpha has two sources of raw materials, one at Chicago, Illinois, the other at Louisville, Kentucky. The Chicago source will be capable of supplying 300 shipments per year; Louisville has a 400-shipment capacity. An additional source of raw materials must therefore be opened to meet the anticipated raw material needs of the plants. Preliminary screening by Alpha has narrowed the choice to two attractive alternatives—Columbus, Ohio, and St. Louis, Missouri. Each of these sites would be capable of supplying 200 shipments annually. Alpha has decided to make its selection on the basis of minimizing transportation costs. Estimates of the cost per shipment from each source to destination are shown in the cells of the matrix in Table 6.4.

The cost analysis for Alpha Company proceeds in two stages. The first stage finds the lowest cost obtainable if the Columbus source were added to the existing network. The second stage determines the minimum cost possible if the St. Louis source were chosen. The results of these two analyses are compared, and the most favorable alternative is then selected. A final solution of this analysis for Alpha is shown in Figure 6.4.

If Columbus is selected, minimum annual shipping costs will be $120,000. This occurs if 100 shipments go from Chicago to Evansville (costing $200 each), 200 shipments from Chicago to Fort Wayne (costing $200 each), 100 from Louisville to Evansville ($100 each), 300 from Louisville to Lexington ($100 each), and 200 shipments from Columbus to

[7]The simplex method of linear programming has also proved useful in location analysis. For an example of implementation for locating two new industrial production facilities, see R. F. Love and L. Yerex, "An Application of a Facilities Location Model in the Prestressed Concrete Industry," *Interfaces* 6, no. 4 (August 1976), 45–49.

Table 6.4 Sources, destinations, and costs of raw material shipments

Source	Evansville	Lexington	Fort Wayne	Number of Shipments Available from Source
Chicago	$200	$300	$200	300
Louisville	100	100	300	400
Columbus	300	200	100	200
St. Louis	100	300[a]	400	200
Number of shipments needed by destination	200	300	400	

[a]Cost to transport one shipment from St. Louis to Lexington.

Fort Wayne ($100 each). These optimal shipment quantities are shown beneath the diagonal lines in part (a) of Figure 6.4. This shipping plan satisfies the raw material needs of all three plants and fully uses the capacities of all three raw materials sources. Any different patterns of source-to-destination shipments will result in higher annual shipping costs.

Part (b) of Figure 6.4 shows that if St. Louis is selected, the minimum cost shipping pattern will incur $140,000 of annual costs. Columbus is therefore the preferred raw materials location site.

FIGURE 6.4
Evaluation of system transportation costs for two raw materials sources

(a)
If Columbus is selected destination

Source	Evans-ville	Lexing-ton	Fort Wayne	Shipments available
Chicago	$200 / 100	$300	$200 / 200	300
Louisville	$100 / 100	$100 / 300	$300	400
Columbus	$300	$200	$100 / 200	200
Shipments needed	200	300	400	

Minimum total annual cost = $120,000

(b)
If St. Louis is selected destination

Source	Evans-ville	Lexing-ton	Fort Wayne	Shipments available
Chicago	$200	$300	$200 / 300	300
Louisville	$100	$100 / 300	$300 / 100	400
St. Louis	$100 / 200	$300	$400	200
Shipments needed	200	300	400	

Minimum total annual cost = $140,000

Notice that the linear programming (LP) formulation differs from the previous simple median model approach in two fundamental ways:

1. Number of alternative sites. The median model assumes that all locations in geographic space are eligible for selection as the new location. Linear programming, in contrast, considers only a finite number of alternative sites that are preselected from preliminary feasibility studies.
2. Direction of transportation movements. The simple median model assumes that all shipments move on rectangular coordinates. The LP procedure does not.

Simulation

Although several quantitative models like the ones we've discussed can handle location problems of limited scope, many real world problems are more complex than our examples. Some systems have multiple sources shipping to numerous plants; they in turn ship finished goods to warehouses from which further shipments are made to retailers. Multiechelon (multilevel) production-distribution systems such as these pose formidable problems. Even with the simplest revision of this system, adding or deleting one network component, the combinational aspects of the problem make it computationally difficult to evaluate. More realistically, we may wish to consider more drastic changes, such as a total revision of the warehousing network. With problems of this complexity, no optimal solution is possible. Instead, approximation techniques like computer simulation are used.

BEHAVIORAL IMPACT IN FACILITY LOCATION

Our previous discussions of models focused on the *cost* consequences. But costs are not the whole story, and models simply don't consider any aspects of a problem that are nonquantifiable. New locations require that organizations establish relationships with new environments and employees, and adding or deleting facilities requires adjustments in the overall management system. The organization structure and modes of making operating decisions must be modified to accommodate the change. These hidden "system costs" are usually excluded from quantitative models, and yet they are very real aspects of the location decision.

Cultural Differences

The decision to locate a new facility usually means that employees will be hired from within the new locale. It also means that the organization must establish appropriate community relations to "fit into" the locale as a good neighbor and citizen. To be successful at these endeavors, the organization must recognize the differences in the way people in various ethnic communities, and urban, suburban, and rural areas react to new businesses. Managerial style and organizational structure must adapt to the norms and customs of local subcultures. Each individual's disposition toward accepting responsibility, exercising independence of thought and initiative, style of interpersonal interaction with others, and lifelong goals and aspirations are tempered by local environmental elements. Employees' acceptance of superior-subordinate relationships and varying degrees of authoritarianism may vary with subcultures, as do their life goals, beliefs about the role of work, career aspirations, and perceptions of opportunity, which result in different on-the-job behaviors and talents. Such differences have implications not only for managerial style but for staffing, training, and job mobility as well.

At the international level, there are even greater cultural differences. Compare, for example, the Japanese work tradition with that of Western industrial society.[8] Japanese workers are often guaranteed lifetime employment. Management decisions usually are group rather than individual decisions. Individual compensation is determined by length of service, number of dependents, and numerous factors apart from the employee's productivity. Obviously operations managers in Japan face a very different set of managerial problems from their U.S. counterparts. Wage determination, employee turnover, hiring, and promotion practices are not at all the same.

The European social system, as another example, has resulted in more of a "managerial elite" in their organizations than in those in the United States. Because of education, training, and the socialization process, including a lifelong exposure to a relatively rigid class system, lower subordinates have not been prepared to accept participative managerial styles. This has resulted in organizational forms that are more authoritarian/centralized than participative/decentralized.

By recognizing cultural differences, we can anticipate special problems if we decide to locate in another society. It is not simply a matter of duplicating a highly refined manufacturing process from the United States somewhere else. Merely transferring tools and equipment is not adequate. To operate the physical facility, managerial techniques and skills, in proper mixture, must be borrowed from the culture, and so must the cultural assumptions that are needed to make them work. Differences in social settings, occupations, and other cross-cultural variables will impose diverse management orientations.[9] Clearly, the economic, political, and cultural makeup of a society has far-reaching effects on the technological and economic success of multinational locational decisions.[10]

---

[8]J. B. Keys and T. R. Miller, "The Japanese Management Theory Jungle," *Academy of Management Review* 9, no. 2 (April 1984), 342–53.

[9]L. R. Gomez-Mejia, "Effect of Occupation on Task Related, Contextual, and Job Involvement Orientation: A Cross-Cultural Perspective," *Academy of Management Journal* 27, no. 4 (December 1984), 706–20.

[10]For issues in international operations, see W. Skinner, *Manufacturing in the Corporate Strategy* (New York: John Wiley & Sons, 1978), chaps. 15–17.

Job Satisfaction

In recent years managers have been very concerned about employee job satisfaction because it has an impact on how well the organization operates.[11] Although no consistent overall relationship between job satisfaction and productivity seems to exist, other important relationships have been found. As compared with employees with *low* job satisfaction, those expressing *high* job satisfaction exhibit the following characteristics:

1. Lower labor turnover
2. Less absenteeism
3. Less tardiness
4. Fewer grievances

These four factors can have substantial impact on both costs and disruptions of operations. But how is job satisfaction related to facility location? There is some evidence that satisfaction is related to community characteristics such as community prosperity, small town versus large metropolitan locations, and the degree of unionization. Accordingly, a company with facilities in multiple locations can expect variations in employee satisfaction due to attitudinal and value-system variations across locational sites.[12]

Consumer Considerations

For many organizations, location planning must emphasize consumer behavior and proximity to customers. If your primary product is to provide a service to the public, locational convenience for the customer may be the prime consideration. Theaters, banks, supermarkets, and restaurants heavily emphasize customer convenience when choosing a location. In fact, convenience of location itself is often considered to be the product offered by some firms. For these reasons the location decision may be regarded as a marketing function instead of a production/operations responsibility, especially as it affects revenues rather than costs.

SUMMARY

This chapter highlighted the problems of planning for capacity and location of facilities, noting that they are interrelated, because the decision to change capacity often involves the location of new facilities or the dislocation of existing ones. Problems of selecting a location require consideration of how costs and revenues will be affected. Preliminary studies are needed to gather information from many sources to identify feasible sites. We discussed detailed studies using models to evaluate cost consequences of alternative locations. Some of these models are simula-

---

[11]See R. M. Steers, *Introduction to Organizational Behavior* (Santa Monica, Calif.: Goodyear Publishing Co., Inc., 1981), Chap. 13.

[12]See S. P. Robbins, *Organizational Behavior*, 2nd ed. (Englewood Cliffs, N.J.: Prentice Hall, 1983), 50–67.

tion models, which can be constructed to include many types of costs in complex multilevel production-distribution systems, and simple median and linear programming models, which are particularly useful when there are substantial transportation costs among multiple facilities in a system.

We saw that throughout the process of identifying and evaluating alternatives, management must consider the behavioral implications of location. The revenues of many service organizations depend upon a location featuring customer convenience and accessibility. Organizations having less direct contact with the consuming public must recognize potential differences in employee behavior that can arise at various locations. In the various regions within a country, different life styles and value orientations are necessarily carried over into the workplace, and these differences affect on-the-job behavior and overall organizational performance. Subcultural differences have implications for both job design (conversion technology) and managerial style.

At the international level, we discussed how cultural differences limit locational alternatives in other countries. At the very least, production/operations managers must recognize that locating in another country usually involves more than a simple transplanting of technology, and they must try to uncover any "hidden" problems. The skills and environmental support required to operate may be scarce or nonexistent, or cultural differences may inhibit efficient operations, to name just a couple of potential difficulties that present quite a complex challenge to the operations manager.

CASE

Porta-Putt, Inc.

Porta-Putt, Inc., manufactures and distributes gasoline-powered outboard motors for boats. One of their three plants, the St. Louis assembly plant, is obsolete. The Los Angeles and Chicago assembly plants were recently renovated. Rather than continue operation in St. Louis, management is considering the possibility of finding a new location for the third plant. This is an opportune time, because in two years the new Denver distribution warehouse will be opened. Since the new assembly plant could be the primary supplier of motors to the Denver warehouse, the new plant could be located to minimize shipping costs, which are a substantial part of Porta-Putt's operating costs.

Two types of shipping costs are incurred at the St. Louis plant. First, raw materials and subcomponents used in assembling the motors are shipped from Minneapolis and Seattle to the St. Louis facility. Then, after final assembly, the St. Louis plant ships the finished products to the Denver distribution center. Figure 6.5 shows the geographic locations of the three facilities that ship to or from the St. Louis facility. Table 6.5 summarizes the annual number of standard loads shipped between St. Louis and each of the other three sites. The cost of shipping a standard load is estimated to be $.10/mile.

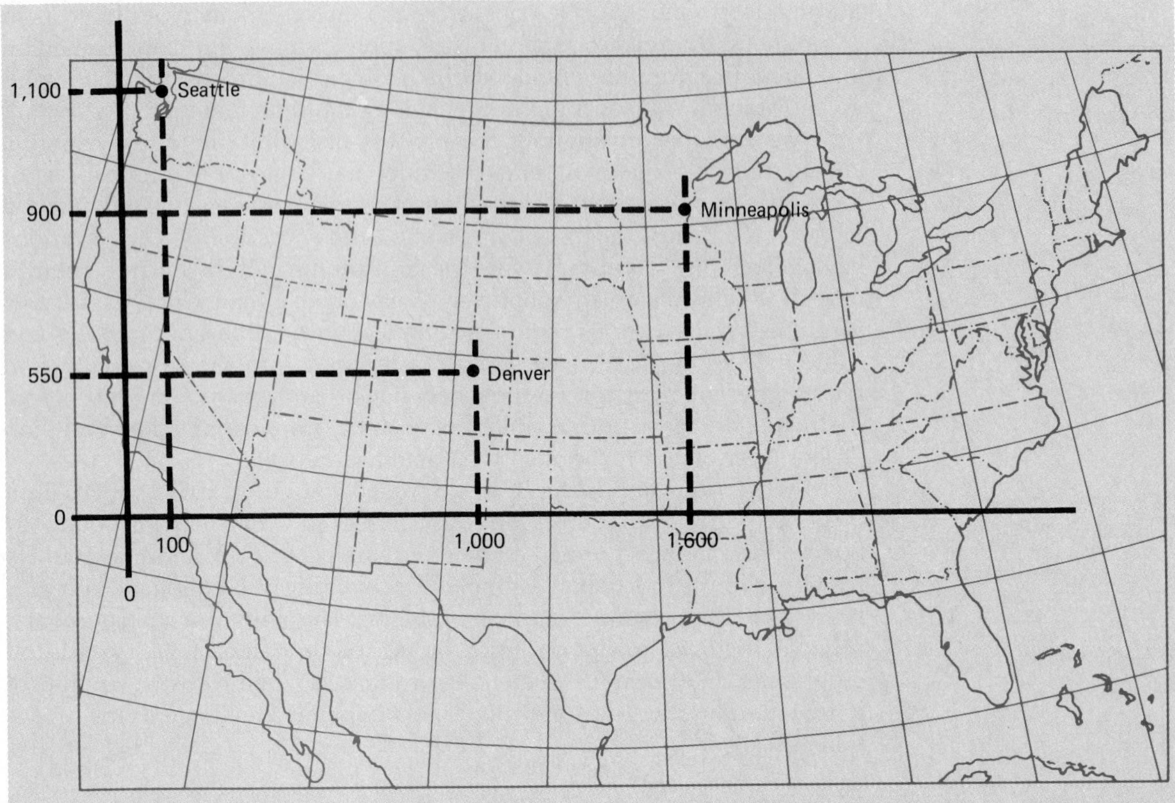

FIGURE 6.5
Porta-Putt, Inc.

Table 6.5 **Shipments between the St. Louis plant and other Porta-Putt**

Existing Facilities	Annual Number of Standard Loads	Coordinates of Existing Facility x	y
Denver	10,000	1,000	550
Seattle	8,000	100	1,100
Minneapolis	4,000	1,600	900

Management would like to find a location that would minimize the potentially high annual transportation costs. At the same time, however, there is some hesitation about moving away from metropolitan St. Louis, the original assembly facility established 35 years ago. Porta-Putt's experienced work force has survived many work methods and assembly line changes. From these refinements has evolved an intricate assembly operation that efficiently produced quality motors—until recently, when the plant became technologically obsolete. The vice president, who must make the relocation decision, feels that he should tell the St. Louis employees they might lose their jobs, but so far he has only discussed this possibility with several managers there. When the idea of relocation was introduced, these managers were dismayed at the prospect of leaving the St. Louis area. Present an analysis of the major factors in this decision and recommend a location.

REVIEW AND DISCUSSION QUESTIONS

1. Although facility location is a planning decision, it has implications for decisions in the organizing and controlling subfunctions. Explain.
2. Outline the factors that should be considered in locating a nuclear generating plant. List these factors in order of priority to show each's importance to the decision.
3. Contrast the location problems of a manufacturing firm and a supermarket, showing the relevant considerations they share and those that differ.
4. Discuss the possible reasons for changing the location of an emergency services system, such as an urban fire fighting company.
5. Suppose for economic reasons you wish to locate your manufacturing facility in a small community that currently seems to be unfavorably disposed toward your industry. What strategies might you employ before making your decision?
6. Discuss the primary limitations of the simple median model. How important to the location problem are these limitations?
7. The simple median model is appropriate for some location problems; linear programming is appropriate for others. Identify the conditions of the location problem that would lead you to select one model over the other.
8. What aspects of different subcultures should be considered in locational analysis?
9. If you expand your existing company by opening a new division in a foreign country, should the new division be staffed by local personnel or by personnel imported from the parent organization? Explain.

PROBLEMS

Solved Problems

1. Location A would result in annual fixed costs of $300,000, variable costs of $63/unit, and revenues of $68/unit. Annual fixed costs at location B are $800,000, with variable costs of $32/unit, and revenue of $68/unit. Sales volume is estimated to be 25,000 units/year. Which location is most attractive?

   A cost-volume-revenue analysis is helpful for evaluating the two alternatives. The break-even points are found from:

$$BE = \frac{\text{fixed cost}}{\text{revenue/unit} - \text{variable cost/unit}}$$

$$BE_A = \frac{\$300{,}000}{\$68 - 63} = 60{,}000 \text{ units}$$

$$BE_B = \frac{\$800{,}000}{\$68 - 32} = 22{,}222 \text{ units}$$

At the expected demand of 25,000 units, profits (loss) for the alternatives are:

	Alternative	
	A	B
Revenue	\$1,700,000	\$1,700,000
Costs		
Total variable	1,575,000	800,000
Total fixed	300,000	800,000
Total costs	1,875,000	1,600,000
Profit (loss)	(175,000)	100,000

Location B is most attractive, even though annual fixed costs are much higher than for A.

2. A site is sought for a temporary plant to supply cement to three existing construction sites: downtown, at a mall, and at a suburb. The locations of the existing sites and the loads to be delivered to each are as follows:

Delivery Site	Grid Location (miles)		Number of Loads Required	Delivery Cost/ Load/Mile
	East	North		
Downtown	20	10	22	\$10
Mall	10	40	43	\$10
Suburb	40	20	36	\$10
			Total = 101	

Find the best site for the cement plant. What total shipping cost will result?

Using the simple median model, the median load is 51. To find the best east location we begin at mile zero on the grid and proceed eastward to the location that receives the 51st load (see Figure 6.6). At the first grid location used (mile 10), 43 loads go to the mall. At the next location eastward (mile 20), 22 loads go to downtown and at this location the median (51st) load will have been delivered. Hence, the optimal east location (E*) is mile 20. In a similar fashion, the median load in the northern direction is delivered at mile 20 to the suburb site (N* = 20). The resulting shipment costs, \$22,300, are shown in the following table:

Delivery Site	Distance (miles) from cement plant			Cost/Mile/ Load (C_i)	Number of Loads (L_i)	Cost $C_i \times D_i \times L_i$
	$\|E - E^*\|$	$\|N - N^*\|$	Total (D_i)			
Mall	$\|10 - 20\| = 10$	$\|40 - 20\| = 20$	30	\$10	43	\$12,900
Downtown	$\|20 - 20\| = 0$	$\|10 - 20\| = 10$	10	10	22	2,200
Suburb	$\|40 - 20\| = 20$	$\|20 - 20\| = 0$	20	10	36	7,200
					Total =	\$22,300

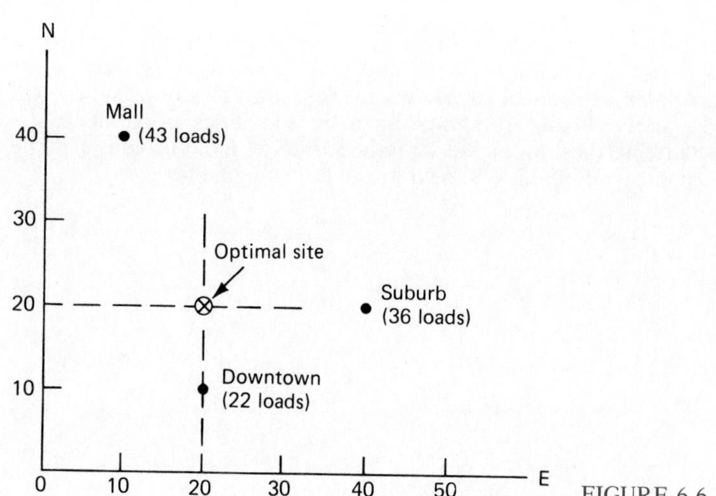

FIGURE 6.6

Reinforcing Fundamentals

3. Bubble Breweries has two distribution warehouses on Highway 70. Warehouse A, located at mile zero, receives 3,000 standard beer shipments annually from the brewery. Warehouse B, located at mile 1,200, receives 1,000 standard shipments annually from the brewery. For these shipment patterns, what would be the better brewery location for minimizing annual transportation costs to warehouses?

4. Ontario Dairies, Ltd., is considering where to locate dairy processing centers to prepare milk products for regional markets in Canada. Locations and milk volumes are given below. Transportation costs, $.50/mile/100 pounds, are uniform throughout the area. Use the simple median model to find the best location. *Show your work.*

Location	Coordinate Location (miles)[a]	Milk Processing (100,000 pound units)
London, Ont.	N/S/E/W = 0	200
Cochrane, Ont.	W = 20, N = 400	300
Toronto, Ont.	E = 120, N = 20	800
Montreal, Queb.	E = 340, N = 80	200

[a]N is North, S is South, E is East, W is West.

5. Bigtown is trying to find the best location for a master solid waste disposal station. At present, four substations are located at the following coordinate (x, y) locations: station 1 (40, 120), station 2 (65, 40), station 3 (110, 90), and station 4 (10, 130). The number of loads hauled monthly to the master station will be 300 from station 1, 200 from station 2, 350 from station 3, and 400 from station 4. Use the simple median model to find the best location.

6. Suresnap fishing reels require variable production costs of $12/unit. Fixed costs are $200,000 for first shift operations, which have a capacity of 30,000 reels. Distributors purchase reels for $20 each. Suresnap can double capacity by operating a second shift at an additional semifixed cost of $80,000. Using a schematic model, evaluate the alternative levels of plant operation.

7. First National Bank is considering the location of a branch central processing facility (CPF) to perform check processing and other paperwork operations for four existing branch banks in its northeastern market area. This new facility will not be open to the public. Figure 6.7 shows the current facilities' proximity to the existing main bank (which is shown as zero on the axis). The monthly volume to be processed from each branch bank is shown in the following table:

Bank	Volume (1,000 items)
A	50
B	60
C	10
D	100

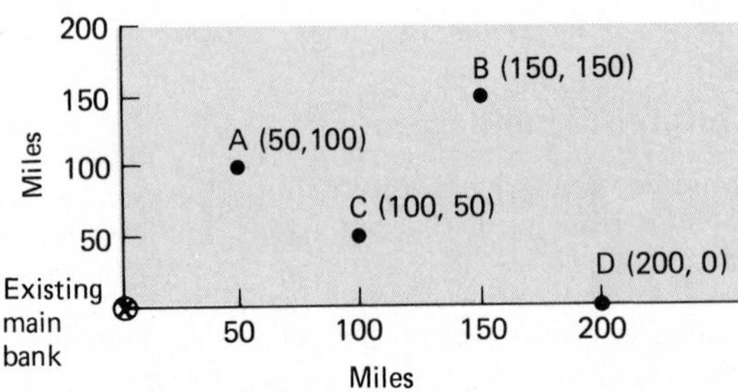

FIGURE 6.7

The existing main bank wants to move all of this dollar volume to the new CPF location.

(a) Locate the CPF using the simple median model. Show the CPF on the graph. Show your work.

(b) The actual cost of transportation is $100/1,000 items processed per mile. What will be the cost savings for processing branch C work at the CPF rather than at the existing main bank?

Challenging Exercises

8. A company has conducted a comprehensive study of five cities, one of which will be selected as the site for a new facility. Annual operating costs for each city are estimated as follows:

Annual operating costs ($ millions)

City	Labor	Transportation	Local Taxes	Power	Other
1	0.90	0.10	0.17	0.21	0.16
2	1.10	0.08	0.20	0.29	0.11
3	1.20	0.07	0.25	0.25	0.12
4	0.85	0.12	0.19	0.18	0.16
5	0.75	0.14	0.17	0.23	0.18

For each community, the company compiled subjective ratings of several important attributes:

Attribute

City	Community Receptivity	Labor Availability	Transportation Quality	Quality of Life
1	very good	good	fair	acceptable
2	fair	very good	acceptable	fair
3	good	fair	outstanding	good
4	fair	outstanding	acceptable	very good
5	very good	acceptable	fair	outstanding

(a) On the basis of annual operating costs, which site is best?
(b) Devise a method for quantifying the intangible factors, and integrate them with the cost data into overall evaluation measures. Which site is best now?

9. Highline Enterprises manufactures its products at plants in Los Angeles and Chicago. Shipments are then sent to customers in Denver, Seattle, and New York. The Los Angeles plant produces a maximum of 50 shipments annually, and the Chicago plant produces a maximum of 70 shipments. Costs/shipment from Los Angeles are $1,000 to Denver, $900 to Seattle, and $1,600 to New York. A shipment from Chicago costs $800 to Denver; $1,300 to Seattle; and $1,000 to New York. Next year, demand is expected to be for 60 shipments at Denver, 40 at Seattle, and 80 at New York. Highline will build a new plant at either Dallas or Knoxville, and the plant will have an annual capacity of 60 shipments. At Dallas, manufacturing costs will average $100,000/shipment; the manufacturing cost at Knoxville will be $80,000. Shipment cost from Dallas is $600 to Denver; $1,000 to Seattle; and $1,400 to New York. From Knoxville a shipment to Denver is $900; to Seattle, $1,200; and to New York, $700.
(a) Set up this problem in a linear programming framework.
(b) Outline the specific kinds of information you would expect from the linear programming model.
(c) What relevant information for this decision would not be provided by the model?

10. United American Savings and Loan has three processing centers (Newburg, Central, and Wilmont) for 27 branch locations. A sudden increase in demand for item processing has come about due to a new service—a customer draft on account, which is similar to a personal checking account in a commercial bank.

United American had closed the Newburg processing center since the facilities at Wilmont and Central had enough capacity on one shift to handle demand. Now either the Wilmont facility must go to a second shift or the Newburg facility must be reopened. Revenue is expected to average $.20 per item processed at each facility.

The Wilmont facility has been operating with fixed costs of $500,000 and variable costs of $.10, with an annual first shift capacity of 10 million items. Starting a second shift would increase variable costs for items processed on that shift to either $.12 or $.14, with probabilities of .6 and .4, respectively. Second shift annual capacity would be 10 million items.

The Newburg facility can be reopened for fixed costs of either $100,000 or $50,000, with probabilities of .3 and .7, respectively. Unit variable costs are expected to be $.12, and capacity is 7 million items annually.

As vice president of operations, you must *prepare a recommendation* for expanding capacity for an upcoming meeting with the president. In your analysis, *prepare a decision tree* for the president depicting this situation and a *rough graph* of costs and revenues for various volumes.

11. Revise the simple median model to reflect differences in transportation cost rates for loads flowing between the new facility and several existing facilities.
12. A company has three existing warehouses to which it will ship furniture from a new factory whose location must be decided. The factory will receive raw materials from its wood supplier and its fabric supplier. The annual number of shipments, shipment costs, and the locations of the suppliers and warehouses are shown below. Where should the factory be located to minimize annual transportation costs?

Existing Facility	Number of Loads/Year To or From Factory	Cost/Load/Mile	Coordinate Location (miles)	
			x	y
Wood supplier	120	$8	100	400
Fabric supplier	200	6	800	700
Warehouse 1	60	5	300	600
Warehouse 2	40	5	200	100
Warehouse 3	70	5	600	200

Utilizing the QSOM Computer Software

13. Reconsider Problem 12. What if building two new smaller factories is an alternative to having one large new factory? (Assume each of the two new factories consumes one-half the total inputs and ships one-half the total outputs). What if three new smaller factories, each dedicated to supplying a warehouse, is an additional alternative? (Assume each factory consumes input resources in proportion to the factory's share of total company output). Prepare your recommendations with supporting data.

GLOSSARY

Break-even analysis Graphical or algebraic representation of the relationships among volume, cost, and revenues in an organization.

Job satisfaction Employee perceptions of the extent to which their work fulfills or satisfies their needs.

Labor turnover A measure of the stability or change in the organization's work force; the net result of employee terminations and entrances.

Location of a facility Geographic site at which a productive facility is situated.

Simple Median Model A mathematical procedure for finding a facility location that minimizes transportation costs of a network of facilities.

Subculture Regional or ethnic variations of a culture.

Value system Individual's beliefs or conceptions of what is desirable, good, and bad.

SELECTED READINGS

Aly, A. A., and D. W. Litwhiler, Jr., "Police Briefing Stations, A Location Problem," *AIIE Transactions* 11, no. 1 (March 1979), 12–22.

Buffa, E. S., *Meeting the Competitive Challenge*. Homewood, Ill.: Richard D. Irwin, 1984, 65–82.

Cole, J. J., and E. J. Bardi, *The Management of Logistics* (2nd ed.). St. Paul, Minn.: West Publishing Company, 1980.

Love, R. F., and L. Yerex, "An Application of a Facilities Location Model in the Prestressed Concrete Industry," *Interfaces* 6, no. 4 (August 1976), 45–49.

Schmenner, R. W., "Look Beyond the Obvious in Plant Location," *Harvard Business Review* 57, no. 1, (January–February 1979), 126–32.

Skinner, W., *Manufacturing in the Corporate Strategy*. New York: John Wiley, 1978.

SUPPLEMENT TO CHAPTER 6

LINEAR PROGRAMMING: THE TRANSPORTATION METHOD

The transportation (or distribution) method is a special form of the general linear programming problem and must meet the general characteristics noted in the supplement to Chapter 5. Additionally, the transportation method is applicable to problems with the following characteristics:

1. *Sources*. A quantity of resources exists at a finite number of "sources," and these resources are available for allocation.
2. *Destinations*. A finite number of "destinations" exists, each of which needs to be supplied with a specified quantity of resources that are available from the sources.
3. *Homogeneous units*. From the viewpoint of the destinations, the available resources are homogeneous; that is, a unit of resource supplied by one origin (source) is equivalent to a unit supplied by any other origin.
4. *Costs*. The cost of allocating a unit of resource from each origin to each destination is known and constant.

Although problems meeting the conditions above can be formulated and solved by the simplex method, the transportation method is less cumbersome. The generalized transportation format consists of a source-destination matrix with m distinct sources (rows), each of which has RA_i units of resource available and n destinations, each in need of RN_j units of resource. The cost of allocating one unit of resource from source i to destination j is C_{ij}. The problem is to allocate resources from sources to destinations so that the total cost of allocations for the system is minimized. The restrictions are:

1. All destination needs must be met.
2. No source may allocate more units than it has available.
3. Negative quantities cannot be allocated.

The objective, then, is to minimize total cost:

$$\begin{aligned} TC = {} & C_{1A}X_{1A} + C_{1B}X_{1B} + \ldots + C_{2A}X_{2A} \\ & + C_{2B}X_{2B} + \ldots + C_{mA}X_{mA} + C_{mB}X_{mB} \\ & + \ldots + C_{mn}X_{mn} \end{aligned}$$

where X_{ij} is the number of units allocated from i to j, subject to the restrictions (constraints) noted above.

The Transportation Method

See the Alpha Processing Company example (page 206), which we will use to illustrate the transportation method. Alpha Processing's two raw material sources send shipments as needed to the various plants. The addition of a new raw material source at Columbus, Ohio, is being considered. We focus on this one alternative. Shipment costs, plant requirements, and source availabilities are summarized in Figure S6.1.

A five-step procedure is used to find the set of allocations that minimize total shipment costs:

1. Frame the problem so that the total number of shipments available equals the number of shipments needed.
2. Create an initial feasible solution.
3. Evaluate the existing solution for possible improvement.
4. Modify the existing solution.
5. Repeat steps 3 and 4 until no further improvement is possible.

1. Ensure That Availability Equals Requirements In Figure S6.1, the number of shipments available at the three sources (900) is equal to the number needed by the destinations. Later we show how to adjust the matrix when this equality does not exist.

2. Create an Initial Feasible Solution A *feasible solution* is one in which the needs of all destinations are filled and the capacities of all sources are fully used. Many initial solutions are possible. By convention, we use the northwest corner rule to create an initial solution here. Allocate as many shipments as possible into the northwest cell of the matrix. In this example, 200 units can be allocated from RMS_1 to P_1.

Destination

Cost/shipment is the dollar amount in each cell

Source	P_1	P_2	P_3	Shipments available
RMS_1	\$200 / 200	\$300 / 100	\$200	300
RMS_2	\$100	\$100 / 200	\$300 / 200	400
RMS_3	\$300	\$200	\$100 / 200	200
Shipments needed	200	300	400	900 / 900

FIGURE S6.1
Transportation matrix for Alpha-Processing Company, adding the Columbus raw materials source (RMS_3)

Thereafter, allocations are made to adjacent cells to the east or south of the northwest corner. As shown in Figure S6.1, the next allocation would be 100 shipments from RMS_1 to P_2. At this stage the requirements of P_1 have been met and the shipping capacity of RMS_1 has been fully utilized. The third assignment is 200 shipments from RMS_2 to P_2. Next, 200 shipments go from RMS_2 to P_3. Finally, 200 shipments are assigned from RMS_3 to P_3. These shipments are recorded beneath the diagonals in the appropriate cells. Overall, the pattern of shipments in the matrix flows generally from the northwest to southeast. This is done without regard to the costs involved. The resulting initial solution is feasible because all restrictions in the problem have been met. If this pattern of shipments is used, the annual cost will be as follows:

$$TC = \$200 \times 200 + \$300 \times 100 + \$100 \times 200 + \$300 \times 200 + \$100 \times 200 = \$170{,}000$$

3. Evaluate the Existing Solution Would a different shipping pattern reduce total cost? This question can be answered by using the *stepping stone procedure* for evaluating alternative solutions.

First, the number of used cells in the existing solution must be considered. These are the cells in which shipping assignments have been made. In general, the stepping stone procedure requires that there be $(m + n - 1)$ used cells, where $m + n$ equals the number of row and column constraints, respectively. In Figure S6.1, there are three row restrictions (one for each source) and three column restrictions (one for each destination), for a total of six. Therefore, the $(m + n - 1)$ requirement is met, and we can proceed with the stepping stone procedure. Later we consider how to proceed if the number of used cells is not equal to $(m + n - 1)$.

Using the existing solution as a starting point, we evaluate changing the unused cells one at a time to see how the costs would be changed. If several of these cells offer cost improvements, the most attractive one is selected, and the existing solution is modified accordingly. If none of these cells offers a cost improvement, the existing solution is optimal and the analysis ends.

We begin by evaluating the unused cell RMS_2 to P_1. If one shipment is allocated to this cell, the shipments in cell RMS_1 to P_1 must be reduced to 199. Otherwise, the P_1 column restriction (200 shipments) would be violated. Next, shipments from RMS_1 to P_2 must be increased from 100 to 101 so that the RMS_1 row restriction is met. Finally, the shipments from RMS_2 to P_2 must be reduced from 200 to 199. By making these changes, we have fully satisfied the row and column restrictions. It is important to notice what has happened from a systems viewpoint. By making a change in allocations to *one* cell (RMS_2 to P_1), we need to make subsequent adjustments in *other* cells in the network so that the overall system adheres to the constraints. The cells requiring adjustment are shown in part (*a*) of

Figure S6.2. The arrows indicate the *path* of cell adjustments for the four affected cells. Notice the pattern of alternating pluses and minuses from cell to cell throughout the path. A minus indicates that shipments are reduced in that cell; a plus means that shipments are increased to balance the network. This evaluation path is not arbitrarily selected; it is *unique.*

When the number of used cells in the existing solution equals $(m + n - 1)$, there is a unique evaluation path for each unused cell in the matrix. The evaluation path *always* consists of one unused cell and several used cells. The used cells in the path are called the *stepping stones.*

How does one find the unique stepping stone path? Beginning in the unused cell (to be evaluated), move onto any used cell (call it stepping stone 1, SS_1). Then rotate 90 degrees from SS_1 onto SS_2. From SS_2 rotate 90 degrees onto SS_3, and continue this process until a 90 degree rotation from SS_i leads back to the original unused cell from which the movements began. This series of rotations is clearly portrayed as a square path for cell $RMS_2 - P_1$.

If these changes are made, how will costs be affected? Relative to the existing solution, costs will be affected as follows: Costs will increase by \$100, since a new shipment is made into cell $RMS_2 - P_1$; costs in cell $RMS_1 - P_1$ will decrease by \$200, since one less shipment is made here; an additional shipment is made to cell $RMS_1 - P_2$, thus raising costs by \$300; and costs in cell $RMS_2 - P_2$ will decrease by \$100. Adding together all the increases and decreases, the overall net effect is a cost increase of \$100. This cell evaluation, summarized in part (a) of Figure S6.2 shows that this cell is unattractive and does not offer a desirable alternative solution. We now proceed to evaluate the other unused cells.

The stepping stone path for evaluating unused cell $RMS_1 - P_3$ consists of $(RMS_1 - P_3) \rightarrow (RMS_2 - P_3) \rightarrow (RMS_2 - P_2) \rightarrow (RMS_1 - P_2)$. The clockwise direction of movement on this path, shown in Part (b) of Figure S6.2, is irrelevant; it could just as well have been counterclockwise. This unique path shows that overall costs will be *reduced* by \$300 if a shipment is made from RMS_1 to P_3. Instead of changing the existing solution to obtain this cost savings, we first evaluate all other unused cells to see if even greater cost savings are possible.

The stepping stone paths have been evaluated for each of the two remaining unused cells. Parts (c) and (d) show that costs will increase if shipments are made to either $RMS_3 - P_1$ or $RMS_3 - P_2$.

As you can see, only one of the four unused cells in the original solution, cell $RMS_1 - P_3$, offers any cost reduction.

4. Modify the Existing Solution The original solution is modified by allocating shipments into cell $RMS_1 - P_3$. Furthermore, since \$300 of cost savings result for each shipment, we will allocate as many as possible. Examination of part (b) of Figure S6.2 reveals that 100 shipments, at most, can be allocated, since no more than 100 can be removed from cell $RMS_1 - P_2$. Therefore, 100 units will be added to $RMS_1 - P_3$, and appropriate

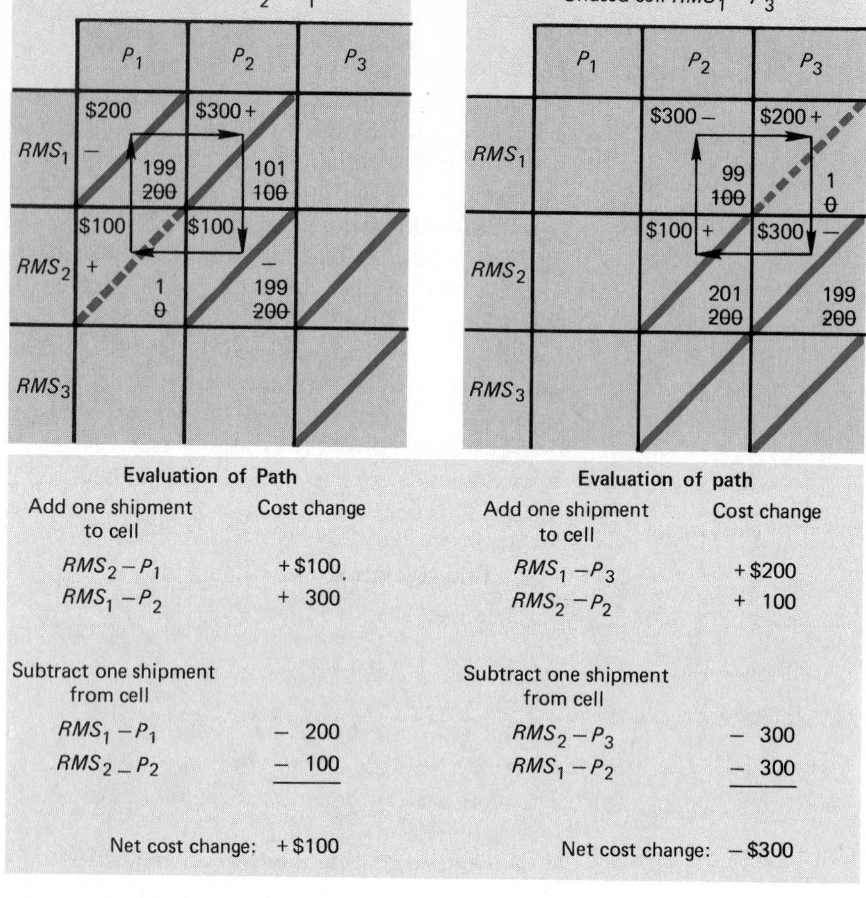

(a)
Unused cell RMS2 − P1
P1
P2
P3
RMS1
$200
−
199
200
$300 +
101
100
RMS2
$100
+
1
0
$100
−
199
200
RMS3
Evaluation of Path
Add one shipment to cell
Cost change
RMS2 − P1
+ $100
RMS1 − P2
+ 300
Subtract one shipment from cell
RMS1 − P1
− 200
RMS2 − P2
− 100
Net cost change: + $100
(b)
Unused cell RMS1 − P3
P1
P2
P3
RMS1
$300 −
99
100
$200 +
1
0
RMS2
$100 +
201
200
$300
−
199
200
RMS3
Evaluation of path
Add one shipment to cell
Cost change
RMS1 − P3
+ $200
RMS2 − P2
+ 100
Subtract one shipment from cell
RMS2 − P3
− 300
RMS1 − P2
− 300
Net cost change: − $300

FIGURE S6.2
Evaluating unused cells

adjustments will be made in cell shipments on the rest of the evaluation path. This course of action will result in a cost savings of ($300/shipment) × (100 shipments) = $30,000. The modified solution is shown in Figure S6.3, part (a).

5. Reevaluate and Modify The first revised solution is now treated as a new problem in which steps 3 and 4 are repeated. Applying the stepping stone procedure, we find that only one cell ($RMS_2 - P_1$) offers any cost reduction. This desirable change is highlighted in Figure S6.3, part (b). Therefore, a second revised solution is created by allocating as many shipments as possible, 100, into $RMS_2 - P_1$ (see Figure S6.4).

Evaluation of the unused cells in Figure S6.4 shows that no further cost reduction is possible. The optimal solution has been found. If the Columbus, Ohio, raw material source is added to the existing network, the best shipping pattern is to send 100 shipments from RMS_1 to P_1, 200 from RMS_1 to P_3, 100 from RMS_2 to P_1, 300 from RMS_2 to P_2, and 200 from RMS_3

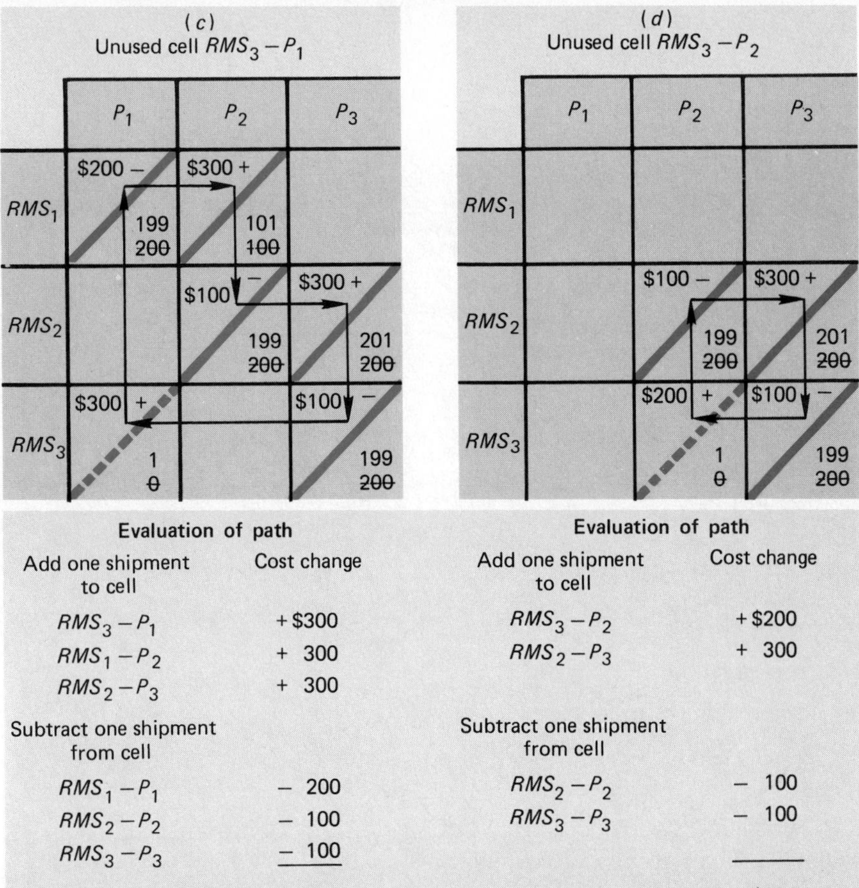

FIGURE S6.2
(cont.)

FIGURE S6.3
Assignment revisions for Alpha Processing Company

(a)
First revised solution

	P_1	P_2	P_3	
RMS_1	$200 / 200	$300	$200 / 100	300
RMS_2	$100	$100 / 300	$300 / 100	400
RMS_3	$300	$200	$100 / 200	200
Needed	200	300	400	900 / 900

$$
\begin{aligned}
TC &= +(\$200) \times (200) + (\$200) \times (100) \\
&\quad + (\$100) \times (300) + (\$300) \times (100) \\
&\quad + (\$100) \times (200) \\
&= \$140{,}000
\end{aligned}
$$

(b)
Evaluation of unused cells in first revised solution

	P_1	P_2	P_3	
RMS_1		+ $300		
RMS_2	–$200			
RMS_3	+ $200	+ $300		

	P_1	P_2	P_3	Available
RMS_1	\$200 100	\$300 (+\$100)	\$200 200	300
RMS_2	\$100 100	\$100 300	\$300 (+\$200)	400
RMS_3	\$300 (+\$200)	\$200 (+\$100)	\$100 200	200
Needed	200	300	400	900 / 900

TC = (\$200) x (100) + (\$200) x (200) + (\$100) x (100) + (\$100) x (300) + (\$100) x (200)
= \$120,000

FIGURE S6.4
Second revised (optimal) solution for Alpha Processing Company

to P_3 when *RMS*'s are Chicago, Louisville, and Columbus, and *P*'s are Evansville, Lexington, and Fort Wayne.

Some Additional Considerations

Inequality of Availability and Requirements We said earlier that the transportation method can be applied only when the resources available equal the resources required. In the Alpha Company example, 900 shipments are needed and 900 are available. If the problem had originally stated that only 800 shipments were required by the destinations, an additional fictitious destination would be created and added to the matrix. This new dummy plant, P_4, would become a column with a requirement of 100 shipments, and the adjustment would provide the necessary equality. A zero cost coefficient would be inserted in each cell of the dummy column to reflect the fact that assignments in these cells are fictitious, having no real cost. The use of a dummy row or column, whichever is needed, is equivalent to the use of slack variables in the simplex method.

Degeneracy A condition called *degeneracy* exists in a transportation problem when the number of used cells is less than $(m + n - 1)$. Degeneracy can occur at the initial or at intermediate stages of the problem. When degeneracy exists, a unique stepping stone path cannot be identified for evaluating an unused cell. A standard procedure for overcoming degeneracy cells for placing an arbitrarily small, fictitious assignment called *theta* (θ) in one of the currently unused cells. The cell with *theta* is then treated as if it were a used cell during this stage of the problem. *Theta* is not, however, a real assignment, and it does not result in any real cost. When a *theta* is needed, it can be added to any empty cell, but time can be saved by adding it to an empty cell that will allow as many unused cells as possible to be evaluated. *Theta* remains in the matrix until it is subtracted out, or until a real allocation is made into its cell. It then disappears from the problem.

Maximization Problems Sometimes the problem has a maximization rather than minimization objective. The same procedure is used in either case. In a maximization problem, the cell evaluations have a reverse interpretation. When maximizing, a positive cell evaluation indicates that further improvement is possible in that cell. A negative evaluation indicates that the cell offers an undesirable change.

Alternative Optimal Solutions The final optimal solution may not be unique. Alternative optimal solutions exist whenever any unused cells have zero cell evaluations. A zero evaluation means that although the existing solution mix can be changed, the criterion value will not change.

REVIEW AND DISCUSSION QUESTIONS

1. In general, how do you decide which cost elements to include in or exclude from the cells of a transportation LP problem?
2. What problem characteristics must exist to enable the use of the transportation method of LP?
3. Explain what is happening when you use the stepping stone procedure for cell evaluation.
4. What is meant by the property of *homogeneity?* Why is it important?
5. Identify the similarities and differences of the transportation and simplex methods of LP.
6. What is the significance of having $(m + n - 1)$ used cells in solution? Will an optimal solution have $(m + n - 1)$ used cells?
7. Describe the northwest corner rule as a method for obtaining an initial feasible solution. Are there other ways of getting an initial feasible solution? Explain.
8. What conditions must exist to enable you to know an optimal solution has been found? That an alternative optimal solution exists?
9. If total resources available are unequal to the total required, what adjustments must be made in formulating the problem?
10. Why are dummy cells assigned a cost coefficient of zero? Can nonzero cost coefficients be used? Explain.
11. For an optimal solution matrix, give an economic interpretation of the cell evaluations.
12. What is the significance of degeneracy in transportation LP problems?
13. What types of locational problems can be aided by the transportation method of LP?

PROBLEMS

Reinforcing Fundamentals

1. Consider the following problem, in which costs are recorded for allocating one unit from each source to each destination:

Source	Destination A	B	C	Maximum Units Available
1	$1	$3	$2	275
2	2	4	1	325
3	3	2	3	300
Minimum units requested	350	400	150	

(a) Use the northwest corner rule to obtain an initial feasible solution.
(b) What is the cost of this initial solution?
(c) Find the minimum cost solution.
(d) What is the optimal allocation pattern, and what is its cost?
(e) Is there an alternative optimal solution?

2. Suppose the data matrix in Problem 1 contained profit figures rather than costs. Find the profit maximizing solution.

3. The costs of shipping a unit from each source to each destination, along with the rim requirements, are shown below.

Source	Destination A	B	C	D	Source Availability (units)
1	$7	$10	$8	$5	728
2	6	4	9	7	475
3	3	6	5	8	775
Destination requirements (units)	226	675	351	455	

(a) Develop an initial feasible solution using the northwest corner rule.
(b) Find the optimal solution.
(c) Interpret the optimal solution.

4. Following are the source availabilities, destination requirements, and costs of assigning a unit from each source to each destination:

Source	Destination A	B	C	Source Availability (units)
1	$4	$7	$3	250
2	5	6	2	150
3	3	7	5	250
4	6	1	4	200
Destination requirements (units)	350	300	200	

Develop an initial feasible solution using the northwest corner rule, and find the optimal solution.

5. Bill's Gravel Company operates three gravel pits from which loads of gravel are shipped to various construction sites. Pit 1 has a monthly capacity of 100 loads; 85 loads can be delivered from pit 2, and pit 3 can supply 145 loads each month. Requests for deliveries next month have come from four construction sites, site A (131 loads), site B (77 loads), site C (49 loads), and site D (104 loads). Bill's profits depend on which pit is used to supply each construction site.

Profit/load of gravel

	Construction Site			
From Pit	A	B	C	D
1	$24	$30	$27	$32
2	29	19	21	36
3	26	29	20	18

What should Bill do?

Challenging Exercises

6. Set up Problem 1 in a simplex format.
7. Refer to Problem 9 at the end of Chapter 6. Solve the problem using the transportation method. Which site should be selected, Knoxville or Dallas? Explain.
8. A company has factories at cities V, W, and X. Management will add an additional plant at city Y or Z, with an annual capacity of 500,000 units of output. Capacities of existing plants are 722,000 at V, 510,000 at W, and 808,000 at X. City Y is attractive because labor costs will average only $5.10/unit, compared with $5.40 at city Z. Unit labor costs are $5.25 at V, $6.30 at W, and $5.70 at X. The factories annually ship output to wholesalers in cities A (615,000 units), B (961,000 units), and C (914,000 units), with shipping costs as follows:

Average cost of shipping 1 unit to wholesaler

From Factory	A	B	C
V	$1.00	$1.50	$1.25
W	1.25	1.30	1.10
X	0.90	1.15	1.35
Y	1.05	0.95	1.00
Z	0.95	0.80	1.10

Which site, Y or Z, is most attractive?

SELECTED READINGS

Anderson, D. R., D. J. Sweeney, and T. A. Williams, *An Introduction to Management Science* (3rd ed.). St. Paul, Minn.: West Publishing Company, 1982.

Bierman, H., Jr., C. P. Bonini, and W. H. Hausman, *Quantitative Analysis for Business Decisions* (6th ed.). Homewood, Ill.: Richard D. Irwin, 1981.

7

Layout Planning

Layout planning and machine or assembly line balancing have always been given priority in our operations.

World competition and technological advancements have forced significant changes in our layout planning process. We are utilizing computer-aided layouts for increased productivity and alternate design analysis. Computer software packages are used to determine total cost relationships, for example, the materials department's most effective combination of "move and stores" and reduction of in-process material cost.

Participative management processes and employee involvement have become an integral part of effective layout planning.

"Selling" new projects and effective implementation are the results of sound layout practices reflecting the everchanging workplace environment.

Utilization of the tools for layout planning discussed in this chapter are basic to understanding and optimizing the operations layout function.

William W. Willoughby
Manager, Engineering Support
BOC Powertrain
General Motors Corporation
Flint, Michigan

Mr. Willoughby's comments demonstrate that successful operations depend upon the physical layout of facilities. Flows of materials, productivity, and human relationships are all involved in the internal arrangement of the conversion facility. As we shall see, some modeling techniques are useful for layout planning, and behavioral factors must be considered too. Let's begin by finding out just what layout planning is.

LAYOUT CONCEPTS

To see how layout planning affects operating costs and effectiveness, we have to examine how different types of layout designs apply in different situations.

Types of Manufacturing and Service Operations

The operations function in both manufacturing and service organizations can be divided into two basic types, intermittent and continuous, depending on the degree of product standardization and volume of output.

Intermittent Operations Intermittent manufacturing is conversion with production characteristics of low product volume, general purpose equipment, labor-intense operations, interrupted product flow, frequent schedule changes, large product mix, and made-to-order products. Services with these same characteristics (e.g., automobile repair facilities) are also classified as intermittent conversion operations.

Continuous Operations Continuous conversion operations are featured by high product volume, special purpose equipment, capital-intense operations, small product mix, and standardized products made to inventory.

Basic Layout Designs

A layout design is the location or configuration of departments, work stations, and equipment that constitutes the conversion process. It is the spatial arrangement of the physical resources that is used to create the product.

We discuss three basic layout designs: process-oriented, product-oriented, and fixed-position. These designs are differentiated by the types of work flows they entail; the work flow, in turn, is dictated by the nature of the product. Table 7.1 summarizes some of the characteristics that differentiate basic layouts from one another.

Process Layout Process-oriented layouts are appropriate for intermittent operations when work flows are not standardized for all units of output. Unstandardized work flows occur either when a variety of different products is produced or when one basic type of product with many possible variations is made. In a *process layout,* the processing work centers or departments are grouped together according to the type of function they perform. Distribution warehouses, hospitals and medical clinics, universities, office buildings, and job shop facilities are often designed in this manner. Figure 7.1 shows a process layout for a medical clinic. Similarly, a manufacturing layout could have process departments or equipment groupings such as welding, heat treating, painting, and so on.

Table 7.1 Characteristics of layout designs

Aspect of the Conversion Process	Product-Oriented	Process-Oriented	Fixed-Position
Product characteristics	Layout geared to producing a standardized product, in large volume, at stable rates of output	Layout for diversified products requiring common fundamental operations, in varying volume, at varying rates of output	Low volume, each unit often unique
Product flow pattern	Straight line of product; same sequence of standard operations on each unit	Diversified flow pattern; each order (product) may require unique sequence of operations	Little or no product flow; equipment and human resources brought to site as needed
Human skills requirement	Tolerance for performing routine, repetitive tasks at imposed pace; highly specialized work content	Primarily skilled craftsmen; can perform without close supervision and with moderate degree of adaptability	High degree of task flexibility often required; specific work assignments and location vary
Supporting staff	Large administrative and indirect support staff for scheduling materials and people, work analysis and maintenance	Must possess skills for scheduling, materials handling, and production and inventory control	High degree of scheduling and coordinating skills required
Material handling	Material flows predictable, systematized and often automated	Type and volume of handling required is variable; duplication of handling often occurs	Type and volume of handling required is variable, often low; may require heavy-duty general purpose handling equipment
Inventory requirements	High turnover of raw material and work-in-process inventories	Low turnover of raw material and work-in-process inventories; high raw materials inventories	Variable inventories due to lengthy production cycle can result in inventory tieups for long periods
Space utilization	Efficient utilization of space, high rate of product output per unit of space	Relatively low rate of output per unit of facility space; large work-in-process requirements	For conversion within the facility, a low rate of space utilization per unit of output may occur
Capital requirements	High capital investment in equipment and processes that perform very specialized functions	Equipment and processes are general purpose and feature flexibility	General purpose equipment and processes that are mobile
Product cost components	Relatively high fixed costs; low unit direct labor and materials costs	Relatively low fixed costs; high unit costs for direct labor, materials (inventory) and materials handling	High labor and materials costs; relatively low fixed costs

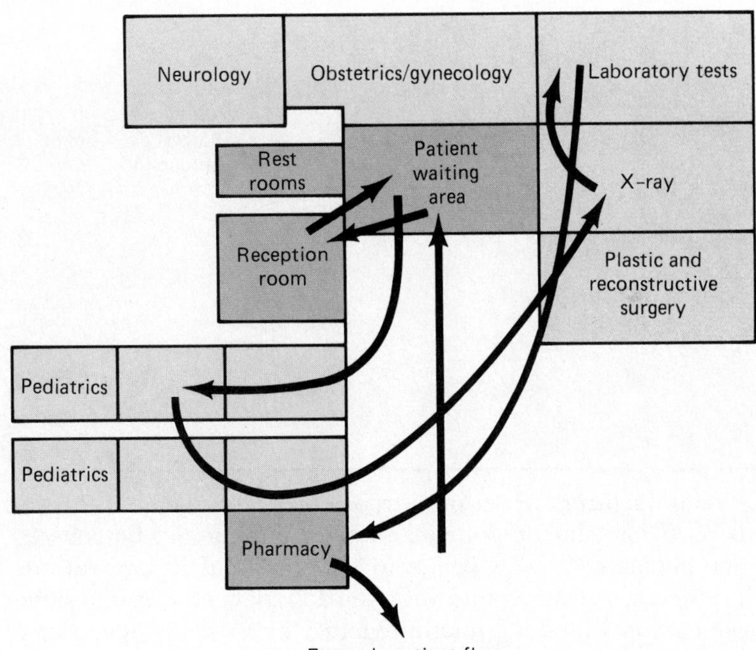

FIGURE 7.1
Process layout for medical clinic

Product Layout Product-oriented layouts are used when one standardized product is being produced, usually in large volume. Each of the units of output requires the same sequence of operations from beginning to end. In *product layout,* work centers and equipment are therefore ideally arranged in a line to provide the specialized sequence of operations that will result in product buildup. Each work center may provide one highly specialized part of the total buildup sequence. Automatic carwashes, cafeteria serving lines, mass medical exams for military recruits, automobile assembly, and beverage bottling plants use product-oriented layouts. Figure 7.2 illustrates a product layout organized to provide the fixed sequence to build up, from beginning to end, a manufactured product. Figure 7.3 illustrates a familiar product layout, an automated carwash.

Fixed-position Layout Fixed-position layouts are necessary when, because of size, shape, or any other characteristic, it isn't feasible to move the product. In *fixed-position layout,* the product remains in one location; tools, equipment, and human skills are brought to it, as needed, to perform the *appropriate stages of buildup.* A home plumbing repair operation in which resources are brought to the service site is an example. Layouts for building ships, locomotives, and aircraft are often of this type, as are agricultural operations, in which plowing, planting, fertilizing, and harvesting are performed as needed in the fields.

Combination Layouts Often pure layouts do not exist, and a combination layout must be used. This is most common for process and product combinations.

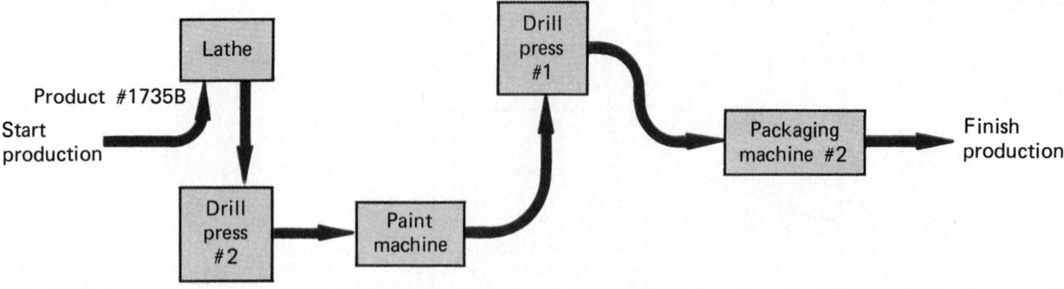

FIGURE 7.2
Product layout in manufacturing

EXAMPLE Refrigerator manufacturers use a process-oriented arrangement to produce various parts and subcomponents. Metal stamping may be consolidated into one department, all types of welding in another, and various heat-treating processes grouped into yet a third work center. At the same time, all these components are brought together in assembly operations, especially for final assembly of the product. The final assembly operations are designed on a product-flow or product-oriented basis.

Differences Among Basic Layout Designs

Does it really matter what type of basic design is selected? Yes. The appropriate layout depends upon many factors (see Table 7.1 for some examples).

FIGURE 7.3
Product layout of carwash

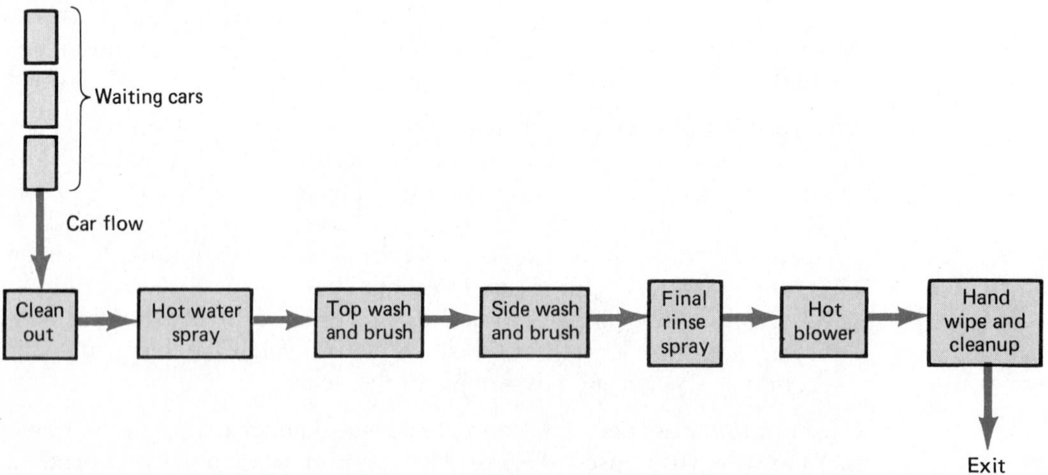

DEVELOPING THE PROCESS LAYOUT: MODELS AND BEHAVIOR

Process Layout Models

Many kinds of models are useful in layout planning. Mathematical analysis can help managers conceptualize the problem; computer models can provide quick approximations of good layouts; and physical models (templates and scale models, among others) can help us visualize the physical aspects of layouts.

EXAMPLE In designing and constructing a new manufacturing facility in Kentucky, an initial task was to list all equipment for a boiler room, which was to be attached to the main building. This task had to be done first, because only after the room had been sized could the price be negotiated with the general building contractor. First, the floor dimensions and heights of all boilers, air compressors, water pumps, and similar equipment were obtained. Second, templates were cut to scale. Third, alternative layouts were tried until a reasonable layout was found. Upon review, an experienced maintenance foreman pointed out that to "rod-out" (clean) the boilers, a wall would have to be knocked out. To avoid having to knock a wall out, the boilers were turned in another direction on the template. A reasonable layout and size were decided upon, and the boiler room was constructed accordingly.

Graphic and Schematic Analysis Perhaps the most common layout technique is the use of *templates,* two-dimensional cutouts of equipment drawn to scale. These cutouts are moved about by trial and error within a scaled model of the walls and columns of the facility. This technique is used for all three types of layouts—process, product, and fixed. Similarly, microcomputer graphics can visually display tentative layouts on a cathode-ray tube, and modifications can be made by keyboard manipulations.

A Load-distance Model In a process-oriented facility, diversified products are processed, jobs flow in various day-to-day patterns, and a relatively high amount of material must be handled. The manufacture of a special-order tool may require that it move through as many as 20 different work centers as buildup progresses from raw materials to finished form. All this movement costs money. People and equipment must be on hand, and space must be available for storing the product in between work centers. Since transporting adds no value to the product, managers seek layout designs to minimize unnecessary flows among departments.

The most commonly used quantitative model for process layout tries to *minimize total movement* by considering not only the *number* of interdepartmental moves of a product but also the *distances* over which

Table 7.2 Flow matrix showing estimated number of loads, L_{ij} per planning period among all pairs of departments

		Department				
		1	2	3	4	5
	1		(220)	130	400	370
Loads moved between departments 1 and 2	2		—	0	400	470
	3			—	150	400
	4				—	100
	5					—

the moves are made. In this model, we minimize the criterion C where

$$C = \sum_{i=1}^{N}\sum_{j=1}^{N} L_{ij}D_{ij} \tag{7.1}$$

where N = the number of work centers
L_{ij} = the number of loads or movements of work between work centers i and j
D_{ij} = the distance between work centers i and j

The criterion C being minimized may be viewed as a cost by assuming all load-distance moves have constant unit costs. If unit costs are unequal, equation 7.1 can be modified by multiplying $L_{ij}D_{ij}$ by K_{ij}, where K_{ij} is the cost to move a unit load a unit distance between work centers i and j.

We must begin by estimating the number of loads, L_{ij}, expected to be moved among all pairs of departments during an appropriate planning horizon, say one year. These estimated annual volumes of movements can be summarized in a flow matrix like that in Table 7.2.[1]

The next step is to determine the distances, D_{ij}, among all pairs of departments. The distances depend on the relative locations you assign to the departments in the layout design. Begin the design process by proposing an initial layout configuration; departments are assigned to available spaces. Then, using equation 7.1, measure the effectiveness of the initial configuration. Finally, modify the initial layout so that you can increase effectiveness by reducing transport costs. Repeat this process until you can find no further improvement.

Actually, the cost effectiveness of each possible design need *not* be fully calculated with equation 7.1. Although many different designs are possible, many of them are equivalent, or nearly so, from a transport cost viewpoint, and they need not be calculated separately. Consider the

[1]The flow matrix in Table 7.2 is appropriate when the *direction of flow* between departments is immaterial. In some situations, however, a load from i to j may be more or less costly than a load moving from j to i. In these cases, an expanded flow matrix must be developed to identify the direction of flow. For a discussion of this expanded treatment, see Elwood S. Buffa, *Modern Production/Operations Management,* 6th ed. (New York: John Wiley & Sons, 1980).

situation shown in Figure 7.4. Six work centers could be assigned to six available areas in these three different ways, among others. From a geometric viewpoint, the three configurations are nearly equivalent. In each design, these pairs of departments are located as close to one another as possible: 1–2, 2–3, 4–5, 5–6, 1–4, 2–5, 3–6. Therefore, the evaluation criterion needs to consider only the flows between *nonadjacent* departments, 1—3, 1—6, 3—4, 4—6. *This means that the L_{ij} D_{ij} computations following the initial evaluation for a layout design can be reduced just to those with nonadjacent flows.* The procedure is directed trial and error, and optimality is not guaranteed.

EXAMPLE

Greenwich Supply Company is a wholesale warehouse distribution facility. It receives orders from building contractors for kitchen cabinets and appliances. Inventories are stored in the warehouse and retrieved, as needed, to fill each order. All products for an order are transported by forklift truck to a centralized area where they are packaged for shipment to the contractor. Each completed order is then moved by forklift from the packing area to the shipping and receiving dock. We will evaluate the warehouse layout to see if it can be modified to reduce materials handling costs.

The existing facility layout is diagrammed in Figure 7.5. Section 1 is the shipping and receiving dock, and section 9 is the current packing area. The other 14 sections are storage areas for different types of appliances and cabinets.

Materials handling flows occur between the packing area and the other 15 sections. Loads are hauled to area 1 from only one source, section 9. All other loads flow from the remaining sections *into* section 9. The location of the shipping and receiving dock is fixed; it cannot be relocated. All other sections are eligible for relocation.

Records for the last two years reveal that the average annual load flows from departments 2 through 8 to department 9 are 2–500, 3–80, 4–320, 5–140, 6–150, 7–160, and 8–330; from departments 10 through 16 to 9 are 10–250, 11–100, 12–140, 13–240, 14–100, 15–240, and 16–500. The load flow from department 9 to department 1 is 2,500. We now use equation 7.1 to calculate the effectiveness of the existing layout. Table 7.3 shows the calculations for both adjacent and nonadjacent loads. The existing layout has a load distance rating of 12,300.

To improve the layout, we try to move those departments with heavy load flows closer together. Department 9, for example, can be moved closer to the shipping dock. We could also relocate department 16 closer to the packing area, and department 14 could be relocated to a more remote setting. A revised layout incorporating these and other changes is shown in Figure 7.6.

Overall, the layout analysis has reduced load movements by 34 percent.

1	2	3
4	5	6

4	5	6
1	2	3

4	5	3
1	2	6

FIGURE 7.4
Different but equivalent layout configurations

Some Limitations At best, our analysis provides a starting point, a layout that can be modified to account for additional complexities. Often the sizes and/or shapes of all departments cannot be uniform. Special restrictions may be imposed by aisle requirements, limited access to work areas, different types of materials handling methods, and electrical and plumbing requirements. Other process considerations may require, for example, that noisy operations not be adjacent to audio-testing areas sensitive to noise, or that operations that create contaminants should not be near expensive instruments sensitive to dirt or dust. In addition, the model we have used can require lengthy computational efforts, particularly when the number of departments and combinations of interdepartmental flows become large. For these reasons, alternative types of layout analysis are often used.

Computer Models Many computer-based layout models have been developed. We will briefly discuss only one of them, CRAFT, the Computerized Relative Allocation of Facilities Technique.[2] CRAFT is a heuristic procedure; it rearranges departmental locations in an attempt to find configurations that reduce the materials handling costs. The idea is to obtain a *satisfactory* layout design by evaluating thousands of alternative layout patterns quickly on a computer.

CRAFT can handle facilities consisting of up to 40 work centers of different shapes and sizes, and individual work centers that are either movable or immovable for purposes of relocation. These features take into account realistic restrictions imposed by the construction of buildings. CRAFT also considers differences in types and costs of materials handling among work centers. To use CRAFT, the analyst must provide an initial layout configuration, a load matrix identifying the volumes of materials flows among all departments, and a transport cost matrix identifying the cost of transporting a load between departments.

The evaluation procedure uses a criterion similar to equation 7.1. After calculating the effectiveness of the initial layout, CRAFT exchanges the locations of pairs or triplets of departments. The effectiveness of each exchange is evaluated, the best of these exchanges is adopted, and the entire process is repeated. When total materials handling costs can be reduced no further or when a specified number of repetitions has been reached, the best available solution is printed out as a layout.

A recent extension of CRAFT layout systems allows for multiple types

[2]Elwood S. Buffa, Gordon C. Armour, and Thomas Vollmann, "Allocating Facilities with CRAFT," *Harvard Business Review* 42, no. 2 (March–April 1964), 136–58; and Philip E. Hicks and Troy E. Cowan, "CRAFT-M for Layout Rearrangement," *Industrial Engineering* (May 1976), 30–35.

of spaces to be considered.[3] By modifying equation 7.1 to allow for multiple objectives, the inclusion of actual architectural design elements is possible in the layout. In an office setting, for example, representations of individual work stations, circulation areas, and the positioning of walls and doorways are allowed. This extension provides the operations manager with additional levels of detail in layout planning and illustrates the continued use of computers and modeling to improve operations.

Behavioral Aspects of Process Layout

Operations managers must consider individual and group behavior when planning a process-oriented layout. The layout specialist's problem-solving ability, which is necessary for developing the final design, is a form of individual behavior. Also, the layout design, once implemented, can affect both employee relationships and group behavior and customer behavior and satisfaction.

Behavior in Layout Design The layout designer's role seems to have changed with the introduction and increasing use of computer heuristics. Are these computer approaches superior to the traditional designs that people developed? Some studies suggest that they may not be. A study by Scriabin and Vergin found that people developed more economical designs than did three of the more widely publicized computer-based design models.[4] This was true for both large and small layout problems. Although modern technologists assume that computer models are superior to humans' designs, the experimental results do not support this assumption. The researchers offer the following possible explanation of their findings:

> It may well be that in problems of larger size the ability of man to recognize and visualize complex patterns gives him an edge over the

[3]F. Robert Jacobs, "A Layout Planning System with Multiple Criteria and a Variable Domain Representation," *Management Science* 33, no. 8 (August 1987), 1020–34.

[4]Michael Scriabin and Roger C. Vergin, "Comparison of Computer Algorithms and Visual Based Methods for Plant Layout," *Management Science* 22, no. 2 (October 1975), 172–81. For different results and conclusions, see Thomas W. Trybus and Lewis D. Hopkins, "Human vs. Computer Algorithms for the Plant Layout Problem," *Management Science* 26, no. 6 (June 1980), 570–74.

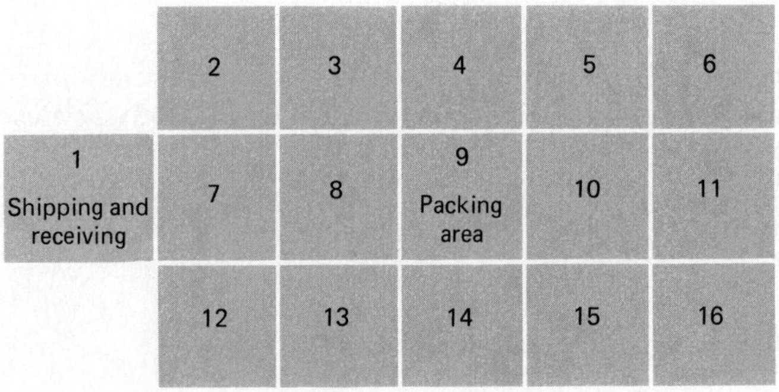

	2	3	4	5	6
1 Shipping and receiving	7	8	9 Packing area	10	11
	12	13	14	15	16

FIGURE 7.5
Existing layout of Greenwich Supply Company's relative locations of product storage areas (aisles omitted)

Table 7.3 Calculation of existing layout effectiveness

Adjacent Departments

Adjacent Departments	Unit Distance Between Departments (D_{ij})	Number of Loads Between Departments (L_{ij})	Loads Times Distance ($L_{ij}D_{ij}$)
3–9	1	80	1 × 80 = 80
4–9	1	320	1 × 320 = 320
5–9	1	140	1 × 140 = 140
8–9	1	330	1 × 330 = 330
10–9	1	250	1 × 250 = 250
13–9	1	240	1 × 240 = 240
14–9	1	100	1 × 100 = 100
15–9	1	240	1 × 240 = 240

$$\sum_{i=1}^{N}\sum_{j=1}^{N} L_{ij}D_{ij} \text{ for}$$

Movements between adjacent departments = 1,700

Nonadjacent Departments

Nonadjacent Departments	Unit Distance Between Departments (D_{ij})	Number of Loads Between Departments (L_{ij})	Loads Times Distance ($L_{ij}D_{ij}$)
2–9	2	500	500 × 2 = 1,000
6–9	2	150	150 × 2 = 300
7–9	2	160	160 × 2 = 320
11–9	2	100	100 × 2 = 200
12–9	2	140	140 × 2 = 280
16–9	2	500	500 × 2 = 1,000
9–1	3	2,500	2,500 × 3 = 7,500

$$\sum_{i=1}^{N}\sum_{j=1}^{N} L_{ij}D_{ij} \text{ for}$$

Movements between nonadjacent departments = 10,600

Total effectiveness for all departments = 1,700 + 10,600 = 12,300

essentially mechanical procedures followed by the computer programs. Such an explanation is supported by experience in other types of problem solving.[5]

Perhaps some combination of human and computer interaction may lead to even better results.

[5]Scriabin and Vergin, "Comparison of Computer Algorithms," 179.

Effectiveness

Adjacent Departments		Nonadjacent Departments	
Departments	$L_{ij}D_{ij}$	Departments	$L_{ij}D_{ij}$
9–1	2,500	3–9	320
2–9	500	5–9	420
4–9	320	6–9	450
8–9	330	7–9	320
10–9	250	11–9	400
16–9	500	12–9	420
		13–9	480
		14–9	400
		15–9	480
Subtotal = 4,400		Subtotal = 3,690	

Total effectiveness = 4,400 + 3,690 = 8,090

Improvement over initial layout = 34.2%

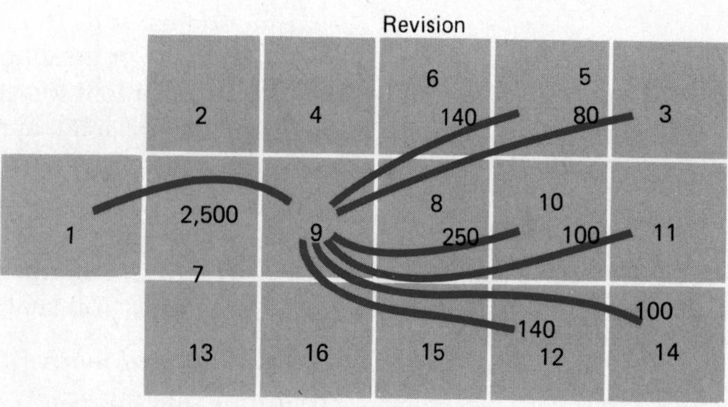

FIGURE 7.6
A revised layout with effectiveness ratings computed

Individual and Interpersonal Behavior of Employees We know that our environment affects how people feel about themselves and react toward others. The layout design can either help or hinder employees' relationships with one another. Spatial arrangements have an impact on employee satisfaction, internal motivation, and performance.[6] Layout also facilitates or impedes professional interaction among employees.

Process layouts result in departmentalization of activities according to skills. Each skill or craft group establishes norms and group affiliations that determine the kinds and amounts of productive efforts its members make. Often these norms are compatible with official standards set by management, but at other times they are not. A redesigned layout may inadvertently disrupt existing group relationships. Employee reactions to these changes may be adverse, and absenteeism, employee turnover, and labor relations problems may all increase. Realignment of loyalties may lead to conflicts among groups. As a result, *the manager of the entire operation must be particularly skilled at intergroup coordination.*

Customer Behavior For some organizations, the customer-producer interaction creates special problems, especially when the customer is present in the facility and takes part in the conversion process. In medical, dental, and legal facilities, welfare agencies, supermarkets, and banking businesses, individual customers (clients) have differing needs, and they may be "processed" through different departments accordingly. The layout can affect not only the quality and speed of service, but customer

[6] Randall S. Schuler, Larry P. Ritzman, and Vicki Davis, "Merging Prescriptive and Behavioral Approaches for Office Layout," *Journal of Operations Management* 1, no. 3 (February 1981), 131–42.

satisfaction as well. In a full-service bank facility, for example, the layout for such daily transactions as withdrawals, deposits, and money orders must be convenient for quick processing of walk-in customers. At the same time, areas for loan applications must be both quickly accessible and private. Data processing facilities and maintenance and administrative offices can be placed in more remote locations. Overall, the facility must provide a balance between easy, quick service and customer convenience and satisfaction on the one hand and efficient flows of materials and information for internal operations on the other.

Measuring Subjective Criteria Sometimes subjective criteria, rather than obvious quantitative indicators, are a dominant consideration. If so, we may use a revision of our previous layout criterion to accommodate such judgmental factors. In equation 7.1, L_{ij} could be used as a subjective priority indicator instead of the number of loads between two departments. Early in the design phase of layout, management can use an arbitrary scale, say between 1 and 10, to rate the importance of having two departments located close together. A rating of 10 indicates the most importance; 1, the least importance. After rating the importance of proximity for all pairs of departments, management can summarize the resulting priorities in a matrix. This L_{ij} matrix can then be used in equation 7.1, and the layout procedure can proceed as we described it earlier. This procedure provides a systematic way of using subjective priorities, including behavioral phenomena, in layout analysis.

DEVELOPING THE PRODUCT LAYOUT: ASSEMBLY LINE MODELS AND BEHAVIOR

Organizations that produce large volumes of a single product can gain economic benefits from a product-oriented (assembly line) layout. Early in the twentieth century, Henry Ford revolutionized an industry and the U.S. economy by mass producing automobiles. Since each car was identical, the entire buildup sequence could be predetermined in careful detail. Each task was minutely studied by engineers and managers to find ways to do it more quickly and at lower cost. Better work methods, specialized equipment and tools, and extensive employee training were used to reduce performance times. This, then, was the basic concept of the Ford assembly line. The product layout is as applicable today as it was in 1913. Later, we examine some contemporary behavioral considerations that were of minor concern at the beginning of the century.

Product Layout Models

Graphic and Schematic Analysis Assembly lines are most often designed and laid out by industrial engineers. Historically, they have used trial-and-error manual techniques and templates, drawings, and graphical procedures to develop initial designs and then improve them. For large facilities with many tasks and work centers, no mathematical procedures ensure finding the best possible design. Consequently, the quality of the design depends upon the experience and judgment of qualified designers.

Heuristics in Product Layout Mathematical and computer-based heuristic models can offer some assistance in obtaining a quality design. They can rapidly identify and evaluate alternative designs, far more than can be evaluated manually or intuitively. These rules are developed as much by observation and experimentation as they are by theory, and they are often specially adapted for a specific layout problem.

Defining the Design Problem The fundamental problem of layout planning for assembly lines is to find the number of workstations (workers) and the tasks to be performed at each station, so that a desired level of output is achieved. All of this is to be accomplished in such a way that excessive input resources are minimized.

Notice several important points in this definition. First, the design focuses on achieving a desired level of productive capability (output capacity). Second, if tasks are to be assigned to workstations, the *sequence* of tasks must be considered. Which tasks must be done first, and which ones may follow? Third, the definition emphasizes our concern with attaining desired output *efficiently*, without using unnecessary input resources.

Capacity, Sequencing, and Efficiency Let's illustrate these ideas by using an example.

EXAMPLE A manufacturer is developing plans for a facility to make aluminum storm windows. The desired minimum output capacity is 320 windows/day. The operations manager has obtained the tentative assembly line layout design shown in Table 7.4 and Figure 7.7. The manager wishes to know if this is a good design and if better designs are possible.

This is a good design if:

1. It meets the desired output capacity
2. The sequence is technically feasible
3. It is an efficient line

FIGURE 7.7
Diagram for storm window assembly line

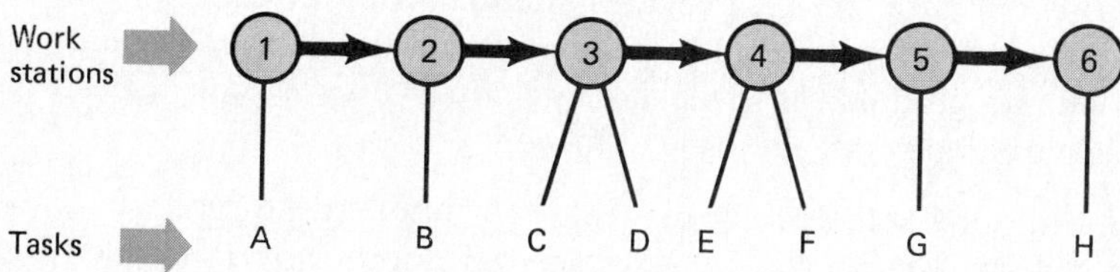

Table 7.4 Initial assembly line design for assembly of aluminum storm windows

Work Station	Preceding Workstation	Task to Be Performed at Workstation	Task Definition	Must Follow (predecessors)	Task Time (seconds)
1	—	A	Assemble frame	—	70
2	1	B	Install rubber molding	A	80
3	2	C	Insert frame screws	A	40
		D	Install frame latch	A	20
4	3	E	Install frame handle	A	40
		F	Install glass pane	B, C	30
5	4	G	Cover frame screws	C	50
6	5	H	Pack window unit	D, E, F, G	50
					380

1. Is Capacity Adequate? Capacity is determined by the longest time required from among all the workstations. From Table 7.4 we know that the work done at station 1 requires 70 seconds, and station 2 requires 80 seconds. Station 3 consists of two tasks—inserting frame screws (C) and installing the frame latch (D). Thus, the work done at station 3 requires 60 (40 + 20) seconds. The times required for stations 4, 5, and 6 are 70, 50, and 50 seconds, respectively. The longest time, then, is needed at station 2 (80 seconds), since a unit spends fewer than 80 seconds at every other station. Since every unit passes through all stations, and each must spend 80 seconds at station 2, station 2 is the *bottleneck operation,* the station that restricts the rate of flow off the line. A finished window assembly will flow off the end of the line every 80 seconds. This length of time is called the *cycle time* of the line.

With a cycle time of 80 seconds, how many windows are produced daily? It depends on the length of a working day. If the operation runs for one 8-hour shift each day, the available productive time each day is 28,800 seconds (8 hours × 3,600 seconds/hour). Therefore, maximum daily output can be determined by calculating as follows:

$$\begin{aligned}\text{Maximum daily output (number of units)} &= \frac{\text{Available time per day}}{\text{Cycle time required/unit}}\\ &= \frac{28{,}800 \text{ seconds/day}}{80 \text{ seconds/unit}}\\ &= 360 \text{ units/day}\end{aligned}$$

We see, then, that since it can generate more than the required 320 units daily, this assembly line design provides adequate output capacity.

There is an alternative method for determining whether capacity is adequate. We can calculate the *maximum allowable cycle time* if desired capacity (320 units per day) is to be achieved.

$$\text{Maximum allowable cycle time to meet desired capacity} = \frac{\text{Available time/day}}{\text{Desired number of units/day}}$$

$$= \frac{28{,}800 \text{ seconds/day}}{320 \text{ units/day}}$$
$$= 90 \text{ seconds/unit}$$

This calculation shows that any design with a cycle time of 90 seconds or less will provide the desired capacity. Designs with cycle times in excess of 90 seconds will not be of adequate capacity.

2. Is the Sequence of Tasks Feasible? We will assume that the proposed sequence of tasks is feasible. We will return to this question soon.

3. Is the Line Efficient? The proposed design has six stations, each manned by one employee. All six workers are paid daily wages for 8 hours. How much of our employees' time is spent on productive effort, and how much on idleness? It depends on the pace of the line that management selects. The pace can be set anywhere between the cycle times of 80 and 90 seconds. In Table 7.5, we have calculated the efficiency of labor utilization for cycle times of 90 and 80 seconds.

As you can see, idleness is higher for the 90-second cycle, and labor utilization is more efficient for the 80-second cycle. Daily idleness is 10 labor hours for the 80-second cycle. If the hourly wage is $10, each day $100 is paid for idleness. These excessive costs would eventually have to be passed on to the customer by appropriate price setting.

Balancing the Line How can the cost of idleness be reduced? Perhaps the eight elementary tasks (A to H in Table 7.4) can be reassigned so that work assignments are more evenly distributed in terms of time. If productive times required at all stations were equal, we could have no idle time, and the line would be perfectly balanced. The design problem of

Table 7.5 Calculation of labor utilization efficiency for proposed 80- and 90-second lines

	Station							Utilization of Employees
	1	2	3	4	5	6	Total Time/Cycle	(efficiency)
	Efficiency for 90-second cycle time (seconds)							
Productive time (task time) expended each cycle	70	80	60	70	50	50	380	380 ÷ 540 × 100 = 70.4%
Available employee time each cycle (cycle time)	90	90	90	90	90	90	540	—
Idle time each cycle	20	10	30	20	40	40	160	160 ÷ 540 × 100 = 29.6
	Efficiency for 80-second cycle time (seconds)							
Productive time (task time) expended each cycle	70	80	60	70	50	50	380	380 ÷ 480 × 100 = 79.2
Available employee time each cycle (cycle time)	80	80	80	80	80	80	480	—
Idle time each cycle	10	0	20	10	30	30	100	100 ÷ 480 × 100 = 20.8

finding ways to equalize performance times at all stations is called the *line balancing problem.* Our procedure for improving the design uses six steps:

1. Define elemental tasks.
2. Identify precedence requirements.
3. Calculate the minimum number of work stations needed.
4. Apply an assignment heuristic for specifying the work content at each station.
5. Calculate effectiveness and efficiency.
6. Seek further improvement.

For the previous example (aluminum storm window facility), we have already taken the first step, defining elemental tasks, and shown them in Table 7.4.

The second step tells us that elemental tasks cannot be done in just any order. Certainly the window units, for example, cannot be packed until they are completely assembled. These precedence relationships are listed in Table 7.4 under the heading "Must follow (predecessors)."

Once the desired line output is specified, we can calculate the *theoretical minimum number of stations* that are required, the third step in our procedure:

$$\begin{aligned}\text{Theoretical minimum number of stations} &= \frac{\text{Total work content (time)/unit} \times \text{Desired number of units/day}}{\text{Total productive time available/day}} \\ &= \frac{380 \text{ seconds/unit} \times 320 \text{ units/day}}{(28{,}800 \text{ seconds/day})} \\ &= 4.22 \text{ stations} \qquad (7.2)\end{aligned}$$

Since we are dealing in whole stations, at least five stations are needed. The *actual* design may use more than the minimum number of stations; it depends on the types of precedence relationships that exist in the problem. The initial design in Table 7.4 uses six stations.

The fourth step involves applying an assignment heuristic. The designer must now assign eight tasks to five or more stations. Several combinations of task-to-station assignments are possible. For larger problems with thousands of tasks and hundreds of stations, we often use heuristics. We will apply a longest-operation-time heuristic to find a balance for the 90-second cycle time.

The steps in the *longest-operation-time (LOT) rule* are:

LOT 1. Assign remaining tasks to the next station according to the length of task operation time; the eligible task with the longest time is assigned first. Maintain precedence relationships.

LOT 2. After assigning a task to a station, determine how much unassigned time remains at the station.

LOT 3. Determine whether other eligible tasks can be assigned to the station. If so, make the assignment. Maintain precedence relationships. If not, return to LOT 1 and add a new station. Continue until all tasks have been assigned to stations.

To apply the rule, we first array the tasks in descending order of operation time. Task sequence with operation times parenthetically in seconds is B (80), A (70), G (50), H (50), C (40), E (40), F (30), and D (20).

In LOT 1 we try to assign B to station 1, since B has the longest time. However, B is ineligible because it must follow A (precedence requirement). In fact, A *must* be assigned to station 1 before any other task becomes eligible for assignment. After A is assigned to station 1, 20 seconds of unassigned time remains (LOT 2). Using LOT 3, we see that D is the only eligible task that can be assigned to this station. B, C, and E all meet the precedence requirements, but their operation times exceed the unassigned time (20 seconds) at station 1. Therefore, station 1 consists of tasks A and D for a total of 90 seconds operation time.

Now we add station 2. B has the longest operation time (80 seconds) among the eligible unassigned tasks. B is therefore assigned to station 2. Using LOT 2, we find that 10 seconds (90 − 80 = 10) of unassigned time remain at this station. Since all other tasks require more than 10 seconds, none is eligible to be added to station 2.

To the third station we may assign C or E. We arbitrarily select C, with an operation time of 40 seconds. Remaining unassigned time at station 3 is therefore 50 seconds (90 − 40 = 50). Then E and G become eligible at this station. Since G has the longest operation time, it is assigned. Thus station 3 consists of tasks C and G with a total performance time of 90 seconds (40 + 50 = 90).

This entire process, carried to completion, is summarized in Table 7.6. The procedure has resulted in a five-station assembly line consisting of the work elements shown in Figure 7.8.

Table 7.6 Assigning tasks to stations using the longest-operation-time heuristic achieving a 90-second cycle time

Heuristic Steps	Station	Eligible Tasks	Task Selected for Assignment	Task Operation Time (seconds)	Unassigned Time Remaining at Station (seconds)	Remaining Eligible Tasks for This Station
1	1	A	A	70	20	D
2	1	D	D	20	0	none
3	2	B,C,E	B	80	10	none
4	3	C,E	C	40	50	E,F,G
5	3	E,F,G	G	50	0	none
6	4	E,F	E	40	50	F
7	4	F	F	30	20	none
8	5	H	H	50	40	none

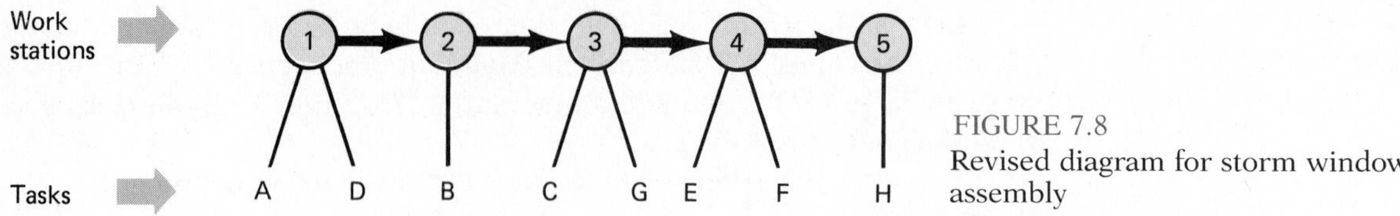

FIGURE 7.8
Revised diagram for storm window assembly

The design is *effective* if it meets the desired capacity—if the output goal is accomplished. Its *efficiency* is measured by the labor utilization measure described earlier. In the fifth step, we want to check both measures of performance. In the previous section, we balanced to achieve the maximum allowable cycle time (90 seconds). The design is shown in Figure 7.9, along with calculations of efficiency and effectiveness. The design is more efficient than the one presented to the operations manager in our example earlier in this chapter.

At this stage, we may be able to improve a design by trial and error, step 6 of our procedure. In addition, many other heuristics may be used instead of the longest-operation-time approach. Several computerized heuristics are available, and since different heuristics can lead to different designs, you may wish to try more than one approach.

There are occasions when output capacity and efficiency can be increased by deviating from the procedures we have presented. *Task sharing,* for example, occurs when there are three stations manned by separate operators, all of whom have some idleness each cycle. By eliminating one operator, we can reduce idleness by letting the remaining two take turns doing the task at the third station. Other improvements are possible if more than one person can be assigned to a single station. Finally, if the desired output level exceeds the line capability, further work analysis may be helpful. Bottleneck operations may be reexamined by time study, or methods improvements may be sought to reduce task time.

FIGURE 7.9
Assembly line design for 90-second cycle

	Stations and tasks					Effectiveness (goal accomplishment) One unit every 90 seconds, or 320 units/day	Efficiency (utilization of employees)
	1 AD →	2 B →	3 CG →	4 EF →	5 H		
Time required/unit (seconds)	90	80	90	70	50 →	Total = 380 seconds	380 ÷ 450 X 100 = 84.4% utilization
Productive time available/ unit at each station (seconds)	90	90	90	90	90 →	Total = 450 seconds	70 ÷ 450 X 100 = 15.6% idleness
Idle time/cycle at each station (seconds)	0	10	0	20	40 →	Total = 70 seconds	

Behavioral Aspects of Product Layout

The major behavioral issues in product-oriented layouts revolve around employee satisfaction, motivation, boredom, and productivity. Historically, the assumption has been that ever-increasing job specialization would lead to increased labor productivity. Experience has shown this assumption to be true up to a point. Sometimes routinization leads to job dissatisfaction, absenteeism, and higher employee turnover. Often employees feel that as jobs become more highly specified, something gets "lost"; the work tends to become meaningless. Responses to these problems include quality circles and job enlargement, enrichment, and rotation, all of which are discussed more thoroughly in Chapter 8.

COMPARATIVE APPROACHES TO REPETITIVE MANUFACTURING: IMPLICATIONS FOR LAYOUT

The preceding forms of layout reflect the approach to operations that has dominated manufacturing thought in Western societies for decades. More recently, however, a different approach by the Japanese has proven its competitive effectiveness in repetitive manufacturing and, consequently, is receiving considerable attention by Western firms as they seek to regain their competitive positions today.

Repetitive Manufacturing: Push or Pull?

Repetitive manufacturing processes are those that produce many units of one product or of several models of one basic product. This occurs commonly in such industries as appliances, toys, and automobiles.[7] Units of a given model can be visualized as progressing in a flow-oriented process through stages of product buildup. It may begin with fabrication of the basic components that are then built into subassemblies that are, in turn, combined in final assembly. The decisions of when and how many units to produce at each stage of processing vary considerably depending on the choice of a "push" versus a "pull" system for planning and control.

Push Versus Pull[8] The traditional Western perspective emphasizes a "push" orientation toward getting production through the manufacturing system. This emphasizes nonstop adherence to a predetermined production schedule derived from anticipated demand for the products. We preplan when final assembly will occur and, working backward toward earlier stages, we identify when subassemblies, fabricated parts, and purchased materials will occur to provide the scheduled quantity of finished outputs. Thus, once the schedule is set into motion, the work at each stage proceeds in large lots or batches and, when completed, the subcomponents are either sent to the next department or are delivered to a

---

[7]For a discussion of repetitive manufacturing, see Richard J. Schonberger, "The Transfer of Japanese Management Approaches to U.S. Industry," *Academy of Management Review* 7, no. 3 (July 1982), 479–87.

[8]Push versus pull systems are discussed in greater detail in Robert W. Hall, *Zero Inventories* (Homewood, Ill.: Dow Jones-Irwin, 1983).

storage area (inventory) where they wait for retrieval when needed by the users at the next stage of processing. After a work center has met the schedule, its obligation to succeeding stages is fulfilled. Its subsequent activities are relatively independent of the other work centers because of the cushion of inventories it has provided. Thus the units progress in batches that are pushed through successive stages of buildup until, finally, the required quantity of completed product units is fulfilled.

The "pull" system of planning and control, popular in Japanese manufacturing, is quite different. It emphasizes simplicity, flexibility, and close coordination among work centers in repetitive manufacturing. Although final assembly schedules are developed, the manufacturer recognizes that actual demand will vary from what was anticipated and, consequently, is prepared to adapt production as these variations occur. The Japanese orientation is toward assembly-to-order rather than assembly-to-schedule. The upstream activities (subassembly, fabrication, purchasing of materials) are geared to match the final assembly needs for a relatively limited range of products. Consequently, the what and when of production in upstream departments is highly variable and is governed by what the downstream departments need. The subassemblies and component parts are thus "pulled" through the system by actual end-item demands in the specific models, sizes, or color combinations of the product demanded by consumers. The idea is that if units aren't needed now, don't produce them now or ahead of time; when they are needed, be prepared to create them rapidly in the required quantity.

This austere vision of inventory is exemplified by the Toyota Kanban (card) system.[9] Here, inventory is closely controlled at minimum levels by using a manual two-card system. One kind of card (conveyance kanban), similar to a requisition, authorizes the withdrawal of a container of materials from a supplying work center to a using work center. A second card (production kanban) authorizes production of a container of materials to replace those that were withdrawn earlier. Each item of material in the production process has a prescribed number of containers in circulation at any one time. In addition, a container has in it a prescribed quantity (say, four units) of its designated material. By choosing the number of containers and the standard quantities in them, inventories are carefully and visibly controlled on the shop floor. By reducing the number of cards circulating between two interacting work centers, in-process inventories approach zero and the needed parts arrive just in time. As a result, there is an absence of inventories (raw materials, component parts, final products); stockless production is a major feature of the "pull" system of planning and control.

[9]The kanban system is discussed in Richard J. Schonberger, *Japanese Manufacturing Techniques* (New York: The Free Press, 1982). See also Robert W. Hall, *Zero Inventories* (Homewood, Ill.: Dow Jones-Irwin, 1983).

Operations Characteristics in Push Versus Pull Systems

The design and operation of a conversion system take on quite a different flavor, depending upon whether it is geared toward a push or a pull orientation. The two approaches impose different types of equipment, machinery, and maintenance policies, as well as inventory postures, worker skills, support staffs, and management abilities. For each of these areas, the push versus pull contrasts are summarized in Table 7.7.

Push System To accomplish its scheduled production in nonstop flows, the push system emphasizes predesigned and relatively fixed assembly line balances using dedicated single-purpose machines with high output capabilities. Abundant supplies of work-in-process inventories between stages facilitate nonstop production runs once they're started in downstream departments. Materials handling equipment shuttles parts and components to work areas from supplying departments or storage depots when scheduled by the materials control staff. The workers at receiving stations perform their specialized tasks repetitively on all units in the production lot. Work center management focuses on ensuring that the station is manned and has materials available and on motivating employees to meet scheduled output commitments. Long production runs avoid expensive setup and changeover costs.

Pull System Emphasizing flexibility and simplicity, the pull system adopts less expensive, smaller, adaptable machines rather than one big one. Intricate tools and attachments permit rapid equipment changeovers as required for different models at each station. The goal of lotless (stockless) production in assembly is reflected in the closeness of work stations; this permits each unit of product to be passed to the next station when it is completed, rather than accumulating in large batches after each stage. This gives station-to-station visibility of work progress, and it eliminates in-process inventories, inventory storage areas, inventory conveyance equipment, and materials control staff.

Diligent workers are the preeminent resource in the system. In addition to making the product itself, these workers adjust their own equipment for quick changeovers to different models. When low product demand warrants the shutdown of their production line, they are reassigned to other lines, or work on redesigning their own work stations and equipment to improve the production process or to do preventative maintenance. The pull system also demands more floor-level leadership from its foremen, who must exercise problem-solving skills in balancing and rebalancing production line work daily to meet frequent demand variations rather than adhering to nonstop predetermined schedules.

Workplace Layout: The U-Shape The emphasis on flexibility in pull systems is exemplified by the use of U-shaped, as opposed to straight-line, layouts. Consider, for example, the 13-station production work center in Figure 7.10. Suppose incoming materials are available to produce a small batch, for example, 5 units, of one product. If the 13 stations are positioned

Table 7.7 Characteristics of contrasting approaches to repetitive manufacturing

Operations Characteristics	Push System (United States)	Pull System (Japan)
Major orientation	Balanced nonstop flows to meet predetermined schedule.	Flexibility and simplicity in responding quickly to actual demand.
Machines	Use single specialized machines with production capacities in excess of anticipated needs. Large capital investment in machine and special tooling to perform a single purpose repeatedly.	Multiple copies of smaller, simpler, less expensive, and perhaps slower machines with specially developed flexible tooling to facilitate shutdown, startup, and changeovers to different product models. Tools and attachments located conveniently at machine site to simplify setups and changeovers.
Material handling equipment	Extensive reliance on elaborate devices to move large lots or batches of raw materials, components and subassemblies between work stations and inventory storage areas.	Minimal use of conveyance equipment. Frequent use of manual transfer of components from worker to worker by locating work stations close together and producing in small batches or one at a time.
Inventory posture	Extensive work-in-process inventories accumulate between work stations and stages of production. Produce large runs of components to spread high setup costs across many units, to avoid expensive changeovers, to hedge against equipment failures, and to compensate for defective components.	Avoid excessive inventories. In general, the prevailing view is that inventories are dysfunctional because they mask or hide production problems. Produce only what is needed as it is needed. Instead of producing ahead of need, produce just in time in small batches (or one at a time) as frequently as necessary.
Relationships with suppliers	Supply contracts often awarded on basis of price competition among suppliers who are geographically dispersed. Relationships between buyer and suppliers is transient. Materials purchased and delivered in large quantities and stored until used.	Close, long-lasting, and team-like supplier-buyer relationships. Close purchase-delivery coordination, frequently on short notice in variable quantities, with suppliers located near customer's facility.
Manpower utilization	Features task specialization and strict division of labor in fixed work assignments with limited task scope. Limited transfer of employees across jobs with different work content and variety. Employees oriented toward performing specialized tasks on many units of one product with emphasis on keeping the line running.	Flexible labor orientation toward a broader scope and view of work responsibilities. Concerned with discovering and correcting process weaknesses to ensure error-free production of every unit of product. Make equipment changeovers and setups of their own work stations as needed to produce varieties of product models. Limited hiring and layoffs by transferring employees to diverse jobs as demand at their own workplace fluctuates. Production lines stop until any problems are corrected through efforts and ingenuity of works.

Operations Characteristics	Push System (United States)	Pull System (Japan)
Support staff	Extensive investment in staff personnel for preproduction design of equipment, facilities, line balancing to a planned output rate, and job design for efficiency. Attempt to design production problems and bottlenecks out of the system to meet anticipated output levels. Extensive use of staffs for planning and controlling inventories, materials flows, and product quality during production. Foremen on production lines that are dedicated to a single product model ensure that each work station has the materials and people to meet the scheduled output. Foremen responsible for motivating a large number of employees.	Emphasis on improving production processes during as well as before production. Joint problem solving by engineering, workers, and managers as needed to address and resolve each problem as it arises. Foremen provide floor-level leadership for problem-solving and frequent rebalancing of lines in response to variable demands for mixed models of product. Constant emphasis on improving quality and reducing inventories and setup times. Strive for a single production line that can produce mixed models by rapid changeovers to meet market demand.

compactly, one or two workers can quickly set up all the machines without much wasted travel time between stations. Once production begins on the 5-unit lot, the worker at location A can perform operations 1–3 and 11–13 on all the units, while the worker at B performs operations 4–10. As you can see, the U-shape offers more options for flexible work assignments than does a straight-line layout. A worker can operate both sides of the parallel legs or adjacent stations. When the demand for this work center's output declines, one operator alone can do the work at all 13 stations. When demand rises, the lone worker can be joined by another to respond rapidly with more output. The trick is to decide how many workers to use,

FIGURE 7.10
U-shape layout for a workstation

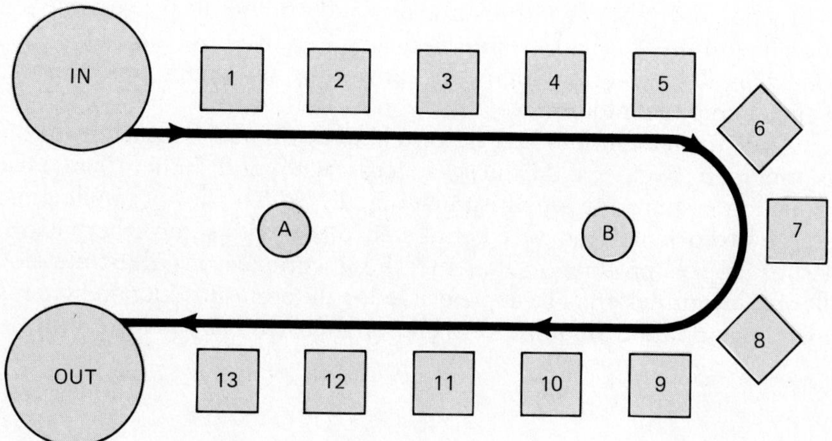

how to distribute the work load, and what size the small batches to be produced in each lot should be.

Relationship to Competitive Focus and Strategy

On the basis of competitive experience during the past decade, Japanese successes with the pull system are vivid evidence of its effectiveness as a competitive weapon. Its dominant success has been in situations that feature the repetitive manufacturing of a relatively modest variety of models, sizes, styles, or color combinations of one basic product. By intensively focusing their manufacturing skills on a limited product line, they develop fast and flexible responses to market demand, high product quality, and reduced inventory costs, all with lower investments in plant facilities and equipment. This exemplifies how the production function can be designed and focused to provide an advantage in a company's competitive strategy.

SUMMARY

Layout decisions are made only periodically. Since they have long-run consequences, they must be planned carefully. The layout design ultimately affects the cost of producing goods and delivering services for many years into the future. We discussed three traditional, basic layout formats: process, product, and fixed-position. Process layouts are arranged in such a way that work centers or departments are grouped together according to the type of function they perform. Product layouts arrange work centers and equipment in a line so that a specialized sequence of operations will result in product buildup. In a fixed-position layout, the product remains in one location, and resources are brought to it.

For process and product (assembly line) layouts, the design begins with a statement of the goals of the facility. Layouts are designed to meet these goals. After initial designs have been developed, improved designs are sought. This can be a cumbersome and tedious task because the number of possible designs is so large. For this reason, quantitative and computer-based models are often used to assist the designer. The models for process and product layouts are distinctly different: process models generally minimize load (volume)–distance moved relationships, and product models generally focus on minimizing idle labor time through line-balancing techniques.

Aside from the traditional views, a newer orientation in facility layout has emerged from the Japanese success with pull rather than push production systems for repetitive manufacturing. The layout implications of these two orientations were contrasted, along with some other characteristics of the production system. These comparisons illustrate how different layout designs are appropriate for different production systems, depending upon the organization's chosen focus and competitive strategy.

CASE

Sonographic Sound Systems, Inc.

SSS is a small local manufacturer of high-quality phonographs. For two years, SSS has produced its most popular portable phonograph on an eight-hour shift at a rate of 84 units/day. Management is satisfied with existing plant capacity but is concerned about the labor efficiency of its main assembly line. Fred Regos, operations manager, has asked his industrial engineer to recommend a redesign of the existing assembly line, because the vice president has established a goal of increasing labor utilization without decreasing output rate. This goal is consistent with the broader goal of a cost reduction of 10 percent for the production facility.

The assembly line currently has seven stations in which a total of ten tasks are performed. The task descriptions, times, and precedence relations are as follows:

Task	Description	Immediate Predecessors	Task Time (minutes)
A	Load chasis frame	—	1
B	Insert gear assembly on frame	A	2
C	Install electric motor on frame	A	4
D	Assemble turntable stem to gear assembly	B	2
E	Install rubber bearing assembly onto gear assembly	B	1
F	Mount, fit, and fasten turntable mechanism to stem	D	5
G	Interconnect gear and motor assemblies	C and E	1
H	Install turntable	F and G	3
I	Install tone arm assembly	G	4
J	Install and fasten cover	H and I	3

The existing assembly line and personnel are:

Station	1	2	3	4	5	6	7
Work content	A and B	D and E	C and G	F	H	I	J
Worker	Alice	Tom	Bill	Debbie	Sam	Corice	Ike

All employees have been with SSS two years or more. Tom finds that he has time on his hands and enjoys chatting with Alice. In all his time at SSS, Sam has never worked at another station. Although Bill doesn't like to perform task G, he takes great pride in his skill at doing C. Clorice and Ike agree that their jobs tend to get boring.

What changes would you recommend to Fred Regos? What reactions to these changes would you expect from the line employees?

REVIEW AND DISCUSSION QUESTIONS

1. Give examples of organizations that have predominantly product, process, and fixed-position layouts.
2. Compare and contrast the characteristics of intermittent and continuous conversion operations.
3. Describe and illustrate the significant relationships among the capacity and layout decisions.
4. What relationships exist between the layout and location decisions?
5. To what extent do the quantitative layout models consider behavioral factors?
6. Compare the manual and quantitative models for product-oriented (assembly line) layout design. What are the advantages of each kind of model?
7. Identify and describe the different models used to assist the layout designer.
8. Identify the primary behavioral factors involved in process-oriented layout design. Give examples.
9. Explain the essential features of CRAFT, a computerized layout model.
10. Identify the primary behavioral factors involved in product-oriented (assembly line) layout design. Give examples.
11. Compare the manual and quantitative models for process layout design. What are the advantages of each kind of model?
12. Compare differences in design strategies for developing an initial layout design (for a new facility) and for developing a revised layout design (for an existing facility).
13. Some would contend that employees generally should not have a major voice in layout design. Others argue that the layout should be developed in a participative manner, with major involvement by employees. Discuss this issue.
14. Explain how and why the push versus pull system for planning and control affects facility layout design.
15. Compare and contrast major aspects of employee behaviors under push versus pull systems for repetitive manufacturing.

PROBLEMS

Solved Problems

1. The assembly line design shown in Figure 7.11 provides the desired output rate for an eight-hour shift. Calculate the following: total work content, maximum eight-hour output, theoretical minimum number of stations, efficiency and idleness of the line.
2. Seven departments (see Figure 7.12) will receive incoming parts from the factory's receiving dock, which can be located at either position A or position B in the facility. The number of loads per month is shown in parentheses. Which position is best, A or B?

Reinforcing Fundamentals

3. A vacuum cleaner manufacturing company incurs a variable cost of \$50/unit produced and receives revenues of \$70/unit. Two alternative layout designs are being considered for finished goods storage and shipment. The first alternative would involve loading the products directly into trucks for shipment at a large loading facility near the end of the assembly lines. Annual fixed costs of operation of the large truck fleet would be \$350,000; materials handling costs would be \$150,000.

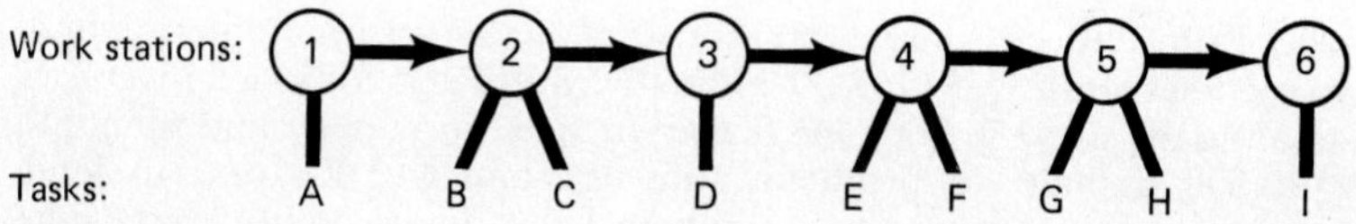

Work stations: (1) → (2) → (3) → (4) → (5) → (6)

Tasks: A | B C | D | E F | G H | I

Task times (minutes): = 4   1.5 1.5   3.5   1.5 2.5   2 1.5   4

Total work content/unit = 4 + 1.5 + 1.5 + 3.5 + 1.5 + 2.5 + 2 + 1.5 + 4

= 22 minutes/unit

$$\text{Maximum daily output} = \frac{\text{available time/day}}{\text{cycle time/unit}} = \frac{480 \text{ minutes/day}}{4 \text{ minutes/unit}} = 120 \text{ units/day}$$

$$\text{Theoretical minimum number of stations} = \frac{\text{Work content/unit} \times \text{Desired units/day}}{\text{Total productive time available/day}} = \frac{22 \times 120}{480} = 5.5 \text{ (or 6 whole stations)}$$

$$\text{Efficiency/cycle} = \frac{\text{Productive time/cycle}}{\text{Available time/cycle}} = \frac{22 \text{ minutes}}{6 \text{ stations} \times 4 \text{ minutes/station}} = \frac{22}{24} = 91.6\%$$

$$\text{Idleness/cycle} = \frac{\text{Idle time/cycle}}{\text{Available time/cycle}} = \frac{0 + 1 + .5 + 0 + .5 + 0}{24} = \frac{2}{24} = 8.4\%$$

FIGURE 7.11

A	1 (90)	B
2 (60)	3 (30)	4 (50)
5 (40)	6 (90)	7 (70)

FIGURE 7.12

Departments 1, 3, and 6 are ignored in the analysis since each of them is equidistant from A or B.

For A				For B			
Receiving Department	Unit Distance from A	Number of Loads	Loads Times Distance	Receiving Department	Unit Distance from B	Number of Loads	Loads Times Distance
2	1	60	60	2	2	60	120
4	2	50	100	4	1	50	50
5	2	40	80	5	3	40	120
7	3	70	210	7	2	70	140
		Total =	450			Total =	430

The B location offers lower cost.

The second alternative, a large warehouse near the assembly area, would result in a truck fleet costing $170,000 annually; average additional inventory carrying costs annually of $150,000; $45,000 each year to manage and maintain inventories; $20,000 damage to products annually; and $10,000/year to load, operate, and maintain the conveyance equipment from the assembly area to the warehouse.

Existing fixed costs of operation (in addition to the two layout alternatives) are $400,000/year. What impact, if any, do the layout designs have on the company's break-even volume of operation?

4. The university library is considering a new location for department 6, the book purchase processing department. Library staff would like to change departments 6 and 2, 2 being the social science reference staff. Given estimates as shown, what would be the impact of this change?

Effectiveness (monthly book loads)

Department	Department					
	1	2	3	4	5	6
1	—	100	0	100	200	0
2	—	—	0	0	0	0
3	—	—	—	10	100	0
4	—	—	—	—	0	100
5	—	—	—	—	—	0
6	—	—	—	—	—	—

Current layout

1	2	3
6	5	4

5. Work centers A through L, tentatively located as shown, have the load shipments in the load-flow chart.

Inter-department flows (units/year)

From	To				
	D	G	H	I	J
A	300	600	—	—	200
C	600	300	200	—	400
E	100	—	—	—	500

Layout (tentative)

A	B	C	D
E	F	G	H
I	J	K	L

(a) Assuming $1 transportation cost/unit-distance for each load, find a good layout.

(b) Suppose cost/unit-distance is $4 for each load from work center E and is $1 for each load from A and C. Find a good layout.

6. A small printing shop wishes to locate its seven departments in a one-floor building that is 40 units wide and 50 units long. Department sizes are as follows:

Department	Length (units)	Width (units)
Layout	10	10
Cutting	20	10
Shipping	10	10
Supply storage	20	15
Printing	25	20
Binding	20	20
Art	20	20

The average annual number of loads flowing between departments is expected to be:

From Department	To Department: Layout	Cutting	Shipping	Supply Storage	Printing	Binding	Art
Layout	—	—	—	—	—	—	—
Cutting	—	—	—	100	—	400	—
Shipping	—	—	—	500	—	—	—
Supply storage	—	600	100	—	400	100	—
Printing	—	—	—	—	—	1,200	100
Binding	—	100	1,000	—	200	—	—
Art	—	100	—	—	100	—	—

What is your layout recommendation?

7. In considering a new office layout, a designer obtained importance ratings for locating service groups near one another. On a scale of 1 (low importance) to 10 (high importance), service group proximity ratings were as shown in Table 7.8.

   Assume the overall space is three units wide and three units long; all service group areas are of equal size, one unit by one unit. What is your recommended layout design?

Table 7.8 Importance of close proximity among service groups

Service Group	Design	Estimating	Accounting	Computer	Records	Sales Engineers	Management
Maintenance	—	—	—	—	—	—	—
Library	9	—	—	—	—	2	—
Design	—	8	—	8	7	10	7
Estimating	—	—	4	—	2	10	4
Accounting	4	—	—	6	10	5	3
Computer	—	—	—	—	2	6	3
Records	—	—	—	—	—	5	—
Sales engineers	—	—	—	—	—	—	8

8. Given the following tasks and requirements for an assembly line, what is the maximum daily output and efficiency?

Task	Performance Time (minutes)	Immediate Predecessors
A	5	F
B	2	F
C	3	E, G
D	7	A, B
E	8	D, H
F	4	—
G	6	D
H	3	D

9. Consider the following production line in which work elements A to H must be performed in alphabetical order:

Work center	1	2	3	4	5	6
Work elements	A, B	C	D, E	F	G	H
Element time (minutes)	2, 1.5	4	2, 2	3	2.5	3

   (a) Identify the bottleneck operation.
   (b) What is the minimum cycle time?
   (c) Assuming an eight-hour work day, what is the maximum daily output?
   (d) If the line uses one employee per station, how many hours of idle time exist daily? How many hours of productive time?
   (e) Calculate the efficiency of the line.

10. For a food processing plant, the following data on the task precedence relationships exist. Assume the tasks cannot be split.
   (a) What is the theoretical minimum cycle time?
   (b) Balance the line using the longest-operation-time rule. Use the theoretical minimum cycle time.
   (c) Calculate the efficiency of the balanced line.

Task	Performance Time (minutes)	Immediate Predecessors	Task	Performance Time (minutes)	Immediate Predecessors
A	3	—	E	2	A
B	6	A	F	4	C, B
C	7	A	G	5	C
D	5	A	H	5	D, E, F, G

Challenging Exercises

11. A group of physicians is considering forming a new medical clinic in a single-story facility in a suburban area. Although design plans are just underway, they have decided to have service departments with these relative sizes (space requirements):

Service Department	Size (square feet)	Service Department	Size (square feet)
Laboratory	600	Neurology	600
Plastic surgery	600	Pediatrics	1,800
Patient waiting area	600	Pharmacy	400
Ob./gyn.	800	X-ray	600

The number of patients moving among pairs of departments during each month is expected to be:

Department	Lab	Plastic Surgery	Waiting	Ob./Gyn.	Neurology	Pediatrics	Pharmacy	X-ray
Lab	—	20	50	100	80	200	—	200
Plastic surgery	—	—	70	—	10	—	20	5
Waiting	—	—	—	400	100	900	—	50
Ob./gyn.	—	—	—	—	—	50	40	50
Neurology	—	—	—	—	—	10	20	80
Pediatrics	—	—	—	—	—	—	150	200
Pharmacy	—	—	—	—	—	—	—	30

The physicians are not yet concerned with the overall configuration of the building, just so all departments are on one floor. There is a direct relationship between number of patients and patient walking distances. What relative department locations do you recommend for minimizing patient flows (walking distances)?

12. An assembly line must be established to include the following tasks:

Task	Time (seconds)	Immediate Predecessors	Task	Time (seconds)	Immediate Predecessors
A	120	—	F	20	E
B	50	A	G	90	H
C	40	B	H	60	A
D	80	C, F	I	30	A
E	100	A	J	60	D, G, I

(a) Construct a precedence diagram for the tasks.
(b) To balance the line to a 120-second minimum cycle time, what is the theoretical minimum number of workstations?
(c) Use the longest-operation-time rule to balance the line to a 120-second cycle.
(d) What is the efficiency of the line?

13. For the data in Problem 12, redo Parts c and d using the shortest-operation-time rule. Using the largest-number-of-follower-tasks rule (the task with the largest number of follower tasks).

14. A toy company, Electro-Play, Inc., is interested in balancing a production line that will manufacture an electronic football game to compete with the successful pocket-calculator size model of Mattel. Tasks, performance times, and precedence relationships are shown:

Task	Performance Time (seconds)	Immediate Predecessors	Task	Performance Time (seconds)	Immediate Predecessors
A	40	—	G	10	C
B	20	A	H	10	E
C	15	B	I	10	E
D	60	—	J	5	F, G, H, I
E	20	D	K	10	J
F	10	C			

(a) Construct a precedence diagram for the tasks.
(b) To balance the line with a 60-second minimum cycle time, what is the theoretical minimum number of work stations? A seven-hour day is worked.
(c) Balance the line with the longest-operation-time (LOT) rule, balancing to a 60-second cycle.
(d) What is the efficiency of the line?
(e) Many of the behavioral problems in assembly line balancing also apply to the more general problem of job design. What suggestions might you offer if you wanted to incorporate job enlargement/enrichment into the balanced line given above?

15. Able Manufacturing has an opportunity to bid on a contract to produce an electronic assembly. Able could use excess assembly capacity at its main production facility. The contract would require delivery (within two years) of 30,000 units. Able's methods engineers suggest an assembly line consisting of nine tasks:

Task	Performance Time (minutes)	Immediate Predecessors	Task	Performance Time (minutes)	Immediate Predecessors
A	2	G	F	4	G
B	6	G	G	3	I
C	2	B, D	H	2	C, E
D	5	A, F	I	4	—
E	3	D			

Assembly would occur on one shift with average productive time of 7½ hours per employee daily (allowances for breaks, fatigue, shutdowns, etc.). There would be 22 productive days monthly. Direct labor costs are \$9/hour; variable overhead is estimated at 10 percent of direct labor; direct materials are \$12/unit; initial tooling for the project is \$100,000, and semifixed costs of manufacturing for the assembly line are estimated at \$7,000/month. Able desires a 15 percent profit margin on selling price for such contractual commitments. Should Able submit a bid and, if so, at what selling price?

Utilizing the QSOM Computer Software

16. Reconsider Problem 6. What if a proposed materials handling system will save 50 percent of the current handling costs on each load flowing from the binding department? Prepare your recommendations with supporting data.
17. Reconsider Problem 14. What if the line is balanced to cycle times other than the 60-second cycle? Prepare a report on the effects of various cycle times with supporting data.

GLOSSARY

Bottleneck operation Of all assembly line workstations, the one that requires the longest operation time.

Cycle time Elapsed time between completed units coming off the end of an assembly line.

Elemental task The smallest work task that can be assigned to a workstation.

Fixed-position layout Facility arrangement in which the product remains in one location; resources are brought to the product location to perform the appropriate stages of buildup.

Heuristic Simplification procedure in which a set of rules is systematically applied; results in the discovery of a satisfactory problem solution.

Job analysis Minute study of a task in an effort to eliminate unnecessary activity and find ways to do the task faster and cheaper.

Kanban A card system used for controlling the movement and production of materials on the shop floor in a stockless manufacturing system.

Layout design Location or configuration of departments, workstations, and equipment that constitute the conversion process; spatial arrangement of the physical resources used to create the product.

Line balancing Assigning tasks to assembly line stations so that performance times are equalized as much as possible.

Longest-operation-time rule (LOT) A line-balancing heuristic that gives top assignment priority to the task having the longest operation time.

Predecessor task A task which must be performed prior to performing another (follower) task.

Process layout Arrangement of facility so that work centers or departments are grouped together according to the type of function they perform.

Product layout Arrangement of facility so that work centers and equipment are in a line; provides specialized sequence of operations that will result in product buildup.

Pull system A manufacturing system that makes parts only when needed by the users of those parts; thus the parts and materials are drawn or pulled through the system by user demand for them.

Push system A manufacturing system that makes parts to meet a predetermined schedule and then sends them forward to the next stage or to inventory storage to await further processing.

Repetitive manufacturing Processes that produce many discrete (whole) units of one product or many discrete units of different models of a basic product.

Stockless production Manufacturing systems that strive to operate without work-in-process inventories; also referred to as *lotless production* and *just-in-time systems.*

SELECTED READINGS

Buffa, Elwood S., Gordon C. Armour, and Thomas Vollmann, "Allocating Facilities with CRAFT," *Harvard Business Review* (March–April 1964), 136–58.

Francis, Richard L., and John A. White, *Facility Layout and Location*, Englewood Cliffs, N.J.: Prentice Hall, 1974.

Hall, Robert W., *Zero Inventories*. Homewood, Ill.: Dow Jones-Irwin, 1983.

Hicks, Philip E., and Troy E. Cowan, "Craft-M for Layout Rearrangement," *Industrial Engineering* 8, no. 5 (May 1976), 30–35.

McLeavey, D. W., and S. L. Narasimhan, *Production Planning and Inventory Control*. Boston: Allyn & Bacon, 1985, chap. 12.

Ritzman, Larry, John Bradford, and Robert Jacobs, "A Multiple Objective Approach to Space Planning for Academic Facilities," *Management Science* 25, no. 9 (September 1979), 895–906.

Schonberger, Richard J. *Japanese Manufacturing Techniques*. New York: Free Press, 1982.

———"The Transfer of Japanese Manufacturing Management Approaches to U.S. Industry." *The Academy of Management Review* 7, no. 3 (July 1982), 479–87.

Schuler, R. S., L. P. Ritzman, and V. Davis, "Merging Prescriptive and Behavioral Approaches for Office Layout," *Journal of Operations Management* 1, no. 3 (February 1981), 131–42.

Trybus, Thomas W., and Lewis D. Hopkins "Human vs. Computer Algorithms for the Plant Layout Problem," *Management Science* 26, no. 6 (June 1980), 570–74.

PART III ORGANIZING THE CONVERSION SYSTEM

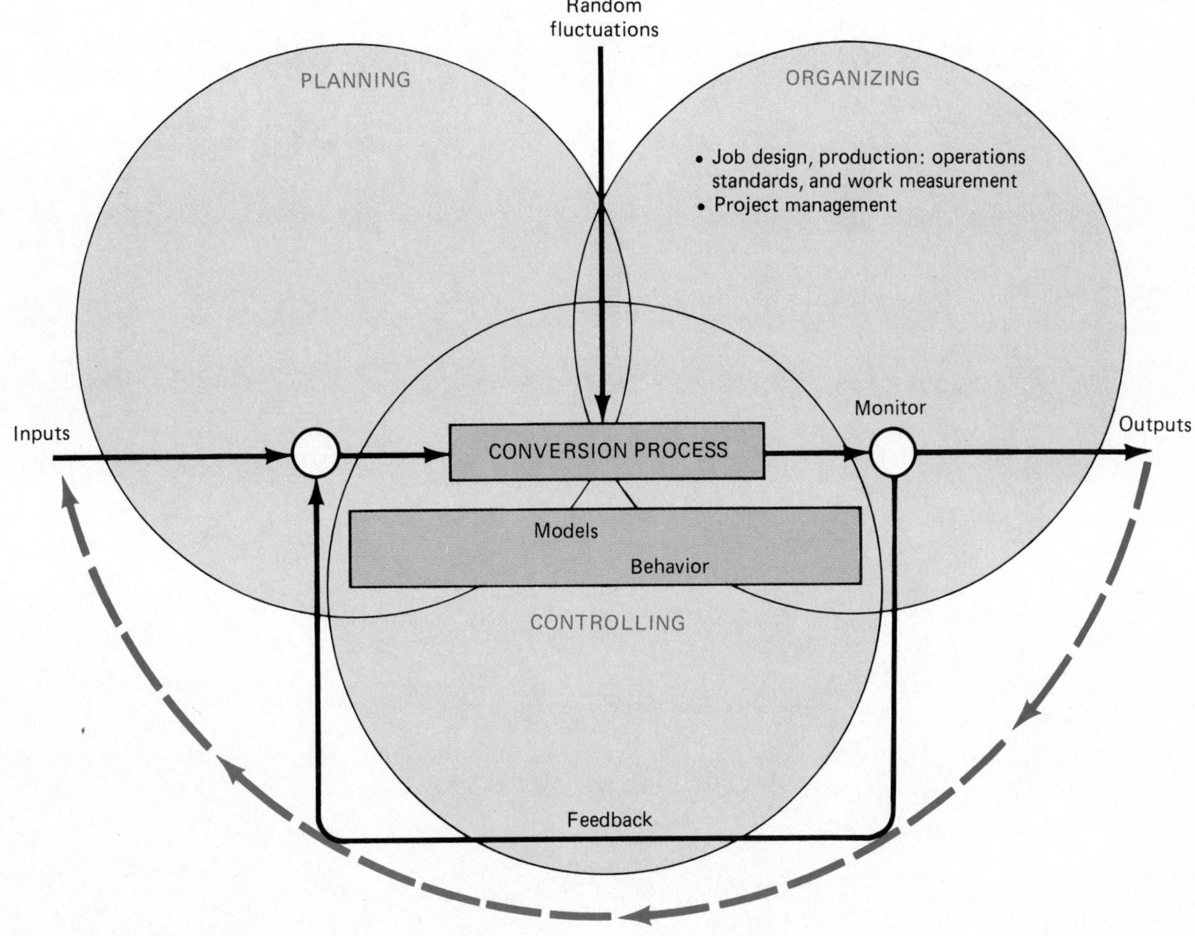

Production and operations management activities

8

Job Design, Production and Operations Standards, and Work Measurement

Job design, job standards, and work measurement have always been important to 3M Company. Job design in particular is becoming ever more important and, I believe, is the most critical.

In 3M, the behavioral human factors element of job design is gaining in recognition and has resulted in the creation of a separate human factors resource group for the corporation. I am glad to see that this chapter recognizes the importance of this factor. Job design must also be considered in the very beginning of product design, for we have too often designed products for end users without much thought for good manufacturability and resultant consistent quality.

In 3M Company, we have found that in labor-intensive areas, work standards and work measurement together increase productivity approximately 20%. As the chapter points out, many companies overlook or neglect this important element of operations. While money has to be spent to *develop* standards and measure the work, and money must continue to be spent to *maintain* these standards and measurement, 3M has found that this always pays off. The return on investment is generally more than 3:1. Work standards and work measurement must be evaluated carefully for their effect on quality—factors often overlooked in the past.

A challenge for operations management in the future is to develop effective design, standards, and measurement for white-collar jobs. Although difficult, this is not impossible. Because of automation and other productivity measures, the percentage of blue-collar workers in 3M, and in business as a whole, is gradually declining. As a result, improvement of white-collar productivity is becoming increasingly important and needs to be seriously addressed. I believe much can be accomplished in this area through applying the principles and methods described in this chapter.

C. W. Pipal
Staff Vice President
3M Company
St. Paul, Minnesota

It is encouraging to see a successful, established company like 3M benefit so much from applying the essentials of this chapter. Although we know many companies utilize traditional engineering approaches with contemporary behavioral modifications, the productivity increases of 20 percent and return on investments of up to 3:1 cited by Mr. Pipal are eye-catching. We hope this encourages you to grasp the fundamental issues and techniques we are discussing here.

This chapter focuses on people at work. The basic building block in a manufacturing or service organization is the *job,* a group of related tasks or activities that need to be performed to meet organizational objectives. Jobs are then grouped into larger units called *departments,* and departments are grouped into such basic functions as *marketing, engineering,* and *production.* Consider an example. The elements of placing a washer on a bolt, placing a nut on a bolt, and tightening the nut firmly with an automatic wrench constitute a *task.* Repeating this and similar tasks constitutes a *job* in the motor assembly *department,* which is in the *production function* of an organization that finances, markets, and produces washing machines.

Two basic developments have characterized organizations in modern industrialized societies. First and most significant was scientific management's focus on the logic of the production process, particularly people and machines at work on a job. This follow-up of Adam Smith's concept of labor specialization has led to establishment of logical approaches to job design, individual and group standards for performance, and techniques for measurement of work. A good bit of the development in industrial engineering over the last century has been devoted to this rational, scientific, and logical approach to job analysis.

More recently, human relations and behavioral science studies of jobs have come about. The development of the behavioral approach has tended to moderate scientific management's rational approach to jobs. The behavioral approach has provided clear evidence that people have multiple needs, feelings, and personal goals that are not always consistent with job designs, standards, and performance measures obtained from using traditional rational techniques. Clearly, the modern production and operations manager must be aware of and respond to the worker as an individual.

In job design, we use methods analysis to establish the general work flow in the facility. Once the general work flow has been established, specific jobs can be detailed. After the jobs have been designed, a standard needs to be established to ensure that the jobs are being performed properly. Establishing a standard, however, requires an understanding of work measurement. We want to emphasize that work measurement *follows* methods analysis. Only after we have established the proper method for getting the job done (job design) can we be concerned about measuring it (setting the standard through measurement). Obviously, setting a standard for an existing job and then redesigning it constitute wasted effort. Let's begin our discussion of these three related areas with the one that comes first, job design.

JOB DESIGN

In production and operations, job design follows the planning and designing of product, process, and equipment. Job design specifies the content of each job and determines the distribution of work within the organization. Just as an architect can build (design) a house many different ways with many different materials, so can a manager build (design) a job with many different parts (elements). A combination of creativity and adherence to basic goals is critical to both the architect and the manager.

Traditional Engineering Dimensions of Job Design

Often managers, responsible for many subordinates and equipment, feel overwhelmed by details. Couldn't we be more efficient if we improved our jobs? But how can we improve them when we hardly know what the jobs consist of? One answer to the managers' dilemma is offered by the scientific approach. It urges managers to:

1. Identify the general operations problem area and the jobs that seem to be contributing to or causing the problem
2. Carefully analyze and document how the work is currently being performed (Established industrial engineering techniques are available to assist in analysis and documentation.)
3. Analyze the content of individual jobs and job elements
4. Develop and implement new work methods

Often jobs can be broken apart, separated into elements. If the elements are assigned to different workers, each worker can perform fewer elements but can perform them faster and perhaps under more specialized conditions (e.g., with special tools or work benches). This basic concept, *specialization of labor,* has been very effective in increasing operating efficiency in manufacturing; it has been less effective, however, in the service industries.

Work Methods Analysis Aids To help the manager or a staff analyst study a job once a problem has been identified, certain techniques have been developed. One of these uses *operation charts* to analyze the job into elementary motions of the right and left hands—reaching, carrying, grasping, lifting, positioning, and releasing, for example. Often a time scale is placed in the middle of the operation chart so that it is clear how much time is taken by each hand to perform the associated motion. Operation charts are appropriate for routine, repetitive, short cycle tasks performed on low to moderate production volumes.

Activity charts divide operations into the major task segments performed by the worker and the machine and separate them by a vertical time scale. In this way, the analyst can easily compute the percentages of productive and idle time and concentrate on methods of reducing idle time for the worker and/or the machine. Activity charts are appropriate for routine, repetitive tasks with worker-machine interaction. The activity chart in Figure 8.1 illustrates how a punched deck of computer cards is

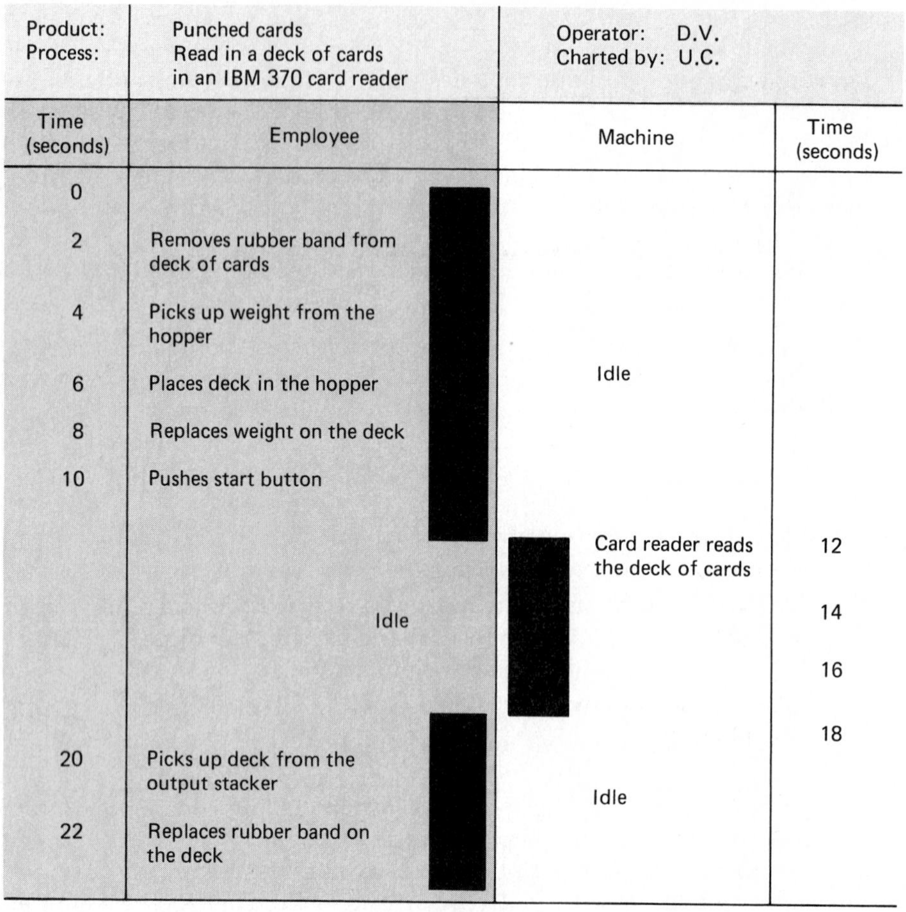

Product: Process:	Punched cards Read in a deck of cards in an IBM 370 card reader	Operator: D.V. Charted by: U.C.	
Time (seconds)	**Employee**	**Machine**	**Time (seconds)**
0			
2	Removes rubber band from deck of cards		
4	Picks up weight from the hopper		
6	Places deck in the hopper	Idle	
8	Replaces weight on the deck		
10	Pushes start button		
		Card reader reads the deck of cards	12
	Idle		14
			16
			18
20	Picks up deck from the output stacker	Idle	
22	Replaces rubber band on the deck		

Summary

	Employee		Machine	
	Time (seconds)	%	Time (seconds)	%
Work	14	63.6	8	36.4
Idle	8	36.4	14	63.6

FIGURE 8.1
Employee-machine activity chart

loaded and unloaded by a card reader. In this example, the analyst might improve efficiency by focusing on the first 10 seconds of idle machine time, the second 10 seconds of idle worker time, and the last 3 seconds of idle machine time.

Flow process charts analyze interstation activities, attempting to portray the flows of the overall production process. To capture this flow, analysts classify each movement of the product through the conversion process into one of five standard categories: operation, transportation, storage, inspection, or delay. Flow process charts are appropriate for visualizing the sequential stages of the conversion process. They help reveal unnecessary product movements or duplication of effort whose elimination would improve efficiency. Flow process charts provide a broader level of analysis than the preceding methods; many jobs are examined, but none in depth. The five categories of product movement are:

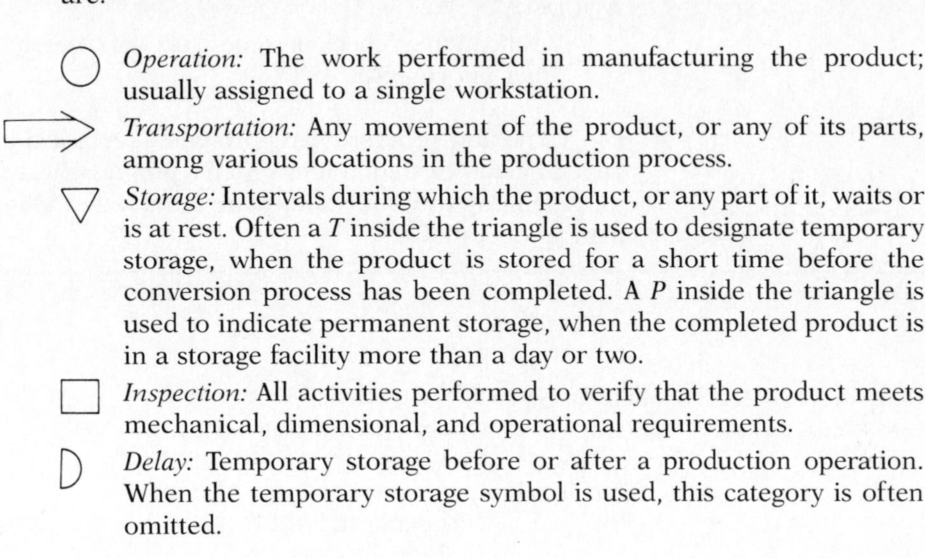

Operation: The work performed in manufacturing the product; usually assigned to a single workstation.

Transportation: Any movement of the product, or any of its parts, among various locations in the production process.

Storage: Intervals during which the product, or any part of it, waits or is at rest. Often a *T* inside the triangle is used to designate temporary storage, when the product is stored for a short time before the conversion process has been completed. A *P* inside the triangle is used to indicate permanent storage, when the completed product is in a storage facility more than a day or two.

Inspection: All activities performed to verify that the product meets mechanical, dimensional, and operational requirements.

Delay: Temporary storage before or after a production operation. When the temporary storage symbol is used, this category is often omitted.

EXAMPLE A study was conducted to document current library operations in the technical processing function of a major resource library.[1] The purpose of the study was to provide a basis for specification of computer automation systems in technical processing. Figure 8.2 is a typical product process chart. The following excerpt from the report illustrates this service sector application of traditional job design techniques.

"*Materials Flows and Procedures* This section presents the operations of the University of Missouri-Columbia Elmer Ellis Library's Technical Services Division in considerable detail. Because of the extensiveness of this description, a summary of the processing of materials is presented . . . The summary takes the form of "product process charts" and "floor diagrams" describing the general operations and movements undergone by the broader categories of library materials. The "station" identifiers heading each column of the process charts refer to desk locations as marked on the accompanying floor diagrams.

"Product process charts are in common use for describing processing of industrial materials, and they provide a convenient means of summarizing the numerous flow diagrams . . . The charts are easy to read once the following symbols and corresponding meanings are understood:

---

[1]S. Craig Moore, Everett E. Adam, Jr., Edward P. Miller, Daniel W. Doell, and Louis E. Fruend, *Library Studies Project*—Vol. I., *Project Summary,* and Vol. II, *Technical Services in the UMC Library System* (Columbia: University of Missouri, 1973). See pp. 12–15, Vol. II.

◎ Point of origination

◯ Operation performed on an item or group of items

○ Movement of an item or group of items from one location to another

▽ Delay

◇ Verification or check of some aspect of the item against a standard or other information

"The flow process charts presented technical procedures in enough detail that computer systems programmers could proceed with programming procedures for computers rather than continue with manual operations.[1]"

FIGURE 8.2
Product process chart of library operations

Source: S. Craig Moore, Everett E. Adam, Jr., Edward P. Miller, Daniel W. Doell, and Louis E. Fruend, *Library Studies Project:* Vol. I, *Project Summary,* and Vol. II, *Technical Services in the UMC Library System* (Columbia: University of Missouri, 1973). See pp. 12–15, Vol. II.

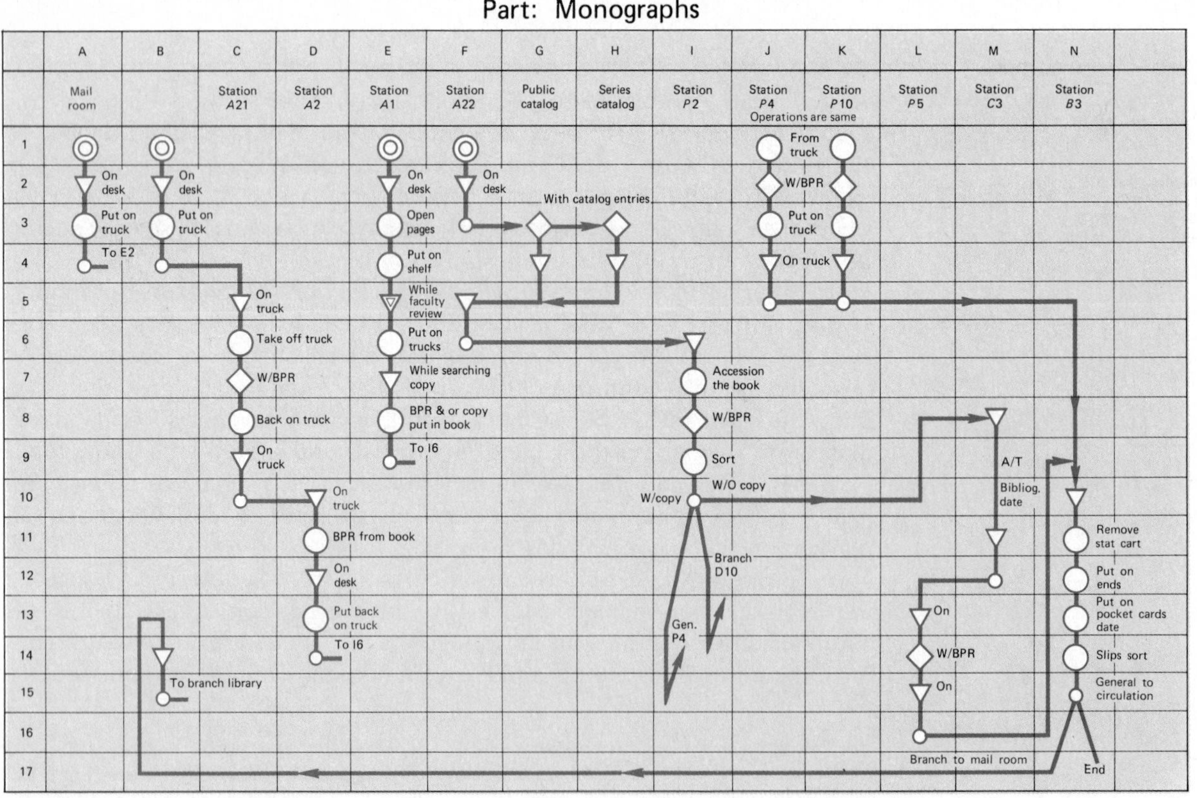

Table 8.1 Traditional engineering work methods aids in job design

Activity	Analysis Method
Routing, repetitive tasks with short cycle times and low to moderate production volumes; stationary worker at a fixed work place	Operations charts, principles of motion economy
Routine, repetitive tasks with long cycle times and moderate to high production volumes; worker interacts with equipment or other workers	Activity charts, worker-machine charts, gang process charts
Overall conversion process; interactions of workers, workstations and work units; flow of work	Process charts, flow diagrams

Table 8.1 summarizes the application of these techniques to various kinds of work activities. In the table, two terms are mentioned for the first time: *gang process charts,* which trace the interaction of several workers and one machine, and *principles of motion economy.* Principles of motion economy are general guidelines for analyzing and improving work arrangements, the use of human hands and body, or the use of tools to increase efficiency and reduce fatigue. Table 8.2 lists several principles of motion economy, many of which can be applied to both shop and office work.

Worker Physiology Over the years considerable effort has been devoted to studying people's physiology as it relates to their work. Statistics on reaching range, grip strength, lifting ability, and many other physiological factors have been reasonably well documented. Workplace arrangements, job design, and equipment design all require consideration of physiological factors. An industrial engineering handbook is a good source of information on the physiological capabilities of workers.

Working Environment The working environment is extremely important in designing jobs. Temperature, humidity, and air flow all affect work. If you've ever tried to mow grass or move furniture on a hot, humid day, you know how much harder high temperatures make your job. The same is true for less physically demanding work—typing, writing, and studying. The latter tasks, while easier at temperatures a little warmer than those that are best for manual tasks, are harder when temperatures are very high than when temperatures are moderate. A comfortable temperature might range from 65°F to 80°F (26.4°C to 38.4°C), the lower temperatures better for physically demanding work.

Similar to temperature, we know noise, light intensity, and many other environmental variables affect productivity. They also affect health and safety. Recognizing the lack of national uniformity in working conditions, Congress passed the Williams-Steiger Occupational Safety and Health Act of 1970 (OSHA). The act, which covers every employer with one or more employees in a business concerned with commerce, establishes

Table 8.2 Principles of motion economy

Using the Human Body the Way It Works Best

1. The work should be arranged to provide a natural rhythm which can become automatic.
2. The symmetrical nature of the body should be considered:
   a. The motions of the arms should be simultaneous, beginning and completing their motions at the same time.
   b. Motions of the arms should be opposite and symmetrical.
3. The human body is an ultimate machine and its full capabilities should be employed:
   a. Neither hand should ever be idle.
   b. Work should be distributed to other parts of the body in line with their ability.
   c. The safe design limits of the body should be observed.
   d. The human should be employed at its "highest" use.
4. The arms and hands as weights are subject to the physical laws and energy should be conserved:
   a. Momentum should work for the person and not against them.
   b. The smooth continuous arc of the ballistic is more efficient.
   c. The distance of movements should be minimized.
   d. Tasks should be turned over to machines.
5. The tasks should be simplified:
   a. Eye contact should be few and grouped together.
   b. Unnecessary actions, delays, and idle time should be eliminated.
   c. The degree of required precision and control should be reduced.
   d. The number of individual motions should be minimized along with the number of muscle groups involved.

Arranging the Workplace to Assist Performance

1. There should be a definite place for all tools and materials.
2. Tools, materials, and controls should be located close to the point of use.
3. Tools, materials, and controls should be located to permit the best sequence and path of motions.
4. Gravity feed bins and containers can deliver material close to the point of use.
5. The workplace should be fitted to the task and to the human.

Using Mechanical Devices to Reduce Human Effort

1. Vises and clamps can hold the work precisely where needed.
2. Guides can assist in positioning the work without close operator attention.
3. Controls and foot-operated devices can relieve the hands of work.
4. Mechanical devices can multiply human abilities.
5. Mechanical systems should be fitted to human use.

Source: Frank C. Barnes, "Principles of Motion Economy: Revisited, Reviewed, and Restored," *Proceedings of the Southern Management Association Annual Meeting* (Atlanta, Ga., 1983), p. 298.

strict health and safety standards by encompassing existing codes and adding to them. Publications describing the program are available from local OSHA area directors; they describe the act's purpose as follows:

> . . . to assure as far as possible every working man and woman in the Nation safe and healthful working conditions and to preserve our human resources. . . .[2]

[2]U.S. Department of Labor, Occupational Health and Safety Administration, *All About OSHA*, OSHA publication no. 2056, p. 3.

How is OSHA to implement this mandate? Congress was specific:

- By encouraging employers and employees to reduce hazards in the workplace, and start or improve existing safety and health programs
- By establishing employer and employee responsibilities
- By authorizing OSHA to set mandatory job safety and health standards
- By providing an effective enforcement program
- By encouraging the states to assume the fullest responsibility for administering and enforcing their own occupational safety and health programs that are to be at least as effective as the federal program
- By providing for reporting procedures on job injuries, illnesses, and fatalities[3]

Although OSHA's success depends significantly on voluntary compliance, the program does provide enforcement measures and information to employers to help them understand and obey the law. OSHA inspectors now have the capability of identifying employers with the "worst" safety records and inspecting those locations first.[4] OSHA officials have accepted a "worst-first" scheduling rule. As best we can judge, inspections are based on a combination of worker complaints, target industries, random inspection, and worst-first analysis.

Behavioral Dimensions of Job Design

In the past, industrialized societies have used economic criteria as their primary guides in designing jobs. We agree that economic criteria are still paramount. We mustn't forget, though, that behavioral implications in job design can and do influence performance. To ignore these concepts is to bypass the opportunity to add further economic benefits to those we obtain through traditional approaches. After World War II managers and behavioral scientists, developing an interest in industrial jobs in which workers had the "blue-collar blues," developed *job rotation* and *job enlargement* techniques as responses to an overemphasis of scientific management. More recently *job enrichment* and the *redesign of job characteristics* have added to our abilities to improve jobs. Keeping in mind that our goal is to add further economic benefits, let's examine each of these behavioral ideas.

Job Rotation Sometimes we cannot eliminate undesirable aspects of a job by redesigning or automating it. An excellent way to approach such a job is to move employees into it for a short period of time and then move them out again.

---

[3]Ibid.

[4]For initial development of the "worst-first" scheduling concept, see Everett E. Adam, Jr., "Priority Assignment of OSHA Safety Inspectors," *Management Science* 24, no. 15 (November 1978), 1642–49.

Have you ever worked the graveyard shift (from midnight until 8:00 A.M.)? Many people find it undesirable. Such service organizations as police and fire departments and hospitals, however, must have people on duty around the clock, and workers are moved into and out of the graveyard shift. Just as employees can move in and out of a shift that is undesirable, *they can be rotated in and out of jobs that are undesirable*. Even though there is no change in job content, rotating employees among different jobs can reduce boredom and monotony by exposing the employee to a broader perspective of the entire production process.

Job Enlargement Job enlargement proponents argue that we have simplified and routinized jobs to the point where they are so specialized that workers perceive them to be monotonous; workers are bored and dissatisfied. Because of boredom and job dissatisfaction, many workers withdraw from the organization, which has high levels of tardiness, absenteeism, and turnover. If managers would enlarge jobs by adding tasks, additional stimuli would reduce the ill effects of too simplified, too specialized jobs. Figure 8.3 illustrates the assumptions behind job enlargement.

Our conceptualization of an enlarged job offers the employee four opportunities:

1. Variety, the opportunity to use a variety of skills
2. Autonomy, the opportunity to exercise control over how and when the work is completed
3. Task identity, the opportunity to be responsible for an entire piece or program of work
4. Feedback, the opportunity to receive on-line information[5]

The nature and content of a job may be changed through job enlargement in two basic ways. First, more tasks of a similar nature and skill level can be added. If a job consists of tightening one nut on one bolt, for example, it could be redesigned to consist of tightening four different nuts on four different bolts. The job would then be enlarged horizontally. Second, other tasks of a different nature but similar skill level may be added. Instead of tightening one nut on one bolt, the worker could

[5]J. R. Hackman and E. E. Lawler, "Employee Reactions to Job Characteristics," *Journal of Applied Psychology*, Monograph 55 (1971), pp. 259–86.

FIGURE 8.3
Assumptions behind job enlargement

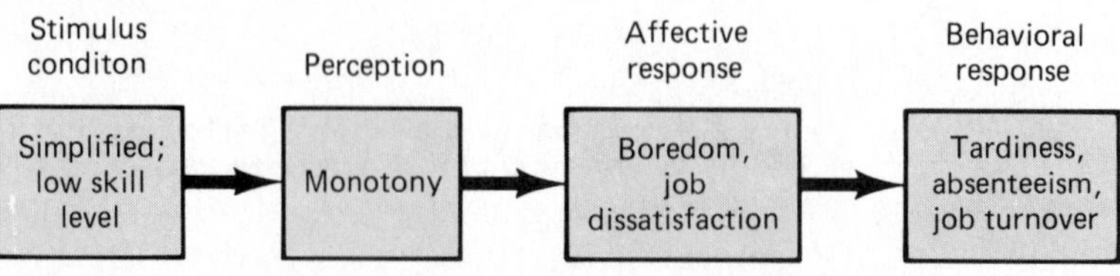

assemble two pieces of metal and a piece of plastic, tighten a nut and bolt to hold the assembly together, and walk to a storage area to get more nuts and bolts. The job would then be enlarged vertically.

EXAMPLE In a regional library, a job analysis was performed on all positions. The five circulation clerks' duties included working at the circulation desk, shelving books, and maintaining a particular part of the general collection (records, films, or young adult periodicals). The analyst discovered that the clerks found maintaining part of the collection the most rewarding and important part of their jobs. The routine, repetitious duties consisted of merely receiving and checking out books.

After their jobs had been redesigned, circulation clerks continued to perform their old duties of shelving books and maintaining a special part of the general collection, but they also began to perform some of the duties formerly done by a page. Time at the circulation desk was not allowed to exceed two hours at any one time, and total time at the desk was normally no more than four hours a day. This essentially vertical redesign resulted in increased job satisfaction and reduced job turnover.

Attempts to enlarge blue-collar jobs, however, provide mixed results. It seems clear that for routine, repetitive jobs with total job cycle times below one and one-half to two minutes, there is some chance of improved performance through job enlargement.[6] Other studies have reported improved satisfaction from job enlargement without performance changes. Perhaps these job satisfaction gains, which quite frequently result in decreased organization withdrawal, will turn out to be the primary, or at least the most consistent, benefit that can be attained from systematic job enlargement programs.

Job Enrichment *Job enrichment* is verticle expansion, similar to vertical job enlargement, yet different in that managerial tasks are added (rather than similar tasks in job enlargement). Job enrichment presumes that many jobs are so highly specialized that operative workers can no longer visualize how their work contributes to the organization goals.

EXAMPLE A manufacturing vice president for a leading foods manufacturer visited a class in beginning operations management and explained how job enrichment worked at his organization. The company was brand labeling corn flakes for a larger grocery chain, and the buyers were at the corn flakes plant for the day. Two production workers were selected and brought directly into a conference room where boxes of both competitors' and the company's corn flakes were available. These workers were asked, "Why are our corn flakes as good or better than others?" They answered by

[6] Maurice Kilbridge and Leon Webster, "An Economic Model for the Division of Labor," *Management Science* 12, no. 6 (February 1966), B255–69.

crunching various brands on the table and explaining in detail their jobs and quality control.

Two benefits resulted from this. First, the buyers were impressed with the workers' knowledge. Second, and most important, the workers returned to the workplace enthused about their contribution, and they spread this enthusiasm to other workers in their group. They related their contribution in "selling the product." The operative workers' jobs were more meaningful to them, and their attitudes toward their jobs were improved.

Many managers feel that the goals of job enrichment and increased efficiency are not only compatible; they are necessary partners. They argue that it's impossible to sustain productivity without the conscious satisfaction that job enrichment helps create.

Two conditions need to be established for effective job enrichment:

1. Management must supply information on goals and performance that previously was not available to the workers.
2. A proper *organizational climate* has to be established for success. Primarily, this climate does not imply excessive control of individual behavior in the organization.

These two conditions can be met by reorienting traditional management thinking:

1. Every employee must be viewed as a manager. Each must get involved in the management activities of planning, organizing, and controlling his or her own job. This is the basic goal of job enrichment.
2. The organization should strive to make work like play—to make the job fun. If a worker's job can be designed so that it offers the rewards that a game does—visible and meaningful goals, immediate feedback, group cohesiveness, and people who are there because they want to be—then workers will enjoy their jobs. We've designed too many of these rewards out of jobs; we can design them back in.[7]

Job Enrichment at General Foods The manufacturing vice president in the previous example told our class that his company's interest in job enrichment stemmed directly from a competitor's experience. In 1968 General Foods (the competitor) built a pet food plant in Topeka, Kansas, with the intent of emphasizing new behavioral techniques that would develop skills, create challenging jobs, and encourage teamwork. The new job design focused on several basic features: autonomous work groups,

[7]M. Scott Myers, *Every Employee a Manager* (New York: McGraw-Hill Book Co., 1970), pp. 47–49; 70.

challenging job assignments, job mobility and learning rewards, information availability, self-government, status symbols, and evaluation.[8]

There were some start-up pains, but the first 18 months of the job enrichment effort generally yielded positive results. Fixed overhead costs were 33 percent lower than those of existing plants; quality rejects were reduced by 92 percent; the safety record was outstanding compared with other company plants; morale was high; absenteeism was 9 percent below the industry norm; and turnover was far below average.

Job Design in Sweden In the late 1960s and early 1970s, Saab and Volvo experimented with varying degrees of job enlargement, job rotation, job enrichment, and production team procedures.[9] The results, though mixed, were generally positive. At one Volvo automobile assembly plant, for example, management combined job rotation and enrichment by having workers follow the same auto body through several workstations. The job cycle time was increased six- or sevenfold, to some 20 minutes. Job turnover, the primary target for reduction, was in fact reduced from 40 to 25 percent. Absenteeism, however, nearly doubled. Increased absenteeism was attributed to government legislation enacted during Sweden's then current economic slowdown; it allowed workers to stay off the job with little or no effect on salary.

Partial Solutions in Job Design Although not every job can be enriched, there are many partial solutions for jobs that are hard to enrich, particularly routine, boring, and otherwise undesirable jobs. Table 8.3 offers a few suggestions.

As is true with job enlargement, studies of job enrichment aren't conclusive. Those that have been done have generally concentrated on jobs lending themselves to enrichment. It is clear that if pay or supervision is a source of dissatisfaction, job enrichment will likely fail.[10] Some workers don't accept the middle-class values and goals inherent in job enrichment; they "don't want to be a manager." For some workers, enrichment might reduce social interaction, a result many workers would find undesirable. And many employees prefer a low level of required competency, high security, and relative independence to the increased responsibility and growth that job enrichment implies.

Job enrichment does have promise, though, and has been successful in some situations. We simply want to caution you against accepting this behavioral technique *in place of* sound work measurement and traditional

---

[8]R. E. Walton, "How to Counter Alienation in the Plant," *Harvard Business Review* (November–December 1972), pp. 70–81.

[9]Andrew S. Szilagyi, Jr. and Marc J. Wallace, Jr., *Organization Behavior and Performance,* 2nd ed. (Santa Monica, Calif.: Goodyear Publishing Co., 1980), pp. 173–77; W. F. Dowling, "Job Design in the Assembly-Line: Farewell to the Blue Collar Blues?" *Organizational Dynamics* (Spring 1973), pp. 51–67; and C. H. Gibson, "Volvo Increases Productivity Through Job Enrichment," *California Management Review* (Summer 1973), pp. 64–66.

[10]Raymond J. Aldag and Arthur P. Brief, *Task Design and Employee Motivation* (Glenview, Ill.: Scott, Foresman and Company, 1979), p. 101.

Table 8.3 **Partial job design solutions for jobs that cannot be enlarged or enriched**

Job Characteristics	Partial Solutions to Job Design
Routine, repetitive, boring, hot, noisy, generally undesirable	Use the job as an entry job in the organization, with the understanding that the employee will be there only a short time. Occasionally a worker might even want to remain in the job.
	Post the job daily. Often you will get a few daily volunteers who are looking for a change but don't want the job permanently.
	Employ the mentally handicapped, fitting them carefully to these types of jobs. They often make excellent employees when adequately trained and properly matched to a job.
	Employ part-time workers. Especially if full-time work is not available, part-time workers are often happy to do work that they would dislike on a full-time basis.

job design procedures. A possible supplement? Yes. A replacement? We think not.

Redesign of Job Characteristics and Participation Recent research in job design suggests that certain *core dimensions* of jobs can be redesigned to improve performance. These include task variety, task identity, task significance, task autonomy, and feedback. Conceptually, we can redesign these core dimensions so that they allow for individual differences in people's reactions to and feelings about their jobs. Researchers have not yet been able to answer some basic questions about job redesign. How do we identify and measure individual characteristics? Can we directly relate these characteristics to observed (not perceived) job performance? Research is still preliminary, but it does suggest that *individual differences* have a significant impact on the effectiveness of any job redesign effort.[11] We'd like to point out, however, that when jobs are redesigned, you should expect resistance to change of some magnitude and intensity. Often, the general feeling is, "I know this job better than you do; who are you to be changing it?" It is much easier to bring about meaningful change in jobs if you involve the workers or at least give them the opportunity to *participate* in the change process.

[11]See Andrew D. Szilagyi, Jr. and Marc J. Wallace, Jr., *Organizational Behavior and Performance,* 2nd ed. (Santa Monica, Calif.: Goodyear Publishing Co., 1980), pp. 160–68; Raymond J. Aldag and Arthur P. Brief, *Task Design and Employee Motivation* (Glenview, Ill.: Scott, Foresman and Company, 1979), pp. 81–105; Jon L. Pierce and Randall B. Dunham, "Task Design: A Literature Review," *The Academy of Management Review* 1, no. 4 (October 1976), pp. 83–97; and J. Richard Hackman, Greg Oldham, Robert Janson, and Kenneth Purdy, "A New Strategy for Job Enrichment," *California Management Review* 17, no. 4 (Summer 1975), pp. 57–71.

EFFECTIVE JOB DESIGN: COMBINING ENGINEERING AND BEHAVIORAL APPROACHES

On the one hand we have suggested traditional industrial engineering techniques for designing jobs, techniques that are an outgrowth of the scientific management approach. Yet on the other hand we suggest behavioral approaches to job design, most of these having been developed as a part of more recent organizational behavior research. What, then, is best? Let's try to relate these two approaches conceptually by looking at Figure 8.4.

As you study Figure 8.4, you will see that *both* traditional engineering and behavioral job design techniques are used to obtain the expected outcomes, accomplishment, and positive employee feelings. But no matter

FIGURE 8.4
Effective job design

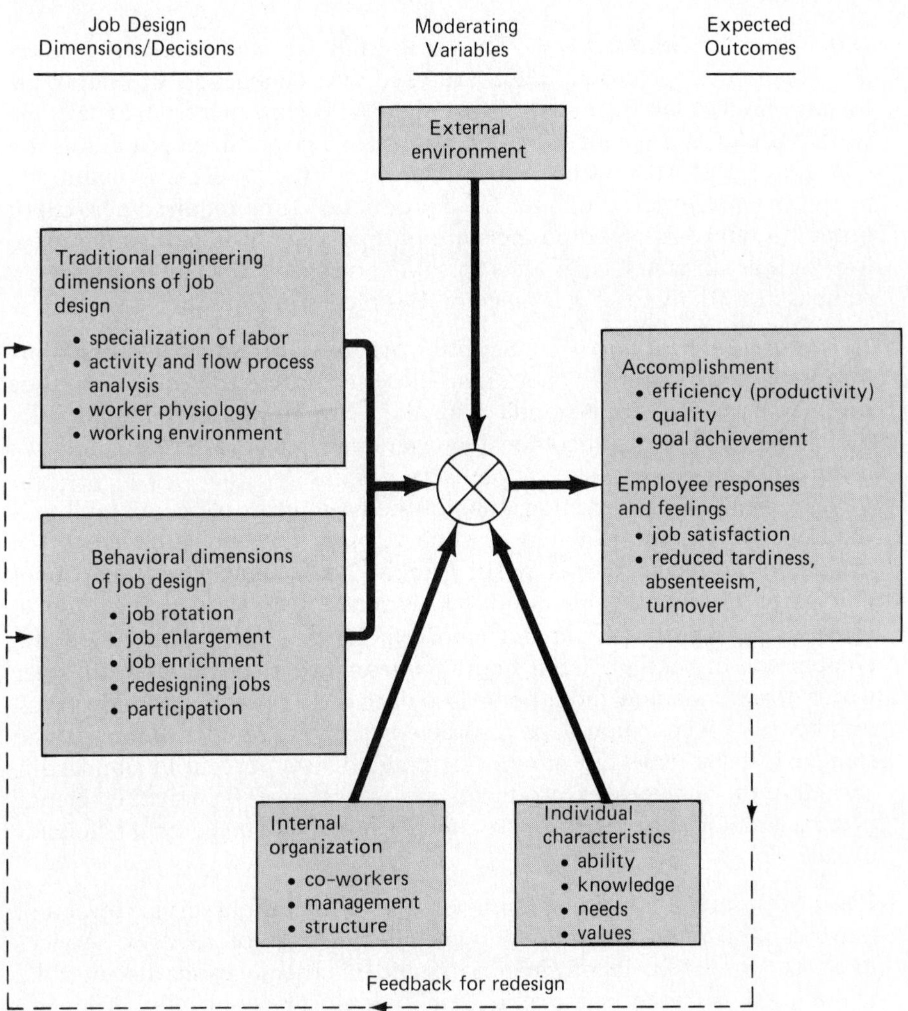

how well engineering and behavioral job design is done, the outcomes depend upon the external environment, the actual organization, and individual employee characteristics. These variables moderate or intervene between *job design* and *desirable outcome,* thus making effective job design highly complex as Figure 8.4 suggests.

PRODUCTION AND OPERATIONS STANDARDS

In the conversion process, to produce effectively and efficiently, management must establish goals for evaluating actual performance before the conversion process begins. These goals are translated into standards. A production and operations standard is a criterion established as a basis for comparison in measuring or judging output. The standard can be set for quantity, quality, cost, or any other attribute of output, and it is the basis for control.

Standards at Various Levels in the Organization

Individual Job Standards The terms *standard, labor standard, production standard,* and *time standard* are used interchangeably in operations management. A labor standard is simply what is expected from an average worker under average working conditions for a given time period. It is the concept of a "fair day's work." A standard set at the lowest level within the organization is expressed in terms of production time required per unit of output or, conversely, output per unit of time. A candy-making operation, for example, in which coconut is sprinkled on soft chocolate might have a standard of .01 minutes per piece or 100 pieces per minute.

Departmental Standards Several workers may perform as a unit, thus forming a team assembly operation. These teams and the equipment they use may have one group standard for the team output. By adding all the individuals and teams together, managers can set department standards for quality, quantity, costs, and delivery dates.

In production/operations, one of the basic units of accountability is the department; the foreman or supervisor of the department is often evaluated in terms of his or her ability to manage the department efficiently. Frequently this evaluation is made against an expectation to operate at or near 100 percent labor efficiency. (*Labor efficiency* is the comparison of "actual" labor hours to "standard" labor hours.) In other words, for every actual labor hour used directly in operations, an expected number of pieces should be produced; this expected number is the standard. If the expected number is attained, 100 percent of standard is earned. If more pieces are produced, a greater than 100 percent efficiency occurs, and if fewer pieces are produced, a less than 100 percent efficiency is earned.

Plant Standards At the plant, works, or comparable service level unit (such as a hospital or a school), a specified volume of goods or services must be produced; labor, materials, and overhead standards must be maintained, and at the same time their costs must be controlled. If you are familiar with cost accounting systems, you realize the need for accurate cost systems for labor, materials, and overhead. Likewise, quality levels must be maintained commensurate with product objectives. The point is clear—operations managers have multiple goals, and they must react to them with multiple standards.

Surprisingly, labor time standards are used much less uniformly in the *service sector* than they are in hard goods manufacturing. Since the service sector is generally more labor intense, it could benefit most from labor time standards. If you, as an emerging operations manager, find yourself employed in the service sector, you have an opportunity to bring great benefits to the largest labor sector of the economy by applying these scientific management techniques.

Uses of Standards

As a basis for making operating decisions, (labor) time standards are used to evaluate the performance of workers and facilities and for predicting, planning, and controlling operations (see Table 8.4).

Consider two uses of time standards in Table 8.4, formulating standard costs and cost estimating. Standard costs are computed in accounting as follows:

$$\text{Standard cost} = \text{Standard usage} \times \text{Standard labor rate} \tag{8.1}$$

The standard usage is the industrial engineering established time (labor) standard; the standard labor rate is the accepted labor rate for the labor force that will be performing the work. If the standard usage, the labor standard, is incorrectly established, the standard cost will be in error. Standard costs are compared with actual costs giving a labor efficiency variance where

$$\text{Actual costs} = \text{Actual usage} \times \text{Standard labor rate} \tag{8.2}$$

and

$$\text{Labor efficiency variance} = \text{Standard costs} - \text{Actual costs} \tag{8.3}$$

Table 8.4 **Uses of time (labor) standards**

Evaluating Performance	Predicting, Planning, and Controlling Operations
Evaluating individual performance; subsequent compensation	Aggregate planning of work force levels and production rates
Evaluating department performance; subsequent supervisor compensation	Capacity planning and utilization
Evaluating process design, layout, and work methods	Scheduling operations; time sequencing jobs
Estimating expense and revenue streams in equipment evaluation as alternatives are compared	Cost estimating of products and production lots
Formulating standard costs	Planning types of labor skills necessary and budgeting labor expenses

Key operation management performance evaluation decisions are based on labor efficiency variances, so it is important for data in calculating the variance to be correct. The following example illustrates how an error in establishing the labor standard carries through to the labor efficiency variance.

EXAMPLE A manufacturing firm introducing a new product set a preliminary labor standard at 10 units/hour. The standard labor rate is $8/hour in the plant where the part is to be produced. During the third month of production, 800 units were produced using 90 labor hours. The labor efficiency variance is calculated as:

$$\begin{aligned} \text{Standard cost} &= (.10 \text{ hours/unit})\ (800 \text{ units})\ (\$8/\text{hour}) \\ &= \$640 \\ \text{Actual cost} &= (90 \text{ hrs})\ (\$8/\text{hour}) \\ &= \$720 \\ \text{Labor efficiency variance} &= \$640 - \$720 = -\$80 \end{aligned}$$

Management was somewhat concerned about the negative variance but decided to have industrial engineering thoroughly check the labor standard before taking corrective action. Engineering recommended the standard be established at 12 units/hour; this was done. The labor efficiency variance was recalculated as:

$$\begin{aligned} \text{Standard cost} &= (0.0833 \text{ hour/unit})\ (800 \text{ units})\ (\$8/\text{hour}) \\ &= \$533.12 \\ \text{Labor efficiency variance} &= \$533.12 - \$720 = -\$186.88 \end{aligned}$$

The labor standard was in error by 20 percent (from 10 to 12 units/hour). This resulted in more than doubling the unfavorable variance (from $−80 to −$186.88). Management now set out to find causes for the more unfavorable variance.

Formal and Informal Standards

The actual work standard may vary considerably from the scientifically established industrial engineering standard. There is no escaping the impact of the informal organization, with its own communication network, system of authority, leaders, and work standards. Operations managers should not ignore the informal organization. Rather, they must attempt to influence the informal organization to communicate its work standards and at the same time attempt to influence the acceptance of formal standards by the informal work group.

WORK MEASUREMENT

A labor standard tells what is expected of an average worker performing under average job conditions. The critical questions in establishing a labor standard are:

1. How do we determine who is an "average" worker?
2. What is the appropriate performance dimension to be measured?
3. What scale of measurement should be used?

After answering these questions, you can use work measurement techniques to establish labor time standards. *Work measurement* is the determination of the degree and quantity of labor in production/operations tasks.

The Average Worker

People vary not only in such physical characteristics as height, arm span, and strength, but in their working pace as well. To determine a labor standard, we need to find an "average worker." But how do we do that? Usually, the best thing to do is observe several workers and estimate their average performance. We need to trade off the costs of sampling and the costs of inaccurate standards. The more workers sampled and studied, the closer the performance standard should be to true "average" performance and the costlier sampling. There are also costs associated with inaccurate standards; they can lead to tolerating inefficiencies, result in distorted product costs, and affect all the uses of standards we listed in Table 8.4. In trading off the costs of sample size and the costs of inaccuracy, we can find a range of reasonably low total costs.

The concept of an average worker brings up yet another point. Once average performance rates have been determined, the performance standard remains to be set. Should the standard be set at the average of total performances for the group or at a level at which almost all the group can be expected to reach the standard? Table 8.5 shows a hypothetical situation in which workers are divided into five performance categories. Should the standard be set at 22.25 units per hour, the mean, or at 14 units per hour, a number that 95 percent of the workers can be expected to reach? Arguments for both sides are obvious. Some engineers feel that quoting a minimum standard, the second choice, encourages poor performance. They prefer to have about one-half the workers seeking but not attaining 100 percent of the standard; that is, they suggest setting the standard at the mean performance. Others feel that standards should be attainable by 90 to 95 percent of the workers. Both approaches can be used effectively.

Table 8.5 Distribution of 100 workers sampled

Number of Workers Sampled	Performance in Units/Hour	Frequency of Total Workers	Cumulative Frequency of Workers	Complementary Cumulative Frequency of Workers
5	10–14	0.05	0.05	0.95
20	15–19	0.20	0.25	0.75
45	20–24	0.45	0.70	0.30
25	25–29	0.25	0.95	0.05
5	30–34	0.05	1.00	0.00

Performance Dimensions

When establishing work standards, management generally considers *quantity* to be the primary performance to be measured and *quality* the secondary standard. Quantity is usually measured as pieces per time period in manufacturing and service units per time period in service industries. A lumber sawing operation, for example, might have standard performance set at 1,200 pieces sawed per hour; a bank teller might have standard performance measured and set at 24 customers served per hour. Quality standards are often set as a percent defective—defective units divided by total units, all multiplied by 100. The key points in determining dimensions of performance are:

1. The dimension must be specified before the standard is set.
2. The standard and subsequent actual performance dimension must both be measurable.

Measurement Scales

Our discussion of work measurement uses a scale in which the normal performance is scaled at 100 percent, as illustrated in Figure 8.5. If performance is 25 percent above normal, the worker is producing at 125 percent of the normal scale. You can find a more detailed discussion of scaling in many industrial engineering texts.

Accuracy

How accurately can a work standard be set? Obviously, experienced raters can set a standard more accurately than can inexperienced raters. Although even experienced raters make errors, the standards they set are generally found to have lower variability than standards set using only historical data. We recommend that you use raters for work measurement, although you must be aware that because setting a standard is not a finely developed scientific procedure, there are bound to be some errors.

Work Measurement Techniques

There are six basic ways of establishing a time (work) standard:

1. Ignoring formal work measurement
2. Using the historical data approach
3. Using the direct time study approach

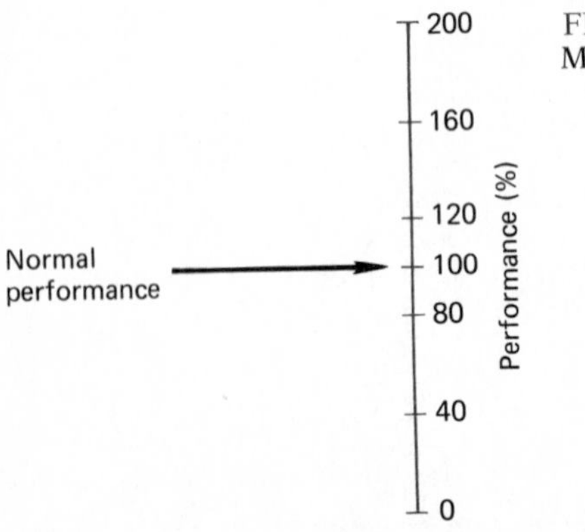

FIGURE 8.5
Most common work measurement scale

4. Using the predetermined time study approach
5. Using the work sampling approach
6. Combining approaches 2 through 5

Ignoring Formal Work Measurement For many jobs in many organizations, especially in the labor-intense service sector, formal labor standards are simply not set at all. The issue of a fair day's work for a fair day's pay is ignored. Even though there is no explicit basis for criticism, workers may be blamed for poor performance and inefficiency. Often because management has not established a work (time) standard, some informal standard is established by default. Since this informal standard generally compares unfavorably with those set by other techniques, we do not recommend ignoring formal work measurement.

Historical Data Approach This method assumes that past performance represents normal performance. In the absence of other formal techniques, some managers use past performance as their main guide in setting standards.

What are the advantages of this method? Basically, it is quick, simple, inexpensive, and probably better than ignoring the questions of establishing a work standard at all. The major disadvantage, as you can reason is that the past might not at all represent what an average worker could perform under average working conditions.

Direct Time Study Approach Often called a *time study,* a *stopwatch study,* or *clocking the job,* this technique is certainly the most widely used method for establishing work standards in manufacturing. Perhaps you have observed a job being studied by an industrial engineer, clipboard and stopwatch in hand.

How does direct time study work? We won't go into the fine points here, but basically there are six steps in the procedure:

1. Observe the job being timed. This technique depends upon direct observation and is therefore limited to jobs that already exist. The job selected should be standardized, in terms of equipment and materials, and the operator should be representative of all operators.
2. Select a job cycle. Identify the work elements that constitute a complete cycle. Decide how many cycles you want to time with a stopwatch.
3. Time the job for all cycles. Workers behave in varying ways when their performances are being recorded; common reactions are resentment, nervousness, and slowing the work pace. To minimize these effects, repeated study, study across several workers, and standing by one worker while studying a job somewhere nearby, perhaps in another department, can be helpful.
4. Compute the normal time based on the cycle times.
5. Determine allowances for personal time, delays, and fatigue.

6. Set the performance standard (standard time) as the sum of observed normal time and determined allowances (the sums of steps 4 and 5).

Another way to state step 6 in the procedure above is:

$$\text{Standard time} = \frac{\text{Normal time}}{1 - \text{Allowance fraction}} \tag{8.4}$$

where

$$\text{Normal time} = \text{Average cycle time} \times \text{Rating factor} \tag{8.5}$$

$$\text{Average cycle time} = \frac{\Sigma \text{ Time recorded to perform an element}}{\text{Number of cycles observed}} \tag{8.6}$$

$$\text{Allowance fraction} = \text{Fraction of time for personal needs, unavoidable work delays, fatigue}$$

and

$$0 \leq \text{Allowance fraction} \leq 1.0$$

EXAMPLE The time study of a machinery operation yielded cycle times of 8.0, 7.0, 8.0, and 9.0 minutes. The analyst rated the worker observed as 90 percent. The firm uses a 15 percent allowance factor. Computing the standard time,

$$\text{Average cycle time} = \frac{8.0 + 7.0 + 8.0 + 9.0}{4} = 8.0 \text{ minutes}$$

$$\text{Normal time} = (8.0)(.90) = 7.2 \text{ minutes}$$

$$\text{Standard time} = \frac{7.2}{(1 - 0.15)} = \frac{7.2}{.85} = 8.47 \text{ minutes}$$

The standard time for this machinery operation would be set at 8.47 minutes, which is greater than the average cycle time observed adjusted for the rating factor (90 percent) and the allowance fraction (15 percent).

Industrial engineers frequently use a rating factor when timing jobs. In essence the engineer is judging the worker as 85 percent normal, 90 percent normal, or some other rating depending on his or her perception of "normal." Obviously, ratings of this kind depend on subjective judgments.

EXAMPLE A laboratory research study required that a routine, repetitive task be designed so that quantity and quality could easily be measured. A collating task similar to such industrial jobs as collating sheets of paper for a promotional mailing, interleaving ash trays and paper in a packing operation, or collating papers for filing by an office file clerk was devised. For this collating task, a male worker took an IBM data processing card from each of six boxes, examined each card for keypunching errors, and sequenced the cards in order, one from each box. A sequence of six good cards made one good unit. The worker then stepped to another table and placed the unit in a box of good units. If an error card was found, the worker placed the error card in an error box and returned to obtain a good card from the box in which he had found the error card. The study required that he repeatedly collate good units of six cards for several hours.

A time study was made by observing five different workers for 20 cycles each. A cycle consisted of starting at box one, completing a unit, and returning to box one. The average time for each worker is expressed as an observation and shown in the table. Workers were observed without their knowledge; the average overall cycle time was 0.2247 minutes/cycle. (Another way of stating the standard would be at 4.4503 units/minute or, more commonly, 267 units/hour).

Direct time study for the quantity standard (expressed in minutes/cycle)

Observation	Single Card	Six Cards	Average Time
1	.0286	.1610	.1966[a]
2	.0255	.1540	.2287
3	.0166	.2089	.2804
4	.0276	.1616	.1831
5	.0292	.2096	.2345
Average	.0255	.1790	.2247

[a]Average of performance times for 20 cycles.

One question arises from this example. Why was the sample made up of five workers and 20 cycles? It was judged that this sample was of sufficient size to give a reasonably accurate estimate of average time at a reasonable cost; in direct time study there is an accuracy/cost tradeoff.

Predetermined Time Study Approach For jobs that are not currently being performed but are being planned, the predetermined time study approach is helpful in setting standards. Predetermined time studies can also be applied to existing jobs as an alternative to using direct time study methods. The bases of this technique are the stopwatch time study and time study from films. Historical data for tens of thousands of people making such basic motions as reaching, grasping, stepping, lifting, and standing have been accumulated. These motions have been broken down into elemental actual times, averaged by industrial engineers into predetermined standards, and published in table form. The procedure for setting a predetermined time standard is:

1. Observe the job or think it through if it is yet to be established. If you are observing the job, it is best to use a typical machine, representative materials, and an average worker performing the job correctly.

2. Record each job element. Do not be concerned about elemental times; just thoroughly document all the motions performed by the worker.
3. Obtain a table of predetermined times for various elements and record the motion units for the various elements. Motion units are expressed in some basic scale (a Therblig scale is often used) that corresponds to time units.
4. Add the total motion units for all elements.
5. Estimate an allowance for personal time, delays, and fatigue in motion units.
6. Add the performance motion units and allowance units for a standard job motion unit together and convert these motion units to actual time in minutes or hours. This total time is the resulting predetermined time standard.

This procedure is illustrated by reexamining the collating task we discussed earlier.

The primary advantage of predetermined time studies is that they eliminate nonrepresentative worker reactions to direct time studies. Workers don't slow the pace or get nervous, because the standard is set away from the workplace in a logical, systematic manner. The basic disadvantage of this technique is encountered early in its use. If some job elements are not recorded, or if they are recorded improperly, future timing won't be accurate. If job elements can't be properly identified and set forth in a table, they must be evaluated with the direct time study approach.

Work Sampling Approach *Work sampling* does not involve stopwatch measurement, as do many of the other techniques; instead, it is based on simple random sampling techniques derived from statistical sampling theory. Its purpose is to estimate what proportion of a worker's time is devoted to work activities. It proceeds along the following steps:

1. Decide what conditions you want to define as "working" and what conditions you want to define as "not working." Not working consists of all activities not specifically defined as working.
2. Observe the activity at selected intervals, recording whether a person is working or not.
3. Calculate the proportion of the time a worker is engaged in work *(P)* with this formula:

$$P = \frac{x}{n} = \frac{\text{(Number of observations in which working occurred)}}{\text{(Total number of observations)}} \tag{8.7}$$

With this calculation the manager can estimate the proportion of time a worker is engaged in work activity; this proportion can then be used as a performance standard.

EXAMPLE For the collating job, a predetermined time standard was set. Table 8.6 shows the motions of the right and left hands, provides a code, and shows the TMU (time measurement unit) motion units. This technique is called *methods time measurement* (MTM) and is a widely accepted predetermined time study approach. The MTM procedure allows one to observe the task, breaking it down into movements that have been studied in depth and that have a predetermined average time. The MTM chart in Table 8.6 was broken into several blocks for clarity.

Table 8.6 Methods time measurement chart for the quantity standard

Right Hand	Code	TMU	Code	Left Hand
		14.2	R12D	Reach to cards
		3.5	G1B	Grasp a card
		10.6	AP2	Apply pressure to separate
		3.5	T45S	Turn card
		13.4	M12B	Move to focus eyes
Transfer card from other hand	G3	5.6		
Subtotal		50.8		Subtotal
Multiplied by 6		304.8		Multiplied by 6
		5.6	G3	Transfer cards from other hand
		13.4	M12B	Move to final box
		4.0	D1E	Disengage cards
		15.0	WP(1)	Walk to start again
Subtotal		342.8		Subtotal
Error allowance		3.2		Error allowance
Subtotal		346.0		Subtotal
		51.9		15 percent personal, fatigue, and delay allowance
Total TMU		397.9		Total TMU

Notice toward the bottom of Table 8.6 the error allowance (placing an error card in the error box) and the allowance for personal needs (fatigue and unavoidable delay). The time allowance for personal needs, fatigue and unavoidable delays is a standard industrial engineering allowance. Fifteen percent, a widely used allowance, is assumed for this task.

Since one TMU equals 0.00001 hours, the total MTM time per cycle, 397.9 TMU, is converted directly to .23874 minutes/cycle. This is 4.188 units/minute, or 251 units/hour.

EXAMPLE A library administrator was concerned about the percent of time that a circulation clerk spent with patrons at the desk. Circulation activity included only those times when a clerk was engaged in assisting a patron at the circulation desk. The information clerk working at a nearby desk was asked to record once every half-hour for a week whether or not the circulation clerk was "working." Results were as follows:

Day	Number of Observations	Number of Circulation (working) Observations
Monday	16	8
Tuesday	15	8
Wednesday	20	12
Thursday	16	10
Friday	16	10
Total	83	48

The proportion of the time spent in the circulation activity, as defined by the administrator, was

$$P = \frac{x}{n} = \frac{48}{83} = .578$$

The administrator concluded that the proportion was low enough to add other clerical activities to this job.

Work sampling can also be used to set production standards; the procedure is similar to the one used in direct time studies. We can determine normal times as shown below (equation 8.8) and calculate standard times according to equation 8.4.

$$\text{Normal time} = \frac{\text{Total study time} \times \begin{array}{c}\text{Percent of time}\\ \text{employee observed}\\ \text{working}\end{array} \times \begin{array}{c}\text{Performance}\\ \text{rating}\\ \text{factor}\end{array}}{\text{Number of pieces produced}} \tag{8.8}$$

The work sampling approach to job measurement is particularly adaptive to service sector jobs—jobs such as those in libraries, banking, health care, insurance companies, and government. A good deal of the accuracy of this technique depends upon sample size.

By including a concept called *rating* or *leveling performance*, you can extend work sampling to include output standards. Once a job has been studied, the analyst must decide whether the worker's performance was average, above average, or below average. If the analyst decides performance was average, no adjustment is made. If the analyst decides the worker is above average (measured as units/time period), his or her rate is multiplied by a factor less than one; if the employee was working below average, the rate is leveled to average by multiplying the observed performance by a factor greater than one.

Disadvantages of work sampling include the engineer's or manager's objectivity, studying only a few workers, and "working" as a broad concept, not easily defined with precision. There are, however, some obvious advantages with work sampling. It is simple, easily adapted to service sector and indirect labor jobs, and an economical way to measure performance. In short, work sampling is a useful work measurement technique if it is used with discretion.

Combining Work Measurement Techniques Which work measurement technique should you use? In practice, they are used in combination, as cross-checks. One common practice is to observe a job, write down in detail all the job elements, and set a predetermined time standard. Then one can check the history of performance on this or similar jobs to verify that the predetermined standard is reasonable. To provide a further check, the job by elements and in total can be time studied. The point is clear: No one work measurement technique is totally reliable. Because of the high skill level required in setting the standard, we recommend a cross-check whenever possible.

EXAMPLE For the collating task we discussed earlier, the predetermined time standard was .2383 minutes/collation cycle. This was cross-validated by direct time study, which provided a standard of .2247 minutes/cycle. Finally, according to a previous study that used this task but under slightly different working conditions, actual historical times in the similar task were .1954 minutes/cycle. The first two times cross-validated quite closely, and the historical standard was reasonably close, so the predetermined time standard was adopted.

An apparent oversite in the direct time study is the omission of the 15 percent allowance used in the predetermined method. If this allowance is deleted from the predetermined method, the predetermined time is .2076, which is similar to the historical time.

Work Measurement for White-collar Workers Among the work measurement techniques presented, which appear most suitable for white-collar workers? Since white-collar jobs are typically labor intense and minimally automated, the same measurement techniques employed in the service sector would seem appropriate. We suggest a combination of historical data and work sampling. When predetermined time study can be used—on more routine white-collar jobs—it can be a useful approach too.

Current Usage of Work Measurement A comprehensive 1976 survey of U.S. and Canadian industries asked a simple question, "Are you using

Table 8.7 **How standards are established**

Technique	Percent of Time Used
Time study	89.5
Predetermined approaches	
Standard data	61.4
Predetermined time standard system	32.2
Estimate based on historical experience	44.2
Work sampling	21.3
Others	3.0

Source: Robert S. Rice, "Survey . . . ," page 21. Reprinted with permission from *Industrial Engineering magazine,* July 1977. Copyright Institute of Industrial Engineers, 25 Technology Park/Atlanta, Norcross, GA 30092.

work measurement and, if you do, for what purposes?"[12] This study was compared with a similar survey *Factory* magazine had conducted in 1959. Of the nearly 1,500 usable responses to the 1976 study, 89 percent reported they were using work measurement. This contrasts sharply with the 1956 survey, in which only 71 percent of the 785 respondents reported using work measurement. Correspondingly, the later study found 53 percent of the respondents used work measurement to measure employee performance, compared with only 20 percent in the earlier study. In the 1976 study, work measurement was also used for estimating and costing (89 percent), establishing wage incentives (59 percent), and production scheduling (55 percent). As the study makes clear, this traditional scientific management technique is by no means "dead" or "outdated" in industry; rather, it is apparently quite useful.

Another dimension of the more recent survey involves setting standards. The question was asked "What conditions trigger revision of a standard?" The most frequent reasons were changes in methods and materials (75 percent of respondents checked), low performance due to a tight standard (65 percent checked), and high performance due to loose standards (54 percent checked). The respondents were also asked, "How are standards established?" From Table 8.7 we see time study to be the most popular technique (used 89.5 percent of the time). The percentages do not add to 100 percent, since often more than one technique is used to set a standard, as we advised earlier.

In this chapter thus far, we have addressed the advantages and disadvantages of each work measurement technique. In light of the apparent advantages, why aren't all organizations using work measurement? We find the answer in the opinion of the 1,500 survey respondents —43 percent listed shortage of qualified specialists as an obstacle, 23 percent listed measurement as uneconomical, 25 percent stated measurement as impractical, and 21 percent said management is not interested. There is a career opportunity here for you, should you be interested in work measurement.

[12]Robert S. Rice, "Survey of Work Measurement and Wage Incentives," *Industrial Engineering* 9, no. 7 (July 1977), 18–31.

COMPENSATION

In their desire to motivate employees, sustain high performance levels, and obtain job satisfaction, production and operations managers establish compensation systems and practices for jobs. Compensation typically is either a commonly used conventional approach (resulting in a fixed hourly or monthly wage) or an incentive system (resulting in a variable wage). Table 8.8 summarizes such systems.

What do pay systems accomplish in operations? Managers view compensation as a way to influence behavior, whereas employees see it as a reward. Because of these different perspectives, the compensation approaches don't always provide the intended motivation, performance, satisfaction, and loyalty. Systems should be matched to objectives. If the organization values job experience, a seniority-based system might be best. Yet this might frustrate high achievers who would prefer incentive or merit-based systems. There seems to be a reemerging interest in incentive systems of all types, but especially organization-wide (or plant-wide) systems called *productivity gain-sharing*. These are modifications of traditional plans, such as Lincoln or Scanlon plans, that have been available for some time.[13] These compensation plans pay for group performance increases, usually sharing gains between the company and the employees equitably.

Table 8.8 Summary of conventional and incentive pay systems

Conventional Systems	Incentive Systems
Job-based—Employee paid on the basis of job characteristics; all employees on this job are given a single rate of pay.	*Individual*—Employee paid solely on the basis of measured performance; higher performance is tied directly and objectively to higher pay.
Seniority-based—Employee paid on the bases of job characteristics and length of service; all employees on this job are given a single *range* of pay. Those with higher seniority are positioned higher in the range.	*Group*—All employees in a work group are paid on the basis of the performance of that group.
Merit-based—Employee paid on the bases of job characteristics and performance; all employees on this job are given a single *range* of pay. Those that perform more meritoriously are positioned higher in the range.	*Organization-wide*—Employee paid for some aspect of the organization-wide, measurable performance; cost savings or profit-sharing bonuses, awarded as supplements to conventional or other primary pay systems, are examples.
Mixed-based—Employee paid on the bases of job characteristics and some combination of seniority, merit, and other.	

Source: Charles N. Greene, Everett E. Adam, Jr., and Ronald J. Ebert, *Management for Effective Performance.* (Englewood Cliffs, N.J.: Prentice Hall, 1985), p. 118.

[13]Lincoln and Scanlon plans can be found, for example, in Richard I. Henderson, *Compensation Management: Rewarding Performances,* 4th Ed., (Reston, Va.: Reston Publishing, 1985).

SUMMARY

This chapter highlighted work organization as a key function in production/operations management. This requires the manager to design jobs, establish job standards, and perform work measurement. In practice, methods analysis (job design) is followed by work measurement (establishing the job standard through measurement).

We noted that traditional engineering approaches to job design have emphasized the use of operation charts, activity charts, flow process charts, and principles of motion economy. But it has been shown that consideration must also be given to worker physiology and environmental conditions, as these affect job design. Such behavioral concepts as job rotation, enlargement, enrichment, and redesign of job characteristics were shown to enhance productivity and satisfaction. We learned that if managers use both traditional modeling and contemporary behavioral concepts in designing jobs, the results may be more efficient and effective performance than could be provided by either alone.

Emphasized was the importance of standards. After the job has been designed, individual, department, and plant job standards must be established. Standards are used for evaluating the performance of employees and facilities and predicting, planning, and controlling operations.

Although work measurement techniques do not provide perfect accuracy, they were shown to be considerably more accurate than other alternatives, including total reliance on management's judgment. Several methods of work measurement were mentioned; they include using historical data, direct time study, predetermined time study, and work sampling. In practice, several techniques are used in combination to cross-validate the work that is measured.

CASE

First National Bank

Lock-box operations in a large commercial bank process accounts receivable for customers. First National Bank has a major commitment to lock-box operations and is currently the regional processor for several major oil companies and national retailers, one of the larger credit card companies, and dozens of smaller regional companies. Customers of these companies mail their payments directly to First National, using a special zip code. Theoretically, First National is able to intercept the payment (shorten the mail time), process the paperwork, and credit the firm's account—all within a day from the time it receives the payment.

Lock-box operations are becoming a problem for First National. Every day it receives thousands of bills and payments for hundreds of accounts. Over the last few months, there have been as many as three days' backlog in work-in-process. First National is in jeopardy of losing two national accounts to competitor regional banks, which are outperforming it (a typical major oil company might use four banks geographically dispersed about the country). First National has assigned a "breakthrough" team to set performance standards and study jobs within this department.

The key employee appears to be the account processor, a person who opens incoming mail, verifies payment with the bill, records payment by account number, separates payments and bills, and delivers each for further processing. The account processor must also encode the payments (usually checks) and send them to check processing so that they can clear the bank and First National can receive credit for the money it has credited to the national account customer.

The team performed both a direct time study and work sample for the account processor job, with the results shown below. The bank uses a 15 percent allowance factor in all clerical jobs.

Management is concerned that setting a standard now will further damage performance. In fact, the day after the direct time study, 14 of the 35 second-shift workers were absent, a number much higher than the normal 10 percent. Jan Holms, an informal group leader who was one of the workers studied, told the analyst the company would "pay for this pressure." She was one of those absent the next day.

Frank Waring, the operations vice president, would like to change the entire work flow orientation, dissolving the lock-box department as it is now organized and grouping lock-box and other operations functions by customer rather than product. Frank's counterpart at Citibank recently wrote an article for the *Harvard Business Review* explaining that bank's success with a customer account focus, and Frank was most impressed. Although this seems like an appropriate time to consider such a move, Frank is not gathering the support he had anticipated from his team of management subordinates.

Direct time study data—processor job

Cycle Time (minutes) Processor 1	2	Number Times Observed Processor 1	2
0.5	0.5	1	2
0.7	0.7	3	4
1.0	1.0	5	3
1.3	1.5	2	1
1.5	2.0	1	1

Performance ratings: Worker 1 85%
Worker 2 80%

Work sampling data—processor job

	Worker 1	Worker 2
Number payments processed	322	296
Length of time observed (hours)	8	8
Performance rating	85%	80%
Idle time	25%	30%

REVIEW AND DISCUSSION QUESTIONS

1. Explain the difference between job design and production/operations standards.
2. Discuss the relationship between work measurement and methods analysis. Which typically follows the other? Why?
3. Contrast operation charts, activity charts, and flow process charts.
4. Contrast conventional, fixed-rate compensation systems with incentive systems. As a beginning management trainee, which would you prefer? Why?
5. Explain how traditional engineering and behavioral job design can actually be used together (see Figure 8.4).
6. Contrast job enlargement and job enrichment. Are they mutually exclusive?
7. Discuss the assumptions behind job enlargement.
8. Explain how departmental and plant standards differ from individual job standards. Provide an example of each from an organization of your choice.
9. Select two uses of time (labor) standards. Explain how the time standard could help a municipal police department in a city of 40,000 persons for the two uses you have selected.
10. Explain the predetermined time study approach to work measurement.
11. Why would combinations of work measurement approaches be a good strategy in establishing a standard?
12. Discuss the current use of work measurement. What do you conclude?
13. Why are production/operations standards important?

PROBLEMS

Solved Problems

1. In a candy factory a direct time study was made of the chocolate melting and pouring operation. Two inexperienced industrial engineers and one experienced engineer each made the study simultaneously. They agreed precisely on cycle times (shown below) but varied on rating the work. The experienced engineer rated the worker 100 percent, and the other engineers rated the worker 80 percent and 110 percent. The firm uses a 15 percent allowance factor.

Cycle Time (minutes)	Times Observed
25	1
29	2
30	2
31	1

(a) Determine the standard time using the experienced industrial engineer's judgments.

(b) Find the standard times using the data of each inexperienced engineer. What is your interpretation when compared to Part a? Are you sure the experienced engineer is correct? What could be done to enhance consistency in analyst performance ratings?

Rating the worker at 100%:

$$\text{Normal time} = \frac{25 + (29)(2) + (30)(2) + 31}{6} = 29 \text{ minutes}$$

$$\text{Standard time} = \frac{29}{1 - .15} = 34.12 \text{ minutes}$$

Rating the worker at 110%:

Normal time $= 29 \times 110\% = 31.90$ minutes

$$\text{Standard time} = \frac{31.90}{1 - .15} = 37.53 \text{ minutes}$$

Rating the worker at 80%:

Normal time $= 29 \times 80\% = 23.20$ minutes

$$\text{Standard time} = \frac{23.2}{1 - .15} = 27.29 \text{ minutes}$$

Obviously, considerably different standard times are derived for different ratings. Although an experienced engineer could be wrong, we have more confidence in an experienced person. We could enhance consistency by training. Training firms and short courses are available for use.

2. As a cargo loader for Southeastern Airlines, you are charged with the responsibility of setting a time standard (in minutes) for uploading refrigerated unitized loads. The following study was conducted over 300 hours with 900 uploading performed.

Composite Performance Rating	Activity	Times Observed
80	Manually check and lift unitized load onto trailer	100
100	Tow loaded trailer with tractor to aircraft	300
120	Check electrical contacts holding pins and safety wires (called *wiring out;* this time will be reduced by 50 percent by an additional inspection during manufacture of the containers)	400
90	Correct any malfunctioning observed during wiring out	100
110	Load unitized load into plane bay with automatic lift	400
140	Return tractor and trailer to warehouse	300
	Personal or idle time	400

Official Southeastern personal time allowance is 10 percent of total eight-hour work day *unless otherwise stated;* it is not otherwise stated here.

$$\text{Average observed time/uploading} = \frac{300 \text{ hours}}{900 \text{ uploading}} \times 60 \text{ minutes/hour}$$
$$= 20 \text{ minutes/uploading}$$

Normal Minutes/Uploading

$$20 \times \frac{100}{2000} \times .80 = 8.0 \text{ minutes}$$
$$20 \times \frac{300}{2000} \times 1.00 = 3.0 \text{ minutes}$$
$$20 \times \frac{400}{2000} \times 1.20 \times 0.50 = 2.4 \text{ minutes}$$
$$20 \times \frac{100}{2000} \times .90 = .9 \text{ minutes}$$
$$20 \times \frac{400}{2000} \times 1.10 = 4.4 \text{ minutes}$$
$$20 \times \frac{300}{2000} \times 1.40 = 4.2 \text{ minutes}$$

Total normal time minutes/uploading 15.7 minutes

$$\text{Standard time} = 15.7 \text{ minutes/uploading} \times \frac{100}{100 - 10} = 17.44 \text{ minutes/uploading}$$
$$= .29 \text{ hours/uploading}$$

Reinforcing Fundamentals

3. An experienced industrial engineer conducted a direct time study for an acid mixing operation. The analyst found cycle times as shown below, rated the worker observed as 90 percent, and used the firm's 10 percent allowance factor. Determine the standard time.

Cycle Time (minutes)	Times Observed
1.7	3
1.7	4
1.9	2
2.1	1
2.2	1

4. A speciality wood products company in eastern Kentucky manufactures handmade miniature wooden dogs. This Dandy Dogie product line is hand carved, varnished, labeled, and boxed, all by the same person. But there are wide variances in quality and performance times, which management is no longer willing to accept. In the hope of establishing a standard time, management has done a direct time study focusing on the two-inch walnut beagle. The results are shown below. For now, carving is being eliminated from the study. The firm's allowance factor is 10 percent. Establish a standard time for the remainder of the job.

	Cycle Observed (minutes)				
Job Element	1	2	3	4	Performance Rating
Varnish	5	4	5	4	105%
Label	0.5	0.4	0.3	0.5	95
Box	2	2	1	2	95

5. American Commerce's labor standard for over-the-road truck drivers is 320 miles/8-hour shift. Current wages are $8/hour under a nationwide contract. The assigned drivers from the Cleveland terminal logged 31,525 miles the first week of April and recorded 822 hours of work. A no overtime policy is in existence for Cleveland-based drivers.
   (a) What is the labor efficiency variance for the first week of April?
   (b) The American Commerce shop steward (driver union representative) contends that since the drivers log primarily noninterstate miles, the standard should be 10 percent less, or 288 miles/day. Operating management would like a comparative labor variance for the first week in April. What do these labor variances actually mean to management?
6. A farming conglomerate has a large cow-calf operation. The manager expects the hay crew to place 1,750 bales of hay in the barn daily during harvest. The contract costs for labor only are $180/day (for a crew of four). In the past four days 8,100 bales have been harvested. What is the farm manager's labor efficiency variance for the hay crew? Would you suggest any action based on this figure?
7. Direct time study for a task resulted in the following times, expressed in minutes per cycle.

Observation	Average Time
1	1.321
2	1.411
3	1.704
4	1.175

A predetermined time standard was set at 2,128 TMU/cycle, which converts to 1.275 minutes/cycle. What time standard would you recommend? Justify your choice.

8. Develop an employee/machine activity chart to show how a multipage term paper should be copied on a coin-operated photocopy machine. Use a layout diagram. Assume there are ample coins and that the stack of pages is prepared (unstapled) at the start of the task.

9. Job analysis and methods study reveal that during an eight-hour workday a man-machine operation typically experiences various unavoidable delays totaling 40 minutes and one equipment setup changeover of 20 minutes. Operators need 20 minutes for personal time and take two 15-minute coffee breaks. Standard time per operation cycle (to produce one unit) is 10 minutes. How many units are produced by an operator who produces at 85 percent of standard? At 115 percent of standard?

10. A student is facing midterm exams and decides to start the semester's first real studying. After one day in the library, the student is dismayed to find that at the rate of present studying, he will not be ready to take the exams until four days after they are over. A friend volunteers to do a work sampling study and finds the following:

Two-hour Time Period	Times Observed	Number of Studying Observations
1	12	9
2	21	10
3	9	4

As a percentage, what is the proportion of time spent studying?

11. Filing clerks in a state department of welfare were considered to be filing any time they had a paper in their hands. The following seven days of observations were selected at random over the past month. What proportion of the time is spent in filing? What work measurement approach is this? How might one alternatively define filing?

Day	Times Observed	Number of Filing Observations
1	12	8
2	19	12
3	10	5
4	23	14
5	15	10
6	12	9
7	17	11

Challenging Exercises

12. Several laboratory technicians in a hospital are primarily responsible for running the highly automated "Chemistry 12" blood profile test. An experienced technician was work sampled on this job over a two-week period (70 hours). The lab technician produced 412 blood samples. The analyst studying the job found that the technician was working 60 percent of the time and idle the rest. Some idleness was due to waiting for the automated equipment to complete analysis. The performance rating was 85 percent, but the analyst was uncertain about this because of the automated equipment. Allowances are set at 10 percent.

(a) Determine a standard time for a standard blood profile.

(b) How could the analyst be more certain about the performance rating?

13. A manufacturer is considering the purchase of one of two types of equipment, type A or type B, to perform an operation. Initial equipment cost is $10,000 for either A or B. Operating costs are estimated as follows:

	A	B
Maintenance (per month)	$750	$500
Supplies (per unit)	—	.052
Operator (per hour)	9	9

The equipment manufacturers both arranged for experimental demonstrations, in which stopwatch time studies of operator/machine performance for five cycles were measured. Demonstrations revealed the following time in minutes:

	Cycles for A					Cycles for B				
Activity	1	2	3	4	5	1	2	3	4	5
Load machine	0.32	0.29	0.28	0.31	0.30	0.30	0.27	0.25	0.22	0.21
Machine time (machine paced)	2.73	2.61	2.68	2.71	2.63	2.62	2.57	2.59	2.51	2.54
Unload machine	0.14	0.10	0.09	0.12	0.11	0.12	0.09	0.10	0.11	0.09
Inspect product	1.21	1.08	1.29	1.15	1.20	0.92	0.94	0.86	0.79	0.87
Apply label to product[a]	—	—	—	—	—	0.05	0.04	0.05	0.05	0.04

[a]Label application is automatic for A and manual for B.

The time study expert rated the operator as performing at 115 percent of normal on equipment A and 110 percent of normal on B during the observation cycles. It is estimated that operators will receive two 15-minute coffee breaks daily. Unavoidable delays are estimated to be 40 minutes for A and 25 minutes for B during an 8-hour day. Evaluate the two alternatives and justify your recommendation of A or B.

14. A post office mail room receives mail and cancels the postage stamps. After the application of appropriate work simplification techniques, you take a direct time study of the simplified job and obtain the following elemental times in minutes:

	Job Element	Cycle 1	2	3	4	5
Empty mail bags	1	.16	.31	.14	.15	.16
Straighten mail	2	.60	.60	.60	.60	.60
Carry trays to reader	3	.34	.36	.35	.37	.38
Cancellation machine	4	.50	.50	.50	.50	.50
Empty trays	5	.24	.24	.48	.27	.25

You further determine the following information about this job:

(1) Job elements 2 and 4 are machine-controlled and cannot be speeded up by the operator.
(2) You observed two irregular occurrences while timing the job. These are the elemental times, which vary from the average of all readings by more than 20 percent of each element's average.
(3) You rated the operator at 120 percent when he was working.
(4) Management and the worker's union have negotiated the following allowances for this job:
   Personal—30 minutes/day
   Unavoidable delay—40 minutes/day
   Fatigue—10 percent of the normal time
(5) An operator on this job earns $5/hour.
(6) Material cost per unit is $.50.
(7) Total overhead cost is added in at a rate of 150 percent of the sum of direct labor and material cost.

(a) How many pieces should each operator produce during an eight-hour shift?
(b) What is the total standard cost per piece?

15. Assume you, as a bank officer, have your bank tellers count out $100 in denominations of six $10 bills, seven $5 bills, and five $1 bills. The purpose of this operation is to supply your bank's night teller IV service with this bankpack. Suppose a continuous stopwatch time study yielded the following data:

Element	Cycle (minutes, cumulative) 1	2	3	4	5	6	7	8	Peformance Rating (%)
(1) Count 6—$10	.12	.66	1.24	1.95	3.26	3.91	4.52	5.05	110
(2) Count 7—$5	.27	.84	1.40	2.12	3.41	4.08	4.66	5.21	115
(3) Count 5—$1	.38	.96	1.51	2.20	3.52	4.18	4.74	5.29	105
(4) Count $100	.56	1.09	1.80	2.41	3.80[a]	4.36	4.94	5.48	110
(5) Place stocks in chute[b]	—	—	—	3.13	—	—	—	—	90

[a]Teller had to recount because of error.
[b]Occurs about once every ten cycles.

The allowances for this job are set at 15 percent of the workday (eight hours).

(a) What is the normal time for this job?
(b) What is the standard time for this job?
(c) What is the standard output in terms of $100 bundles/hour?
(d) How long (in terms of work hours) would it take to package 500 packs, if the tellers assigned to the job worked at a 115 percent pace on the average?

GLOSSARY

Activity chart Divides operations into major task segments performed by workers and machines; times them to determine idle and productive times; appropriate for routine, repetitive tasks with worker-machine interaction.

Direct time study A work measurement technique that involves observing the job, determining the job cycle, stopwatch timing the job cycle, and computing a performance standard.

Flow process chart Analyzes interstation activities to capture the flows of products through the overall production process.

Gang process chart Traces interaction of several workers and one machine.

Job Group of related tasks or activities that need to be performed to meet organizational objectives.

Job design Specifies the content of each job and determines the distribution of work within the organization.

Job enlargement Procedure of redesigning jobs or modifying work content to provide greater stimulus variety, autonomy, task identity, and feedback for the worker.

Job enrichment Procedure of redesigning work content to give more meaning and enjoyment to the job by involving employees in planning, organizing, and controlling their work.

Job rotation Movement of employees into a job for a short period of time and then out again.

Operation chart Analyzes and separates the motions of the right and left hands to determine how much time is taken by each hand for a job; appropriate for routine, repetitive, short cycle tasks.

OSHA Williams-Steiger Occupational Safety and Health Act of 1970; develops standards, penalties and enforcement procedures for job-related safety and health.

Predetermined time study A work measurement technique that involves observing or thinking through a job, recording job elements, recording preestablished motion units, and computing a performance standard.

Principles of motion economy General statements focusing on work arrangements, the use of human hands and body, and the use of tools.

Standard A criterion established as a basis for comparison in measuring or judging output.

Work measurement The determination of the degree and quantity of labor in product tasks.

Work sampling Work measurement technique that involves defining the condition "working," sampling the activity over time, and computing proportion of time the worker is engaged in "work."

SELECTED READINGS

Aldag, Raymond J., and Arthur P. Brief, *Task Design and Employee Motivation.* Glenview, Ill.: Scott, Foresman, 1979.

Barnes, Frank C., "Principles of Motion Economy: Revisited, Reviewed, and Restored," *Proceedings Southern Management Association.* Atlanta, Ga., 1983, pp. 297–99.

Barnes, R. M., *Motion and Time Study: Design and Measurement of Work* (6th ed.). New York: John Wiley, 1968.

Nadler, Gerald, *Work Design: A Systems Concept* (rev. ed.). Homewood, Ill.: Richard D. Irwin, 1970.

Pierce, Jon L., and Randall B. Dunham, "Task Design: A Literature Review," *The Academy of Management Review* 1, no. 4 (October 1976), 83–97.

Rice, Robert S., "Survey of Work Measurement and Wage Incentives," *Industrial Engineering* 9, no. 7 (July 1977), 18–31.

Szilagyi, Andrew S., Jr., and Marc J. Wallace, Jr., *Organizational Behavior and Performance* (2nd ed.). Santa Monica, Calif.: Goodyear Publishing Co., 1980.

U.S. Department of Labor, Occupational Health and Safety Administration, *All About OSHA.* OSHA publication No. 2056.

9

Project Management

In Prentice Hall's college production department, our products are books, complicated books, books headed for the college market. Each book is a "project" which appears on the production editor's desk as a large pile of manuscript pages, a combination of typed copy, tear sheet copy of art and text from previous editions, figures drafted by the author, other illustrations, and front and back matter material. These disparate elements are sent off in different directions for various treatments and must appear bound within covers and ready for sale approximately ten months later.

Planning for the production of a college text involves decisions about the book's specifications (size, color, paper, covers); design (complexity and level, typefaces, art); permissions (where and in what languages the book will sell); composition (setting the type); printing, and binding. Scheduling involves overlapping time frames so that some tasks can be done at the same time (editing and establishing costs, for example), while other tasks that depend on prior events occur later (paging and indexing, for example); and the schedule must end at a time advantageous to sales. Planning and scheduling for a specific book take place at a launch meeting, where activities are identified, the sequencing is established, and a time is set for each activity within the overall ten-month limit. The book's advance through the schedule is recorded and adjustments made as necessary. The production editor at Prentice Hall is able to carry a considerable number of books at the same time, very efficiently, thanks to the production schedule.

Susan J. Fisher
College Book Editorial Production
Prentice Hall
Englewood Cliffs, New Jersey

PROJECT PLANNING

Project Defined

Ms. Fisher's commentary emphasizes a project orientation for creating and launching Prentice Hall's new products into the marketplace. The production editor plans, organizes, and controls the progress of each project (book) according to its unique production requirements. Project management in this environment is a way of life that calls for the coordination of numerous and diverse activities that are all interrelated. Project planning and scheduling are involved, and these require certain technical and behavioral considerations.

A project is a one-shot set of activities with a definite beginning and ending point. The activities must be done in a particular order (they have precedence relationships). The key concept that differentiates project planning from other key types of planning and scheduling is that each project is a unique entity with a one-time occurrence.

EXAMPLE Gordon's Department Store has an annual employees' picnic in June. The picnic has been set for Sunday, June 14, and will begin at 4:00 P.M. and end at 9:00 P.M. Activities that must be planned for this project include publicity; providing ice cream, soft drinks, games, and prizes; arranging for a potluck meal; obtaining a facility (location); and coordinating the evening's activities.

Project Planning and Scheduling

Project planning includes all activities that result in developing a course of action about a specific project. *Goals* for the project, including resources to be committed, completion times, and results, must be set and their priorities established. Actual work responsibilities must be identified and assigned. Time estimates and resources required to perform the work activities must be *forecast* and *budgeted.*

Project *scheduling,* in contrast to project *planning,* is more specific. Scheduling establishes times for the various phases of the project. In project scheduling, the manager considers the many activities of an overall project and the tasks that must be accomplished and relates them coherently to one another and to the calendar.

EXAMPLE Slick Wilson, a first-semester freshman at State, is receiving advice from his sophomore roommate on how to study for finals, which start in two weeks. Slick, who has ignored the entire problem until now, is advised to list all his courses and estimate how much time he needs to study for the final in each course. Next, Slick's roommate suggests that he should look in the final exam schedule. When he has determined the order in which he must take his finals, Slick should study for the first one first, the second one next, and so on until he has prepared for all his exams. Slick follows this advice, and he decides that upon completion of the last final, he will throw the schedule away and forget about finals, school, and his introduction to project scheduling.

The *project* in this example is to study for finals. The *beginning point* is now, two weeks before his first final. The *ending point* is clear: When Slick steps in to take the last final. The project *activities* are studying for various courses. These activities must be *time sequenced against one another,* so that Slick can be prepared for his finals in the order he has to take them, and they also have to be *time sequenced against a calendar.* Viewing final exam preparation as a project, you might use project management to improve the scheduling of your study time at the end of this semester.

PROJECT SCHEDULING MODELS

There are various methods for scheduling projects. In this section we look at two simple project scheduling models—Gantt charting and the Program Evaluation and Review Technique (PERT). Both are schematic models, but PERT also has some mathematical model adaptations.

Gantt Charts

A *Gantt chart* is a bar chart that shows the relationship of activities over time. Project activities are listed down the page and time across the page.

Figure 9.1 shows a Gantt chart developed for a student preparing for final exams. The project activities are studying for exams in English, history, math and psychology. Math is broken into two subactivities —studying new concepts since the last exam and studying material on exams one and two for review. By examining the horizontal time axis, we see that all activities must be completed in three and one-half weeks.

Table 9.1 shows some common Gantt chart symbols. An open bracket indicates the scheduled start of the activity, and a closing bracket indicates the scheduled completion. Studying English 1, for example, is scheduled to start at the beginning of week 1 and end after one and one-half weeks. The heavy line indicates the currently completed portion of the activity. For English 1, one of the one and a half weeks of studying has been completed. Finally, the caret at the top of the chart indicates current time

Table 9.1 Gantt chart symbols

Symbol	Symbol Meaning
[	Start of an activity
]	End of an activity
[——]	Actual progress of the activity
v	Point in time where the project is now

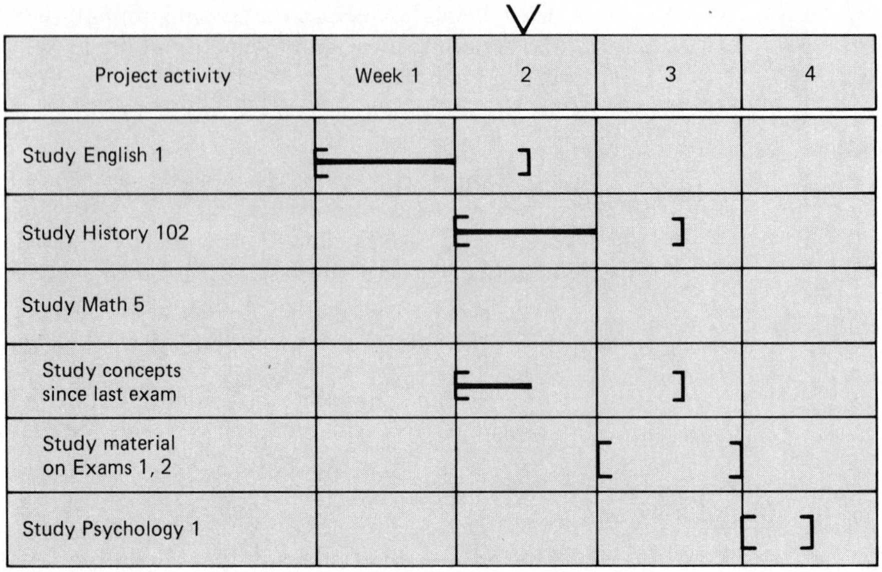

Project activity	Week 1	2	3	4
Study English 1				
Study History 102				
Study Math 5				
Study concepts since last exam				
Study material on Exams 1, 2				
Study Psychology 1				

FIGURE 9.1
Gantt chart for project scheduling

on the time scale (one and one-half weeks after starting). Students can use this chart to visualize their progress and to adjust their study activities.

One of the strengths of project scheduling with Gantt charts is the simplicity of the schematic model. In the construction example below, contractors, foremen, and company management could readily read and understand the model.

EXAMPLE A new manufacturing facility, which required a large expenditure in plant and equipment, was built in Kentucky. The general contractor had had previous project experience, but the largest of his projects had been about half this size. He had never used formal scheduling techniques. To help him, the company representative drew up Gantt charts. These charts included both an overview chart listing major general and subcontractor activities and more detailed charts for critical activities from the overview chart. The charts forced the general contractor to plan in a way he hadn't done before. Later, the company representative saw him using the charts to communicate with his foremen and subcontractors.

The Gantt charts were also valuable for the company representative, a recent business school graduate. The process of constructing the chart provided an understanding of project activities, their precedence relationships, and how in real time the project would be completed by the target date. The charts were a critical model for subsequent project control.

Network Modeling

Network modeling allows us to address project scheduling a little more formally than we can with the Gantt chart. Although network models are based on rigorous theory and precise definitions, we discuss only a few terms and concepts here.

Figure 9.2 illustrates the essential features for network modeling. A *node* is a circle on the graph that designates the beginning and/or ending of an arc; there are six nodes in Figure 9.2. An *arc* is the arrow that begins at one node and ends at another; arcs in Figure 9.2 are 1–2, 1–3, 2–4, 2–5, 4–6, 5–6, and 3–6. On an arc, the arrowhead defines direction; the head is at the ending point. Arc 1–2, for example, begins at node 1 and is completed at node 2. By convention, the diagram is constructed to flow generally from left to right, but arrow *length* is of no significance.

The purpose of the diagram is to depict precedence relationships among the arcs. *Precedence* is indicated at each node; all arc arrowheads (which lead into the node) must be completed before new arcs may begin (before an arrow from the node can begin). In Figure 9.2, for example, arc 1–2 precedes arcs 2–4 and 2–5 but does not precede arc 1–3. Arcs 1–2 and 1–3 are parallel arcs with no precedence relationship.

Program Evaluation and Review Technique (PERT)

Development of PERT Program Evaluation and Review Technique (PERT) was developed for the U.S. Navy in 1958 for planning and control of the Polaris project. The results of using PERT in that application, in which some 3,000 contractors were involved, is generally reported to have reduced by two years the project completion time for the Polaris nuclear submarine project. In both government and industry today, PERT is widely used.

A similar modeling approach called the *Critical Path Method* (CPM) is also used by business and government. Since CPM and PERT are nearly equivalent, we will concentrate on only one of the two, PERT.[1]

[1]Computer software programs available for network analysis are presented in Larry A. Smith and Joan Mills, "Project Management Network Programs," *Project Management Quarterly*, June 1982, 18–29.

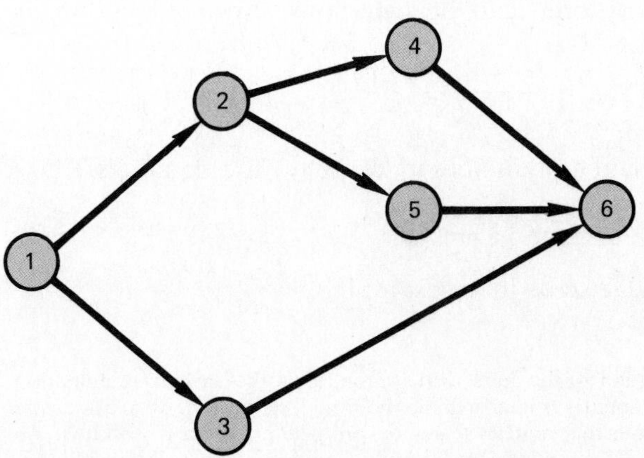

FIGURE 9.2
Network of nodes and arcs

Application of PERT First we should clarify when PERT may be used. If your situation lacks the following features, PERT application will have little benefit. First, the scheduling problem must be a project with identifiable activities. Second, the project and activities must all have clear starting and ending points. Third, PERT is most beneficial for projects that are complicated by having many interrelated tasks. Fourth, PERT is good for projects with alternative possible arrangements and sequences of activities and time durations.

The Language of PERT Basically, the PERT language is a vocabulary of simple symbols and terms. As described in Table 9.2, key symbols include the *activity* designation, the *event* designation, and the *critical path.* Since the critical path requires the longest time through the network, management should watch it most closely to avoid unnecessary project delays.

Logic of PERT How does PERT work? It works by following these steps:

1. All activities in the project must be clearly identified.
2. The sequencing requirements among activities must be designated.
3. A diagram reflecting the sequence relationships must be constructed. (See Table 9.3 for typical sequence relationships.)
4. Time estimates for each activity must be obtained.
5. The network is evaluated by calculating the critical path and other project performance data. The evaluation creates the schedule and plan for subsequent control.
6. As time passes and actual experience is recorded, the schedule is revised and reevaluated.

Time estimates are obtained from either past data or the experience of those responsible for completing a particular activity. Optimistic (t_o), pessimistic (t_p), and most likely (t_m) times must be estimated so that the expected (average) activity time can be calculated from the following equation:[2]

$$t_e = \frac{(t_o + 4t_m + t_p)}{6} \tag{9.1}$$

To calculate the variance of an activity time, we use equation 9.2.

$$\sigma_e^2 = \left(\frac{t_p - t_o}{6}\right)^2 \tag{9.2}$$

Let's use the five PERT steps in an example.

[2]Equation 9.1 is an approximation of the Beta distribution, as is the variance calculation discussed next. Although these equations approximate the Beta distribution, we are unaware of empirical evidence suggesting that activity times on projects are Beta distributed. We accept these formulas based on practices and intuitive appeal, rather than evidence concerning the actual distribution of activity times.

Table 9.2 **PERT glossary**

Symbol	Term	Meaning
	PERT	Program Evaluation and Review Technique
→	Activity	A work component needed to be accomplished; a task within the overall project that has a definite beginning and ending point. The activity consumes time. The length of the arrow representing the activity has no meaning.
○	Event	A node in the network that designates the beginning and/or ending of activities. A point in time.
○→○	Network	Combination of nodes and arcs that describes the logic of the project. There is one definite starting and ending point for the entire project.
	Critical path	The path through the network consisting of several activities whose total activity times are the longest of any path through the network. The most pressing, dangerous, risky path through the network. Usually denoted by heavy lines or dashed lines through the activities on that path.
	Critical path time	Total time of all activities on the critical path.
t_e	Expected time of an activity	Expected completion time of an activity. The time estimate with a 50-50 chance of being over- or underachieved. The mean time for the activity.
t_o	Optimistic time	Time estimate for fast activity completion. There is very little chance (for example, 1 in 100) of completing the activity in less than that time. Will occur only under rare favorable conditions.
t_p	Pessimistic time	Estimated time in which there is very little chance (for example, 1 in 100) of completing the activity in more than that time. Will occur only under rare unfavorable conditions.
t_m	Most likely time	Estimated time that is the single best guess for activity completion. The "mode" of the distribution of activity times; the most likely time.
T_E	Earliest expected time	Summation of t_e times up to that event. Calculated at an event. Earliest time expected to complete all previous activities.
T_L	Latest allowable time	Latest time an activity can be started that still allows the project to be completed on time. Calculated at an event that designates the start of an activity.
T_s	Slack time	Difference between T_E and T_L; the amount of freedom or latitude available in deciding when to start an activity without jeopardizing the timely completion of the overall project. $T_s = T_L - T_E$.
-	Dummy activity	A fictitious activity with no actual time. Necessary occasionally to preserve network logic.

EXAMPLE *The Long-Term Care situation.* Long-Term Care, Inc., is a Professional II nursing home aspiring to become a Professional I nursing home. It wants to provide the ultimate in nursing care for patients, but because of recent federal regulations it will need a new, specially designed facility. The administrator at Long-Term Care, Inc., has been so busy with current operations that she has not had time to generate an overall project schedule.

The first thing the administrator must do is to identify all activities. The administrator prepares the following list of long-term care activities:

A. Perform pilot services for six patients in new facility.
B. Build the facility.
C. Install all equipment and furnishings.
D. Recruit nursing home staff.
E. Train nursing home staff.
F. Pass safety inspection of Municipal Building Authority.

Table 9.3 Precedence relationships in PERT

Network	Meaning
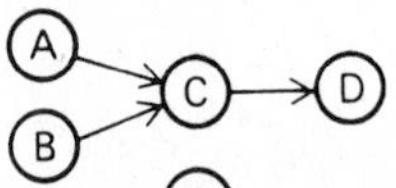	Represents activities AB, BC, and CD, where activity CD may not begin until both AC and BC have been completed. Activities AC and BC may occur concurrently and are called *parallel activities.*
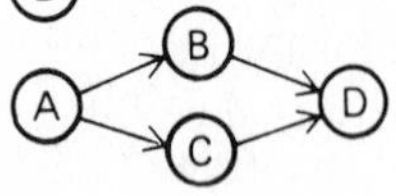	BD may not begin until AB is completed. CD may not begin until AC is completed. AB–BD and AC–CD are *parallel paths.* However, AC does not have to begin at the same instant that AB begins, although it *may.* Similarly, BD does not have to be completed at the same instant that CD is completed, although it may. Similarly, BD may be completed before AC is completed.
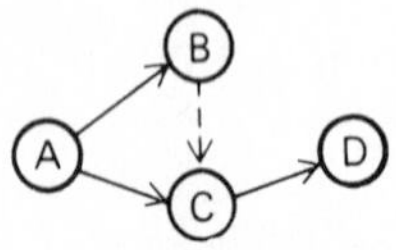 OR 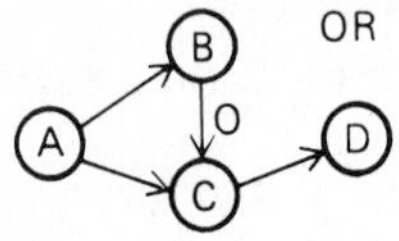	BC is a *"dummy"* activity, used when necessary to preserve the logic of the network. It may be represented in two ways, as shown. A dummy activity requires no time. The use of a dummy allows all activities to have unique identities. Activity CD cannot begin until activities AB and AC are completed. This network has two paths: AB–BC–CD and AC–CD.

Are these activities in the proper sequence? Suppose, as consultants, we encourage the administrator to establish clear precedence relationships. After some thought she identifies the necessary sequence of activities as shown in Table 9.4.

Table 9.4 Long-Term Care sequencing of activities

Activity	Predecessors' Activity	Time Estimates (weeks) t_o	t_m	t_p
B. Build facility	None	20	24	30
F. Safety inspection	B	2	3	4
C. Install equipment	B	8	16	20
D. Recruit staff	None	2	2	3
E. Train staff	D	4	5	6
A. Perform pilot	C, E, F	4	5	9

Figure 9.3 accomplishes step 3 of PERT—diagramming the sequence relationships. Then an arbitrary coding scheme was adopted to create node identification numbers. Note that there must be a node to *begin* (node 10) and to *end* (node 60) the project.

A dummy activity is required in the diagram because activity A, which also can be called activity 50–60, must be preceded by activities E, C, and F. The only way we can logically arrange those precedents and have unique arc identities is to use the dummy activity, 40–50. Look at node 50. Before activity 50–60 can begin from the node, activities 20–50, 30–50, and 40–50 must be completed. If we didn't use the dummy, activities C and F would both begin at node 20 and end at node 50; they would not have unique identities.

Our next step is to get the administrator to establish time estimates for each activity. Where can she find these times? She can ask building contractors, equipment manufacturers, and her own staff for their estimates of recruitment, training, and pilot program times. Time estimates are provided above.

Next we perform step 5, finding the critical path, critical path time, and slack times. First we must calculate, using equation 9.1, the expected time, t_e, for each activity. For activity 10–20 (activity B), this calculation is as follows:

$$t_e = \frac{(t_o + 4t_m + t_p)}{6}$$

$$= \frac{[20 + 4(24) + 30]}{6} = 24.3 \text{ weeks}$$

Similar calculations are made for each activity, and the expected times are shown next to the arrows in Figure 9.4.

Which of the paths is the longest through the network? There are three paths: 10–20–40–50–60, 10–20–50–60, and 10–30–50–60. The total expected time for the first path is (24.3 + 3.0 + 0 + 5.5), or 32.8 weeks; for the second path (24.3 + 15.3 + 5.5), 45.1 weeks; and for the third path (2.1 + 5.0 + 5.5), 12.6 weeks. Therefore, the critical path is 10–20–50–60, and the critical path time is 45.1 weeks. In Figure 9.4, we have shown the critical path on the PERT diagram.

Figure 9.4 also shows the earliest expected times (T_E) and latest allowable times (T_L) *at each event,* allowing us to calculate the *event slack,* the extra time available at each event if we arrive as soon as possible and

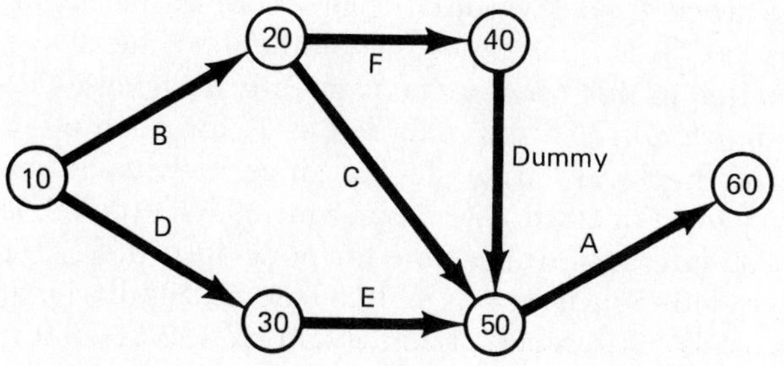

FIGURE 9.3
PERT diagram for Long-Term Care, Inc.

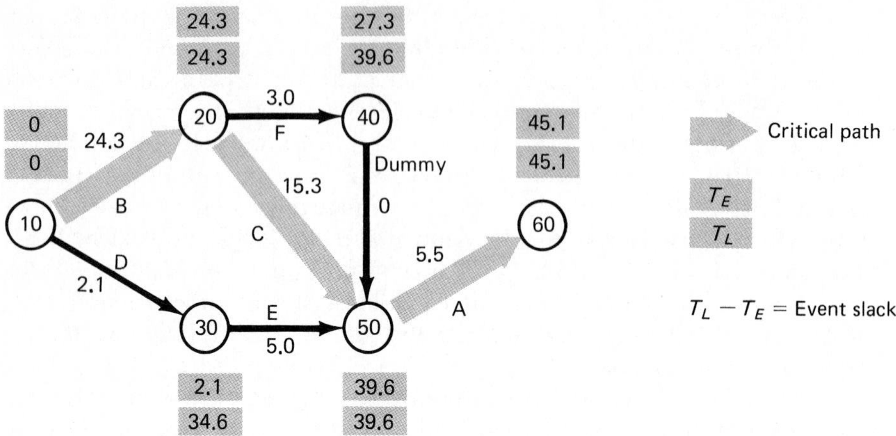

FIGURE 9.4
Critical path and event slacks for Long-Term Care, Inc.

leave as late as possible and still be able to finish the Professional I nursing home facility on time. First we calculate the earliest expected time (T_E) for each node in the network beginning with node 10. To calculate T_E for a node, calculate the sum of all previous t_e values up to that node on that path. T_E for node 10, set for convenience to time zero, occurs when the project starts. At node 20, T_E is equal to the preceding T_E plus the t_e of activity 10–20 (24.3 weeks). Thus, T_E at node 20 is (0 + 24.3), or 24.3. At node 40, T_E is 27.3 weeks, the sum of all t_e values for activities 10–20 and 20–40. Alternatively, T_E at node 40 is the sum of T_E at node 20 and the t_e of activity 20–40, or (24.3 + 3.0). Notice that T_E at event 50 is 39.6. The sum of all t_e values for the path 10–20–40–50 is 27.3, and the sum of t_e values for path 10–30–50, an alternative way to get to event 50, is 7.1. The sum of t_e values for the other alternate path, 10–20–50, is 39.6. Since T_E represents the earliest expected completion time of *all* activities up to that node, it must be 39.6 weeks until we arrive at event 50, rather than 7.1 or 27.3 weeks. Continuing in this manner, T_E for event 60 is 45.1 weeks, the earliest expected completion time for the entire project. As we have shown, T_E calculations begin at the front end (the source) of the network and continue on through until all T_E values for the entire network have been determined.

The reverse procedure is used for the T_L calculations. We begin at the end of the network and proceed backward, node by node, to the beginning. First consider node 60. Its earliest expected completion time is 45.1 weeks. If it can be completed in that time, we conveniently designate 45.1 as the *latest permissible finish time*. This is recorded as T_L for node 60 in Figure 9.4. Next we work backward to node 50. Since activity 50–60 requires 5.5 days, event 50 must occur no later than time 39.6 if event 60 is to occur by time 45.1. The latest allowable time for node 40 is the T_L for node 50 less t_e for activity 40–50 (39.6 − 0 = 39.6 weeks). Similarly, at node 30, T_L equals T_L at node 50 minus t_e of activity 30–50 (39.6 − 5.0 =

34.6 weeks). T_L for node 20 requires special consideration; two activities must be considered, 20–40 and 20–50. First let's consider activity 20–40. T_L for node 20 equals T_L for node 40 minus t_e of activity 20–40 (39.6 − 3.0 = 36.6 weeks). Next, for activity 20–50, T_L for node 20 equals T_L for node 50 minus t_e of activity 20–50 (39.6 − 15.3 = 24.3 weeks). The *smaller* of these two T_L choices for node 20 is selected. Thus, T_L for node 20 is 24.3 weeks. Had we chosen T_L of 36.6, event 50 could not occur by its latest permissible time of 39.6. Following the same logic, we find T_L for node 10 is zero.

Now we can calculate the event slack, which is $T_L - T_E$ for each event. If we look at Figure 9.4, we see that event slack is zero for most events. Event 30, however, has slack of 34.6 − 2.1 = 32.5 weeks, and event 40 has slack of 39.6 − 27.3 = 12.3 weeks. Why does slack equal zero at events 10, 20, 50, and 60? *Because slack will always be zero on the critical path.* This is why that path is critical; there is no "fool-around," or slack time.

We may recruit workers for activity 10–30 as soon as we start the building (10–20). If we start then, in 2.1 weeks we can expect to be finished recruiting workers. What is the very latest we need to start training the workers for activity 30–50? We must have the project completed in 45.1 weeks less 5.5 weeks for pilot runs and 5.0 weeks for training. Therefore, we must begin training no later than at 45.1 − 5.5 − 5.0 = 34.6 weeks. *The slack time at event 30 is therefore the difference between latest start and earliest start* (34.6 − 2.1 = 32.5 weeks). Since management attention and resources may be shifted to the critical path from paths that have a good bit of slack, this is an important concept.

Time/Cost Tradeoffs Managers often want to reduce critical path times, even if it costs extra money to make the reductions. PERT/cost procedures can be used to reduce critical path times. Although we won't discuss these formal methods here, we consider basic time/cost tradeoff concepts.

Projects contain two kinds of time-related costs: *Indirect project costs* include overhead, facilities, and resource opportunity costs that can be eliminated if the project is shortened. Monthly overhead costs of maintaining a house trailer at a construction site, for example, might be $1,100 per month for heat, light, telephone, clerical help, and other *indirect* construction costs. A second kind of cost is the *activity direct cost* associated with expediting (speeding up) the project. These expediting costs include overtime work, hiring extra labor, retaining an expeditor, long-distance telephone calls, and leasing more equipment.

The essence of the time/cost tradeoff is allocating resources (spending money) to reduce project time only to the point where further direct cost expenditures equal indirect project cost savings. Beyond this point, the cost of expediting exceeds the benefit of reduced indirect project costs. The procedure for such an analysis in PERT is straightforward:

1. *Obtain cost estimates.* For each activity, determine indirect project costs and expediting costs per time period ($/day, $/week).

2. *Determine crash times.* For each activity, find the shortest possible activity time.
3. *Identify activities on the critical path.*
4. *Evaluate the PERT network.* Reduce the critical path (CP) activity times by observing these restrictions: Begin expediting the CP activity with the least expediting cost, continuing to the second least costly, and so on to the most costly, or until one of the following occurs:
   (a) The target expedited time has been reached.
   (b) The resources for expediting ($) have been exhausted.
   (c) The indirect project costs are less than the expediting costs for each activity on the critical path.

In this procedure, you must be careful to keep an eye on the critical path. As the original path is reduced, other paths may also become critical. Should two or more paths have to be expedited simultaneously, the procedure may become too costly. We look at an example to illustrate this procedure.

EXAMPLE The facilities manager of Home State Insurance Company's new office wing finds that the air conditioning unit is not functioning after the normal May trial. The compressor is out and the fan is out because the system was improperly wired. After much discussion, the general contractor has agreed to replace the whole system. Of course, the manager wants to know how quickly the job can be done. He has collected data as summarized in Table 9.5.

The manager has decided to construct a PERT diagram to assist in planning the work by finding the critical path and critical path time. He also intends to spend $400 expediting if it is economical to do so.

The facilities manager is experienced in PERT diagramming and constructs the diagram in Figure 9.5. The critical path is comprised of activities A, D, G, H, and I with a critical path time of 19 days. Steps 1 through 3 have been completed in our cost/tradeoff analysis.

To reduce the critical path time according to step 4–1, the manager can expedite only activities A at $50/day for possibly 1 day and G at $120/day for 4 possible days. Activity A is reduced for 1 day at a cost of $50. The critical path has still not changed, but project completion time has been reduced to 18 days. G is reduced by 2 days at a cost of $240. Now two paths become critical: path 1–2–5–6–7–8 and path 1–2–4–6–7–8. Up to this point, project completion time has been reduced to 16 days. The manager has spent a total of $50 + $120 + $120, or $290 of the $400 allowable for expediting. To reduce one more day, he must spend $120 on G and $80 on F (the cheaper of C and F) simultaneously. Therefore, to take the fourth day from the project, he must spend an additional $120 + $80, or $200. He cannot do so, since total expenditure would exceed the $400 budget limit.

Table 9.5 Home State Insurance Company data

Activity	Immediate Predecessor(s)	Expected Duration (t_e)(days)	Standard Deviation (σ_e)(days)	Minimum Duration (crash time) (days)	Cost/Day Expedite
A. Place order	—	3	1	2	$ 50
B. Pull old compressor	A	4	0	2	100
C. Remove old fan	A	6	0	4	200
D. Build new unit	A	4	3	4	—
E. Remove old unit	B	5	5	2	400
F. Modify duct work	C	3	2	2	80
G. Ship new unit	D	7	1	3	120
H. Install new unit	F, G	3	2	3	—
I. Start up new unit	E, H	2	1	2	—

Probabilistic PERT PERT can be used to estimate the probability of completing a project within some desired length of time. We do this by considering the variance (σ_e^2) as well as the mean (t_e) of the activity times. In using probabilistic PERT, we make the two assumptions that activity times are statistically independent and that project completion time is normally distributed. The independence assumption allows us to add the activity variances to obtain a total project variance. The normality assumption lets us use the normal distribution in our analysis.

The mean of the distribution of project completion time is the sum of the individual t_e values on the critical path; it is the expected critical path time. The total variance for the critical path is the sum of the individual critical path activity variances:

$$\sigma_{cp}^2 = \sum_{e=1}^{n} \sigma_e^2 \tag{9.3}$$

FIGURE 9.5
Home State Insurance Company PERT diagram

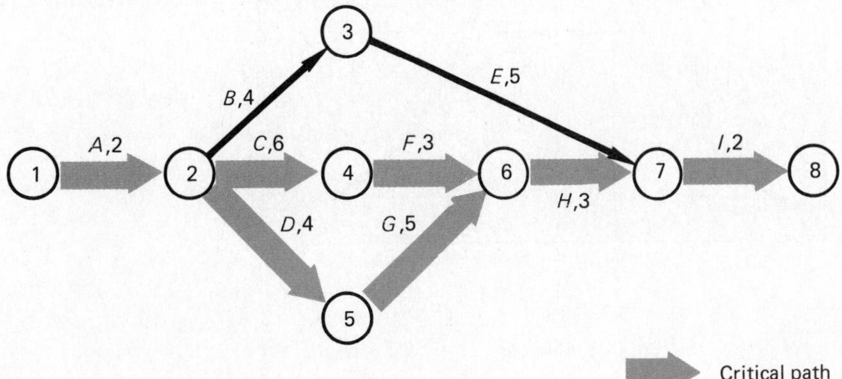

Consider the Home State Insurance Company example. In the data for Home State Insurance (Table 9.5), the standard deviations for the critical path activities were 1 for A, 3 for D, 1 for G, 2 for H, and 1 for I. From equation 9.3, we see the critical path variance (σ^2_{cp}) is:

$$\sigma^2_{cp} = \sum_{e=1}^{5} \sigma^2_e$$
$$= 1^2 + 3^2 + 1^2 + 2^2 + 1^2$$
$$= 16$$

The critical path probability distribution, then, has a mean (the critical path time) and standard deviation:

$$\mu_{cp} = 19 \qquad \sigma_{cp} = 4$$

Suppose now that the facilities manager wants the project to be completed by July 5, which is 16 days away. Using X to represent project completion time, he wants to find the probability

$$P(X \leq 16)$$

This is illustrated in Figure 9.6. We can find the standard deviate, Z, by

$$Z = \frac{X - \mu_{cp}}{\sigma_{cp}}$$
$$= \frac{16 - 19}{4} = -0.75$$

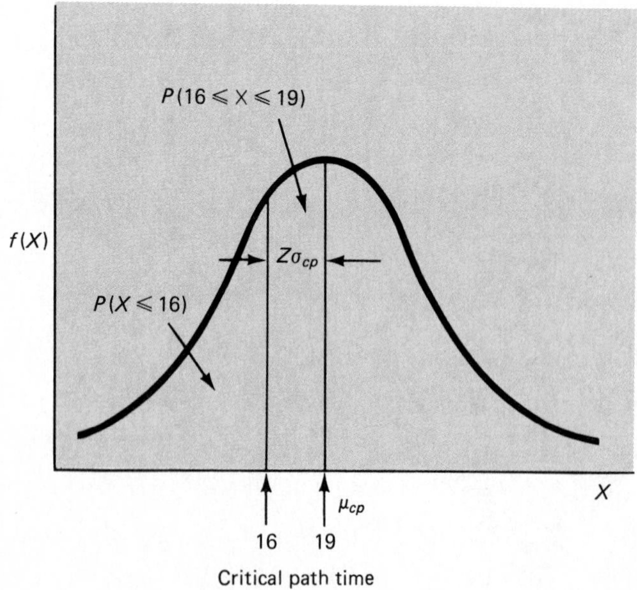

FIGURE 9.6
Critical path time and variance for Home State Insurance Company

In the normal table (Appendix Table A) in the appendices, we find for $Z = -0.75$ the corresponding probability of 0.2734, which is the $P(16 \leq X \leq 19)$. Subtracting from the mean,

$$P(X \leq 16) = 0.5000 - P(16 \leq X \leq 19)$$
$$= 0.5000 - 0.2734$$
$$= 0.2266$$

The chance of finishing the project by July 5 is only about 22.7 percent. The manager might now want either to expedite or to generate some contingency plan.

Limited Resources PERT assumes that there are sufficient resources available to complete simultaneously all activities that are scheduled. This is often not the case. If there are conflicts, limited amounts of labor, for example, some rule is needed to allocate resources among competing activities.[3] Although there are models for approaching this problem, we have observed some heuristics that are generally used in practice:

- Schedule the shortest activity first.
- Schedule the activity with the lowest variance (most certain) first.
- Schedule the jobs for a particular organization unit (division, department) first.
- Schedule the activity with the least amount of total slack first.

MANAGING THE PROJECT

Project management, unlike routine functions that are repeated, presents some special challenges that require somewhat different talents and a unique management style. Getting the project launched and overseeing its completion have both technical and behavioral dimensions as we see next.

Planning and Controlling the Project

In contrast to our previous examples, most major projects pose real challenges for their planning, progress monitoring, and control. Project management is assisted in these duties by two methodologies—work breakdown structures and progress reporting.

Work Breakdown Structure The *work breakdown structure* (WBS) is a methodology for converting a large-scale project into detailed schedules for its thousands of activities. The WBS is a level-by-level breakdown of project modules. The overall project is subdivided into major subcomponents that, in turn, are further subdivided into another lower level of more detailed subcomponent activities, and so on. Eventually, all the

[3]For a review of the limited resources case, see E. W. Davis, "Project Scheduling Under Resource Constraints—Historical Review and Categorization of Procedures," *AIIE Transactions* 5, no. 4 (December 1973), 297–313.

tasks for every activity are identified, commonalities of detailed activities are discovered, and unnecessary duplication of activities can be eliminated.

After the WBS is developed, it can be used to create segments of the network structure which, ultimately, are combined into the PERT network for the project. Let's examine the WBS methodology in an example.

EXAMPLE Long-Term Care, Inc. intends to expand into a new, specially designed facility. Now, however, the administrator wants a more realistic project analysis rather than the simplified preliminary analysis shown earlier. Consequently, the consultants developed a WBS that reveals several types and levels of activities that were omitted in the preliminary study of the project. Figure 9.7 shows selected portions of the WBS; only five of the level 3 activities are shown, and all activities below level 3 are omitted from the diagram. Some of the tasks for three of these activities are listed for future reference. In planning for level 2, some new activities were added that had been overlooked in the preliminary study—certification and long-term financing. At level 3, two special equipment needs were identified as were three different kinds of professional staff personnel.

The administrator used the WBS to create segments of the network structure. From level 3, for example, she identified linkages among the tasks for therapist procurement and the installation of the two special equipment systems. As Figure 9.8 shows, the cardio-stress analyzer (2) cannot be calibrated until the hydro-muscular bath (1) is installed because

FIGURE 9.7
Work breakdown structure for Long-Term Care project

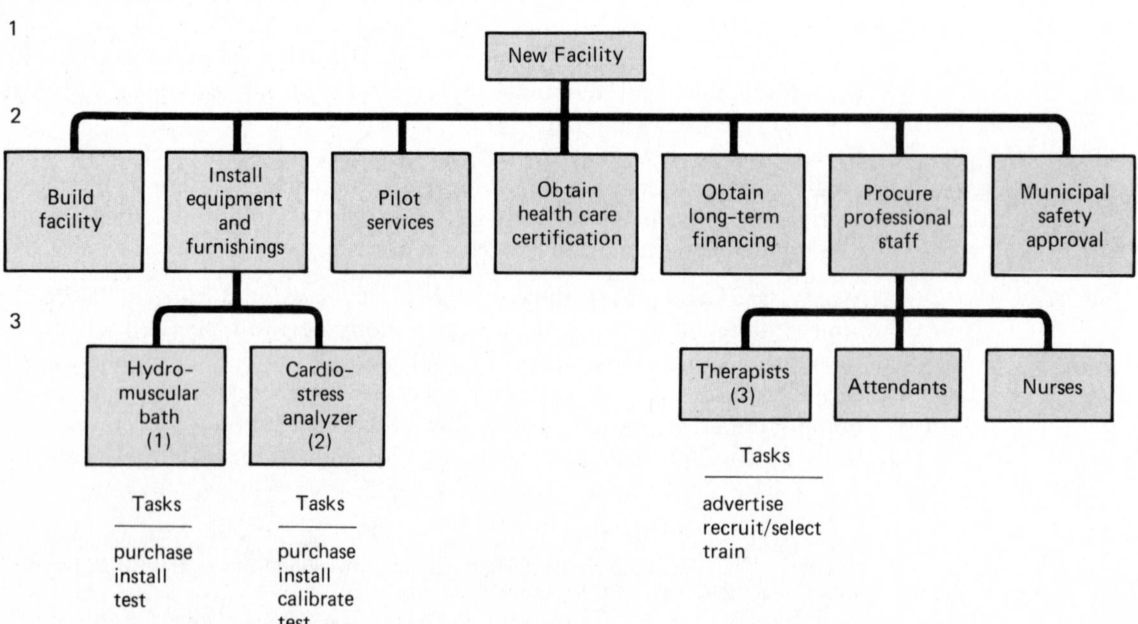

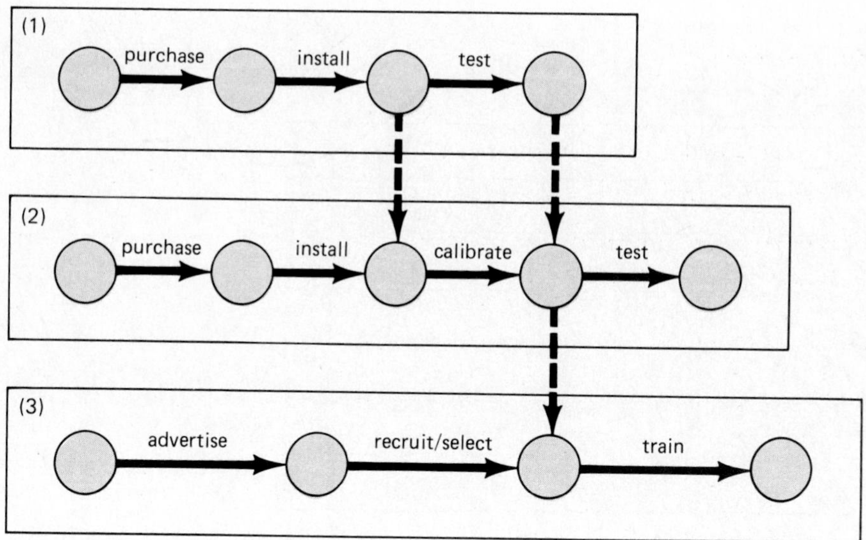

FIGURE 9.8
Creating network segments from work breakdown structures for Long-Term Care project

the two systems work together. Similarly, the analyzer (2) must be tested after the bath testing is completed. Although therapists (3) can be recruited earlier, their training cannot begin until the analyzer (2) is fully calibrated; therapist training in this instance is geared toward the special equipment in this facility.

By following the procedure in the example the administrator developed a complete PERT network (not shown) involving some 300 activities for the facility project. Start and finish dates for the activities were estimated along with their costs. From these data she developed project budgets which would enable her to monitor the project, stage by stage, as it progressed.

Progress Reporting Project management involves more than just planning; it also requires progress monitoring and taking corrective action when activities deviate from schedules or costs get out of line. Progress reporting assists in these control efforts by showing cost variances (actual versus budgeted) and time variances (actual versus scheduled) during the life of the project. Figure 9.9 shows how these time and cost variances can be consolidated into a visual progress report.

After the project began in January, the actual costs of work completed (ACWC) were tallied, month by month, into a cumulative total. As of the end of November (now), actual costs are $365,000 for all work completed. How do the actual costs compare with the budgeted costs for those same activities? The budgeted costs for work completed (BCWC) have been consistently lower than actual costs; cost overruns have been experienced.

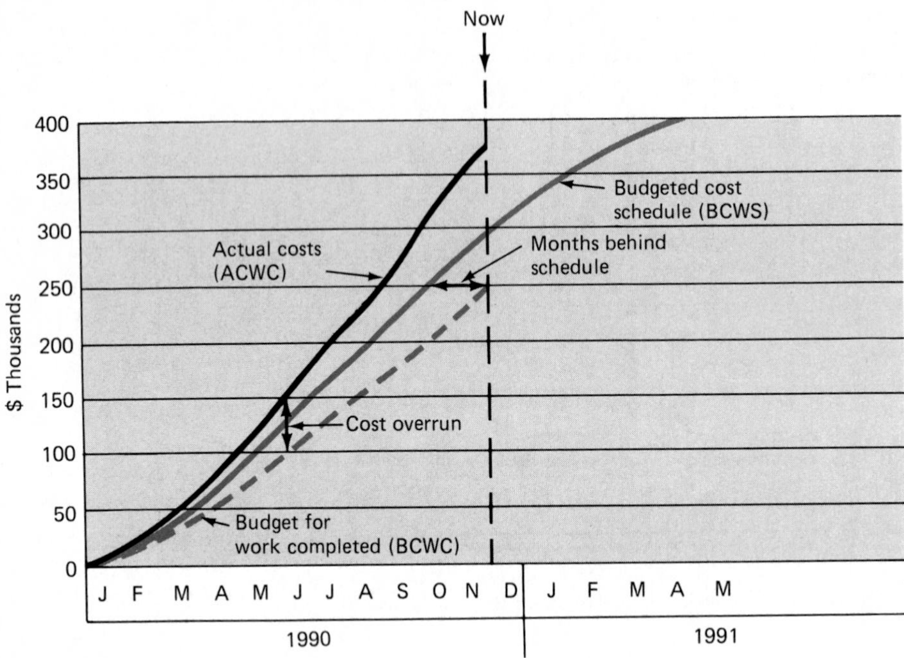

FIGURE 9.9
Progress report for a project

At the end of June, for example, the cumulative overrun for all work completed was about $60,000, as indicated by the vertical distance between the ACWC curve and the BCWC curve. Corrective action is needed to contain the high cost variance.

The progress report also shows the budgeted cost for work scheduled (BCWS) in the project. These are the time-phased expenditures that were budgeted when the project was planned. If the activities had progressed as planned, expenditures would have occurred as indicated by the BCWS curve. At the end of November, however, actual progress is lagging behind scheduled progress. The horizontal distance between the BCWS line and the BCWC line indicates the project is nearly two months behind schedule in terms of work completed versus work scheduled to date. Again, adjustments in work progress are required if the project is to be completed on schedule.

Behaviors in Implementation

Aside from the technical aspects of projects, their success usually depends on organizational abilities as well. Some adjustments of the organization's structure are commonplace, as are the behavioral adjustments of managers and subordinates in project settings.

Matrix Organization The matrix organization is a team approach to special projects. When the teams are established, the organization's structure departs from the conventional functional basis for departmentalization. Figure 9.10 illustrates a project organization using this matrix concept. In this example, the "home" departments of the various team members are functional: engineering, production, and marketing, depending upon what skills are required for the particular project. Thus the organization's structure becomes a matrix of functional areas (the horizontal dimension of the matrix) and projects (the vertical dimension).

Today, project teams enjoy widespread acceptance in many of our major industries. They are especially effective in large companies that emphasize new product development and rapid launching of new products in the marketplace.

Several factors seem to have been responsible for this trend toward project organization and project management. Rapid technological changes forced organizations to minimize development lead times, reduce costs, and avoid obsolescence. These pressures resulted in the need for a kind of organization that could cut across functional areas. The matrix (project) organization fills that need. Engineers, scientists, technicians, market specialists, and other skilled personnel can be effectively and efficiently loaned from their "home" organization unit into another unit for periods of time, thus avoiding duplicating skills and saving unnecessary costs to the organization.

Behaviors in a Project Environment

Project managers must not only be competent technically but must also be skilled in analysis, interpersonal relations, and decision making. Let's briefly examine a few key behaviors within project teams.

Communication Project leaders must be able to communicate freely with both team members and line employees who are not regular team members. Within the immediate project team, communication is frequent and often involves intensive collaboration. Short daily meetings, written

FIGURE 9.10
Matrix (project) organization chart

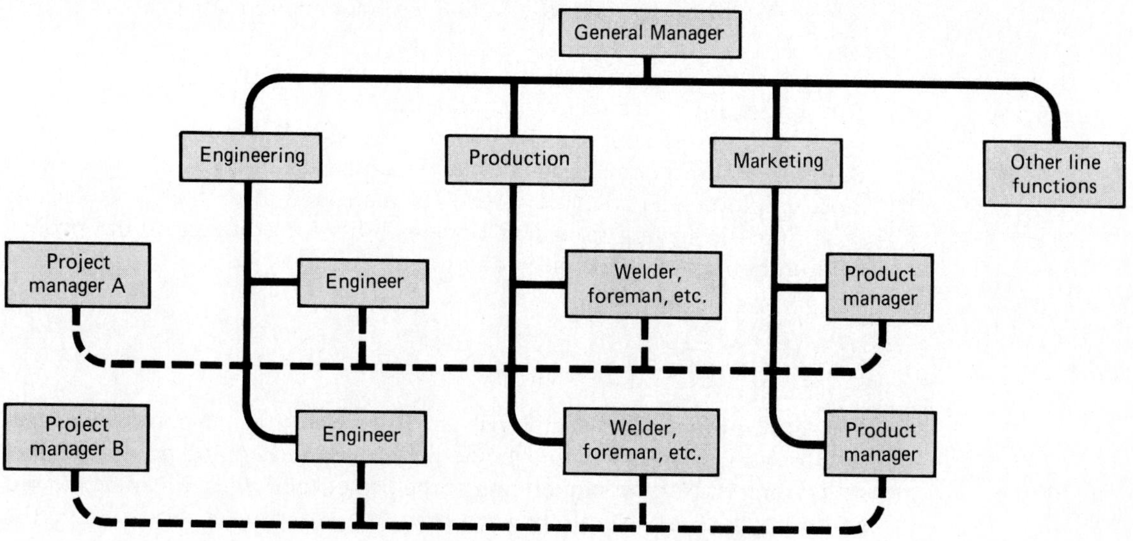

correspondence, and one-on-one problem-solving sessions are often necessary for the sorts of tasks required of project teams. The nonroutine, diverse, often ill-structured tasks that project teams engage in require flexible relationships and communication to avoid duplication of effort and costly project delays.

Motivation The several motivators that can be used by a project leader are not substantially different from those available to other managers. Key motivators can be either extrinsic or intrinsic rewards. One difficulty in project environments is that project managers may not have sufficient latitude to give monetary rewards to employees working on the project. They may be able, however, to see that monetary rewards such as incentives for cost control and completion time are given to full-time project team members. Many other teams rely more on intrinsic rewards for member satisfaction. These rewards include satisfaction from project tasks accomplished, pride in quality workmanship, pleasure from job flexibility, and pride in the team effort. All of these can be fostered and encouraged by managers in most projects.

Group Cohesiveness As the size of the project team and the overall group increases, group cohesiveness decreases. The higher a group ranks in organization status (measured by project importance, skills required, and job flexibility), the more cohesive the group tends to be. If group members' social, economic, or psychological needs are met by a group, they tend to feel strong ties to the group. The more a project team fills these needs, the more cohesive the team. Finally, management pressures for group members to work in close proximity to one another under stress conditions usually contribute to group cohesiveness.

Overall, the more cohesive the group, the better the chances a project can be completed on budget and on time. Because of both the diversity of team members and the one-shot nature of the project, group cohesiveness is difficult to obtain in project teams. But project teams that exhibit cohesiveness have an increased chance of achieving their primary goals.

Project Organization Advantages and Disadvantages

Perhaps the one overriding advantage of project organization is that by grouping people and tasks, the organization can tackle unusual project opportunities on short notice. There are disadvantages too, however. Building and dispersing project teams can be upsetting to the routine of most employees. Furthermore, project managers often feel considerable constraints in having to accept responsibility for completing the project without being given line authority to control it.

SUMMARY

Project planning includes all those activities resulting in a course of action for a one-shot venture with specific beginning and ending points. Project scheduling is the time sequencing of the project activities. It can be viewed as a subphase of overall project planning. In project scheduling, the activities of the project are identified and related to one another and to the calendar.

Techniques for project scheduling include Gantt charts and PERT analysis. Gantt charts are visual aids whose strength lies in their simplicity and ease of understanding. Program Evaluation and Review Technique (PERT) analysis is an application of basic network analysis. Activities, represented as network arcs, are related sequentially to one another and represented schematically. Such statistics as critical path time, critical path variance, and event slack are calculated to enhance the value of PERT analysis as a basis for project control. Other useful variations include cost/time tradeoff analysis and probabilistic PERT.

Planning for and monitoring the project is aided by work breakdown structures and progress reporting. Organizing, by creating a project-oriented organization, focuses on a matrix approach to grouping jobs. In a situation somewhat unique to projects, the project manager assumes responsibility for project goals without commensurate authority over line activities. Thus the project manager needs skills in communication, coordination, motivation, and maintaining a cohesive project work group.

CASE

Electran Manufacturing, Ltd.

Electran Manufacturing, Ltd., is a diversified manufacturer in two primary fields, electronic applications and transportation equipment. In the transportation field, Electran products are in the forefront of technological applications, especially in terms of electrical circuitry and component packages. Electran management takes great pride in its technological leadership and has decided to retain earnings to support a substantial research and development (R&D) effort.

Currently 74 persons are employed full-time in the R&D division, and at any one time at least twice that many more are involved to some degree in R&D projects. These employees are assigned primarily to line operations in such functional areas as engineering, finance, marketing, and production.

Electran organizes its R&D effort by functional area within the division. Engineers, scientists, and technicians are grouped separately. Additionally, within each of these technical specialties, employees are grouped and housed together. Electrical engineers, mechanical engineers, and metalurgical engineers, for example, are each grouped and located together. Projects rotate from group to group, depending upon what work needs to be accomplished. There is a department head for each of the engineering, science, and technical support areas, and three additional project managers have individual project responsibility. There is considerable pressure on project managers for project completion, but they have limited control over staff within the R&D division and even less control over the approximately 150 employees who assist in product development on an occasional basis. The R&D division manager has recently read a brief article about matrix organization. He wonders if matrix organization might be helpful in relieving some of the burden from his project managers and in enhancing division productivity.

One of the three project managers is trying to grasp the basis of PERT. He has assembled the following data for a project soon to be started. He wants to establish a PERT diagram for the project, determine the earliest completion date from project start using expected times, and find the minimum cost plan. This project manager doesn't know whether he has enough data to proceed; even if he does have enough data, he doesn't know how to analyze them and apply the results.

Activity	Immediate Predecessors	Expected Time (days)	Cost/Day to Expedite
A–B	—	2	$100
A–C	—	4	80
A–D	—	5	70
B–E	A–B, A–C	3	100
E–F	B–E	6	150
F–H	E–F	2	50
D–H	A–D	11	100
H–I	F–H, D–H	1	100

The project manager has budgeted $200 for expediting should he want to use it.

REVIEW AND DISCUSSION QUESTIONS

1. Differentiate between project and other types of planning.
2. Explain how project planning and project scheduling relate.
3. Provide an example, not given in this chapter, of a project. Describe the project, identifying the beginning and ending points, the activities, and the time sequencing of the activities against one another and the calendar.
4. Discuss how a Gantt chart can be used as a scheduling tool. What type of model is a Gantt chart?
5. PERT has characteristics of both a mathematical model and a schematic model. Explain.
6. Explain how the scheduling and cost performance of a project might be measured. When might such a measure be useful?
7. Discuss the key behaviors that occur within project teams. In your discussion, explain who the people are who exhibit each behavior, and explain the possible consequences of such behavior on project goal accomplishment.
8. Contrast the advantages and disadvantages of project organization.
9. Provide the features that a situation should present before PERT may be used.
10. In PERT, the terms are important. Explain the difference between an activity and an event. What is a critical path?

11. Present the logic of PERT. (How does PERT work?)
12. Explain how a time/cost tradeoff could exist in a project involving the construction, staffing, and opening of a new clubhouse at an existing country club.
13. Managers often complain that statistical analysis is too complicated. Suppose that although your supervisor exhibits such an attitude, he likes PERT. In minimally technical terms, explain the advantages of probabilistic PERT to your supervisor and try to convince him or her to accept it.
14. Your project is to design and build an insulated dog house for your favorite Collie. Show how to use a work breakdown structure to develop the project network.

PROBLEMS

Solved Problems

1. Compute the values for the earliest expected times (T_E) and the latest allowable times (T_L) for the network shown in Figure 9.11. The expected time is shown beside each activity.

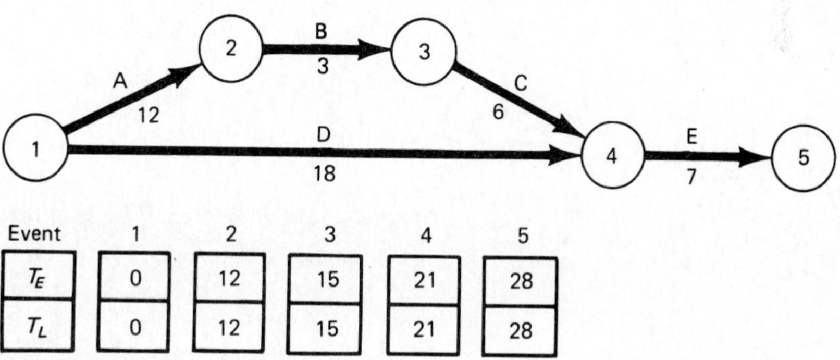

FIGURE 9.11

2. Determine the expected completion time and the variance of completion time for the network shown in Figure 9.12 (the optimistic, most likely, and pessimistic time estimates are shown for each activity).

1 (4, 6, 8) 2 (7, 11, 13) 3 (8, 10, 14) 4

FIGURE 9.12

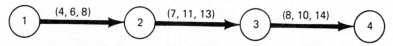

activity:	1–2	2–3	3–4
t_e:	$\frac{4 + 4(6) + 8}{6} = 6.00$	$\frac{7 + 4(11) + 13}{6} = 10.67$	$\frac{8 + 4(10) + 14}{6} = 10.33$
σ_e^2:	$\left(\frac{8 - 4}{6}\right)^2 = 0.4444$	$\left(\frac{13 - 7}{6}\right)^2 = 1.000$	$\left(\frac{14 - 8}{6}\right)^2 = 1.000$

network: expected completion time = 27.00 weeks; variance = 2.444.

Reinforcing Fundamentals

3. A veterinarian would like to put drains for collecting animal waste and a septic tank in his animal shelter. He has identified the following activities and estimated their times (in days): planning (4), obtaining contractor (7), excavating (3), laying drainage tile (2), concrete work (4), landscaping (3). All activities are sequential except for laying the drainage tile and concrete work which may be done at the same time but must be done after excavation.
   (a) Prepare a Gantt chart.
   (b) Prepare a PERT chart.
   (c) Which chart do you believe would be most useful on this project? Why?
4. Given the following PERT diagram (Figure 9.13) with times in days:
   (a) Compute the values for the earliest expected times (T_E) and the latest allowable times (T_L).
   (b) Find the event slack at event 2.
   (c) The penalty cost per day for each day over 15 days is $10. The costs of expediting, for those activities that allow it, are:

Activity	Expediting Cost/ Day	Maximum Days That Can Be Reduced by Expediting
2–4	$ 7	2
3–4	6	1
4–5	15	3

   Which activities (and by how many days), *if any*, would you expedite?

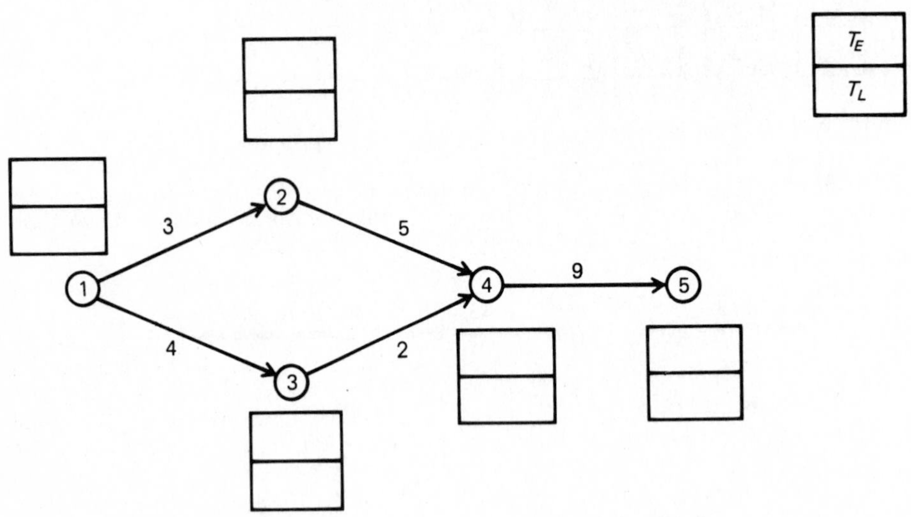

FIGURE 9.13

5. Given the PERT activities in Figure 9.14:
   (a) What is the critical path?
   (b) Construct a Gantt chart for this project.
   (c) Examine the activity variances. Which path through the network would you suggest that the project manager watch most closely? Why?

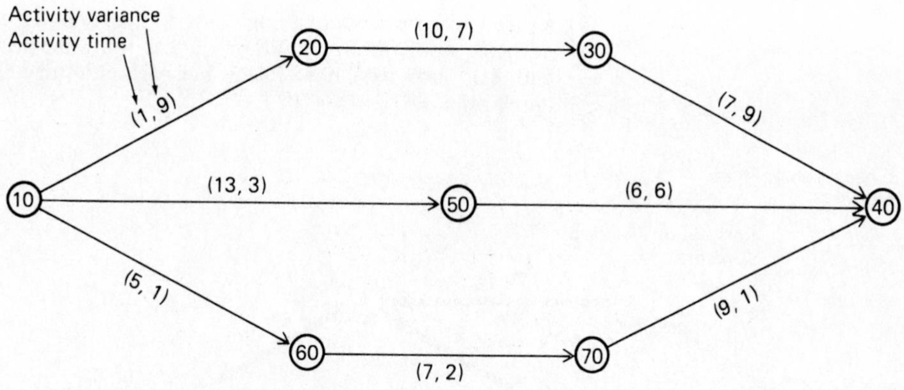

FIGURE 9.14

6. Given the following data (Figure 9.15):

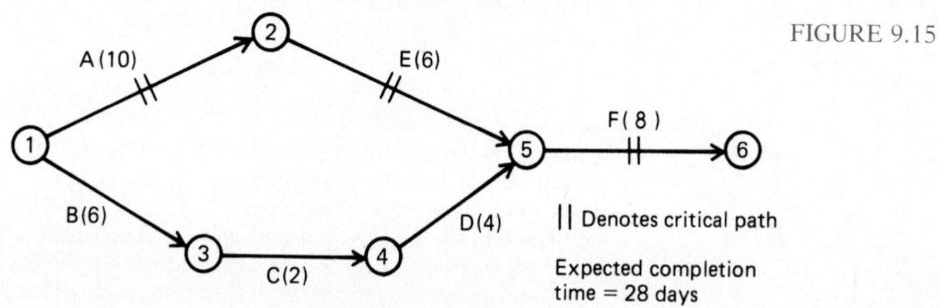

FIGURE 9.15

Activity	Expected Duration (days)	Cost/Day to Expedite	Minimum Duration (days)
A	10	$50	6
B	6	30	3
C	2	—	2
D	4	40	2
E	6	80	4
F	8	100	5

(a) What is the minimum expected completion time of the project (for an "allcrash" solution) and the associated expediting cost?
(b) Identify all activity durations and expediting costs that minimize total expediting costs while still providing the minimum expected completion time for the project.

7. For the data given in Problem 6, identify all possible expected project durations and the minimum total expediting costs of each. Develop a graph of this relationship, and identify the activity durations and the critical path activities for each point on the graph.

8. Consider the research and development project PERT diagram shown in Figure 9.16.
(a) Find the critical path and critical path time.
(b) What is the probability that the project will take more than 21 days to complete?

(c) A new activity is being considered. The activity, economic evaluations of pesticide application, would precede activity DC and follow activities AB, AD, and AE. Draw the new PERT network. Identify the new activity on your network.

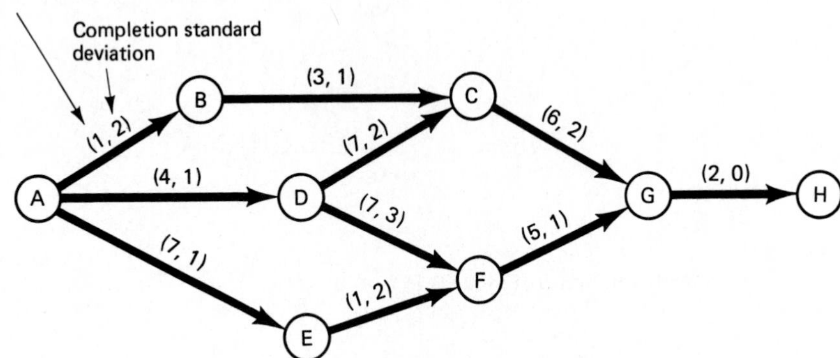

FIGURE 9.16

9. A market research project for Trademark Greeting Cards (TGC) is being planned as shown below. For the market research manager,
   (a) Construct a PERT diagram.
   (b) Explain the critical path concept and what the critical path is for this project.
   (c) Analyze costs and recommend action. The project has fixed costs of \$100/day; that is, each day the completion time is shortened from the expected time, the firm saves \$100.

Activity	Immediate Predecessors	Expected Completion Time (days)	Minimum Expedited Time (days)	Expedited Cost/Day
1	—	10	5	\$80
2	1	20	15	65
3	2	25	15	40
4	2	20	15	70
5	3, 4	15	13	90
6	5	15	10	105
7	1	60	45	30
8	6, 7	5	4	85

10. A public accounting firm has described an audit program at a bank in terms of activities and events and has calculated the expected activity times (t_e) and their variances (σ^2_e) as shown (e.g., activity 10–20 has $t_e = 8$ and $\sigma^2_e = 3$). The activity times are in days in the PERT network (Figure 9.17).
    (a) Find the critical path and the mean critical path time for the audit program.
    (b) If activity times are assumed to be independent and normally distributed, what is the probability that the audit is completed in 22 days or fewer? Of what value is this information to a partner in the firm?
    (c) What can you tell about activity 30–60 as it relates to the critical path?
    (d) What is the event slack at event 50? Why?

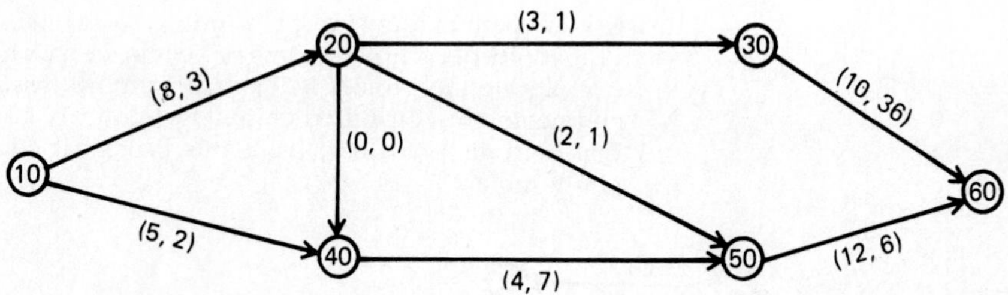

FIGURE 9.17

11. For an R&D project, the PERT network in Figure 9.18 was constructed. Activity times are in months.

(a) What is the critical path?

(b) What is the event slack at event 30? What does that mean?

(c) Two activities have to be added due to a change in project definition. An activity of two months must precede the entire project, and an activity of two months must precede activity 10–30. What impact, if any, will this have on the critical path and on the event slack at event 30?

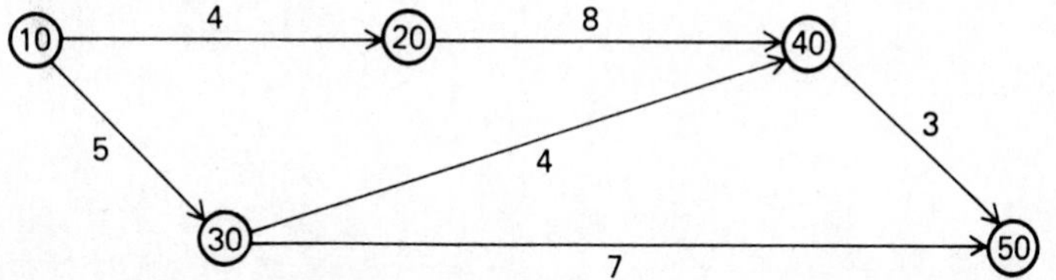

FIGURE 9.18

Challenging Exercises

12. A short project has data as shown in the table below.

(a) Construct a PERT diagram. Calculate the critical path time, and clearly designate the critical path.

(b) Calculate the earliest expected time, the latest allowable time, and slack time at each event. Why is slack time always zero at each event on the critical path?

(c) Assuming independent activities that are normally distributed, what is the probability of completing the project in 19 days or fewer?

(d) If you chose to expedite only one activity, which would you choose? Why?

Activity	Immediate Predecessors	Expected Time (days)	Variance	Cost/Day to Expedite	Maximum Days That Can Be Expedited
A	—	6	2	$100	3
B	—	11	9	50	1
C	—	13	5	200	2
D	A	6	4	—	—
E	C, F, G	4	4	300	1
F	D	4	1	150	1
G	B	7	3	200	2

13. A project manager for Electromagnet, Inc., has constructed the PERT network shown in Figure 9.19. Assist the manager by determining the following:

(a) Critical path and critical path time
(b) Probability of completing this project in 11 days or fewer and the probability of completing the project in 13 days or more (assuming independent activities and normally distributed completion times)
(c) Expected gain (or loss) from this project if completed, given the following payoff table:

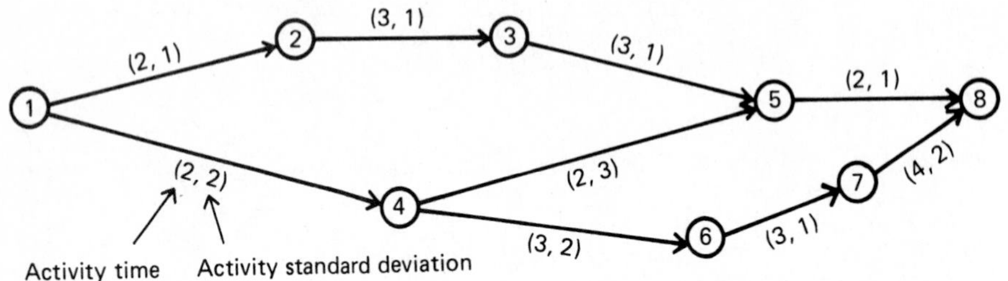

FIGURE 9.19

	State of Nature		
Alternatives	Finish 11 Days or Fewer	Finish in 12 Days	Finish 13 Days or More
Complete the project	+$800	+$200	−$100
Don't start the project	$0	$0	$0

14. A computer programming team has divided a project in terms of activities and events and has calculated expected activity times (t_e) and their variances (σ^2_e) as shown in Figure 9.20. (For example, activity 10–20 has a t_e = 8 and σ^2_e = 3.) The activity times are in days in the PERT network.
    (a) Find the critical path and the mean critical path time for the project.
    (b) If activities are assumed to be independent and normally distributed, what is the probability that all computer programming is completed in 17 days or fewer?
    (c) Your goal is a lower project completion time. If you can spend $500 and reduce activity 50–80 one day or $600 and reduce activity 60–80 two days, which, if either, should you do?

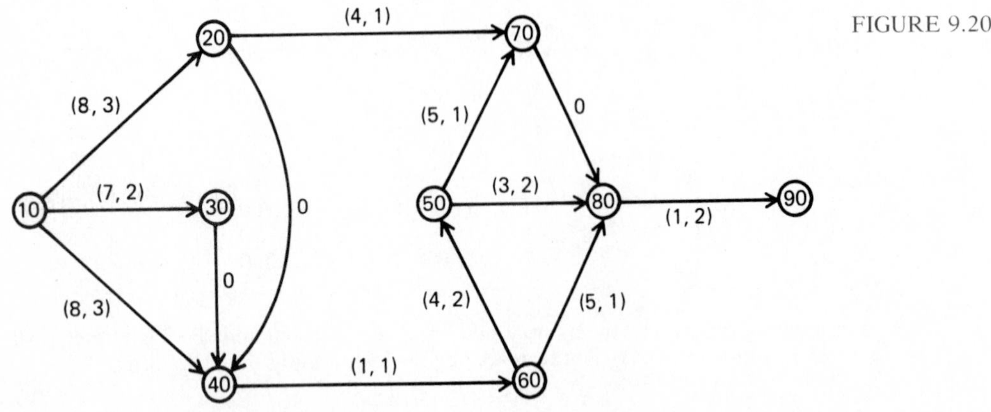

FIGURE 9.20

(d) If the project requires more than 19 days, a penalty of $300/day is assessed on the programmers. If the project finishes in fewer than 19 days, a bonus of $300/day is given to the programmers. What is the expected payoff to the programmers?

15. Temple Hospital is designing and implementing a wage incentive program. Included are the activities of this project and other project information. Activity times are independent and normally distributed.
(a) Construct a PERT network and mark the critical path.
(b) What is the probability of completion in more than 15 weeks?
(c) You have $1,000 to spend expediting. Where would you spend it? Why?

Activity	Immediate Predecessors	Expected Time (weeks)	Expected Standard Deviation	Minimum Expected Time	Cost/ Week to Expedite
Project planning 1–2	—	3	1	3	—
Job analysis 2–3	1–2	5	2	2	$ 500
Performance analysis 2–4	1–2	4	2	2	500
Market wage survey 2–5	1–2	7	3	6	300
Structure internal wage program 3–5	2–3, 2–4	3	2	2	1,000
Finalize incentive program 5–6	2–5, 3–5	4	2	4	—

Utilizing the QSOM Computer Software

16. Project data for a building renovation (time in days) is shown below. Each activity that has a most likely time of 6 days or more can have its pessimistic time reduced by one day if you are willing to expend the resources to do so. Your client wants the renovation completed in 34 days or less and will pay you $1,000 bonus for each day saved. You will be penalized $500 for each day in excess of 34 days. How much are you willing to pay to reduce the pessimistic times?

Activity	Immediate Predecessors	Time Estimates: Optimistic	Most Likely	Pessimistic
1–2	—	2	3	4
1–3	—	4	6	8
1–4	—	7	9	11
2–3	1–2	3	4	5
2–4	1–2	5	7	9
2–5	1–2	8	10	12
2–6	1–2	14	17	20
3–5	1–3, 2–3	7	9	11
3–6	1–3, 2–3	12	15	18
3–7	1–3, 2–3	8	11	14
4–5	1–4, 2–4	6	8	10
5–6	2–5, 3–5, 4–5	4	5	6
5–8	2–5, 3–5, 4–5	8	10	12
6–8	2–6, 3–6, 5–6	5	7	9
7–8	3–7	7	9	11
8–9	5–8, 6–8, 7–8	3	4	5

GLOSSARY

Arc In networks, the arrow that begins at one node and ends at another.

Matrix organization An organization that combines functional and project bases for groupings of organization units.

Node In networks, a circle that designates the beginning and/or ending of an arc.

PERT Program Evaluation and Review Technique; a project-scheduling technique that is an application of network modeling.

PERT activity Work needed to be accomplished; designated by an arc.

PERT critical path The path through the network consisting of several activities whose total activity times are the longest of any path through the network.

PERT event A point in time on the project; designated by a node; designates the beginning and/or ending of activities.

PERT slack time Event slack or time latitude for activity performance that still allows the project to finish on time.

Probabilistic PERT A modification of PERT to consider the variance (σ^2) and the mean (t_e) of the activity times.

Progress reporting A methodology for monitoring the time and cost variances during the progress of a project.

Project A one-shot set of activities, a project venture, with a definite beginning and ending point.

Project planning All activities that result in developing a course of action for a one-shot venture with a specific beginning and ending point.

Project scheduling Time sequencing of activities in a project.

Work breakdown structure A methodology for the level-by-level breakdown of a project into successively more detailed subcomponents.

SELECTED READINGS

Cleland, D. I., and D. F. Kocaoglu, *Engineering Management.* New York: McGraw-Hill, 1981.

Davis, E. W., "Project Scheduling Under Resource Constraints—Historical Review and Categorization of Procedures," *AIIE Transactions* 5, no. 4 (December 1973), 297–313.

Moder, J. J., C. R. Phillips, and E. W. Davis, *Project Management with CPM, PERT, and Precedence Diagramming* (3rd ed.). New York: Van Nostrand Reinhold, 1983.

Smith, Larry A., and Joan Mills, "Project Management Network Programs," *Project Management Quarterly* (June 1982), 18–29.

Weist, J. D., and F. K. Levy, *A Management Guide to PERT/CPM* (2nd ed.). Englewood Cliffs, N.J.: Prentice Hall, 1977.

PART IV SCHEDULING CONVERSION SYSTEMS

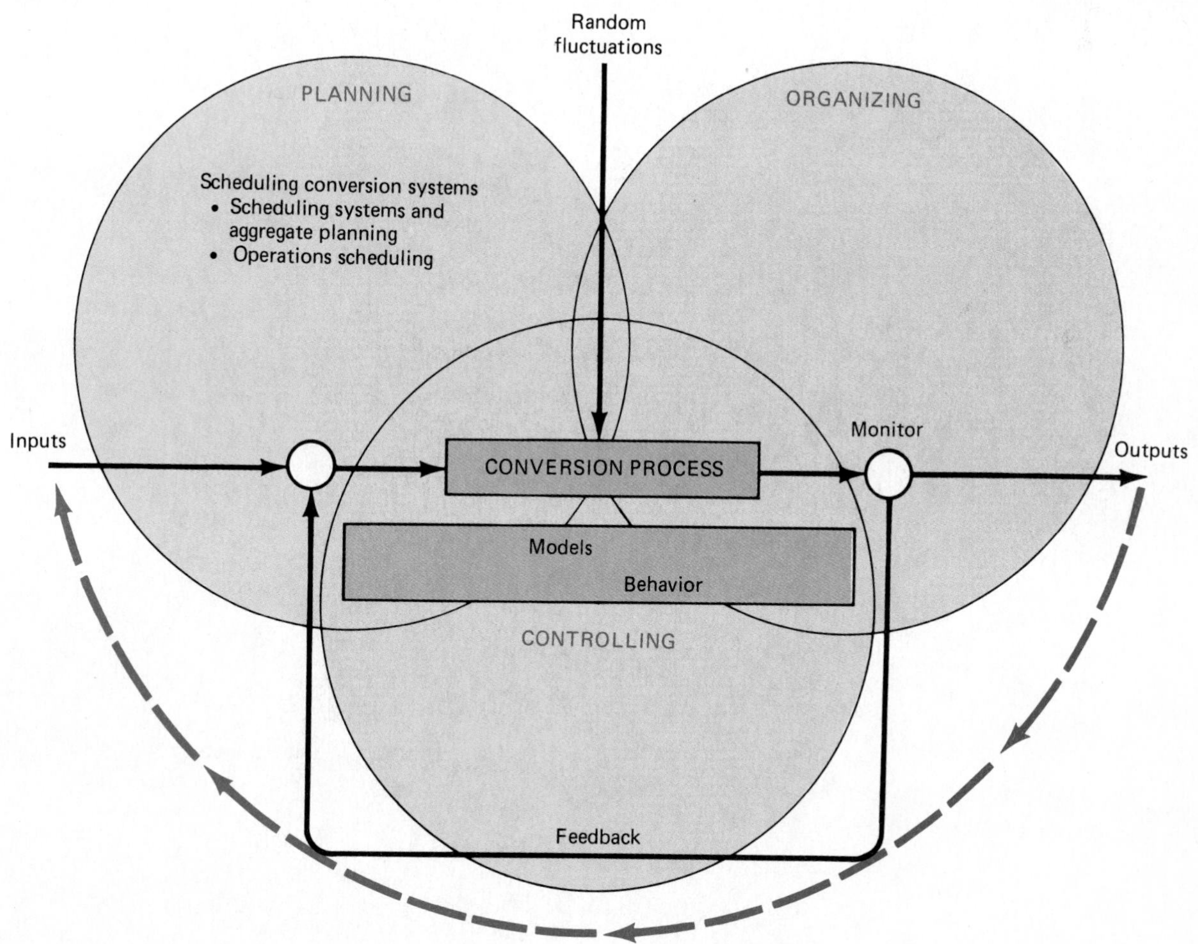

Production and operations management actvities

10

Scheduling Systems and Aggregate Planning

Because the aircraft manufacturing industry is highly sensitive to fluctuating demands and to the corresponding cost impacts of these fluctuations upon the production environment, a thorough knowledge of the fundamentals of scheduling systems and operations by management is essential to our competitive position. A stable work staffing level is a major goal of our aggregate planning process because of the added costs associated with erratic variation of these levels. Even minor changes resulting in job transfers multiply to many changes in a highly skilled and unionized environment. McDonnell Douglas Canada Ltd. utilizes several methods to maintain the delicate balance between the flexibility required with regard to market schedule demands and long-term production planning to maintain competitive cost. The use of suitable long-term planning horizons, effective use of inventories, reassignment of employees, and level loading through finite capacity planning are some of the methods used to temper the impact of changes.

In an industry in which as many as 20,000 different parts (some of them used in large quantity multiples) are incorporated into a single aircraft component with very long detailed part flow times relative to other industries, a disciplined approach to planning and scheduling systems is required.

Garret G. Ackerson, President
McDonnell Douglas Canada Ltd.
Toronto, Ontario, Canada

Imagine yourself in charge of a large facility, such as McDonnell Douglas Canada Ltd., that houses many types of equipment and people. How should you use these potentially productive resources during the next six months, year, or even longer? Your answer to this question, as indicated in

Mr. Ackerson's introductory comments, will directly affect the success of your organization. One source of guidance is provided through operations planning and scheduling systems. After presenting an overview of these systems, we will concentrate on two particular elements, aggregate planning and master scheduling, showing how they are used in both manufacturing and service operations.

OPERATIONS PLANNING AND SCHEDULING SYSTEMS

Operations planning and scheduling concerns the volume and timing of outputs, the utilization of operations capacity, and balancing outputs with capacity at desired levels for competitive effectiveness. The management systems for doing all of this involve various hierarchical levels of activities that fit together from top to bottom in support of one another, as shown in Figure 10.1. Note that the time orientation ranges from long to short as we progress from top to bottom in the hierarchy. Also, the level of detail in the planning process ranges from broad at the top to detailed at the bottom.[1]

In this chapter we focus on the aggregate production and capacity plan and its decomposition down to the level of master production scheduling and rough-cut capacity planning. Let's begin with an overview of the entire system.

Overview of the Operations Scheduling and Planning System

The Business Plan The *business plan* is a statement of the organization's overall level of business activity for the next 6 to 18 months. Developed at the top executive level, the plan is based on forecasts of general economic conditions, anticipated conditions of the industry, and competitive considerations; it reflects the company's strategy for competing during the coming year(s). It is usually expressed in terms of outputs (dollar volume of sales), quarterly or sometimes monthly, for each of its broad product groups but not for the specific items or individual products within each group. It also may specify the overall inventory and backlog levels to maintain during the planning period.

The business plan, in a sense, is an agreement between all functional areas—finance, production, marketing, engineering, R&D—regarding the level of business activity and product groups they are committed to support. It is not, at this level, concerned with all the details and specific timing of the actions for executing the plan. Instead, it determines a feasible general posture for competing to achieve its major goals. The resulting plan guides the lower-level, more detailed decisions.

Aggregate Production (Output) Planning This plan is the production portion of the business plan and addresses the *demand side* of its overall activities by showing the outputs it will produce, expressed in numbers of units of its product groups or families. Since various product groups may

[1]Hierarchical planning and decisions are discussed in H. C. Meal, "Putting Production Decisions Where They Belong," *Harvard Business Review* 62, no. 2 (March–April 1984), 102–11.

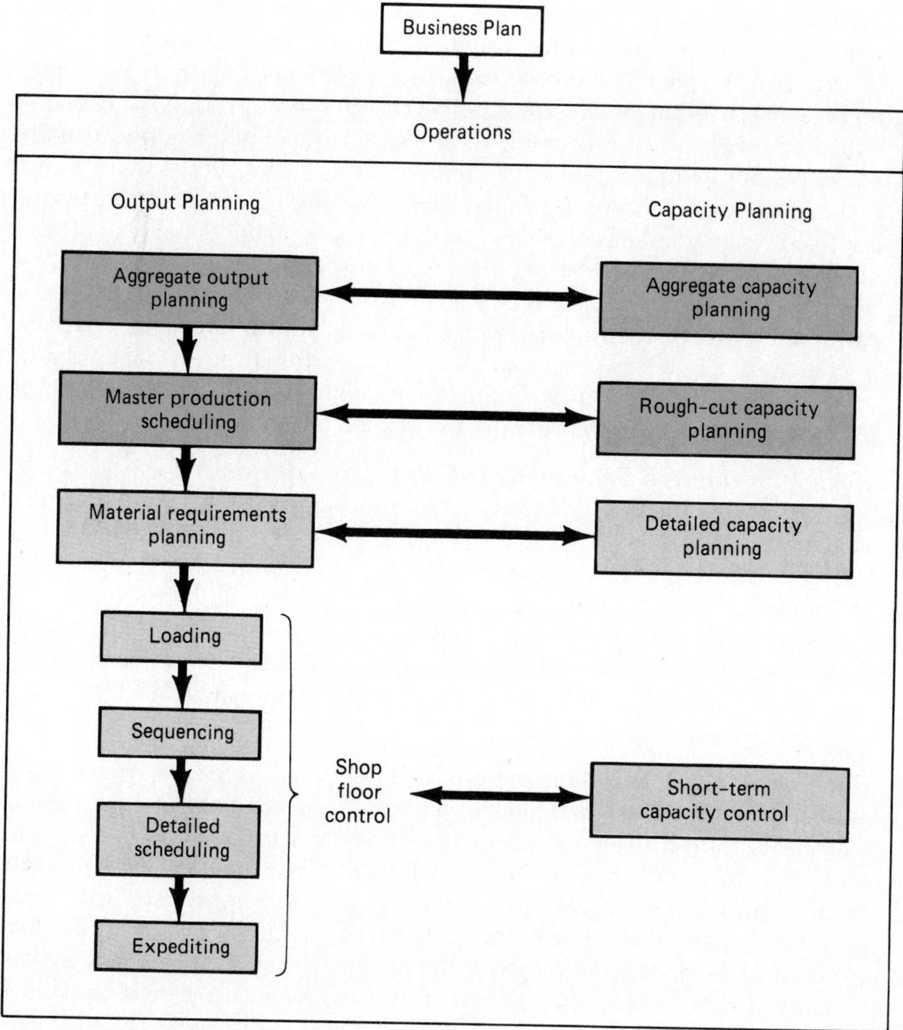

FIGURE 10.1
The operations planning and scheduling system

be produced at diverse plants, facilities, or manufacturing divisions, each of them needs its own production plan. The division's aggregate output plan covers the next 6 to 18 months on a weekly or monthly basis. Planning at this level ignores such details as how many of each individual product, style, color option, or model to produce. The plan recognizes the division's existing fixed capacity and the company's overall policies for maintaining inventories and backlogs, employment stability, and subcontracting.

Capacity Planning Any statement of output intentions isn't useful unless it is workable and feasible. This is the role of aggregate capacity planning—to keep capacity utilization at desired levels and to test the feasibility of planned output against existing capacity. Thus, it addresses *supply-side* questions of the division's ability to meet the demand. Capacity and output must be in balance as indicated by the arrow between them in Figure 10.1. Capacity planning translates production output plans into *input* terms to *approximate* how much of the division's production capacity will be needed and consumed. A product group, for example, usually consumes some logical blocks of capacity such as labor hours of assembly or machine center hours for fabrication. Although their basic capacities are fixed, management can manipulate the short-term capacities of these blocks by the ways they deploy their work force, by subcontracting or by using multiple work shifts to adjust the timing of overall outputs. As a result, the aggregate planning process balances output levels, fixed capacity constraints, and temporary capacity adjustments to meet demand and utilize capacity at desired levels during the coming months. The resulting plan sets limits on the master production schedule.

Master Production Scheduling (MPS) The purpose of *master scheduling* is to meet the demand for individual products in the product group. This more detailed level of planning *disaggregates* the product groups into individual products and indicates when they'll be produced. The MPS provides an important linkage between marketing and production. It shows when incoming sales orders can be scheduled into production and, upon completion, when each shipment is scheduled to be sent to the customer. Thereby, it provides realistic order promising that takes into account current backlogs when new sales orders are booked.

Rough-Cut Capacity Planning (RCCP) *Rough-cut capacity planning* (sometimes called *resource requirements planning*) is done in conjunction with the tentative master schedule to test its capacity feasibility before the MPS is finally settled. This step ensures that a proposed MPS doesn't inadvertently overload any key department, work center, or machine, prohibiting the MPS from being implemented. Although the check can apply to all work centers, it is typically performed on the critical ones that are most likely to pose bottlenecks in the manufacturing process. It is a quick and inexpensive way to find and correct gross discrepancies between the capacity requirements (in direct labor hours, for example) of the MPS and available capacity.

Material Requirements Planning (MRP) The master schedule is the driving force for the *material requirements planning* (MRP) system or any other type of materials and inventory planning system. As discussed in Chapter 14, MRP shows the time-phased requirements for materials order releases and receipts that enable the master production schedule to be implemented.

Detailed Capacity Planning (DCP) *Detailed capacity planning,* also called *capacity requirements planning,* is a companion process used with MRP to identify in detail the capacity required to execute the material plan. At this level, more accurate comparisons of available and needed capacity for scheduled work loads are possible. DCP is discussed in Chapter 14.

Shop Floor Control *Shop floor control* emphasizes coordination of weekly and daily actions that get jobs done. Individual jobs are assigned to machines and work centers (loading), the sequence of processing the jobs for priority control is determined, start times and job assignments for each stage of processing are decided (detailed scheduling), and materials and work flows from station to station are monitored and adjusted (expediting). Coordinating all of these activities into smooth flows, especially when unplanned delays and new priorities arise, often calls for last-minute adjustments of outputs and capacities (short-term capacity control).

With this background on the entire production planning and scheduling process, let's take a closer look at aggregate planning and master scheduling.

BASIC CONCEPTS IN THE AGGREGATE PLANNING PROCESS

Developing an aggregate production plan involves four basic considerations: the concept of aggregation, the goals of planning, the use of forecasts of aggregate demand, and the options for adjusting short-run capacity.

Concept of Aggregation

To develop an aggregate plan, first identify a meaningful measure of output. This presents no problem for organizations with a single product because their outputs are measured directly by the number of units they produce. Most organizations, however, have several products, and a common denominator for measuring total output may not be so easy to find. A brewery manager, for example, can plan capacity in terms of gallons of beer produced, ignoring for the moment how that capacity will be subdivided among various types of beer and packaging alternatives. A steel producer can plan in terms of tons of steel, and a paint producer, gallons of paint. Service organizations such as urban transit systems may use passenger miles as a common measure, health care facilities use patient visits, and educational institutions often use faculty-to-student contact hours as a reasonable measure.

A meaningful measure can usually be found by identifying product groups or families of individual products that, although different from one another, share common production processes or consume similar basic resources. Five models of electronic pocket calculators or six models of outboard boat motors are examples of two such product groups. In these cases it may be reasonable to plan in terms of producing so many units of "the representative" calculator or of maintaining inventories of so many units of "the typical" outboard motor in the product group. You can see, then, that organizations strive for an overall measure of output that makes sense in the context of their unique production process and product mix.

Goals for Aggregate Planning

The aggregate plan must simultaneously satisfy a number of goals. First, it has to provide the overall levels of output, inventory, and backlogs that are dictated in the business plan. If the business plan calls for inventory buildups in anticipation of a major promotional campaign, the aggregate plan should offer the appropriate production support. Similarly, the plan must respond to seasonal sales variations or reductions of order backlogs if called for by the business plan.

A second aggregate planning goal is to use the facility's capacity in a manner consistent with the organization's strategy. Underutilized capacity can be an expensive waste of resources. Therefore, many firms plan for a level production rate close to full capacity for efficient operations. Other companies, however (e.g., those competing on the basis of superior product quality or flexible service to customers), keep a cushion of excess production capacity for quick reactions to sudden surges in market demand. We can see, then, how the desired level of capacity utilization depends on the company's strategy.

Finally, the plan should be consistent with the company's goals and policies regarding its employees. A firm may emphasize employment stability, especially where critical job skills are scarce, and therefore be reluctant to hire or lay off employees. Other firms without such goals change employees freely as the output level is varied throughout the aggregate planning horizon.

Forecasts of Aggregate Demand

The benefits to be gained from aggregate planning efforts depend on forecasting capabilities. The forecasting models we have presented in Chapter 3 can be used to forecast demand for product groups as well as individual product demands for the planning horizon. These forecasted patterns of aggregate (group) demand are necessary information inputs to aggregate planning.

Interrelationships Among Decisions

Often plans for aggregate output are developed for periods of 6 to 18 months into the future. Why does the plan cover such a long time span? Because week-to-week and month-to-month actions are not independent of one another. In fact, they are closely interrelated, since management actions and decisions in one month determine which alternatives are available in subsequent months. Therefore, managers must consider the future consequences of current decisions.

EXAMPLE

As manager of a refrigerator manufacturing facility, you wish to plan the level of output for February. At the end of January you observe 100 finished refrigerators left over in inventory. Twenty assemblers were on the payroll in January, each earning a salary of $1,600/month. On average, each assembler is capable of producing 10 refrigerators/month. You have just been informed that 200 refrigerators will be demanded by customers during February. Since you already have 100 units in inventory, you decide to produce exactly 100 more units during February so you can meet the February demand of 200 units. Since only 10 assemblers are required to produce February's planned output, you lay off 10 assemblers at an average layoff cost of $400/worker. One month later you face a similar decision. Consumer demand for refrigerators in March is estimated to be 300 units. Since no refrigerators are left in inventory from February, the entire 300 units for March must be produced during March. To accomplish this, you must hire 20 additional assemblers at the beginning of March so that the work force (30 assemblers) can produce the required 300 units. The cost of hiring and training assemblers averages \$300/assembler, and inventory costs are assumed to be negligible.

This is an example of planning with a one-month time horizon. If each month is treated separately and independently for planning purposes, what costs would result? Table 10.1 shows us.

Let's look at the same example using a two-month planning horizon. At the end of January you find out that demand is expected to be 200 units in February and 300 units in March. With this information you develop the plan (in Table 10.2) for both February and March. This plan calls for retaining all 20 assemblers for February and March and thereby avoiding the layoff and hiring costs of the first plan. This cost savings was accomplished by looking into the future and considering not only next month's expected demand but the demand for the following month as well. As you can see, aggregate plans should be developed not to minimize costs in each individual period but in the long run, since minimizing costs in the short run can turn out to be expensive in the long run.

Table 10.1 Total cost using a one-month planning horizon

Planned Decisions and Costs	February	March	Total
Number of employees	10	30	40
Units of output	100	300	400
Wages (costs)	10 × \$1,600 = \$16,000	30 × 1,600 = \$48,000	\$64,000
Layoff (costs)	10 × \$400 = \$ 4,000	\$ 0	\$ 4,000
Hiring (costs)	\$ 0	20 × \$300 = \$ 6,000	\$ 6,000
Total (costs)	\$20,000	\$54,000	\$74,000

Table 10.2 Total cost using a two-month planning horizon

Planned Decisions and Costs	February	March	Total
Number of employees	20	20	40
Units of output	200	200	400
Wages (costs)	20 × \$1,600 = \$32,000	20 × \$1,600 = \$32,000	\$64,000
Layoff (costs)	\$ 0	\$ 0	\$ 0
Hiring (costs)	\$ 0	\$ 0	\$ 0
Total (costs)	\$32,000	\$32,000	\$64,000

We have seen that short time horizons can be undesirable. However, can we select a horizon that is too long? From a practical standpoint, the answer is yes. By enlarging the planning horizon, we dramatically increase the number of possible alternative plans. The costs of computation and the time required to find the best plan can become prohibitive. Also, forecasts of future demand usually become less accurate as we look farther into the future, and plans based on highly inaccurate forecasts may be of little value.

STRATEGIES FOR DEVELOPING AGGREGATE PLANS

An Aggregate Plan for a Manufacturer

Let's apply these basic concepts to develop an aggregate output plan using a simple graphical or manual approach. The goal is to find a cost-effective plan that meets expected demand over a 12-month horizon.

EXAMPLE Go-Rite Company is a make-to-stock wagon manufacturer whose primary product group consists of three models of wagons. The annual business plan, based on marketing's sales forecasts, calls for wagon sales totaling $6,840,000 with quarterly sales as follows in row 1:

	Quarter			
	1	2	3	4
Forecasted sales ($) for all product groups	$1,080,000	2,640,000	1,960,000	1,160,000
Units (wagons)	27,000	66,000	49,000	29,000
Labor hours	21,600	52,800	39,200	23,200

The business plan was translated into manufacturing terms (units and labor hours) using historical conversion factors. First, the typical wagon contributes $40 to sales revenue so the approximate number of wagons per quarter is shown in row 2. Since output on average is 10 wagons/day for each production employee (or .8 labor hours/wagon), the estimated labor-hour requirements are shown in row 3. Forecasts of product-group demand (Figure 10.2) reflect a major peak in the spring and a minor peak in the fall. Lowest demand occurs during the winter months.

The first step in the analysis is to determine the productive requirements this demand pattern places on the facility. At first glance, May appears to be the peak month, with 24,000 units demanded. The actual number of available productive days must also be considered, however. Because of an annual vacation shutdown, for example, August has only 11 productive days. The output rates per available productive day are shown

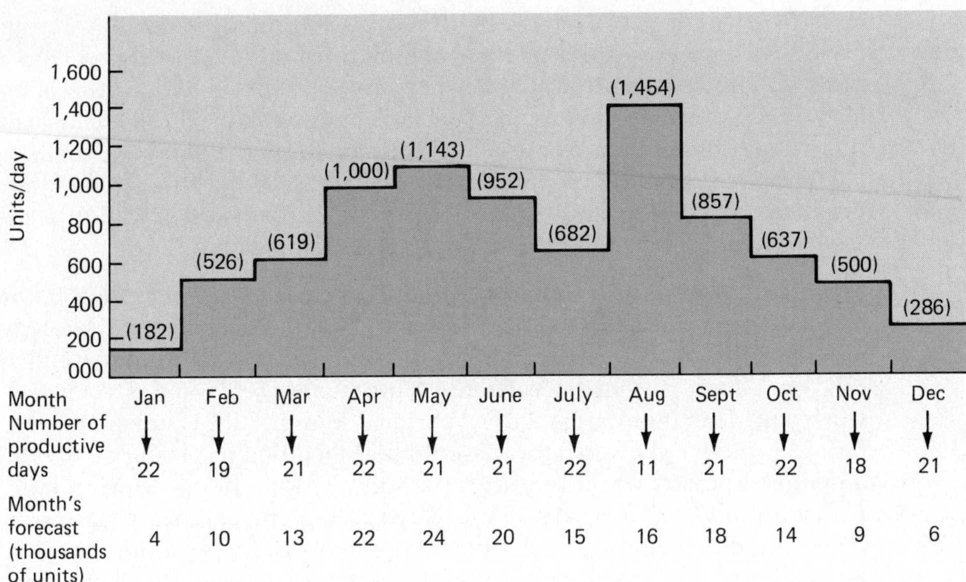

FIGURE 10.2
Output rate per productive day when monthly production meets monthly demand

in Figure 10.2. Let's examine three "pure strategies" that the planner could use to cope with these wide swings in monthly demand.

Three Pure Planning Strategies

Several short-term capacity adjustments can be used to absorb monthly demand fluctuations. Common in make-to-stock organizations are three of these adjustments—work force size, inventories, and work force utilization. Any one of these can be varied to meet demand variations without consideration of the other two (thus they can be called *pure strategies*). Usually, however, some combination of the three is better than using just one. In addition to these internal adjustments, manufacturers often use subcontractors, rented or leased equipment, and other external resources for responding to periods of heavy demand.

Strategy 1: Vary the Number of Productive Employees in Direct Relation to Monthly Output Requirements From historical data, management can estimate the average productivity per employee and thus determine the number of employees needed to meet each month's output. When required monthly output declines, employees can be laid off. As monthly demand increases, the work force can be increased accordingly. In our example, output average per employee is 10 wagons/day. Therefore about 18 employees would be needed in January, 53 in February, 62 in March, and so on.

Several disadvantages are obvious in this strategy. The wide swings in employment levels cause very high hiring and layoff costs. Also, indirect costs of training new employees, decreases in employee morale during periods of layoff, and the like are common. In addition, required work skills may not be readily available when they are needed. When fairly long lead times are needed to procure special employee skills, these hiring lead times and training periods must be accounted for in the planning horizon. Furthermore, sometimes community reactions to such a strategy are negative. Finally, this strategy is not feasible for companies with guaranteed wage and other hiring and layoff agreements with unions.

Strategy 2: Maintain a Constant Work Force Size but Vary the Rate of Work Force Utilization Suppose, for example, we chose the strategy of employing 70 workers per month throughout the year. On an average, this work force would be capable of producing 700 wagons each day. During the lean months (January, February, March, July, October, November, December), the work force would be scheduled to produce only the amount forecasted, resulting in some idle working hours. During high-demand months (April, May, June, August, September), overtime operations would be needed to meet demand. The work force would therefore be intensely utilized during some months and underutilized in other months.

A big advantage of this strategy is its avoidance of the hiring and layoff costs associated with strategy 1. But other costs are incurred instead. Overtime, for example, can be very expensive, commonly at least 50 percent higher than regular-time wage rates. Furthermore, there are both legal and behavioral limits to the amount of overtime that can be worked. When employees work extensive amounts of overtime, they tend to become inefficient and job-related accident rates increase.

Idle time also has some subtle drawbacks. During slack periods, employee morale can diminish, especially if the idle time is perceived to be a prelude to future layoffs. Opportunity costs also result from idle time. When employees are forced to be idle, the company forgoes the opportunity of getting units of output that could have been produced. Although wages are paid, some potential output has been lost forever.

Strategy 3: Allow Inventories to Fluctuate in Response to Demand Variations Finished goods inventories in make-to-stock companies can be used to cushion the response to demand fluctuations. A fixed number of employees, selected so that little or no overtime or idle time is incurred, can be maintained throughout the planning horizon. Producing at a constant rate, output will exceed demand during slack demand periods, and finished goods inventories will accumulate. During peak periods, when demand is greater than productive capabilities, the demand can be supplied from inventory. This planning strategy results in fluctuating inventory levels throughout the planning horizon.

The comparative advantages of strategy 3 are obvious: stable employment, no idle time, and no expensive overtime. What about disadvantages? First, inventories of finished goods (and other supporting inventories) are not cost-free. Inventories tie up working capital that could otherwise be earning a return on investment. Materials handling costs, storage space requirements, risk of damage and obsolescence, clerical efforts, and taxes all increase with larger inventories. Backorders can also be costly. Customers may not be willing to tolerate backordering, particularly if alternative sources of supply are available; sales may be lost, and customer ill will may negatively affect future sales potential. In short, there are costs for carrying too much or too little inventory.

A Graphical Method for Aggregate Output Planning

Usually, none of the pure strategies is best by itself; a mixture of two or three is better. The various alternative plans or "mixtures" involve tradeoffs. One way to develop and evaluate these alternatives is by using a *graphical planning procedure*. The graphical method is convenient and relatively simple to understand, and it requires only minor computational effort. To use the graphical method, follow these steps:

1. Develop a graph showing cumulative production days for the entire planning horizon on the horizontal axis and cumulative units of product on the vertical axis. Plot the cumulative demand data (forecasts) for the entire planning horizon.
2. Select a planning strategy, and determine the proposed production output for each period in the planning horizon. Calculate and plot on the graph the cumulative output for this tentative plan.
3. Compare expected demand and proposed output; plot both on the same graph. This comparison identifies periods of excess inventories and periods of inventory shortages.
4. Calculate the costs for this plan.
5. Modify the plan, attempting to meet aggregate planning goals by repeating steps 2 through 4 until a satisfactory plan is established.

We will demonstrate steps 1 through 4 for three different aggregate plans. The fifth step, additional modification, is left for you to do as an exercise. Since step 4 requires cost data, the next example section contains cost estimates obtained from Go-Rite's accounting and engineering department.

EXAMPLE

Inventory carrying costs are \$1/unit for each month that the wagon is carried in inventory. Inventory costs are based on the average level of inventory for the month. Costs are incurred for changing the company's production rate. When the production rate is increased, additional employees must be hired and trained. When the production rate is reduced, some employees must be laid off and/or idle time occurs. The larger the change in production rate (increase or decrease), the greater the cost incurred. Table 10.3 shows the costs of changing production rates by different amounts. Production rates are expressed in terms of units (wagons) per day. It is assumed for initial planning purposes that the daily production rate, once selected, will be used every day for the entire month. The company places a high cost on backorders and lost sales, a cost so high that management wants a plan in which cumulative output at least meets expected demand throughout the planning horizon. The facility's maximum capacity is 100 employees (1,000 wagons/day) on a single shift. Capacity can be temporarily increased by using overtime with additional costs of $4/unit.

A Plan with Level Production We'll develop a plan that meets all the requirements above and that does so by using a constant output (production) rate with no hiring, layoffs, idle time, or overtime. Step 1 of our procedure, plotting cumulative forecasted demand, is done in Figure 10.3.

Table 10.3 Estimated cost for changing production rates from month to month

Change in Daily Production Rate from Previous Month in Units (increase or decrease)	Estimated Cost of Changing Production Rate
1–200	$ 4,000
201–400	10,000
401–600	18,000
601–800	28,000

For step 2, we have specified a planning strategy consisting of a constant average production rate for each day. When we plot cumulative production day by day for this strategy, it appears as a straight line on the graph (see Figure 10.3). The line begins at the origin (zero units of output) and rises steadily to the right as cumulative output increases. Go-Rite's cumulative output line should be steep enough always to meet or exceed cumulative demand requirements to avoid lost sales and backorders. If the production curve is too steep, however, excessive inventories are accumulated. The desired line passes through the origin (point A) and the outlying point (point B) on the cumulative demand curve.[2] The cumulative production output described by this line meets our planning requirements: Beginning on the first day production commences at a constant daily rate and total output exceeds total demand until the end of September (point B). At the end of September, units produced to date equal the total demanded to date. Thereafter, output exceeds expected demand for the remainder of the planning horizon. What is the daily production rate? Point B represents 180 cumulative days of production and 142,000 cumulative units of output (from Figure 10.2). Thus,

[2]Passing the line through point A assumes no beginning inventory exists. If there are finished units on hand at the beginning of the planning horizon, the amount should be marked on the vertical axis and that mark, rather than point A, is the beginning point of the output line on the graph.

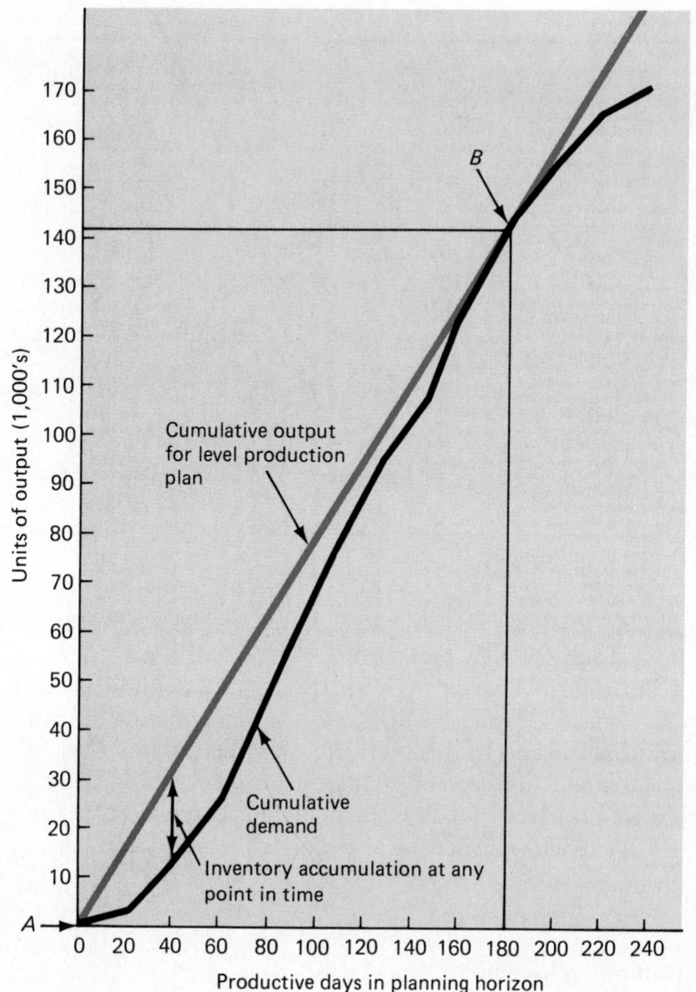

FIGURE 10.3
Aggregate output plan and forecasted demand

$$\frac{142{,}000 \text{ units}}{180 \text{ days}} = 790 \text{ units/day (approximately)}$$

The resulting monthly plans are shown in Table 10.4. Since 790 units are produced each day, and since each employee can average 10 units/day, 79 employees are needed. Since the daily production rate is unchanged from month to month, there are no production rate change costs. The average monthly inventories total 120,405 units for the year. Therefore, inventory costs are about \$120,405 (\$1/unit/month).

A Plan That Closely Follows Demand One alternative to producing at a constant rate is a plan in which monthly output is geared to meeting expected monthly demand. This is sometimes called a *chase plan* because the output rate is chasing (closely following) the demand rate. In this case, the cumulative output curve coincides with the cumulative demand curve. Therefore, the daily production rates are those shown earlier in Figure

Table 10.4 Monthly plan for level production rate

Month	Days	Output Rate/Day	Output	Demand	Beginning Inventory	Net Additions (subtractions) to inventory	Ending Inventory	Average Monthly Inventory (beginning and ending)/2
Jan	22	790	17,380	4,000	0	13,380	13,380	6,690
Feb	19	790	15,010	10,000	13,380	5,010	18,390	15,885
Mar	21	790	16,590	13,000	18,390	3,590	21,980	20,185
Apr	22	790	17,380	22,000	21,980	(4,620)	17,360	19,670
May	21	790	16,590	24,000	17,360	(7,410)	9,950	13,655
June	21	790	16,590	20,000	9,950	(3,410)	6,540	8,245
July	22	790	17,380	15,000	6,540	2,380	8,920	7,730
Aug	11	790	8,690	16,000	8,920	(7,310)	1,610	5,265
Sept	21	790	16,590	18,000	1,610	(1,410)	200	905
Oct	22	790	17,380	14,000	200	3,380	3,580	1,890
Nov	18	790	14,220	9,000	3,580	5,220	8,800	6,190
Dec	21	790	16,590	6,000	8,800	10,590	19,390	14,095
								120,405

10.2. The resulting plan is shown in Table 10.5. Since monthly inventories are trivial, inventory costs for this plan are very low and backorders or stockouts are not permitted. The daily production rate is changed each month. February's rate is 345 units per day greater than January's. From Table 10.3, we know that the cost of this increase is approximately $10,000. Similarly, we can calculate the cost of changing output rates for all the months in the planning horizon. Further costs are incurred for overtime work in May and August when production exceeds the fixed capacity of 1,000 units/day.

Table 10.5 Monthly plan for variable production rate (chase plan)

Month	Days	Change in Production Rate	Output Rate/Day	Output	Demand	Beginning Inventory	Net Additions (subtractions) to inventory	Ending Inventory	Average Inventory
Jan	22		182	4,004	4,000	0	4	4	2.0
Feb	19	+345	527	10,013	10,000	4	13	17	10.5
Mar	21	+ 92	619	12,999	13,000	17	(1)	16	16.5
Apr	22	+381	1,000	22,000	22,000	16	0	16	16.0
May	21	+143	1,143	24,003	24,000	16	3	19	17.5
June	21	−191	952	19,992	20,000	19	(8)	11	15.0
July	22	−270	682	15,004	15,000	11	4	15	13.0
Aug	11	+772	1,454	15,994	16,000	15	(6)	9	12.0
Sept	21	−597	857	17,997	18,000	9	(3)	6	7.5
Oct	22	−220	637	14,014	14,000	6	14	20	13.0
Nov	18	−138	499	8,982	9,000	20	(18)	2	11.0
Dec	21	−213	286	6,006	6,000	2	6	8	5.0
									139.0

An Intermediate Plan As we have seen, excessive inventories and changes in production rates can be costly. Let's develop a plan that changes production rates only occasionally instead of every month. The plan in Table 10.6 calls for a constant production rate of 548 units/day during January, February, and March. This rate is boosted to 1,000 units/day from April through July. Output is then decreased to 689 units/day for the remainder of the year. The inventory cost of this plan would be $1/unit inventoried, or $67,276. Production rate changes would cost $18,000 for the March–April change and $10,000 for the July–August change, for a total of $28,000.

Comparing the Plans The three plans are evaluated on the basis of total cost for the planning horizon. We have done this in Table 10.7. The level production plan has high inventory costs and no overtime or rate change costs. The plan that varies production rate to meet demand has negligible inventory costs, high rate-change costs, and some overtime costs. These plans exemplify two of the pure strategies discussed earlier. The third (intermediate) plan incurs substantial costs of inventories and rate changes but has the lowest total cost. This plan reflects a mixed strategy, using moderate (not extreme) amounts of inventory and production rate changes to absorb demand fluctuations.

Our example shows why the aggregate planning process is sometimes called *production smoothing*. As demand decreases to lower levels, it is cheaper to decrease production rates (occasionally) than to continue to build up excessive inventories. If there is any one generalization that can be made about aggregate planning, it is this: *When planning production, smooth out the peaks and valleys to meet uneven demand because extreme fluctuations in production are generally very costly.*

Table 10.6 Intermediate plan

Month	Days	Change in Production Rate	Output Rate/Day	Output	Demand	Beginning Inventory	Net Additions (subtractions) to inventory	Ending Inventory	Average Inventory
Jan	22		548	12,056	4,000	0	8,056	8,056	4,028
Feb	19		548	10,412	10,000	8,056	412	8,468	8,268
Mar	21	+452	548	11,508	13,000	8,468	(1,492)	6,976	7,722
Apr	22		1,000	22,000	22,000	6,976	0	6,976	6,976
May	21		1,000	21,000	24,000	6,976	(3,000)	3,976	5,476
June	21		1,000	21,000	20,000	3,976	1,000	4,976	4,476
July	22	−311	1,000	22,000	15,000	4,976	7,000	1,976	8,476
Aug	11		689	7,579	16,000	11,976	(8,421)	3,555	7,776
Sept	21		689	14,469	18,000	3,555	(3,531)	24	1,790
Oct	22		689	15,158	14,000	24	1,158	1,182	603
Nov	18		689	12,402	9,000	1,182	3,402	4,584	2,883
Dec	21		689	14,469	6,000	4,584	8,469	13,053	8,818
									67,276

Table 10.7 **Operating costs for three plans**

	Plan		
Type of Cost	Level Production Rate	Variable Production Rate (chase)	Intermediate
Overtime	$ 0	$ 31,988[a]	$ 0
Inventory	120,405	139	67,276
Production rate change	0	112,000[b]	28,000
Total cost	$120,405	$144,127	$95,276

[a]May: 143 units/day × 21 days × $4/unit × $12,012. August: 454 units/day × 11 days × $4/unit = $19,976.

[b]From data in Tables 10.3 and 10.4

Capacity Planning

In evaluating the capacity *feasibility,* we see differences among Go-Rite's three aggregate plans. Neither the level plan nor the intermediate plan exceeds the facility's daily maximum capacity of 1,000 units. The chase plan, however, exceeds maximum capacity in May and August and, accordingly, overtime or second-shift operations would be needed.

In terms of capacity *utilization,* the level plan consistently uses 79 percent of maximum capacity. The chase plan's utilization, in contrast, varies from only 18 percent up to 145 percent during the year. The intermediate plan uses 55 to 100 percent of maximum capacity. If these levels of utilization are unsuitable, either the demand for its products must be stimulated (to gain higher capacity utilization) or the capacity must be adjusted.

MASTER SCHEDULING AND ROUGH-CUT CAPACITY PLANNING

The next step in the planning process is master production scheduling, which translates the aggregate plan into operational production schedules for individual products. As we illustrate the master scheduling concepts, we'll use the intermediate aggregate plan (Table 10.6) for the Go-Rite Company.

Disaggregation of Aggregate Plans

As contrasted with aggregate plans, the master schedule is more detailed —it deals with individual products (not just product groups) and when they'll be produced week-by-week. How should our aggregate output be subdivided among each of the products we produce? What mix of these products should comprise our aggregate inventories? This process of translating aggregate plans into plans for individual products is called *dissaggregation,* a problem that has received surprisingly little formal attention until recently.[3] As a result, the dominant practice today involves disaggregation by cut-and-fit or trial-and-error procedures. Using forecasts of individual product demands, trial amounts of each product are scheduled week by week. The resulting weekly totals of output are then compared against aggregate requirements, checked for their capacity feasibility, and revised accordingly. You can see all of these steps in the discussion below as we develop a master schedule for the Go-Rite Company.

Developing a Trial Master Production Schedule

The master scheduler in our Go-Rite example has obtained forecasts of weekly demands for the three wagon models (A, B, C). These forecasts, coupled with known customer orders, result in the forecast demands shown in Table 10.8 (forecasts beyond 16 weeks are omitted here for brevity). Each of the 16 weeks is 5 working days and thus, the forecasts (44,970 wagons) cover the next 80 days and match closely with the aggregate plan's overall demand of 45,000 wagons.

Next, a trial master production schedule is developed (Table 10.9). We can see that some of all three models are scheduled for production during the first week since no beginning inventories are available and Go-Rite's aggregate plan calls for no stockouts. After week 1, the master scheduler settles on a general pattern of producing wagons A and C in the same weeks while B is often produced alone. Through experience, by trying various combinations, the scheduler hopes to meet product demand, avoid excessive production setup costs, maintain appropriate aggregate inventory levels, and do all of this within planned capacity levels.

How well does this MPS match up with the aggregate plan? The schedule results in cumulative production output levels that exceed cumulative demands, as shown in Table 10.10. In addition, aggregate inventories after 8 weeks and 16 weeks closely parallel the levels sought in the aggregate plan. Thus, the MPS is feasible insofar as the aggregate plan is concerned.

Rough-Cut Capacity Planning

Is the MPS feasible from the standpoint of Go-Rite's production capacity? Let's make some rough (approximate) checks to answer these questions.

We can check overall labor-hour requirements using accounting and engineering data. Suppose Go-Rite's labor standards (standard hours/unit) are 0.88, 0.66, and 1.08 hours for products A, B, and C, respectively.[4] Applying these standards to the 16-week (80-day) schedules, we see in

---

[3]A review of the status of disaggregation is given in L. J. Krajewski and L. P. Ritzman, "Disaggregation in Manufacturing and Service Organizations: Survey of Problems and Research," *Decision Sciences* 8, no. 1 (January 1977), 1–18.

[4]The labor standards for the three types of wagons, when weighted by their historical proportions of total sales, result in an overall standard of 0.8 labor hours/wagon. The proportions of sales for the wagons are 35, 50, and 15 percent for models A, B, and C, respectively: $.35 \times .88 + .5 \times .66 + .15 \times 1.08 = .8$.

Table 10.8 Forecasts of weekly demands (units) for individual products

	Week																
Product	1	2	3	4	5	6	7	8	9	10	11	12	13	14	15	16	Totals
A	160	160	160	160	500	735	735	735	890	930	930	930	1,300	1,545	1,545	1,545	12,960
B	295	295	295	295	940	1,370	1,370	1,370	1,625	1,690	1,690	1,690	2,420	2,910	2,910	2,910	24,075
C	455	455	455	455	500	525	525	525	485	475	475	475	495	545	545	545	7,935
Totals	910	910	910	910	1,940	2,630	2,630	2,630	3,000	3,095	3,095	3,095	4,215	5,000	5,000	5,000	44,970

Table 10.9 Master production schedule (trial): units of output for each product

	Week															
Product	1	2	3	4	5	6	7	8	9	10	11	12	13	14	15	16
A	540	1,740	1,740				1,740	1,740			1,740	1,740		1,800	1,800	1,800
B	1,200			2,740	2,740	1,740			2,740	2,740			3,096	3,200	3,200	3,200
C	1,000	1,000	1,000			1,000	1,000	1,000			1,000	1,000	1,000			

Table 10.10 Cumulative demand and output after 8 weeks and 16 weeks for trial MPS

		Week								Ending Inventory Week 8		Ending Inventory Week 16
Product	Cumulative	1	2	3	4	5	6	7	8		16	
A	demand	160	380	420	640	1,140	1,875	2,610	3,345	4,155	12,960	3,420
	production	540	2,280	4,020				5,760	7,500		16,380	
B	demand	295	590	885	1,180	2,120	3,490	4,860	6,230	2,190	24,075	2,521
	production	1,200			3,940	6,680	8,420				26,596	
C	demand	455	910	1,365	1,820	2,320	2,845	3,370	3,895	2,105	7,935	1,065
	production	1,000	2,000	3,000			4,000	5,000	6,000		9,000	
Scheduled ending inventory from MPS:										8,450		7,006
Desired ending inventory from aggregate plan:										8,468		6,976

Table 10.11 Rough-cut capacity test: Overall MPS labor requirements versus planned capacity

	Labor-hour Requirements (80 days) from MPS		
Product	(1) Units Scheduled	(2) Standard Hours/Unit	(3) = (1) × (2) Total Labor Hours Required
A	16,380	0.88	14,414
B	26,596	0.66	17,553
C	9,000	1.08	9,720
Total MPS requirement = 41,687 hours			
Available labor (from aggregate plan) = 41,581 hours[a]			

[a]548 units/day × 62 days × 0.8 hours/unit + 1,000 units/day × 18 days × 0.8 hours/unit = 41,581 hours.

Table 10.11 that the required labor hours are reasonably close to the planned available labor hours, overall, if employees work at the standard rates.

When discrepancies arise between available and required capacities they must be reconciled by revising the MPS or by adjusting the capacity.[5]

In summary, we can see how the goals of master scheduling and capacity planning become balanced by the process we've described. Capacity planning keeps capacity utilization at desired levels while master scheduling meets product demand.

AGGREGATE PLANNING FOR SERVICE ORGANIZATIONS

Service organizations can also use aggregate planning. The typical service operation, however, is a make-to-order rather than a make-to-stock situation. Consequently, finished goods are not available for responding to demand fluctuations. Instead, backlogs of jobs can be increased or decreased to utilize capacity at desired levels.

Consider a city government's public works department responsible for (1) repairing existing streets and roads (gravel, asphalt, concrete) and drainage systems, (2) building new roads, and (3) removing snow and ice. The department cannot build up inventories of these finished "products." It can, however, retain the proper mixtures of skilled and unskilled labor,

[5]Further methods for rough-cut capacity planning are available in T. E. Vollmann, W. L. Berry, and D. C. Whybark, *Manufacturing Planning and Control Systems* (Homewood, Ill.: Richard D. Irwin, Inc.), 1984. See also D. W. McLeavey and S. L. Narasimhan, *Production Planning and Inventory Control* (Boston: Allyn & Bacon, Inc.), 1985.

equipment, supplies, and the use of subcontractors that will meet the demand for various "products" (services).

EXAMPLE

In the past, the public works department has had an experienced work force of about 400 people and, with an emphasis on stable employment, the director is reluctant to change the number of regular employees. The workers average 2,000 road miles of service/month. This figure is used to estimate the expected productivity of 5 road miles/employee/month, or 0.24 miles/employee/day. Three sources are available for meeting excess demand:

1. The regular work force can work overtime. The overtime premium is 50 percent of the regular $1,500/month wage.
2. Subcontracting to private firms is available at an average cost of $400/road mile. Contracts for these services must be arranged several months in advance.
3. Supplementary labor, up to a maximum of 100 workers, is available from May to September at a salary of $1,200/month. Hiring and layoff costs average $100/supplementary employee.

Among the three types of services, snow removal is given top priority due to its public safety implications. Second priority is on new road construction because the department's crews work closely with subcontractors and the work has to occur under favorable weather conditions. Road repair and maintenance is somewhat variable and less weather-dependent. As the third priority service, it is used to absorb variations in the overall work load as long as the repair backlog doesn't get out of hand.

Currently, the director is evaluating two alternative plans for aggregate output and is dually concerned about their cost and service implications. Although cost minimization is important, effective service to the public is a major concern in this highly visible operation.

Using road miles as the common unit of measurement, the director has obtained last year's aggregate (product group) demand and the demands for each type of service. With the existing 400 employees, the matchup between regular time capacity and demand is shown in Figure 10.4. These data are then used to see how the two new plans would have performed, in terms of job backlogs and costs, if the plans had been in effect last year.

Alternative Plans for Services

The first alternative, plan A, would increase the work force to 480 full-time employees throughout the year. This provides a capacity of 115.2 road miles/day and does not use subcontracting. As shown in Table 10.12, March and April capacities are highly underutilized. However, the backlog at year end is small—less than one-half of one month's work. The ending backlog (967 road miles) could be avoided by subcontracting during June through October.

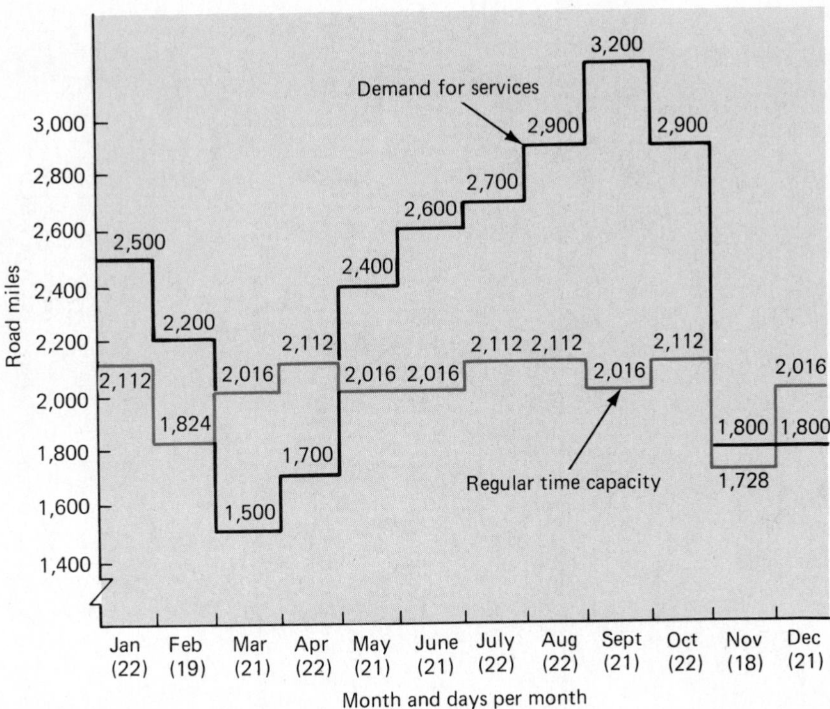

FIGURE 10.4
Monthly demand and capacity for road services

Plan B proposes 400 full-time employees and 100 supplementary workers during May through September, along with subcontracting in the peak months. The supplementary capacity for May through September (Table 10.13) would have reduced peak-season backlogs and left less than one month of unmet demand at year end. Subcontracting for 1,724 road miles during June through November would have satisfied the demand for services by year end.

Comparing the Plans

Plan B, the lowest-cost alternative, accumulates some backlogs of road repair and maintenance in the early months of the year. Plan A, although more costly, avoids backlogs in the early months. It is risky, however, because it adds full-time employees who may have to be released later if future work loads should diminish.

By now the fundamental considerations of the public works department should be clear. See if you can find a good aggregate plan for its operations to assure yourself that you understand this planning procedure.

Additional Models for Aggregate Planning

The graphical technique (model) has the advantages of simplicity, understandability, and no requirement of any special equipment. It can be done easily on a computer or manually. Its primary drawback is that the planner has no assurance that a "best" plan has been developed; it relies on the planner's experience and judgment. Some models, many beyond the scope

Table 10.12 Capacity and cost evaluation for Plan A

Month	Total Demand (road miles)	Repair & Maintenance (road miles)	Snow Removal & New Construction (road miles)	Capacity (road miles)	Backlog (−) from Capacity Shortage Versus Excess Capacity (+) Without Subcontracting (road miles)	Cumulative Backlog (road miles)
Jan	2,500	850	1,650	2,534[a]	+ 34	0
Feb	2,200	870	1,330	2,189	− 11	− 11
Mar	1,500	1,000	500	2,419	+919	0
Apr	1,700	1,150	550	2,534	+834	0
May	2,400	1,300	1,100	2,419	+ 19	0
June	2,600	1,350	1,250	2,419	−181	− 181
July	2,700	1,350	1,350	2,534	−166	− 347
Aug	2,900	1,350	1,550	2,534	−366	− 713
Sept	3,200	1,300	1,900	2,419	−781	−1,494
Oct	2,900	1,150	1,750	2,534	−366	−1,860
Nov	1,800	800	1,000	2,074	+274	−1,586
Dec	1,800	600	1,200	2,419	+619	− 967

Full-time wages = \$8,640,000; Subcontracting costs = \$386,800; Total annual costs = \$9,026,800

[a]480 employees × 0.24 road miles/employee/day × 22 days = 2,534 road miles.

Table 10.13 Capacity evaluation for Plan B

Month	Total Demand (road miles)	Repair & Maintenance (road miles)	Snow Removal & New Construction (road miles)	Capacity (road miles)	Backlog (−) from Capacity Shortage Versus Excess Capacity (+) Without Subcontracting (road miles)	Cumulative Backlog (road miles)
Jan	2,500	850	1,650	2,112[a]	−388	− 388
Feb	2,200	870	1,330	1,824	−376	− 764
Mar	1,500	1,000	500	2,016	+516	− 248
Apr	1,700	1,150	550	2,112	+412	0
May	2,400	1,300	1,100	2,520[b]	+120	0
June	2,600	1,350	1,250	2,520	− 80	− 80
July	2,700	1,350	1,350	2,640	− 60	− 140
Aug	2,900	1,350	1,550	2,640	−260	− 400
Sept	3,200	1,300	1,900	2,520	−680	−1,080
Oct	2,900	1,150	1,750	2,112	−788	−1,868
Nov	1,800	800	1,000	1,728	− 72	−1,940
Dec	1,800	600	1,200	2,016	+216	−1,724

Full-time wages = $7,200,000; Seasonal wages = $600,000; Hiring/layoff costs = $10,000; Subcontracting costs = $689,600; Total annual costs = $8,599,600

[a]400 employees × 0.24 road miles/employee/day × 22 days = 2,112 road miles.
[b]500 employees × 0.24 road miles/employee/day × 21 days = 2,520 road miles.

of this book, have also been used to develop aggregate plans. Sophisticated or simple, all these models share several features. First, they all require the user to specify a planning horizon and obtain aggregate demand forecasts. Second, in every model the decision variables must be explicitly identified. (Decision variables are the factors that can be varied to generate alternative plans—size of work force, production rate, overtime/idle time, inventory level, subcontracting, etc.) Third, the relevant costs must be identified. They include costs of wages, hiring/layoff, overtime, inventory, subcontracting, and so on.

Optimal Models for Aggregate Planning

Linear Programming It is possible to formulate aggregate planning in a linear programming framework.[6] The linear programming procedure then identifies the *optimal* plan for minimizing costs. This plan specifies the number of units of output to produce, how many shifts the manufacturing facility should operate, and how many units of inventory should be carried in each time period. One limitation of linear programming is its assumption of linear costs. As we see later, linear cost relationships are not always accurate representations of actual costs.

Linear Decision Rules A well-known mathematical modeling approach provides a set of equations to calculate the best work force size, production rate, and inventory level for each time period in the planning horizon. This set of equations has become known as the *linear decision rules* (LDRs).[7] The advantages of this procedure are that, like linear programming, it guarantees an optimal solution and saves trial-and-error computations. In addition, it recognizes that some cost relationships may be nonlinear rather than linear. The LDR model has an advantage, then, since it can use both linear and quadratic (nonlinear) cost relationships.

A disadvantage of the LDR model is that it must be custom tailored for each organization. The procedure requires a careful study of a company's cost structure, which must then be expressed in mathematical form. Next, a rather extensive mathematical analysis must be made to come up with the proper linear decision rules for that particular company. Whenever the company's cost relationships change, for example, when salaries increase, the mathematical derivation of the LDRs must be redone.

A Heuristic Approach for Aggregate Planning

A final class of aggregate planning models has evolved in recent years. These methods apply in situations in which management has done aggregate output planning on an intuitive basis. Best known among them

---

[6]The application of linear programming to aggregate planning was pioneered by E. H. Bowman, "Production Scheduling by the Transportation Method of Linear Programming," *Operations Research* 4, no. 1 (February 1956), 100–103. An application of the simplex method to production planning by a truck manufacturer is given by J. A. Fuller, "A Linear Programming Approach to Aggregate Scheduling," *Academy of Management Journal* 18, no. 1 (March 1975), 129–36.

[7]The procedure for developing the LDRs is demonstrated by C. C. Holt, F. Modigliani, J. F. Muth, and H. A. Simon, *Planning Production, Inventories, and Work Force* (Englewood Cliffs, N.J.: Prentice Hall, 1960).

is the *management coefficients model.* This procedure requires obtaining records of past work force, production, and inventory decisions. These data are analyzed by multiple regression techniques to find those regression equations that best fit the historical data. These regression equations are then used to make *future* planning decisions in much the same way that the LDRs are used.

The advantages of the heuristic model are that the model is easy to obtain if sufficient historical data are available and that by reducing the variability in decision making, it can reduce costs. The heuristic model must be applied, however, with great caution. The fact that *past* decision-making tendencies have been successful does not necessarily mean they will be successful when they are applied mechanically to *future* circumstances. Furthermore, this procedure may provide plans that are nowhere near optimal.

Search Procedures

Often it is possible to have a computer search for optimal aggregate plans. The computer does this by trying many combinations of work force and production rates for each period in the planning horizon. Although it explores many possible combinations of these variables, it does not do so randomly. Very specific rules are built into the search procedure to guide the search in a systematic way. The search continues until no further improvement results or until a specified amount of search has been reached.

A disadvantage of computer search is the possibility of obtaining a nonoptimal plan. Although they explore and evaluate a large number of plans, they do not examine *all* possible plans. Thus unlike the mathematical optimization models, the best plan may not be discovered by computer search.

Computer search is probably the most flexible of the optimum-seeking aggregate planning models. Cost functions need not be linear or quadratic, nor do they need to be unchanging over time. Various types of costs and operating constraints can be incorporated in the model. When the tradeoffs for cost and accuracy are considered, the computer search procedures are very attractive approaches to aggregate planning.

Selecting an Aggregate Planning Technique

Few studies have compared the various solution techniques that range from simple graphical techniques to more complex mathematical models. A notable exception is the work of Lee and Khumawala.[8]

Lee and Khumawala compared four models with company decisions for an aggregate planning situation in a capital goods firm having an $11 million annual sales volume. The plant was a typical job shop manufacturing facility in which parts were produced for inventory and then assembled into the final product. A computer simulation was developed that closely followed the firm's operations and allowed the models to be

[8]W. B. Lee and B. M. Khumawala, "Simulation Testing of Aggregate Production Planning Models in an Implementation Methodology," *Management Science* 20, no. 6 (February 1974), 903–11.

compared. Models compared in the study are listed in Table 10.14. (Parametric production planning is another heuristic method.) As you can see, comparative profits clearly favor each model over the existing company decisions. The management coefficients model showed the least improvement, $187,000 (4 percent); the search decision rule showed the greatest improvement, $601,000 (14 percent).

IMPLEMENTING AGGREGATE PLANS AND MASTER SCHEDULES

Unplanned Events

Once the aggregate plan is developed, it must be continually updated as time elapses to take into account unplanned occurrences. Although January's forecasted demand may have been 4,000 units, at the end of January we may find that actual demand is above or below the forecasted amount, and ending inventory for the month may be at some level other than what we expected. Other unexpected events can also disrupt plans. Perhaps the planned output level for the month was not achieved, or perhaps the work force did not produce at its average capability. In any event, unplanned events must be taken into account by reusing the aggregate planning methods we used before, except that we now use actual conditions, instead of planned conditions as input data to the model.

When aggregate plans are updated, we can expect corresponding changes will be needed in the master production schedule. In fact, MPS changes are needed even when the aggregate plan remains fixed. MPS transactions, records, and reports are updated and reviewed periodically as forecasts of individual item demands change, when methods improvements or engineering changes modify the production process and performance times, and when materials delays or equipment failures occur. This periodic review and updating process, called *rolling through time,* exemplifies the dynamic nature of the planning and scheduling activities in operations management.[9]

Behavioral Considerations

Behavioral considerations enter into aggregate planning and scheduling both in the planning process itself and in attempting to implement the plan.

Behavior in the Planning Process Some important behavioral factors arise from the extreme complexity of the planning problem and the capacity limitations of the person who must resolve the planning problem. Consider the time horizon that should be used for optimal planning. In some situations, a long horizon is required, and problem complexities increase accordingly. Do planners adopt a long enough horizon? Some

[9]*Rolling through time* is discussed in T. E. Vollmann, W. L. Berry, and D. C. Whybark, *Manufacturing Planning and Control Systems* (Homewood, Ill.: Richard D. Irwin, Inc.), 1984, Chap. 7.

Table 10.14 Comparative profit performance of selected aggregate planning models

Aggregate Planning Model	Annual Profit
Company decisions	$4,420,000
Management coefficients model	4,607,000
Linear decision rule	4,821,000
Parametric production planning	4,900,000
Search decision rule	5,021,000

Source: William B. Lee and Basheer M. Khumawala, "Simulation Testing of Aggregate Production Planning Models in an Implementation Methodology," *Management Science* 20, no. 6 (February 1974), 906.

experimental research reveals that they do not.[10] Although "short-sighted" plans based on judgment and experience result in operating costs that are higher than they need to be, the use of longer horizons apparently poses a difficult mental task. Fortunately, today's abundance of computers and software offers inexpensive, powerful assistance. Microcomputers with database software and electronic spreadsheets permit desktop convenience for exploring complex planning and scheduling problems quickly, and they're often used to supplement the human elements of the planning process.

Behavioral Considerations in Implementation The implementation of a plan can affect organizational behavior in several ways. It signals the need for actions by other parts of the organization. Purchasing must plan to acquire necessary materials and resources. Arrangements may have to be made for retaining the services of subcontractors. Changes in work force must be closely coordinated with the personnel department so that appropriate human resources are available when needed. In short, the adoption of an aggregate plan initiates decision-making activities throughout the organization.

Implementation of a plan may also affect the organizational climate. Both motivation and job satisfaction can be affected. If the work force is decreased in successive time periods, when layoffs occur, or are anticipated, job security is threatened, and both morale and job satisfaction decrease.

SUMMARY

We discussed in this chapter how operations planning and scheduling systems give coherence to production activities and, overall, direct them toward enhancing the organization's competitive effectiveness. These systems were shown to involve various hierarchical levels of activities that

[10] Time horizon and the effects of irrelevant information in intuitive planning are presented in the study by R. J. Ebert, "Environmental Structure and Programmed Decision Effectiveness," *Management Science* 19, no. 4 (December 1972), 435–45.

fit together from top to bottom in support of one another. The aggregate output plan, which identifies the level of production activity for the next 6 to 18 months, expressed in quantities of product groups, was shown to support the overall business plan. We learned that aggregate capacity planning emphasizes the availability of resources for implementing planned output and the two—planned output and capacity—must be balanced at the aggregate level of analysis.

Next we gave a detailed analysis of master production scheduling, which deals with output and capacity questions in more detail. The master schedule shows week by week how many units of each item or end product are due for completion, based on customer orders and short-term forecasts of demand. Our discussion noted that to ensure the feasibility of MPS, it is developed in conjunction with rough-cut capacity planning. We saw that if scheduled production and capacity are mismatched, either the schedule must be modified or the capacity must be temporarily adjusted. Once settled, the master schedule was seen to be consistent with the aggregate plan from above and capable of guiding the more detailed scheduling activities that are undertaken later in the production process.

CASE

Chemtrol Pharmaceutical

Forecasts of Chemtrol Pharmaceutical's primary product show seasonality of monthly demand as follows (units per month): 400, 300, 500, 600, 500, 600, 500, 400, 200, 200, 300, 300. Currently, 300 units are on hand in finished goods inventory. Historically, the highly skilled work force has averaged one-half unit/person daily when 38 to 48 employees are operating. Average productivity drops to .416 units/person when fewer than 38 employees are working, and it averages .446 units/person with more than 48 employees. Standard materials cost $30/unit. Chemtrol's policy of producing 300 units/month during September through February and 500 units/month from March through August has led to predictable employment patterns for the local labor force. Wage rates average $10/hour, and the company operates an eight-hour shift on each of the 20 working days each month. Costs of hiring and training a new employee are estimated at $2,000; a layoff costs $1,000/employee. Finished goods are costed at 4 percent of the value of an item in inventory per month. Backorders are estimated to cost $15/unit/month.

Arlin Sprang, Production Manager, has been requested to find ways to reduce operating costs by at least 10 percent as part of Chemtrol's overall cost-reduction program. He wants to consider what possible efficiencies might result from alternative production scheduling policies.

REVIEW AND DISCUSSION QUESTIONS

1. Identify the relevant costs that should be considered in developing a plan for aggregate output and capacity.
2. Compare and contrast rough-cut with aggregate capacity planning. How are they similar and different?
3. What factors should be considered in selecting a planning horizon? Explain.
4. Outline the advantages and disadvantages of the three pure strategies of aggregate planning.
5. Compare and contrast three different methods of aggregate planning: graphical, linear programming, and a heuristic approach.
6. What role does forecasting play in the aggregate planning process?
7. Aggregate plans and master production schedules are developed on the basis of demand forecasts. But after the forecasts have been made, actual demand often deviates from the forecasted amount. Explain how the aggregate planning process continues when this happens.
8. Explain how aggregate plans and master production schedules serve as initiators of action in other functional activities of the organization.
9. Demonstrate how aggregate planning and scheduling costs are affected by forecast errors.
10. Discuss similarities and differences in the aggregate planning problems facing service organizations and goods-producing organizations.
11. What problem characteristics cause the master production scheduling problem to be so complex?
12. How might aggregate planning affect job satisfaction?
13. What problem characteristics cause the aggregate planning problem to be so complex?

PROBLEMS

Solved Problems

1. A manufacturer has the following information on its major product:
   Regular-time production capacity = 2,600 units/period
   Overtime production costs = $12/unit
   Inventory costs = $2/unit/period (based on the ending inventory)
   Backlog costs = $5/unit/period
   Beginning inventory = 400 units

Period	Demand (units)
1	4,000
2	3,200
3	2,000
4	2,800

Develop a level production plan that yields zero inventory at the end of period 4. What costs result from this plan?

Period	Demand	Production	Ending Inventory	Regular Production	Overtime Production
0			400		
1	4,000	2,900	− 700	2,600	300
2	3,200	2,900	−1000	2,600	300
3	2,000	2,900	− 100	2,600	300
4	2,800	2,900	0	2,600	300
Average =	3,000				

$$\begin{aligned}\text{Total cost} &= \text{Overtime} + \text{Inventory} + \text{Backlogs}\\ &= (300 \times 4 \times \$12) + (0 \times \$2) + (1{,}800 \times \$5)\\ &= \$23{,}400\end{aligned}$$

2. A chair manufacturer who produces three different models (A, B, and C) has developed a master production schedule for the next five weeks. Historically, worker productivity has averaged 8 units/week for each employee based on the "typical mix" of chairs. The company employs 50 workers. The standard labor hours for chairs are 1.0, 2.0, and 1.5 hours for models A, B, and C, respectively.

Master Production Schedule (units)

Chair	Week 1	2	3	4	5
A	200		200		100
B				200	100
C	100	300	100		

Evaluate the capacity utilization of the MPS.

Schedule of Labor Hours

Chair	Week 1	2	3	4	5
A	200		200		100
B				400	200
C	150	450	150		
Total requirements (hours)	350	450	350	400	300
Total hours available	400	400	400	400	400

Capacity is underutilized in weeks 1, 3, and 5; capacity is inadequate in week 2.

Reinforcing Fundamentals

3. Refer to the data for Problem 1. If you could adjust the beginning inventory (400 units) to any level you choose, what beginning level would minimize the annual operating costs?
4. Refer to the data for Problem 2. Develop a master schedule that improves the capacity utilization under the following conditions: Production during the five-week horizon must include 500, 300, and 500 units of chairs A, B, and C, respectively, and no more than two types of chairs can be scheduled in any week.
5. Reconsider the aggregate planning problem of the Go-Rite Company example presented in this chapter. If the beginning aggregate inventory is 10,000 units (instead of zero), develop a good aggregate plan that uses a level production rate. How would the costs of your plan compare with those of the previous level plan in Table 10.7?
6. Reconsider the aggregate planning problem of the Go-Rite Company example presented in this chapter. If the beginning aggregate inventory is 10,000 units (instead of zero), develop a good aggregate plan that uses a chase strategy. How would your plan's costs compare with those of the chase plan in Table 10.7.
7. Referring to the data in Problem 6, evaluate the capacity feasibility and utilization of the new chase plan.
8. Randolf Corporation has estimated its aggregate demand for the coming year as follows:

Month	Productive Days	Demand (units)	Month	Productive Days	Demand (units)
Jan	22	8,000	July	22	26,000
Feb	19	12,000	Aug	11	16,000
Mar	21	18,000	Sept	21	18,000
Apr	22	20,000	Oct	22	14,000
May	21	28,000	Nov	18	9,000
June	21	25,000	Dec	21	7,000

Currently, there are 100 employees with normal productivity of 12 units/day/employee. Daily capacity can be increased up to 30 percent by working overtime at an additional cost of $2/unit. Regular time salaries average $30/day/employee. Monthly costs of storing units in inventory are $2/unit. Inventory shortages cost $10/unit short. Costs of hiring and training a new employee are $300, and a layoff of an employee costs $200. Additional capacity is available by subcontracting to a local manufacturer at a cost of $8/unit. Currently, Randolf has 5,000 units in inventory. Develop a good plan for next year's aggregate output.
9. An office equipment repair company has sales/service offices throughout North Carolina. The company services such products as typewriters, dictating equipment, photocopiers, and small computers. The following is the demand forecast for the next year in bimonthly groups.

Period	Forecasted Demand (standard units of work)
Jan–Feb	210
Mar–Apr	245
May–June	260
July–Aug	250
Sept–Oct	235
Nov–Dec	220

(a) Prepare a graph of cumulative service units demanded versus cumulative service days, assuming that each two-month period has 43 working days.
(b) Assume that an employee contributes 344 working hours each two months and that each unit requires 30 standard hours to produce. Assuming no overtime or part-time employees, calculate the number of employees required each period.
(c) The company staffs to meet peak demand without overtime, hiring, or firing to meet demand changes. With a current labor rate of $8.25/hour, what will be the bimonthly and annual labor costs? What is the extra cost incurred for this policy?
(d) Cost out an alternative aggregate plan that allows hiring or firing a maximum of twice during the year. For this plan, assume hiring costs equal firing costs and are $2,300/employee hired or fired. Would you recommend this plan over Part c above?

10. Reconsider the two aggregate plans that were developed for the public works department example in this chapter. Prepare for the director your recommendation for a better aggregate plan.

11. Reconsider the master production schedule for the Go-Rite Company example (Table 10.9) in this chapter. Suppose the standard labor hours/unit are .80, .75, and .97 for models A, B, and C, respectively. Perform rough-cut capacity tests of the MPS under these new conditions, and compare your results with those in Table 10.11.

Challenging Exercises

12. Reconsider the Go-Rite Company example in this chapter. Assume that customer backorders are now allowed and the backlog cost is $2/unit/month. Develop a good aggregate plan for wagon production.

13. Reconsider the Go-Rite Company example in this chapter. Suppose three months have elapsed since the initial aggregate planning and during that time actual demand was 5,000 units in January, 12,000 in February, and 14,000 in March. New sales forecasts for April through December are 24,000; 25,000; 21,000; 16,000; 16,000; 18,000; 14,000; 10,000; and 7,000. Develop a revised plan to take into account this recent information.

14. Reconsider the aggregate planning problem of the Go-Rite Company in this chapter, and do the following:
(a) Develop a good plan for the first 3 months of the year, ignoring the remaining months.
(b) Develop a good plan for the first 6 months of the year, ignoring the last 6 months.
(c) Assuming your 6-month plan in part b is fully implemented, develop a good plan for the final 6 months of the year.
(d) Compare the costs of the 3-month, 6-month, and 12-month plans. Explain any differences among them.

15. A manufacturing firm is trying to schedule production for the coming three months. Product demand for each of the next three months is forecasted as 300, 250, and 325 units, respectively. Currently, 95 units are on hand and available in finished goods inventory at the factory. At the end of the three-month scheduling period, the company wants to have 120 finished units available for future demand, and it wants to have supplied enough units to meet all demand (backorders are not allowed). Regular shift operations are capable of producing 200 units/month at a cost of $10/unit. Overtime operations can supply up to 100 units/month at $15 cost/unit. Inventory carrying costs are $2/unit/month for finished goods. Structure this scheduling problem in a transportation linear programming format. Create and interpret an initial feasible solution.

16. Reconsider the master production schedule for the Go-Rite Company (Table 10.9). The master scheduler wishes to do a more detailed job of rough-cut capacity planning to see if the trial schedule is feasible in Go-Rite's four major work centers. The planned labor availability is as follows:

Work Center	Days 1–62 Number of People	Days 1–62 Standard Hours/Week	Days 63–80 Number of People	Days 63–80 Standard Hours/Week
Fabrication	19	760	35	1,400
Welding	16	640	30	1,200
Painting	6	240	10	400
Assembly	14	560	25	1,000

Each wagon is processed through all the work centers and, historically, the total work content in a typical wagon is distributed as follows: 35 percent in fabrication, 30 percent in welding, 10 percent in painting, and 25 percent in assembly. Evaluate the capacity feasibility and utilization in the work centers for the trial MPS.

GLOSSARY

Aggregate capacity planning The process of testing the feasibility of planned output (aggregate) against existing capacity and evaluating overall capacity utilization.

Aggregate output planning The process of determining output levels (units) of a product group over the next 6 to 18 months on a weekly or monthly basis; it identifies the overall level of production outputs in support of the business plan.

Backorders Outstanding or unfilled customer requests for output.

Blocks of capacity Clusters of key resources in the facility that are consumed during the production process; examples include machine time and labor time.

Business plan A statement of the organization's overall level of business activity for the next 6 to 18 months, usually expressed in terms of dollar volume of sales for its various product groups.

Disaggregation The process of translating aggregate plans for product groups into detailed operational plans for individual products.

Graphical method of aggregate planning Two-dimensional model showing the time phasing of demand against aggregate output rates and aggregate capacity.

Linear decision rules (LDRs) Set of equations determining optimal work force and production decisions for aggregate output.

Master production schedule (MPS) Shows week by week how many of each end product are due for completion; developed from customer orders and demand forecasts for each product.

Mixed strategy Aggregate scheduling strategy that incorporates or combines some elements from each of the "pure" aggregate planning strategies.

Product group (family) A set of individual products that share or consume common blocks of capacity in the manufacturing process.

Pure strategy Aggregate planning strategy using just one of several possible means to respond to demand fluctuations.

Relevant costs Those costs that change, or potentially change, depending upon the decision alternative selected.

Rough-cut capacity planning The process of assessing the capacity feasibility of master production schedules.

Shop floor control Activities that execute and control shop operations; includes loading, sequencing, detailed scheduling, and expediting jobs in production.

Work force utilization Extent to which existing work force resources are over- or underutilized relative to their regular time availabilities.

SELECTED READINGS

Berry, W. L., T. E. Vollmann, and D. C. Whybark, *Master Production Scheduling: Principles and Practice*. Falls Church, Va.: American Production and Inventory Control Society, Inc., 1979.

Buffa, E. S., and J. G. Miller, *Production-Inventory Systems: Planning and Control* (3rd. ed.). Homewood, Ill.: Richard D. Irwin, 1979.

Holt, C. C., F. Modigliani, J. F. Muth, and H. A. Simon, *Planning Production, Inventories, and Work Force*. Englewood Cliffs, N.J.: Prentice Hall, 1960.

Krajewski, L. J., and L. P. Ritzman, "Disaggregation in Manufacturing and Service Organizations: Survey of Problems and Research," *Decision Sciences* 8, no. 1 (January 1977), 1–18.

Lee, W. B., and B. M. Khumawala, "Simulation Testing of Aggregate Production Planning Models in an Implementation Methodology," *Management Science* 20, no. 6 (February 1974), 903–11.

McLeavey, D. W., and S. L. Narasimhan, *Production Planning and Inventory Control*. Boston: Allyn & Bacon, 1985.

Meal, H. C., "Putting Production Decisions Where They Belong," *Harvard Business Review* 62, no. 2 (March–April 1984), 102–11.

Vollmann, T. E., W. L. Berry, and D. C. Whybark, *Manufacturing Planning and Control Systems*. Homewood, Ill.: Richard D. Irwin, 1984.

11

Operations Scheduling

First Express, a division of First Tennessee Bank, N.A., provides payment system services to financial institutions and corporations located nationwide. Each night, all across the nation, Federal Express airplanes fly to Memphis, and while Federal Express employees are sorting packages, First Express employees are sorting checks. Upon completion of the process and according to schedule, the airplanes fly from Memphis back to the originating cities and both the checks and packages are delivered to their appropriate destinations.

First Express provides this service because of the time value of money. When a check drawn on a Miami bank is deposited in a Seattle bank, the check must be sent from Seattle to Miami. The time the check is in transit is called *float*. Reducing the float time creates opportunities for a financial institution to produce additional business or produce income for itself. Let's assume the above mentioned check is for $10 million and that normally it takes two days from the time it is deposited in the Seattle bank until it is paid by the Miami bank. If a service can clear the check in one day, rather than two, the real value at today's rates is nearly $2,700. To the Seattle bank, this could be income that flows directly to the bottom line.

First Express provides this service. Intensive job shop and work center scheduling is required by many different organizations if the desired results are to be achieved. The financial institution in Seattle must process and deliver the check to Federal Express before the plane departs. The plane must arrive in Memphis on time and be off-loaded rapidly.

First Express's operation consists of receiving, sorting, reject processing, outbound packaging, and reconciling. The inbound area requires more manpower initially as the boxes arrive quickly and receive priority sequencing at this point. This heavy work load moves to other departments as the evening progresses. Consequently, work schedules must accommodate each work center's highs and lows.

Personnel on the inbound side are cross-trained and shifted to outbound later in the work cycle. Each step of this process is dependent on the successful completion of the preceding one. We have a narrow processing window; slackness in one area cannot be made up in another. With such little room for error, our employees must work quickly and accurately.

Packages arrive at First Express from 11:00 P.M. till 1:30 A.M. and begin to leave our facility at 2:05 A.M. The packages are loaded into the Federal Express airplanes and flown to the destination city. Upon arrival in the city, a Federal Express employee immediately delivers the package to our clearing bank. The delivery must occur before that bank's deposit deadline or the "speed up" in the availability of funds will not occur.

Many variables must be appropriately managed to provide our service. Every night, First Express puts into practical operation the concepts provided in this chapter.

Walter W. Stafeil
Senior Vice President & Manager
First Express
Memphis, Tennessee

As Mr. Stafeil's comments indicate, the operations at First Express have direct and visible consequences for their customers. Success at First Express depends on the ability to manage complex intermittent operations systems. In this chapter we examine the nature of intermittent systems and introduce some concepts, models, and behavioral considerations that enter into planning their use.

WHAT ARE INTERMITTENT SYSTEMS?

Conversion systems can be broadly classified as either continuous or intermittent, depending on the characteristics of the conversion process and the product or service. A *continuous* or *assembly-type system* is one in which a large or indefinite number of units of a homogeneous product is being produced. Intermittent systems, on the other hand, produce a variety of products one at a time (in which case they are custom made) or finite numbers of different products in batches to customer order. Many conversion facilities are neither strictly intermittent nor solely continuous but a combination of both.

Manufacturing

In a manufacturing context, *intermittent systems* are traditionally referred to as *job shops*. As work orders arrive, the work load on the facility increases. Some work centers may be idle at the same time that others are severely overloaded. A work center may experience a large buildup of to-be-done orders awaiting processing. When one order is completed, the equipment may have to be reset or adjusted before the next order can be processed. The challenge is to manage these flows of orders through the shop.

The *sequence* in which waiting jobs are processed is important in determining the efficiency and effectiveness of the intermittent system. Sequencing determines the amount of job lateness, costs incurred for setup and changeover, delivery lead times, inventory costs, and the degree of congestion in the facility. Indeed, the scheduling of intermittent systems poses a challenging problem for operations managers.

Services

Intermittent systems exist in goods-producing and in-service organizations. Intermittent service systems frequently offer provided-to-order services. In restaurants offering meals served to customer order and in automobile repair shops, for example, conversion systems are similar in concept to those in manufacturing job shops.

INTERMITTENT SCHEDULING CONCEPTS AND PROCESSES

As with continuous and assembly operations, the overall stages of planning in Figure 11.1 apply to job-shop operations as well. Guided by the business plan, aggregate planning reveals overall levels of planned output and capacity utilization as we discussed in Chapter 10. Then, customer orders and forecasts for specific products are incorporated into a master production schedule for the weeks and months ahead. This master schedule feeds the material requirements planning system (discussed in Chapter 14), or any other type of materials planning procedure, that identifies when the products and components are due for completion. Then a transition occurs in the planning process; its emphasis shifts to even more detailed, day-to-day scheduling and control activities called *shop floor control*. As we discuss these activities in the context of job-shop operations, you'll see how they supplement the production plans and how they direct shop operations toward desired results. We discuss these concepts primarily in the context of manufacturing, yet for the most part, they can be generalized to services as well.

Overview of the Scheduling and Control Process

After production plans reveal when specific items and products are needed, there still remain some tasks for translating them into operational terms for their implementation on the shop floor. Included among these are loading, sequencing, detailed scheduling, expediting, and input/output control.

Loading Each job may have its unique product specification and, hence, its routing through various work centers in the facility. As new job orders are released, they are assigned or allocated among the work

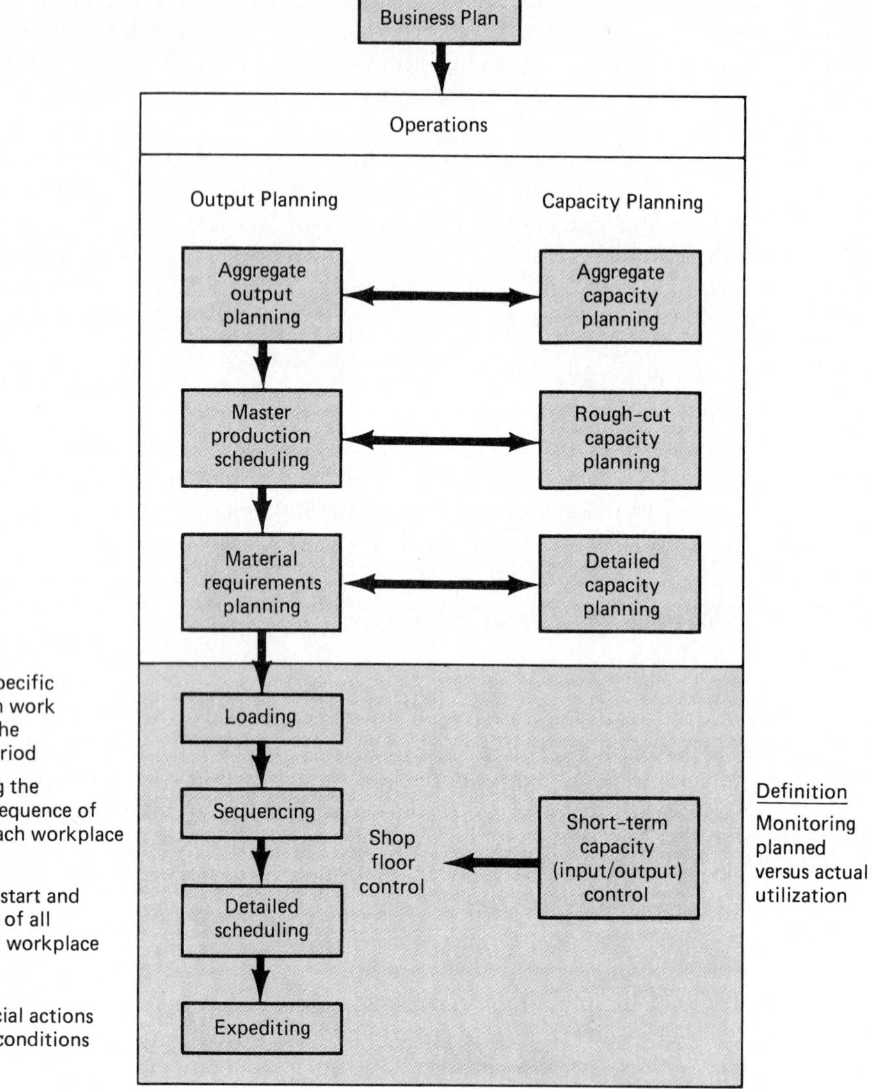

FIGURE 11.1
The operations planning and scheduling system

centers, thus establishing how much of a load each work center must carry during the coming planning period, known as *loading* (sometimes called *shop loading* or *machine loading*).

Sequencing This stage establishes the priorities for jobs in the queues (waiting lines) at the work centers. Priority sequencing specifies the order in which the waiting jobs are processed; it requires the adoption of a priority sequencing rule, a concept we discuss later.

Detailed Scheduling Calendar times are specified when job orders, employees, and materials (inputs), as well as job completion (outputs), should occur at each work center. Detailed dates and times are usually not specified until loading and sequencing have been completed. Using estimates of processing durations and due dates for all jobs, schedulers can establish their beginning and ending dates and develop the detailed schedule.

Expediting In tracking a job's progress, special action may be needed to keep it moving through the facility on time. Manufacturing or service operations disruptions—equipment breakdowns, materials inavailabilities, last-minute priority changes—that cause deviations from plans and schedules sometimes necessitate expediting an important job on a special-handling basis.

Input-Output (Short-Term Capacity) Control Production plans and schedules call for certain levels of capacity and output for a work center, but its actual utilization may differ from what was planned. We can monitor actual versus planned utilization of the work center by using input-output reports and, when discrepancies exist, we can make adjustments to control the utilization at desired levels.

Let's take a closer look at each of these activities to see what they involve and how they relate to one another.

LOADING

Given the existence of several work centers capable of processing new customer orders, which jobs should be assigned to which centers? We know from the production schedule what products are due for completion and when. Furthermore, we have each item's routing so we know which work centers might be involved. Although even the best production schedule creates imbalanced loads, either too heavy or too light, we can still manipulate and manage them at reasonable levels. Two basic approaches for doing so, infinite and finite loading, are in use today. We will present infinite loading in the next section, but delay our discussion of finite loading. To best understand finite loading, you'll need an understanding of priority scheduling and detail scheduling. Therefore, we'll address finite scheduling as a separate section after those topics are presented.

Infinite Loading

With *infinite loading systems,* jobs are allocated to work centers without regard to the work center's capacity; jobs are loaded from the production schedule into the work center as if its capacity were unlimited. With either manual or computer-based systems, Gantt charts and visual load profiles can be helpful for evaluating the current loadings.

The Gantt Load Chart This graphical procedure is shown in Figure 11.2. The aircraft repair facility has four work centers through which five

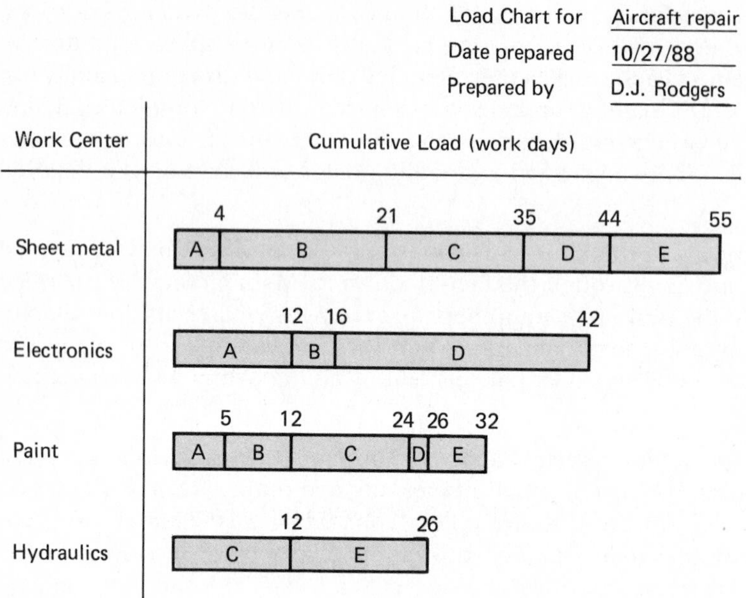

FIGURE 11.2
Gantt load chart for aircraft repair facility

jobs (open orders) must be processed. Aircraft A, B, C, D, and E require sheet metal work; A, B, and D are the only aircraft needing electronics work. The chart shows the total estimated work load that the open orders require at all work centers. Thus, 55 days of cumulative work lie ahead of the sheet metal center; the paint center faces a 32-day load, and so on. The chart does not specify which job will be completed at which time, nor does it show the sequence in which the jobs should be processed.

The Gantt load chart offers the advantages of ease and clarity in communicating important shop information. It does have some important limitations, however. Since the chart is a deterministic device, it does not convey the variabilities of task duration, equipment (including breakdowns), and human performance times, any of which can cause the estimated load to be inaccurate. Also, the chart is static and must be updated periodically to account for new job arrivals and revised time estimates for existing jobs.

The Gantt chart signals the need for reassigning resources when the load at one work center becomes too large. Employees from a low load center may be temporarily shifted to high load areas, or, alternatively, excessive load buildup may be alleviated by temporarily increasing the size of the work force. Multipurpose equipment can be shifted among work centers. If the waiting jobs can be processed at any of several work centers, some of the jobs at high load centers can be reassigned to low load centers. Later we will show how the Gantt chart can be applied to detailed scheduling as well as to loading.

Visual Load Profiles Open job orders are assigned completion dates from the production schedule and, with infinite loading, they're loaded into the work center according to their due dates. Since loading ignores its capacity, the work center can be underloaded or overburdened with waiting jobs in future periods. A visual load profile, like those shown in Figure 11.3, reveals the matchup between the work load and the capacity.

For a manual scheduling system in Part (a) of the figure, the load consists of open orders that have been released to the work center. The load for week 1 exceeds capacity, but the future loads are well within weekly capabilities.

In a computer-based scheduling system, such as time-phased MRP, planned order releases and scheduled receipts, in addition to open orders, can be projected into the load profile as shown in Part b, of the figure. Doing so, we see that projected loads for weeks 3, 4, and 6 exceed capacity, even though the loads for the open orders are feasible.

When confronted with critical overloads, we can try to shift some of the overload to alternative work centers or routings. Or, we can use *lot splitting,* whereby a job order is split and only part of it is processed now and the rest is deferred until later. Still another alternative is *operations splitting:* Part of the job is processed at one work center, and the rest is done in another, similar work center.

Loading with the Assignment Algorithm Occasionally a special case of the linear programming algorithm can be useful for assisting in the loading problem. It can be used when the number of jobs equals the number of work centers or machines on which the jobs must be processed.

This method requires that each machine be assigned one and only one job. Furthermore, some criterion must be chosen to evaluate the "goodness" of the assignments. The person loading may wish to assign in

FIGURE 11.3
Infinite loading for a work center: visual load profiles

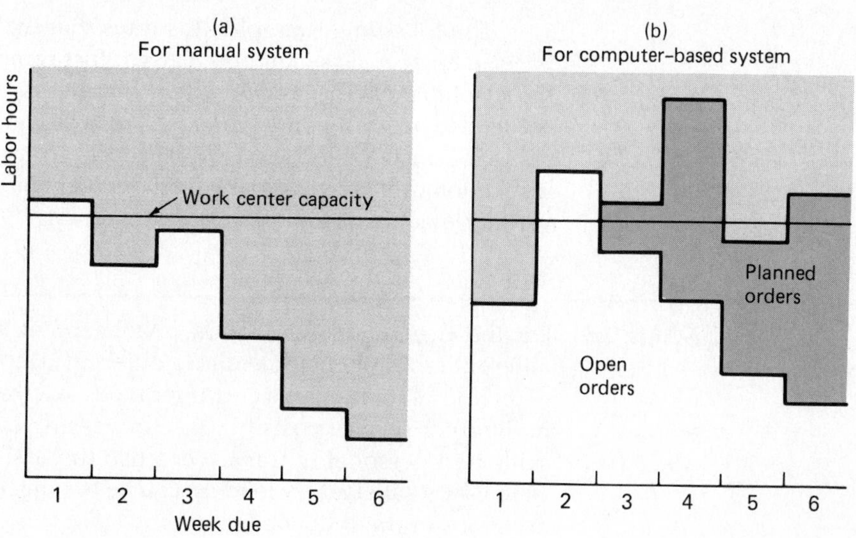

such a way that profit is maximized, operating cost is minimized, or completion time is minimized. Finally, this method is *static;* it indicates a situation at one point in time. However, jobs might be arriving continuously.

Often there are conflicts, in that there is not always a best load center (such as a machine) for each job. Perhaps two jobs could best be run on one load center, but the load center can only process one job. The assignment algorithm is used to resolve this problem. It involves four simple steps that consider the *opportunity costs* of different assignments.

1. *Column reduction.* Subtract the lowest cost in each column from every cost element in that column. Do this for every column. This new matrix of *opportunity costs* is now used in the next step.
2. *Row reduction.* Subtract the lowest cost in each row from every cost element in that row. Do this for every row. This new matrix of opportunity costs is now used in the next step.
3. *Cover the zeros.* Cover all the zero elements in the matrix with horizontal and/or vertical lines. Find the *minimum* number of lines necessary to cover all zeros. If the number of lines required is equal to the number of machines available, an optimal solution has been reached. The optimal assignments are found by examining the zero elements in the matrix. If the number of lines is less than the number of machines, go to step 4.
4. *Create new zeros.* Begin with the matrix and the lines from step 3. Find the smallest uncovered cost element (not covered by a line) and subtract it from all uncovered cost elements, including itself; add it to all cost elements at the line intersections. All other cost elements remain unchanged. Now erase all horizontal and vertical lines and return to step 3.

The following example illustrates that the assignment algorithm can be used for service sector application. Just remember to make analogies to the machine (server) and job (item or person processed). These processes could also be used in assigning jobs to typists in a word processing center, assigning inspection tasks to inspectors in a government health service inspection unit, and assigning farm workers to farm work centers that have varying machine/labor skill requirements.

EXAMPLE

For the Beef Eater Restaurant, management must decide how to direct different types of customers into different waitress service areas. Management knows that various customer types/waitress combinations will result in different service costs because of varying customer traits and waitress skills and personality traits. Let's use the assignment technique to illustrate how a satisfactory loading can be arranged when costs for Beef Eater are given in the following matrix:

Customer Type	Waitresses		
	Sally	Wanda	Bertha
1	$12.90	$11.90	$12.10
2	15.30	15.50	14.30
3	13.90	13.90	13.00

Our first matrix would be for column reduction, the second for row reduction.

	S	W	B
1	0	0	0
2	2.40	3.60	2.20
3	1.00	2.00	0.90

→

	S	W	B
1	0	0	0
2	0.20	1.40	0
3	0.10	1.10	0

The minimum number of lines required to cover all zeros is 2, a number that does not equal the numbers of servers. (Servers are analogous to machines and customers to jobs in the algorithm.) We proceed to step 4.

	S	W	B
1	0	0	0.10
2	0.10	1.30	0
3	0	1.00	0

The minimum lines now equal the number of servers and the optimal solution is:

Customer Type	Waitress	Cost
1	Wanda	$11.90
2	Bertha	14.30
3	Sally	13.90
		$40.10

PRIORITY SEQUENCING

When jobs compete for a work center's capacity, which job should be done next? Priority sequencing rules are applied to all jobs awaiting in the queue. Then, when the work center becomes open for a new job, the one with the highest priority is processed next.

Choosing the Right Sequencing Rule

Many different sequencing rules are available as we'll soon see, and the logical questions are "Which one should I select?" and "What difference does it make?" Your choice is important because a sequencing rule that performs well on one dimension, say on minimizing inventories, may not do so well on another dimension such as minimizing production setup costs. Some major criteria are the following:

- Setup costs
- In-process inventory costs
- Idle time, percent
- Percentage of jobs late
- Average job lateness
- Standard deviation of job lateness
- Average number of jobs waiting
- Average job completion time
- Standard deviation of job completion time

Three of the criteria (setup costs, in-process inventory costs, and station idle time) are primarily concerned with internal facility efficiency. The more these are minimized without jeopardizing service to customers, the better the use of limited resources and chances for improved profitability. Three of the criteria (percentage of jobs late, average job lateness, and variance of job lateness) are more customer- or service-oriented than internally oriented. To the extent that these criteria increase, service to customers deteriorates. Finally, three of the criteria (number of jobs waiting, average job completion time, and variance of job completion time) reflect both a customer service and internal efficiency orientation that are hard to separate. It is difficult, if not impossible, to find a sequencing rule that best satisfies all these criteria simultaneously.

Some Priority Sequencing Rules

The following rules are representative of the many that are used today in manufacturing and service industries:

- First-come-first-served (FCFS). As its name suggests, incoming jobs or customers are processed in their order of arrival using this rule. It is commonly applied in service industries such as banks, supermarkets, etc.
- Earliest due date (EDD). Top priority is assigned to the awaiting job that has the earliest due date. This rule ignores when the jobs arrive and the amount of operation time each of them requires.
- Shortest processing time (SPT). The job that can be completed in the shortest time at this work center is processed next. The jobs' due dates and order of arrival are immaterial.
- Truncated shortest processing time (TSPT). This rule is the same as

the SPT rule, except that the jobs that have waited longer than some designated truncation time are given highest priority and are processed next.

- Least slack (LS). This rule calculates the slack of each awaiting job and gives highest priority to the one having the least slack. Slack is the time remaining until its due date minus the duration of the operation time for the job. The order of arrival is ignored with this rule.

Let's examine some of these rules to illustrate how they work and to become more familiar with their terminology. We'll apply them to the five job orders awaiting sheet metal operations in the aircraft repair facility we discussed earlier. Customers submitted these job orders during the past week. Rather than evaluating all of the 5! or 120 different possible sequences for these five jobs, let's evaluate the sequences created by the FCFS and SPT rules.

First-come-first-served (FCFS) Sequencing In a sense of fairness to the customers, let's consider a first-come-first-served (FCFS) sequencing rule. Say that job orders arrived alphabetically, and that customers requested that their sheet metal work be completed at the times listed under Job Due Date in Table 11.1.

The job flow time for this processing sequence measures the length of time each job spends in the system to complete that job. Thus, flow time includes waiting time and processing time for each unit. Job B, for example, waits 4 days while A is being processed and then takes 17 days operation time itself. Job B is therefore to be completed in 21 days, its flow time.

Our FCFS sequencing rule results in the following:

1. *Total completion time.* All jobs will have been completed in 55 days.
2. *Average completion time.* The average number of days a job spends in the system is 31.8. This figure is calculated by summing the flow times for all jobs and dividing by the number of jobs:

$$(4 + 21 + 35 + 44 + 55) \div 5 = 31.8$$

Table 11.1 Sequencing data for a first-come-first-serve (FCFS) priority rule

Job Sequence	Job Operation Time (days)	Job Flow Time	Job Due Date
A	4	4	6
B	17	21	20
C	14	35	18
D	9	44	12
E	11	55	12
	55		

3. *Average number of jobs in the system.* The average number of jobs in the system from the beginning of the sequence through the time when the last job is finished is 2.89. For the first 4 days, 5 jobs are in the system; for the next 17 days, 4 jobs are in the system; for days 22 to 35, 3 jobs are in the system, and so forth. There are 55 total days for the sequence. Hence,

$$[5(4) + 4(17) + 3(14) + 2(9) + 1(11)] \div 55$$
$$= 2.89 \text{ jobs in the system/day}$$

4. *Average job lateness.* The average lateness of the jobs is 18.6 days. The lateness for each job is obtained by comparing its flow time with its due date. Thus, job A is completed at day 4; since its due date is day 6, there's no lateness. Job B is completed at day 21, and its due date is day 20; this job is one day late. Similarly, lateness for jobs C, D, and E is 17, 32, and 43 days, respectively. Average lateness is:

$$(0 + 1 + 17 + 32 + 43) \div 5 = 18.6 \text{ days}$$

The FCFS sequencing rule has the advantage of simplicity, and in some respects it provides a sense of "fair play" from the customer's viewpoint. However, some other rules are more desirable from the productive system's viewpoint.

Shortest Processing Time (SPT) Consider the shortest processing time (SPT) rule: sequence the orders according to processing time, and assign highest priority to the order with the shortest processing time.

The SPT rule yields the data in Table 11.2 and the following performance by using the sequence A, D, E, C, B:

1. *Total completion time.* All jobs will have been completed in 55 days.
2. *Average completion time.* The sum of flow times is (4 + 13 + 24 + 38 + 55) = 134. Average completion time is 134 ÷ 5 = 26.8 days.
3. *Average number of jobs in the system.* Over the entire span of 55 days, 5 jobs are in the system (waiting or being processed) for 4 days while job A is being processed; 4 jobs are in the system while job D is being

Table 11.2 Sequencing data for a shortest processing time (SPT) priority rule

Job Sequence	Job Operation Time (days)	Job Flow Time	Job Due Date
A	4	4	6
D	9	13	12
E	11	24	12
C	14	38	18
B	17	55	20

processed for 9 days, and so on. Thus, the average number of jobs in the system each day is:

$$[5(4) + 4(9) + 3(11) + 2(14) + 1(17)] \div 55 = 2.44 \text{ jobs}$$

4. *Average job lateness.* The days late for each job in this sequence are 0, 1, 12, 20, and 35 days, respectively. Average lateness is:

$$(0 + 1 + 12 + 20 + 35) \div 5 = 13.6 \text{ days}$$

Characteristics of the Sequencing Rules

When we compare the performance of FCFS and SPT, we see that SPT is superior. Although total completion time is 55 days for both sequences, SPT offers a lower average completion time. This means that inventories are tied up to a lesser extent, and quicker service can be provided to customers. With SPT, the average number of jobs in the system is reduced; this reduction can lead to less shop congestion and lower inventory levels. Finally, since average lateness in deliveries to customers is reduced, overall service is improved.

The superior performance of the SPT rule in our example was not an accident. For jobs to be processed in one work center, it is consistently superior to other rules; it is optimal for minimizing average completion time, average number of jobs in the system, and average job lateness.

Among the five rules cited, only two—EDD and LS—are based on the *due date*. This feature is especially useful in MRP scheduling systems because the MRP outputs identify scheduled receipts in weekly or even daily time periods that become the due dates for batches of component items.

Sequencing Through Multiple Work Centers

Our discussion of sequencing, up to this point, has focused on processing jobs through a single work center and, for this simple problem, optimal analytical solutions are possible. Most facilities, however, aren't faced with having several jobs to be processed at a single work center; they have many jobs to be done on multiple (often as many as a hundred) centers. Furthermore, not all jobs are going to follow identical routings; some pass through a few work centers; others pass through many. As jobs arrive at facilities in a variety of patterns, they are routed diversely. Thus the composition of waiting jobs at a work center may change continuously, and priority sequencing becomes a dynamic ongoing process.

For instances like these, optimal analytic solution procedures do not exist. One approach by mathematicians and operations researchers has been to apply queueing theory to jobs as they form waiting lines (queues) in advance of being served (processed). The strength of queueing theory is that it provides optimal solutions. Application of queueing theory is severely limited because the mathematical complexity becomes insurmountable once such assumptions as arrival times and service times are relaxed from a few well-known distributions (exponential and Poisson, for example) to more realistic empirical distributions.

Simulation of Intermittent (Job-Shop) Systems

The basic procedures of simulation we discussed in the supplement to Chapter 10 can be used to evaluate various sequencing rules in job-shop facilities. The following outline shows the components and procedures that are included in a simulation approach to modeling an intermittent system. Simulation offers advantages for evaluating system performance as compared with tampering directly with the job shop itself.

1. *Shop configuration.* The number of work centers in the shop must be specified in the model.
2. *Job arrivals.* One segment, or module, of the model is needed to generate the arrivals of new jobs entering the system. The pattern and timing of simulated arrivals can be based on historical patterns previously experienced by the facility. During the simulation, the Monte Carlo technique can be used to select at random the time of the next job arrival based on the data pattern supplied by the simulation designer.
3. *Job classification.* Once a new job arrives, its processing requirements or routing must be established. Again, historical data can reveal patterns of processing (routing) requirements that may be built into the model. When a new simulated job arrives, its routing is determined in the simulator, using the Monte Carlo technique.
4. *Processing times.* In the simulator, the time required to process a job at a work center can be determined based on historical service time patterns supplied by the simulation designer. Often, the service (processing) time for a job is randomly selected from a service time distribution that is representative of that work center. The Monte Carlo technique is used for this purpose.
5. *Specification of shop performance parameters.* The designer specifies the shop performance characteristics of interest. Such statistics might include percent of idle time at each center, length of job queues throughout the system, average waiting times for jobs, value of inventories in process, measures of job lateness, and measures of job flow times through the system.
6. *Specification of sequencing rule.* The priority sequencing rule to be tested is selected and built into the model.
7. *Simulation.* The simulation is conducted over time (this is called a *simulation run*). It is executed by generating new job arrival times, determining their routings, loading them to the appropriate work centers, sequencing them by use of the priority rule, and creating the representative service times for each job at each center. This simulation is done for a large number of job arrivals, say 10,000 or more. When a job is finished at one center, it is placed in the waiting line at the next center in its routing to await processing there. When a work center finishes one job, it is free to begin servicing one of the jobs in its waiting line. The awaiting job with highest priority (based on the

sequencing rule) is selected for processing next on the open work center.

8. *Recording shop performance parameters.* After all jobs have been processed, the resulting shop performance statistics are recorded and saved for later evaluation and comparison. The simulation run has been completed.
9. *Replication.* At this point, the original sequencing rule can be replaced with an alternative rule in the model. Then, with all other model components unchanged, the simulation can be repeated. The shop performance characteristics from the second run can be compared with those of the first run to determine which of the two sequencing rules performs better. Systematic replications can be made for any number of different rules.

Simulation Results for Job Completion Time One study tested ten different priority dispatching rules in six different job-shop configurations using computer simulation.[1] The results are based on processing over 2 million simulated jobs through the system. Our main interest in the results has to do with the *job completion characteristics* of the rules, an important concern to shop managers. Job completion time is commonly measured in two ways: as the *average* processing or flow time of jobs through the system; and as the *dispersion of job* flow times through the system (measured by a standard deviation or variance).

The simulation study found, among the ten rules that were tested, that average (mean) flow time per job was lowest (0.99) for the SPT rule, and for the other rules it was as high as 2.54. The standard deviation of flow time ranged from 1.55 to 5.43 for the various rules. Although the standard deviation of flow time was lower for two of the other rules, SPT did well on this dimension also. These results are not surprising when you consider how the SPT rule works. Since the job selected for processing next is the one with the smallest expected completion time, this job doesn't have to wait long in the queue; its flow time (waiting plus processing time) is low.

Simulation Results for Job Lateness and Work-in-process Inventories Using a computer simulation, another researcher examined how well 39 different priority rules performed in terms of job lateness and in-process inventories in the facility.[2] In terms of percentage of jobs late (that is, jobs not completed by due date), SPT performed far better than most other rules tested. Using several measures of work-in-process, this same study found that the SPT rule was not optimal for minimizing work-in-process,

---

[1]See Y. R. Nanot, "An Experimental Investigation and Comparative Evaluation of Priority Disciplines in Job Shop-Like Queueing Networks" (Ph.D. dissertation, UCLA, 1963).

[2]See R. W. Conway, "Priority Dispatching and Job Lateness in a Job Shop," *Journal of Industrial Engineering* 16, no. 4 (July–August 1965), 228–37, and idem, "Priority Dispatching and Work-in-Process Inventory in a Job Shop," *Journal of Industrial Engineering* 16, no. 2 (March–April 1965), 123–30.

although its performance was still relatively good. The optimal rules are called *compound rules.* They require somewhat more complex calculations than does the SPT rule. These compound rules are a weighted combination of the SPT and other rules, all combined into one.[3] In short, the SPT, although not optimal, performed well, and it did so without requiring the extensive calculations necessary in the more complex rules.

Sequencing Procedures for Other Criteria

Some additional sequencing procedures are available for more specialized situations. First we examine sequencing for situations where setup costs are the primary consideration. Next we look at a procedure that minimizes the completion time for the last job through two successive work centers.

Setup Dependence Sometimes the dominant consideration at a workstation is the setup, or changeover, cost for processing the different jobs. Table 11.3 shows that overall setup costs for the aircraft repair facility depend on the sequence in which the five jobs are processed. These data show the setup cost when job *j* is processed after job *i*. It assumes that job A is already being processed and jobs B, C, D, and E remain to be done. If we choose job B to follow A, a high setup cost ($29) is incurred. If job D follows A, the setup cost is only $18. Which sequence of all jobs minimizes total setup costs?

The Next Best Rule (NB) One heuristic solution approach, the next best (NB) rule states, "Given that job *i* is being processed, select next the unassigned job *j* for which setup cost is minimum." For example, if job A is currently being processed, job D would be selected next, since it has the lowest setup cost following job A. After job D, job C or E ($10 setup cost) would be selected next. The NB rule would yield two sequences:

Sequence	Cost
NB_1: A–D–C–E–B	$18 + 10 + 26 + 18 = $72
NB_2: A–D–E–C–B	$18 + 10 + 16 + 35 = $79

NB_1 is preferred, since its cost is lower than NB_2. This NB_1 sequence is not optimal. An enumeration of all 24 possible sequences shows that the optimal sequence is A–D–E–B–C, with a cost of $60. However, NB_1 may be considered *satisfactory,* especially if we are dealing with larger problems for which complete enumeration of all alternatives is not feasible.

In this example, sequence NB_2 happens to be identical to the SPT (shortest processing time) sequence. In general, however, the NB and SPT

[3]For examples of combination rules, see E. LeGrande, "The Development of a Factory Simulation Using Actual Operating Data, in *Readings in Production and Operations Management,* ed. E. S. Buffa (New York: John Wiley & Sons, Inc., 1966); also J. C. Hershauer and R. J. Ebert, "Search and Simulation Selection of a Job-Shop Sequencing Rule," *Management Science* 21, no. 7 (March 1975), 833–43.

Table 11.3 Matrix of setup costs

		Follower Job j				
		A	B	C	D	E
Predecessor	A	\$0	\$29	\$20	\$18	\$24
Job i	B	0	0	14	19	15
	C	0	35	0	37	26
	D	0	15	10	0	10
	E	0	18	16	40	0

sequences are not expected to coincide. If they do not, you must choose between the two rules. Your choice depends on the relative importance you place on costs of machine setup (NB) as opposed to the value of gaining overall shop effectiveness (SPT).

Sequencing Through Two Work Centers Imagine that you have a set of awaiting jobs, all of which have to be processed through two successive work centers. If you wish to sequence the jobs to minimize the completion time for the last job through the process, an optimal procedure for doing so is available.

Suppose the five jobs, A through E in the aircraft repair facility must each pass through the sheetmetal center and then through the paint center. We wish to find the sequence that minimizes completion time of the last job. The processing time for each job in each center is shown in Table 11.4.

Since there are five jobs, there will be five positions in the processing sequence. These steps tell how to allocate the jobs to the five positions in the sequence:

1. Determine the minimum of all the processing times, PT_{ij}.
2. If the minimum PT_{ij} is associated with work center 1, place the corresponding job in the earliest available position in the sequence; if the minimum PT_{ij} is associated with work center 2, place the corresponding job in the latest remaining position in the sequence.
3. Cross out both times of the job just assigned to omit that job from further consideration. Cross out the PT_{ij} for the job i just assigned, across all work centers, j.
4. Now return to step 1 and repeat the procedure by identifying the minimum of all remaining PT_{ij}.

Using the data from Table 11.4, the assignments proceed as follows:

1. PT_{D2} is the minimum, 2 days.
2. Since PT_{D2} is associated with center 2, job D is assigned to the last (fifth) position in the sequence.

Table 11.4 Processing times (in days) for jobs in two work centers[a]

Job	Work Center 1 (sheet metal)	Work Center 2 (paint)
A	4	5
B	17	7
C	14	12
D	9	2
E	11	6

[a]PT_{ij} = processing time of job i in center j, where i = A, B, C, D, E, and j = 1, 2.

3. Since job D has been assigned, its times are crossed out, and only jobs A, B, C, and E require further consideration.
4. (Return to step 1). Of the remaining eight PT_{ij}, $PT_{A1} = 4$ is the smallest. Since it is associated with center 1, job A is assigned to position 1 in the sequence. Then the times for job A are crossed out, and only jobs B, C, and E have yet to be assigned to remaining positions 2, 3, and 4 in the sequence.
5. (Repeat). Of the remaining six PT_{ij}, $PT_{E2} = 6$ is minimum. Since it is associated with center 2, job E is assigned to the last available position in the sequence (position 4).

Continuing in this manner, we find that the desired sequence turns out to be A–C–B–E–D. The time-phased flow of this job sequence is shown graphically in Figure 11.4. Completion of job D, the last job in the sequence, occurs in 57 days, the minimum. It is important to remember that this rule applies when all jobs must be processed *in the same order on both work centers,* first on center 1, then on center 2.

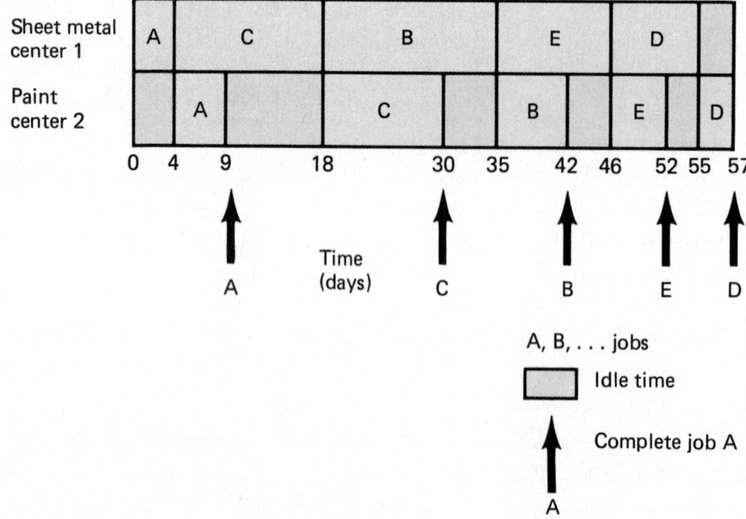

FIGURE 11.4
Work flow for sequencing five jobs in two centers in sequence A–C–B–E–D

In concluding our coverage of sequencing, you should note two of its overriding features. First, an abundance of sequencing methods is available; they can affect shop performance in different ways. Second, in choosing among these methods you should carefully evaluate them in terms of the criteria that are of greatest importance for your organization's competitive posture.

DETAILED SCHEDULING

Having discussed the loading and sequencing levels of intermittent systems scheduling, let's examine how the supplementary scheduling is accomplished. This process provides the detailed schedule required by operating personnel so that they know when to start what job and when it should be finished.

Gantt Scheduling Charts We previously showed a Gantt load chart. Another version of the Gantt chart can be helpful for visualizing detailed scheduling of orders. Figure 11.5 is an example; it shows one possible processing schedule for jobs A through E in the aircraft repair facility. Each pair of brackets denotes on the time scale the estimated beginning and ending of the activity enclosed within it at each work center. The solid bars beneath the brackets show the cumulative work loads that currently exist at each work center. Overall, then, 55 days of job processing, 2 days of setup, and 19 days of idle time constitute the 76-day sheet metal schedule. As work is completed, the "Time now" arrow moves to the right, and a heavier or color-coded line may be used between the schedule brackets to denote work actually accomplished. Scheduled and completed work can thus be compared.

FIGURE 11.5
Gantt chart for order scheduling (job sequence: A–C–B–E–D)

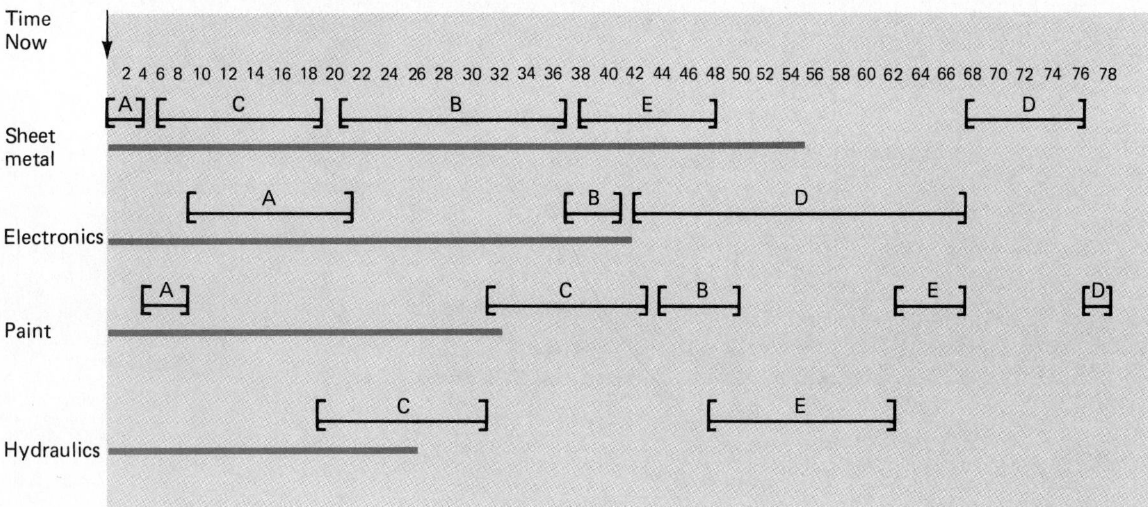

FINITE LOADING

Finite loading is an alternative scheduling technique that combines into a single system the loading, prioritizing, and detailed scheduling activities that we discussed individually above. In contrast to infinite loading, finite loading systems start with a specified capacity level for each work center and a listing of potential work orders (jobs). The work center's capacity is then allocated unit by unit (e.g., labor hours) to the work orders by simulating job starting times and completion times. Thus, the system creates a detailed schedule for each job order and each work center based on the centers' finite capacity limits. Jobs are allocated to the centers according to their capacities hour by hour and day by day into the future. The resulting finite capacity load profile would resemble the one shown in Figure 11.6.

The priority sequencing rule is built into the simulator. Since inputs to the simulator (e.g., from an MRP system) specify job due dates (not start times nor completion times), the jobs can be loaded using either a forward or a backward scheduling procedure, as we see next.

Forward Scheduling

Forward scheduling (or set forward) is commonly used in job shops where customers place their orders on a "needed-as-soon-as-possible" basis. Forward scheduling determines start and finish times for the next priority job by inserting it into the *earliest* available time slot and, from that time, determines when the job will be finished in that work center. Since the job and its components start as early as possible, they will typically be completed before they are due at subsequent work centers in the routing. Consequently, the set-forward procedure accumulates in-process inventories that sit throughout the facility until they're needed at subsequent stations. While these excessive inventories are a drawback, *forward scheduling is simple to use, and it gets jobs done in shorter lead times, overall, than does the backward scheduling procedure.*

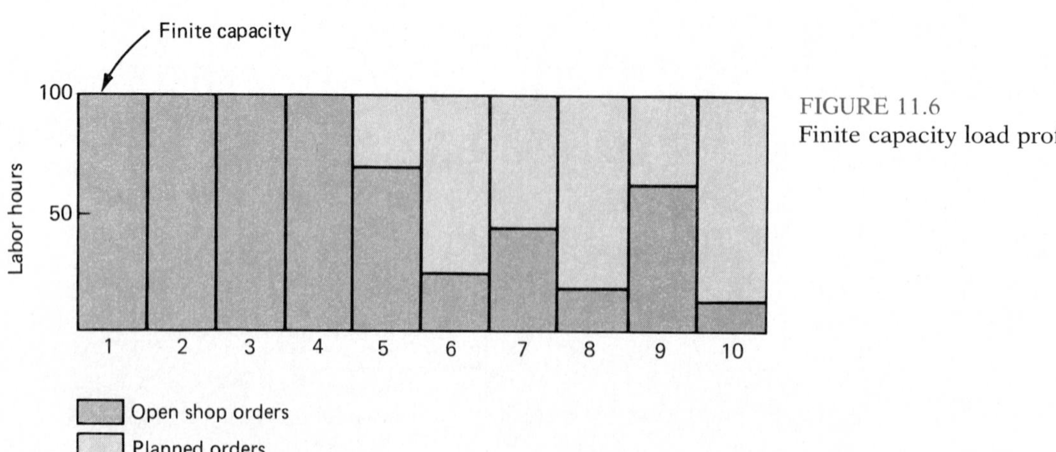

FIGURE 11.6
Finite capacity load profile

Backward Scheduling Another method, often used in assembly-type industries and in job shops that commit in advance to specific delivery dates, is *backward scheduling* (or set backward). It inserts the next priority job into the *latest* open time slot that will enable its completion just when it is due, but not before. Then the job's start time is determined by setting back from this finish date. *By scheduling jobs and parts as late as possible, the backward procedure minimizes inventories since the components aren't produced until they're needed by subsequent workstations.* To gain these inventory efficiencies, however, a price is paid: Bills of materials and lead-time estimates must be accurately maintained for all work centers or else the system breaks down, due dates are violated, and delivery service to customers deteriorates.

EXAMPLE The Hi-speed Machining Company has received two job orders, A and B, both of which require processing at machines 1 and 2. The first-come-first-served rule is used to assign priorities to jobs, which are coded alphabetically as to their order of arrival. The operations sequences are given below in the routings for the two jobs, both of which are due after 8 hours. Each machine is available for 8 hours every day, and no other jobs are currently scheduled on them. Develop schedules for the jobs using the forward and backward procedures.

Route Sheet: Job A			Route Sheet: Job B		
Operations Sequence	Machine	Operation Time (hours)	Operations Sequence	Machine	Operation Time (hours)
1	1	2	1	1	2
2	2	3	2	2	3
3	1	1			

The forward technique first schedules top-priority job A as early as possible; its first operation is for 2 hours on machine 1 (as circled in Figure 11.7). Then it is scheduled in hours 3 to 5 on machine 2. Job A finishes on machine 1 in hour 6, its earliest possible finish time. Next job B is scheduled into the remaining open times as early as possible. First it goes into machine 1 in hours 3 and 4. Then its second operation, on machine 2, is scheduled for hours 6 through 8.

The backward technique starts by scheduling the highest-priority job so that it finishes at its due time. Therefore, job A's latest operation is scheduled into machine 1 for hour 8. Then its preceding operation is scheduled as late as possible, hours 5 through 7 in machine 2. Similarly, operation 1 is scheduled for hours 3 and 4 in machine 1 for job A. Now job B is scheduled for its last operation, at machine 2, in hours 8, 4, and 3. Its first operation is then assigned to machine 1 for hours 1 and 2.

You can see that the two procedures yield entirely different schedules

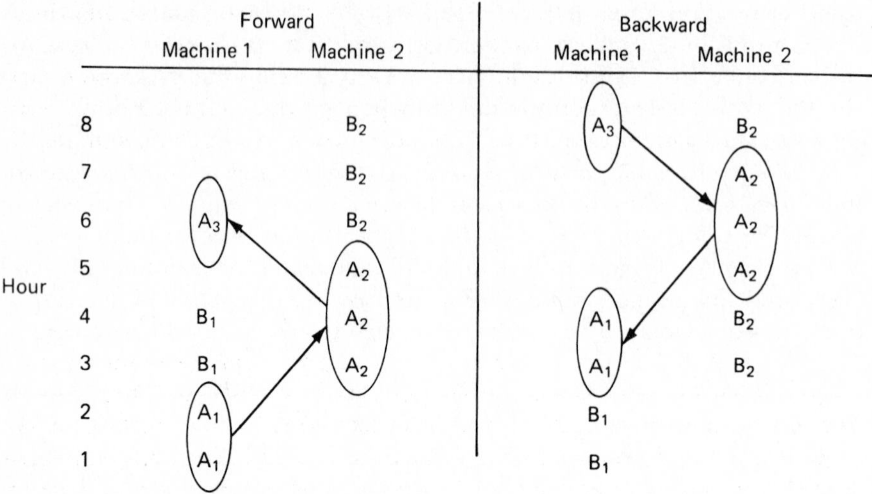

FIGURE 11.7
Forward and backward schedules for Hi-speed Machining Company

for the two machines. In this example both jobs can be completed by their due times, but this is often not the case, and job lateness, especially for lower-priority jobs, will be the result. In our forward schedule, excess inventories accumulate; job A finishes two hours early and the first operation on job B finishes one hour before it is needed at machine 2. In the backward schedule, job B is interrupted at machine 2 after hour 4 to allow the higher-priority job A to pass through. Then job B resumes in hour 8.

Using Finite Versus Infinite Loading

Finite loading has some drawbacks that lead its critics to conclude that it is an inappropriate control technique. Its planned schedules for the work centers often become obsolete from unanticipated materials delays and inaccurate processing time estimates at feeder work centers. Consequently, the finite loading simulation has to be rerun (updated) frequently, and these run costs are much greater than the low costs of sequencing by priority rules for infinite loading systems. Advocates of finite loading, however, claim they get more accurate capacity load estimates for the very short term, the next few days, than they get from the infinite loading-sequencing-detailed scheduling procedure.

EXPEDITING

Let's say that we have accomplished all the activities we've discussed so far. We have finished loading, sequencing, and detailed scheduling. But we are not done yet. Disruptions may prohibit our plans from being implemented to some extent. Necessary materials or manpower may not be available at the right times as planned; equipment may break down; a particularly important customer may desire special treatment. Any of these and other contingencies may cause disruptions and result in rescheduling, a form of corrective action that is part of the *control* process. If the progress of a job is unsatisfactory, the job may be *expedited*. Special attention is devoted to it, and priorities may be shifted at work centers to "hustle the job through" ahead of others. Certainly expediting is sometimes necessary; but caution should be exercised lest it tend to be overused.

INPUT-OUTPUT (SHORT-TERM CAPACITY) CONTROL

Control reports from input-output analysis are helpful for monitoring each work center's performance. They enable us to evaluate over time how well the available capacity is being utilized. In Table 11.5, labor-hour requirements for new jobs into the work center for each week were recorded in the first row as "planned input." The work center's "planned output" is the weekly work rate (hours of capacity to be expended) that was chosen by management. In Table 11.5, we see that planned outputs exceed planned inputs, reflecting management's intentions to decrease the work center's backlog, week by week, from the beginning level of 300 units at week 0 down to 100 units (labor hours) by week 4.

OPTIMIZED PRODUCTION TECHNOLOGY (OPT)

An alternative to the production planning and scheduling approaches previously presented in this chapter is OPT (Optimized Production Technology), a computer-based system for planning production, materials needs, and resource utilization. It was first introduced in the United States

Table 11.5 Input-output report for work center 100 (report prepared after week 4)

	Standard Hours/Week				
	1	2	3	4	5
Planned input	400	350	350	300	300
Actual input	400	350	350	300	
Cumulative deviation (actual-planned)	0	0	0	0	
Planned output	450	400	400	350	300
Actual output	440	410	405	330	
Cumulative deviation (actual-planned)	−10	0	+5	−15	
Planned backlog[a]	250	200	150	100	100
Actual backlog	260	200	145	115	

[a]Backlog at time 0 = 300 units.

in 1979 by Creative Output Inc., a consulting firm in Milford, Connecticut.[4] The key feature of OPT is its emphasis on carefully utilizing bottleneck work centers (people or machines) in shop operations. The OPT philosophy recognizes that managing bottlenecks is the key to successful performance; total system output can be maximized, and in-process inventories can be reduced.

The OPT software consists of four modules: (1) BUILDNET; (2) SERVE; (3) SPLIT; and (4) OPT. The starting module, BUILDNET, creates a product network that identifies the shop situation. It includes definitions of how each product is made (its buildup sequence, bill of materials, and routing through the shop), the product's time requirements (setup, run time, schedule delay), the capacity availability of each resource (work center, machine, worker), and the order quantities and due dates of work orders in the shop. The initial purpose of SERVE is to create a tentative processing schedule for the awaiting jobs in the shop. Later, it creates a more refined schedule. The crucial information obtained from this initial schedule is an estimate of the percentage utilization of the various shop resources.

The SPLIT module separates critical from noncritical resources based on their percentage utilizations in the initial schedule. Resources that are near or above 100 percent utilization are the bottleneck operations. These bottlenecks, and the operations that follow them in the product buildup sequence, are the "critical" operations; all others (those with lower percentage utilizations) are "noncritical." The OPT module reschedules the critical part of the network using a forward scheduling procedure that considers the finite capacities of resources. After the critical part of the network is scheduled (in the OPT module described above), the procedure cycles back to the SERVE module to reschedule the noncritical resources (work centers or machines).

The OPT package consists not just of software, but of consulting services and training for implementation as well. The specific details of the procedure, especially of SERVE and OPT (the detailed scheduling modules), are proprietary (not published and available to the general public). Consequently, detailed comparative evaluations of its performance with that of other systems are not available.

SELECTED BEHAVIORAL ELEMENTS IN INTERMITTENT SYSTEMS

Operations managers are keenly aware of some prominent behavioral considerations in intermittent systems. These factors are *part of* the system, and they arise from two sources: the sheer technical complexities

[4]See F. R. Jacobs, "OPT Uncovered: Many Production Planning and Scheduling Concepts Can Be Applied With or Without the Software," *Industrial Engineering* (October 1984), pp. 32–41. See also R. E. Fox, "OPT—An Answer for America—Part IV," *Inventories & Production* 3, no. 2 (March–April 1983).

of having large numbers of jobs at various stages of completion, and the organization of and role relationships in the system. Although these two sources of behavioral considerations are interrelated, we consider them separately.

Complexity of Job Status

When you must decide how to process a few jobs through a small number of work centers, your problem is manageable. When the number of jobs increases to hundreds or thousands, each with different routings among hundreds of processing stations, however, your problems are magnified many times. Not only must you process all these jobs, you want to satisfy customers with on-time deliveries, and you want to do so smoothly and efficiently. A single individual is incapable of accomplishing all this. Our limited mental capacities prohibit total awareness of current job status and how that status changes over time. For these reasons, the tools presented earlier have great value to managers of intermittent systems. Gantt load charts and scheduling charts, although simplistic in concept and appearance, serve as memory supplements. For decision making, priority sequencing rules play a similar role. By systematically applying priority rules, we get the simplified process we need. Although the rules do not ensure optimal system performance, they do help achieve satisfactory performance, and they are usually better than alternative approaches, including human intuition.

System Organization and Role Relationships

A more pervasive set of problems emerges when one considers the entire intermittent system and the relationships among its subcomponents. The behaviors of individual employees, groups, and work centers or departments must all be integrated in an effective system. Some factors affecting these behaviors can be identified.

Individual Characteristics You may remember that intermittent systems, as compared with continuous flow systems, contain a high degree of task variety. Different types of employee skills and work orientations are necessary. Generally, jobs in intermittent systems are already "enlarged"; work content varies, and a higher degree of employee responsibility is emphasized in executing the tasks. In hiring, managers seek employees who have high skill levels and who can work independently without a great deal of supervision. Through monetary reward systems, by facilitating group relationships, and through various methods of allocating work among employees, management can create a working environment that enhances the security and fulfills the social needs of its employees. Fulfilling these needs increases motivation in job performance.

Group Characteristics In discussing facility layout (Chapter 7), we pointed out that intermittent systems consist of departments or work centers sharing common processes. A facility might have three departmental groupings consisting of machining, painting, and photography, for example. In these different departments are found different skill or craft groups, and group affiliations are often established. There are three reasons for these group affiliations: command structure, physical proximity, and shared craft interest. As a *formal* basis for group affiliation among machinists, for example, the organizational structures may specify that all machinists report to a machining foreman. Departmental members must communicate and interact with one another to some extent in accomplishing departmental tasks. Second, the physical proximity of machinists in the facility, since they usually work near one another, tends to facilitate interaction and communication, both work-related and personal. Since this is likely to occur on a regular basis, strong group bonds may form. Finally, the existence of an important shared interest, the craft or skill of the department employees, provides a basis for interaction. Unions facilitate this last affiliation; it is likely that in a unionized facility of any size, more than one union will represent differing groups of employees.

The existence of a work group has significant implications for the operations of the system. Although the employees in a group usually adopt a set of shared norms and strive toward satisfying member needs, the group goals may or may not be consistent with organizational goals. Group norms can strongly influence the kinds and amounts of productive activities of its members, especially in highly cohesive groups. When the goals of these cohesive groups are consistent with management's goals, the groups tend to produce at higher levels.

Centralized Versus Decentralized Decision Making The decentralized scheduling system provides an important dimension of managerial discretion for the first-line supervisor: *The supervisor decides which employees will work on which job orders.* This type of action prerogative doesn't exist in more centralized systems. In an environment in which wages are hourly and fixed, the decentralized system might be one of the few devices directly available to the supervisor for rewarding and motivating employees. In the more centralized systems, job assignments are often made on a relatively depersonalized basis by the production control center. Any gains from better interdepartmental coordination could be offset by losses in intradepartmental dissatisfaction and/or productivity.

In many companies, bargaining between subordinates and foremen for job assignments is a traditionally accepted interpersonal process. Without it, the prestige attributed to the supervisors' role and the respected skilled workers' esteem may both diminish. Unless other adjustments are made, the diminution of the process could lead to frustration and defensive behavior by supervisors and subordinates alike, followed by a decrease in productivity and quality.

SUMMARY

Intermittent systems have several distinctive characteristics. The types of processes, job orders, work flows, and human skills contrast sharply with those of continuous, or mass-production, systems. Generally, intermittent systems have to deal with diversified customer requests and irregular work flows. The intermittent scheduling process involves aggregate planning, master scheduling, materials planning, loading, priority sequencing, detailed scheduling, expediting, and input-output control.

Concentrating on shop floor control, we showed how infinite loading systems allocate incoming jobs to work centers and how Gantt charts and visual load profiles help evaluate current loadings. The assignment algorithm was also presented for loading in special circumstances. Then, the question of how to sequence jobs through the loaded work centers was considered. We saw how some rules performed well on selected dimensions but not so well on others. Then, the processes of detailed scheduling, expediting, and input-output control were described and linked together with the sequencing and loading processes.

Finite loading systems, those having integrated loading, sequencing, and detailed scheduling processes, were presented as an alternative to infinite systems. Finally, we concluded with some behavioral considerations of both individuals and groups for intermittent systems operation.

CASE

Newtone

In 1962 Bill Withers began to make custom furniture full time in his garage. Bill's work had been admired by friends and neighbors, who often asked him to make special pieces for them. In 1965, he leased a previously used facility and expanded his operations by hiring 2 additional skilled workers, a woodworker and a leather specialist. By 1968, Newtone was incorporated and had 11 employees.

Today, Newtone serves a custom furniture market covering the northwestern region of the United States. Bill Withers, the president, has a staff of 37 employees. Custom-made furniture is the sole product line, and the company has prided itself on high quality and timely delivery services. Organizationally, Newtone has sales, purchasing, shipping, and design departments. Internal processing departments include wood framing, wood preparation, wood finishing, metal finishing, leather, glass, plastics, and cloth fabrics.

This past year 250 to 300 jobs were processed in the facility on any given day. Although product quality remains high, on-time deliveries have deteriorated; the average job seems to be four to seven weeks late. Bill Arnold, an employee since 1967 and a special assistant to the shop manager, does the shop loading. His job also includes coordinating the overall shop efforts with those of the sales and design departments. He recently compiled data (shown in the table below) on waiting job orders for a typical day.

Detailed scheduling of orders has always been the responsibility of the three shop foremen. Larry Cline is foreman of the wood preparation, framing, and finishing departments. Isaac Trumbolt has the leather department and cloth fabrics. Willie Heft is foreman of three departments: metal, glass, and plastics.

Bill Withers is concerned about job lateness. He feels deteriorating customer service might well affect future sales. He has requested George Herring, whose primary experience has been coordinating a new physical distribution system, to analyze the current situation and recommend changes. George is uncertain which factors he should consider and how to proceed with the problem.

Work Center	Number of Orders Waiting to Be Processed	Number of Shop Operations Required on Waiting Orders						Lateness Status of Waiting Jobs			
								On Time or Ahead (number of jobs)	Lateness (weeks)		
		3	4	5	6	7	8		1–2	3–5	6 or More
Wood framing	314	63	69	47	44	44	47	261	44	9	—
Wood preparation	409	98	86	74	45	57	49	61	147	119	82
Wood finishing	223	65	60	45	29	20	4	22	34	78	89
Metal finishing	71	—	7	32	25	7	—	55	16	—	—
Leather	157	—	—	44	61	23	29	135	19	3	—
Glass	63	19	22	16	6	—	—	63	—	—	—
Plastics	106	48	37	21	—	—	—	106	—	—	—
Cloth fabrics	198	—	41	74	53	30	—	133	45	20	—

REVIEW AND DISCUSSION QUESTIONS

1. What is a job shop (intermittent system)?
2. Outline and describe the critical parameters of the job-shop scheduling problem.
3. Identify elements of human behavior that are affected by job-shop scheduling.
4. Is job-shop scheduling a planning activity or a control activity? Explain.
5. Four levels of the shop floor control are loading, sequencing, detailed scheduling, and input-output control. What are the distinctions among these four activities?
6. What are priority sequencing rules? Why are they needed?
7. Discuss the advantages and limitations of using the Gantt load chart and visual load profiles.
8. Discuss the significance of maintaining data integrity in computerized scheduling systems.
9. How does a Gantt chart for detailed scheduling differ from a Gantt load chart?
10. Why do most organizations settle for priority rules yielding satisfactory, rather than optimal, system performance?
11. Outline and discuss major differences between finite and infinite loading.

PROBLEMS

Solved Problems

1. Five jobs await processing on a machine. The setup costs, shown below, depend on the sequence in which the jobs are processed. Apply the next best rule to determine the sequence for these jobs if job I is processed first.

Setup Costs (dollars)

Predecessor Job	Follower Job				
	I	II	III	IV	V
I	—	1,300	100	900	300
II	1,000	—	200	700	600
III	100	500	—	1,100	900
IV	500	800	900	—	400
V	800	200	600	300	—

Sequence: I–III–II–V–IV
Cost: \$100 + 500 + 600 + 300 = \$1,500

2. Jobs A, B, and C arrived in alphabetical order and are given priority on a first-come-first-served basis. The routings and operation times are shown below. Develop schedules for the jobs on the machines using the forward scheduling procedure.

	Route Sheet: Job A		Route Sheet: Job B		Route Sheet: Job C	
Operations Sequence	Machine	Time (hours)	Machine	Time (hours)	Machine	Time (hours)
1	I	2	II	2	I	3
2	II	3	III	1	III	4
3	III	1	I	3	II	1

		Forward Schedule: Machine		
		I	II	III
Hour	13		C	
	12			C
	11			C
	10			C
	9			C
	8	C		
	7	C		
	6	B		A
	5	B	A	
	4	B	A	
	3	C	A	B
	2	A	B	
	1	A	B	

Reinforcing Fundamentals

3. Jobs arriving at Joanna's Downtown Upholstery Shop are processed and due as shown.

Waiting Orders by Number (in order of arrival)	Estimated Processing Time (days)	Due Date (days from now)
317	12	20
318	11	20
319	14	18
320	2	8

(a) How many processing sequences are available for these four jobs?
(b) Apply the first-come-first-served priority sequencing rule, calculating average job lateness. Now apply the shortest processing time rule, and find the average job lateness. Which rule is better for average job lateness? Will that always be the better rule for any data?

4. Given the following data for jobs awaiting processing at a work center, calculate system performance using first-come-first-served, last-come-first-served, and shortest processing time sequencing rules.

Waiting orders (in order of arrival)	P	Q	R	S	T
Processing time (days)	10	4	16	8	7
Due date (days from now)	20	14	26	18	17

5. Suppose, for the waiting jobs in Problem 4, setup costs are incurred for processing the next job after finishing any other job at the work center.

Setup Costs (dollars)

Predecessor Job	Follower Job				
	P	Q	R	S	T
P	—	120	90	80	30
Q	100	—	20	70	60
R	10	50	—	100	80
S	50	90	80	—	40
T	80	70	60	60	—

Assuming job P is being processed now, apply the next best (NB) sequencing rule and determine the resulting total setup cost. How does this setup cost compare with that of the SPT rule?

6. Arline Industries is an intermittent manufacturing facility, processing jobs to customer order. Currently, eight open orders are awaiting processing. All jobs must be processed at the same facility.

Waiting orders (in order of arrival)	A	B	C	D	E	F	G	H
Processing time (days)	23	16	5	31	11	20	2	27
Due date (days from now)	28	35	15	40	30	45	8	50

(a) Develop a Gantt load chart for the facility.
(b) How many different processing sequences are possible?
(c) Develop a visual load profile for infinite loading; the work center's capacity is five days of processing per week.

7. (a) Apply the first-come-first-served (FCFS) priority sequencing rule to the Arline facility in Problem 6. Calculate total completion time, average completion time, average number of jobs per day in the system, and average job lateness.
(b) Apply the shortest processing time (SPT) rule, and perform the same calculations as in Part a.

8. Apply the last-come-first served (LCFS), earliest due date (EDD), and least slack (LS) rules to the Arline facility in Problem 6. Compare these results to those in Problem 7.

9. Data Systems, Inc., processes all incoming jobs through two successive work centers, A and B (each job goes first through A, then through B). Five jobs await processing.

	Job				
	S	T	U	V	W
Processing time in A	14	3	22	31	7
Processing time in B	8	9	4	17	12

Assign a job sequence that minimizes the completion time of the last job processed. What is the total flow time for this sequence?

10. Ten new projects await processing by Environmental Impact Affiliates. Each job requires an empirical research evaluation before it can be assessed by the legal advisor. All projects must be evaluated empirically and legally. Estimates of processing times (days) for the empirical and legal phases are:

Project	A	B	C	D	E	F	G	H	I	J
Empirical phase	20	18	7	30	10	20	3	25	14	24
Legal phase	7	21	36	9	12	17	8	22	17	12

(a) Develop a Gantt load chart for the work centers (empirical and legal).
(b) Find the processing sequence that minimizes the completion time of the last project processed.
(c) Draw the Gantt chart for order scheduling based on the results for Part b.
(d) What is the completion time of the last project to be processed?

11. First National Bank has four new tellers with varying skills who are to be assigned to the main bank or one of the branches. The criterion for assigning tellers to locations is minimized customer waiting time. An index of customer waiting time is shown in the table below for each of four locations and varying teller skills. Make teller assignments, using the assignment technique, that will minimize the index of overall waiting time. What is the total waiting time index for the optimal assignment?

Location	Teller			
	A	B	C	D
Main Bank	40	60	30	90
Southwest Branch	60	30	60	60
Clearwater Branch	80	60	40	40
Northgate Branch	70	50	60	40

Challenging Exercises

12. Architectural Design Associates has six jobs to be assigned to six architects. The expected effectiveness of each architect on each job has been estimated on a rating scale from 1 to 100; a rating of 1 is high effectiveness, and 100 represents low effectiveness. Make the six assignments that will maximize overall effectiveness.

	Effectiveness Ratings					
Job	Louise	William	Ken	Mary	Carl	Patricia
1	33	40	19	24	58	36
2	57	61	8	29	3	24
3	25	56	12	20	10	14
4	44	72	22	37	47	27
5	62	42	31	20	10	33
6	49	33	30	15	22	41

13. At McFilly Corporation, eight jobs await processing at a single facility. After one job is finished, facility setup costs are incurred before the next job can be processed. Setup costs depend on the processing sequence.

Waiting orders	A	B	C	D	E	F	G	H
Processing time (days)	23	16	5	31	11	20	2	27
Due date (days from now)	28	35	15	40	30	45	8	50

Facility Setup Costs (dollars)

Predecessor Job	Follower Job							
	A	B	C	D	E	F	G	H
A	—	15	15	20	10	25	15	20
B	15	—	5	10	20	15	5	10
C	5	20	—	30	15	10	10	10
D	25	10	15	—	25	5	5	15
E	20	25	15	30	—	10	30	20
F	30	15	20	25	35	—	10	15
G	15	30	5	10	25	5	—	35
H	10	5	15	20	10	25	10	—

(a) Assuming job G is currently being processed, determine the minimum cost sequence for processing the remaining jobs.

(b) For the sequence obtained in Part a, calculate total completion time, average completion time, average number of jobs per day in the system, and average job lateness.

(c) Assuming job G is processed first, calculate setup costs for the processing sequence obtained by applying the SPT rule to the remaining jobs.

14. Jobs A, B, and C arrive at a work center in alphabetical order and are given priorities on a first-come-first-served basis. The routings and estimated operation times through this work center's three machines are shown below. Develop schedules for the jobs on the machines using the forward and the backward scheduling procedures. The jobs' due times are hour 10 for A, hour 16 for B, and hour 14 for job C. How much job lateness results? How much excess inventory results?

	Route Sheet: Job A		Route Sheet: Job B		Route Sheet: Job C	
Operations Sequence	Machine	Time (hours)	Machine	Time (hours)	Machine	Time (hours)
1	1	3	II	3	I	4
2	II	3	III	2	III	4
3	III	2	I	2	II	2

15. Reconsider Problem 14. Now, however, suppose job priorities are based on the SPT rule (not on the FCFS). Develop forward and backward schedules, and compare the results to those for Problem 14. Now, instead of the SPT priorities, use earliest due date (EDD) priorities to develop forward and backward schedules; compare these results with your earlier results.

16. For the data in Problem 10, suppose that each project must pass through both processing phases but does not have to be processed through them in any particular order. A project may go through either the empirical or the legal phase first, and then go through the other phase. Assume the projects are received in alphabetical order. Job due dates are: 60 for A, 75 for B, 32 for C, 85 for D, 70 for E, 95 for F, 25 for G, 110 for H, 130 for I, and 97 for J. Determine the processing sequence for the projects using the following sequencing heuristic:

(1) Assign an awaiting project to a work center whenever the work center becomes available.

(2) If both work centers become available simultaneously, the next assignment is made to the empirical research phase.

(3) At each work center, unstarted projects have priority over projects that have completed one phase of processing.

(4) Awaiting projects are assigned to work centers on a first-come-first-served basis.

(a) Determine the sequence in which projects are processed and completed.

(b) Calculate total completion time, flow times, average completion time, and average job lateness for the sequence obtained in Part a.

(c) Determine the sequence in which projects are processed and completed, using the following sequencing heuristic:

(1) Assign a project to a work center whenever the work center becomes available.

(2) If both work centers become available simultaneously, the next assignment is made to the empirical research phase.

(3) Projects are assigned to work centers on the basis of processing time; the awaiting project with the shortest processing time (SPT) is given highest priority, regardless of whether it has completed one phase of processing.

(d) For the sequence obtained in Part c, calculate total completion time, flow times, average completion time, and average job lateness.

(e) Compare the results of Parts b and d.

Utilizing the QSOM Computer Software

17. Z-Mat Manufacturing, Inc., utilizes a job shop in which three jobs—A, B, and C—are performed. Machines 1 and 2 are required for the operations. Job A must first be processed on machine 1 for 3 days and then on machine 2 for 7 days. Job B is processed on machine 2 for 11 days. Job C is processed on machine 2 for 2 days and then on machine 1 for 6 days. The due dates for Jobs A, B, and C are 6, 9, and 12 days, respectively.

Using QSOM's Job-shop scheduling program with shortest processing time as the primary rule and first-come-first-served as the tie breaker, determine maximum completion time, mean completion time, maximum waiting time, mean waiting time, and mean lateness for completing jobs A, B, and C.

18. To demonstrate the power and utility of QSOM for job-shop scheduling, consider this situation, which is more complex than chapter examples.

In one particular machine shop, four distinct jobs are processed on three different machines (1–cutting, 2–grinding, 3–boring), as shown below.

Job	Operations/Job	Machine Sequence (routing)	Process Times (days)	Due Dates (days)
A	3	1–2–3	2–1–1	7
B	3	2–3–1	10–8–6	16
C	3	1–3–2	4–7–1	4
D	3	3–2–1	8–1–6	17

Using SPT as the primary rule and FCFS as the tie breaker, with the QSOM job-shop scheduling program determine maximum completion time, mean completion time, and maximum waiting time for completing jobs A, B, C, and D.

GLOSSARY

Assignment algorithm A particular version of linear programming used to assign jobs to facilities such that a specific criterion is optimized.

Detailed scheduling Determining start times, finish times, and worker assignments for all jobs at each workplace.

Expediting Tracking a job's progress and taking special actions to move it through the facility.

Flow time Total time that a job is in the system; the sum of waiting and processing times.

Gantt chart A graphical procedure showing work loads and/or scheduled activities on a time scale.

Input/output control A procedure for monitoring actual versus planned utilization of a work center's capacity.

Load Cumulative amount of work (open orders or planned orders) currently assigned to a work center for future processing.

Queue A waiting line.

Routing The processing steps or stages needed to create a product.

Sequence rule A systematic procedure for assigning priorities to jobs, thereby determining the sequence in which jobs will be processed.

Setup cost Cost of revising and preparing a facility or department for processing a job.

Shop floor control Procedures for the detailed execution of production plans for jobs at work centers on the shop floor.

Visual load profile A graph showing the time-phased load from open or planned job orders on the work center.

Work center A facility, set of machines, or workstation that provides a service or transformation needed by a job or a customer order.

SELECTED READINGS

Conway, R. W., W. L. Maxwell, and L. W. Miller, *Theory of Scheduling.* Reading, Mass.: Addison-Wesley, 1967.

Fox, R. E. "OPT—An Answer for America—Part IV." *Inventories & Production* 3, no. 2 (March–April 1983).

Hershauer, James C., and Ronald J. Ebert, "Search and Simulation Selection of a Job-Shop Sequencing Rule," *Management Science* 21, no. 7 (March 1975), 833–43.

Jacobs, F. R., "OPT Uncovered: Many Production Planning and Scheduling Concepts Can Be Applied with or without the Software," *Industrial Engineering* (October 1984), pp. 32–41.

McLeavy, D. W., and S. L. Narasimhan, *Production Planning and Inventory Control.* Boston: Allyn & Bacon, 1985.

Vollmann, T. E., W. L. Berry, and D. C. Whybark, *Manufacturing Planning and Control Systems* (2nd ed.). Homewood, Ill.: Richard D. Irwin, 1988.

Weeks, J. K., and J. S. Fryer, "A Methodology for Assigning Minimum Cost Due-Dates," *Management Science* 23, no. 8 (April 1977), 872–81.

PART V CONTROLLING THE CONVERSION SYSTEM

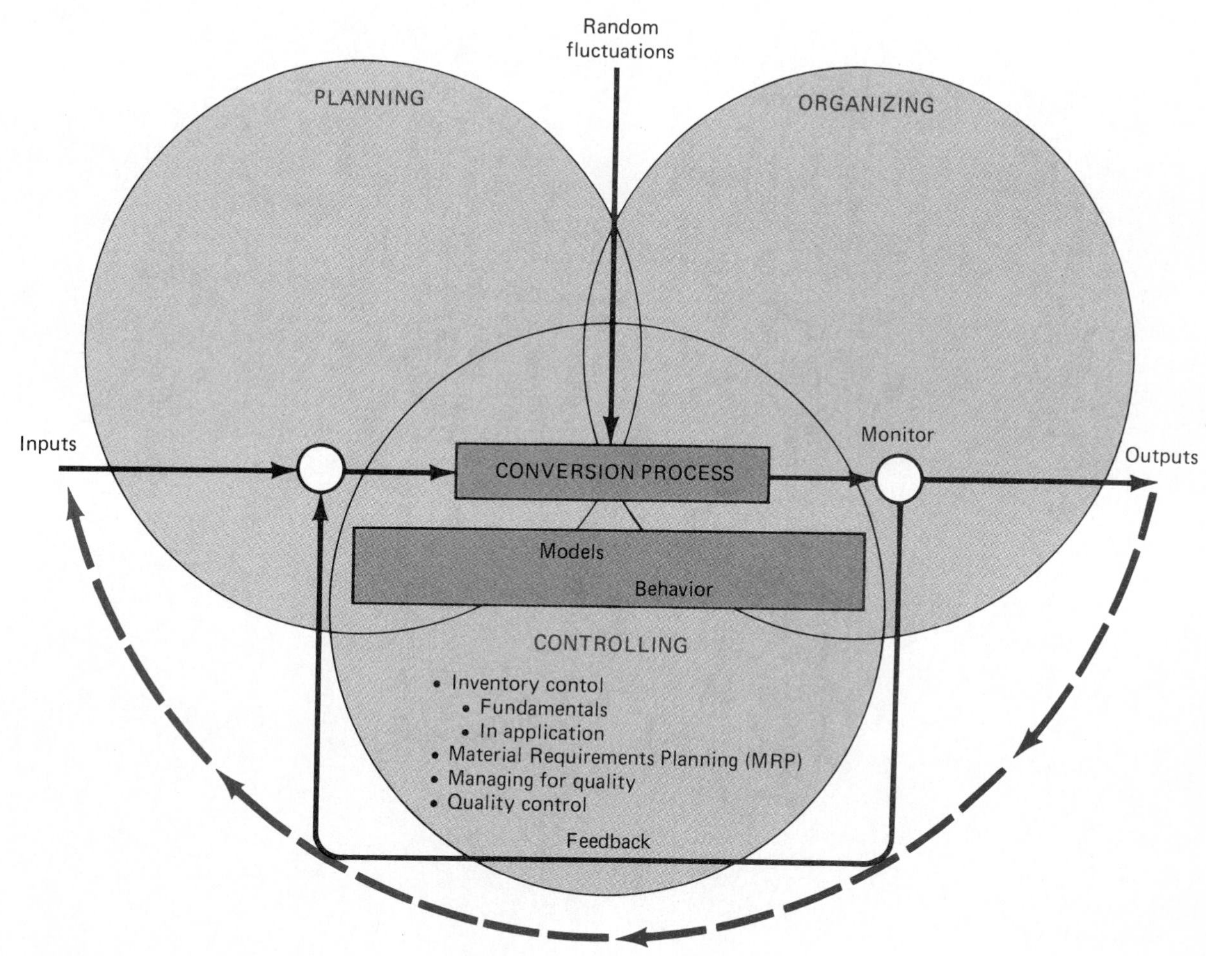

Production and operations management activities

12

Inventory Control Fundamentals

Inventory control is a subject of vital importance to almost every type of business, whether production- or service-oriented; it touches almost every facet of our water and electric utility. Raw materials such as coal and fuel oil must be scheduled and stockpiled for the production of electricity. Operating supplies such as hydrogen, chlorine, and fireside treatment chemicals must be delivered and on hand in the proper quantities for the operation of the power plant and the water treatment plant. Large stocks of materials such as poles, wire, valves, and pipe must be kept to operate, maintain, and expand the extensive distribution system required to deliver electricity and water to the customer. If the proper materials are not available when needed, construction crews will not be able to extend service to new customers in a timely fashion. During a loss of power or water pressure, the lack of a proper repair part could mean that a customer might be without service for an extended period of time. On a daily basis, even stocks of blank forms and envelopes must be kept on hand for the preparation of monthly bills.

Since the health and welfare of a community is involved, it would be easy to take the approach that large volumes of everything must be kept on hand to ensure that there will never be a shortage. But customers also like low rates, and the value of inventory on hand can easily exceed 5 percent of the annual revenues of the utility. Thus the proper balance must be struck to provide proper inventory with the minimum financial impact on the customer.

Richard E. Malon
Water and Light Director
City of Columbia
Columbia, Missouri

Production/operations managers are responsible for operations cost control. One critical cost of operations is investment in raw materials, supplies, work-in-process, and finished products not yet shipped. If this investment becomes excessive, the results are high capital costs, high operating costs, and decreased production efficiency when too much space is used for inventory. Although these costs are apparent for manufacturing, it is easy to believe that service organizations do not have such inventory costs. Electricity is, after all, an "invisible" service we simply use when we turn on a switch. Yet, as Mr. Malon so aptly illustrates, inventory control is crucial to both efficiency and cost control in the generation and delivery of electricity and water to consumers who expect their public utility to provide good service at reasonable rates.

Operations managers usually develop a plan specifying desired levels for materials, and they organize jobs to carry out this plan. Because of environmental influences, however, actual performance often does not conform to planned performance, and managers must exercise material (or inventory) control. Operations managers must monitor output, compare actual with planned output, and take corrective action through feedback mechanisms. This discussion is illustrated in the figure immediately preceding this chapter, where we are reminded again that inventory control relates closely to planning and organizing.

In most other functional production/operations areas, there is more of a balance between modeling and behavioral considerations than there is in inventory control. Inventory theory and modeling have been developed so thoroughly by applied mathematicians that one often is left in awe at the level of model sophistication. In this and the next chapter, we will focus on fundamental modeling, the richest approach for learning the basics of inventory control.

DEMAND AND CONTROL SYSTEM CHARACTERISTICS

Independent and Dependent Demand

Previously we made the distinction between independent and dependent demand (Chapter 3). This chapter and the next reflect inventory control systems for independently demanded items, that is, for items that are unrelated to one another. Before we turn to basic inventory concepts, let's briefly examine the elements of a control system in more detail than we have previously. Understanding control is important for managing inventories, but equally so for quality and overall cost control as well.

Elements of a Control System

Controlling is a process by which some aspect of a system is modified to achieve desired system performance. A homeowner, for example, may lower the thermostat setting at night to hold monthly heating bills within a budgeted amount. A manufacturer of luggage may decide to purchase leather from a new supplier when it discovers that present suppliers are providing inferior leather. The purpose of the control process is to cause

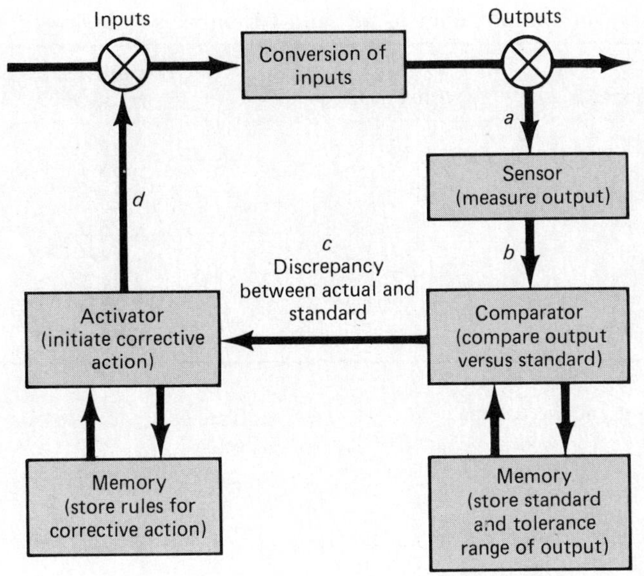

FIGURE 12.1
Elements of the control subsystem

the system to run true to its objectives. Control is not an end itself but rather a means to an end—improving system operation.

Conceptually, many kinds of systems—biological, social, mechanical, political, and economic—have control subsystems that share certain elements. These include system inputs, outputs, a sensor, a comparator, a memory, and an activator. The relationships among these subsystem elements are shown in Figure 12.1.

Information flows are essential to a control system. Without them, a system simply cannot exist—or if it does, it is certainly inoperable. In Figure 12.1, the information segments a through d comprise an information feedback loop. This feedback is the basis for all control systems. Information from the output side of the conversion process is transformed and fed back into the input side in a steady flow. In this way, management is continually able to compare actual performance with planned results.

Although we may be unaware of them, control systems operate around us all the time. When the pupils in your eyes enlarge or contract as light intensity changes, your body is using a control system. When your automatic thermostat turns on the furnace because the room is cooler than you want it to be, it is operating a control system. Look again at Figure 12.1, and see if you can identify the subcomponents of these or other control systems.

INVENTORY CONCEPTS

Inventory Defined

Inventories play a major part in the economy of the United States, as Table 12.1 shows. These data alone suggest that operating managers should find inventory management a fruitful area for cost control. From the firm's

Table 12.1 U.S. Gross National Product (GNP) and Inventories ($ billions)[a]

Year	GNP	Inventories	Inventories as a % of GNP
1950	$1,203.7	$278.1	23.1%
1960	1,665.3	370.0	22.2
1970	2,416.2	571.1	23.6
1975	2,695.0	673.0	25.0
1978	3,115.2	761.0	24.4
1982	3,166.0	768.4	24.3
1984	3,520.4	821.2	23.3
1986[b]	3,702.4	841.0	22.7

[a]Dollars are adjusted for 1982 value.
[b]Annual rate includes fourth quarter estimate.
Source: Economic Report of the President, January 1987, pp. 246, 265.

viewpoint, inventories represent an investment; capital is required to hold materials at any stage of completion.

Inventory is stores of goods and stocks. In manufacturing, inventories are called *stockkeeping items* and are held at a stock (storage) point. Stockkeeping items usually consist of:

- Raw materials
- Work-in-process
- Finished products
- Supplies

Inventory control is the technique of maintaining stockkeeping items at desired levels. In manufacturing, since the focus is on a physical product, emphasis is on materials and material control; in the service sector, the focus is on a service (often consumed as generated), and there is very little emphasis on materials or stocks.

EXAMPLE First National Bank is a commercial bank with full line services. The typical individual account includes various transactions: checking, savings, lock boxes, and loan transactions. Focusing on the teller operation, one has difficulty distinguishing among raw material, work-in-process, and finished goods inventories. The technical operation is to convert labor and material into the service of caring for money. The service is consumed as it is generated. Such materials as deposit slips, withdrawal slips, and loan payment coupons are more like operating supplies than raw materials. The accounting service depends upon properly completed slips and coupons; they could be viewed as work-in-process. Customer statements awaiting mailing could be viewed as finished goods (services).

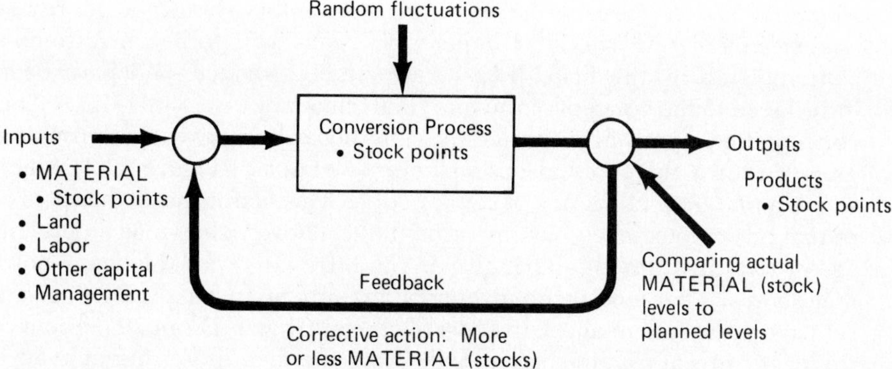

FIGURE 12.2
The conversion process: materials conversion

In service-oriented organizations that are not so highly labor-intense, inventories assume more importance. Community blood banks must keep inventories of blood types; military organizations and transit systems maintain inventories of equipment and replacement parts. In local department stores, inventories must be substantial to encourage sales. Production/operations management focuses on conversion of inputs into outputs of goods or services. This conversion process is reexamined with emphasis on material input in Figure 12.2. Note that there may be stock points at the input (raw material), conversion (work-in-process), and output (product) stages.

Why Inventories?

The fundamental reason for carrying inventories is that *it is physically impossible and economically impractical for each stock item to arrive exactly where it is needed exactly when it is needed.* Even were it physically possible for a supplier to deliver raw materials every few hours, for example, it could still be prohibitively expensive. The manufacturer must therefore keep extra supplies of raw material inventory for use when they're needed in the conversion process. Other reasons for carrying inventories are summarized in Table 12.2.

Table 12.2 Why organizations carry inventory

Level	Reason
Fundamental (primary)	Physical impossibility of getting right amount of stock at exact time of need
	Economical impracticality of getting right amount of stock at exact time of need
Secondary	Favorable return on investment
	Buffer to reduce uncertainty
	Decouple operations
	Level or smooth production
	Reduce material handling costs
	Bulk purchases

Return on Investment and Turnover Inventory should be viewed as an investment and should compete for funds with other investments contemplated by the firm. If you have studied finance, you have been introduced to the concept of the marginal efficiency of capital (MEC). This concept holds that a firm should invest in those alternatives that provide a greater return than capital costs to borrow. Look at Figure 12.3, which shows a marginal efficiency of capital curve. This figure shows the rates of return on various inventory investment alternatives (shown as a percentage of total investment alternatives). The MEC curve for this firm shows that about 20 percent of the inventory investment alternatives will give a return on investment above the cost of capital. That is, about 20 percent of the firm's inventory alternatives will bring the firm more money than it would have to spend if it borrowed money. These 20 percent of investments should be accepted. The 80 percent of the investment alternatives that would bring in less than the cost of capital should be rejected. Inventory investment alternative A in Figure 12.3, for example, is an acceptable investment. If inventory cannot compete on this same basis with other uses of funds (plant, equipment, land, advertising, bonds, etc.), inventory should be reduced until it becomes an attractive alternative for the firm.

Both manufacturing and service firms are interested in return on investment or return on assets employed. Return on assets is profits divided by assets. With a little thought we realize: (profits/assets) =

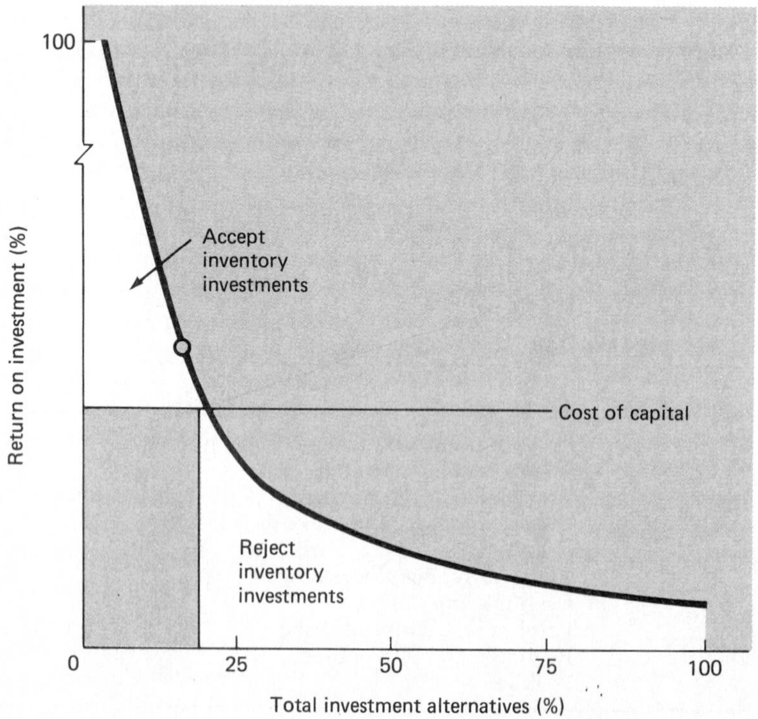

FIGURE 12.3
Typical marginal efficiency of capital curve (MEC)

(profits/sales)(sales/assets). Profits/sales is markup and sales/assets is turnover. Now we see that one way to improve return on investment is to increase turnover. We want to sell those assets that are inventory over and over again in a reasonable time frame. One way to do this is to keep the assets in inventory low, thus improving the chance of high inventory turnover.

Buffer Stock When demand is unusually variable, some protection is needed against the prospects of high stockout costs. Inventory can be used to "buffer" against such uncertainties. Likewise, procurement *lead time,* the time between ordering and receiving goods, is not always constant. Buffer stocks can be used to protect against stockouts from uncertain demand during procurement lead times.

Decoupling Inventories are also useful when they *decouple* operations, when they break operations apart so that one operation's supply is independent of another's supply. This decoupling function serves two purposes. First, inventories are needed to reduce the dependencies among successive stages of operations so that breakdowns, material shortages, or other production fluctuations at one stage do not cause later stages of operations to shut down. Figure 12.4 illustrates this concept in a diecasting firm. A second purpose of decoupling through inventories is to let one organization unit schedule its operations independently of another. In automobile manufacturing, for example, engine buildup can be scheduled separately from seat assembly, and each can be decoupled from final automobile assembly operations through in-process inventories.

Production Smoothing Inventories can also assist in leveling production. When we examined aggregate planning and scheduling in Chapter 10, we noted that products can be built through slack demand periods and used in peak demand periods. Thus high costs of production rate and work force level changes can be avoided.

Material Handling In some manufacturing and service operations, material handling costs can be reduced by accumulating parts between operations. This is particularly true of intermittent systems, since they involve less automation of material handling than do continuous systems.

FIGURE 12.4
Decoupling of operations by using inventory

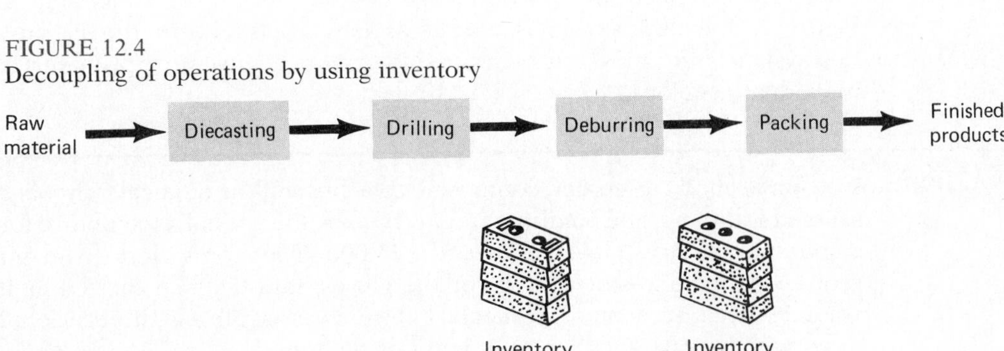

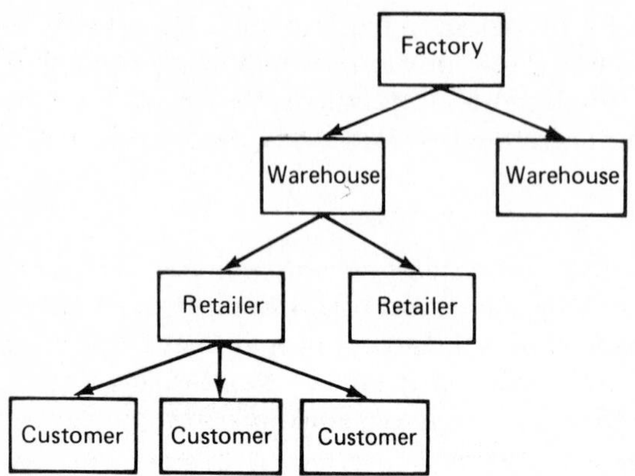

FIGURE 12.5
Multiechelon inventory systems

Parts can be accumulated and inventoried in tote boxes or baskets and transported by handjack dollies or forklift trucks much more economically than they can be carried by hand. In continuous manufacturing, automated material handling systems, rather than larger work-in-process inventories, are designed to reduce overall handling costs.

Bulk Purchases With bulk purchases, quantity discounts can be arranged, thus providing a cost advantage of inventories. If firms practice economies of scale in production by producing large volumes, or if a firm's transportation costs are lower for bulk shipments, those firms often offer quantity discounts.

Inventory System Concepts

Multistage Inventories When parts are stocked at more than one stage in the sequential production process, there are multistage inventories. Figure 12.4 illustrates several stages of production in a diecasting facility. Since there is interaction between inventory items in the various stages (raw material, diecastings, drilled parts, etc.), it is a difficult problem to establish balanced inventory levels at each stage and for the system overall. Our treatment in this chapter focuses on inventory at a single stage, with little consideration of interactions of the various stages. Materials requirements for successive stages are discussed in Chapter 14.

Multiechelon Inventories In inventory systems, multiple institutional levels are involved in converting raw materials into consumer products; each level is called an *echelon*. Multiechelon inventories, illustrated in Figure 12.5, include products stocked at the various levels in the distribution system. Our introductory discussion centers on inventory problems at individual echelons.

EXAMPLE In a large medical center composed of a hospital, a medical school, a school of nursing, and auxiliary research units, the annual expenditure for disposable surgical gloves exceeded $75,000. The stores clerk, who set reorder points and stock levels for the gloves, said that she carried high volumes because demand to central stores was erratic, with occasional large withdrawals. Further examination uncovered two additional echelons of glove inventory in the hospital: stocked gloves on the hospital floor or wing housing a surgery room and stocked gloves in the doctors' and nurses' offices and desks. Thus, demand in central stores was buffered by storerooms near surgery, and storerooms were buffered by emergency supplies in offices.

Reaction to Demand Changes The system should *not* have to react to rising demand by changing inventories in direct proportion to the increase in demand. As the hospital example illustrates, this is sometimes a complication in a multiechelon inventory structure. One statistical study of inventory-sales ratios in selected firms in Australia and the United States concluded that *an increase in demand can be serviced by a less than proportional increase in inventories.*[1] The converse is also true: When demand decreases, inventories cannot be decreased in direct proportion. Many firms became aware of this concept firsthand in the 1974–1975 and 1980–1982 recessions. As demand weakened during these periods, many firms reduced their inventories too much and suffered substantial production cost increases as a result.

The Operating Doctrine

Operations managers must make two basic inventory policy decisions: *when* to reorder stock and *how much* stock to reorder. These decisions are referred to as the *inventory control operating doctrine.*

The time to reorder is called the *reorder point.* A system signal, usually a predetermined inventory level, tells clerical or other responsible personnel when it is time to reorder stocks. The amount that should be reordered is called the *order quantity. The inventory level that signals the need to reorder and the reorder quantity selected are economic decisions at the heart of the operations manager's inventory control function.* Although the manager may not actually operate the control system, he or she is responsible for setting the operating doctrine.

Inventory Systems

Q/R Inventory System One practical way to establish an inventory system is to keep count of every item issued from stores and place an order for more stock when inventories dwindle to a predetermined level, the reorder point. The order is fixed in size (volume), size having been predetermined. Figure 12.6 illustrates two such Q/R inventory systems. In the system on the left, the demand for inventories, the usage rate, is known and constant. Replenishment inventories are assumed to be received at the stock point the moment they have been ordered. Notice that at the beginning of the time axis (far left), an order seems just to have arrived. As time goes by, inventory is steadily depleted until a level of R_1 units is reached. At R_1, the reorder point (also called the *trigger level*), another order is placed for Q_1 units from the supplier. These units arrive at the instant they are ordered. Procurement lead time is zero. The usage pattern is then repeated, and at level R_2, quantity Q_2 is ordered. In a simple case

---

[1]See J. M. Samuels and D. J. Smyth, "Statistical Evidence on the Relationship Between a Company's Sales and Its Inventories," *International Journal of Production Research* 6, no. 3 (1968), 249–56.

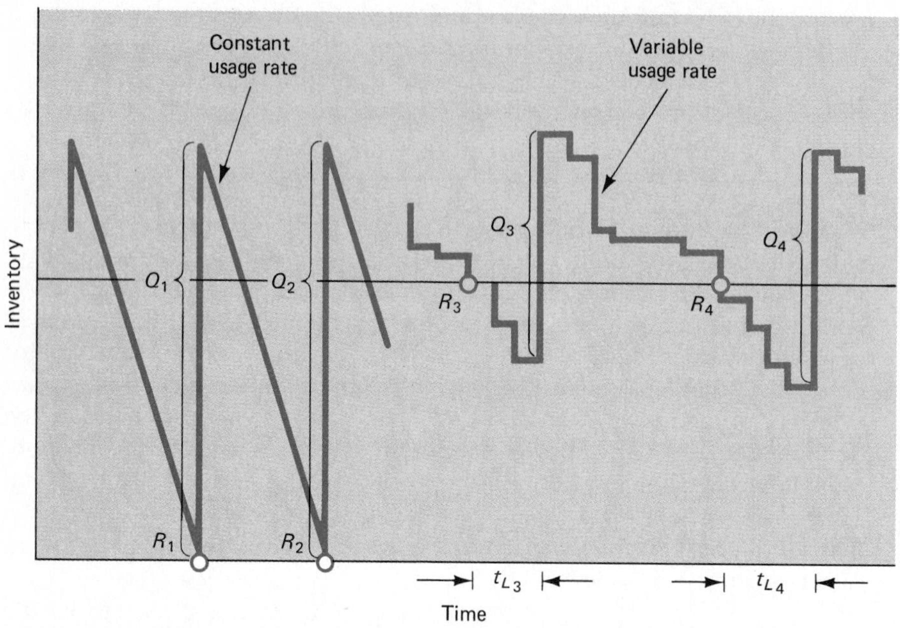

FIGURE 12.6
Q/R inventory systems

like this, there would be no need to carry buffer stocks; delivery is instantaneous, and the demand for the inventory item is known for certain. Thus R_1 is set at zero units.

In a Q/R system, both the reorder quantity and the reorder point are fixed. For Figure 12.6, then, $R_1 = R_2$ and $Q_1 = Q_2$.

A second and slightly more complex inventory situation is shown at the right of Figure 12.6. Usage (demand) is variable; we do not know in advance how rapidly inventory will be depleted. As before, $R_3 = R_4$ and $Q_3 = Q_4$; however, as you can see, somewhat different procedures are used to determine their values. It is difficult to establish the most economical operating doctrine when demand varies, as it does here, and even more difficult when lead time varies too. Since lead time is the time between placing and receiving an order, it is shown as t_{L_3} and t_{L_4} on the graph. When either demand or lead time varies, the time interval between orders varies—but the order quantity always remains constant.

Periodic Inventory System Another practical inventory control method is to examine inventories only at set time intervals, periodically, and to then reorder an amount equal to some preestablished base stock level. As Figure 12.7 illustrates, the level of inventory is examined at times T_1 and T_2, and orders are placed for quantities Q_1 and Q_2. The base stock level and the time between orders, t_1 and t_2, are set by operations management and comprise the inventory system's operating doctrine. In the periodic system $t_1 = t_2$, but Q_1 does not necessarily equal Q_2. Although Figure 12.7 shows constant demand within any one review period and zero lead time, these conditions could be relaxed and still allow the periodic inventory system concepts to be retained.

In this book, we emphasize Q/R systems. Although we concentrate on determining economic order quantities and reorder points, however, remember that the procedures are similar for the periodic system. Economic order quantity in the Q/R system and base stock levels in the periodic system determine how much to order; reorder point in the Q/R system and time between orders in the periodic system determine when to order.

INVENTORY COSTS

In operating an inventory system managers should consider only those costs that vary directly with the operating doctrine in deciding when and how much to reorder; costs independent of the operating doctrine are irrelevant. Basically, there are five types of relevant costs:

1. Cost of the item itself
2. Costs associated with procuring the stocks
3. Costs of carrying the stock items in inventory
4. Costs associated with being out of stock when units are demanded but are unavailable
5. Operating costs associated with data gathering and control procedures for the inventory system

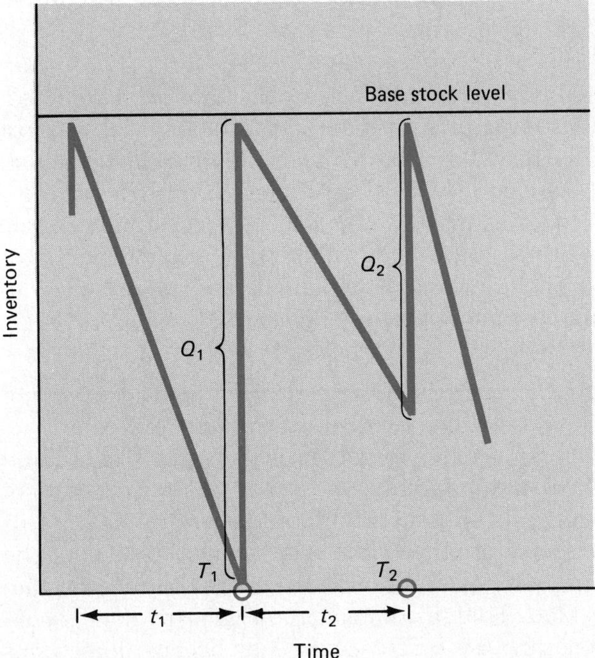

FIGURE 12.7
Periodic inventory system

Often these five costs are combined in one way or another, but let's discuss them separately before we consider combinations that may be used in different inventory situations.

Cost of Item

The *cost,* or *value,* of the item is the sum paid to the supplier for the item received or the direct manufacturing cost if produced. It is normally equal to the purchase price. In some instances, however, transportation, receiving, or inspection costs, for example, may be included as part of the costs of the item. If the item unit cost is constant for all quantities ordered, the total cost of purchased goods needed during the planning horizon is irrelevant to the operating doctrine. (We show in this chapter's supplement how it drops out of the total cost equation when we model this situation.) If the unit cost varies with the quantity ordered, a price reduction called a *quantity discount,* this cost is relevant.

Procurement Costs

Procurement costs are those incurred by placing a purchase order or are incurred as setup costs if manufactured. These costs vary directly with each purchase order placed. Procurement costs include costs of postage, perhaps telephone calls to the vendor, labor costs in purchasing and accounting, receiving costs, computer time for record keeping, and purchase order supplies.

Inventory Carrying Costs

Carrying, or *holding, costs* are the real out-of-pocket costs associated with having inventory on hand. Typical out-of-pocket costs include insurance, warehouse rental, heat, light, taxes, and losses due to pilferage, spoilage, or breakage. Another opportunity cost, while not an out-of-pocket cost, must be considered—the cost incurred by having capital tied up in inventory.

Stockout Costs

Stockout costs, associated with demand when stocks have been depleted, take the form of lost sales costs or backorder costs. When sales are lost because of stockouts, the firm loses both the profit margin on actual unmade sales and customer good will. If customers take their business elsewhere, future profit margins may also be lost. When customers agree to come back after inventories have been replenished, they make backorders. Backorder costs include loss of good will and money paid to reorder goods and notify customers when goods arrive.

EXAMPLE A customer at First National Bank had two unpleasant banking experiences this year. First, he went to a teller to get six rolls each of dimes and quarters. At this drive-in banking facility, the teller was out of rolls of dimes; she substituted two rolls of nickels but could spare no more. This forced the customer to make another stop at a competitor bank. The second experience was an attempt to obtain an $8,000 commercial rate loan to purchase some land. The customer agreed to provide adequate stocks and bonds as collateral but was refused the loan because loan funds were not available, not because he was a bad risk. The customer received the loan at a competitor bank and thereafter did all his banking at the competitor.

As this example shows, stockouts can and do occur in the service industries as well as in manufacturing. Stockouts can result in lost service opportunities, lost interest or profit, and lost customer good will.

Cost of Operating the Information Processing System

Whether by hand or by computer, someone must update records as stock levels change. In those systems in which inventory levels are not recorded daily, this operating cost is primarily incurred in obtaining accurate physical counts of inventories. Frequently, these operating costs are more *fixed* than variable over a wide quantity (volume) range. Therefore, since fixed costs are not relevant in establishing the operating doctrine, we will not consider them further.

Cost Tradeoffs

Our objective in inventory control is to find the *minimum cost operating doctrine* over some planning horizon. We need to consider all relevant costs—the cost of the item, procurement costs, carrying costs, and stockout costs. Using an annual planning horizon, these costs can be expressed in a general cost equation:

Total annual relevant costs	=	Cost of the item	+	Procurement costs	+	Carrying costs • Cycle stocks • Buffer stocks	+	Stockout costs • Lost sales • Backorders	(12.1)

Each of the costs in the equation can be expressed in terms of order quantity and reorder point for a given inventory situation. The solution method is then to *minimize* the total cost situation. This can be accomplished graphically; by tabular analysis using trial and error; or by using the calculus, the most accurate method. Using the calculus, operations researchers have developed a wide range of optimal formulas, which vary with changes in the actual inventory situation.

Graphically, the minimization of this equation consists of cost tradeoffs. For a simple model in which costs of purchased goods (items) and stockouts are irrelevant, the tradeoff is between only two cost components—procurement and carrying costs (see Figure 12.8). Notice that annual carrying costs increase with larger values of order quantity, Q. This is logical; large values of Q result in large average inventory levels and, therefore, large carrying costs. Likewise, when Q increases, fewer orders must be placed during the year and annual ordering costs decrease. Therefore, as shown in Figure 12.8, procurement costs decrease as carrying costs increase. There is a *cost tradeoff* between the two. If we add the costs graphically, we obtain a total cost curve. The optimal order quantity is the point at which annual total cost is at a minimum, Q^* in this case. For more complex cost situations, the cost curves become difficult to graph and analyze tabularly, *but the cost tradeoff concepts remain the same.*

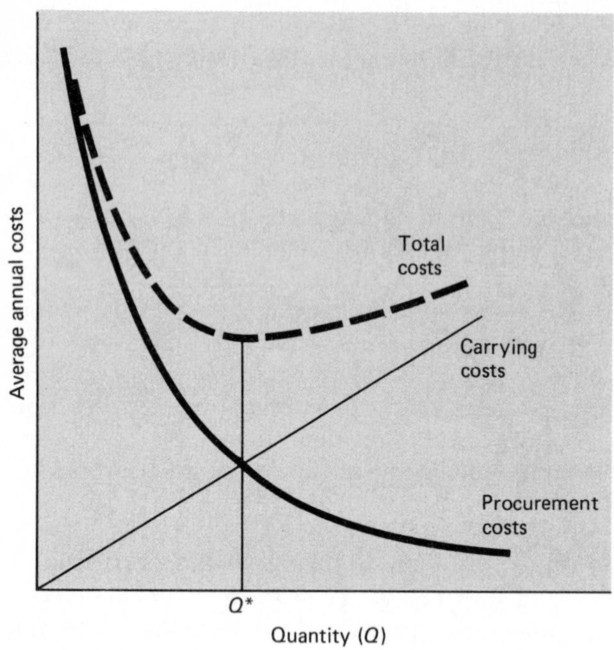

FIGURE 12.8
Cost tradeoffs in inventory control

INVENTORY MODELING

The methodology for modeling inventory situations is straightforward. The purpose is to derive an operating doctrine, and four simple steps are involved.

1. Examine the inventory situation carefully, listing characteristics and assumptions concerning the situation.
2. Develop the total annual relevant cost equation in narrative.
3. Transform the total annual cost equation from narrative into the shorthand logic of mathematics.
4. Optimize the cost equation, finding the optimum for how much to order (order quantity) and when to reorder (reorder point).

As mentioned in our discussion of inventory systems, we will develop models only for the Q/R system, although the general methodology holds for the periodic system as well. Remember, too, that inventory situations can be classified as either *deterministic* (variables are known with certainty) or *stochastic* (variables are probabilistic). In this chapter we discuss two deterministic models, especially the simple lot size formula, saving our discussion of a third deterministic model and stochastic models until the next chapter.

Variables in Inventory Models For model development and discussion, we will use the following notation:

D = Annual demand in units
Q = Quantity ordered
Q^* = Optimal order quantity
R = Reorder point
t_L = Lead time
S = Setup or procurement cost per order
I = Carrying charge per unit, expressed as a percentage rate
C = Cost of the individual item; the purchase cost per item
K = Stockout cost per unit out of stock
P = Production rate; units per period of time
d_L = Demand per unit of time during lead time
D_L = Demand during lead time; total demand during lead time
TC = Total annual relevant costs

DETERMINISTIC INVENTORY MODELS

The Simple Lot Size Formula

The earliest derivation of what is often called the *simple lot size formula* was developed by Ford Harris in 1915.[2] Apparently, it was again independently derived by R. H. Wilson, who popularized it. In his honor, it is sometimes referred to as the *Wilson formula.*

This inventory situation assumes that

1. Inventory is being controlled at one point (in a stockroom or in raw materials, for example)
2. Demand is deterministic and at a constant known rate per year
3. No stockouts are allowed
4. Lead time is constant and independent of demand
5. Purchase cost per unit is fixed

To simplify the case even further, lead time can be assumed to be zero; that is, delivery is instantaneous.

What does the total annual relevant cost (TC) equation look like? Let's modify equation 12.1 to fit this situation:

$$\text{Total annual relevant costs} = \text{Procurement costs} + \text{Carrying costs} \quad (12.2)$$

Stockouts do not occur, and the annual cost of purchased goods is excluded, since the purchase price per unit is fixed. Only those costs that can be affected by our choice of Q are included. Expanding equation 12.2,

$$TC = \begin{pmatrix}\text{Cost of}\\\text{ordering}\end{pmatrix}\begin{pmatrix}\text{Number of}\\\text{orders}\\\text{placed/year}\end{pmatrix} + \begin{pmatrix}\text{Cost of}\\\text{carrying}\\\text{1 unit}\end{pmatrix}\begin{pmatrix}\text{Average}\\\text{number of}\\\text{units carried}\end{pmatrix} \quad (12.3)$$

$$= S\begin{pmatrix}\text{Number of}\\\text{orders placed/year}\end{pmatrix} + IC\begin{pmatrix}\text{Average number}\\\text{of units}\end{pmatrix}$$

[2]Ford Harris, *Operations and Cost* (Chicago: A. W. Shaw Company, 1915), pp. 48–52.

The number of orders placed per year can be expressed in terms of annual demand and order quantity. Since

$$\text{Annual demand} = \left(\begin{matrix}\text{Quantity ordered}\\ \text{in each order}\end{matrix}\right)\left(\begin{matrix}\text{Number of orders placed/}\\ \text{year}\end{matrix}\right) \quad (12.4)$$

then

$$\text{Number of orders placed/year} = \frac{\text{Annual demand}}{\text{Quantity ordered in each order}} = \frac{D}{Q}$$

How can we determine the average inventory per year? Look again at the constant usage situation in Figure 12.6. What is the maximum inventory, the highest that inventory will ever be? It is the order quantity, Q. What is the lowest inventory? Since we reorder when the stock is fully depleted, the lowest is zero. This pattern, in which inventories vary from maximum to minimum and then back to maximum, is called a *cycle*. For *any one cycle*, the average inventory would be

$$\text{Average inventory/cycle} = \frac{\text{Maximum inventory} + \text{Minimum inventory}}{2} = \frac{Q + 0}{2} = \frac{Q}{2}$$

Think about the several cycles of inventory orders in Figure 12.6. The average for any *one* of these cycles is $Q/2$, but what is the average inventory per year? It is still $Q/2$. *Average inventory is time independent.*

EXAMPLE Morrison, Inc., orders new trays and issues them to various cafeterias from central stores. If Morrison orders 1,000 trays eight times a year, what is the *annual average inventory* in trays, presuming all the assumptions for the simple lot size formula hold? The average inventory for the first, second, and so on to the eighth cycle would be 1,000/2, or 500. Try to picture the cycling of inventories eight times and the annual effect of this cycling. For the *entire year,* the maximum would be 1,000 and the minimum 0, and the uniform usage would produce an average inventory of 500 new trays.

Substituting our expressions for the number of orders placed per year and average inventory into equation 12.3, our total cost equation becomes

$$TC = S\frac{D}{Q} + IC\frac{Q}{2} \quad (12.5)$$

From this total cost equation evolves the formula for the optimal order quantity, the quantity at the low point of the total cost curve in Figure 12.8:

$$Q^* = \sqrt{\frac{2DS}{IC}} \tag{12.6}$$

Since delivery is instantaneous, the reorder point should be set at the lowest point possible, zero, to avoid carrying excess stocks. The operating doctrine, then, is

$$\text{Order } Q^* = \sqrt{\frac{2DS}{IC}}$$
$$\text{At point } R^* = 0$$

If you want to see how the calculus is used in this derivation, read the supplement at the end of this chapter.

EXAMPLE Our Redeemer Catholic Church orders candles periodically, and delivery is essentially instantaneous. Annual demand, estimated to be 180 candles, is constant. Candles cost \$8/dozen; the cost of placing the order is estimated to be \$9; and the annual carrying charge is estimated to be 15 percent of the candle cost. What quantity should the priest order, and when should he reorder? Calculate the economic order quantity:

$$Q^* = \sqrt{\frac{2DS}{IC}}$$

$$= \sqrt{\frac{2\left(\frac{180}{12}\right)(9)}{0.15(8)}}$$

$$= \sqrt{225}$$

$$= 15 \text{ dozen}$$

The priest should order 15 dozen. Since delivery is instantaneous, he should order only upon depleting stock, which happens exactly once a year. The operating doctrine is $Q^* = 15$ dozen candles at the point $R^* = 0$.

In our example, the priest is ordering periodically, perhaps intuitively. Possibly he considers that the reasonable cost of candles (\$8/dozen) and the high cost of placing an order (\$9) mean that he needn't order very frequently. This raises an important question. How *sensitive* are costs to optimal order quantity? When he's intuitively ordering candles, how far away from optimal order quantity could the priest be and still have relatively low costs? Let's examine the sensitivity of the simple lot size formula.

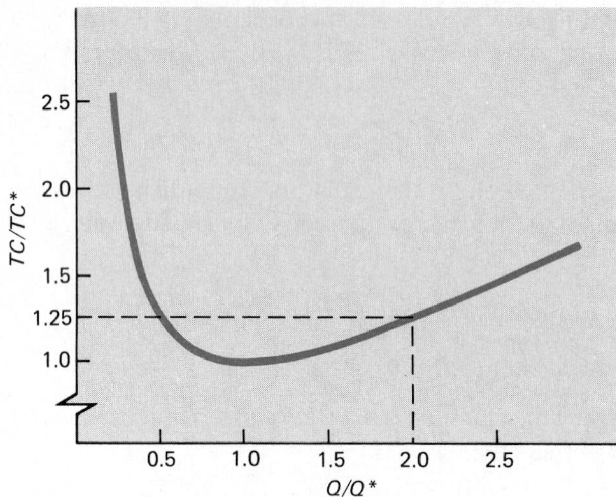

FIGURE 12.9
Inventory sensitivity—simple lot size case

Source: G. Hadley and T. M. Whitin, *Analysis of Inventory Systems* (Englewood Cliffs, N.J.: Prentice Hall, 1963), p. 36.

Model Sensitivity We can compare the sensitivity of total costs (TC) for any operating system with the total costs for an optimal inventory system (TC^*) by using the ratio TC/TC^*. To do this, we compute TC/TC^* as a function of Q/Q^*.

$$\frac{TC}{TC^*} = \frac{S\frac{D}{Q} + IC\frac{Q}{2}}{S\frac{D}{Q^*} + IC\frac{Q^*}{2}} \qquad (12.7)$$

Substituting $Q^* = \sqrt{2DS/IC}$ into equation 12.7 and solving algebraically, we find the general relationship

$$\frac{TC}{TC^*} = \frac{1}{2}\left[\frac{Q^*}{Q} + \frac{Q}{Q^*}\right] \qquad (12.8)$$

Note that the total cost ratio in this equation is expressed solely in terms of Q and Q^*. If our existing order quantity (Q) is very close to optimal (Q^*), the ratio TC/TC^* is slightly larger than unity. As Q departs farther from Q^*, we expect TC/TC^* also to grow. Graphically, the relation between Q/Q^* and TC/TC^* for the simple lot size case (equation 12.7) is shown in Figure 12.9. Note the flatness of the curve around the minimum point, 1.0 on each axis. If actual Q is off from the optimal in either direction by a factor of two, costs are increased by only 25 percent. This has important practical implications. For cases that fit the assumptions of the simple lot size model, improving ordering rules won't save much money. Correcting an ordering rule, even one far from optimal, might not result in a very large dollar savings.

EXAMPLE Thompson Tooling has a Department of Defense contract for 150,000 bushings a year. Thompson orders the metal for the bushings in lots of 40,000 units from a supplier. It costs $40 to place an order, and estimated carrying costs are 20 percent of the item cost, \$0.15. Thompson wants to know what the percent variation their order quantity is from optimal and what this variation is costing them, if anything. Finding optimal order quantity.

$$Q^* = \sqrt{\frac{2DS}{IC}}$$

$$= \sqrt{\frac{2(150{,}000)(40)}{0.2(0.15)}}$$

$$= 20{,}000$$

Comparing optimal order quantity with current order quantity, Q:

$$\frac{TC}{TC^*} = \frac{1}{2}\left(\frac{Q^*}{Q} + \frac{Q}{Q^*}\right)$$

$$= \frac{1}{2}\left(\frac{20{,}000}{40{,}000} + \frac{40{,}000}{20{,}000}\right)$$

$$= 1.25$$

This calculation shows that even though order quantity deviates from optimal by 20,000 units, or 100 percent, the costs are only 25 percent higher than optimal. The excess (marginal) costs of the nonoptimal order quantity can be found as follows:

$$\text{Marginal costs} = 0.25\ (TC^*)$$

$$= 0.25\left(S\frac{D}{Q^*} + IC\frac{Q^*}{2}\right)$$

$$= 0.25\left(\frac{40(150{,}000)}{20{,}000} + \frac{0.2(0.15)(20{,}000)}{2}\right)$$

$$= 0.25\ (300 + 300)$$

$$= \$150$$

Alternatively,

$$TC^* = S\frac{D}{Q^*} + IC\frac{Q^*}{2}$$

$$= \frac{(40)(150{,}000)}{20{,}000} + \frac{(0.20)(0.15)(20{,}000)}{2}$$

$$= 300 + 300$$

$$= \$600$$

and

$$TC_{\text{actual}} = \frac{(40)(150{,}000)}{40{,}000} + \frac{(0.20)(0.15)(40{,}000)}{2}$$

$$= 150 + 600$$

$$= \$750$$

Marginal cost of the nonoptimal policy is \$750 − \$600, or \$150.

Notice from this example that for annual purchases valued at \$22,500, even though order quantity was off *100 percent,* the cost to Thompson Tooling was only an additional \$150. You may also note that for the TC^* calculation, ordering costs are equal to carrying costs, each being \$300. This is just what we illustrated graphically earlier.

Gradual Replacement Model

Sometimes, part of the delivery is instantaneous upon ordering, but the rest of the units are sent little by little over time. When the order is placed, the supplier begins producing units, which are supplied continuously to the purchaser. While these units are being added into inventory (causing it to grow), customers are drawing units out of inventory (causing it to diminish). Consider the case in which replenishment rate (P) exceeds withdrawal rates (D). After some time, the order quantity has been produced, and net inventories have increased. The inventory level, however, never reaches the same high level as the simple lot size model, the order quantity. This situation is illustrated in Figure 12.10. During the time t_p, the slope of inventory accumulation is not vertical, as it was in the simple lot size model. This is the case because the entire order is not received at one time. Since $P > D$, during the time t_p inventory is consumed as well as built up, and this situation continues until the initial order quantity, Q, has been produced and delivered. At that point, inventory is at its maximum. Thereafter, during time t_d, demand occurs while the process used for production is idle or shifts to other jobs. At the end of time t_d, another order for Q is placed, production startup is instantaneous, and the cycle repeats. The order for the entire lot is filled continually over time, not immediately as was the case with the simple lot size model.

Still applying the other assumptions of the lot size model, the total annual cost equation for this model is the same as equation 12.2:

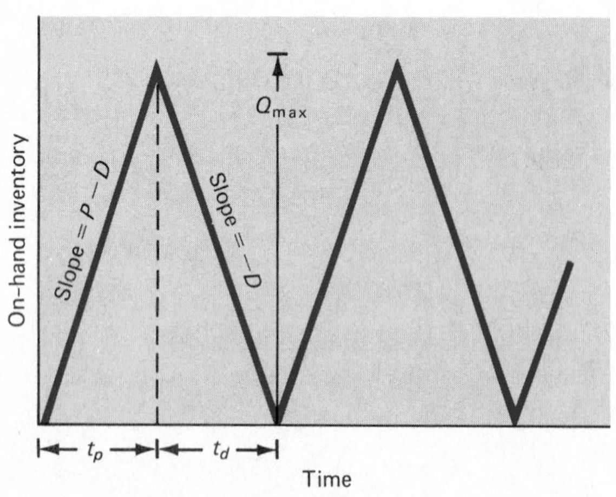

FIGURE 12.10
Gradual replacement (finite production rate) inventory situation

$$\begin{matrix}\text{Total annual} \\ \text{relevant costs}\end{matrix} = \text{Procurement costs} + \text{Carrying costs}$$

It can be written as follows:

$$TC = S\frac{D}{Q} + IC\begin{pmatrix}\text{Average number} \\ \text{of units}\end{pmatrix}$$

As we have noted, maximum inventory never reaches Q but is somewhat less. Therefore, average inventory carried will not be $Q/2$. Realizing that the positive slope of the graph is $P - D$ and the negative slope is $-D$, we can find the maximum inventory, Q_{max} from

$$\text{Slope} = \frac{\text{Rise}}{\text{Run}}$$

$$P - D = \frac{Q_{max}}{t_p}$$

But the length of time required to produce a lot is:

$$t_p = \frac{Q}{P}$$

Substituting

$$P - D = Q_{max} \div \frac{Q}{P}$$

$$Q_{max} = (P - D)\frac{Q}{P} = Q\left(\frac{P - D}{P}\right)$$

Average inventory is then

$$\begin{matrix}\text{Average} \\ \text{inventory}\end{matrix} = \frac{\text{Maximum inventory} + \text{Minimum inventory}}{2}$$

$$= \left(\frac{Q(P - D)}{P}\right) + 0 \div 2$$

$$= \frac{Q}{2}\left(\frac{P - D}{P}\right)$$

The total cost equation to be minimized for the gradual replacement correction case is:

$$TC = S\frac{D}{Q} + IC\left[\frac{Q}{2}\left(\frac{P - D}{P}\right)\right] \tag{12.9}$$

which yields

$$Q^* = \sqrt{\frac{2DS}{IC}\left(\frac{P}{P - D}\right)} \tag{12.10}$$

Since production and resupply begin instantaneously, the optimal reorder point would again be at $R^* = 0$. Note that for this operating doctrine, the formula for Q^* is identical to Q^* for the simple lot size model (equation 12.6) except for the *finite correction factor* $[P/(P - D)]^{1/2}$. Will this finite correction result in Q^* being greater here than in the simple lot size formula? Examine the factor and remember that $P > D$.

In the next example, an order should be placed for 1,414 salads when there are no salads on hand. When 1,414 salads are ordered, it takes about 11.5 days to produce them and about 17 days to consume them. A salad must be kept fresh for 5.5 days. What type of salads are these? Fruit? Lettuce? The manager should therefore question whether it is feasible to meet the restriction. This situation illustrates for us how inaccurate costs or an inappropriate inventory model can distort reality. As the example shows, however, you should always make validity checks in applying inventory or other models to production/operations situations.

EXAMPLE A large hotel serves banquets and several restaurants from a central kitchen in which labor is shifted among various stations and jobs. Salad consumption (demand) is virtually constant and known to be 30,000 salads/year. Salads can be produced at a rate of 45,000/year. Salads cost $0.40 each, and it costs $4 to set up the salad line. Carrying costs of salads, high because of spoilage, are estimated to be 90 percent of the cost of a salad. No stockouts are allowed. The hotel would like to establish an operating doctrine for salad preparation.

First, we can set the reorder point at $R^* = 0$, because labor can be shifted to the salad operation instantaneously, and the production rate is greater than the demand rate. Finding Q^*,

$$Q^* = \sqrt{\frac{2DS}{IC}\left(\frac{P}{P - D}\right)}$$

$$= \sqrt{\frac{2(30{,}000)(4)}{0.9(0.4)}\left(\frac{45{,}000}{45{,}000 - 30{,}000}\right)}$$

$$= \sqrt{2(10)^6}$$

$$= 1{,}414$$

Lead Time in Deterministic Models

Deterministic models can easily be adjusted for lead times known with certainty. The reorder point is calculated:

$$R^* = \text{Buffer stock} + \text{Demand during lead time} \qquad (12.11)$$

$$= 0 + (\text{Lead time})\ (\text{Demand/unit time}) \qquad (12.12)$$

$$= t_L d_L$$

The reorder point is now set and shown in Figure 12.11. Note that total demand during lead time, D_L, is lead time times demand per unit time. At R^*, an order will be placed for Q^* units. The actual order for quantity Q^* will arrive t_L later. During the time between ordering and arrival, d_L units will be demanded, and inventory will be reduced accordingly.

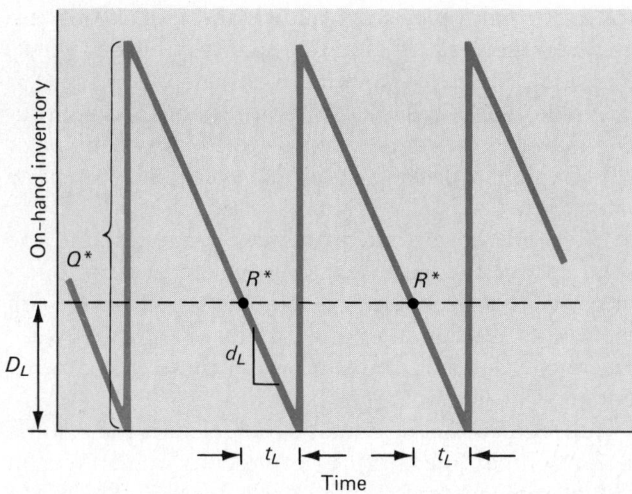

FIGURE 12.11
Reorder points with lead times

EXAMPLE A hamburger chain has a local retail outlet that uses 730 cases of six-ounce paper cups annually. Ordering costs are \$15; carrying costs are 30 percent of average inventory investment; and a case costs \$12. Delivery lead time is known with certainty to be five days. Establishing the optimal operating doctrine,

$$
\begin{aligned}
Q^* &= \sqrt{\frac{2DS}{IC}} = \sqrt{\frac{2(730)(15)}{0.3(12)}} \\
&= 77.99 \\
&= 78 \\
R^* &= t_L d_L \\
&= 5d_L \\
&= 5\left(\frac{730}{365}\right) \\
&= 10
\end{aligned}
$$

The operating doctrine would be to order 78 cases when stocks on hand reach 10 boxes.

SUMMARY

In this chapter we illustrated that inventories are necessary for a number of reasons, the fundamental one being that it is physically impossible and economically impractical for every stock item to be delivered exactly when it is needed. In controlling inventories, we discussed that it is necessary to establish an operating doctrine, that is, policy decisions concerning *when* to replenish stocks and *how much* stock to replenish; these decisions, are usually made within the framework of either a quantity/reorder (Q/R) inventory system or a periodic inventory system. In our analysis of the Q/R system, we noted that when stock is depleted to an established reorder point, a predetermined quantity is ordered. In the periodic system, after an established time interval has passed, stock is replenished up to a predetermined base stock level.

We defined the inventory costs that are relevant in selecting the operating doctrine—the cost of the item, costs associated with procurement, costs of carrying the item in inventory, and costs associated with being out of stock when units are demanded. Formally or informally, we learned that inventory control decisions must consider these cost components and their tradeoffs.

For inventories with deterministic demands and lead times, some helpful models were presented: the simple lot size formula (Wilson formula) and the gradual replacement (finite correction) model. When demand and lead times are known, we noted that there is no need to carry buffer stock, since stockouts will never occur. This simplifies the models considerably.

REVIEW AND DISCUSSION QUESTIONS

1. Identify and describe the elements of control systems. Use a schematic diagram to assist in your discussion.
2. Give an example of a nonorganizational control system in science or engineering. Identify its goal, its control elements, and its information flows.
3. Give an example of an organizational control system. Identify its goals, its control elements, and its information flows.
4. Differentiate between multistage and multiechelon inventories. Must you have only one or the other? Explain.
5. What is meant by the inventory operating doctrine? In the operating doctrine, why are *two* decisions necessary?
6. Contrast the periodic and quantity/reorder inventory system operating doctrines.
7. Explain the steps in the modeling methodology for inventory situations. Why is the understanding of this methodology important to the practicing manager?
8. Define inventory control in the context of an automobile repair facility employing four mechanics. For any technical terms used in your definition, provide examples.
9. Refer to Figure 12.2 (the materials conversion process). For a general purpose farming operation, provide one example of a material item for each stock point.
10. Why are inventories necessary? Discuss.
11. What kinds of items should be selected when managers are attempting to improve inventory systems? Why?
12. Explain the cost tradeoffs of equation 12.5 in essay form, using a graph if it is helpful.
13. Explain how the situation of the finite production (gradual replacement) rate inventory differs from the simple lot size situation. What impact does the cost of the item have on each situation? Explain.
14. In deterministic inventory models, total costs are relatively insensitive to deviations from the optimal operating doctrine. Explain.

PROBLEMS

Solved Problems

1. A television manufacturer requires 24,000 two-centimeter-long pieces of wire every month for assembly. Ordering costs are estimated at $42, and the cost of carrying is 25 percent of the unit price, which is $.08. Assuming delivery is instantaneous, find the reorder point and economic order quantity.

$$D = (24{,}000)\,(12) = 288{,}000 \text{ pieces/year}$$
$$S = \$42$$
$$I = 25\%$$
$$C = \$0.08$$
$$Q^* = \sqrt{\frac{2DS}{IC}} = \sqrt{\frac{(2)\,(288{,}000)\,(\$42)}{(.25)\,(\$0.08)}} = 34{,}779.3$$

There should be 34,780 pieces/order; $R^* = 0$.

2. The Ohio State University location of McDonald's uses 120 six-ounce paper cups each day. McDonald's plans to be open 360 days a year. The cups cost $.10/dozen; ordering costs are $5/order; and carrying costs are 50 percent of the item cost (since space is a premium).
   (a) Find the economic order quantity if delivery is instantaneous.
   (b) Currently, cups are ordered every 30 days. Relate current ordering quantity, optimal order quantity, current total costs, and optimal total costs. What does this mean?

Solution (for Part a) $D = (120 \div 12)(360) = 3{,}600$ dozen

$$S = \$5$$
$$I = 50\%$$
$$C = \$.10$$
$$Q^* = \sqrt{\frac{2DS}{IC}} = \sqrt{\frac{2(3600)(\$5)}{0.50(\$.10)}} = 848.53 = 849 \text{ dozen}$$

Solution (for Part b) Current order quantity (Q) = 3600 ÷ 12 = 300 dozen

Current total costs:
Ordering costs = $5 × 12 (orders) = $60
Carrying costs = $.05 × 150 (average inventory) = $7.50
Total current costs = $67.50

Costs when using Economic Order Quantity (EOQ):
Ordering costs = $5 × (3600 ÷ 849) = $21.200
Carrying costs = $.05 × 424.5 = 21.225
Total costs – EOQ method = $42.425

Obviously, McDonald's can save $25.075 by using the EOQ method rather than the current operating policy, a savings of more than 37% from current costs.

Reinforcing Fundamentals

3. A local bakery, Harry's, orders 100 50-pound bags of flour every three months.
   (a) What is the average inventory for three months (in bags)?
   (b) What is the average inventory for a year (in bags)?
   (c) What is the average monthly inventory (in pounds)?
4. Delicious Donut Shop requires 50 bags of flour every three months. The costs of ordering are $12/order placed, and a carrying charge of 22 percent of the flour

cost. A bag of flour costs $27. Flour can be delivered virtually instantaneously from a local warehouse. Determine the operating doctrine for a quantity/reorder point inventory system.

5. The owner of Delicious Donut Shop (see Problem 4) has been ordering 100 bags of flour at one time.
   (a) What percentage is the owner away from optimal order quantity? How much is this deviation costing per year?
   (b) Considering the total cost of flour per year, what can you conclude about deviations from optimal order quantity? Should the owner continue to investigate similar situations? Why or why not?

6. Use the graphical method to estimate Q^* for the following situation, in which delivery is instantaneous and usage rate is constant throughout the year.

$$D = 10{,}000 \text{ units}, \; R = 0 \text{ units}$$
$$I = .25, \; C = \$100/\text{unit}$$
$$\text{Procurement cost/order} = \$50 + \$.50/\text{unit in the order}$$

7. A textile manufacturer is interested in optimally determined inventories for cutting operations for a children's product line. The production manager would like to establish the optimal reorder point and order quantity for each item in the line. Garment 78A201, a typical product, is demanded uniformly throughout the year, total demand being 14,000 items. The production rate is 2,000 items/month. Sewing, the operation following cutting, is staffed to meet annual demand exactly. Setup costs for cutting are $240, and the cost of carrying one item for a year is $.50. Since cutting and sewing are done in the same plant, delivery of cut items to sewing is essentially instantaneous. Determine the cutting operation operating doctrine for garment 78A201.

8. A missile manufacturer requires a particular electric wired subassembly for final assembly. Annual subassembly demand is 480 "wire bundles"; order costs are $85; carrying costs are 75 percent of average inventory investment; and bundles cost $1,125 each. Delivery time is known with certainty to be 21 days. Establish the optimal operating doctrine.

9. Buster's Inc. is interested in the economical order quantity for a production subassembly that is currently purchased from another company. The final assembly made by Buster's is for a parent company, under an annual contract, with the year's demand set at 75,000 units. Two purchased subassemblies are required for one final assembly. The cost of a subassembly is $13, and the cost of placing an order with the supplier is $27. The annual inventory holding charge is $4. Trinidad currently orders 1,000 units at one time. Can you save them any money by recommending a new order quantity? If so, how much can they save and what quantity should they order?

Challenging Exercises

10. Ward Paper Box Company supplies a particular candy box to Russell Stover Candy Company, delivering 200 one-pound candy boxes/day. The machine that produces these boxes has a capacity of 1,000 boxes/day. In the past, Ward has always run the machine one day a week to satisfy the weekly demand of 1,000 cartons over a 5-day work week (50 weeks a year). Setup costs are $100/run, and carrying costs are $.05/box/day.
    (a) Find the economic order quantity for this candy box.
    (b) What is the cost savings in a year by ordering the economic order quantity rather than following current policy?

11. A fast-food outlet uses 180 breakfast paper cartons/day. The outlet plans to be open 365 days a year. The cartons cost $.20/dozen; ordering costs are $5/order; and carrying costs are 70 percent of the item (since space is a premium).
    (a) Find the economic order quantity if delivery is instantaneous.

(b) Currently, cartons are ordered every 14 days. Relate current ordering quantity, optimal order quantity, current total costs, and optimal total costs. What does this mean?

12. A dairy that supplies a large number of retail outlets uses a certain ingredient at the rate of 1,500 pounds a day, 250 days a year. Delivery is virtually constant and requires two days. A two-day usage of safety stock is set by management and cannot be changed. Ordering costs are $40/order, and the cost of carrying inventory charge is $0.001/pound/day. Determine

(a) the economic order quantity,

(b) the reorder point,

(c) the maximum inventory level, and

(d) the total annual carrying costs.

13. Often variances for production are computed and the results are used for subsequent production control.

(a) Compute the raw material price and usage (quantity) variance and the direct labor quantity variance for Milton Industries' key product, shown below. State the variance as favorable or unfavorable.

(b) For each measure in Part a, would you take action as a manager? Why or why not?

(c) Write the general formula you used to compute this variance. (Note: We did not provide a formula in this chapter.)

	Standard for 1,000 Units	Actual for 1,000 Units
Raw materials:		
Price	$1.20/pound	$1.40/pound
Quantity	1 pound/unit	1,100 pounds
Direct labor:		
Price	$6.00/hour	$6.00/hour
Quantity	2.37 hour/unit	2,172 hours

14. A missile manufacturer (see Problem 8) is investigating setting up a "bundle wiring" room and manufacturing the wire bundles for production. This would bring 480 items currently purchased at $1,125 "in house," generating some $540,000 of business a year. The method of production under investigation produces a maximum of 4 bundles/day over a 250-day year. Cost per item produced is estimated to remain at $1,125 each, but items can be delivered when they are produced rather than in the previously determined lot size. Ordering costs are expected to fall to $30/order, with carrying costs remaining 75 percent of inventory investment. The $1,125/item cost estimate would cover all fixed costs of the new production line and variable costs for this item only.

(a) For the Economic Order Quantity (EOQ) of Problem 8, find the total annual inventory cost when the items are purchased.

(b) Establish the EOQ for the manufacturer producing the wire bundle in house.

(c) For the EOQ in Part b, find the total annual inventory cost.

(d) Which do you recommend—purchase or produce? Why? What qualitative factors did you consider in your decision?

Utilizing the QSOM Computer Software

15. An auto parts outlet sells 120 spark plugs weekly and operates year-round less two weeks for holidays. The plugs cost $7/dozen, and the cost of placing an order is $12. Carrying costs are 30% of item cost. Using QSOM's inventory theory program and assuming delivery is instantaneous, determine the EOQ, R^*, and order interval.

16. A general contractor uses 50,000 pounds of Portland cement each month. The 100-pound bags cost $8 each, and the contractor pays $15/order. Carrying costs are 25% of unit cost. Top management estimates that the shortage cost per bag per year would be $10, should such a situation occur. The supplier fulfills all orders in one month. Using QSOM's inventory theory program, determine the EOQ, reorder point, and the order interval for this contractor.

GLOSSARY

Buffer stocks Inventories to protect against the uncertainties of unusual product demands and uncertain lead times.

Carrying costs Real out-of-pocket costs associated with having inventory on hand; include opportunity costs, heat, light, breakage, and taxes.

Decoupling Use of inventories to break apart operations so that one operation's supply is independent of another's supply.

Inventory Stores of goods and stocks.

Inventory control Technique of maintaining stock-keeping items at desired levels.

Lead time Time between ordering and receiving goods.

Multiechelon inventories Products stocked at various levels (factory, warehouse, customer) in a distribution system.

Multistage inventories Parts stocked at more than one stage in the sequential production process.

Operating doctrine Basic inventory policy decisions made by operations managers concerning when to reorder stocks and how much stock to reorder.

Periodic inventory system Operating doctrine of replenishing stocks up to a base stock level after an established time period has elapsed.

Procurement costs Costs of placing an order, including postage, telephone calls to vendor, labor, and computer costs associated with purchasing.

Q/R inventory system Operating doctrine of replenishing stocks by ordering an economic order quantity (Q) when the reorder point (R) is reached.

Stockout costs Costs associated with demand when stocks have been depleted; generally lost sales or backorder costs.

SELECTED READINGS

Buffa, E. S., and R. G. Miller, *Production-Inventory Systems: Planning and Control,* (3rd ed.). Homewood, Ill.: Richard D. Irwin, 1979.

Hadley, G., and T. M. Whitin, *Analysis of Inventory Systems.* Englewood Cliffs, N.J.: Prentice Hall, 1963.

Harris, F. W., *Operations and Costs.* Chicago: A. W. Shaw Company, 1915.

Starr, M. K., and D. W. Miller, *Inventory Control: Theory and Practice.* Englewood Cliffs, N.J.: Prentice Hall, 1962.

SUPPLEMENT TO CHAPTER 12

OPTIMIZATION AND INVENTORY CONTROL

In this supplement we briefly present several optimization concepts from the calculus and relate them to inventory control. The calculus concepts will not be thoroughly understood by the reader who has never been exposed to the calculus; they are stated to provide a brief review for those understanding the basics of classical optimization.

The only inventory case derived here is the simple lot size formula, the first inventory model presented in the chapter. The derivation is started where the chapter stopped; development of the model terms are not repeated.

Classical Optimization

The Derivative The concept of a derivative is to differentiate with respect to a variable. Differentials that are required for this supplement are:

$$
\begin{aligned}
d(a) &= 0 \\
d(ax) &= a\,dx \\
d(x + y - z) &= dx + dy - dz \\
d(x^n) &= nx^{n-1}dx
\end{aligned}
$$

where a represents a constant and x, y, and z are variables.

Let's find the first derivative of the expression $y = 3x^2 + x - 3$ with respect to the variable x:

$$
\begin{aligned}
\frac{d(Y)}{dx} &= \frac{d}{dx}(3x^2) + \frac{d}{dx}(x) - \frac{d}{dx}(3) \\
&= 6x + 1
\end{aligned}
$$

In this example, each of the differentials is used to find the first derivative, $d(y)/dx$. The second derivative is found by taking the derivative of the first derivative:

$$
\begin{aligned}
\frac{d^2(y)}{dx^2} &= \frac{d}{dx}(6x) + \frac{d}{dx}(1) \\
&= 6
\end{aligned}
$$

Optimization In the calculus, the derivative is taken to find the value of the decision variable that gives the largest or smallest value of a criterion function. The general procedure is to take the first derivative of a function with respect to a decision variable and set the result equal to zero. The equation is then solved for the decision variable in terms of the other parameters in the equation. To determine whether the optimal point is a maximum or a minimum, the second derivative is taken. If the second derivative is positive, the optimal point is a minimum. If the second derivative is negative, the optimal point is a maximum. If the second derivative is zero, the point is an inflection point.

In the previous example,

$$\frac{d(y)}{dx} = 6x + 1$$

The optimal value of x is found by setting this equation equal to zero and solving for x:

$$0 = 6x + 1$$
$$x = -\frac{1}{6}$$

When the second derivative was found, it was +6. Therefore, $x = -1/6$ is a minimum point.

Partial Derivatives The object of a partial derivative is to hold all variables as constants except the one that is being differentiated. We partially differentiate, viewing all other variables as constants rather than variables.

For example, if $y = zx^3 - x^2 + 2x$, let's find the first partial derivative of y with respect to x. To do this, we treat z as though it were a constant and differentiate:

$$\begin{aligned}\frac{\delta y}{\delta x} &= \frac{\delta}{\delta x}(zx^3) - \frac{\delta}{\delta x}(x^2) + \frac{\delta}{\delta x}(2x)\\ &= z\frac{\delta}{\delta x}(x^3) - \frac{\delta}{\delta x}(x^2) + 2\frac{\delta}{\delta x}(x)\\ &= 3zx^2 - 2x + 2\end{aligned}$$

Optimizing the Simple Lot Size Formula The total cost equation for the simple lot size formula was developed to be:

$$\begin{aligned}TC &= CD + S\frac{D}{Q} + IC\frac{Q}{2}\\ &= CD + SDQ^{-1} + \frac{IC}{2}Q\end{aligned}$$

Taking the partial derivative of total cost with respect to order quantity, Q:

$$\frac{\delta(TC)}{\delta Q} = 0 + (-SDQ^{-2}) + \frac{IC}{2}$$

Setting the first derivative equal to zero, and solving for Q:

$$\begin{aligned}0 &= \frac{-SD}{Q^2} + \frac{IC}{2}\\ \frac{SD}{Q^2} &= \frac{IC}{2}\\ Q^* &= \sqrt{\frac{2DS}{IC}}\end{aligned}$$

Checking the second derivative to assure a minimum of the cost function:

$$\begin{aligned}\frac{\delta^2(TC)}{\delta Q^2} &= \frac{\delta}{\delta Q}\left(-\frac{SD}{Q^2}\right) + \frac{\delta}{\delta Q}\left(\frac{IC}{2}\right) = -(-2)\frac{SD}{Q^3} + 0\\ &= \frac{2DS}{Q^3}\end{aligned}$$

a positive value results, thus assuring a minimum. Notice that the term CD, the item cost, dropped out of the first equation in the first derivative. This illustrates that this cost component is constant with regard to changes in order quantity.

Again, we can see the power of the logic in calculus, but you need not be overwhelmed if you cannot follow all the mathematics. Clearly, the logic of mathematics is useful when applied to the many rational problems in productions/operations.

PROBLEMS

1. For the following total cost (TC), find the optimal order quantity, Q^*. A is a constant. Is this a minimum or a maximum cost point? Why?

$$TC = (27 + A)Q + \frac{100}{Q} + 274$$

2. Given a (Q/R) item control system in which:
(a) Delivery is instantaneous.
(b) The vendor quotes a price (c) as twice the variable charge (V) plus the ratio of the fixed charge (F) divided by the order quantity (Q).
(c) The inventory storage rate (i) is applied to the value of the *maximum* inventory.
(d) No stockouts are permitted.
(e) The demand per year (d) and the cost of ordering per order (S) are both known. Define any additional notation used.
(1) Explain the basic approach one should take in proceeding to analyze this type of system. Determination of the *optimal* operating doctrine is the goal.
(2) Write a verbal total cost equation for the entire system.
(3) Solve the system for the optimal operating doctrine (Q^* and R^*).

13

Inventory Control Applications

Stockless production, discussed in part of this chapter, goes by various names—*just-in-time production, zero inventories,* and others. Perhaps all the names are misnomers because the real goal is excellence in manufacturing, and a better description would be *total production system.* Reducing inventory is only one of the methods used to direct constant attention to detailed problems—product engineering, quality, process engineering, layout, setup times, tooling, maintenance, and many others. A full review of stockless production is like relearning Manufacturing 101 from a different point of view—problem solving in an atmosphere of constant improvement.

Development through stockless production means taking advantage of every possibility to improve through standard, repetitive operations. A base of knowledge and experience is necessary for this development, just as good fundamentals are important in the development of any athletic team. Developing people takes first priority, followed by development of the production process, and as a result a smooth system of material flow emerges as testimony to a long program of improvement in many areas.

Robert W. Hall
Professor of Operations Management
Indiana University
Indianapolis, Indiana

Professor Hall brings to our attention that applying inventory fundamentals calls on management to become involved in the total production system. Before we examine stockless production and the application issues Professor Hall raises, let's look at a few inventory situations that are slightly more complex and realistic than those in the last chapter.

DETERMINISTIC INVENTORY MODELS

Quantity Discounts

Each of us has purchased consumer goods in larger volumes than immediately needed so that we could pay a lower unit price (dollars per pound, per gallon, etc.). When demand is known for certain, delivery is instantaneous (no stockouts) and item cost varies with volume ordered; the result is a modified simple lot size situation called the *quantity discount case*. Although the concept of quantity discounts is also applicable to other inventory situations, for our introductory treatment we will modify only the simple lot size situation discussed in Chapter 12.

Figure 13.1 illustrates the quantity discount concept, the basis of which is examination of price breaks. As volume ordered (Q) increases, the supplier can often produce and ship more economically. To encourage volume purchases, the supplier shares the economies of scale with the customer. In Figure 13.1, the solid lines represent average annual costs for various feasible order quantities. Note, however, that the solid lines are *discontinuous* at the price breaks; for different ranges of Q values, different cost curves apply.

In the operating doctrine for quantity discounts, reorder point is still at zero inventory, since delivery is assumed to be instantaneous. The general procedure for determining the reorder quantity starts by checking the lowest cost curve for an optimal Q. If that is unsuccessful, each higher cost curve is systematically checked until optimal is found. Follow these steps:

1. Calculate the economic order quantity (EOQ) using the simple lot size formula for the lowest unit price.
2. Determine if the EOQ in step 1 is feasible by determining whether it is in the quantity range for that price. *If it is feasible,* stop here.

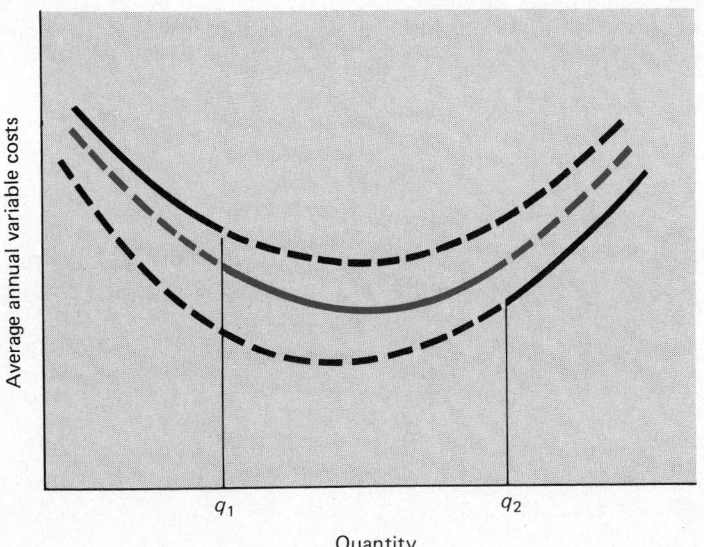

FIGURE 13.1
Quantity discounts

Compute the total cost for this quantity, compute the lowest total cost at each price break, and choose the quantity with the lowest total cost.

3. If the EOQ in step 1 is not feasible, compute the total cost for the lowest *feasible* quantity for the lowest unit price.
4. Perform the first and second steps for the next higher unit price. If there is a feasible solution, stop and follow the procedure in step 2. If not, perform the third step. The "best" price/quantity to date is for the *lowest total cost* of all costs evaluated in step 3.
5. Repeat step 4 until a feasible solution is found or all prices are evaluated. If no feasible optimal quantity is found with the EOQ, choose the price break with the lowest total cost.

Essentially, this procedure finds the lowest cost point on the lowest cost curve, checks feasibility, and if nothing is feasible, computes a cost at the price break that allows a feasible solution. Then we move to the next highest cost curve (see Figure 13.1) and repeat the procedures. In this way, all *minimum cost* EOQ's will be calculated, and all price breaks will eventually be checked, provided an optimal feasible solution is not discovered earlier. As in all inventory operating doctrines, the optimal order quantity is the *quantity that offers the lowest total cost.* An example should help clarify this procedure.

EXAMPLE

Consider an inventory situation in a medical center where disposable sanitary packs are ordered in boxes of 5 dozen/box. Annual demand is 400 boxes; the cost of placing an order is $12; and the inventory carrying charge is 20 percent. There are two price breaks; price per box is $29 for 1 to 49 boxes, $28.50 for 50 to 99 boxes, and $28 for an order of 100 or more boxes.

To determine the optimal quantity, we begin on the lowest cost curve and compute Q for a price of $28 per box.

$$Q = \sqrt{\frac{2DS}{IC}} = \sqrt{\frac{2(400)(12)}{.2(28)}} = 41.40$$

$$= 41 \text{ boxes}$$

Since 100 or more boxes must be ordered to realize a price of $28 per box, our $Q = 41$ is not feasible. Computing the total cost at the lowest feasible quantity, 100, we get

$$TC = CD + S\frac{D}{Q} + IC\frac{Q}{2}$$

$$= 28(400) + 12\left(\frac{400}{100}\right) + .2(28)\left(\frac{100}{2}\right)$$

$$= \$11{,}528$$

Moving to the next highest curve,

$$Q = \sqrt{\frac{2DS}{IC}} = \sqrt{\frac{2(400)(12)}{.2(28.5)}} = 41.04$$
$$= 41 \text{ boxes}$$

The price of $28.50 is for a volume of 50 to 99 boxes, so $Q = 41$ is not feasible. Computing the total cost at the first feasible quantity (50) in this range, we obtain,

$$TC = CD + S\frac{D}{Q} + IC\frac{Q}{2}$$
$$= 28.50(400) + 12\left(\frac{400}{50}\right) + .2(28.50)\left(\frac{50}{2}\right)$$
$$= \$11{,}638.50$$

Moving to the next highest and last cost curve,

$$Q = \sqrt{\frac{2DS}{IC}} = \sqrt{\frac{2(400)(12)}{.2(29)}} = 40.68$$
$$= 41 \text{ boxes}$$

This is a feasible quantity, since $29 is the price for a volume of 1–49 units. Now we must compute the total cost for $Q = 41$:

$$TC^* = CD + S\frac{D}{Q^*} + IC\frac{Q^*}{2}$$
$$= 29(400) + 12\left(\frac{400}{41}\right) + .2(29)\left(\frac{41}{2}\right)$$
$$= \$11{,}835.97$$

Comparing all total costs, we see that the lowest total cost is $11,528 for an order quantity of 100. Therefore the operating doctrine for disposable sanitary packs is

$$Q^* = 100$$
$$R^* = 0$$
$$TC^* = \$11{,}528$$

For the disposable sanitary packs, the quantity discount overcame higher carrying costs. The total of ordering and carrying costs were $328.00 for $Q = 100$, $238.50 for $Q = 50$, and $235.97 for $Q = 41$. However, the quantity discount of $1 per box for 400 boxes (comparing $Q = 100$ with $Q = 41$) overcame the additional $92.03 in ordering and carrying costs, making $Q = 100$ the more attractive choice.

In Chapter 12 and in the quantity discount situation above, we explained several deterministic models. In reality we rarely encounter the simplified conditions shown in these models. Let's now relax the deterministic conditions and examine some models of a more practical nature, stochastic inventory models.

STOCHASTIC INVENTORY MODELS

Variable Demand, Variable Lead Time, Variable Demand During Lead Time

Variable Demand For simple inventory models, we assumed that future demand is known with certainty. Generally, however, this is not the case; demand must be estimated. The most common way to estimate demand is to collect data about past experiences and forecast future demand based on that data. Here is a summary of the most recent seven days' demand for a part used in manufacturing:

Actual Daily Demand (units)	Number of Occurrences (days)	Relative Frequency of Occurrence
1–200	3	42.8%
201–400	2	28.6
401–600	1	14.3
601–800	1	14.3
	7	100.0%

In the conventional method for measuring usage, we calculate (1) the average usage rate from historical data, and (2) the standard deviation of usage about the average. In the data for the manufacturing part, the usage rate intervals are very wide; each interval covers a 200-unit range. To obtain some very approximate indicators of the demand pattern, we calculate the mean and standard deviation of these data using only the midpoints of the intervals. Average, or expected, demand is calculated as 300 units/day $\{[100\ (3) + \ldots + 700(1)] \div 7\}$ with variability in demand calculated as a standard deviation of 214 units $\{[3\ (100 - 300)^2 + \ldots + (700 - 300)^2] \div 7\}^{1/2}$. Figure 13.2 illustrates the frequency distribution of daily demand.

Lead Time Like demand, lead time is often uncertain rather than constant. If it is uncertain, the length of lead time takes on some distribution. Extending our manufacturing part example, we find that the distribution of lead times is

Actual Lead Time (days)	Number of Occurrences	Relative Frequency of Occurrence
2	2	28.6%
3	3	42.8
4	2	28.6
	7	100.0%

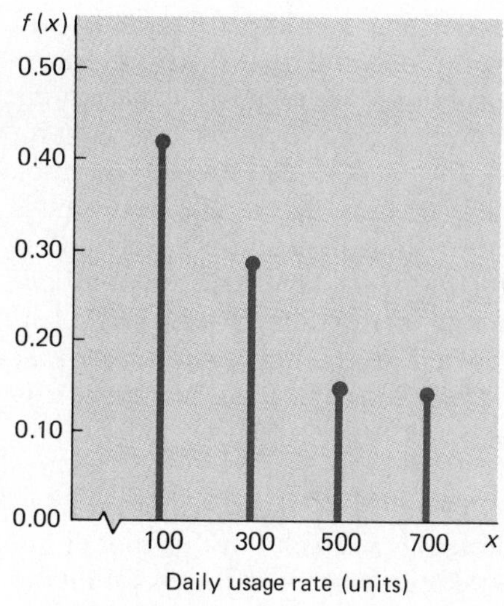

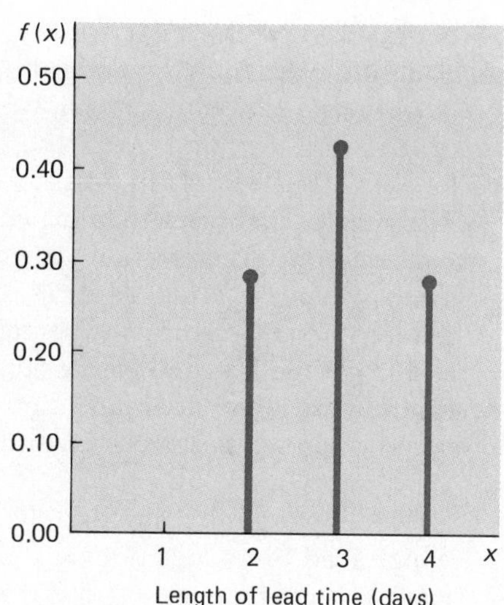

FIGURE 13.2
Relative frequency distribution of daily usage and lead times

The expected lead time and standard deviation of lead time are 3 days and 0.75 days, respectively, with the relative frequency shown in Figure 13.2.

Demand During Lead Time The two sources of demand variation during lead time, the length of lead time itself, and the demand per time period of lead time interact to determine *demand during lead time*. For our example we can determine "expected demand during lead time" (average demand). For the manufacturing part:

$$\begin{array}{c}\text{Expected demand}\\ \text{during lead time}\end{array} = (300 \text{ units/day})\ (3 \text{ days}) = 900 \text{ units}$$

If we had the lowest demand for each day (100) of the shortest lead time (2), we would have a low demand during lead time of 200 units. Likewise, if the most demanding condition prevailed, highest demand per day (700) and longest lead time (4), demand during lead time would be 2,800 units.

As you can see, between these extreme points, there can be various levels of demand. We can calculate all possible combinations of the duration of lead time and daily demand and see what values are possible for demand during lead time. We can also calculate the probabilities of these demands and use them to construct a probability distribution of demand during lead time. For larger problems involving many classification intervals of demand and lead time, hand calculations become tedious. An alternative method for generating the distribution of demand during lead time is to *simulate* the operation of the inventory system over time on the computer. By drawing a lead time, drawing a demand, computing a demand during lead time, and repeating the process dozens of times, we could classify the data into a distribution of lead-time demands and compute a mean and standard deviation to describe that distribution.

Figure 13.3 illustrates how inventory levels are affected by variations in lead-time demand. After the first reorder point, R_1, expected demand and expected lead time occur. After R_2, the second lead time, t_{L_2}, occurs. Although t_{L_2} is shorter than expected, daily demand during the lead time is considerably greater than expected; thus, overall lead-time demand is greater than expected. After R_3, both lead time, t_{L_3}, and daily demand are different from what was expected; demand is much lower than expected, and lead time is much greater than expected. As the figure shows, the two random variables, demand and lead time, interact. This interaction is common in actual inventory situations.

A Model for Variable Demand and Constant Lead Time, with Specified Service Level

Now let's examine a moderately complex quantity/reorder point model in which lead time does not vary, but demand is variable. In this model, we want to find an operating doctrine that takes into account the possibility of a stockout. We want to establish buffer stocks that are adequate for providing a specified level of protection for service to customers when demand is uncertain.

We'll define a few additional variables to those defined in the previous chapter:

$$\mu = \text{random variable representing demand during lead time}$$
$$\sigma_\mu = \text{standard deviation of demand during lead time}$$

FIGURE 13.3
Q/R model with varying demand and lead times

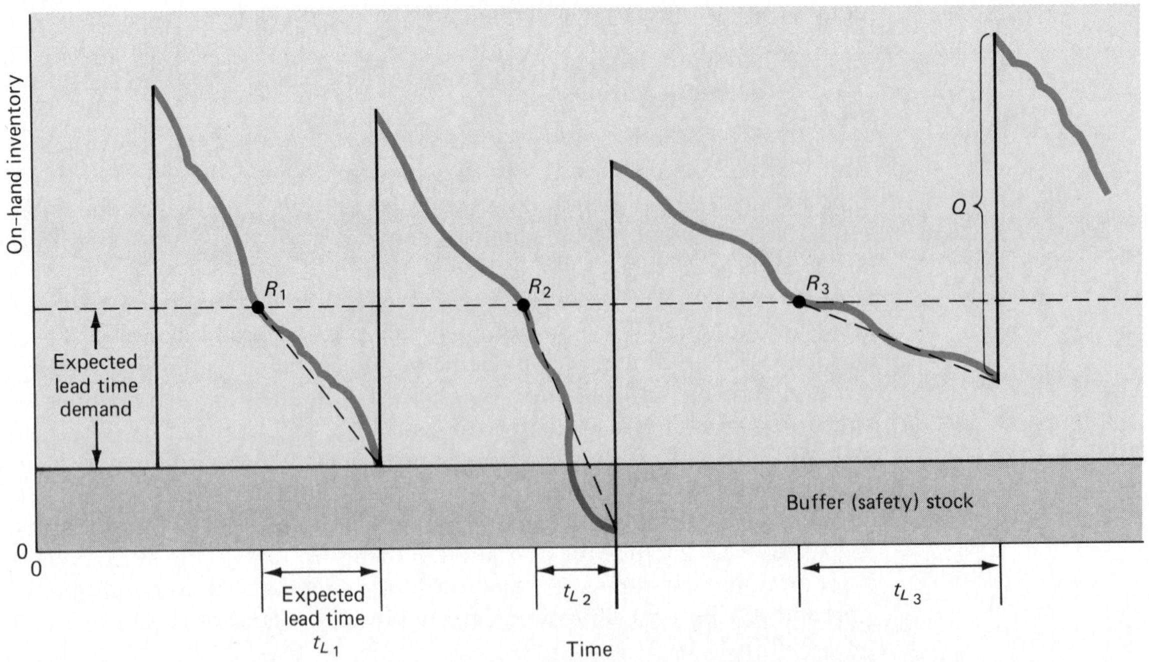

$\bar{\mu}$ = expected lead-time demand
$\bar{d}$ = average daily demand
$\bar{\sigma}_d$ = standard deviation of daily demand
$\bar{D}$ = expected annual demand
B = buffer stock
z = number of standard deviations needed for a specified confidence level

Look closely at the first cycle in Figure 13.3. Several relationships exist. First, we can see that the expected lead-time demand ($\bar{\mu}$) plus the buffer stock (B) equals the reorder point (R_1). This general relationship holds:

$$R = \bar{\mu} + B \qquad (13.1)$$

Second, we know that if lead time (t_L) is constant, which it is for the model being developed, expected lead-time demand equals expected demand times lead time:

$$\bar{\mu} = \bar{d}t_L$$

We also know that the buffer stock is the *protection* for the service level specified, $z\sigma_\mu$ units. Buffer stock is z standard deviates of protection for a given *variability* of demand during lead time. Substituting, the reorder point for our operating doctrine is now:

$$R = \bar{\mu} + B$$
$$R^* = \bar{d}t_L + z\sigma_\mu \qquad (13.2)$$

The order quantity is simply the simple lot size formula with expected annual demand substituted for annual demand:

$$Q^* = \sqrt{\frac{2\bar{D}S}{IC}} \qquad (13.3)$$

The use of average demand in equation 13.3 is appropriate for this model regardless of the shape of the demand distribution. Because of its variable nature, demand may take on many shapes. It may be a very unconventional empirical distribution, or it may be normally distributed, Poisson distributed, or negatively exponentially distributed. You may not be familiar with all of these distributions; we mention them only because they have been found to be reasonable representations of demand at various levels of production-wholesale-distribution systems. There is some evidence, for example, that the normal distribution describes many inventory situations at the production level; the negative exponential describes many of the wholesale and retail levels; and the Poisson describes many retail situations.[1]

[1]Buchan and E. Koenigsberg, *Scientific Inventory Control* (Englewood Cliffs, N.J.: Prentice Hall, 1963).

EXAMPLE Daily demand for product EPD101 is normally distributed with a mean of 50 units and a standard deviation of 5. Supply is virtually certain with a lead time of six days. The cost of placing an order is \$8, and annual holding costs are 20 percent of the unit price of \$1.20. A 95 percent service level is desired for the customers who place orders during the reorder period. Backorders are allowed. Once stocks are depleted, orders are filled as soon as the stocks arrive. There are no stockout costs. We can assume sales are made over the entire year.

Determining the operating doctrine, we calculate order quantity as follows:

$$Q^* = \sqrt{\frac{2\bar{D}S}{IC}} = \sqrt{\frac{2(50)\,(365)\,(8)}{.2(1.20)}}$$
$$= 1{,}103$$

From the normal distribution, a 0.95 confidence level gives $z = 1.645$ (see Appendix A). Thus

$$R^* = \bar{d}t_L + z\sigma_\mu$$
$$= 50(6) + 1.645\sigma_\mu$$

From statistics, we know that for an independent variable the total variance is the sum of the individual variances. The variance of demand during lead time is as follows:

$$\sigma_\mu^2 = \sum_{i=1}^{6} \sigma_i^2 = 6(5)^2$$
$$\sigma_\mu = \sqrt{6(5)^2} = 12.2$$

Therefore,

$$R^* = 50(6) + 1.645(12.2)$$
$$= 300 + 20 = 320 \text{ units}$$

Our operating doctrine is to order 1,103 units when we reach an order point of 320.

In our example for product EPD 101, the operating doctrine accomplishes two things. First, it results in economical levels of cycle stocks because our choice of Q^* provides a proper balance between ordering costs and inventory carrying costs throughout the year. Second, it provides the desired level of customer service during lead times while we are waiting to receive a replenishment order from our suppliers. As illustrated in Figure 13.4, the 320 units we have on hand when we place an order provide a 95 percent assurance of being able to meet customer demand until the new shipment is received. We expect only 300 units to be demanded, but we carry an extra 20 units of buffer stock to provide the

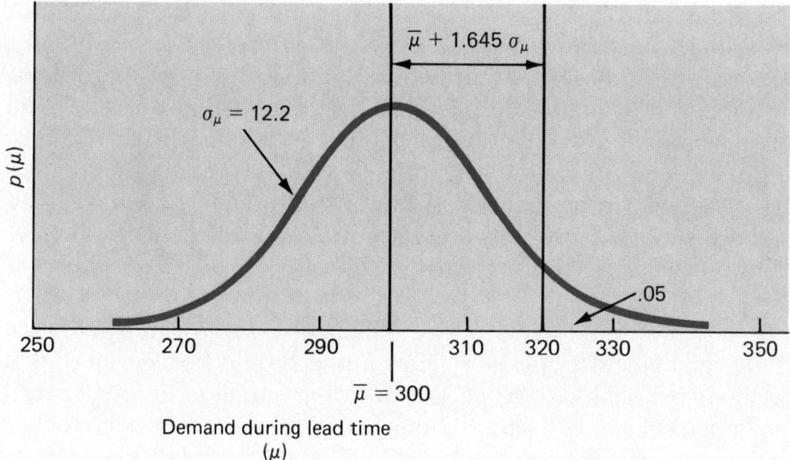

FIGURE 13.4
Distribution of demand during lead time when lead time is six days and daily demand is normally distributed with mean of 50 units and standard deviation of 5 units.

desired service level. How much do we pay to obtain this extra level of production? Our average inventory levels for the year are 20 units higher than they otherwise would have been. Therefore, the annual cost of carrying buffer stock is:

$$\begin{aligned} BIC &= (20 \text{ units})(.20)(\$1.20/\text{unit}) \\ &= \$4.80 \end{aligned}$$

Expected Stockout Cost and Expected Number of Stockouts At times demand is expressed as an empirical distribution, and lead time is constant. When this is the case, the density function, $f(x)$; the cumulative function $F(x)$; and the complementary cumulative function, $(1-F(x)$, can readily be found. *The complementary cumulative function is also the probability of a stockout if that demand occurs.* The expected stockout cost, a key calculation in the total inventory cost, would be the expected probability of a stockout times the stockout cost for stockout costs that are incurred regardless of the number of units short. The concept of the complementary cumulative can also be used to set buffer stocks for the allowable number of stockouts per year. The expected number of stockouts for any demand level is found by multiplying the number of orders in a year (D/Q) times the probability of a stockout. If the stockout cost is cost per unit short, then the calculation of stockout costs is more complex.

Variable Demands and Lead Times The basic procedure for finding operating doctrines when *both* daily demands and lead times vary is a convergence procedure; we use directed trial and error. For the quantity/reorder point model, we compute an order quantity assuming constant demand. Then we calculate a reorder point using the order quantity we have just computed. We then use this reorder point to revise the previous estimate of order quantity and recalculate the reorder point. Eventually, the order quantity and reorder point converge upon their optimal values. Another approach for considering two distributions is an analytical calculation: complete enumeration of a joint probability distribution for demand during lead time. Similarly, one could use computer simulation to generate the joint probability distribution.[2] Although a detailed treatment of these models is beyond our introductory treatment, we believe you should be aware of their existence.

A Single Period Model for Perishable Products and Services

Products News vendors, produce managers, and owners of meat markets all must face the question "How much should I order, given that the product is perishable?" When the ordering situation is for the next period only, the critical costs are the shortage costs of being understocked (C_u) and the costs of being overstocked (C_o). The news vendor, manager, or owner is faced with minimizing overall costs when demand is not known with certainty.

Equation 13.4 suggests that the person ordering a perishable product or service should stock at that fractile (portion) of demand, the critical fractile (CF), where the ratio of the shortage cost to the sum of shortage and overstock costs is met.

$$CF = \frac{C_u}{C_u + C_o} \tag{13.4}$$

The *critical fractile* is the service level that maximizes profits for the perishable goods case.

EXAMPLE A magazine shop owner has four different retail locations. A popular monthly magazine varies uniformly from 500 to 1,200 copies for demand at all stores combined. Ordering is centralized and magazines can be moved easily from store to store. The magazines cost \$125/hundred and sell for \$2.25 each. When purchased in lots at this price, the publisher accepts no returns. What should be the ordering quantity for the next period?

$$\begin{aligned} CF &= \frac{C_u}{C_u + C_o} \\ &= \frac{(\$2.25 - \$1.25)}{(\$2.25 - \$1.25) + \$1.25} \\ &= \frac{1.00}{1.00 + 1.25} = \frac{1.00}{2.25} \\ &= 0.444 \end{aligned}$$

The manager would experience a loss in profit of \$1.00 (\$2.25 − \$1.25) if

[2]See Jack R. Meredith and Thomas E. Gibbs, *The Management of Operations* (New York: John Wiley & Sons, 1980), pp. 437–44, for generating joint probability distributions.

he orders too few, but a loss of $1.25 if he orders too many. He should stock at 0.444 of the difference between 500 and 1,200 copies.

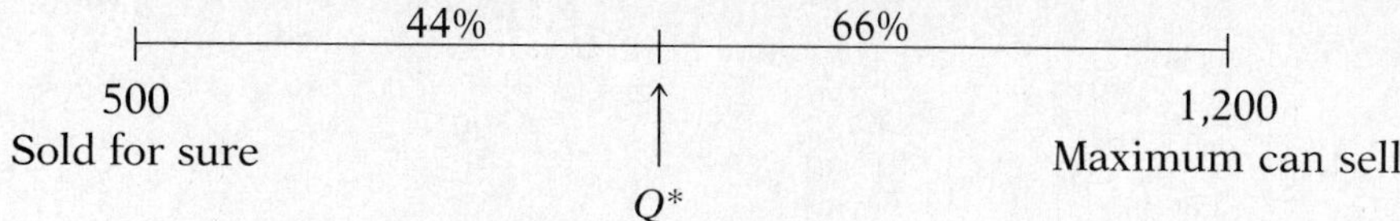

The economic order quantity (Q^*) is then

$$\begin{aligned} Q^* &= 500 + 0.444\ (1{,}200 - 500) \\ &= 500 + 310.8 \\ &= 810.8 \end{aligned}$$

Since orders must be in lots of 100, the closest to optimal would be to order 800 copies of the magazine for next month.

Services This ordering rule holds for single service orders, just as for products. Consider, for example, the capacity planning question for service vendors such as accountants, cleaning services, and hotels. "How much capacity should be ordered for the next period if we know past demands, costs, and profits?" The assumption is that demand cannot be stored, just as in the perishable goods case.

EXAMPLE The owner of a motel, with 32 rooms is trying to determine whether to build an addition or incur stockouts, referring customers to competitors when demand exceeds supply. The cost of maintaining a hotel room averages $15/day. A typical room rents for $45/night. Capacity is currently 32 rooms. During the last six months, demand has averaged as follows:

Daily Rooms Demanded	Number of Occurrences (days)
0–20	90
21–30	50
31–40	32
41 or more	10
	182 days

The critical fractile, or optimal service level, is calculated as follows:

$$\begin{aligned} CF &= \frac{(\$45.00 - \$15.00)}{(\$45.00 - \$15.00) + (\$15.00)} \\ &= \frac{\$30}{\$45} = 0.667 \end{aligned}$$

The demand distribution should be met up to the 0.667 fractile of the distribution to optimize profit. The fractiles are as follows:

Demand	Number of Occurrences	Cumulative Number of Occurrences	Cumulative Fractile
0–20	90	90	0.494
21–30	50	140	0.769
31–40	32	172	0.945
41 or more	10	182	1.000
	182		

It is optimal to have a capacity of rooms that falls between 0–20 rooms and 21–30 rooms (0.667 is between 0.494 and 0.769). If 20 rooms were available, that demand would be met 49.4 percent of the time; if 30 rooms were available, that demand would be met 76.9 percent of the time. Since the motel currently has 32 rooms, its capacity should not be increased.

INVENTORY CONTROL IN APPLICATION

Concepts for the Practitioner

Dynamic Inventory Levels The simple lot size formula

$$Q^* = \sqrt{\frac{2DS}{IC}}$$

illustrates that the relationship between demand (D) and order quantity (Q^*) varies with the square root of demand. Table 13.1 illustrates this relationship for several demand levels. Note that as demand increases 100 percent, inventory order quantity, and subsequently maximum inventory levels, increase only 41 percent. *Demand changes should not cause rapid, wide fluctuations in inventory.* If operations managers find in application that work-in-process and finished goods inventories are building rapidly, the problem may very well be caused by scheduling and loading difficulties, not by increases in demand.

Table 13.1 Relationship between demand and order quantity in the simple lot size situation: example demands

Demand	Change in Demand	Order Quantity	Change in Order Quantity
1,000	—	$31.62\sqrt{2S \div IC}$	—
1,500	50%	$38.73\sqrt{2S \div IC}$	22%
2,000	100	$44.72\sqrt{2S \div IC}$	41
3,000	200	$54.77\sqrt{2S \div IC}$	73
4,000	300	$63.24\sqrt{2S \div IC}$	100

Service Level *Service levels,* or treatment policies for customers when there may be stockouts, can be established and measured in several different ways. In this chapter we have focused on one measure—the probability that there will be a stockout (of any size) during a lead time or cycle. Firms utilize at least two more common measures:

1. Ratio of the number of *customers* receiving the product to the number of customers demanding the product
2. Ratio of the number of *units* supplied to the number of units demanded

Suppose four customers each demanded 100 units and demand was met. When a fifth demanded 200 units, however, demand was not met. Service level as a customer ratio in this case is 4/5, or 80 percent serviced; service level as a unit ratio is 400/600, or 67 percent serviced. Our example in Figure 13.4 used the number of units as the service level criterion. Whether a firm uses a customer or a unit ratio depends on what use management wants to make of buffer stocks. As an operations manager, you must make sure that marketing and general management understand the way service level is being measured so that internal disagreements can be minimized.

Saving Money in Inventory Systems

Suppose your first assignment on your first job is to evaluate the current inventory system and procedures at a major distribution center for a national company. Where would you begin? What would you do? In this section, we hope to provide you with a general guide toward saving money in inventory systems. Table 13.2 provides an overview of situations you might find in practice and the operating guides you could follow. There are two new concepts in the table—blanket rules and classifying by ABC.

Blanket Rules *Blanket rules* are general rules such as "always carry a month's supply on all items," "reorder when you take out the last case of any item," and "don't order any inventory that won't fit in this room." These rules almost always give one the opportunity to evaluate the rule in light of the economics of total annual inventory costs.

ABC Classification Let's examine ABC classification closely as it holds considerable promise as a cost-saving technique. When an organization's inventory is listed by dollar volume, generally a small number of items account for a large dollar volume, and a large number of items account for a small dollar volume.

The ABC inventory concept divides inventories into three groupings—an A grouping for those few items with large dollar volume; a B grouping for items with moderate unit and dollar volume; and a C grouping for the large number of items accounting for a small dollar volume. The A group might contain, for example, about 15 percent of the items, the B group 35 percent, and the C group 50 percent.

Table 13.2 **A general guide for saving money in inventory control**

Inventory Situation	Operating Guides
No priority for inventory items	Classify by ABC; examine high dollar volumes first, low dollar volumes last.
Blanket rules applied	Challenge on cost basis by examining items and families of parts; justify by return on investment.
Stochastic (variable) demand and lead times	Obtain estimates of mean and variance of demand, lead time, and especially demand during lead time; adjust buffer stocks, reorder point, and order quantity to avoid continued overstock or understock situations.
High stockout costs	Identify high stockout cost items by questioning staff; adjust buffer stocks on cost tradeoff basis.
Safety stocks	Evaluate reasons for safety stocks; levels should be based on demand, lead times, and cost tradeoff among ordering, carrying, and stockout costs; do not set intuitively.
Decoupling operations	Justify in-process inventory levels as basis for cost reductions and efficiency in operations; reduce levels if too much inventory results in inefficiencies due to space limitations.
Raw material and finished goods inventory	Examine physical inventories carefully; accept obsolescence write-offs but reduce future obsolescence through more careful scheduling and control; coordinate closely with purchasing on raw materials and marketing on finished goods inventories.

Table 13.3 **Example annual usage of inventory by value**

Item Stock Number	Annual Dollar Usage	Percent of Total Value
2704	$125,000	46.2%
1511	90,000	33.3
0012	32,000	11.8
2100	15,500	5.8
0301	6,200	2.3
0721	650	0.2
8764	525	0.2
7402	325	0.1
3520	300	0.1
	$270,500	100.0%

Table 13.3 lists a number of stock items according to decreasing dollar usage, and Table 13.4 groups these items into an ABC classification. The A items comprise 79.5 percent of the total dollar volume, the B items 17.6 percent, and the C items only 2.9 percent. Notice, however, that the A items are only 22.2 percent of the total items, the B items 22.2 percent, and

Table 13.4 Example ABC grouping of inventory by value

Classification	Item Stock Number	Annual Dollar Usage	Percent of Total Dollar Usage	Number of Items	Percent of Total Number of Items
A	2704, 1511	$215,000	79.5%	2	22.2%
B	0012, 2100	47,500	17.6	2	22.2
C	0301, 0721, 8764, 7402, 3520	8,000	2.9	5	55.6
Totals		$270,500	100.0%	9	100.0%

the C items 55.6 percent. Figure 13.5 graphically illustrates the dollar value classification for this example.

If you are trying to reduce costs in an inventory system, which class would you concentrate on? The high dollar volume group, the A class, should receive your attention first. One of the major costs of inventory is annual carrying costs, and your money is invested largely in class A. Tight control, sound operating doctrine, and attention to security on these items would allow you to control a large dollar volume with a reasonable amount of time and effort. Items in this class are usually either high unit cost items or high volume items with at least moderate costs. Class C items, the bulk of all items, should have carefully established but routine controls.

Inventory Control Procedures

Inventory control procedures vary in complexity and accuracy from the absence of any noticeable control to computerized systems for distribution and production. In between these extremes are simple visual controls, the

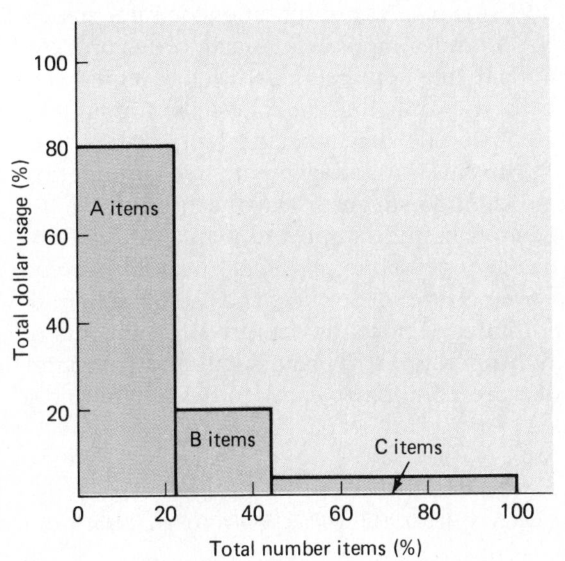

FIGURE 13.5
Example ABC inventory classification: percent inventory value versus percent of items

two-bin system, and cardex systems. We briefly examine here two of the systems—a cardex file and IBM's computerized MAPICS system. In a following section we discuss the Japanese just-in-time and kanban systems. The two-bin system, which needs no extended explanation, consists simply of filling two bins with units of the same item. One bin is used first; when it is empty, the quantity necessary to replenish the empty bin is reordered, and stock from the second bin is used.

Cardex File System The cardex file system has variations, but the essential features are:

1. There is a card for every stock item; the cards are filed on a rotating drum or file cabinet in a central location.
2. On the top of each card is the computed operating doctrine. The supply source (vendor) may be listed here also.
3. A ledger comprises the balance of the card. It states beginning inventory, orders placed, orders received, issues from stores, and current inventory levels. Each time a transaction is made, an entry with the corresponding date is recorded. When physical inventories are taken, cards are adjusted to reflect current actual inventories.

Even though simplicity is the main advantage, we find remote terminal access computer facilities with central processing capabilities have made this cardex procedure obsolete for multilocation distribution and manufacturing firms. Computers are less costly than cardex systems. Cardex files are still useful, however, for small and medium-sized organizations with limited computer access, even though microcomputers offer a good alternative for the progressive, small business owner.

IBM's MAPICS The Manufacturing Accounting and Production Information Control System (MAPICS) is a series of modules for information and control in manufacturing.[3] Modules include financial, order processing and accounting, and manufacturing applications as well as a guide for implementation planning. The key module for control is that on manufacturing applications. It includes product data management, material requirements planning (MRP), inventory management, and production costing and control applications. IBM suggests that the benefits of the inventory management application include improved plant productivity, reduced time required by inventory personnel, reduced inventory investment and storage space, improved customer service, and establishment of the basic inventory data and status reports as required for successful application of MRP. Production/operations managers will find computer firms' representatives and software companies eager to help them find a system that will fit their needs.

---

[3]See IBM's *Manufacturing Education Guide*, GH30-0241-0, and the *MAPICS Features Education Manual*, SR30-0369-1 (Atlanta, Ga., 1979).

Quantity/Reorder Versus Periodic Inventory Systems

To practice independent demand item inventory control, production/operations managers must select either a quantity/reorder (Q/R) system or periodic inventory system. (Within an organization of any size, both systems exist, but in different settings.) The following points might assist you in making this decision.

1. *The periodic system requires less manpower to operate than the Q/R system.* In the Q/R system, each item must be counted as it is issued or demanded. In the periodic system, no person is required in the inventory area except at the end of the period, when a physical inventory must be taken. The periodic system is especially good for raw material and supply inventory systems for which tight security is not necessary.
2. *The periodic system requires less calculating time than the Q/R system.* In the Q/R system, each issue or demand from stock must be subtracted to obtain net inventory. If this is not done, a reorder point might be skipped. *Systemic costs,* the costs of running the system, are generally less with the periodic system.
3. *The periodic system may require more buffer stock to protect against uncertainties of demand and lead time.* If the quantity/reorder point and corresponding base stock level/reorder time are set mathematically, in a minimum cost framework, there is no advantage to one system over the other. However, often in the periodic system, the reorder time is set to correspond with a nonoptimal weekly or monthly physical inventory resulting in higher costs.
4. *The periodic system can result in more stockouts when unusually high demand occurs.* When one or more successive unusually large demands occur, because the Q/R system keeps track of a net inventory with each unit demanded, it can react more quickly.

JAPANESE APPROACH TO INVENTORY MANAGEMENT

The Japanese have experienced substantial gains in overall manufacturing productivity during the past 25 years (see Chapter 2), and those gains have come in part from their approach to inventory management. It is quite difficult to explain Japanese manufacturing techniques without considering automation, behavior, inventory, process design, quality, and scheduling. We will try to summarize succinctly what others believe to be the inventory concepts the Japanese follow and how they make these concepts work to reduce costs.[4] But let's start with a brief review of the principles underlying their approach to manufacturing.

[4]This section on Japanese inventory systems relies on a number of sources, major sources being Robert W. Hall, *Zero Inventories,* © 1983, Dow Jones-Irwin, Homewood, Ill.; and Richard J. Schonberger, *Japanese Manufacturing Techniques: Nine Hidden Lessons in Simplicity* (New York: The Free Press, 1982).

Japanese Manufacturing and Inventory

Professor Robert W. Hall, Indiana University, suggests these cornerstones to the Japanese manufacturing system.

1. Produce what the customer desires.
2. Produce products only at the rate the customer wants them.
3. Produce with perfect quality.
4. Produce instantaneously—with zero unnecessary lead time.
5. Produce with no waste of labor, material, or equipment; every move has a purpose so there is zero idle inventory.
6. Produce by methods that allow for the development of people.[5]

Quite similarly, Richard J. Schonberger identifies nine simple—yet hidden—lessons from the Japanese.[6] These lessons focus on management technology, just-in-time production, total quality control, behavioral techniques, plant configurations, flexibility, purchasing, self-improvement of work quality, and striving for simplicity in all things.

How Japanese Manufacturing Ideally Works Throughout this book, we have made recommendations for approaching these aspects of operations management in the United States. With the exception of managing for quality (Chapters 15 and 16), you now have the background to understand and evaluate what follows. Although our example is oversimplified, the Japanese approach to manufacturing would ideally be as follows.

First, identify the customer's needs. Find out what the customer requires in terms of quantity, quality, and schedule. Know as much about the customer's needs as he or she does. Second, obtain the exact amount of material needed for today and process it piece by piece. The first person in the manufacturing process must perform his or her job and hand the piece to the next person. The piece must be correct or there will be delays all the way down the line. If there is an error and the next person can't use the piece, it should be handed back with admonishment; it should be clear, though, that there is a willingness to help solve any problems so this won't happen again. There is no in-process inventory. Everything currently being made is needed by the customer, so no finished goods inventory exists.

Quality is perfect. Waste cannot be hidden—poor products that are 2, 3, or 4 percent defective cannot be made and put in storage to be sorted later. Finally, everyone is expected to be involved in discovering how to simplify the job, and management strives to aid all employees in accomplishing this goal. Cooperation, teamwork, and a striving for consensus in all decisions are foremost in management's mind.

Stockless/Just-in-Time Production It is suggested the key element in Japanese manufacturing is "stockless" production. Everything is ordered,

---

[5]Hall, *Zero Inventories*, p. 2.

[6]*Schonberger, Japanese Manufacturing Techniques.* Each lesson is a chapter in the book.

Table 13.5 Results of stockless production programs in Japan

Company	Duration of Program (years)	Inventory Reduction (% of original value)	Throughput Time Reduction (% of original value)	Labor Productivity (% increase)
A	3	45%	40%	50%
B	3	16	20	80
C	4	30	25	60
D	2	20	50	50

These data were collected in late 1981 by Professor Jinichiro Nakane, Waseda University, Tokyo. The companies did not wish to be identified. The figures represent rough management estimates, as the rounded figures suggest. Labor productivity is estimated as sales in yen adjusted for inflation divided by *total* employees.

The superior progress of Company B may be somewhat illusory, since it was thought to be in the worst condition when starting stockless production.

None of these companies had more than two months in raw material plus work-in-process inventory when they began the program. All had some version of quality circles and quality improvement programs in place when they began, so the measurements of improvement have a high base point from which to index improvement.

Improvements are still taking place at each of these companies, and all of them are perhaps Class B at this point. Stockless production is a condition of constant improvement. All the companies anticipate more and more progress on these goals unless overtaken by a business disaster.

Source: Hall, *Zero Inventories,* 24.

made, and delivered just when needed. Production is "just-in-time."[7] There is a necessary linkage between stockless production and quality —every item must be made correctly just in time and every time. This is a key element in productivity gains. There is no waste. Therefore labor, material, and tools are all used productively.

What can this stockless production do for a company? Table 13.5 illustrates that the results are spectacular for four selected companies; benefits include savings in inventory, improvement in meeting schedules, and increased labor productivity.

The concept of zero inventories is very appealing, but we know that this approach is not always economically or practically feasible. Consider, however, the results of moving closer to this goal. Removing in-process inventory is much like dredging a channel in a river—the level of the water is reduced when underwater obstacles are removed. There are no deep pools anymore. Protection is gone, but the flow is much smoother,

[7]For a synopsis of stockless/just-in-time systems, see Richard A. Schonberger, "Some Observations on the Advantages and Implementation Issues of Just-in-Time Production Systems," *Journal of Operations Management* 3, no. 1 (November 1982), 1–11; and Jinichiro Nakane and Robert W. Hall, "Manufacturing Specs for Stockless Production," *Harvard Business Review* 61, no. 3 (May–June 1983), 84–91.

ideally reaching a situation of an even flow with minimum depth (inventory level) for navigation (production).

Kanban *Kanban* (pronounced kahn-bahn) literally translated means "visible record."[8] Generally we think of kanban as a card. In manufacturing, it is a card that is attached to a basket or container containing an order for production. What is produced fits into that container—no more, no less—and is always of excellent quality. The container card is the scheduling system, and this card system "pulls" manufacturing parts through the plant. The traditional U.S. and European inventory system is a schedule-based system. The order release "pushes" items through the plant. With kanban, the customer's order is filled without guesswork or excesses.

Schonberger explains what is needed to make kanban work:

> Kanban provides parts when they are needed but without guesswork and therefore without excess inventory resulting from bad guesses. But there is an important limitation to the use of kanban. Kanban will work well only in the context of a just-in-time (JIT) system in general, and in the context of the setup time/lot size reduction feature of JIT in particular. A JIT program can succeed without a kanban subsystem, but kanban makes no sense independently of JIT.[9]

Inventory Turnover One method of judging the effectiveness of an inventory system is to measure inventory turnover—the number of times total inventory turns over (is sold) in a time period. Generally speaking, the more rapidly inventory turns (cost of goods sold ÷ average dollar inventory), the more profitable the firm. This is true until some minimum inventory level necesary to support sales is reached. This minimum inventory will vary; it is generally higher for a retail sales outlet than for a custom machinery manufacturer.

To illustrate how inventory turnovers vary, consider a 1982 survey of 40 U.S. high technology companies with $25 million to $2 billion in annual sales.[10] Across all 40 companies, annual inventory turns for 1982 averaged 2.91. This ranged from 2.72 for the computer systems companies to 3.72 inventory turns for telecommunication companies. Individual companies varied from 0.96 to 5.61 inventory turns for all companies in the survey. Examining five years of annual survey data, the authors found the higher growth firms (in annual sales dollar increases) had slightly higher inventory turns. Companies with higher sales backlogs also experienced higher inventory turns, as might be expected.

Although we cannot make a direct comparison with foreign competi-

---

[8]For details on kanban, see Schonberger, "The Kanban System," *Japanese Manufacturing Techniques,* 219–38.

[9]Ibid., p. 221.

[10]Pittiglio, Rabin, Todd, and McGrath Consulting Company, "Inventory Performance for High Technology Industries—1982," *Production Inventory Management Review* 3, no. 6 (June 1983), 27–30.

Table 13.6 Comparison of manufacturing inventories[a]

Company	Days On Hand	Annual Turnover[d]
Toyota Motor Company (1980)[b]	4.0	62
Tachikawa Spring Company (1982)[c]	3.3	75
Jidosha Kiki (1982)[c]	3.2	78
Kawasaki Motorcycle—Japan (1981)	3.2	78
Kawasaki USA (active parts—1982)	5.0[e]	50[e]
Tokai Rika[b] (1982)[c]	3.7	68
American competitors (1981)	10–41	6–25[e]

[a]Manufacturing inventory is defined as raw material, parts, and work-in-process. It does not include finished goods. The companies using stockless production typically count the manufacturing inventory at the end of each month. Estimates of the American companies were made by materials managers of the companies at a meeting of the American Production and Inventory Control Repetitive Manufacturing Group in June 1981. The estimate of days on hand at Kawasaki USA was made by the inventory manager.

[b]Figures include inventory on consignment at small suppliers.

[c]These companies are among the larger suppliers of the Japanese auto industry.

[d]Annual turnover and days on hand are related by

$$\text{Turnover} = \frac{250 \text{ days/year}}{\text{days on hand}}$$

The Japanese companies typically state inventory in days on hand, the American ones by a turnover ratio. American reaction at first is that the amount of money required for inventory is minuscule. That is true, but recall that inventory levels are really an indicator of the degree to which the production process itself has become flexible and free of breakdowns and rework. The financial impact of that is enormous, but it is not explicitly identified as a separate item in the financial statements.

[e]Figures are estimates.

Source: Hall, *Zero Inventories,* 31.

tors for the survey above, a Japanese survey suggests that, based on annual inventory turnover, American competitors are being outperformed. As Table 13.6 indicates, the Japanese firms are turning inventory 50–78 times, whereas their American competitors are in the 6–25 range; this is indeed a substantial difference.

Jidosha Kiki Company Ltd. Professor Hall provides an excellent set of examples from Japanese manufacturing companies. Although Toyota is perhaps the most documented success story, we believe Jidosha Kiki Company Ltd. also provides a good example. In the data of Table 13.7 note how inventory, productivity, quality, and setup times all improve together. We certainly have a great deal to learn from Japanese inventory management, and we encourage those interested in manufacturing management to pursue this topic more thoroughly.

BEHAVIORAL PITFALLS IN INVENTORY CONTROL

Rational Decision Making Establishing the inventory operating doctrine involves a decision process that is rational, logical, and unemotional.

Table 13.7 **Development of stockless production at Jidosha Kiki Company Ltd.**

	Start of Program 1976	1981	
Inventory (days on hand)			
Raw material	3.1	1.0	
Purchased parts	3.8	1.2	
Work-in-process	4.0	1.0	
Finished goods	8.6	3.7	
	19.5	6.9	
Productivity index	100	187	
Defect rates			
From suppliers	2.6%	0.11%	
Internally (cumulative)	0.34%	0.01%	
Setup times			
Over 60 minutes	20%	0%	
30–60 minutes	19%	0%	
20–30 minutes	26%	3%	
10–20 minutes	20%	7%	
5–10 minutes	5%	12%	Single-digit setups
100 seconds–5 minutes	0%	16%	Single-digit setups
Under 100 seconds	0%	62%	One-touch setups

These data were taken from a briefing by Jidosha Kiki executives during a visit July 2, 1982. Jidosha Kiki, which supplies brakes and steering gear to the auto industry, learned its methods from Toyota, and their system is very similar. They began a very clear conversion to this kind of thinking with a "revolution" in 1976, and the results have been very good for them. Jidosha Kiki has a few large presses. Most of the rest of their equipment is small, light, flexible metalworking equipment.

The extremely low amount of raw material, purchased parts, and finished goods results from the truck delivery system of Japan, described later. Jidosha Kiki executives were unsure if these levels would be further reduced, but they were certain that additional in-plant improvement could further reduce work-in-process to 0.5 days on hand.

Source: Hall, *Zero Inventories*, 30.

As operations managers, you should be aware that people making inventory decisions interject their own biases and individual traits into the decision-making process from time to time. The people you work with are complex, with wants and desires of their own, and they should not be expected to behave like machines. The inventory management *process* is rational, but the people involved in the process are not always rational.

Feedback Operations managers must monitor inventory levels and make adjustments within the production planning and control process when they discover that actual output deviates from planned output. These adjustments might well involve decisions to build inventory, reduce inventory, or change inventory procedures and operating doctrines. There can be no *control in* inventory without three activities:

1. Monitoring of performance and inventory levels
2. Feedback to decision makers comparing actual performance and material usage with planned performance and usage
3. Adjustment of inputs to the conversion process, especially the capital inputs of inventory

Feedback should include status reports, prepared manually or by the computer, as well as visual feedback obtained by touring the facility. There is no good substitute for walking through the conversion process yourself —whether your organization is a bank, a restaurant, a school, or a manufacturing facility—so you can compare your first-hand observations with planned conditions and quickly make adjustments for discrepancies you may find.

Inventory Policy Often, top management adjusts aggregate inventory levels. These manufacturing and operations policy decisions should be well grounded in cost analysis. We caution top executives against making frequent and drastic inventory policy changes, as they might inadvertently increase overall production costs.

Individual Risk-taking Propensity As you probably know from your own experience, people vary considerably in their tendencies to take chances. Some people thrive on taking risks; others are risk-averse. Any banker can tell you that among checking account customers are a certain percentage who keep far too many cash reserves in low interest-bearing accounts because they are afraid of future uncertainty. Operating managers can also be risk-averse. In their overreactions to the possibility of a stockout, they may carry excessive buffer stocks.

On the other hand, some people are high rollers, risk takers. As operations managers or supervisors, people who take excessive risks are just as damaging to inventory control as are people who are too risk-averse. They may allow inventory levels to vary drastically and cause stockouts, high costs, and adverse effects in other operations subsystems. Individual propensity to take risks within the organization's inventory control procedures should be assessed carefully. Extreme behaviors are costly to operations.

SUMMARY

In this chapter we continued our discussion of inventory control and stochastic (variable) inventory models, which are required when demand, lead time, or both are variable. We stressed that the operations manager is most interested in the distribution of demand during lead time, a critical factor in establishing buffer stocks and the reorder point.

We saw that money can be saved in inventory systems by evaluating the ABC classification, blanket rules, stochastic demand and lead times, high stockout cost items, safety stocks, decoupled operations, and raw material and finished goods inventory.

This chapter listed numerous inventory control procedures for practical application, among them the cardex file system and IBM's MAPICS. Especially highlighted was the Japanese concept of stockless production (just-in-time) which seems to work well in reducing inventories. One feature, kanban, provides discipline to shop-floor control of inventories, a continuing problem in any inventory system.

Primarily, inventory control is a rational process that lends itself to logical procedures. Behavioral pitfalls in inventory control involve the irrationality of decision makers, lack of control, poorly established inventory policies, and the variability in people's propensity to take risks.

CASE

Good Shepherd Home

The Good Shepherd Home is a long-term care facility with an 80-bed capacity located in San Mateo, California. Mr. Scott, the administrator, is concerned about rising food costs. He questions whether administration is as efficient as it might be and realizes that food, a "raw material" for his food services, has increased in price significantly. Mr. Scott decides to investigate food services more closely.

Analyzing last month's purchased items, Mr. Scott summarizes a random selection of items. Mr. Scott wonders what interpretation he should make about these typical items. He has looked at 100 stock items and is considering tighter controls on the 40 stock items that resulted in 400 quantities (dozens, cases, pounds, etc.) being ordered.

Good Shepherd Typical Inventory Items

Number of Stock Items	Quantity Ordered	Total Cost	Average Inventory
3	50	$3,500	$1,200
12	150	2,500	900
20	200	1,500	600
40	400	2,000	200
25	200	500	100

Of particular interest is a problem with a perishable good, bread. Since the home has residents from independent living units eating at the home irregularly, bread demand is uneven. Bread is delivered daily and is used that day for table meal service only; the day-old bread is salvaged for dressing and similar items. Scott estimates the cost of bread to be $.75/loaf and the cost of day-old bread to be $.25/loaf. Scott says, "We should not be out of fresh bread at the table. Although man cannot live by bread alone, it is very important to our residents. I put a high cost on being out of bread—considerably more than the cost of a loaf. In fact, I think every time we run out of bread, it costs a dollar per loaf short in good will lost from our residents."

Knowing Mr. Scott feels this way, the food services supervisor has a standing order for 30 loaves/day and twice that amount on Sunday. The demand for bread the last two weeks is shown below.

Good Shepherd Bread Demand

Week 1		Week 2	
Day	Bread Demand	Day	Bread Demand
Mon	20	Mon	19
Tue	15	Tue	27
Wed	21	Wed	20
Thu	30	Thu	32
Fri	31	Fri	27
Sat	19	Sat	16
Sun	42	Sun	39

In conversation with Mr. Scott, the supervisor says, "I recently heard about cost tradeoffs in food service inventory. I don't really see what item cost, carrying cost, ordering costs, and stockout costs have to do with proper nutrition. I try to buy good quality foods and spend less than $5/day on food for each resident. That's my objective."

Mr. Scott has heard about cost tradeoffs too, but he wonders what they mean and how they could assist in a nursing home environment. To try to understand this better he talked to his bookkeeper. The supervisor says that she knows with certainty that demand for hamburger over a menu cycle is 200 pounds. Furthermore, the bookkeeper estimates it costs $12 to place an order and 20 percent of the hamburger cost to carry hamburger in inventory. Hamburger costs $1.55/pound. The dietitian says a menu cycle lasts two weeks, and Good Shepherd currently orders hamburger every week. Mr. Scott is puzzled by all this.

REVIEW AND DISCUSSION QUESTIONS

1. Explain three common ways to measure and establish service levels, giving an example of each.
2. What is meant by the ABC classification? How might an organization's inventory be analyzed using the ABC classification?
3. In Figure 13.1, why are the lines dotted? Will the optimal cost always be at the lowest point on a cost curve? Why or why not?
4. Inventory control is a rational process in which decisions are often made irrationally. Explain.

5. Given a probability distribution of demand and a distribution of lead time, what alternatives exist for finding the probability distribution of demand during lead time? Select one alternative and explain how it works. Why is the distribution of demand during lead time important?
6. For Figure 13.3, explain how lead time and demand vary. What impact does such variation have on buffer stocks, if any?
7. Suppose a directive comes to a manufacturing facility from the controller strongly suggesting a 35 percent across-the-board reduction in inventory levels. The plant manager asks you to assist him in explaining the need for inventories in manufacturing. What points would you make in favor of having inventories to assist the plant manager in answering the controller?
8. Select two general areas in which money might be saved in inventory control, and explain how you would plan a cost study for each.
9. Discuss the advantages and disadvantages of the periodic inventory system compared with the quantity/reorder inventory system.
10. Explain the concept of inventory turnover. How do American companies compare with Japanese companies based on inventory turnover? Discuss.
11. A nonbusiness student comments, "What is the big deal about Japanese manufacturing? I like their products; they do what I want done. Are they really different in their manufacturing ways from American companies?" How would you respond? Explain.
12. In Japan manufacturing setup time, inventory, quality, and the way employees behave all interact. Explain why this is so.
13. Compare the U.S. "push" scheduling/inventory system to the Japanese "pull" system. What is the role of kanban in the Japanese system?
14. Relate individual propensity for risk taking to decision making in inventory control.

PROBLEMS

Solved Problems

1. Actual daily demand and lead-time distributions are given below. What is expected demand during lead time? What is the minimum that demand during lead time will ever be?

Actual Daily Demand (units)	Number of Occurrences	Actual Lead Time (days)	Number of Occurrences
1–5	2	2	2
6–10	6	3	3
11–15	2	4	2

To find expected demand during lead time, we need first to find expected demand and expected lead time.

$$\text{Expected demand} = \frac{3(2) + 8(6) + 13(2)}{10} = 8 \text{ units/day}$$

$$\text{Expected lead time} = \frac{2(2) + 3(3) + 4(2)}{7} = 3 \text{ days}$$

$$\text{Expected demand during lead time} = 8 \times 3 = 24 \text{ units}$$

The minimum that demand during lead time will ever be is 3 units/day × 2 days = 6 units (not using midpoints for daily demand it *could* be 1 × 2 = 2 units).

2. Daily demand for mini wheels, a popular toy, is normally distributed with a daily mean of 60 cases and a standard deviation of 10 cases. Supply is virtually certain, with a lead time of three days. The cost of placing an order is $6, and annual holding costs are 20 percent of the unit price of $1.20. We want a 90 percent service level at our warehouse for customers who place orders during the reorder period. Service level is the probability that there will be a stockout of any size during lead time. Backorders are allowed. Once stocks are depleted, orders are filled as soon as the stocks arrive. We can assume orders arrive 200 days throughout the year. Determine the operating doctrine for mini wheels.

$$\bar{d} = 60 \text{ cases/day} \qquad t_L = 3 \text{ days}$$
$$S = \$6 \qquad \sigma_d = 10 \text{ cases}$$
$$I = .20 \qquad Z = 1.282 \text{ for 90\% service level}$$
$$C = \$1.20$$

Orders arrive 200 days throughout the year.

$$Q^* = \sqrt{\frac{2DS}{IC}} = \sqrt{\frac{2(60)(200)(\$6)}{.20(\$1.20)}} = 774.59 = 775 \text{ cases}$$
$$\sigma_\mu = \sqrt{3(10)^2} = 17.32$$
$$R^* = \bar{d}t_L + Z\sigma_\mu = 60(3) + 1.282(17.32) = 180 + 22.20 = 203 \text{ cases}$$

The operating doctrine for mini wheels is to order 775 cases when the on-hand inventory reaches 203 cases.

3. A Christmas tree supplier has evaluated weekly demand for November–December over the last seven years. Demand appears normally distributed with a mean of 350 trees demanded weekly and a standard deviation of 200. To assure a fresh supply and maintain a reputation for quality, trees are cut weekly in anticipation of demand. A Christmas tree sells for an average $6.00 wholesale locally and can be salvaged, if not sold locally, by shipping out of state at an average revenue of $2 each (sold "not freshly cut"). Cost to raise and harvest a tree is $3.75. What should be the weekly ordering (harvesting) quantity for the upcoming Christmas season?

$$CF = \frac{C_u}{C_u + C_o}$$

If understocked, the lost sale cost is revenue less harvesting, $2.25, ($6.00 – $3.75). If overstocked, the cost is harvesting less salvage, $1.75 ($3.75 – $2.00).

$$CF = \frac{2.25}{2.25 + 1.75} = \frac{2.25}{4.00} = 0.5625$$

The optimal harvesting level will have 56.25 percent of the normal curve to the left of this stocking level. From Appendix A, we find that the area of the normal curve to be at $Z = 0.157$. Shown graphically in Figure 13.6, we need to find x, the ordering level.

$$x = \mu + Z\sigma$$
$$= 350 + 0.157\ (200) = 350 + 31.4 = 381.4$$

The supplier should harvest 381 trees a week, given these data, to optimize profits.

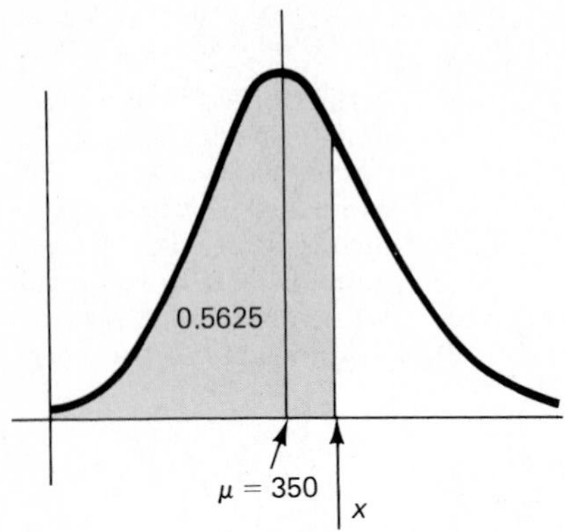

FIGURE 13.6

Reinforcing Fundamentals

4. A bookstore orders blue books (exam booklets) in boxes of one gross. Annual demand is even throughout the year and known with certainty to be 600 boxes. Lead time is known to be exactly one month. The cost of placing an order is $16, and annual carrying charges are 36 percent. The wholesaler gives the bookstore a quantity discount as follows:

Quantity (boxes)	Price/Box
1–49	$7.50
50–99	7.35
100 or more	7.00

Establish the economic operating doctrine.

5. Actual daily demand and lead-time distributions are given below. What is expected demand during lead time? What is the minimum that demand during lead time will ever be?

Actual Daily Demand (units)	Number of Occurrences	Actual Lead Time (days)	Number of Occurrences
20–40	4	1	3
41–60	3	2	2
61–80	3	4	2

6. An electrical motor housing has an annual usage rate of 75,000 units/year, an ordering cost of $20, and annual unit carrying charge of 15.4 percent of the unit price. For lot sizes of fewer than 10,000, the unit price is $.50; for 10,000 or more, the unit price is $.45. Delivery lead time is known with certainty to be two weeks. Determine the optimal operating doctrine.

7. Daily demand for a manufactured part is normally distributed with a daily mean of 80 cases and a standard deviation of 30 cases. Supply is virtually certain, with a lead time of three days. The cost of placing an order is $15, and annual holding costs are 20 percent of the unit price of $6.50. We want a 90 percent service level at our warehouse for customers who place orders during the reorder period. Service level is the probability that there will be a stockout of any size during lead time. Backorders are allowed. Once stocks are depleted, orders are filled as soon as the stocks arrive. We can assume orders arrive 200 days throughout the year. Determine the operating doctrine for this part.

8. The daily demand for a component assembly item is normally distributed with a mean of 80 and standard deviation of 7. Furthermore, the source of supply is reliable and maintains a constant lead time of four days. If the cost of placing the order is $30 and annual holding costs are $.60/unit, find the order quantity and reorder point to provide a 80 percent service level. Service level is the probability that there will be a stockout of any size during lead time. Unfilled orders are filled as soon as an order arrives. Assume sales occur over the entire year.
9. A florist orders flowers weekly. Demand for carnations varies uniformly from 8 to 20 dozen a week. Carnations cost $6/dozen and sell for an average price of $12/dozen, some sold individually and some sold in arrangements. Salvage is virtually zero after a week's storage. Establish the ordering quantity for carnations. Explain your results in terms the florist will understand.
10. Daily demand for pickles for a local chain of fast-food restaurants is normally distributed with a mean of 30 jars and a standard deviation of 7. Supply is virtually certain with a lead time of two days; the cost of placing an order is $2.50, and annual holding costs are 80 percent of the unit price of $.60/jar. A 98 percent service level is desired. Service level is the probability that there will be a stockout of any size during lead time. The restaurant chain serves 365 days a year.
   (a) Determine the operating doctrine for ordering pickles.
   (b) Construct graphs similar to Figures 13.3 and 13.4 to portray this situation.
   (c) What is the annual cost for pickle buffer stocks? Does this cost seem reasonable for a 98 percent service level?
11. For the fast-food restaurant chain in Problem 10, suppose that exactly the same situation exists for coffee as did for pickles, except that coffee costs ten times as much per can as do pickles per jar.
   (a) What is the operating doctrine for coffee?
   (b) What is the annual cost for coffee buffer stocks?
   (c) What conclusions can you reach concerning the effect price has on operating doctrine and buffer stocks (by comparing your answer with that of Problem 10)?
12. For the fast-food restaurant chain in Problem 10, suppose that exactly the same situation exists for chocolate syrup as did for pickles, except that chocolate syrup demand is 30 cans/day with a standard deviation of 28 cans.
   (a) What is the operating doctrine for chocolate syrup?
   (b) What is the annual cost for chocolate syrup buffer stocks?
   (c) What impact does the variability of demand (the standard deviation) seem to have on buffer stocks (by comparing your answer with that of Problem 10)?
13. Bilson, Inc., purchases all metal needed in bar stock form. With an annual demand of 4,000 units, a purchase ordering cost of $80, and storage costs of 20 percent of the unit cost, what is the optimal order quantity given these price breaks:
   (a) 0–299, $50/unit
   (b) 300–499, $40/unit
   (c) 500 or more, $30/unit.

Challenging Exercises

14. The demand per period for an important inventory item seems to have the following probability distribution:

Demand (D)	Probability of Demand Occurring
5	.4
6	.2
7	.1
8	.3

All stock to meet the demand for a period must be acquired at the start of the period. The product costs $5/unit and sells for $8/unit. Any leftover units at the end of a period must be disposed of as "seconds" at a selling price of $4/unit. On the other hand, if the stock becomes depleted, there is no cost associated with the shortage.

(a) Under the conditions noted above, will it be more profitable to stock six or seven units at the start of each period?

(b) If there were a cost associated with a shortage and a probability of a shortage for each demand level, how would you modify Part a?

15. Demand for the local daily newspaper at a newsstand is normally distributed with a daily mean of 210 copies and standard deviation of 70. A newspaper sells for $.25 cents and costs $.20 to purchase. Day-old newspapers are very seldom requested, and therefore they are destroyed upon receipt of the next day's paper. What should the newsstand's daily order be to maximize profits?

16. A bank purchases promotional ball point pens for $4 each. The company that supplies the pens suggests that if the imprinted pens were ordered in twice the quantity, a 25 percent discount could be arranged. At present the bank orders 100 pens every two months. Ordering costs are $12, and the bank's cost of money is 15 percent. What ordering policy should be followed? Show your analysis to support your decision.

17. A family of products in the Economize line of a hardware producer are so similar that they are grouped and viewed as one product. Daily demand for this group is normally distributed with a mean of 20 and a standard deviation of 10. Supply is virtually certain with a lead time of five days. The cost of placing an order is $27.50, and holding costs are 20 percent of the group product price of $94. Management wants a 90 percent service level for customers who place orders during the reorder period. Service level is the probability that there will be a stockout of any size during lead time. Backorders are allowed. Once stocks are depleted, orders are filled as soon as the stocks arrive. Assume sales are made over the entire year.

(a) Find the reorder point.

(b) Draw an on-hand inventory versus time graph of this inventory situation, placing the correct reorder point on the graph and identifying data given or calculated where possible.

18. At McDonald's on the Ohio State University campus, six-ounce paper cups are used at a rate of 120 cups/day and are ordered in lots of 850 dozen. McDonald's is open 360 days a year. After several months on the job, a business school student (employee) finds that lead time is virtually a constant three days, not instantaneous as was previously assumed, and that daily demand varies with a mean of 120 cups and a variance of 36 cups. The manager desires to run out of cups once every six months or less (an average of two times a year). Establish an operating doctrine for management.

19. You find yourself, as operations manager of a group of stock market analysts for a small brokerage firm, faced with the following problem. The company's market research group suggests you "follow" (analyze) some "risky" stocks, as some customers desire this kind of investment. They estimate maximum demand from any one "high risk taker" to be in any one month:

Number of Risky Stocks Demanded	Probability of This Number Being Demanded
2	.30
4	.20
5	.10
6	.30
8	.10

They also assess a cost associated with not having the number of risky stocks demanded to be $100 (loss of customer possibilities). Furthermore, you know that your unit costs per month (C) to "follow" stocks are:

$$C = \begin{cases} \$25D \text{ for } D \leq 4 \\ \$15D \text{ elsewhere} \end{cases}$$

where D is the number of risky stocks demanded. How many risky stocks should you "follow" each month?

20. A bank is evaluating teller capacity. Daily demand for teller services is as shown below. The cost of not serving a customer or having the customer leave angry because of a long wait is estimated to be high and should be avoided. The cost of having a teller and facility is $75/day. A teller typically generates $250/day in revenue. Develop a decision rule for the bank to follow in comparing current capacity with the most economical capacity.

Daily Average Number of Tellers Busy (demanded)	Number of Occurrences Observed
0	0
1–2	13
3–4	21
5–6	10
7 or more	6

21. You have a product with average weekly sales of 600 units. By looking at past demand records, you find that the demand pattern has followed the distribution below:

Demand Above	Percent of the Time
400 units/week	100
450	90
500	79
550	64
600	50
650	22
700	8
750	3
800	0

The cost of carrying an item on inventory for one year is $1.30. There is a fixed cost of ordering of $72 for every order placed. Lead time is constant at one week. The stockout policy has been set to allow two stockouts a year on average. Determine the order quantity and the safety stock that will minimize the variable costs.

22. Wendy's is interested in analyzing the ordering policy for some perishable items, including tomatoes. The daily demand for crates of tomatoes is shown below.

Daily Demand Tomatoes (crates)	Probability This Number Being Demanded
2	.3
4	.4
6	.1
7	.1
9	.1

This cost of ordering tomatoes is small, estimated to be $.25 for a crate; a crate costs an average of $24. If we carry tomatoes, our cost of capital is 20 percent of the item cost. The average shelf life to us of tomatoes is one day with zero salvage value. If a crate that is not on hand is demanded, the cost of being out of tomatoes is estimated to be $100. Lead time is known with certainty to be one day. To simplify ordering, management will only order lots of 2, 4, 6, 7, or 9 crates. Establish an optimal operating doctrine for Wendy's, which operates 365 days a year.

Utilizing the QSOM Computer Software

23. The manager of a health food outlet has determined that demand for her all-natural yogurt is approximately 20 quarts/week. The store operates 50 weeks/year. Her ordering costs are $25, and due to limited freezer space, carrying costs are $10/quart/year. The supplier offers 3 price breaks: Price/quart is $3.00 for 1–39 quarts; $2.90 for 40–79 quarts; $2.80 for 80–119 quarts, and $2.70 for 120 or more quarts of yogurt. By means of QSOM's deterministic discount analysis submenu of the inventory theory program, determine the economic operating doctrine for the health food outlet. Use the "all units discounts" computer program option in the analysis.

24. A retailer has estimated that monthly demand for stone-washed jeans is 65 pairs. His ordering costs are $35, and carrying costs are $5/pair/year. The supplier offers 2 price breaks: $15/pair for 1–49 pairs, $14/pair for 50–99 pairs, and $13/pair for orders of 100 or more.

(a) Using QSOM's deterministic discover analysis submenu of the inventory theory program, establish the economic operating doctrine for this retailer. Use "all units discounts" in the analysis.

(b) Now assume that ordering costs drop to $15 and the supplier alters his discounts in the following manner: $15.00/pair for 1–49, $14.50/pair for 50–99, and $14.00/pair for 100 or more. How does this affect the economic operating doctrine?

(c) Refer back to the original data. Ordering costs are further reduced to $10, but as a result of fire losses in the warehouse, carrying costs skyrocket to $60/unit/year. How does this influence the economic operating doctrine? Why? (Use the original discount scheme.)

GLOSSARY

ABC classification Inventory division with three groupings, an A grouping for a few items with a large dollar volume, a B grouping for items with moderate volume and moderate dollar volume, and a C grouping for items with a large volume and small dollar volume.

Cardex file Manually operated system when an inventory card represents each stock item with transactions kept on the card.

Individual risk-taking propensity Degree to which individuals tend to take or avoid chances.

Kanban Japanese term meaning "visible record"; a card attached to a container; contains an order.

Lead-time demand Units of stock demanded during lead time; can be described by a probability distribution in stochastic situations.

MAPICS Manufacturing and Accounting Production Information Control System; IBM's computerized common data base manufacturing information system.

Quantity discounts Policy of allowing item cost to vary with the volume ordered; usually the item cost decreases as volume increases due to economies of scale in production and distribution.

Service level Treatment policy for customers when there are stockouts; commonly established either as a ratio of *customers* served to those demanding or a ratio of *units* supplied to those demanded.

SELECTED READINGS

Brown, R. G., *Decision Rules for Inventory Management.* New York: Holt, Rinehart & Winston, 1967.

Buchan, J., and E. Koenigsberg, *Scientific Inventory Control.* Englewood Cliffs, N.J.: Prentice Hall, 1963.

Buffa, E. S., and J. G. Miller, *Production-Inventory Systems: Planning and Control* (3rd ed.). Homewood, Ill.: Richard D. Irwin, 1979.

Hadley, G., and T. M. Whitin, *Analysis of Inventory Systems.* Englewood Cliffs, N.J.: Prentice Hall, 1963.

Hall, Robert W., *Zero Inventories.* Homewood, Ill.: Dow Jones-Irwin, 1983.

IBM, Manufacturing Accounting and Production Information Control System (MAPICS). Manufacturing Education Guide and MAPICS Features Education manual. (Order numbers GH30-0241-0 and SR30-0369-1). Atlanta, Ga., 1979.

Meredith, Jack R., and Thomas E. Gibbs, *The Management of Operations.* New York: John Wiley, 1980.

Sasser, W. E., R. P. Olson, and D. D. Wyckoff, *Management of Service Operations.* Boston: Allyn & Bacon, 1978.

Schonberger, Richard J., *Japanese Manufacturing Techniques: Nine Hidden Lessons in Simplicity.* New York: Free Press, 1982.

Starr, Martin K., and D. W. Miller, *Inventory Control: Theory and Practice.* Englewood Cliffs, N.J.: Prentice Hall, 1962.

Stevenson, William J., *Production/Operations Management.* Homewood, Ill.: Irwin, 1982.

14

Material Requirements Planning

As a real life practitioner I can assure you that you are about to enter one of the most exciting chapters in this book. MRP has become a centerpiece for all manufacturing systems. The key to successful production and operations management in a manufacturing company is the balancing of requirements and capacities. It's that simple and yet very challenging.

We at Hallmark Cards produce hundreds of products. About half of our annual sales volume consists of cards and the other half a wide variety of "social expression" products ranging from party goods, puzzles, pens, and pencils to mugs and stickers. In our card area, we produce 32 million cards a week. Without MRP, we would be totally out of control. This informative chapter will be one of the keystones of your professional career. To understand it is essential and to practice it can be a lot of fun. Remember what you are trying to do: Meet the needs of your customers. How? By having the product available when it is wanted. In production management, we do this by knowing in advance what our requirements are now and in the future and planning ahead to have the capacity available. We at Hallmark know this and practice it. It's not a theory—it's the real world.

Al Sondern
Corporate Vice President
Hallmark Cards, Inc.
Kansas City, Missouri

Mr. Sondern's remarks give clear evidence that managing conversion systems effectively entails attention to materials management, including materials procurement, coordinating materials availability, and controlling materials utilization. As a practitioner he recognizes that the complexities of producing numerous different products can cause confusion, inefficiencies, and inferior customer service. Management is better able to control in such an environment if it gets the timely and accurate information it needs. A material requirements planning (MRP) system, the topic of this chapter, can provide this vital information.

PLANNING FOR MATERIALS NEEDS

In recent years material planning systems have replaced reactive inventory systems (discussed in Chapters 12 and 13) in many organizations. Reactive systems ask, "What should I do *now*?," whereas planning systems look ahead and ask, "What will I be needing in the *future*? How much and when?"

Reactive systems are simpler to manage in many respects but have serious drawbacks, especially their high inventory costs and low production delivery reliability. The newer way, the planning system, is more complex to manage, but it offers numerous advantages. It reduces inventories and their associated costs because it carries only those items and components that are needed—no more and no less. By looking ahead to ensure that all materials are available when needed for product buildup, it reduces order processing delays. By setting realistic job completion dates, it gets jobs done on time, order promises are kept, and production lead times are shortened.

The increased customer service and other advantages come at a cost, however. They require an information system with accurate inventory and product buildup information. They also require a realistic master production schedule (MPS) to specify when various quantities of end items will be completed. Finally, and perhaps most important, they require a certain *discipline*, a commitment by schedulers, supervisors, managers, and shop floor employees to make the system work. Once MRP job priorities and schedules are set, they must be adhered to. When discrepancies between planned progress and actual job progress arise, actions are needed to adjust the system and cause the plans to materialize. The key to getting this employee commitment resides in the honesty of the system—keeping it accurate and believable.

Demand Dependency

Demand dependency is an important consideration in choosing between reactive and planning systems. Recall from Chapter 3 that demand dependency is the degree to which the demand for some item is associated with the demand for another item. With *independent demand*, demand for one item is unrelated to the demand for others. In the *dependent demand* situation, if we know the demand for one item, we know the demand for one or more related items. If, for example, the demand for an end product is known, we can calculate how many of its subcomponents are needed—their demand is directly dependent on the end-item demand.

In the past, industry used reactive inventory control systems (such as reorder point–reorder quantity) as the mainstay, ignoring the dependent versus independent distinction. More recently, however, we've learned that inventory planning systems such as MRP are more beneficial than reactive systems for dependent demand items. We don't need large safety stocks for them because we usually know exactly how many dependent items will be needed. Furthermore, we don't need to accumulate excessive cycle stocks of dependent items in advance of when they're needed. Our MRP systems use accurate information about components as substitutes for excessive inventories of those components.

APPLYING MRP AS A SCHEDULING AND ORDERING SYSTEM

MRP is a system of planning and scheduling the time-phased materials requirements for production operations. As such, it is geared toward meeting the end-item outputs prescribed in the master production schedule as shown in Figure 14.1. It also provides outputs, such as due dates for components, that are subsequently used for shop floor control. Once these MRP outputs are available, they enable us to estimate the detailed capacity requirements for the production work centers. MRP's role in coordinating these activities becomes evident as we examine its objectives and structure in greater detail.

MRP Objectives and Methods

MRP systems are intended to provide the following:

1. *Inventory reduction.* MRP determines how many of a component are needed and when to meet the master schedule. It enables the manager to procure that component as it is needed, thereby avoiding costs of continuously carrying it and excessive safety stocks in inventory.
2. *Reduction in production and delivery lead times.* MRP identifies which of many materials and components needs (quantity and timing), availabilities, and actions (procurement and production) are needed to meet delivery deadlines. By coordinating inventories, procurement, and production decisions, it helps avoid delays in production. It prioritizes production activities by putting due dates on customer job orders.
3. *Realistic commitments.* Realistic delivery promises can enhance customer satisfaction. By using MRP, production can give marketing timely information about likely delivery times to prospective customers. Potential new customer orders can be added to the system to show the manager how the revised total load can be handled with existing capacity. The result can be a more realistic delivery date.
4. *Increased efficiency.* MRP provides close coordination among various departments and work centers as product buildups progress through them. Consequently, production can proceed with fewer indirect personnel, such as materials expeditors, and with fewer unplanned

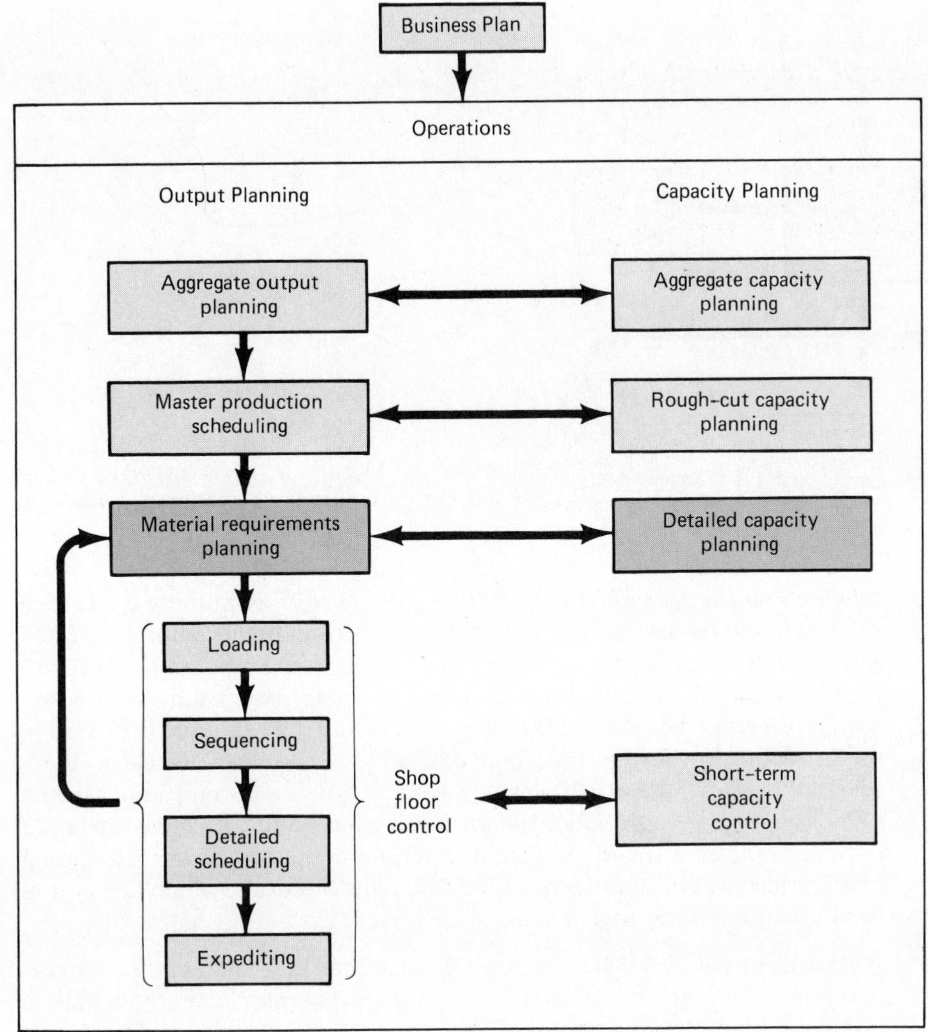

FIGURE 14.1
The operations planning and scheduling system

production interruptions because MRP focuses on having all components available at appropriately scheduled times. The information provided by MRP encourages and supports production efficiencies.

MRP System Components

Figure 14.2 shows the basic components of an MRP system. Three major information elements are mandatory in the MRP system: a master production schedule, an inventory status file, and a bill of materials file for product structure. Using these three information sources, the MRP processing logic (computer program) provides three kinds of information outputs about each product component: order release requirements, order rescheduling, and planned orders. Let's examine each of these elements in more detail.

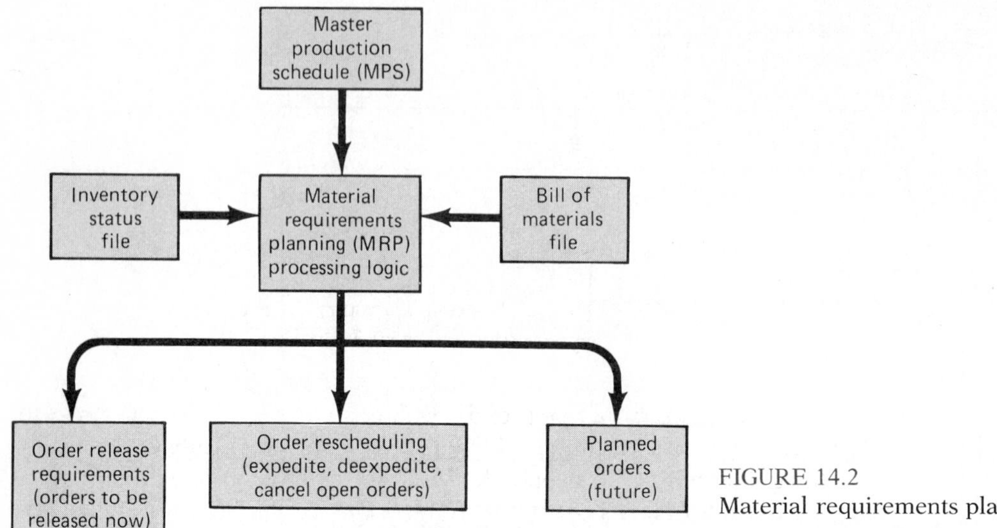

FIGURE 14.2
Material requirements planning system

Master Production Schedule (MPS) The MPS is initially developed from firm customer orders or from forecasts of demand before the MRP system begins to operate; it becomes an input to the system. Designed to meet market demand, the MPS identifies the quantity of each end product (end item) and when it needs to be produced during each future period in the production planning horizon. Orders for replacement (service) components for customers in the field are also entered as end items in the MPS. The MPS then provides the focal information for the MRP system; it ultimately governs the MRP system's recommended actions on the timing of materials procurement and subcomponents buildups, which are geared to meeting the MPS output schedule.

Bill of Materials (BOM) The BOM identifies how each end product is manufactured, specifying all subcomponent items, their sequence of buildup, their quantity in each finished unit, and which work centers perform the buildup sequence in the facility. This information is obtained from product design documents, work flow analysis, and other standard manufacturing and industrial engineering documentation.[1]

The primary information to MRP from the BOM is the *product structure*, an example of which is shown in Figure 14.3. One unit of end product A requires one unit each of subcomponents B and C. The product structure for end product D requires one E and one F. Subcomponent E is created from one B and two units of item C.

In MRP terminology, A and D are *upper-level end items;* the subcomponents are *lower-level items*. By precisely identifying the levels in the product structure, we clearly show the relationships among the

[1]The central role of the bill of materials in MRP is discussed in Joseph A. Orlicky, George W. Plossl, and Oliver W. Wight, "Structuring the Bill of Material," *Production and Inventory Management* 13, no. 4 (1972), 19–42.

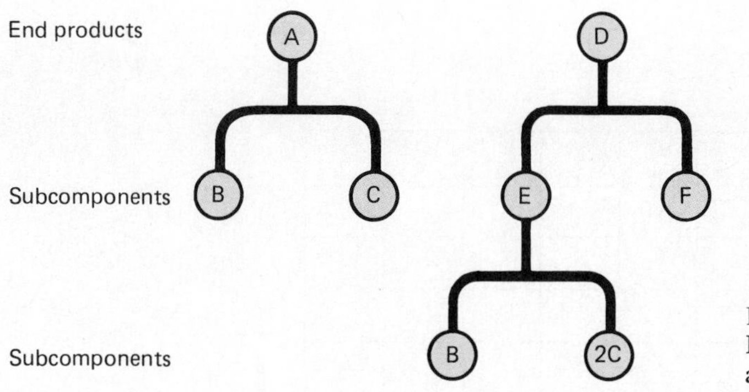

FIGURE 14.3
Product structures for two assembled products

component items in all our end products. Each item in the product structure is given a unique identification number. Subsequently, by knowing the master schedule for end items, MRP can schedule and time-phase the orders for the correct lower-level component items in the product structure.

Inventory Status File The system must retain an up-to-date file of the inventory status of each item in the product structure. This file provides accurate information about the availability of every item controlled by MRP. The system uses this information to maintain an accurate accounting of all inventory transactions, both actual and planned. The inventory status file contains the identification number, quantity on hand, safety stock level, quantity disbursed (allocated), and procurement lead time of every item. The time needed to procure an item, once an order for it is initiated, is taken into account when deciding when to place an order for that item.

The MRP Processing Logic The MRP processing logic accepts the master schedule and determines the components schedules for successively lower-level items throughout the product structures. It calculates for each of the time periods (typically one-week periods) in the scheduling time horizon how many of that item are needed (gross requirements), how many units from existing inventory are already available, the net quantity we must plan on receiving in new shipments (planned order receipts), and when orders for the new shipments must be placed (planned order releases) so that all materials arrive just when needed. This data processing continues until it has determined the requirements for all items that will be used to meet the master production schedule.

Management Information from MRP The MRP output gives a report, similar to the example in Figure 14.4, for each item in the product structure. The example report shows that 400 units of this item are needed (gross requirements) in week 4 and another 500 are needed in week 8. No outstanding orders were previously placed, so there are no units of this item scheduled for receipt as of this time. There are, however, 50 uncommitted units of the item already available in inventory, and these will go toward meeting the week 4 requirements. Consequently, there are

Item identification: #3201-Mounting bracket
Lead time: 3 weeks
Report date: week 0

		Week 1	Week 2	Week 3	Week 4	Week 5	Week 6	Week 7	Week 8
Gross requirements					400				500
Scheduled receipts									
Available for next period	50	50	50	50					
Net requirements					350				500
Planned order receipts					350				500
Planned order releases		350				500			

FIGURE 14.4
An MRP report for one item

Table 14.1 Selected terminology of MRP component records

Allocated: The quantity of an item's on-hand inventory that has been committed for use and is not available to meet future requirements.

Gross requirements: The overall quantity of an item needed at the end of each future time period to meet planned output levels. Planned output for end items is obtained from the master production schedule. Planned output for lower-level items is obtained from the MRP system.

Scheduled receipts: The quantity of an item that will be received at the beginning of a time period from suppliers as a result of orders that have already been placed (open orders).

Available: The quantity of an item expected to be available at the end of a time period for meeting requirements in future time periods. This includes scheduled receipts plus planned order receipts minus gross requirements for the period, plus available items from the previous period.

Net requirements: The net quantity of an item that must be acquired to meet the scheduled output for this period. It is calculated as gross requirements minus scheduled receipts for the period minus available items from the previous period.

Planned order receipts: The quantity of an item that is *planned* to be ordered so that it would be received at the beginning of this time period to meet net requirements for this period. The order has not yet been placed.

Planned order release: The quantity of an item that is *planned* to be ordered and the planned time period for releasing this order that would result in the order being received when needed. It is the planned order receipt offset in time by the item's lead time. When this order is placed (released), it becomes a scheduled receipt and is deleted from planned order receipts and planned order releases.

net requirements of 350 units for week 4 and 500 units for week 8. To meet these net requirements, the report indicates we should plan on receiving 350 units in week 4 and a 500-unit order in week 8. Since this particular item has a three-week procurement lead time, the first order must be placed (released) in week 1 and the second order in week 5.

This report clearly identifies what procurement actions are required to keep production on schedule. It also gives suppliers advanced notification of the demands that will be placed on them in the future. As end-item demands change with the passage of time, modifications in the master schedule will dictate corresponding adjustments of lower-level requirements. Weekly updating, for example, will revise the previous schedules and may indicate that an order must be received earlier (expedited) or that a previously placed order can wait until later (deexpedited) or even be cancelled. As you can imagine, this information system is especially valuable when there are many end items with hundreds or thousands of related subcomponents that must be coordinated among numerous suppliers and departments. Table 14.1 defines some of the key terminology used in the MRP system and its component records.

The MRP Computational Procedure

The MRP computational procedure uses the input information to calculate the current records for each component and item as illustrated in the following example.

EXAMPLE

Consider a company that makes kitchen chairs. Their simplest chair, model H, has two frame components, one for the seat and the front legs and another for the backrest and rear legs. To assemble the seat to the front legs, a worker needs four fasteners (see Figure 14.5). Similarly, to assemble the backrest and rear legs, a worker needs four more fasteners. The two frame subassemblies (F and G) are then attached to each other with four more fasteners. When the two subassemblies are combined, the chair assembly is complete.

Figure 14.6 shows the *product structure* tree and component information including item identification, requirements for one parent item, lead time, and description. Each item in the product structure is categorized by a *level code*. The completed chair, item H, is the high-level item (level 0). Level 1 items are those whose parent is item H; these include items E, F, and G. Items A, B, C, D, and E are the individual components in level 2. Finally the lowest level (level 3) items are raw materials (RM) for the level 2 components.

Figure 14.7 shows a material requirements plan for shipping of 500 chairs in eight weeks, and 50 units each of items A and D in three weeks for replacing and repairing chairs in the field (raw materials have been omitted from the figure).

Without concerning ourselves with how this plan was developed, for the moment, let's concentrate on the information available at the current time for each item. We see that 100 units of H, finished chairs, are on hand prior to week 1. However, we need a safety stock of 50 for unexpected demand. Thus, the net available for meeting the 500 requirement in week 8 is 50. Similarly, 200 units of G are on hand, but 30 units are for safety stock and 60 units were previously allocated to other job orders. Therefore, 110 units are currently available for future allocation.

Information Processing Sequence The MRP processing logic is applied first to the high-level items (end products) in the product structure, then it proceeds to the items on the next lower level. It continues downward, level by level, until it has determined the requirements for all items in the product structure. In the chair assembly example, the completed chair (H) is the "level 0" (high-level) item requiring 500 completed units in week 8. All subsequent information processing is geared toward honoring this schedule. The inventory status file tells us that 50 units of H are currently available from existing inventory; these 50 units are carried forward as available at the end of week 7, resulting in a net requirements listing of 450 additional units of H in week 8. The MRP processing logic then calculates a planned order receipt to occur in week 8 (at the time needed) for 450 units of H. When must this order be placed (released) so that it arrives when it is needed? The processing system answers this question by "offsetting" by the length of the lead time, one week as indicated in the inventory status file for item H. This process is called *lead-time offsetting*. The result is the planned order release at the

FIGURE 14.5
Assembly diagram for chair model H

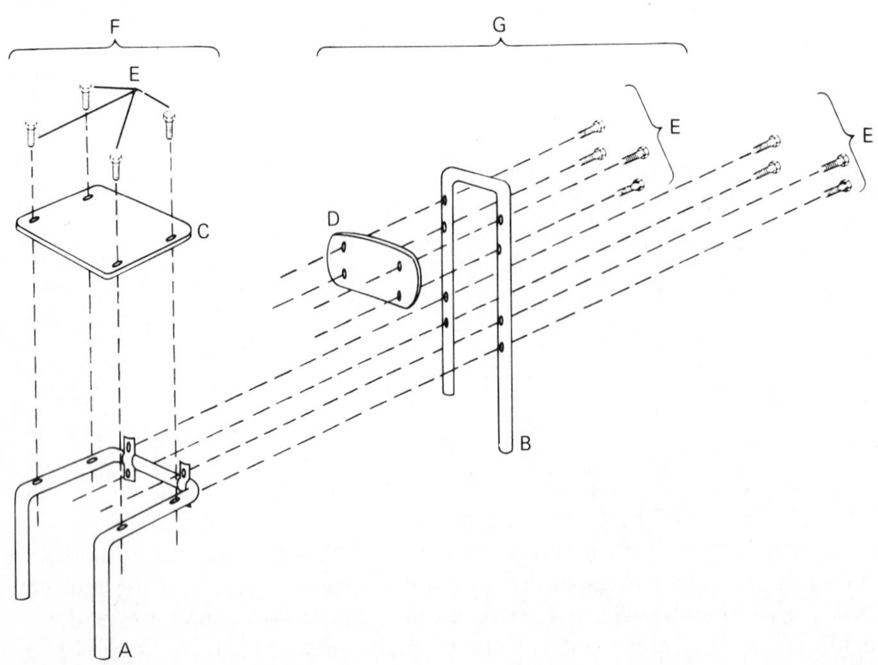

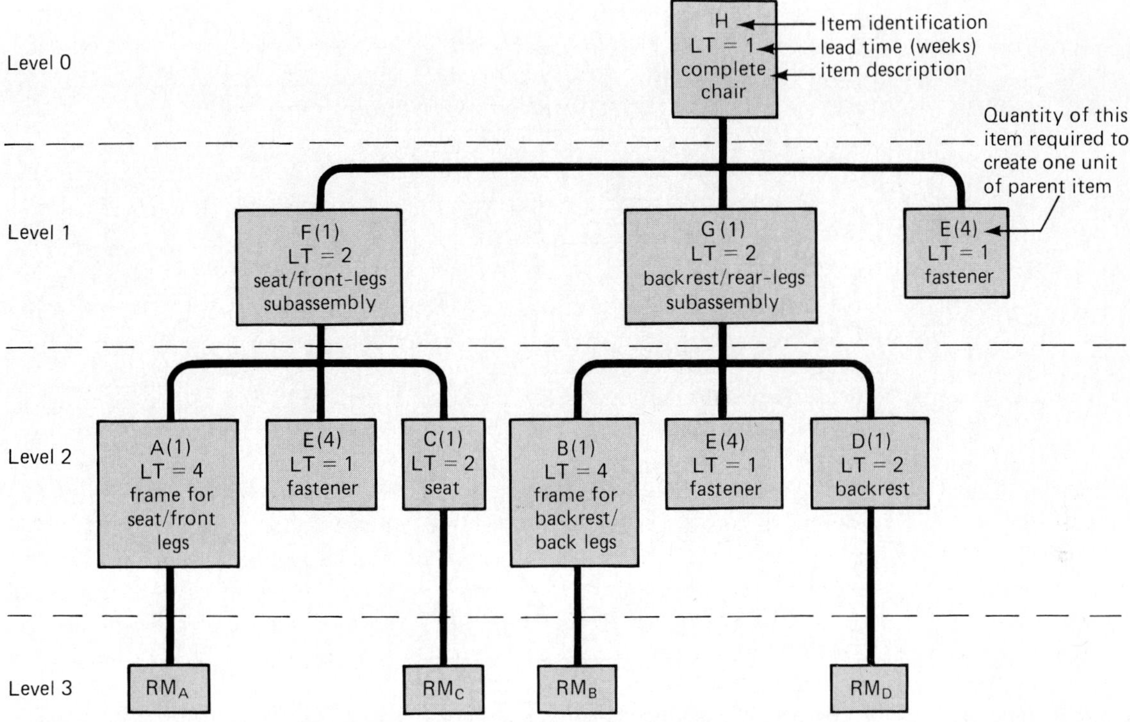

FIGURE 14.6
Product structure tree and item information

beginning of week 7, which, after the one week lead time, will result in a receipt of 450 units at the beginning of week 8.

Having determined requirements for all level 0 items, processing commences on the items in the next, either F or G in the product structure (item E at level 0 is a special case to be discussed soon). Level 1 items are considered next, because they are the only items needed to produce the level 0 item. The gross requirements for components G and F are determined by the planned order releases of the higher-level item H, 450 units in week 7. In general, the gross requirements for a lower-level item must include the planned order releases of the parent item for that time period. Then net requirements for each of F and G can be determined, and planned order receipts can be determined for the period. As was done for H, lead times are offset for F and G to determine planned order releases. The processing logic now proceeds to the next lower level of the product structure and determines requirements for each of items A–E. Then, raw materials requirements are determined.

Indented Bill of Materials To do its level-by-level calculations, MRP processing logic obviously needs information about an end item's relationship to all its subcomponents. The indented bill of materials provides this information. Our model H chair (the end item) has an indented bill of materials (see Table 14.2) with the same information as its product

(Assumes lot-for-lot ordering)

Item ID	Low level code	Lead time (weeks)	On hand	Safety stock	Allocated			Week 1	Week 2	Week 3	Week 4	Week 5	Week 6	Week 7	Week 8	
H	0	1	100	50	0	Gross requirements									500	from MPS
						Scheduled receipts										
						Available	50	50	50	50	50	50	50	50	0	
						Net requirements									450	
						Planned order receipts									450	lead time offset
						Planned order releases								450		
G	1	2	200	30	60	Gross requirements								450		
						Scheduled receipts										
						Available	110	110	110	110	110	110	110	0		
						Net requirements								340		
						Planned order receipts								340		lead time offset
						Planned order releases						340				
F	1	2	52	30	20	Gross requirements								450		
						Scheduled receipts										
						Available	2	2	2	2	2	2	2	0		
						Net requirements								448		
						Planned order receipts								448		
						Planned order releases						448				
A	2	4	50	20	30	Gross requirements				50		448				
						Scheduled receipts				50						replacement parts ordered from field
						Available	0	0	0	0	0	0				
						Net requirements				0		448				
						Planned order receipts						448				
						Planned order releases		448								
C	2	2	60	20	30	Gross requirements						448				from F
						Scheduled receipts										
						Available	10	10	10	10	10	0				
						Net requirements						438				
						Planned order receipts										
						Planned order releases				438						
B	2	4	150	20	30	Gross requirements						340				from G
						Scheduled receipts										
						Available	100	100	100	100	100	0				
						Net requirements						240				
						Planned order receipts						240				
						Planned order releases		240								
D	2	2	52	20	30	Gross requirements				50		340				from G; replacement parts ordered from field
						Scheduled receipts										
						Available	2	2	2	0		0				
						Net requirements				48		340				
						Planned order receipts				48		340				
						Planned order releases		48		340						
E	2	1	500	300	150	Gross requirements						3152		1800		from H×4; from G×4 + F×4
						Scheduled receipts										
						Available	50	50	50	50	50	0	0	0		
						Net requirements						3102		1800		
						Planned order receipts						3102		1800		
						Planned order releases					3102		1800			

FIGURE 14.7
Material requirements plan

structure tree, except it's now in a convenient computational format. We can see quickly how many of which components are required at each level for one complete chair.

Product Explosion To create a parent item we often need multiple units of a lower-level item. One unit of H, for example, requires four units of E. Hence, the planned order releases of 450 H in week 7 must be multiplied by four (4 × 450 = 1,800) to determine the gross requirements of E for week 7. This process is called *product explosion* or *bill of materials explosion.*

Low-Level Coding Often a single item exists in the product structures of multiple end items, or it exists in several levels of one product structure. Item E, for example, exists at both levels 1 and 2. To avoid duplicate or multiple requirements calculations for such an item, MRP by convention assigns the item to the lowest coding level in which it occurs in the product structure. Thus, E is treated as a level 2 item; gross requirements are determined from the planned order releases of its parents, items F, G, and H.

Using MRP Outputs for Materials Decisions

From Figure 14.7 we see that to maintain the planned production schedule, planned order releases for items A, B, and D must be acted on in the current week. These cells are the *action buckets.* The action is to release (launch) an order for the quantities in the planned order release/period 1 cell. MRP merely indicates what actions are needed to meet the MPS goal; now management must act to "make things happen"—to cause (control) the productive system to execute so that it gets the results it wants.

Keeping MRP Current in a Changing Environment

MRP is not a static system; it is responsive to new job orders from customers and current shop conditions, as well as changes anticipated for the future. Consequently the MRP system must be updated with current information and, at the same time, it must facilitate stable production operations in the face of continual change. Four aspects of MRP—pegging, cycle counting, updating, and time fences—are vital elements in this dynamic environment.

Table 14.2 Indented bill of materials for Model H chair

Level	Quantity	Part ID	Description
.1	1	F	Seat/front-leg subassembly
..2	1	A	Seat/front-leg frame
..2	4	E	Fastener
..2	1	C	Seat
.1	1	G	Back/rear-leg subassembly
..2	1	B	Back/rear-leg frame
..2	4	E	Fastener
..2	1	D	Back
.1	4	E	Fastener

Pegging Various disruptions occur in materials plans. *Pegging* is a procedure for identifying which components are affected when a change occurs in any single item. Pegging shows the level-by-level linkages of components and their time-phased status in the MRP records. Figure 14.8 is an example; it shows the current records for end item A and for subcomponents B and C at two lower levels in the product structure.

If we discover that the 20 units of C (scheduled receipts) for period 1 cannot be completed, plans for B and A are affected. The planned order release for B (20 units in period 1) should be cancelled because its supporting materials (C) won't be available. Consequently, the planned order release for 20 units of A in period 2 will be futile and should be cancelled unless special action is taken now to obtain the 20 units of B that are required for week 2.

Similarly, if the master scheduler increases week 7's gross requirements for A from 10 to 30 to meet a special customer order, the pegging procedure traces down through the records to identify associated changes at lower levels. The planned order release for A in week 6 is raised from 20 to 30, and the associated requirements for B and C are changed accordingly. The pegging procedure shows exactly which items' plans must be changed.

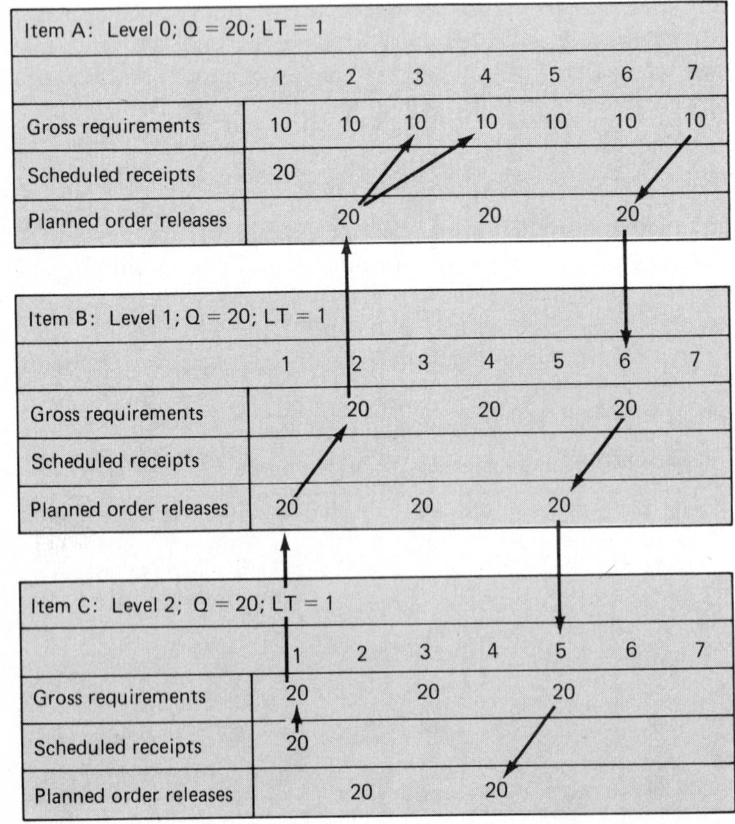

Item A: Level 0; Q = 20; LT = 1	1	2	3	4	5	6	7
Gross requirements	10	10	10	10	10	10	10
Scheduled receipts	20						
Planned order releases		20		20		20	

Item B: Level 1; Q = 20; LT = 1	1	2	3	4	5	6	7
Gross requirements		20		20		20	
Scheduled receipts							
Planned order releases	20		20		20		

Item C: Level 2; Q = 20; LT = 1	1	2	3	4	5	6	7
Gross requirements	20		20		20		
Scheduled receipts	20						
Planned order releases		20		20			

FIGURE 14.8
Pegging the MRP records

Cycle Counting Accurate data records are a must in MRP; otherwise, production schedules can't be maintained, deliveries will be missed, and labor and equipment inefficiencies will result. *Cycle counting* is a procedure for ensuring that on-hand physical inventories correspond to the quantities shown in the MRP records. With cycle counting, components are monitored and counted, including deductions for defective units, at each stage of production and in storage areas on a regular basis. Then the MRP records are updated, weekly or daily, to reflect these actual inventory counts. The subsequent updated records indicate where special adjustments are warranted in production schedules due to excesses and shortages of components at different work centers.[2]

Updating When job orders and other shop transactions occur, the MRP system must be updated. Changes can occur in the master production schedule or the inventory status file (such as revised lead times), or when engineering changes or product redesign modify product structures. Two updating approaches are available—the *regenerative* and the *net change* methods—and they differ in updating frequency. The regenerative approach completely reprocesses the entire set of information and recreates the requirements plan from beginning to end. It reprocesses the production plan at regular intervals, often weekly, and produces a complete, updated plan.

Net change systems, on the other hand, reprocess only those portions of the previous plan that are directly affected by informational changes. They update the production plan each time a change is posted and exploded throughout the system. The updated output contains those parts of previous plans that have changed. To do this, net change systems can require substantial computer access and rather elaborate computer programs. The net change systems do not seem to be as well received by users.

Time Fence As you can see, the dynamics of the MRP environment create potential confusion; if left unchecked, the changes can lead to unstable and erratic shop operations (called *system nervousness*). Stability is gained by using *time fences* in the MRP system. The time fence is incorporated into the MPS and is the shortest lead time from raw material to finished production for an end item. Within this time fence, the MPS is fixed; rescheduling is not allowed, except under unusual circumstances.[3] Thus, for the model H chair (Figure 14.6), the time fence can be found by using the longest normal lead time at each level of its product structure plus the longest lead time for purchased materials (not shown in Figure 14.6). The longest lead times at levels 0, 1, and 2 are 1, 2, and 4 weeks, respectively, so the time fence will be 7 weeks plus the raw materials lead time. Within this time fence, the MPS becomes frozen and the associated order releases are called *firm planned orders*.

---

[2]Various methods for cycle counting are described in T. E. Vollmann, W. L. Berry, and D. C. Whybark, *Manufacturing Planning and Control Systems* (Homewood, Ill.: Richard D. Irwin, Inc., 1984), Chap. 3.

[3]System nervousness and time fences are discussed in D. W. McLeavy and S. L. Narasimhan. *Production Planning and Inventory Control* (Boston: Allyn & Bacon, Inc. 1985), Chap. 8.

Lot Sizing

The MRP system generates planned order releases, which trigger purchase orders for outside suppliers or work orders for internal subcomponent production. Associated with each order is a setup cost—all the costs of placing and receiving an order. This raises the question of how much to order; one must consider the tradeoff of ordering costs and holding costs. Various lot sizing policies are possible. In our example for the model H chair, we assumed *lot-for-lot ordering;* order size equals net requirements for a given period. In MRP systems, economic considerations often result in order quantities that are larger than a single period's net requirements so that holding and ordering costs balance out. The *EOQ technique, the Wagner-Whitin algorithm* (an optimal procedure), and others can be used, some of which are more elaborate and expensive than others.[4]

One lot sizing method, the *part-period method,* does not provide an optimal lot size, but it is a low-cost method that approaches optimality.[5] It generates various order sizes by considering holding versus ordering costs. In the top half of Table 14.3 we see a series of net requirements for an item; in lot-for-lot ordering, this would result in seven separate orders. Assume that ordering cost (setup) per order is $100 and holding cost is $0.50 per part per period, based on ending inventory for that period. Using lot-for-lot orders, the total ordering cost for the horizon is $700, and, if the item is ordered and received at appropriate times, holding cost is zero as shown in the lower half of the table.

Looking at the part-period method, we know that an order must be placed to meet the net requirement of 50 units for week 1. If we increase this order size to include the 80 units needed in week 2, we incur a holding cost of $40 (80 units × $0.50/week) to store the 80 units from week 1 until they are used in week 2. This larger batch is less costly than the alternative of placing two separate orders ($200 ordering costs), so the order size should be increased from 50 to 130 units. Should it be increased even further? If it also included the 40 units needed for period 3, the additional holding costs of $40 (40 units × 2 periods × $0.50/unit/period) would raise cumulative holding costs to $80 for this order. Since this cumulative cost is less than the $100 additional ordering cost, the order size should increase to 170 units. Increasing the order size by still another 90 units (required for week 4) would require carrying these 90 units for three extra weeks at a cost of $135 (90 units × 3 periods × $0.50/unit/period), which would raise cumulative holding costs to $215. Since this $135 exceeds the

[4]See William A. Ruch, "Economic Lot Sizing in MRP: The Marriage of EOQ and MRP" (Paper presented at the 19th Annual Conference, American Production and Inventory Control Society, Atlanta, Ga., October 1976). See also Harvey M. Wagner and Thomson M. Whitin, "Dynamic Version of the Economic Lot Size Model," *Management Science* 5, no. 1 (October 1958), 89–96. A comparative evaluation of various lost sizing and sequencing rules is given in Joseph R. Biggs, "Heuristic Lot-Sizing and Sequencing Rules in a Multistage Production-Inventory System," *Decision Sciences* 10, no. 1 (January 1979), 96–115. See also E. Steinberg and H. A. Napier, "Optimal Multi-Level Lot Sizing for Requirements Planning Systems," *Management Science* 26, no. 12 (December 1980), 1258–71.

[5]See W. L. Berry, "Lot Sizing Procedures for Requirements Planning Systems: A Framework for Analysis," *Production and Inventory Management* 13, no. 2 (1972), 19–34; Wagner and Whitin, "Dynamic Version of the Economic Lot Size Model."

Table 14.3 Reordering patterns and inventory-related costs for two lot sizing rules

Inventory situation (patterns)									
Period (week)	1	2	3	4	5	6	7	8	
Net requirement	50	80	40	90	0	60	120	80	
Units in order received: (part-period rule)	170	0	0	150	0	0	200	0	
Inventory-related cost for two rules[a]									*Total cost*
Lot-for-lot rule									
Holding cost	0	0	0	0	0	0	0	0	$700
Ordering cost	$100	$100	$100	$100	0	$100	$100	$100	
Part-period rule									
Holding cost	$60	$20	0	$30	$30	0	$40	0	$480
Ordering cost	$100	0	0	$100	0	0	$100	0	

[a]Ordering cost/order = $100; holding cost/item/period = $.50.

$100 ordering cost, we cannot economically justify including these 90 units in the order to be received in week 1. We therefore order 170 units to be received in week 1, and this order meets our requirements for weeks 1, 2, and 3. We must place a subsequent order to meet the requirements of week 4 and future weeks. Table 14.3 shows the order receipts pattern of the part-period method and its resulting costs, as compared with the lot-for-lot method for the example situation. Note that the part-period rule outperformed the lot-for-lot rule by $220 in this example.

DETAILED CAPACITY PLANNING

Each time the MRP system is updated we face the question of whether shop capacity is sufficient to implement the current plans. *Detailed capacity planning* is a technique that addresses this question and it does so in more detail than the rough-cut method we presented in Chapter 10. New information from MRP permits some refinements that were unavailable at the rough-cut level. Let's see how this MRP information is used in detailed capacity planning (also called *capacity requirements planning).*

Reconsider the chair manufacturer that was discussed previously; we'll do a detailed capacity analysis for component A (the frame for seat/front legs) shown in the product structure tree, Figure 14.6. A route sheet (Table 14.4) has been developed for component A; it lists the operations sequence, the work centers, the lead times in each center, as well as the standard setup and run times. This routing information, obtained from engineering and production records, is used for evaluating the capacity requirements for item A.

To visualize the time-phased capacity requirements, we first construct the *operation set-back chart* for the end item, chair model H.[6] The

[6]Set-back charts are described in Vollmann, Berry, and Whybark, *Manufacturing,* Chap. 4.

Table 14.4 Component A: route sheet

Operation Number	Work Center	Lead Time (weeks)	Standard Times (hours) Setup Time/Batch	Operation Run Time/Unit
1	Metal cutting	1	1.0	0.05
2	Metal forming	1	3.0	0.20
3	Drilling	1	0.5	0.04
4	Finishing	1	2.0	0.15

abbreviated chart in Figure 14.9 shows details from the route sheet only for component A; details for the other components are omitted.

We can see from the set-back chart that the future capacity demands on the four work centers by component A depend on the planned order releases of its parent item, component F. It also depends on how many component A's, if any, are already finished and available in inventory. This information is provided in the current MRP record for component A, shown in Figure 14.10. The gross requirements for A were calculated from the planned order releases of its parent item, component F (not shown). We see that planned order releases for A are desired in weeks 1 through 4. Each work center's labor-hour requirements (capacity) created by these planned orders are calculated from the standard time data (Table 14.4) and recorded in Table 14.5.

The resulting capacity requirements take into consideration the projected availability of 10 units of component A for week 5; only 60 net units in week 5, rather than the gross requirement of 70, require metal cutting capacity in week 1. Additional capacity requirements in these same four work centers will arise from component B, the back frame, and from

FIGURE 14.9
Partial operation set-back chart for chair model H

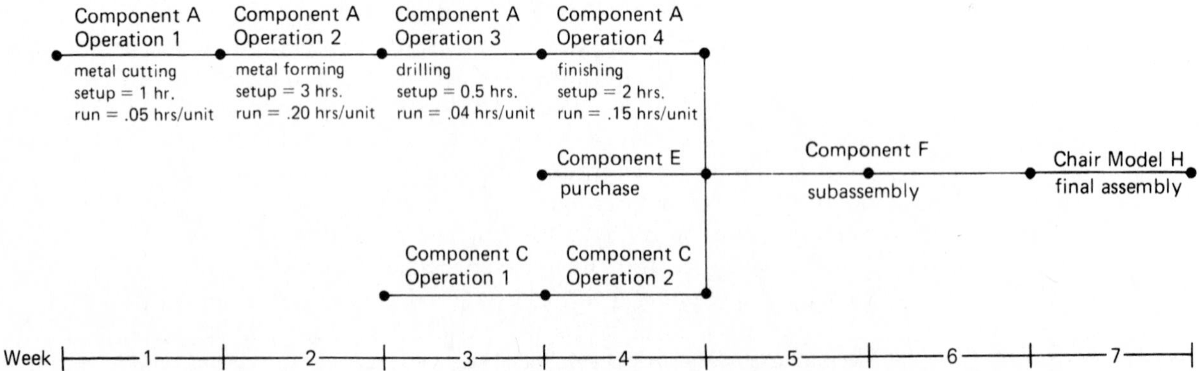

Component A (seat/front frame) LT = 4		Period 1	2	3	4	5	6	7	8
Gross requirements		80	90	90	90	70	70	70	90
Scheduled receipts		70	70	70	80				
Available	70	60	40	20	10	0	–	–	–
Net requirements		–	–	–	–	60	70	70	90
Planned order receipts						60	70	70	90
Planned order releases		60	70	70	90				

FIGURE 14.10
Current MRP record: component A

other chair models in the product line. By combining all the requirements from all sources (products), detailed capacity planning provides accurate estimates of the time-phased capacity demands on the work centers.

LIMITATIONS AND ADVANTAGES OF MRP

The limitations of MRP stem from the conditions that must be met before it can be used. A computer is necessary; the product structure must be assembly-oriented; bill of materials and inventory status information must be assembled and computerized; and a valid master schedule must exist. Another consideration has to do with data integrity. Unreliable inventory and transactions data from the shop floor can wreck a well-planned MRP system. Training personnel to keep accurate records is not an easy task, but it is critical to successful MRP implementation. In general, the system must be believable, accurate, and useful to its users or else it will become an expensive ornament that is bypassed in favor of informal, ad hoc systems.

Table 14.5 Capacity requirements (hours) for four work centers

Work Center	Week 1	2	3	4	5	6	7
Metal cutting	4.0[a]	4.5	4.5	5.5			
Metal forming		15.0	17.0	17.0	21.0		
Drilling			2.9	3.3	3.3	4.1	
Finishing				11.0	12.5	12.5	15.5

[a]1 hour setup + 0.05 hours/unit × 60 units = 4.0 hours.

The dynamic nature of the MRP system is a vital advantage. It reacts well to changing conditions; in fact, it thrives on change. Changing conditions from the master schedule for several periods into the future can affect not only the final required part but also hundreds, even thousands, of component parts. Because the production-inventory data system is computerized, management can make a new MRP computer run to revise production and procurement plans that react quickly to changes in customer demands as reflected in the master schedule.

MRP User Experiences

In 1979, Anderson and Schroeder reported preliminary results of an MRP user study sponsored by the University of Minnesota and the American Production and Inventory Control Society (APICS).[7] Questionnaires were mailed to approximately 1,700 industrial production/inventory control managers. The respondents' ideas about some major characteristics, problems, and benefits of MRP systems are shown in Table 14.6. Some users reported implementation problems—lack of communications about MRP within the company, lack of company expertise, and inadequate support from marketing and manufacturing personnel—all of which were

Table 14.6 **Selected MRP system and environment characteristics (based on user responses)**

Characteristic of System/Environment	Representative Measure of This Characteristic for All Respondents
Use regenerative updating method	70%
Use weekly updating of MPS	57%
Use pegging	55%
Use cycle counting	61%
Have automatic lot sizing by computer	45%
Employ *weekly* time bucket	70%
Initiated MRP system after 1971	76%
Number of weeks in MPS	40 (average)
Installation cost (exclusive of operating cost)	\$424,000 (average)
Estimated eventual system cost (exclusive of operating cost)	\$715,000 (average)
Product data: produce both made to order and to stock	70%
Type of manufacturing: both assembly and fabrication	83%
Number of end items (per plant)	1,546 (average)
Number of parts and components (per plant)	12,445 (average)
Number of levels in bill of materials (per plant)	6.2 (average)

Source: Anderson and Schroeder, "A Survey of MRP Implementation and Practice."

[7]The data in this section are from John C. Anderson and Roger G. Schroeder, "A Survey of MRP Implementation and Practice" (Paper presented at the 10th Annual Conference, American Institute for Decision Sciences, New Orleans, November 1979) and an earlier paper, "A Survey of MRP Implementation and Practice" (MRP Implementation Conference sponsored by the Twin Cities APICS Chapter and the University of Minnesota, Minneapolis, Minn., September 1978). See also J. C. Anderson, R. G. Schroeder, S. E. Tupy, and E. M. White, "Material Requirements Planning Systems: The State of the Art," in eds. McLeavey and Narasimhan, *Production Planning,* 277–91.

viewed as more severe than computer hardware/software problems. When asked for *the* major problem in implementing MRP in their firm, the two most frequent answers were "education of personnel" and "top management support."

Production/inventory control managers rated the accuracy of information in their production processes. These managers felt the least accurate information they had, overall, was on capacity (and capacity planning), market forecasts, and shop floor control. Their most accurate information was bill of materials records; this was followed by master production schedule and inventory records.

Users estimated present and future benefits of MRP as well. They cited greater inventory turnover, reduced delivery lead time, increased success in meeting delivery promises, reductions in internal production adjustments to compensate for unavailable materials, and reductions in the number of materials expediters.

It is evident from the results of this study that MRP is an improvement over previous production planning and control systems for many users. Its applications are growing as operations managers continue to develop better methods for materials management.

MANUFACTURING RESOURCE PLANNING (MRPII)

Historically, most MRP information systems were developed on a segregated basis, rather than as part of a highly integrated information system. More recently, however, other information subsystems throughout the organization have been logically related to the MRP system. Bills of materials data, for example, could be shared with an engineering information system data base; order release and order receipts data could be shared by the order billing and accounts payable information systems; and inventory status data from MRP could become part of marketing and/or purchasing information systems. This type of information integration, in fact, is exactly the impetus for MRPII, the new generation of manufacturing planning and control systems.

Manufacturing resource planning (or "closed loop" MRP) is an integrated information system that steps beyond first-generation MRP to synchronize all the aspects (not just manufacturing) of the business. The MRPII system coordinates sales, purchasing, manufacturing, finance, and engineering by adopting a focal production plan and by using one unified data base to plan and update the activities in all the systems.[8]

As shown in Figure 14.11, the process involves developing from the overall business plan, a production plan that specifies, generally, monthly levels of production for each product line over the next one to five years.

[8]See V. Chopra, "Productivity Improvement Through Closed Loop MRP (Part One)," *Production & Inventory Management Review and APICS News*, March 1982, 18–21. See also V. Chopra, "Productivity Improvement Through Closed Loop MRP (Part Two)," *Production & Inventory Management Review and APICS News*, April 1982, 49–51.

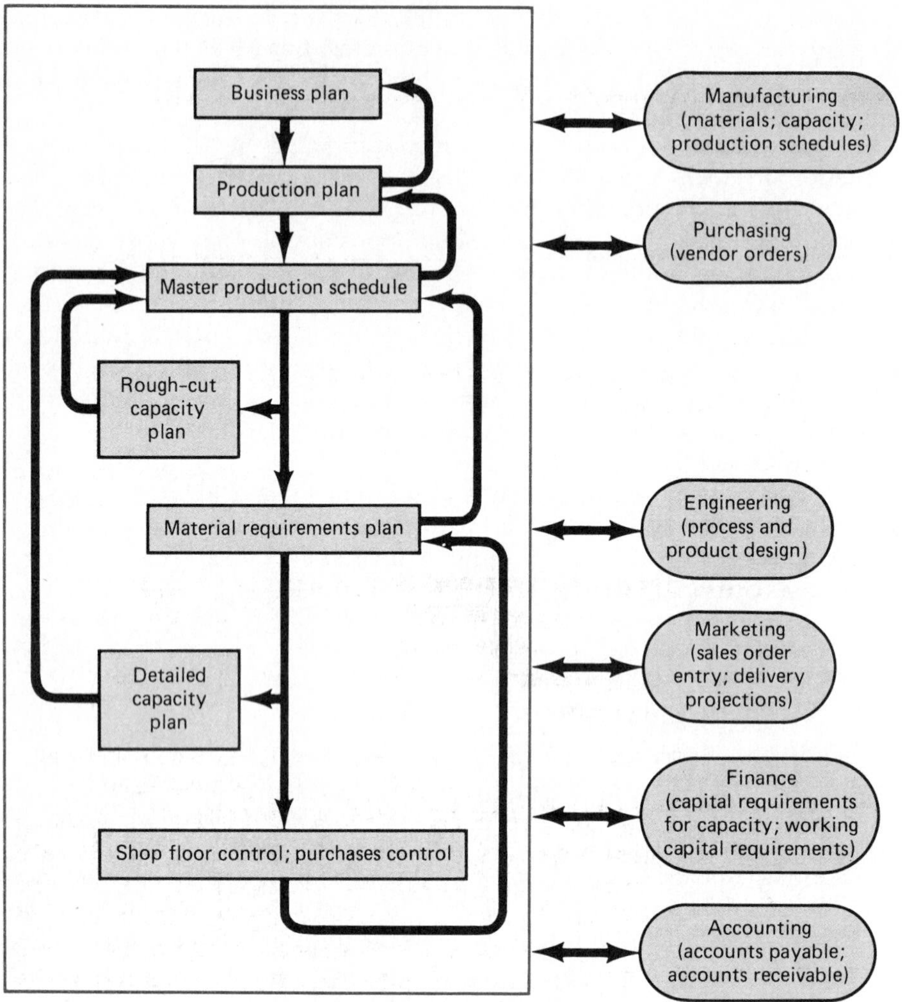

FIGURE 14.11
MRPII: An integrated system for planning and control

Since this production plan affects all the functional departments, it is developed by the consensus of executives for whom it subsequently becomes the "game plan" for company operations. Production is then expected to produce at the committed levels, the sales department is expected to sell at these levels, and finance will ensure adequate financial resources. Guided by the production plan, the master production schedule specifies the weekly quantities of specific products to be built. At this point a check is made to determine whether the capacity available is roughly adequate to sustain the proposed master schedule. If not, either the capacity or the master schedule must be changed. Once settled, the master schedule is used in the MRP logic, as previously described, to create materials requirements and priority schedules for production. Then, a detailed capacity requirements evaluation determines whether the necessary capacity exists for producing the specific components at each work center during the scheduled time periods. If not, the master schedule is revised to reflect the realities of the limited available capacity. After a realistic, capacity-feasible schedule is developed, the emphasis shifts to *execution* of the plan; purchase schedules and shop schedules are generated. From these schedules, work center loadings, shop floor control, and vendor follow-up activities can be determined to ensure that the master schedule is implemented.

One use of the MRPII system is to evaluate various business proposals. If, for example, the output of product X increases by 20 percent in weeks 15 to 20 and that of Y decreases by 15 percent in weeks 10 to 15, how would operations and profitability be affected? The system can simulate how purchases and, hence, accounts payable are affected, when deliveries to customers and accounts receivable occur, what capacity revisions are needed, and so on. The company-wide implications of the proposed change can be evaluated, and the actions of the various departments can be coordinated toward a common purpose.

PURCHASING

Manufacturing, wholesale, and retail firms depend upon the contribution of purchasing (or the procurement function) to secure the materials, supplies, and services to achieve their mission. Most of the companies that use MRP systems rely on purchasing for reliable inputs from outside suppliers. Accordingly, purchasing is an important boundary function that supports operations by acquiring major resources for the conversion process. For manufacturing firms involved in assembly, it is not unusual for the cost of purchased parts and materials to exceed, as a percent of total product cost, the value added internally to the product through manufacturing and assembly. The importance of the purchasing function to the firm's performance and to operations performance is substantial.

Materials management is a term used in manufacturing environments to bring together under one manager all the planning, organizing, and control activities associated with the flow of materials into an organization. *Physical distribution* is an even broader term encompassing materials management *flows into* the organization as well as *storage* and transportation *flows out* as finished products to customers. In the context of operations management, we focus here on the narrower *purchasing function,* which involves providing materials, supplies, and services from outside vendors (suppliers). Accordingly, purchasing is an important boundary function that supports operations by acquiring major resources for the conversion process.

Purchasing Objectives

The objectives of purchasing can be summarized as efficiently providing fairly valued materials, supplies, and services in a timely manner. We view the following objectives as particularly important to operations:

1. *Value.* Value is the combination of price and quality that provides

what is needed technically, at a good competitive price. This does not always translate into low price, although price is certainly a qualifying, if not winning, discriminator for many vendors.

2. *Schedule.* On time, just-in-time delivery. Schedule reliability is crucial.
3. *Investment minimized.* Through careful analysis, the economics of order size, carrying costs, and stockout costs determine the investment level. For example, quantity discounts must justify the larger investment (for a larger order) or investment unnecessarily increases.
4. *Efficient administration.* Included here are executing a low-cost purchasing function, effectively coordinating activities with internal functions (operations, engineering, etc.), and developing and maintaining good external relations with vendors.

Purchasing System

An effective purchasing system must clearly understand the purchase requirements, identify and develop qualified sources of supply, minimize the total cost of supply through careful analysis and decision making, establish price and value, and administer the purchase. Executing these activities involves professional management, good computer resources (microcomputers make item and vendor file maintenance affordable to nearly all), and recognition and support by executives throughout the organization.

Purchasing Requirements Typically, purchasing receives an item requisition that states quantity, description, and the date needed. These internally generated requests are necessary because management allows only purchasing to deal with outside vendors—the proven, most efficient approach for acquisitions. Requisitions, however, are not always clear. Purchasing must seek clarification and understanding. At times this requires facilitating vendor-requisitioner interactions for clarifying specifications and intent.

Sources of Supply Qualified sources of supply are identified from salespersons, personal knowledge, advertisements, requisitioners, executives (higher authorities), trade and industry associations, peers (other purchasing professionals), company records, and many other sources. Still, there are times when vendors must be developed to meet the specific needs of an organization. Quality, reliability, and understanding of one's business are all important requirements. There is much to learn about developing vendor relationships from the Japanese, who develop relationships with fewer suppliers, develop "family" relationships, and make longterm commitments to the supplier.

Cost of Supply Useful approaches for evaluating supply costs include analyzing supply item histories, make-or-buy decisions, value analysis, traditional inventory economic analysis, and discounts. Also useful in cost control are evaluating the unit cost over time through simple historical statistical analysis of prices paid by vendor and evaluating vendor performance. Make-or-buy decisions include issues such as operations capability, need for production secrecy, investments required, volumes, importance to manufacturing, and so on. The analysis balances technical feasibility, capacity, and economic factors. Value analysis determines the required function of the item and then questions everything else, often ascertaining if less-expensive materials could be used. Traditional inventory analysis and quantity discounts were covered in detail in Chapters 12 and 13.

Prices and Value To a great degree, the central function of purchasing is to obtain better prices than if purchasing was totally decentralized. Federal and state laws regulate pricing practices, particularly making illegal price fixing and different pricing for the same item and quantity to different customers. Common sources for prices are lists, quotations, market prices, competitive bids, and direct negotiations.

Administering the Purchase Once specifications, cost evaluation, supplier identification, and price/value have been established, the purchase order is issued. Later receipt (receiving), authorization of payment, record keeping, and in some cases expediting are accomplished. These administrative functions must all be performed efficiently and in a timely manner to support operations, or the benefit of a centralized purchasing function is lost.

SUMMARY

This chapter introduced us to the basics of material requirements planning (MRP) as a material management information system that enables managers to improve operations efficiency, shorten delivery lead times to customers, and reduce inventory levels in many organizations today. We saw that MRP is applicable in environments where end products are produced from many demand-dependent subcomponents, assemblies, and materials with a known and stable sequence of product buildup. With information inputs from bills of material, inventory status files, and the master production schedule, it was illustrated how the MRP processing logic provides time-phased plans for materials procurement and utilization. For each component in the product structure, MRP was seen to show current and planned activities—open shop orders, planned order releases, scheduled receipts—for each period in the planning horizon.

MRP was shown to be especially useful in complex operations where new customer orders are arriving for a variety of products and where shop orders for various parts and components are in different stages of completion. These numerous transactions were accommodated through periodic system updating with accurate shop status data. Discussed were ways to facilitate stable production operations in the face of these continual changes: adopt procedures such as pegging, cycle counting, and time fences. These procedures were shown to enable easy tracing of which components are affected by a change, to ensure that actual materials availabilities coincide with planned amounts, and to freeze the near-term production plans so that imminent shop schedules are more predictable.

CASE

Solar Fabricators, Incorporated

Solar Fabricators, established in 1975, specializes in manufacturing components and supplies for residential construction. Its most successful product line is Solar Seal Window Assemblies, which consists of two independent products, a "main module" (one large standard-size window assembly) and the "secondary module" (a smaller standard-size window assembly). These and the other Solar products, including replacement subcomponents for field servicing, are sold directly to large building and construction contractors throughout the Sunbelt states. The master production schedule for these products calls for gross requirements of 2,000 units in week 12 and 3,000 units in week 16 for the main module; 1,600 units in week 11 and 2,500 units in week 16 for the secondary module; 400 units in week 7 for the installation tool for field needs of the main module, and 600 units in week 4 for the measurement fixture for field needs of the secondary module. For all items, scheduled receipts, available units, safety stock, on-hand units, and allocated units are zero. Solar Fabricators wishes to know which of two lot sizing methods, lot-for-lot ordering or the part-period method, would be most advantageous for its material requirements planning efforts. Production data are given in the accompanying table.

Item ID	Item Level	Item Description	Parent	Quantity Required/ Unit of Parent Item	Source of Supply	Procurement Lead Time (weeks)	Setup or Ordering Cost/Order[a]	Holding Cost/Unit/Week
				Main Module				
A	0	Packaged window set ready for shipping			SFI[b]	1	$ 400	$1.00
B	1	Packing container	A	1	OS	2	100	0.10
C	1	Window set	A	1	SFI	3	2,100	0.80
D	2	Measurement fixture	C	1	OS	3	1,800	0.10
E	2	Installation tool	C	1	OS	2	200	0.05
F	2	Framed window	C	1	SFI	3	1,600	0.60
G	3	Frame screw	F	4	OS	1	300	0.10[c]
H	3	Rubber gasket seal	F	1	OS	3	700	0.10
I	3	Glass panel	F	2	OS	4	1,200	0.30
J	3	Metal frame	F	1	OS	2	600	0.20

Secondary Module								
AA	0	Packaged window set ready for shipping	—	—	SFI	1	$350	$0.80
BB	1	Packing container	AA	1	OS	2	100	0.10
CC	1	Window set	AA	1	SFI	2	700	0.60
DD	2	Measurement fixture	CC	1	OS	3	1,800	0.10
E	2	Installation tool	CC	1	OS	2	200	0.05
FF	2	Framed window	CC	1	SFI	2	1,400	0.50
G	3	Frame screw	FF	4	OS	1	300	0.10[c]
HH	3	Rubber gasket seal	FF	1	OS	3	900	0.10
II	3	Glass panel	FF	2	OS	4	1,400	0.20
JJ	3	Metal frame	FF	1	OS	2	500	0.20

[a]Includes all costs of placing, processing, setup, and receiving an order. A purchase order for multiple items from a single supplier results in a 20 percent reduction of ordering costs per order.

[b]SFI means produced internally by Solar Fabricators; OS means purchased from outside supplier. Items B and BB are purchased from one supplier. Items D and DD are purchased from one supplier. All other items are supplied by different suppliers.

[c]Cost/week for holding 10,000 frame screws in inventory.

REVIEW AND DISCUSSION QUESTIONS

1. Outline the purposes of MRP and explain how an MRP system can achieve these purposes.
2. Identify the basic issues involved in capacity management and describe how these are treated in detailed capacity planning.
3. Find or create example data illustrating inventory-related cost advantages of part-period versus lot-for-lot sizing policies.
4. Compare the cost tradeoffs involved in choosing among the following lot sizing rules: lot-for-lot, EOQ, and the part-period methods.
5. Explain the role of the master production schedule and how it relates to the other elements of an MRP system.
6. What is cycle counting? Explain how and why it is used in MRP systems.
7. Consider a product structure consisting of four levels. Suppose, for one of the lower-level items in the structure, that a cycle count reveals that 10 fewer units are available than is shown in its current MRP record. Show how pegging is a useful procedure for this situation. Why?
8. Identify the pros and cons of frequent versus infrequent updating of MRP systems. What variables should the system designer consider in selecting an updating cycle?
9. How many time periods should be included in the time fence for an end item? Under what conditions should the time fence be violated by master production scheduling changes?
10. What information is needed for detailed capacity planning? Where does this information come from? Show how it is used in a capacity analysis.
11. Of what use are route sheets and operation set-back charts in MRP systems?

12. Within the context of overall planning and scheduling systems for operations, explain the role of MRP.
13. In what ways do material planning systems differ from reactive materials systems? Describe the advantages and limitations of each of these two types of systems.
14. Explain how a discontinuous or lumpy demand pattern can exist for a subcomponent of a parent item, even though the parent item has a smooth demand pattern.

PROBLEMS

Solved Problem

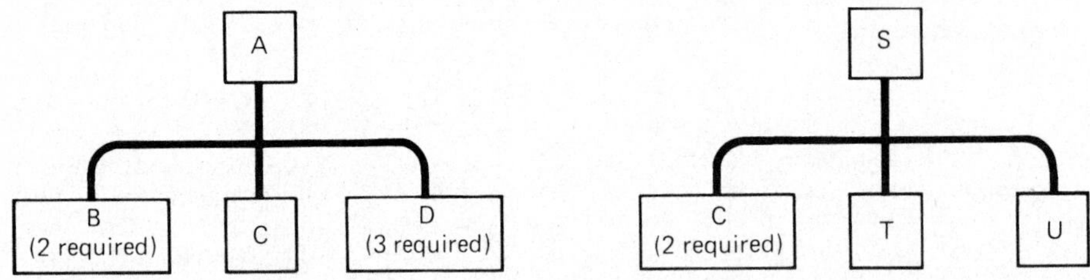

FIGURE 14.12

1. The product structures for end items A and S are shown in Figure 14.12. All items have a one-week lead time. Currently, there are 20 units of A available, 15 units of S, and 90 of C. The standard lot sizes are 50 for A, 35 for S, and 100 for C. The master production schedule calls for 20 units of item A and 15 units of item S for each of the next five weeks. An open order for 100 units of item C is scheduled for receipt in week 1. Create the MRP records for items A, S, and C.

		Week				
Item A		1	2	3	4	5
Gross requirements		20	20	20	20	20
Scheduled receipts						
Available	20	0	30	10	40	20
Planned order releases		50		50		
Item S						
Gross requirements		15	15	15	15	15
Scheduled receipts						
Available	15	0	20	5	25	10
Planned order releases		35		35		

Item C

Gross requirements		120		120
Scheduled receipts		100		
Available	90	70	120	70
Planned order releases			100	

Reinforcing Fundamentals

2. Creative Wood Products manufacturers interior accessories for homes. One of their products, the Trophy Rack, is shown in Figure 14.13. Draw the product structure diagram of the Trophy Rack, label it, and identify the low-level codes for its items.
3. Product 800 is made from two 801 subassemblies, three 802 subassemblies, and two 803 subassemblies. An 801 subassembly consists of two units of component 406 and two units of part 407. The 802 subassembly is made from two units of component 205 and one unit of part 603. An 803 subassembly consists of one part 407, one 950 component, and three 747 subassemblies. A 747 subassembly is made from six units of item 910, three units of item 205, and one unit of 942. Create a product structure tree for product 800, and determine how many units of each component is required to produce 100 units of product 800.
4. Create an indented bill of materials for product 800 using the data in Problem 3.
5. Each unit of end product X requires two units of subcomponent Z. The lead time for X is one week, the standard order quantity is 40 units, and current availability is 30 units. Gross requirements for the next six weeks are 25, 30, 20, 15, 15, and 20 units, respectively. For item Z, lead time is two weeks, standard order quantity is 80 units, and current availability is 90 units. A scheduled receipt for 80 Z's is due in week 1. Develop complete MRP records for X and Z.
6. Route sheets for components A and B are shown below. Planned order releases at the beginning of the current week are 60 units for item A and 40 units for item B. Each work center has an 8-hour capacity each day (5 days/week).
   (a) Create an operations set-back diagram for components A and B.
   (b) Determine the capacity requirements of the planned order releases for the current week.
   (c) In what sequence should the jobs be scheduled at each work center?

Route Sheet: Component A
Lead Time = 1 Week

Operation Sequence Number	Operation Work Center	Lead Time (days)	Standard Times (hours)	
			Setup Time/Batch	Operation Run Time/Unit
1	100	1	2	.1
2	200	1	1	.05
3	100	1	1	.05
4	300	1	2	.15

(Cont.)

Route Sheet: Component B Lead Time = 1 Week				
			Standard Times (hours)	
Operation Sequence Number	Operation Work Center	Lead Time (days)	Setup Time/Batch	Operation Run Time/Unit
1	200	1	2	.15
2	100	1	1	.05
3	300	1	1	.10

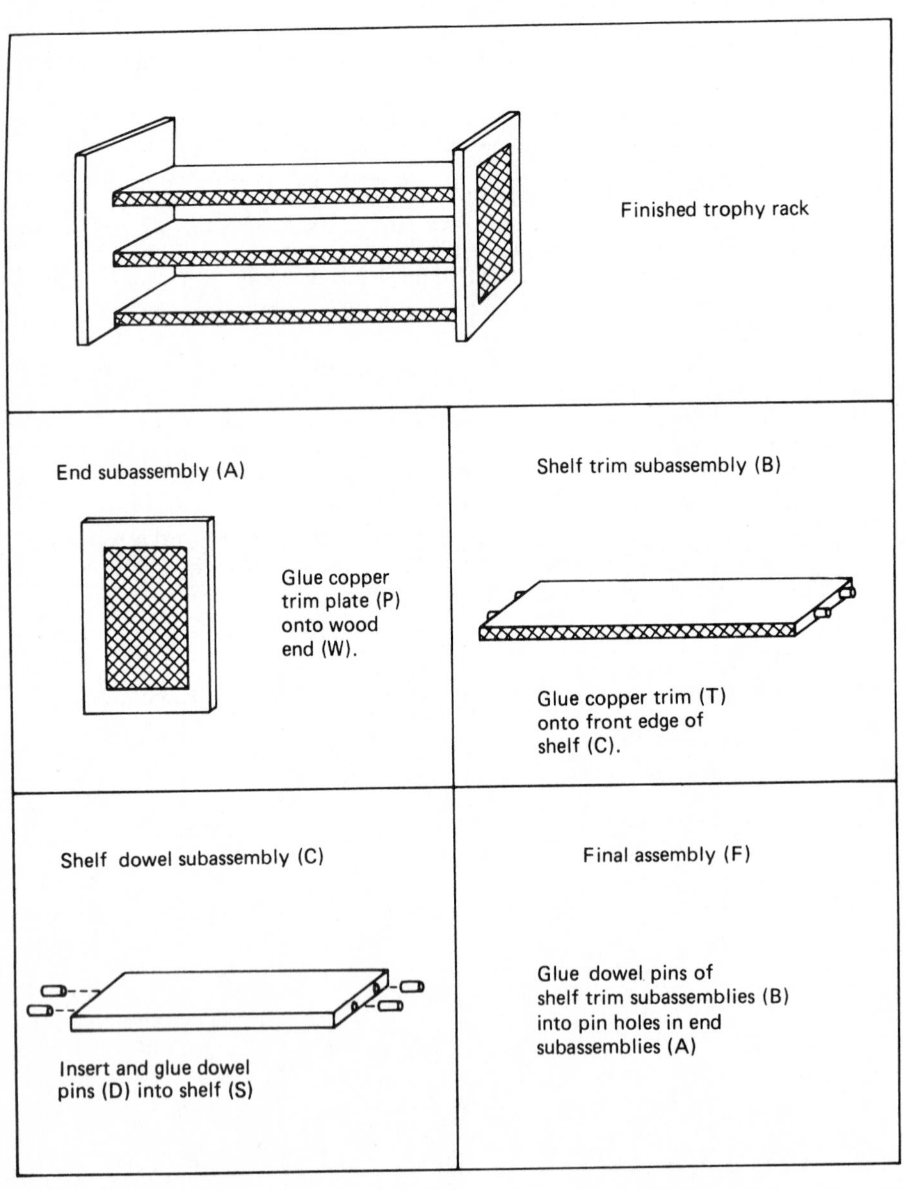
Finished trophy rack
End subassembly (A)
Glue copper trim plate (P) onto wood end (W).
Shelf trim subassembly (B)
Glue copper trim (T) onto front edge of shelf (C).
Shelf dowel subassembly (C)
Insert and glue dowel pins (D) into shelf (S)
Final assembly (F)
Glue dowel pins of shelf trim subassemblies (B) into pin holes in end subassemblies (A)

FIGURE 14.13

7. Product 601 is made from three 740 subassemblies, two 810 subassemblies, and one 900 subassembly. A 740 subassembly consists of one 309 component and two units of part 207. The 900 subassembly is made from two units of component 400 and one unit of part 782. An 810 subassembly consists of one 309 component, one 721 component, and two 682 subassemblies. A 682 subassembly is made from one unit of component 400 and one unit of part 207. Create a product structure tree for product 601 and determine how many units of each component are required to produce 100 units of product 601.
8. Determine the net requirements for items X and Y below:

	Item X	Item Y
Gross requirements	600	50
Scheduled receipts	100	0
Available	0	50
Planned order receipts	0	50
Planned order releases	700	0

9. Patterson Assemblies has a gear assembly that requires part GA211, with material requirements scheduled as shown below. Average demand is 83 units/week, the cost of placing an order (setup) is $200, and the inventory carrying charge is $1.50/unit/week. Holding costs are calculated assuming that average inventory is centered within each week.

Week number	0	1	2	3	4	5	6	7	8
Requirements	—	20	120	80	0	160	194	20	70
Quantity ordered	—								
Beginning inventory	0								
Ending inventory	0								

Using the lot-for-lot ordering rule, complete the MRP record for part GA211. What action needs to be taken if it is now the beginning of period 1? Calculate the total of ordering and holding costs over eight periods.

10. Refer to the data in Problem 9. Using the Wilson EOQ formula (deterministic case), complete the MRP record. Calculate the total of ordering and holding costs over eight periods. What assumption is violated by using the EOQ formula in this case?
11. Refer to the data in Problem 9. Using part-period total cost balancing as an ordering rule, complete the MRP record. Calculate the total of ordering and holding costs.
12. Compare the total costs from the results of Problems 9, 10, and 11. Which rule appears best? Examining the cost components for each rule, briefly explain the difference in the behavior of the various rules.
13. Carcord, Inc., has received an order for 300 units of product G to be completed eight weeks from now. The product structure diagram is shown in Figure 14.14. There is no stock on hand (available) and none on order. Determine the order release data for all necessary orders.
14. For the situation in Problem 13, Carcord has just been advised by the supplier of component L that a delivery delay of two extra weeks is expected because of an equipment breakdown. What impact will this delay have on Carcord's deliveries of product G?

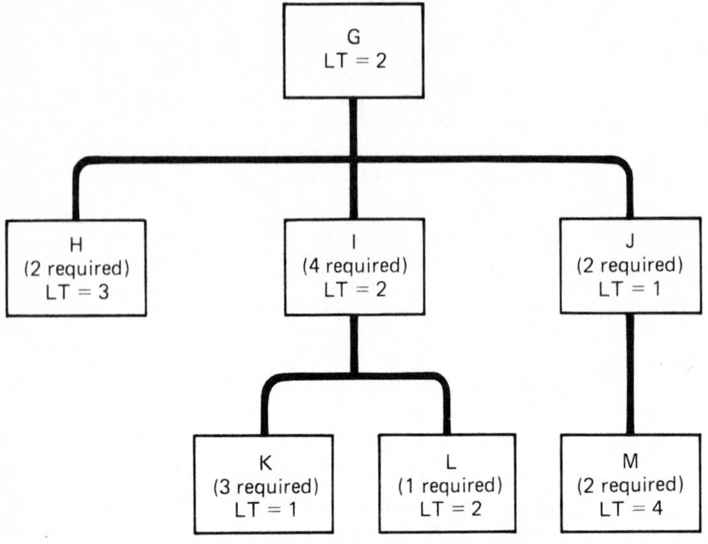

FIGURE 14.14

Challenging Exercises

15. Carcord, Inc., has received an order for 100 units of product 501 with the product structure shown in Figure 14.15. The quantity in parentheses is the number of units of that component that is required by its parent item. There is no stock on hand (available) and none on order. Determine the order release data for all necessary orders.

16. Ambrex, Inc., has received an order for 70 units of product 20 and 50 units of product 40, to be delivered in 12 weeks. The product structures for products 20 and 40 are shown in Figure 14.16. The quantity in parentheses is the number of units of that component that is required by its parent item. Ambrex has on hand (available) 300 units each of components 31 and 37; there is no stock on hand or on order for other components. Determine the sizes and timing of planned order releases necessary to meet delivery commitments for products 20 and 40.

17. After planning for the conditions stated in Problem 16, Ambrex receives a request for an additional order for 50 units of product 40. The Ambrex sales representative wants to know if she can promise delivery within ten weeks, or earlier if possible, to the potential customer. As the production planner, realizing that your assembly operation can, at most, work on assembling 50 units of product 40 at any given time, what is your response to the sales representative's inquiry?

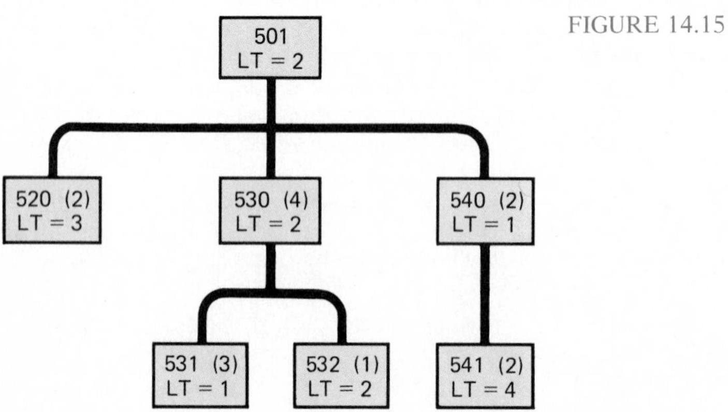

FIGURE 14.15

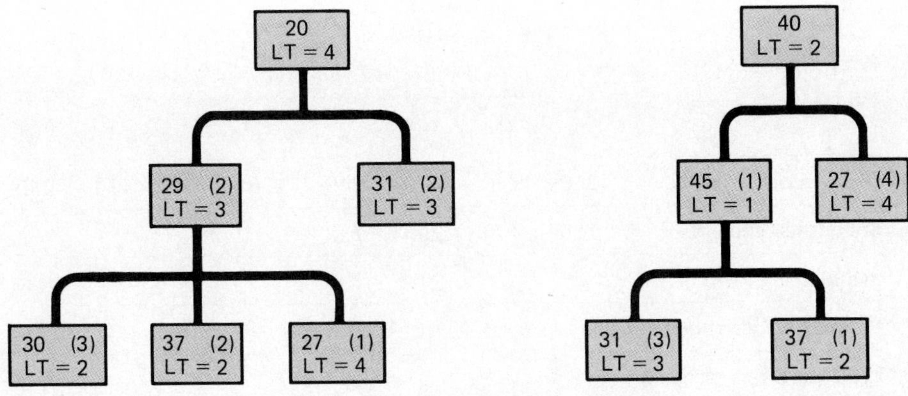

FIGURE 14.16

18. Components A and B are level 2 items in the product structure of the chair shown in Figure 14.6. Their route sheets are shown below along with their current MRP records and status reports on open orders.

Route sheet: Component A: Frame for seat/front legs

			Standard Times (hours)	
Operation Number	Work Center	Lead Times (weeks)	Setup Time/Batch	Operation Run Time/Unit
1	Metal cutting	1	1	.05
2	Metal forming	1	3	.20
3	Drilling	1	.5	.04
4	Finishing	1	2	.15

Route sheet: Component B: Frame for back-rest/back legs

			Standard Times (hours)	
Operation Number	Work Center	Lead Times (weeks)	Setup Time/Batch	Operation Run Time/Unit
1	Metal cutting	1	1	.07
2	Metal forming	1	1	.15
3	Drilling	1	1	.07
4	Finishing	1	2	.12

Current MRP records

Component	Week							
A	1	2	3	4	5	6	7	8
Gross requirements	200	240	240	240	170	170	170	230
Scheduled receipts	170	190	200	230				
Available 140								
Planned order releases								
Lead time = 4 weeks Lot-for-lot ordering								
B								
Gross requirements	200	240	240	240	170	170	170	230
Scheduled receipts	190	200	240	240				
Available 50								
Planned order releases								
Lead time = 4 weeks Lot-for-lot ordering								

Status of open orders

Orders Scheduled for Receipt in Week	Operations Completed as of Now	Operations Remaining
1	1, 2, 3, 4	none
2	1, 2, 3	4
3	1, 2	3, 4
4	1	2, 3, 4

(a) Complete the MRP records for items A and B.
(b) Prepare a capacity requirements report covering the next seven weeks for the four work centers.

19. Foley, Inc., has received an order for 70 units of product A and 50 units of product S, to be delivered in 12 weeks. The product structures for products A and S are shown in Figure 14.17. Foley has on hand (available) 300 units each of components C and E; there is no stock on hand or on order for other components.

(a) Determine the planned order releases for products A and S.
(b) After planning for the conditions stated above, Foley receives a request for an additional order for 50 units of product S. The Foley sales representative wants to know if she can promise delivery within 11 weeks, or earlier if possible, to the potential customer. As the production planner, realizing that your assembly operation can, at most, work on assembling 50 units of product S at any given time, what is your response to the sales representative's inquiry?

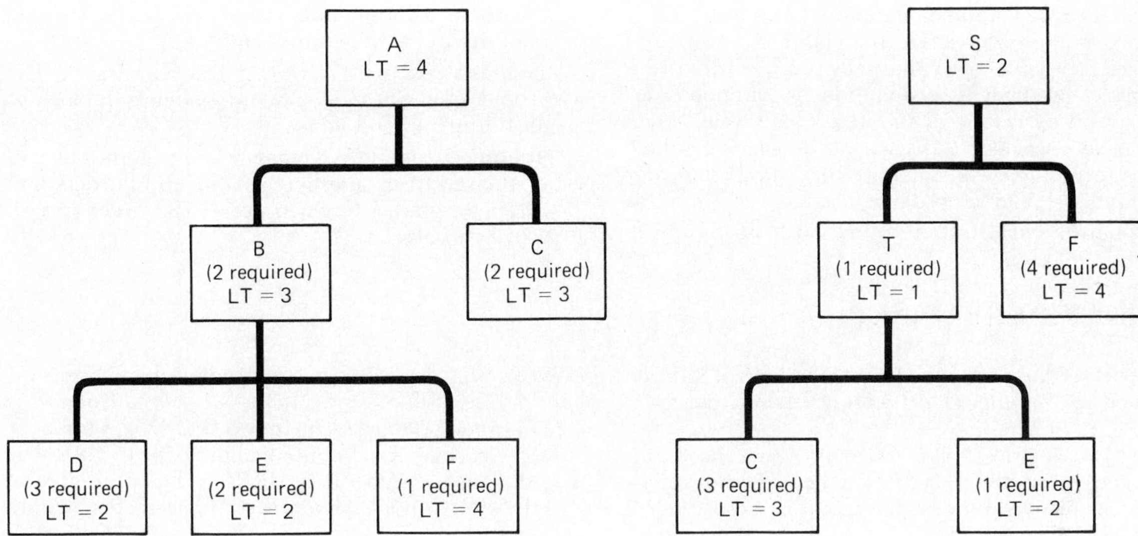

FIGURE 14.17

GLOSSARY

Available Quantity of an item expected to be available at the end of a time period for meeting requirements in future time periods. This includes scheduled receipts plus planned order receipts minus gross requirements for the period, plus amount available from the previous period.

Bill of materials Describes product buildup details of an item, including all subcomponent items, their buildup sequence, the quantity needed for each, and the work centers that perform the buildup sequence.

Dependent demand Relationship between the demand for two or more items; when the demand is known for one item, the relationship tells us the demand for the other item(s).

Detailed capacity planning Iterative process of modifying the master production schedule and/or planned resources to create consistency between capacity and the production schedule.

Gross requirements Overall quantity of an item needed in each future time period to meet planned output levels. Planned output for end items is obtained from the master production schedule. Planned output for lower-level items is obtained from the MRP system.

Inventory status file Complete documentation of the inventory status of each item in the product structure, including item identification, on-hand quantity, safety stock level, quantity allocated, and lead time.

Item level Relative position of an item in the product structure; end items are high-level; preliminary items in the product structure are lower-level.

Lead-time offsetting Process of determining the timing of a planned order release; backing off from the timing of a planned order receipt by an amount equal to the length of lead-time.

Lot-for-lot ordering Lot sizing policy in which order size equals net requirements for the period.

Master production schedule Describes the quantity and timing of each end product to be produced in each future period in the production planning horizon.

Net change system MRP system in which updating the plan involves reprocessing only those portions of the previous plan directly impacted by informational changes.

Net requirements Net quantity of an item that must be procured to meet the scheduled output for this period. It is calculated as gross requirements minus scheduled receipts for the period minus amount available from the previous period.

Part-period method A lot sizing policy that generates varying order sizes by considering holding versus ordering costs.

Planned order receipts Quantity of an item that is *planned* to be ordered so that it will be received in this time period to meet net requirements for the period. The order has not yet been placed.

Planned order release Quantity of an item that is *planned* to be ordered and the planned time period for releasing this order that will result in the order being received when needed. It is the planned order receipt offset in time by the item's lead time. When this order is placed (released), it becomes a scheduled receipt and is deleted from planned order receipts and planned order releases.

Product explosion Determination from the product structure and planned order releases the needed quantities of all subcomponent items.

Product structure A product tree showing the levels and quantities of subcomponent relationships constituting an end item.

Scheduled receipts Quantity of an item that will be received from suppliers as a result of orders that have been placed (open orders). The order has already been placed.

SELECTED READINGS

American Production and Inventory Control Society, *Capacity Planning and Control.* Washington, D.C.: APICS, 1979.

Berry, W. L. and D. Clay Whybark, "Research Perspectives for Materials Requirements Planning Systems," *Production and Inventory Management* 16, no. 2 (1975), 19–25.

"Computer Takes on MRP, Savings Multiply," *Industrial Engineering* 11, no. 3 (March 1979), 26–27.

McLeavey, D. W., and S. L. Narasimhan, *Production Planning and Inventory Control.* Boston: Allyn & Bacon, 1985.

Miller, Jeffrey G., and Linda G. Sprague, "Behind the Growth in Material Requirements Planning," *Harvard Business Review* 53, no. 5 (September–October 1975), 83–91.

Orlicky, Joseph A., *Material Requirements Planning.* New York: McGraw-Hill, 1975.

Peterson, L. D., "Design Considerations for Improving the Effectiveness of MRP," *Production and Inventory Management* 16, no. 3 (1975), 48–68.

Ruch, William A., "Economic Lot Sizing in MRP: The Marriage of EOQ and MRP." Paper presented at the 19th Annual Conference, American Production and Inventory Control Society. Atlanta, Ga., 1976.

Vollmann, T. E., Berry, W. L., and D. C. Whybark, *Manufacturing Planning and Control Systems.* Homewood, Ill.: Richard D. Irwin, 1984.

Wagner, Harvey M., and Thomson M. Whitin, "Dynamic Version of the Economic Lot Size Model," *Management Science* 5, no. 1 (October 1958), 89–96.

Whybark, D. C., and J. Gregg Williams, "Material Requirements Planning Under Uncertainty," *Decision Sciences* 7, no. 4 (October 1976), 595–606.

15

Managing for Quality

At Ford Motor Company we have adopted an operating philosophy to establish and maintain an environment which will result in never-ending improvement in the quality and productivity of products and services throughout the Company, its supply base, and its dealer organizations. The new philosophy requires that the Company improve the quality and productivity of every element of the business from planning through field service. This includes—but is not limited to—all products and services, people relationships, attention to customers' needs, profits, shareholders' investments, and management approaches. In the final analysis, we are "customer-driven."

MISSION

Our mission is to continually improve our products and services to meet our customers' needs, allowing us to prosper as a business and to provide a reasonable return for our stockholders, the owners of our business.

VALUES

- *People:* Our people are the source of our strength. They provide our corporate intelligence and determine our reputation and vitality. Involvement and teamwork are our basic human values.
- *Products:* Our products are the end result of our efforts, and they should be the best in serving our customers worldwide. As our products are viewed, so are we viewed.
- *Profits:* Profits are the ultimate measure of how efficiently we provide customers with the best products for their needs. Profits are required to survive and grow.

GUIDING PRINCIPLES

- *Quality comes first:* To achieve customer satisfaction the quality of our products and services must be our number-one priority.
- *Customers are the focus of everything we do:* Our work must be done with our customers in mind, providing better products and services than our competition.
- *Continuous improvement is essential to our success:* We must strive for excellence in everything we do: in our products, in their safety and value—and in our services, our human relations, our competitiveness, and our profitability.
- *Employee involvement is our way of life:* We are a team. We must treat each other with trust and respect.
- *Dealers and suppliers are our partners:* The Company must maintain mutually beneficial relationships with suppliers, dealers, and our other business associates.
- *Integrity is never compromised:* The conduct of our Company worldwide must be pursued in a manner that is socially responsible and commands respect for its integrity and for its positive contributions to society. Our doors are open to men and women alike without discrimination and without regard to ethnic origin or personal beliefs.

The overall effort must mobilize the entire work force in the pursuit of specific Company goals aimed at satisfying customer requirements for quality, value, and delivery.

John A. Manoogian
Executive Director—Product Assurance
North American Automotive Operations—Ford Motor Company
Dearborn, Michigan

Performance quality is crucial to the long-term survival of most businesses and government organizations. Each of us is aware, in varying degrees, of the international challenge to the North American automobile industry and the impact on quality and value. We thought it appropriate, therefore, to ask Mr. John Manoogian to comment on Ford Motor Company's quality, as he had a significant hand in developing quality strategies and supporting improvement in the 1980s at Ford. It is interesting that he chose to comment on quality in the context of Ford's mission, values, and guiding principles (the first of which is quality). We wanted to share his entire comment as our introduction to Chapter 15, "Managing for Quality." His introduction illustrates that quality is a major part of Ford's business objectives.

MANAGERIAL RESPONSIBILITY IN MANAGING FOR QUALITY

Managing for quality, the subject addressed in this chapter, begins and ends with managerial responsibility. Often there is no great desire on the part of managers to improve quality. Managers seem to be unaware of the urgency of the situation. Nationally, the need for a quality improvement effort seems to be gaining momentum; in fact, there are many barriers to such efforts. In this chapter we want to increase your *awareness* as to the importance of performance quality in operations and in both this and the next chapter to provide you with some alternative *analysis and program choices for improvement.* Should you become involved in, or responsible for, an operations function, the material in this and the next chapter, "Quality Analysis and Control," will help you in your decision making and make you aware of the alternatives available to your organization in seeking quality improvement.

How important is quality to an organization or nation? Peters and Waterman, in the popular management book *In Search of Excellence,* identify quality as a characteristic repeatedly identified in excellent corporations throughout the United States.[1] What about quality in other nations? In thinking about this issue, we return to the Japanese experience since World War II and ask many questions. How can a country of 100 million people achieve worldwide leadership in automobile manufacturing, steel production, shipbuilding, and consumer electronics? How can this be accomplished on an island the same size as California with no national resources except labor? What qualities do consumers admire in Japanese products? The answer is generally the same to these and similar questions—the Japanese understand and provide quality and value in their products.[2] Let's first briefly discuss the quality concept and then focus on managing for improving quality.

PRODUCT QUALITY

Output Quality

In manufacturing a product's important characteristics are specified when it is designed prior to its manufacture. These characteristics are called the *design specifications.* After the product has been produced, we can observe the extent to which it conforms to or deviates from the design specifications. *Product (output) quality is the appropriateness of design specifications to function and use as well as the degree to which the product*

---

[1]Thomas J. Peters and Robert H. Waterman, *In Search of Excellence: Lessons from America's Best-Run Companies* (New York: Harper & Row, Publishers, Inc., 1982).

[2]See Chapter 2 of this book, the sections on productivity and quality and on international productivity; Richard Tanner Pascale and Anthony G. Athos, *The Art of Japanese Management* (New York: Warner Books, 1981); Robert W. Hall, *Zero Inventories* (Homewood, Ill.: Dow Jones-Irwin, 1983); and Richard J. Schonberger, *Japanese Manufacturing Techniques: Nine Hidden Lessons in Simplicity* (New York: The Free Press, 1982).

conforms to the design specifications. Service (output) quality is similarly defined. As you know, output quality can apply to either products or services. We will ask you to make inferences from the discussion of products to service quality in this and the next chapter.

Previously we focused on product and process design. In production and operations, we often have limited affect on design. This is unfortunate, because the job of production focuses on output conformance to design. For the most part, our discussion of quality is about the somewhat narrower operations perspective involving conformance to a design. When there is close conformance between design and output characteristics, there is a high degree of product (output) quality. When there are important discrepancies, there is a low level of quality. Product quality can be seen to fall on a continuum ranging from very low to very high, as Figure 15.1 shows.

There are popular alternative concepts of quality, among these are the following:

- "Quality is fitness for use."
- "Quality is doing it right the first time—and every time."
- "Quality is the customer's perception."
- "Quality provides a product or service at a price the customer can afford."
- "You pay for what you get (quality is the most expensive product or service)."

Although we find each of these views to have merit, they have shortcomings as well. Our judgment is that little is accomplished by arguing over precise quality definitions or slogans. The key to managing for quality lies first in the awareness of the need to improve, and then selecting improvement techniques with the best chance for success. An understanding of product characteristics, product design, and process capability will assist us in becoming aware of quality issues in operations.

Product Characteristics All aspects of the product are not equally important to our customers. Usually, only some of them need be considered when assessing the level of quality. But which aspects are most important? Weight? Size? Shape? Color? Functional performance? *The important product characteristics are determined by the specific market goals of the organization and by the technical requirements of the important stages of the conversion process.* Often we must compromise between these two sources of quality requirements.

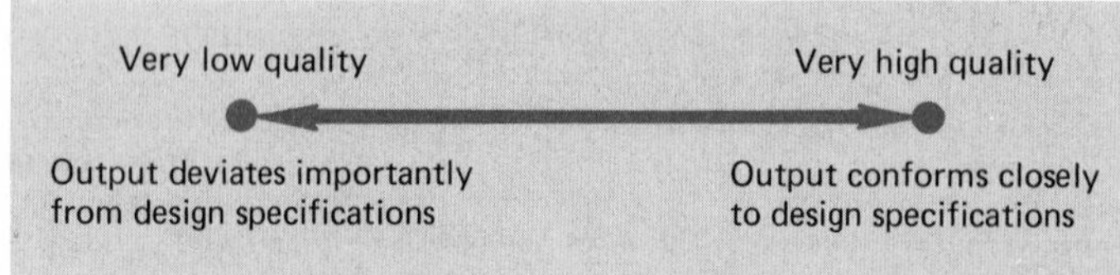

FIGURE 15.1
Degrees of output quality

Design Of two firms producing the same product, one may have to pay high costs to maintain an acceptable quality level, while its competitor can maintain the same quality at a much lower cost. The difference is often a result of the emphasis placed on quality considerations in the design phases of product development, prior to full-scale production. The old adage, "quality is *designed into* the product," holds true. The number of stages in the conversion process, the types of input resources needed, and the types of technical processes required to produce the output are all largely determined in the product design phase.

Process Capability *Process capability* is a quantified statement of *actual product uniformity* under normal working conditions. Instead of measuring various aspects of the process—attributes of the machine, worker, and so forth—one measures the results of the process, the attributes of the product. Process capability then becomes a statement about the *product* uniformity produced from a process. A typical process capability would, for example, state the diameter or length tolerances, scrap or waste material from cutting as a percent of total material inputs, and so forth. A process capability study is conducted over time. From a careful study one is able to determine the natural or inherent variability of the process (the instantaneous reproducibility) and the time-to-time variability. As the manager and employee strive for *continuous improvement,* process capability should change as well.

Of course product and process design does not end when production begins. Design often continues throughout the product life in the form of various redesign activities. These redesign needs are signaled by reliability studies, quality assurance programs, warranty costs, and customer complaints.

MANAGING FOR QUALITY PRODUCTS AND SERVICES

Now that we have an awareness of the quality concept, let's ask how managers actually go about—or should go about—establishing and reaching the quality levels desired. There are several significant steps in effectively managing for quality products and services, as illustrated in Figure 15.2. We have summarized the activities that operations managers must perform in order to establish an overall quality framework, as well as in carrying out the details to achieve the planned level of quality.[3]

The manager must first determine how quality fits into the overall organizational strategy. Then, more specifically, he or she must determine the role that quality will play in the manufacturing (or operations) strategy; the approach used in production or operations should comple-

[3]For an alternative summary view prepared for operations executives and students, see Everett E. Adam, Jr., and Eugene M. Barker, "Achieving Quality Products and Services," *Operations Management Review,* Winter 1987, pp. 1–8.

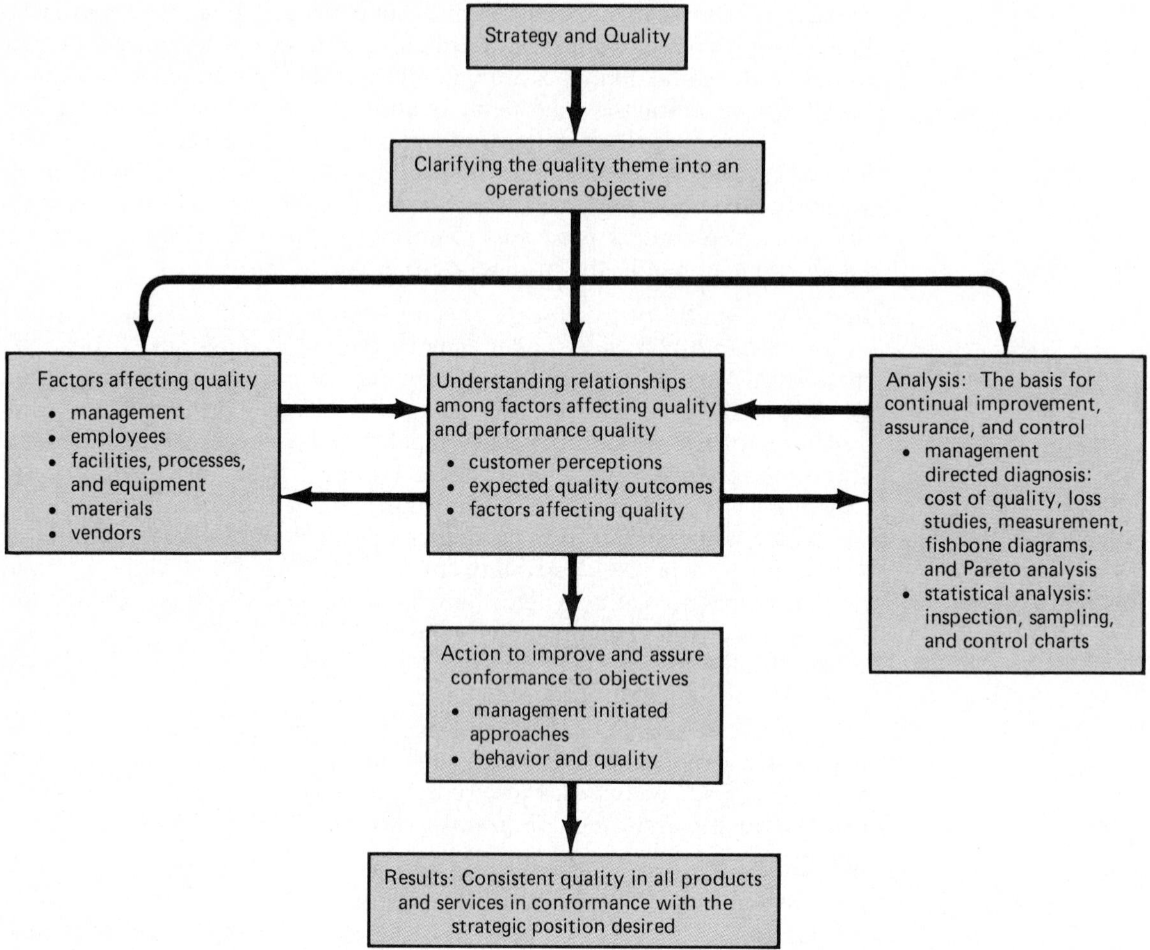

FIGURE 15.2
Managing for quality products and services

ment the overall strategy of the organization. Once this is accomplished, the quality theme must be clarified; it is essential that individuals at all levels within the organization comprehend quality goals.

For any organization there are key elements that affect quality. The effective manager must be able to identify these aspects—they typically include people, facilities, and materials—and seek to understand how they interact in his or her firm.

Once a strategy is developed and communicated and the key variables affecting quality are understood, the conversion function takes place. Products are manufactured. Parts are made. Services are generated. Customers are served. But, how do we know if we *are* conforming to plan? Are we seeking the continual quality improvement desired? With respect to quality, are processes under control? Are quality costs in line with expectations? Fortunately, there is a rich and thorough set of diagnosis and analysis techniques to assist the operations manager in answering these questions. Effective managers have found that statistical techniques, in particular, can be quite useful; these methods are stressed in the following chapter.

Upon completing analysis to identify potential areas for quality improvement, it is necessary to take action and give specific directions to assure performance quality. A variety of programs and techniques exists to help bring behaviors and processes into conformance with expectations. We survey several major programs in this chapter. Finally, we can observe the long-term results: consistent quality in all products and services in conformance with the strategic position desired. Let's now address each major block of Figure 15.2, with particular attention to the quality analysis and action (programs) issues; both are extremely significant in day-to-day operations management.

Strategy and Quality

In developing an operations strategy, market potential (demand) is related to operations capability. As product or service ideas emerge, a general production approach and sales plan are formed. The desired quality level for the product or service is defined. Executives must develop a quality expectation to guide the organization. Quality standards should be set for all activities that support the primary business goals—activities in accounting, finance, engineering, distribution, and administration—as well as for products and services directly consumed by the ultimate customer.

This linkage of strategy with quality is crucial if the firm is to have a consistent purpose. Not only do the Japanese understand the importance of this connection, North American chief executive officers do as well.[4]

EXAMPLE

Japanese manufacturing firms have developed company-wide quality control (CWQC) that has evolved from inspection-oriented quality control (prior to 1945), through a statistical quality control growth phase (1945–1955), through a total quality control growth phase (1955–1970), into what is now CWQC with rapid growth (1970–present). The thrust in a typical Japanese firm is to implement a "process" to promote never-ending improvement in the effectiveness and efficiency of all elements of a business. The goal of CWQC is to mobilize the entire work force in a pursuit of specific company goals aimed at satisfying customer requirements for quality, price, and delivery. The strategy used by an organization accepting CWQC is to improve the effectiveness and efficiency of every element in the business through the use of statistical thinking, managing with facts, and defect and error prevention. Japanese firms accepting CWQC stress these six elements in their approach:

[4]See, for example, comments by the CEOs of Packaging Corporation of American, Texas Instruments Inc., and Caterpillar Tractor Company, respectively: Monte R. Hayman, "PCA Quality," Packaging Corporation of America, 1984; Fred Bucy, "Quality" (Statement released by Texas Instruments, Inc.), October 1982; and Comments to the Shareholders, Lee L. Morgan, Chairman, and Robert E. Gilmore, President, Caterpillar Tractor Company, Annual Report, 1983, p. 5.

1. Quality is first in all business thinking and action.
2. Assure the quality of new product development.
3. Quality must be customer-oriented, not producer-oriented.
4. Consider the next step in any process as the customer.
5. Use a continuing "plan, do, check, action cycle" in all business elements.
6. Respect humanity.[5]

There are certainly many companies that stress quality as a corporate strategy, among them Boeing, Caterpillar, Hewlett Packard, and IBM. For example, a survey of CEOs by a major business publication asked the CEOs for their perception of the American companies with the highest quality products or services. Boeing was the top-rated company by these executives.

Clarifying the Quality Theme

A key to successful quality is first to set a strategy, and then effectively communicate this strategy as a theme to employees and customers. We have seen from several of the examples above the effort CEOs are taking in stressing a theme. As consumers we've seen the media presentations for products: Hallmark's "Mark of Excellence," Ford's "Quality Is Job #1," and General Electric's "Quality Is Our Most Important Product," to name but a few. Internally, companies also go to great lengths to stress the theme, goal, or quality thrust to employees. Some of the alternative "quality" definitions we explored stress this communication issue.

Key Elements Affecting Quality

A systems viewpoint helps us understand the key elements affecting quality. When we view the organization as a system that interacts externally with customers and vendors, we identify two key factors that specify and affect quality at the boundaries of the firm. Customers' desires should be the basis for organization quality objectives. Often in *service-oriented companies,* customers also participate in generating the service—setting quality standards and making sure they are met. Examples include joint participation at self-service gasoline stations, cafeterias, and discount department stores. Customers, to a great extent, serve themselves—and quality can vary widely from individual to individual. It becomes a challenge to design service systems to meet a particular quality level in such a shared labor situation.

Vendors are very important, especially to organizations purchasing a high percentage of their products. Progressive firms are moving toward vendor certification as a means of eliminating incoming inspection. In essence, certification makes the vendor a part of the company team.

---

[5]Company-Wide Quality Control (CWQC)," Report of the NAAO Product Assurance Committee, February 13, 1984.

Within an organization we find that management, employees, material, facilities, processes, and equipment all affect quality. Dr. Joseph Juran and Dr. W. Edwards Deming, specialists on Japanese quality, suggest that as much as 85 percent of the quality problems are *management* problems.[6] Their view is that management, rather than employees, has the authority and tools to correct most quality ills.

As *employees,* most of us have had opportunities to affect quality within an organization. Similarly, as students and professors, we daily see variations in quality. We know that some differences are individually determined. In a production environment, *materials* vary; high-quality materials are easier to work with than low-quality materials, and they often result in a labor savings. The key factor in production is often the degree of *variation*—there should be piece-to-piece consistency within a material lot and in subsequent lots. This is true for material used (inputs) as well as for products and services produced (outputs).

How do *facilities, processes,* and *equipment* affect quality? Tools wear out and break. Roofs sometimes leak and require fixing. Equipment needs to be in good repair so parts are made the same every time.

Understanding Relationships Among Factors Determining Quality

Customer Perceptions A progressive organization should have a well-established strategy for quality; one that is based upon customer perceptions regarding quality. Customer service after the sale of a product is often as important as the quality of the product itself. A customer service audit is one way of identifying customer perceptions concerning quality. This approach is equally meaningful for services and products. It is also useful for all services performed internally (for others in the firm). The following example illustrates how Caterpillar emphasizes quality from a customer perspective.

EXAMPLE Elements of Caterpillar Tractor Company's quality program include:

- Conducting two customer satisfaction surveys following each purchase, one after 300 hours of product use and the second after 500 hours of use
- Maintaining a centrally managed list of product problems as identified by customers from around the world
- Analyzing warranty and service reports submitted by dealers, as part of a product improvement program
- Asking dealers to conduct a quality audit as soon as the products are received and to attribute defects to either assembly errors or shipping damages

---

[6]W. Edwards Deming "On Some Statistical Aids Toward Economic Production" *Interfaces* 5, no. 5 (August 1975), pp 1–15; J. Juran *Upper Management and Quality,* 4th ed. (New York: Juran Institute, Inc., 1981).

- Guaranteeing 48-hour delivery of any part to any customer in the world
- Encouraging dealers to establish side businesses in rebuilding parts to reduce cost and increase the speed of repairs.[7]

Expected Quality Outcomes Throughout this book we have emphasized that people, materials, and processes are blended together to provide products and services for customers. These products and services have a quality attribute, the conformance to expectations. We've emphasized that these expectations should be customer-based rather than manufacturing- or engineering-based.

In reality, manufacturing and operations attempt to conform to internally (engineering or manufacturing) set specifications. The design must ensure that these internally set specifications are consistent with customer expectations. Further, design must also assure that specifications are accurately translated into the language of manufacturing and operations—bills of materials, drawings, route sheets, procedures manuals, job descriptions, and so forth. In manufacturing, this is the work of manufacturing engineering. There must be a customer-product or customer-service linkage, a well-managed interface with clear instructions and feedback to operations (where the work is actually performed). This is equally important for services and manufacturing organizations.

Factor Relationships It is necessary to be more specific than simply stating that people, materials, and processes are interrelated in producing quality products and services. What are the key variables in operations that affect product or service quality?

Although our general answer is "it depends upon the manufacturing or service situation," we need to clarify. The way resources are blended (technology), the relative emphasis of one resource over another (cost structure), and the skills and abilities of people are all crucial. Competition, pride, knowledge—the list can go on and on as to what contributes to quality performance. At this point attempts to definitively model these interrelationships are speculative at best.[8]

It is our opinion that advances in product/service design, statistical thinking, planned change, and selected behavioral interventions hold the most promise for contemporary operations managers attempting to improve quality.

---

[7]Hirotaka Takeuchi and John A. Quelch, "Quality Is More Than Making a Good Product," *Harvard Business Review* 61, no. 4 (July–August, 1983), 139–45.

[8]See, for example, a behavior-technology model of factors affecting quality in Everett E. Adam, Jr., James C. Hershauer, and William A. Ruch, *Productivity and Quality: Measurement as a Basis for Improvement,* 2nd Ed. (Research Center, College of Business and Public Administration, University of Missouri-Columbia, 1986), pp. 144–150.

ANALYSIS FOR IMPROVEMENT, ASSURANCE, AND CONTROL

Management-Directed Diagnosis for Quality

Quality analysis includes diagnosis and improvement techniques. Here we want to discuss diagnosis as a management-directed activity. In the next chapter we learn about statistical analysis as an aid for quality control and improvement.

The Cost of Quality If organizations systematically examined the cost of poor quality, they would be amazed at how expensive it is. As a percentage of total cost of goods sold, poor quality is often well in excess of 20 percent of sales. Where are such high costs located? How can one document these costs? Why haven't otherwise successful companies reduced such costs? These and similar questions can be addressed by examining four broad cost categories: prevention, appraisal, internal failure, and external failure.

Internal failure costs are perhaps the most commonly found and easiest costs to document. Accounting systems support scrap, rework, and similar costs. To a large extent, appraisal costs can also be estimated. In the traditional quality organization in the United States, much of the inspection process is staff and can be reflected as labor costs. This task is more difficult in a progressive, quality-oriented firm where every employee inspects his or her work as part of a job responsibility. However, even in this type of situation, costs can be estimated.

Prevention costs are more difficult to assess. Training, planning, measurement, vendor certification, equipment maintenance, and similar prevention activities can, however, be estimated. External failures —failures of the product or service after it leaves the facility and is being used or consumed—are much more difficult to assess. Field service costs, warrantee claims, and lost sales are all very real.

Although it may be a major effort for the accounting system to construct a cost estimate, the results of such an effort are usually worthwhile. Regardless of the data collection method, *top management will certainly stop and pay attention to a well-constructed and reasonably documented total cost of quality estimate.* It is an effective analysis tool to gain support for quality improvement efforts and expenditures. Evaluating the components of total quality costs can provide the astute operations manager with insight into areas with high potential for improvement.

Quality Costs and Assurance Quality assurance programs commonly involve systematic efforts to assess the overall level of output (final product) quality. They determine current quality levels and trends in these levels, and they make comparisons with the quality levels of competitors. This information is used in product and process redesign, market strategy, and product pricing decisions.

After product standards have been set by management, they must be checked. Since these product standards involve so many aspects of quality control, the costs of quality assurance are high. Prevention, appraisal, and internal and external failure costs previously discussed and outlined in Table 15.1 are all quality assurance costs.

Quality Cost Studies Once the costs of quality are understood, managers may conduct cost (or loss) studies to determine what actions should be taken, if any, to reduce overall costs. Consider, for example, the cost data collected and shown in Table 15.2. For the metal stamping company, the major cost categories are scrap, rework, in-process inspection, and customer returns—all failure and inspection costs. Two items, scrap and rework, account for $559,000 of the $889,700 total quality costs. An examination of prevention costs versus failure would lead one to question if more might not be expended to prevent poor quality and the costs associated with this failure level. A study such as this would be followed by more detailed cost analysis with recommendations for lower, overall costs for the coming six months.

Organizing for Quality

Often, quality control in manufacturing firms is organized in a way distinctly different from the way it is organized in service organizations. Usually, quality control in manufacturing is a staff function established to monitor, police, and assist in corrective action, while in service firms,

Table 15.1 Costs of quality assurance

Prevention (costs associated with design and planning of a quality control program)	Appraisal (costs involved in the direct appraisal of quality both in the plant and in the field)	Internal Failure (costs directly related to the occurrence of defective production within the plant)	External Failure (costs associated with the failure of a product or service in the field)
• QC administration and systems planning • Quality training • Quality planning (QC engineering work) Incoming, inprocess, final inspection Special processes planning Quality data analysis Procurement planning Vendor surveys Reliability studies • Quality measurement and control equipment • Qualification of material	• Testing • Inspection • Quality audits • Incoming test and inspection and laboratory acceptance • Checking labor • Laboratory or other measurement service • Setup for test and inspection • Test and inspection material • Outside endorsements • Maintenance and calibration • Product engineering review and shipping release • Field testing	• Scrap, at full shop cost • Rework, at full shop cost • Scrap and rework, fault of vendor • Material procurement • Factory contact engineering • QC investigations (of failures) • Material review activity • Repair and troubleshooting	• Complaints and loss of customer good will • Warranty costs • Field maintenance and product service • Returned material processing and repair • Replacement inventories • Strained distributor relations

Source: Adapted from J. W. Gavett, *Production and Operations Management* (New York: Harcourt Brace Jovanovich, Inc., 1968), pp. 401–2.

Table 15.2 **Quality costs Metal Stamping Company (six months)**

Quality Cost Category	Annual Quality Cost
Inspection expenses	
Raw material	$ 27,500
In-process and finished goods	111,000
Prevention expense	
Quality improvement project	7,500
Training new employees on quality	13,200
Tooling for quality improvement	3,500
Losses due to failure	
Down press time due to quality	74,000
Scrap	421,800
Rework	137,200
Customer returns	94,000
Total quality costs	$889,700

typically line managers and employees are responsible for quality. One survey of practices in manufacturing quality control had 173 firms responding.[9] Firms were rather uniformly represented by size (number of employees), except for the 30 percent of respondents with 1,001 to 5,000 employees. Two sizes of quality control departments predominated—36 percent of the respondents having 0–9 employees and 34 percent having more than 50 employees. Other department sizes were rather equally distributed.

It would be best, in our judgment, if quality control departments were deemphasized and eventually disbanded. As employees who produce goods and services are trained in statistical processes and are given the tools to improve and control their own outputs, they should be accountable for quality. This shifts the responsibility directly to the source of good quality (as well as errors)—the operative employee and his or her management. With this shift must come management support. The result of this change is inspection at the source of production by the participant in operations. There will no longer be a need for large quality control and assurance departments.

Breakthrough versus Control When seeking quality improvement, a distinction is often made between *sporadic* problems and *chronic* problems. The first are sudden bad changes in the status quo; the second are long-standing bad situations. Techniques for identifying sporadic problems and controlling the underlying processes are addressed in the next chapter. Chronic problems, on the other hand, require scientific problem solving to *breakthrough* to attain a higher quality performance level that the organization has not been able to achieve for a *long time, often years.*[10]

[9]Erwin M. Saniga and Larry E. Shirland, "Quality Control in Practice . . . A Survey," *Quality Progress* 10, no. 5 (May 1977), 30–33.

[10]See J. Juran and Frank M. Gryna, Jr., *Quality Planning and Analysis* (New York: McGraw-Hill Book Company, 1980), Chap. 5.

Arriving at a breakthrough to attaining higher quality requires convincing others of the need, identifying the few vital sources, organizing for new knowledge, analyzing, identifying resistance to change, acting to institute change, and freezing the change into place to gain lasting benefits. This process is very difficult to manage because chronic quality problems are often accepted as a way of life. Managers and employees are unwilling to admit to a better way of doing things, perhaps not even realizing there *is* a better way.

Japanese firms have demonstrated the usefulness of the breakthrough process, halving and then halving again the errors once accepted in manufacturing processes. They willingly aspire to attain levels of quality that many in North America and Europe have accepted as "unattainable." Now many have come to realize that our firms must have breakthroughs for quality so that the firms can remain competitive worldwide.

Measurement of Services Generally, service characteristics are more complex than product characteristics. They are harder to identify and measure. Consequently, measuring and subsequently controlling quality are frequently ignored in services. Although service quality is important, the characteristics that determine customer acceptance are often intangible, complex customer perceptions such as timeliness, employees' attitudes toward customers, and the physical environment where the service is delivered.

One approach has been directed at measurement in services. It describes a measurement procedure that was developed and tested in the Federal Reserve Banking System. The procedure is participative; quality measures are developed by those involved in the delivery of services. A good bit of the overall effort centers on definition—definition of process (system) boundaries, process components, and sources of variation (deviations). Measures are both *quality indicators* (such as number of errors or percent defective) and conceptually innovative *quality productivity ratios* (relating outputs to resource inputs for quality). This measurement procedure has been used in a variety of service functions—personnel, check processing, transfer of funds (banking), data processing, and production planning. Several large and medium-sized commercial banks and manufacturers, including Honeywell, Inc., have reported applications.[11]

Fishbone (Cause and Effect) Diagram

The *fishbone diagram* is a schematic model that provides a picture of the results from analyzing problems (effects) and the causes that contribute to them. Such diagrams are the results of a group effort to solve a problem creatively. These charts are constructed in structured group sessions. Quality problems are often addressed and diagrammed in a quality circle, a small group of co-workers who put forth and address quality and productivity issues relating to their work in an effort to improve group performance. Figure 15.3 illustrates an employee-prepared fishbone dia-

[11]See Adam, Hershauer, and Ruch, *Productivity and Quality*, pp. 152–83, for details of the procedure, case applications, references for personnel and check processing studies, and related studies.

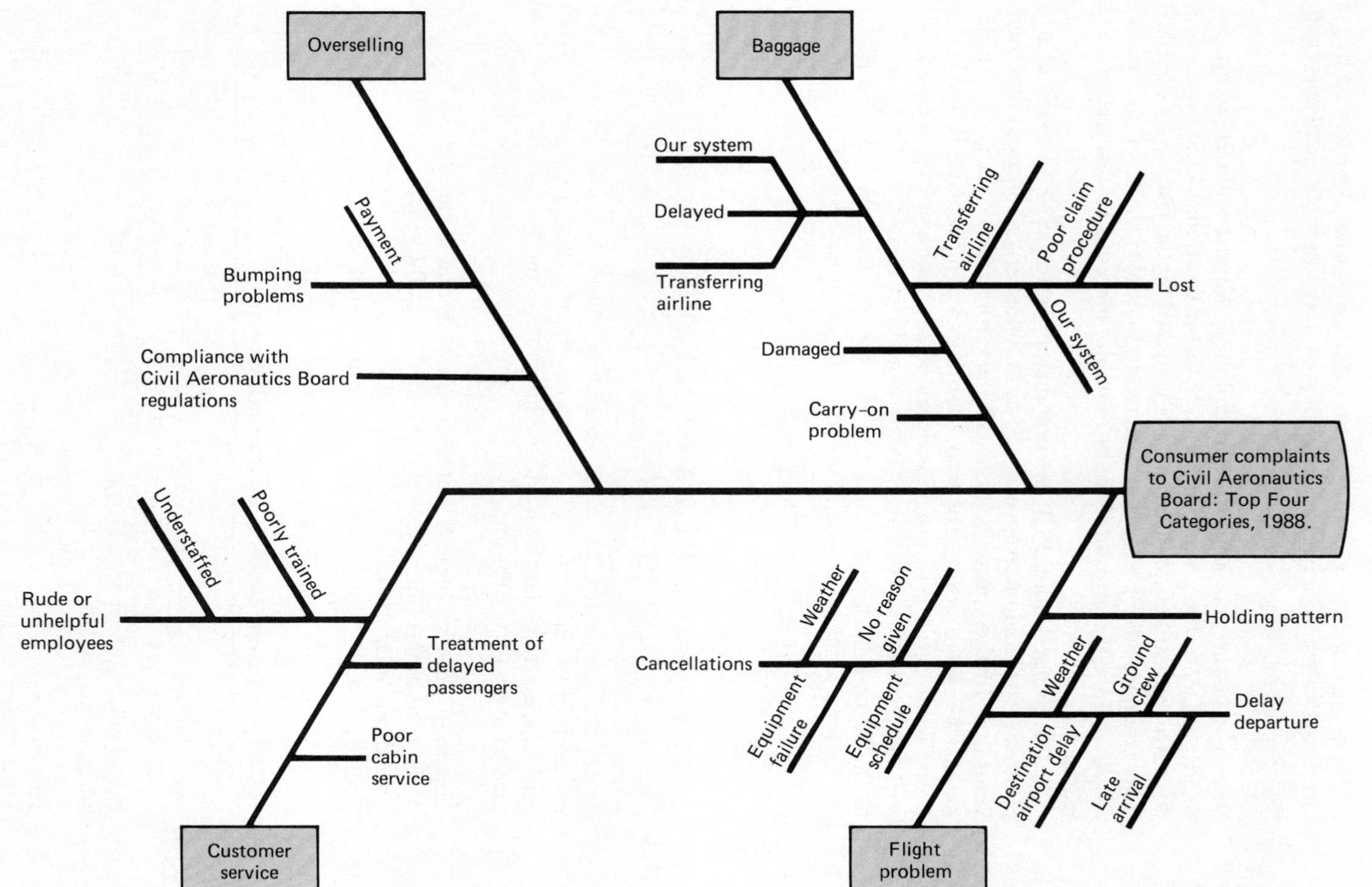

FIGURE 15.3
Cause and effect (Fishbone diagram of airline service quality)

gram for the top four consumer complaint categories experienced by an airline; problems with baggage handling, overselling, flights, and customer service.

Pareto Analysis

Quality costs are not uniformly distributed. Almost without exception, relatively few of the contributors account for the bulk of the costs. This "maldistribution" of quality costs is illustrated by the frequency distribution shown in Table 15.3, often referred to in quality diagnosis as a *Pareto analysis.* If we were to bar graph the table, it would be referred to as a histogram.

Examining Table 15.3 we see that operator errors contribute to photocopying quality costs as much as all other error sources combined. Would a further examination of operator errors show a similar maldistribution of sources of error? Table 15.4 demonstrates this to be so. If we further broke down regular operator large volume jobs in categories such as poor job instructions, inadequate attention to machine, and so forth, we would expect to find a *few vital sources* that primarily contribute to costs, rather than the *many trivial sources* that have a much lesser cost impact.

MANAGEMENT-INITIATED APPROACHES AND ACTIONS TO IMPROVE QUALITY

American companies are taking action to improve quality. Upon what research or premises are these firms developing their approaches? What actions are being taken by leading-edge firms to increase quality? We now turn to these two questions.

Contemporary Management-Initiated Approaches to Improving Quality

The most popular approaches to increasing quality awareness and improvement in the United States are based upon the teaching, writing, and consulting of Dr. W. Edwards Deming, Dr. Joseph M. Juran, and Philip B. Crosby. "Total quality control" programs exemplify the approaches of

Table 15.3 Quality losses in photocopying room

Class of Loss	Annual Quality Loss ($)	Frequency of Loss (%)	Cumulative Frequency of Loss (%)
Operator error	500.00	50.0	50.0
Dirty, spotted drum or glass	225.00	22.5	72.5
Low ink level	125.00	12.5	85.5
Paper misfeed	75.00	7.5	92.5
All other sources	75.00	7.5	100.0

Table 15.4 Operator error quality losses in photocopying

Type of Job	Annual Operator Error Loss ($)	Frequency of Operator Loss (%)	Cumulative Frequency of Operator Loss (%)
Regular operator Large-volume jobs	325.00	65.0	65.0
Irregular (customer) operator	100.00	20.0	85.0
Regular operator Small-volume jobs	50.00	10.0	95.0
Substitute operator	25.00	5.0	100.0

these men in varying blends. Let's briefly discuss each, providing references for the interested reader to pursue further.

Deming's Statistical Thinking Dr. Deming has worked closely with the Japanese since 1950. Rarely has an American received such respect in Japanese business circles. His approaches to quality improvement, analysis, and statistics are widely accepted by Japanese business. In fact, the highest quality award in Japanese industry, the Deming Prize, carries his name. What, then, does he propose?

Dr. Deming lays responsibility for quality improvement at management's doorstep. The *system* is generally the cause for inefficiency and low quality, according to Deming, and it is management's responsibility to *work on the system* (as workers work in the system). Deming's 14 principles stress design of product, specification of the service offered, measurement by simple statistical methods, and action on the causes identified by these methods. He stresses variation as a major manufacturing problem and proposes the use of control charts to assist in evaluating variation. Students of operations management can learn about Deming's philosophy by studying a set of video training tapes offered by the Massachusetts Institute of Technology's (MIT) Center for Advanced Engineering Study or by studying a book by Gitlow and Gitlow.[12]

Juran's Management Processes Through Quality Dr. Juran is a popular author, lecturer, and consultant. For decades, he has presented his views to American managers on management's role regarding quality improvement. Juran has an international background, and his message is managerial in nature. He addresses American management on issues such as rationality, analysis, and management processes in order to get at problems in quality. Although he uses statistical analysis freely, his

[12]W. Edwards Deming, "On Some Statistical Aids Toward Economic Production," *Interfaces* 5, no. 5 (August 1975), 1–15; Myron Tribus, "Deming's Way" (M.I.T. Center for Advanced Engineering Study, April 1982), 8 pages; "Deming's Redefinition of Management" (M.I.T. Center for Advanced Engineering Study, Working Paper); Howard S. Gitlow and Shelly J. Gitlow, *The Deming Guide to Quality and Competitive Position*, (Englewood Cliffs, N.J.: Prentice Hall, 1987).

primary objective is to get top management to help the company's management team develop the *habit of annual improvement.* In Juran's approach, continuing improvement is supplemented with the "breakthrough" sequence, essentially an organized approach to problem identification, analysis, and change based on this analysis, which we presented earlier in this chapter.

Juran has published a number of books, has contributed freely to professional quality journals, and has developed a set of lectures and video tapes to explain his approach. We've had the opportunity to sample each and have found his message to be well thought out and presented in a lively way. The key to the Juran message, again, is that management can and must seek continual improvement. In doing so, quality will improve, along with other performance dimensions. Because competition with other firms and nations is so great, *annual improvement, hands-on management,* and *training* to institutionalize improvement must all fit together in order to meet the competition for quality products and services.[13]

Phil Crosby's Concept of Free Quality As an experienced executive who for 14 years was corporate vice president and director of quality for ITT, Mr. Crosby was involved in the initial phases of "zero defects" programs (presented later in this chapter). He is an active consultant, lecturer, and author of a popular quality book, *Quality Is Free.* The concept of this book, which explains his overall approach, is that

> Quality is free. It is not a gift, but it is free. What costs money are the unquality things—all the actions that involve not doing jobs right the first time. Quality is not only free, it is an honest-to-everything profit maker. Every penny you don't spend on doing things wrong, over, or instead becomes half a penny right on the bottom line.[14]

Phil Crosby Associates (PCA) in Winter Park, Florida, has been involved in educating 20,000 executives from throughout the world concerning quality awareness as a means for improvement. The focus of this training is on conformance to requirements, prevention, the proper attitude toward quality, and measuring quality as a cost of quality. These "absolutes" are put together in an effective presentation package for corporations. Crosby's approach is based on attitudes and awareness; he focuses on management's role in using this approach to improve quality. Whereas Deming and Juran use analysis as a basis for their philosophies, Crosby's approach is behavioral. Evidently, his methods are quite effective. We are aware of individual quality assurance executives, as well as major

[13]Joseph M. Juran, *Upper Management and Quality,* 4th ed. (New York: Juran Institute, Inc., 1983); idem, *Management of Quality,* 4th ed. (New York: Juran Institute, Inc., 1981); idem, *Quality Control Handbook,* 3rd ed. (New York: McGraw-Hill Book Company 1974); idem, Quality Planning and Analysis (New York: McGraw-Hill Book Company, 1980).

[14]Philip B. Crosby, *Quality Is Free* (New York: Mentor, 1979), p. 2. Also see Jay W. Leek, "Quality in Review, the PCA Experience," *Proceedings the World Quality Congress 1984* (Brighton, England, June 1984).

corporations such as IBM, who have had good success with Crosby's approach.

Experiences of Leading-Edge Firms

Although we know of the strides forward made in quality by such companies as American Express, Armco, Citicorp, Firestone, Hewlett Packard, Honeywell, IBM, and McDonnell Douglas Corporation, it is difficult to obtain documented and published details of successful corporate-wide quality programs. However, we do have a few well-documented examples. We now take a closer look at some organizations that have achieved high quality.

Toyota Motor Company Toyota has been a pacesetter for automotive companies throughout the world as a consistently low-cost, high-quality producer. The Toyota concept of stockless production provides high inventory turnover: an annual turnover of working assets of 62 times in 1970, compared with an annual turnover of less than 10 times for typical U.S. firms.[15] Toyota also has several important quality features, including: (1) involvement of the work force in quality and productivity suggestions (quality circles), (2) inspection of supplier plants, and (3) the use of statistical methods and analysis at all levels in the company.

The involvement of the work force can be seen in Table 15.5. Professor Hall notes that the great increase in 1973 resulted from a need to react effectively to the oil crisis. This event jolted Toyota into greater action. Managers should keep in mind that many small savings add up, and some proposals may lead to large savings. Project-by-project teams, often in the form of quality circles, account for many of the formal proposals and implementations. In contrast, we do not perceive this type of pressure as a problem in American industry. We suggest instead that the American worker simply doesn't have the opportunity or the perceived incentive to improve his or her own work. From our understanding of Toyota, it is clear that management must provide that environment.

Table 15.5 Number of annual proposals by workers at Toyota

Year	Total Number of Proposals	Number of Proposals per Person	Acceptance Rate
1965	9,000	1.0	39%
1970	40,000	2.5	70
1973	247,000	12.2	76
1975	380,000	15.3	83
1976	463,000	—	83
1977	454,000	—	86
1978	528,000	—	86
1979	576,000	—	91
1980	859,000	18.7	94

Source: Hall, *Zero Inventories*, 27.

[15] Hall, *Zero Inventories*, 26.

Toyota and Nissan regularly inspect supplier plants. This practice is now being followed by U.S. auto manufacturers.[16] Ford's QI Preferred Quality Supplier Program is an example. Toyota, like many Japanese firms, depends upon workers at all levels to use statistical thinking (as Deming proposes).

Ford Motor Company In addition to employing Dr. Deming as a consultant, Ford has actively pursued the Japanese—and in general the foreign car—quality lead in automobile production. Ford has developed an integrated business strategy to (1) actively pursue product quality improvement, adopting many Japanese quality techniques, and (2) promote and advertise both the commitment to quality and any actual achievements due to product improvement. Quality improvement is stated as the number one business priority at Ford.

Regarding the first part of Ford's strategy, we have had numerous conversations with top Ford executives. They have provided us with materials reflecting Ford's commitment to quality.[17] Ford is in the process of renewing its use of statistical management methods in order to improve productivity and quality. Ford Chairman Donald E. Peterson has endorsed Dr. Deming's 14 points as the foundation for Ford's goal of never-ending improvement in quality and productivity.

The results of Ford's efforts are now being recognized by consumers. In 1987 Ford advertised that they are number one in quality among American automobile manufacturers; they cited independently collected data to support their claim.

Xerox Corporation The segment of Xerox that produces copiers and duplicators has met extremely quick foreign competition, especially from Japanese manufacturers. This competition is directed at gaining market share with low-cost, high-quality products.[18] Xerox's response has been to

- Completely reassess the way they have been doing business
- Learn to deal with issues involving quality and productivity in a different way
- Implement a number of new approaches that will enable long-term competitiveness

Xerox, unique in its industry because it developed the product line that formed the industry, now has a basis for comparison with very *real* competitors who once did not exist. Xerox has three major phases underway:

---

[16]Schonberger, *Japanese Manufacturing Techniques*, 58.

[17]The authors are particularly indebted to Ford executives John A. Manoogian, Executive Director Product Assurance, North American Automotive Operations, and Dick Smith of his staff; James K. Bakken, Corporate Vice-President, Operations Support Staff; and William W. Scherkenbach, Director Statistical Methods.

[18]This section is based on Frank J. Pipp, "A Management Commitment to Quality" (The keynote speech to the 37th Annual Quality Congress, American Society for Quality Control, May 1983).

1. *Competitive benchmarking.* Developing and implementing a continuous process of measuring Xerox products and services against the best and toughest competitors in the world—the best in any industry, not just copiers and duplicators. This led to action resulting in a 21 percent gain in satisfaction in one year.
2. *Employee involvement.* Getting the best from the minds and talents of Xerox employees at all levels. Problem-solving teams, quality circles, changing management style—over one-fourth of Xerox employees are involved in team activities aimed at improvement.
3. *Leadership through quality.* Exposing the very top executives to the work of Drs. Juran and Deming, and attending Phil Crosby's Quality College in Winter Park, Florida, have led to the beginning of a total quality control process in all aspects of the corporation. Top management credibility has been established at Xerox.

From the reaction of Xerox, we see how a U.S.-based company prepares to meet the quality-productivity challenge. We see in Toyota, Ford, and Xerox several similar ideas and a return to the basic concepts and principles of leading worldwide quality experts. Why? Worldwide competition in terms of quality products and services seems to be the driving force.

BEHAVIOR AND QUALITY

The attainment of suitable quality depends upon appropriate human performance when the product or service is being made. In recent years much effort has been devoted to instilling a "quality orientation" in the people who work in the conversion process. Behavioral change procedures directed at changing performance quality *before* rather than after the fact, however, have met with limited success. We will discuss some of these attempts and the inherent behavioral problems that relate to quality in the following few paragraphs.

Quality/Quantity Tradeoffs

Few studies have specifically investigated the relationships between quantity and quality of output. A popular view supported by Dr. Deming and Dr. Juran is that any decrease in quantity would be more than offset by the reduction in waste due to correct performance the first time. A review of the literature suggests there is no simple inherent relationship between these two factors. Especially for such routine, repetitive tasks as typing, bank proofing, or collating, operators tend to emphasize one over the other. If quality improves, quantity decreases; if quantity goes up, quality suffers. For tasks involving more complex and diverse physical and mental processes, the relationships between quantity and quality are not nearly so clear. In these more complex tasks, when does the operator emphasize quality at the expense of quantity? When does the reverse occur? There is no simple answer to our questions. The quantity/quality tradeoff is usually determined by how the conversion processes are designed, staffed, and managed.

Zero Defects

Zero Defects programs, which attempt to improve quality by changing workers' attitudes, were particularly popular in the 1960s and 1970s. Their theme, "Do it right the first time," stresses error-free performance. Unfortunately, however, production/operation processes inevitably result in some undesirable output. Error-free performance is, for most processes, economically and practically infeasible. Although many people assume that errors are made because employees are not conscientious enough about their work, attempts to change employee attitudes have met with very limited success. Banners, slogans, Zero Defect days, and the like generally improve performance only temporarily; in about six months, employees' performance returns to its previous level.

Quality Motivation

The American Society for Quality Control has a quality workbook that stresses some basic concepts for motivating employees. The idea is to apply techniques of motivation and management to obtain improved product quality. Contemporary views include a behavior-performance-reward-satisfaction sequence.[19] Organizations are becoming keenly aware of the alternative pay plans that can shape performance. We have assisted in developing incentive and merit pay systems, for example, that include rewards for good quality.

Behavioral Modification in Quality Control

There have been several attempts to influence performance quality on routine repetitive tasks by employing operant conditioning procedures.[20] Operant conditioning assumes that behavior can be modified by a series of rewards. It appears that performance *quality* is more difficult to change than performance *quantity*. Second, it is clear that financial rewards more often result in improved quality than nonfinancial rewards. Once reasonable quality performance levels have been reached, however, continued financial rewards do not obtain significant additional quality improvement. Third, actual behavior is influenced more greatly by direct rewards than by attitude change procedures. We should be aware, finally, that these procedures provide, at best, mixed results.

EXAMPLE In an attempt to influence quality in a diecasting department of some 36 workers, one company succeeded in obtaining a significant quantity increase but no significant change in quality. Figure 15.4 shows weekly

[19] Charles N. Greene, Everett E. Adam, Jr., and Ronald J. Ebert, *Management for Effective Performance* (Englewood Cliffs, N.J.: Prentice-Hall, 1985), pp. 104–24.

[20] See Everett E. Adam, Jr., "Behavior Modification in Quality Control," *Academy of Management Journal* 18, no. 4 (December 1975), 662–79. This work provides references to the related works of George A. Johnson, William A. Ruch, William E. Scott, Jr., and James B. Shein, all of whom have contributed to quality motivation research. Also see David A. Sprague, Barry Zinn, and Robert Kreitner, "Improving Quality Through Behavior Modification," *Quality Progress* 9, no. 12 (December 1976), 22–24.

changes in the department as the result of a formal program involving weekly individual meetings between the supervisor and each employee. Quantity is measured as percent of standard, and quality is measured by percent defective. Overall, the company, with a $73,000 first-year cost reduction in this department, judged the program successful and implemented it in other departments. The fact remains, however, that quality did not improve, even though emphasis was given to performance quality at least weekly.

Quality Circles

Quality circles (QCs) were initially developed in Japan as employee participative programs to identify the quality variations and then with management to eliminate the source of those deviations. Quality circles in Japan are essentially small groups of employees (perhaps 6 to 12) who meet informally, often in an employee's home to resolve quality-related problems from work. Ideas for solutions are suggested to management, and they work as a team to implement the changes. Employees at all levels in the firm are trained in the basic skills of data charting, sampling, and control. These analytical and statistical skills have become a part of the Japanese general education curriculum and are widely reinforced by industry usage at the level of the operative worker. In 1980, quality control experts estimated that just under a million workers were involved in quality circles in Japan, but only as few as a hundred thousand workers were taking part in the programs in the United States. Those numbers are certainly larger now, as reflected by the increasing interest in the International Association of Quality Circles. The 1984 membership in that organization was estimated at 3,500 quality circle facilitators, primarily from the United States.

Within the United States quality circles have evolved into participative productivity improvement programs which focus on both performance quantity and quality. As in Japan, participation is voluntary.

FIGURE 15.4
Weekly diecasting quality (percent scrap) and quantity (percent performance) performance

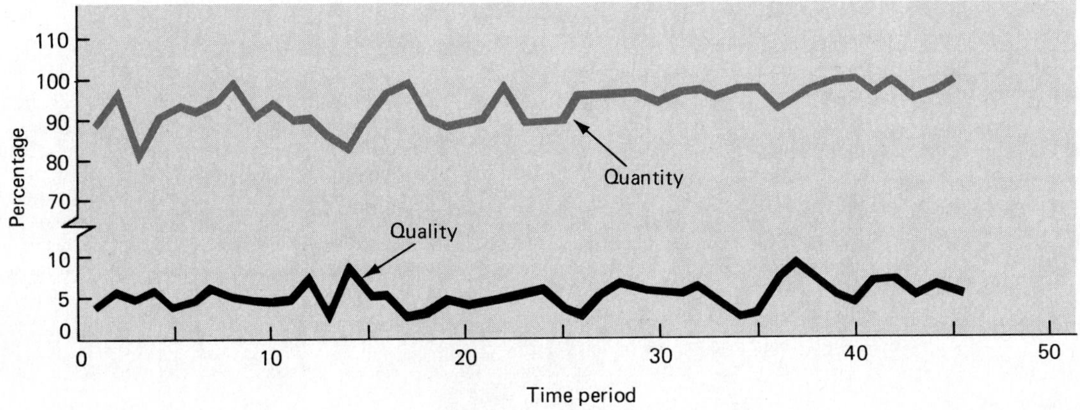

Employees are paid while participating during regular working hours or on overtime. A group leader is selected and trained for the leadership role by the organization. Then the participating group receives training in the methods of problem solving, analysis, and reporting. The group begins meeting to identify problems, collect and analyze the data, recommend solutions, and carry out management-approved changes. Many companies are testing this participative technique in a few locations with an eye toward wider application.[21]

There are very few evaluations of quality circle performance. Most organizations report savings to costs in a range of 3:1 to 6:1, clearly favoring the programs. Others simply accept quality circles as a management participative philosophy without documenting savings. One field study, however, did systematically evaluate QCs' effectiveness.[22] In this study empirical investigation of effective and less-effective quality circles was conducted in nine manufacturing plants of a large, midwestern company. Effective QCs reported higher group cohesion, performance norms, job satisfaction, intrinsic satisfaction, satisfaction with co-workers, self-monitoring, and organization commitment than did ineffective QCs. If an organization values the group's suggestions and values member satisfactions and feelings, the results of this study indicate that quality circles will be effective.

Management Style and Quality Control

Several writers suggest that a participative management style best enhances quality control and improvement efforts.[23] Focusing on the individual, these efforts—many of which are in services—emphasize involvement in setting quality goals, establishing quality measures, and designing jobs for enhanced quality. We have found managers to be increasingly interested in

[21]For example, discussions of quality circles and their applications, see A. V. Feignbaum, "The Internationalization of Quality," *Quality Progress* 12, no. 2 (February 1979) 30–32; Gerald E. Swartz and Vivian C. Comstock, "One Firm's Experience with Quality Circles," *Quality Progress* 12, no. 9 (September 1979) 14–16 (Westinghouse's experience); Charles A. Aubrey, II, and Lawrence A. Eldridge, "Banking on High Quality," *Quality Progress* 14, no. 12 (December 1981), 14–19 (Continental Bank's experience); George Munchus, III, "Employer-Employee Based Quality Circles in Japan: Human Resource Policy Implications for American Firms," *Academy of Management Review* 8, no. 2 (April 1983), 255–61; and John D. Blair and Kenneth D. Ramsing, "Quality Circles and Production/Operations Management: Concerns and Caveats," *Journal of Operations Management* 4, no. 1 (November 1983), 1–10.

[22]Ricky W. Griffin and Sandy J. Wayne, "A Field Study of Effective and Less Effective Quality Circles," *Academy of Management Proceedings 1984*, pp. 217–21.

[23]See John R. Hinrichs, *Practical Management for Productivity* New York: Van Nostrand Reinhold Company, 1978). Hinrichs returned to field sites and interviewed participants in quality improvement studies (see Chapter 2, "Enhancing Product Quality," the original study by E. E. Adam, Jr., and Chapter 6, "Building a Participative Management System to Enhance Product Quality," the original study by F. B. Chaney and K. S. Teel). Also see John C. Shaw and Ram Capoor, "Quality and Productivity: Mutually Exclusive or Interdependent in Service Organizations?" *Management Review* (March 1979), pp. 25–28, 37–39; G. M. Hostage, "Quality Control in a Service Business," *Harvard Business Review* 53, no. 4 (July–August 1975), 98–106; and A. V. Feigenbaum, "Quality and Productivity," *Quality Progress* 10, no. 11 (November 1977), 18–21.

quality, especially in *management techniques* to improve quality. Perhaps this managerial awareness is increasing because of the difficulties encountered recently by such basic U.S. industries as steel and automobiles. International competitors have challenged and sometimes outperformed their U.S. peers concerning productivity and quality.

SUMMARY

In this chapter on managing for quality, we have discussed concepts of product quality, factors affecting quality, management-directed diagnosis, contemporary management approaches to improving quality, and behavioral dimensions in quality. Quality improvement, assurance, and control can be facilitated by management's planning and organizing efforts. Operations managers must provide direction and establish control. However, they must be aware that all of these control procedures are used by people. Quality motivation and behavioral modification techniques are some methods operations managers can use to encourage employees to improve quality. The Japanese have taught us a good bit about high quality—both in analysis and managing people.

This chapter has presented our belief that the most important aspects of an introduction to quality are understanding concepts in quality, being able to apply basic analysis techniques, and understanding that quality improvement is behavioral as well as analytical. Once you have mastered these concepts, you will have a grasp of the fundamentals of quality improvement.

CASE

Fast Break Markets

A small regional supermarket chain, Fast Break Markets, prides itself upon being a high-service, full-line supermarket chain. A typical store has a flower shop, bakery, liquor store, post office, pharmacy, VCR movie rental, and tobacco shop as part of the overall market. Sales have been increasing 20 percent per year in the 1980s, equally increased by in-store sales and from adding new stores.

The table reflects customer complaints systematically collected at three typical stores over two months. The vice president of operations, Max Creach, is astounded by the number of complaints and the different types of complaints. He intends to get the manager of each of the 11 stores to organize the employees to address these complaints. Max would like to analyze the data and then suggest a method for each manager to follow. Although Max has heard of quality concepts such as quality cost studies, breakthrough versus control, fishbone diagrams, and Pareto analysis, he doesn't really know what to suggest to each supermarket manager when they meet Wednesday.

Customer complaints in three stores for two months

Customer Complaint	Number
1. Sanitation	27
2. Courtesy clerk (bagger)	21
3. Product quality	87
4. Product request	105
5. General	58
6. General service level	55
7. Checker	59
8. Human error	27
9. Queueing (waiting line)	33
10. Stock condition	166
11. Prices and price marking	45
12. Policy and procedures	40
13. Parking	18
14. Check cashing	15
15. All other	71
Total	827

CASE

Kitchen Appliance Quality

The production manager for the only facility of a small manufacturer of kitchen appliances is interested in getting management's attention on quality issues. He has allies in the marketing manager and accountant, but little interest from the president and the primary owner, both of whom are interested in production efficiency, sales volume, short-term profits, and growth. The production manager and his allies have the following data, but don't know how to organize the data into an effective presentation. From this information, put together the best case possible to impress management that quality is important and should be stressed.

Data Item	Value (last year)
1. Customer responses to questions about top-selling product last year	a. style—good b. price—excellent c. reliability—poor d. would recommend to friend—no
2. Quality training costs	$ 1,200
Vendor qualification program	500
Field testing	3,500
Purchase quality measurement (calipers, etc.)	400
Scrap, full cost less scrap value	475,000
Inspection in plant	85,000
Field maintenance	15,000
Rework, at full shop cost	1,200,000
Warranty costs	45,000

Returned material processing & repair	375,000
Laboratory testing	3,700
3. Sales	$10,000,000
Total cost of goods sold	7,000,000
Selling and administrative expenses	1,300,000
Total assets in business	3,500,000
4. Percent defective for top-selling product last year	
a. fabrication	7.2%
b. assembly	11.5%
c. finished goods	9.8%
5. Estimated cost due to loss of good will with distributors	
a. late deliveries	$ 50,000
b. poor quality	200,000

REVIEW AND DISCUSSION QUESTIONS

1. If you were to design a portable radio, what product characteristics would you specify as critical for enhancing sales? What characteristics are less important?
2. What product characteristics and quality analysis procedures are important in a dormitory cafeteria? Which of these is most important? Which is least important?
3. Discuss the roles of the cost of quality assurance in quality planning.
4. Explain how strategy and quality interrelate.
5. Explain the interactions among the components in Figure 15.2, "Managing for quality products and services."
6. What is the difference between sporadic problems and chronic problems, and how do these relate to quality improvement?
7. Managerial "breakthrough" is a process or approach to obtaining a higher level of quality. Explain this process.
8. Identify three common errors college freshment make in managing their time. Prepare a fishbone (cause and effect) diagram for these errors.
9. How can Pareto analysis be used effectively as a diagnostic tool in quality improvement? Explain.
10. "If our employees are requested to increase output quality, the quantity of output is going to suffer." Discuss this statement.
11. Is operant conditioning an effective management technique for quality motivation in nonroutine, nonrepetitive tasks? Why or why not?
12. In this chapter the manager is asked to become proficient in quality analysis techniques and is also expected to understand contemporary improvement programs and behavior. Are these expectations inconsistent? Explain.

PROBLEMS

1. It is important to most students to receive a class schedule that meets their academic program and personal needs. Yet student complaints about registration and advisors are often unheard. Problems or complaints could be divided into five categories: (1) unavailable or inadequate professional advice (2) poor registration procedures (3) unavailable classes (4) too few sections for classes, and (5) inadequate information on registration procedures. Prepare a fishbone (cause and effect) diagram reflecting your experiences with these five complaint categories.

2. Consider the five categories in Problem 1. Suppose the average student lost 90 hours of personal time due to these problems over a four-year period. Assume students could receive $5.00/hour working instead of being inconvenienced by poor registration and advice. Prepare a Pareto Analysis for the quality loss in registration and advising, given the data below. Interpret your results, i.e., explain where administrators should focus correction efforts.

Class of Loss	Frequency of Loss (%)
Advising deficiency	20.0
Registration procedures	15.0
Unavailable classes	20.0
Too few sections	30.0
Inadequate procedures	15.0
	100.0

Class of Loss	Frequency of Loss (%)
Too few sections:	
Unable to carpool	5.0
Cannot work part time	20.0
Loss of sleep—early classes	10.0
Cannot get preferred instructor	20.0
Extra summer or semester required	10.0
Unable to fit into schedule—miss education	20.0
Other	15.0
	100.0

3. Quality losses due to employee performance in a fast-food facility were estimated as shown below. Complete a Pareto analysis for this data and interpret your results for management. For the largest dollar loss, prepare a Fishbone diagram with your thoughts on the reason for the loss.

Class of Loss	Dollar Loss One Shift
Prepare too much food—waste	$150.00
Prepare wrong item	35.00
Incorrect order taken	30.00
Wrong change	50.00
Slow service	75.00
Impolite to customer	45.00
Others	100.00
	$485.00

GLOSSARY

Attributes measurement Type of measurement in which a product characteristic is classified into one of two categories: success or failure, accept or reject, and so forth.

Chronic problem A problem that is long-standing and bad (unfavorable); a long-standing adverse quality problem addressed through breakthrough.

Design specifications Detailed requirements of a product specifying its important desired characteristics.

Fishbone diagram A cause and effect diagram; causes that contribute to quality problems (effects) are schematically diagrammed by a group.

Pareto analysis A frequency distribution commonly used to display categories of losses against frequency of the losses.

Process capability Maximum level of output quality performance of a productive process that can occur under ideal operating conditions.

Product quality The appropriateness of design specifications to function and use, as well as the degree to which the product conforms to design specifications.

Quality motivation Application of management motivation techniques to workers to improve quality.

Sporadic problem A problem that is suddenly a bad (unfavorable) change within the status quo; a sudden adverse quality problem addressed through control.

Variables measurement Type of measurement in which a product characteristic is classified according to its degree of conformance on some measurement scale.

Zero defects Formal programs adopted by organizations to change worker attitudes toward quality improvement.

SELECTED READINGS

Adam, Everett E., Jr., and Eugene M. Barker, "Achieving Quality Products and Services," *Operations Management Review* (Winter 1987), pp. 1–8.

Adam, Everett E., Jr., James C. Hershauer, and William A. Ruch, *Productivity and Quality: Measurement as a Basis for Improvement* (2nd ed.). Columbia, Mo.: Research Center, College of Business and Public Administration, University of Missouri, 1986.

Crosby, Philip B., *Quality Is Free*. New York: Mentor, 1979.

Deming, W. Edwards, "On Some Statistical Aids Toward Economic Production," *Interfaces* 5, no. 5 (August 1975), 1–15.

Gitlow, Howard S., and Shelly J. Gitlow, *The Deming Guide to Quality and Competitive Position*. Englewood Cliffs, N.J.: Prentice Hall, 1987.

Griffin, Ricky W., and Sandy J. Wayne, "A Field Study of Effective and Less Effective Quality Circles," *Academy of Management Proceedings* (1984), 217–21.

Hinrichs, John R., *Practical Management for Productivity*. New York: Van Nostrand Reinhold, 1978.

Ishikawa, Kaoru, *Guide to Quality Control* Tokyo, Japan: Asian Productivity Organization, 1976 (11th printing, 1983).

Juran, J., *Upper Management and Quality* (4th ed.). New York: Juran Institute, Inc., 1983.

Juran, J., and Frank M. Gryna, Jr., *Quality Planning and Analysis* (2nd ed.). New York: McGraw-Hill, 1980.

Munchus, George, III, "Employer-Employee Based Quality Circles in Japan: Human Resource Policy Implications for American Firms," *Academy of Management Review* 8, no. 2 (April 1983), 255–61.

Rosander, A. C., *Applications of Quality Control in the Service Industries* (2nd ed.). New York: Markel Dekker, Inc/ASQC Quality Press, 1985.

Takemchi, Hirotaka, and John A. Quelch, "Quality Is More Than Making a Good Product," *Harvard Business Review* 61, no. 4 (July–August 1983), 139–45.

16

Quality Analysis and Control

At Monsanto Chemical Company we are changing corporate culture to more consistently meet agreed-upon customer requirements with each and every business transaction. The mechanism being employed to bring about this change is a Monsanto Quality Improvement Process called Total Quality. The Total Quality Improvement Process is a systematic approach to problem solving that utilizes the teachings of Messrs P. B. Crosby, W. E. Deming, and J. M. Juran.

A key component of the improvement process focuses on the use of statistical methods to achieve process stability. Chapter 16 illustrates how the use of statistical methods can assist in determining the cause of process variations and the steps which can be taken to control these variations.

At Monsanto Chemical Company a high priority for each process, whether it's manufacturing or service, is to achieve process stability. Statistical methods are widely used in making this priority a reality.

As worldwide competition grows, the company that does the best job of consistently meeting agreed-upon customer requirements with minimum hassles and rework will be the company of preference. We are committed to being one of the selected few companies of preference in those areas which we elect to pursue.

Fred L. Thompson
Director, Total Quality
Monsanto Chemical Company,
A Unit of Monsanto Company,
St. Louis, Missouri

The comments by Mr. Thompson give clear evidence of the central role of quality analysis and control in today's competitive environment. Analysis and control are the methods used to implement each organization's quality objectives. You will gain a clearer picture of why and how these tools can be beneficial after being introduced to process capability, statistical process control, inspection, and acceptance sampling. First, however, we examine process variation, one of the most fundamental facts of life in production operations.

PROCESS VARIATION

Variation in all operating systems establishes the need for quality analysis and quality control. We need analysis and control because of the inherent conflict between these two facts:

- Variation (nonuniformity) exists in every operating system; no two units of output are alike.
- The production and use of products and services are most economical when those products are of uniform quality.

Although variation cannot be eliminated, by learning more about it and controlling it, we can increase the number of products from the operating system that conform to usage requirements.

Sources of Variation

The variations in any stage of a conversion process stem from the various sources that constitute the production system—people, materials, machines and equipment, and work methods. We could get uniformity among all the lead pencils we produce if all of the incoming wood had the same texture, strength, and density; if all of the lead and other materials were uniform in each of their characteristics; if the tool setters and equipment operators did not vary in their behaviors throughout the workday; if the equipment ran consistently without tool wear or breakdowns; and if the work environment had constant lighting, humidity, temperature, and so on. However, since uniformity is impossible, the key questions become, "How much variation exists in the processes?" and "What can I do to control the nonuniformity in the processes?"

Measuring Natural Variation: Process Capability

The first step toward control is to *document* the process's capability—its performance under chronic conditions in which sporadic variations do not exist. Many companies simply do not know what their processes are doing, or are capable of doing, and a capability study is a factual basis for gaining such an understanding. The *process capability* study begins by measuring individual units of process output on some key product characteristic, and summarizing the results in a frequency histogram.

Then, the average and standard deviation of the sample units are computed using equations 16.1 and 16.2.

$$\bar{X} = \frac{\Sigma X_i}{N} \tag{16.1}$$

$$S = \sqrt{\frac{\Sigma (\bar{X} - X_i)^2}{N - 1}} \tag{16.2}$$

EXAMPLE Hardness is a critical characteristic of rubber seals for automobile windows. To determine the process capability of seal forming, 90 seals are randomly selected during production. A frequency histogram of the measurements is shown in Figure 16.1. The average hardness, calculated using equation 16.1, is $\bar{X} = 62.56$. The standard deviation, calculated using equation 16.2 with $N = 90$ observations, is $S = 12.97$. The "natural limits" of the process—three standard deviations ($3S$) above and below $\bar{X}$—are also shown.

When sporadic problems are absent, the unit-to-unit variations will be random. Furthermore, most processes have a natural variation pattern that is bell-shaped or normally distributed. So, if the initial histogram is nonnormal, we have reason to suspect that sporadic conditions exist, contrary to the investigator's initial beliefs, and consequently, the measurements may be contaminated and not reflect the process capability. The nonrandom data must be screened out to get a true picture of the process capability. Another reason why the normal distribution is important will be seen later when we construct control charts. At this point we wish merely to emphasize that nonnormality is a signal for caution and further investigation into the process. The data measurements can be tested for the normality assumption by using the Chi-square goodness-of-fit test or by using probability plotting paper.[1]

For the rubber seal example, the distribution in Figure 16.1 appears to be slightly skewed to the left but, overall, seems to approximate the bell-shaped pattern. The mean and standard deviation from the 90 observations are our best estimates of the seal-forming process (the population of individual seals). The "natural limits" (three standard deviations from the average) show that about 99.7 percent of the seals will have hardness values between 23.65 and 101.46 for the chronic condition of the seal-forming process.

[1]See R. C. Pfaffenberger and J. H. Patterson, *Statistical Methods*, 3rd ed. (Homewood, Ill.: Richard D. Irwin, Inc., 1987); see also E. L. Grant and R. S. Leavenworth, *Statistical Quality Control*, 5th ed. (New York: McGraw-Hill Book Company, 1980).

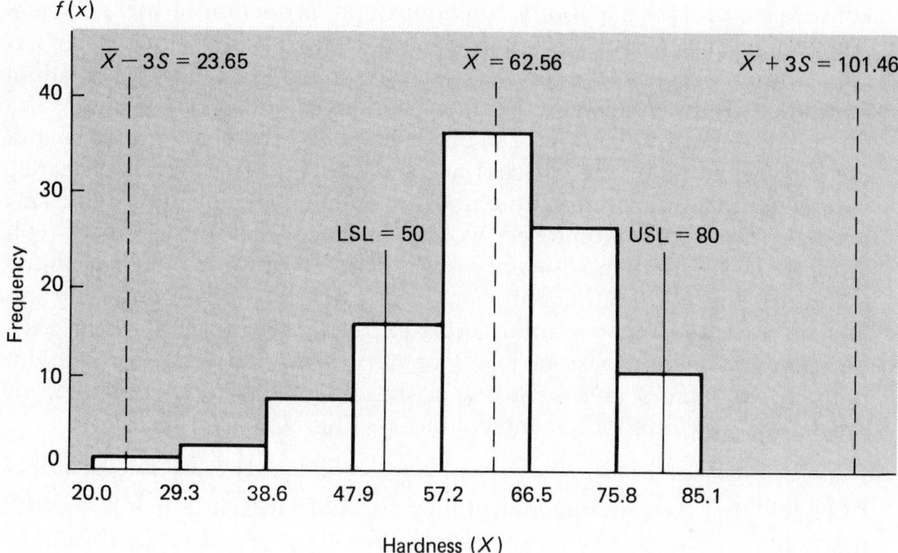

FIGURE 16.1
Frequency histogram of rubber seal hardness for $N = 90$ observations

Specification Limits Capability histograms convey more information about process quality by comparing them with the product's specification limits. *Specification limits* are the boundaries between "good" and "bad" on each characteristic that is important for fitness for use. A customer, for example, may specify the nominal resistance of 17 ohms for an electrical component, with an upper specification limit (USL) of 19 ohms and a lower specificiation limit (LSL) of 15 ohms. Figure 16.2 shows three

FIGURE 16.2
Three process capability conditions

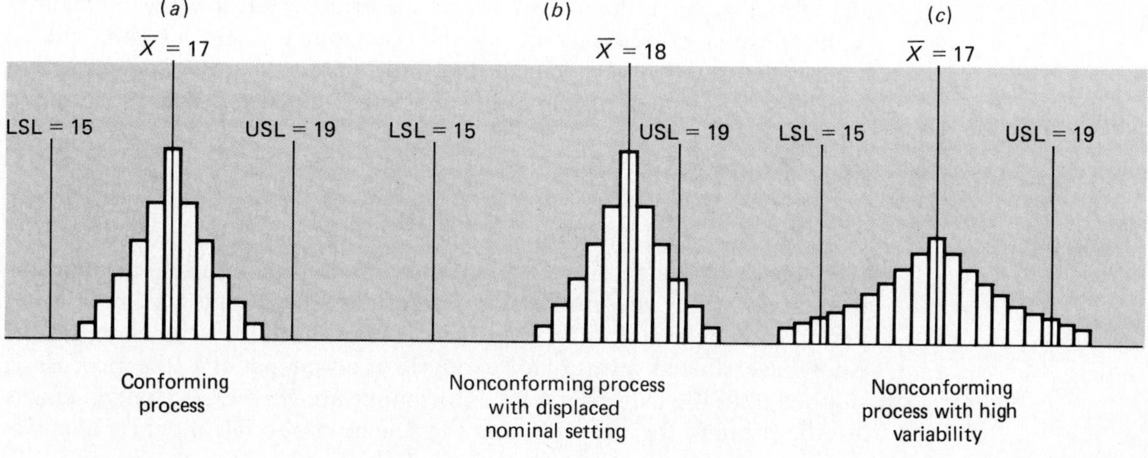

contrasting process capability conditions for production of the electrical component. The chronic condition in part (a) is ideal; the process is conforming because the process output coincides with the nominal resistance, midway between the upper and lower specification limits, and the process variability is low. The process variability in part (b) is low, but the displacement of the process average above the nominal resistance results in nonconforming output above the upper specification limit. This process should be monitored closely because nonconformances will increase if the average resistance shifts further upward or if variability increases. Part (c) has nonconformance due to high process variability. So long as this chronic condition persists, the company will incur costs associated with the existing levels of nonconformance. If, in addition, nonrandom factors arise, causing a shift in the average resistance or raising the variability, nonconformances will grow.

EXAMPLE In Figure 16.1 the lower specification limit (LSL) indicates that seals with hardnesses under 50 are unsatisfactory, based on extensive performance tests in engineering. Similarly, the upper specification limit outlaws seals with hardness above 80. A comparison of the product specifications with the process distribution reveals a significant discrepancy: More than 11 percent (10 units) of the observed seals are under the LSL and more than 5 percent (5 units) are above the USL. Extrapolating further, if the process is normally distributed with an average hardness of 62.56 and standard deviation of 12.97, it can be shown (by using the normal distribution in Appendix Table A) that about 16.6 percent of the seals produced in the future will be under the LSL, and about 8.8 percent will exceed the USL.

The company can estimate the costs associated with this level of product nonconformance and, if justified, determine how to improve the chronic condition of the process through breakthrough and improvement projects.

Process capability analysis, then, describes what the process can do in its chronic condition, and shows how much of the output will be conforming relative to specification requirements. Meanwhile, we need to watch for the onset of nonrandom variations in the process, as we see next.

STATISTICAL PROCESS CONTROL

One approach to controlling nonuniformity, *statistical process control* (SPC), seeks to detect and eliminate nonrandom (sporadic) variations as they arise while the process is operating. The process is monitored periodically by examining sample units of output. If the critical characteristics have shifted away from a purely random pattern, the process is stopped until the causes of nonconformance are corrected. Control charts are the primary tool for SPC, and the selection of control charts depends on the type of measurements that are to be used.

Measuring Variables Versus Attributes

Two different types of measurement, by variables and by attributes, are used in process control. In some situations, we must measure a product characteristic on a continuous scale, such as its length, weight, or volume, all of which are *variables measurements.* Alternatively, *attributes measurement* merely classifies the product into one of two categories (good or bad, success or failure, etc.), depending upon whether the observed product possesses the appropriate characteristic.

Attribute measurements are quicker and easier to make, so they offer more economical data gathering and storage. Variables measurements, however, contain more potential information. Notice, for example, that we could not have constructed the process capability histogram for the rubber seal hardness in Figure 16.1 if we had merely classified each of the 90 sample units as either acceptable or unacceptable. Variables measurements provided the capability data, and they also provide more powerful information for controlling the process.

Control Charts for Variables

Shewhart control charts are the workhorse of statistical process control.[2] The name of the chart comes from Dr. Walter Shewhart of the Bell Telephone Laboratories, who is generally recognized as the "father" of statistical quality control. When a conversion process begins to shift out of control, we would like to know as soon as possible so we can initiate corrective action. Although one would think it would be a simple matter to detect a shift by observation, it usually isn't. Occasionally, random variability in the process may make it seem that process output is bad when actually there has been no basic change. At other times, real shifts are mistakenly attributed to random variability. If a basic change occurs, we want to correct it so we can avoid costs of producing faulty products. On the other hand, we do not want to waste resources trying to correct a process that is already operating properly. To help avoid interpretative errors and detect when real shifts have occurred, quality *control charts* are very useful.

Figure 16.3 shows a control chart for the temperature of a chemical plating operation. This chart has three important parameters, which were determined from historical data: mean (average) temperature, upper

[2]Dr. Walter A. Shewhart, *Economic Control of Quality of Manufactured Product* (New York: D. Van Nostrand Company, 1931).

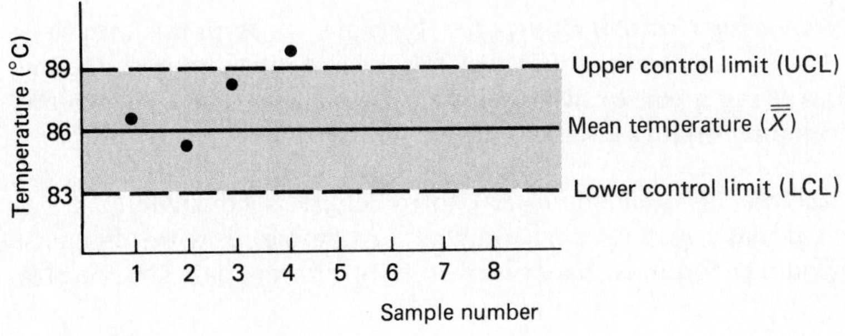

FIGURE 16.3
Example control chart

control limit (UCL), and lower control limit (LCL). In the past, the mean, or average, temperature for the process has been 86°C. The upper and lower control limits have been set at 89°C and 83°C. After the chart had been constructed, four more days of operation transpired. Sample temperature readings for these days were measured and recorded on the chart. Temperature averages for the first two days were near the mean; the third sample average was near the upper control limit. An operations manager could glance at this chart and say, "The process is in control based upon the last three days' performance." The sample average on day 4 is outside the control limits; the average temperature has probably shifted above its historical level of 86°C. Why can we make such a statement? Because of the theory that underlies the control chart, as we see next.

Central Limit Theorem Control charts are based on the statistical concept of the *central limit theorem.* This theorem allows us the convenience of using the standard normal distribution in making judgments about changes in the process we are monitoring. With it, we can conveniently determine the chances that some important characteristic of our process has changed, and we can express these chances explicitly. To use this theorem, we take a randomly selected sample of several units of output from the conversion process. For each unit sampled we measure the critical characteristic, say its length, and compute the arithmetic average of the n observed lengths. We then use this *average* to make our judgments regarding *system performance.* The central limit theorem specifies that if we compute many such averages, they will be approximately normally distributed regardless of the shape of the distribution of individual lengths. The approximation to normality improves, and the standard deviation of the sampling distribution diminishes, as the size of our sample is increased (see Figure 16.4).

The central limit theorum provides an important relationship between the standard deviation S of the distribution of individuals and the standard deviation $S_{\bar{X}}$ of the sampling distribution, as shown in equation 16.3.

$$S_{\bar{X}} = \frac{S}{\sqrt{n}} \tag{16.3}$$

This relationship is helpful because it sometimes saves some cumbersome calculations; if either of the standard deviations (estimated) is known, we can easily calculate the other standard deviation for any sample size (n).

Steps in Developing Control Charts for Averages With this overview of control charts, let's examine the steps for constructing and interpreting them to control the mean or average of a process. The following are the steps in developing quality control charts:

1. Partition the *historical data.* A control chart is constructed from historical data; future performance is compared with this past performance. You must have two distinctly different data sets, one for

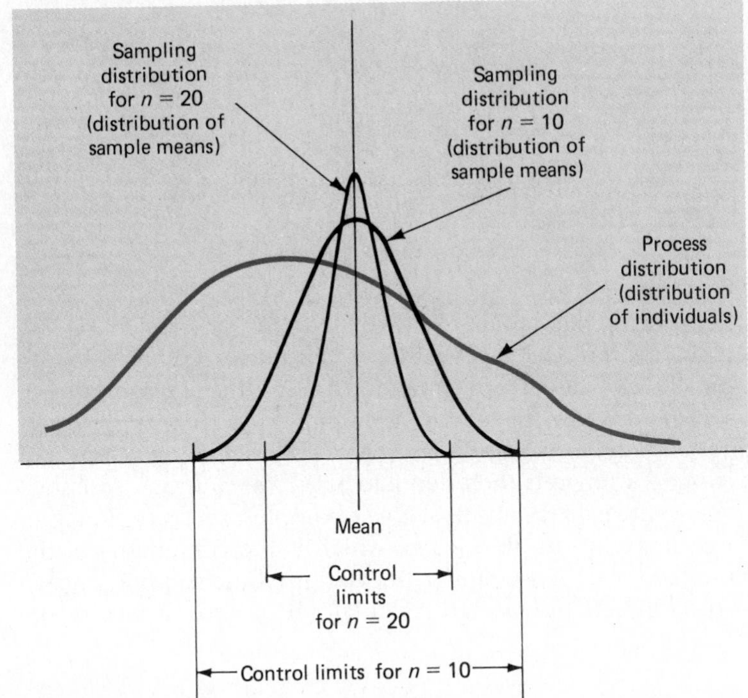

FIGURE 16.4
Two distributions of sample means taken from a process distribution

control chart *construction* and a second to reflect most recent performance.

2. Using the data for control chart construction, *calculate* a process mean and upper and lower control limits. The control limits are based on the sampling distribution.
3. *Graph* the control chart. The chart contains the scaled measurement (on the *y*-axis) versus samples (on the *x*-axis).
4. *Plot* the current or most recent sample average on the chart.
5. *Interpret* the chart to see if (a) the process is in control and no action is required, (b) the process is out of control and an assignable cause should be sought, or (c) the process is in control but trends are occurring that should alert the manager to possible nonrandom conditions.
6. *Update* the control chart. Periodically, the control chart is reconstructed by returning to step 1. You can repartition the data by discarding the oldest historical data and replacing it with historical data collected since the last updating.

Control Charts for Variables

The calculations for the control chart utilize equations 16.4–16.7.

$$\overline{X} = \frac{\sum_{i=1}^{n} X_i}{n} \tag{16.4}$$

$$\overline{\overline{X}} = \frac{\sum_{j=1}^{m} \overline{X}_j}{m} \tag{16.5}$$

$$S_{\overline{X}} = \sqrt{\frac{\sum_{j=1}^{m} (\overline{X}_j - \overline{\overline{X}})^2}{m - 1}} \tag{16.6}$$

$$\text{UCL} = \overline{\overline{X}} + kS_{\overline{X}} \tag{16.7}$$

$$\text{LCL} = \overline{\overline{X}} - kS_{\overline{X}}$$

To calculate a sample average, let X_i be the measured value for ith unit in a sample of size n, and, from equation 16.4, $\overline{X}$ is the average value of these n measurements. Now instead of sampling only once, suppose we sample m times and obtain m sample averages, always picking samples of size n. Each sample average is then denoted as $\overline{X}_j$. We can then calculate the average and standard deviation of these sample averages. Equation 16.5 gives the average of sample means, which is the center line of the control chart for averages. The standard deviation of the sampling distribution, $S_{\overline{X}}$, is used in equation 16.7 to calculate the control limits for the chart.

EXAMPLE Continuing with our earlier example, the automobile company wants to set up a chart for controlling the average hardness of the rubber seals for car windows. The 90 individual hardness measurements consist of 18 samplings in which five seals ($n = 5$) were measured in each sampling. We first find the sample averages, using equation 16.4, as shown in column 3.

Sample (j)	Individual Hardness (X_i: $i = 1 \ldots 5$)	Sample Average ($\overline{X}_j$)
1	65, 70, 60, 50, 65	310 ÷ 5 = 62.0
2	70, 80, 70, 40, 60	320 ÷ 5 = 64.0
.		
.		
.		
17	60, 70, 85, 60, 60	335 ÷ 5 = 67.0
18	55, 75, 80, 40, 55	305 ÷ 5 = 61.0

Then we find the average of the distribution of sample means $\overline{\overline{X}}$ by using equation 16.5:

$$\overline{\overline{X}} = \frac{62.0 + 64.0 + \ldots + 67.0 + 61.0}{18} = 62.56$$

Next we calculate the standard deviation of the sampling distribution using equation 16.6:

$$S_{\bar{X}} = \sqrt{\frac{(62.0 - 62.56)^2 + (64.0 - 62.56)^2 + \ldots + (67.0 - 62.56)^2 + (61.0 - 62.56)^2}{18 - 1}}$$

$$= 5.80$$

Finally, if we want control limits that are three standard deviations ($k = 3$) above and below the mean of the sampling distribution, we apply equation 16.7 as follows:

$$UCL = \bar{\bar{X}} + 3S_{\bar{X}} = 62.56 + 3(5.80) = 79.96$$

$$LCL = \bar{\bar{X}} - 3S_{\bar{X}} = 62.56 - 3(5.80) = 45.16$$

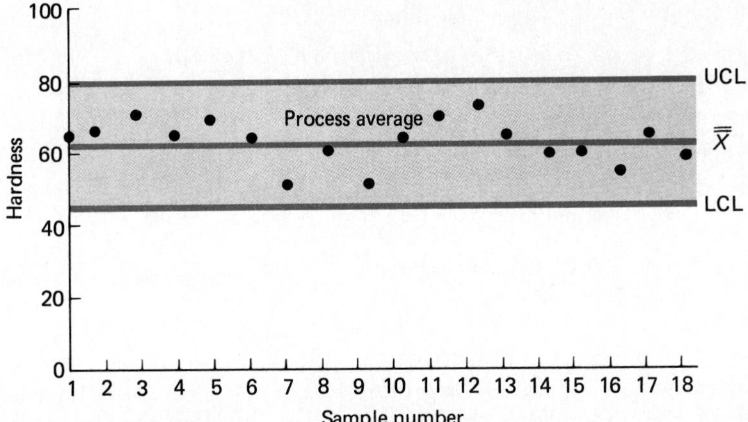

FIGURE 16.5
$\bar{X}$ chart: Control chart for average hardness of window seals

The resulting control chart for average hardness is shown in Figure 16.5.

Although the example uses ($k = 3$) control limits of three standard deviations, which is the dominant industry practice, some applications merit the use of wider or narrower control limits. The real issue is one of risk. Management must decide how certain they want to be that when a process appears out of control, it really is out of control. Managers may desire different degrees of certainty based upon their knowledge of the importance of an error in the process. Three of the many choices available in setting the control limits are to set the limits at ± 1, 2, or 3 standard deviations from the mean. These choices are expressed in terms of standard deviations ($S_{\bar{X}}$) of the sampling distribution shown in Figure 16.6. With narrow control limits ($\bar{\bar{X}} \pm 1S_{\bar{X}}$), there is a reasonable chance that when the process appears to be out of control, it may not actually be out of control (probability .317, or 1 − .683). This probability is equal to the area outside the control limits in part (a) of Figure 16.6. With wide control limits ($\bar{\bar{X}} \pm 3S_{\bar{X}}$), there is little chance of such a sampling error (probability .003). This is the area outside the control limits in part (b); when a sample mean falls outside these limits, the process is very likely out of control.

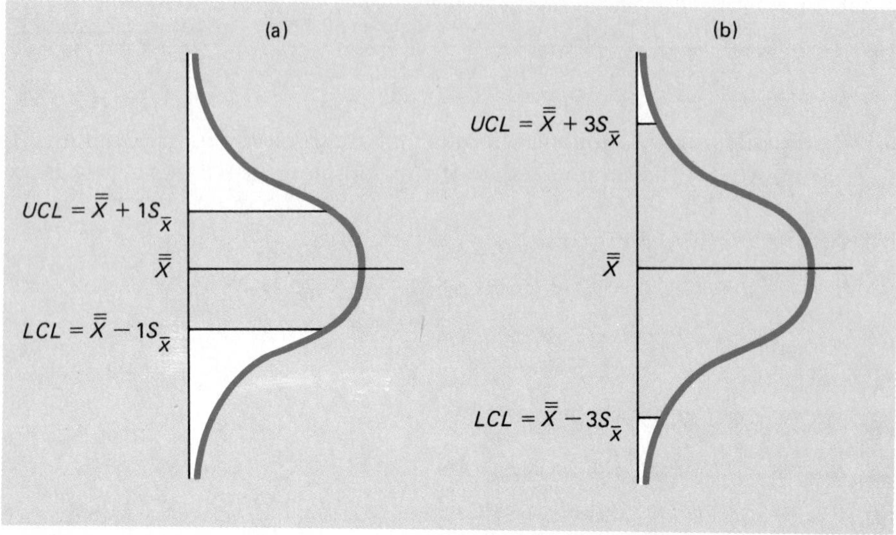

FIGURE 16.6
Probabilities of α error for control limits set at 1 standard deviation (a) and 3 standard deviations (b)

The selection of control limits involves tradeoffs between two types of risks. With the first type, α, called the *producer's risk* or *type I error*, there is a possibility of concluding that the process is out of control when it is actually in a state of statistical control. (This is the same terminology used later in sampling plans.) The producer's risk is reduced by using wide control limits; it is increased by using narrower control limits. The second type of risk, β, the *consumer's risk* or *type II error*, describes the situation in which an out-of-control process is mistakenly adjudged to be in control. This risk increases as the control limits are widened and decreases as they are narrowed. Ultimately, the choice of control limit width must be based on these risks and the costs associated with them. If the costs of undetected shifts are extremely high relative to the costs of correcting the process, narrow limits (lower consumer risk) are appropriate. If the costs of restoring the process to the desired state are very high compared with the costs of producing defective output, wider limits (lower producer's risk) are appropriate.

Simplifying Chart Construction: Tabular Methods If the process we are controlling possesses an important condition, namely, it is normally distributed, we can benefit from tabular methods rather than using equations 16.6 and 16.7 for constructing control charts.[3] The tabular method uses sample ranges, which can be calculated quickly, as substi-

[3]If the process distribution is skewed, a median control chart, instead of an averages control chart, can be used to control the central tendency of the process. See Grant and Leavenworth, *Statistical Quality Control.*

tutes for sample standard deviations to determine the control limits for $\overline{X}$ charts. The first two columns in Table 16.1 give the necessary factors that can be used in the following equations:

$$UCL \text{ for } \overline{X} \text{ chart} = \overline{\overline{X}} + A_2\overline{R} \tag{16.8}$$

$$LCL \text{ for } \overline{X} \text{ chart} = \overline{\overline{X}} - A_2\overline{R}$$

EXAMPLE Using the rubber seal hardness data, the range (R_j) of each sample of five observations ($n = 5$) is calculated as shown below.

Sample (j)	Individual Hardness (X_i: $i = 1 \ldots 5$)	Sample Range (R_j)
1	65, 70, 60, 50, 65	70 − 50 = 20
2	70, 80, 70, 40, 60	80 − 40 = 40
.		
.		
.		
17	60, 70, 85, 60, 60	85 − 60 = 25
18	55, 75, 80, 40, 55	80 − 40 = 40

The average range is

$$\overline{R} = \frac{20 + 40 + \ldots + 25 + 40}{18} = 28.89$$

The control limits, then, using equations 16.8, are calculated as follows:

$$UCL_{\overline{X}} = 62.56 + (0.58)(28.89) = 79.32$$
$$LCL_{\overline{X}} = 62.56 - (0.58)(28.89) = 45.80$$

As you can see, the tabular method yields control limits that are very close to those we previously calculated. Based on the 18 historical sample averages, the process seems to be in a state of statistical control, but averages are not the whole story. What about the variability of the process? The answer to this question is examined next.

Control Charts for Variability Earlier, in Figure 16.2, we saw how increases in process variability can result in nonconforming output. We want to be able to detect changes in variability, and we can do so by using a control chart for the standard deviation or for the range of the process. We restrict our attention to the R chart, a control chart for the range, which is widely used in industry because it is computationally simple, easy to understand, and tabular help (Table 16.1) is readily available. Again, as was the case with the averages chart, the tabular method is applicable only if the process is normally distributed.

The data for the R chart includes the range of individuals in each

Table 16.1 Factors for $\overline{X}$ and R charts (for three-sigma control limits)

Number of Observations in Subgroup n	Factor for $\overline{X}$ Chart A_2	Factors for R Chart	
		LCL D_3	UCL D_4
2	1.88	0	3.27
3	1.02	0	2.57
4	0.73	0	2.28
5	0.58	0	2.11
6	0.48	0	2.00
7	0.42	0.08	1.92
8	0.37	0.14	1.86
9	0.34	0.18	1.82
10	0.31	0.22	1.78
11	0.29	0.26	1.74
12	0.27	0.28	1.72
13	0.25	0.31	1.69
14	0.24	0.33	1.67
15	0.22	0.35	1.65
16	0.21	0.36	1.64
17	0.20	0.38	1.62
18	0.19	0.39	1.61
19	0.19	0.40	1.60
20	0.18	0.41	1.59

Source: Adapted from E. L. Grant and R. S. Leavenworth, *Statistical Quality Control,* 6th ed. (New York: McGraw-Hill Book Company, 1988), p. 670.

sample; each sample range is plotted on the chart. The average range, $\overline{R}$, is also drawn on the chart. The control limits are calculated using equations 16.9 below, along with the appropriate factors D_3 and D_4 from Table 16.1. After the process demonstrates a state of statistical control, subsequent sample ranges can be plotted on the chart. When the new ranges are unusually high or low (outside the control limits), investigation is undertaken to find the cause of the nonrandom behavior in the process.

$$UCL \text{ for } R \text{ chart} = D_4\overline{R} \qquad (16.9)$$
$$LCL \text{ for } R \text{ chart} = D_3\overline{R}$$

EXAMPLE For the rubber seal hardness example, $\overline{R}$ of the 18 sample ranges is 28.89. From Table 16.1, for samples of size $n = 5$, $D_3 = 0$ and $D_4 = 2.11$. The control limits, using equations 16.9, are calculated as follows:

$$UCL_R = (2.11)(28.89) = 60.95$$
$$LCL_R = (0)(28.89) = 0$$

The lower control limit is set at zero on the hardness scale since the D_3 factors from Table 16.1 are zero for all sample sizes below $n = 7$. The 18 sample ranges are plotted on the R chart in Figure 16.7.

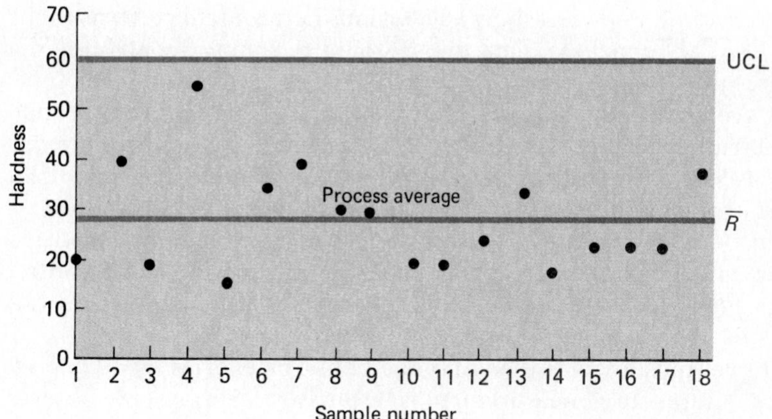

FIGURE 16.7
R chart: Control chart for range of hardness of window seals

Interpreting the Charts Up to this point we have completed steps 1 to 3 in developing control charts; the historical performance has been plotted. But before we can begin using these tools to monitor *future* process behavior, we must first confirm that the historical data reflect the true chronic condition of the process, that only random variation is present. We obtain this confirmation by looking jointly at the two control charts ($\overline{X}$ and R), along with the process capability histogram (Figure 16.1). The comparison is essential because the three diagrams contain different information about the data, and all three must be consistent with one another before we can conclude that the variation in the process is random.

The control charts show the *time-phased* pattern of sample averages and sample ranges. No predictable patterns are evident in the plotted points, and none falls outside the control limits. Consequently, we would like to conclude that the plotted points reflect random variation, but to do so we must first confirm that the process has a normal distribution. Why? Because the tabular factors for the control chart limits, and hence their validity, are based on the assumption of normality. If the process departs from a normal distribution, the control limits in Figures 16.5 and 16.7 are invalid and, consequently, we cannot tell if the process is in a state of statistical control. We validate the normality assumption now by observing that the histogram of individual observations in Figure 16.1 closely resembles, although not perfectly, a normal distribution. A subsequent statistical test for goodness of fit supported the normality assumption. We thus conclude that the control chart limits are valid.

Next we use the control charts to confirm the validity of the histogram in Figure 16.1. The validation is needed because the histogram merely *summarizes* the 90 observations; it may be masking sequential patterns (nonrandom variations). Perhaps, for example, the process average or standard deviation was shifting while the samples were being taken. If so, those shifts might not be evident from looking at the histogram, but the control charts would reveal such patterns. The control charts in

Figures 16.5 and 16.7 do not show any obvious nonrandom patterns in the plottings, so we conclude that the histogram contains only random variations.

Our cross-checking gives us good assurance that the chronic condition of the rubber seal process has been identified. Now, we have created useful tools for statistical process control; we can go on to step 4 and plot future process data on the validated control charts.

Many of the procedures that were described previously for constructing variables control charts are also applicable for constructing control charts for attributes, as we see next.

Control Charts for Attributes

When sample units are classified into one of two categories (good or bad, success or failure, etc.), measurement is by attribute. Suppose we observe a sample of units from some process and classify each as either defective or acceptable. We can calculate the fraction of defective units in the sample and compare it to the historical fraction defective in the process. Such a chart is called a *fraction defectives chart* (or *p chart*). If the sample fraction defective (p) deviates widely from the historic process fraction defective ($\overline{p}$), we may conclude that some change in the process has occurred, that the current fraction defective is either higher or lower than usual. If the process is under control, the sample fraction defective (p) is an estimate of the underlying process fraction defective. Several such sample estimates tend to be normally distributed.

To construct an attribute control chart, we begin by inspecting a sample of n units to determine what fraction of those units is defective. We do this with equation 16.10, where x is the number of defective units:

$$p = \frac{x}{n} \tag{16.10}$$

If this process is repeated, say m times, we get several estimates of fraction defective. Then, using these m estimates of p, we calculate the historical *average* fraction ($\overline{p}$) for the process using equation 16.11.

$$\overline{p} = \frac{\sum_{i=1}^{m} p_i}{m} \text{ or } \frac{\sum_{i=1}^{m} x}{nm} \tag{16.11}$$

The central limit theorem applies for fraction defectives charts in that samples of p values have an approximately normal distribution (unless the sample size is small and $\overline{p}$ is close to zero). The standard deviation of the distribution of p is given by equation 16.12. In this equation, $\overline{p}$ is the average fraction defective, and n is the sample size used in each sample that was taken.

$$\sigma_p = \sqrt{\frac{\overline{p}(1 - \overline{p})}{n}} \tag{16.12}$$

The control limits are calculated from equation 16.13.

$$UCL_p = \bar{p} + k\sigma_p \qquad (16.13)$$

$$LCL_p = \bar{p} - k\sigma_p$$

EXAMPLE A visual inspection for scratches (each unit is judged good or bad) on a decorative paint trim operation produced the following data for last week.

Sample Number (i)	Number of Units Sampled	Number of Defects	Sample Number (i)	Number of Units Sampled	Number of Defects
1	30	5	11	30	5
2	30	4	12	30	7
3	30	4	13	30	4
4	30	5	14	30	5
5	30	7	15	30	4
6	30	4	16	30	5
7	30	5	17	30	5
8	30	6	18	30	7
9	30	4	19	30	6
10	30	5	20	30	4

This week 30 pieces were sampled on each of two occasions. Six pieces were found defective in the first sample, and 9 in the second sample. As operations manager, you are wondering if the process is in control this week.

To find a solution, construct a fraction defectives control chart with two-sigma limits based on last week's typical process performance. Last week's data are used to calculate average fraction defective ($\bar{p}$), the standard deviation of average fraction defective (σ_p), and the control limits (*UCL* and *LCL*). Then plot the percent defective for this week's samples against last week's control chart. The required calculations are shown here.

$$\bar{p} \text{ (for last week)} = \frac{\Sigma x}{nm} = \frac{101}{(30)(20)} = .168$$

$$\sigma_p = \sqrt{\frac{\bar{p}(1-\bar{p})}{n}} = \sqrt{\frac{(.168)(1-.168)}{30}} = .0683$$

$$UCL = \bar{p} + 2\sigma_{\bar{p}} = .168 + 2(.0683) = .305$$

$$LCL = \bar{p} - 2\sigma_{\bar{p}} = .168 - 2(.0683) = .031$$

$$\text{Sample defectives in second week: } p_{21} = \frac{6}{30} = 0.20;\ p_{22} = \frac{9}{30} = .30$$

Now you can construct the resulting control chart as shown in Figure 16.8. Monday's fraction defective is close to the historical process average. Tuesday's sample indicates that the process is still in a state of control. If a future sample falls outside the control limits, the operating manager can

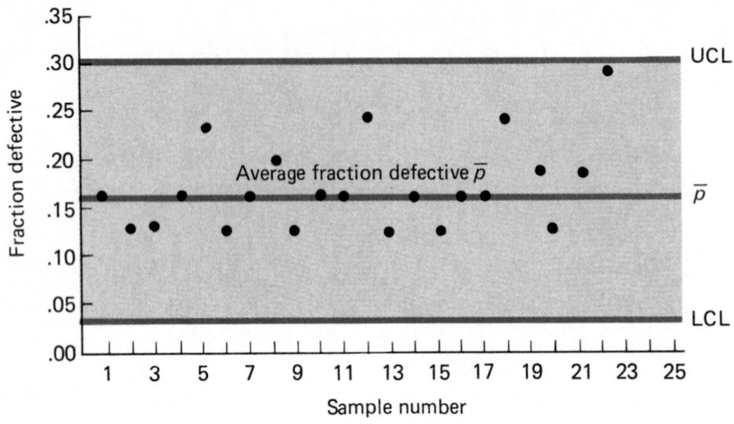

FIGURE 16.8
Fraction defectives control chart (p chart); n = 30

be quite confident (95.4 percent) that nonrandom variation has arisen in the paint trim process.

Although our discussion has focused on fraction defectives charts, other types of attributes control charts, some of which are summarized in Table 16.2, are used in various applications. Examples and methods for using these charts can be found in the quality control references at the end of this chapter.

Other Control Chart Considerations As Figure 16.9 shows, control chart data can form many configurations. Notice that when the process is in its chronic condition, sample observations are randomly scattered around the central value of the chart. When successive sample points form an identifiable pattern or fall outside the control limits, very likely something other than random effects is in operation. Subsequently management should launch an investigation to determine the cause of this nonrandom behavior.

Table 16.2 Types of attributes control charts

Name of Chart	Symbol	Attribute Measured
Fraction defective	p	Fraction of nonconforming units in a sample
Number defective	np	Number of nonconforming units in a sample
Nonconformities	c	Number of nonconformities in one unit of product
Demerit score	D	Weighted sum of demerits for different nonconformities in one unit of product

Source: Adapted from E. L. Grant and R. S. Leavenworth, *Statistical Quality Control,* 6th ed. (New York: McGraw-Hill Book Company, 1988) p. 670.

Step 6 in the construction of control charts, you may remember, is updating the charts. When the charts are periodically updated, they become dynamic rather than static. The control limits and/or the central tendency of the chart change as the process changes over time. Charts must be updated whenever breakthrough and quality improvement projects are implemented, or when any other change occurs in the people, methods, machines, or materials in the process.

After we have identified the product (or process) characteristic to be controlled, we must resolve a number of other design questions. What sample size should be used? How often should a sample be taken? What control limits should be selected? To what degree do we want to emphasize detection and control versus prevention? The answers to these and other design questions are important because they determine both the

FIGURE 16.9
Control chart evidence for investigation

Source: B. L. Hansen, *Quality Control* (Englewood Cliffs, N.J.: Prentice Hall, 1973), p. 65.

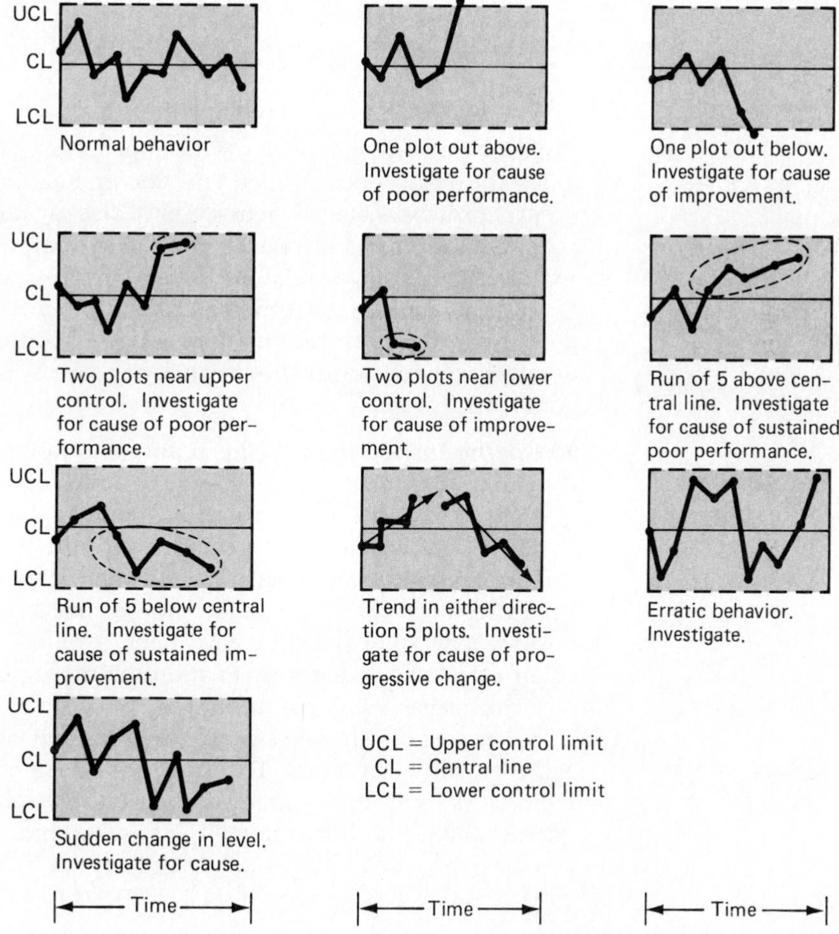

effectiveness and the cost of the control process. Specific answers to these design questions depend to a great extent on the specific organization, on the nature of its processes and products. In general, choices among alternative design parameters involve tradeoffs among opposing costs and risks, and these economic design considerations must be evaluated.

One reason for the increased use of control charts is the growing number of user-friendly and powerful software packages, such as *SQCpack,* that can be used right at the workstations on production or service lines.[4] But even with manual systems, control charts are used in some form in many manufacturing facilities. We have seen them in automobile manufacturing, appliance production, diecasting operations, pet food production, metal stamping, and petroleum refining. More recently, service industries have adopted this useful technique in various settings; accident rates provide measures of goodness of traffic control processes, numbers of robberies as a measure of public safety systems, sickness rates as measures of health care systems, and accident rates as measures of safety in ski slope recreation systems. Banks, hospitals, and other service organizations make use of them too.

INSPECTION

Inspection of raw materials, work-in-process, and finished products provides the basic data needed for documentation and evaluation in the control process. *Inspection,* as we have already implied in our examples, is the observation and measurement of the conversion process outputs and inputs. Inspection can be done either visually or mechanically; its purpose is to see whether the physical characteristics of the good or service conform with specifications. Inspection is commonly divided into three areas: receiving inspection, work-in-process inspection, and finished goods inspection.

Receiving Inspection The quality of outputs from a conversion process can be no better than the inputs from which they are generated, unless excessive costs are first incurred to modify the inputs. Inputs are often built up, over a succession of stages, into the final product. At the end of this progression, we sometimes find that defective inputs used in initial stages result in an unacceptable final product. This requires subsequent costly repair, which could have been avoided. Therefore, management often establishes programs to monitor the inputs prior to their use. At *receiving inspection,* incoming shipments of raw materials subcomponents from vendors or other inputs are observed and evaluated against predetermined quality standards. These materials are often physically separated from work-in-process materials and are only released to operations after passing the initial inspection. It is best to eliminate this activity, moving

[4]*SQCpack: Statistical Quality Control Pack* (Dayton, Ohio: P-Q Systems, 1983).

inspection to the vendor's facility, but only if a working relationship of trust can be established.

Work-in-Process Inspection The employee who produces an item should be responsible for inspecting it to ensure its quality. When there is a felt need for someone other than the line production employee to inspect work, occasionally management inserts special inspection called *work-in-process inspection.* The outputs of one or more stages of production are screened before they are used in subsequent operations. The intensity of inspection depends on the volume of output, the cost of inspecting, and the cost consequences (in subsequent stages) of not inspecting.

An important decision for the operations manager is how many inspection stations to have and where to locate them. A very simple heuristic can be used to help make this decision. Two key factors must be considered, the *percent of defective* output expected at each stage of the conversion process and the *cost* of inspection. Ideally, you would want to inspect at locations where inspection costs are low and percent defective is high. This would give a low cost of inspection per percent defectives detected. We can use a simple three-step procedure for selecting the locations of inspection stations:

1. Identify all stages of the conversion process that are potential locations for inspection stations. Estimate the inspection costs and gather historical percent defective information for these stations.
2. Compute the critical ratio for each potential inspection station:

$$\text{Critical ratio} = \frac{\text{Cost of inspection}}{\text{\% defective}} \tag{16.14}$$

3. Rank the inspection stations by critical ratio. The lowest critical ratio is the most desirable location, the second lowest critical ratio is the second most desirable, and so forth. With limited resources, locate inspection stations until funds are depleted.

EXAMPLE A process has three possible location sites for inspection, A, B, and C. Process percent defectives are 10 percent for site A, 5 percent for site B, and 6 percent for site C. The cost of inspection at site A is \$150, at B is \$200, and at C is \$100. Critical ratios are

$$A = \frac{\$150}{.10} = \$1{,}500$$

$$B = \frac{\$200}{.05} = \$4{,}000$$

$$C = \frac{\$100}{.06} = \$1{,}667$$

Inspection stations should be located first at station A, second at station C, and finally at station B. If funds are limited, locate in that order until funds for inspection are depleted.

Finished Goods Inspection Various testing procedures can be used to determine whether the final product conforms to functional and appearance standards. If it does not, sources of discrepancy must be identified, and corrective measures must be initiated. Finished goods inspection should be a verification stage as the management focus should be *prevention* early in the operations process, not detection at this stage.

ACCEPTANCE SAMPLING

Acceptance sampling is an important statistical application in quality control.[5] It involves the use of systematic plans that prescribe how to sample from finished production and how to use the sampled information to maintain quality at desired levels. It is often used to monitor the quality of incoming materials and parts, or for any other situation that involves making an accept/reject decision about the overall quality of a large shipment or batch of items. As you can see, acceptance sampling, in contrast to ongoing statistical process control, is an "after-the-fact" procedure; it is applied *after* production has ended.

We'll focus on sampling plans as they might apply to receiving inspection. When a large shipment of a purchased item arrives, someone must decide whether to accept or reject the shipment. We have a range of choices from inspecting all units in the shipment to sampling just a few units. A systematic sampling plan can provide the information needed for the accept/reject decision for the entire shipment. Thus the time, effort, and cost of 100 percent inspection are avoided. Of course, there are some risks involved because of possible sampling errors.

Sampling Errors

Two kinds of errors can result from sampling. A shipment of good quality can be mistakenly rejected if a disproportionately large number of defective units from the shipment is selected at random. It is also possible to select at random mostly good units from a shipment of poor quality overall. The first type of risk is α (type I error), the *producer's risk;* the second is β (type II error), the *consumer's risk.* We want a sampling procedure that assures that each of these risks is no greater than a specified chosen level.

Sampling Plan Alternatives

Three classes of sampling plans are most commonly found in industrial applications. With a *single sampling* plan, a randomly selected sample of n units is taken from the shipment, and the quality of each sampled unit is determined. If more than c of the sampled units are nonconforming, the entire shipment is rejected. If c or fewer items are nonconforming, the entire shipment is accepted. Notice that the decision is based solely

[5]See Erwin M. Saniga and Larry E. Shirland, "Quality Control in Practice . . . A Survey," *Quality Progress* 10, no. 5 (May 1977), 32, who found that over 70 percent of responding firms used sampling and control charts. About a third of the respondents judged quality control techniques moderately useful, a third fairly useful, and a third of great consequence. Few rated the techniques of little consequence.

on the results from a single sample of n units. *Double sampling* is a two-stage process in which the first smaller sample may result in a clear accept or reject decision, or in an inconclusive result that calls for a second sampling. After the second sampling, the accumulative sample results from both samples lead to either an acceptance or a rejection. The total number of units needed to make a decision, on average, is smaller with double sampling than with single sampling. *Multiple sampling* is a further extension of the double-sampling concept in which many samples, each of a very small size, may be taken from the shipment until the cumulative sample evidence is conclusive enough to warrant acceptance or rejection. In most applications, the multiple sampling methods require fewer sample units than double sampling plans to arrive at the accept/reject decision. Although double and multiple plans offer the advantage of somewhat less sampling, they are also more cumbersome to design, implement, and understand. These factors may explain why single sampling, which is discussed in greater detail below, is so frequently encountered in practice.

Operating Characteristic Curves

For large shipments consisting of many units, say 5,000, we must determine a sample size (n) and an acceptance number (c) such that we obtain satisfactory assurance that our accept/reject decision, based on the sample, is correct. The choices for n and c determine the characteristics of our sampling plan. Standard procedures are available for determining the sampling plan parameters, n and c, that will meet the performance requirements specified by the user. The performance requirements include the following four items of information: AQL, LTPD, α, and β. AQL is conventional notation meaning "acceptable quality level," or "good quality." LTPD is "lot tolerance percent defective," or "poor quality level." Assigning numeric values to these four parameters is largely a matter of managerial judgment. As soon as their numeric values have been decided, values for n and c can be determined.

EXAMPLE A large medical clinic purchases quantity shipments of pregnancy test kits (PTKs). A shipment contains 10,000 PTKs. It is important that the chemical composition of the PTK shipment be evaluated so that prescribing physicians are assured of valid tests.

Physicians have agreed that a shipment has acceptable quality if no more than 2 percent of the PTKs in it are of incorrect chemical composition. They consider shipments with 5 percent or more defectives to be an extremely bad quality shipment. We want a plan that has a .95 probability of accepting good shipments but only a .10 probability of accepting extremely bad shipments. These performance specifications for the sampling plan are summarized on the left side of Table 16.3. A sampling plan was derived to meet these performance requirements. The plan calls for 308 PTKs to be sampled from each shipment (right side of Table 16.3). If more than ten of these are defective, the entire shipment is rejected. If ten or fewer defectives are found, the shipment is accepted. In this way shipments consisting of 2 percent defectives have only five chances out of 100 of being rejected, whereas shipments with 5 percent defectives have only ten chances out of 100 of being accepted. This sampling plan includes procedures for determining the probability of accepting the shipment if percents defective are between 2 and 5. These probabilities are shown in Figure 16.10.

The curves in Figure 16.10, called the *OC curves* (*operating characteristic curves*), reveal how sampling plans discriminate when used on incoming shipments. If a shipment is of high quality (low percent defectives), a good sampling plan gives us a high probability of accepting the shipment. Shipments of poorer quality (high percent defectives) have a lower probability of being accepted by the plan.

You can see from the uppermost OC curve in Figure 16.10 that the desired probabilities of accepting good and bad quality PTK shipments have been obtained. The second OC curve represents a different sampling plan, $n = 154$ and $c = 5$, that does not meet desired performance specifications; it offers only a .88 probability of accepting good quality shipments, and has a .22 probability of accepting a bad shipment.

***General Effects of* n *and* c** Each sampling plan consisting of n and c has a unique OC curve. Sampling plans with large sample sizes are more discriminating than plans with smaller sample sizes. Figure 16.10 shows OC curves for two sampling plans with different sample sizes and acceptance numbers. For both plans the acceptance number, c, is in constant proportion to n. For plans with larger n's the probability of accepting good quality lots is higher than for plans with smaller n's. Also, for bad quality lots, the probability of acceptance decreases when n is larger. Of course, these benefits are not obtained without incurring the higher inspection costs associated with large sample sizes.

The effect of increasing the acceptance number (for a given value of n) is to increase the probability of accepting the shipment for all levels of percent defective other than zero (Figure 16.11). By using a larger c, we allow shipments with more defectives to pass inspection. As c is decreased, the inspection plan becomes tighter.

Table 16.3 Sampling plan and specifications for PTKs

Performance Specifications	Parameters of Sampling Plan
Good quality (AQL) = .02 or fewer defectives	
Desired probability of accepting a good quality shipment = .95	$n = 308$
Risk: probability of α errors = .05	$c = 10$
Bad quality (LTPD) = .05 or more defectives	
Desired probability of accepting a bad quality shipment = .10	
Risk: probability of β errors = .10	

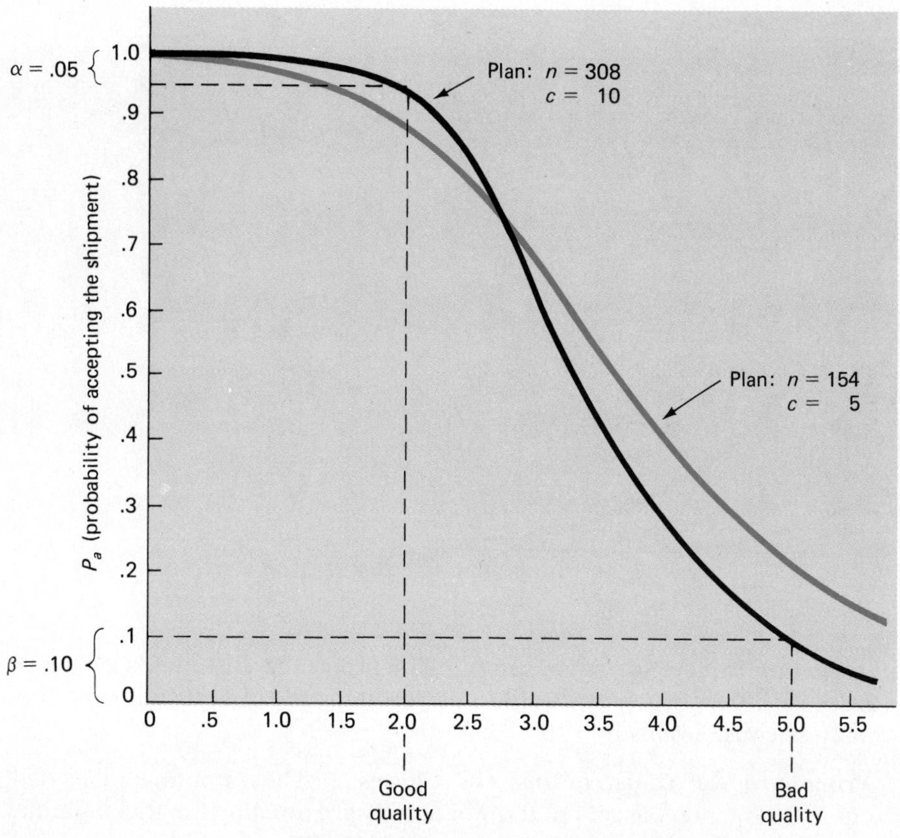

FIGURE 16.10
Probabilities of accepting a PTK shipment (OC curve)

In general, higher values of c allow for "looser" performance, increasing the probability of accepting a shipment with a given level of defectives. Increasing n results in greater confidence that we have correctly discriminated between good and bad shipments. However, inspection costs are also increased with larger values of n. The task of quality management is to find the proper balance between the costs and benefits of alternative sampling plans.

Establishing Policies on Good and Bad Quality Choosing what percents defective constitute good and bad quality is a vital management decision. The sampling plan is designed around this decision. If managers are too stringent in defining good quality, the costs of obtaining (purchasing) such high quality shipments can become exorbitant. At the other extreme, a high percent defective can result in conversion disruptions, high scrap and rework costs, and higher costs of customer ill will. If it's possible to negotiate good and bad quality levels when you're purchasing shipments from suppliers, you can arrange for the vendor's finished goods

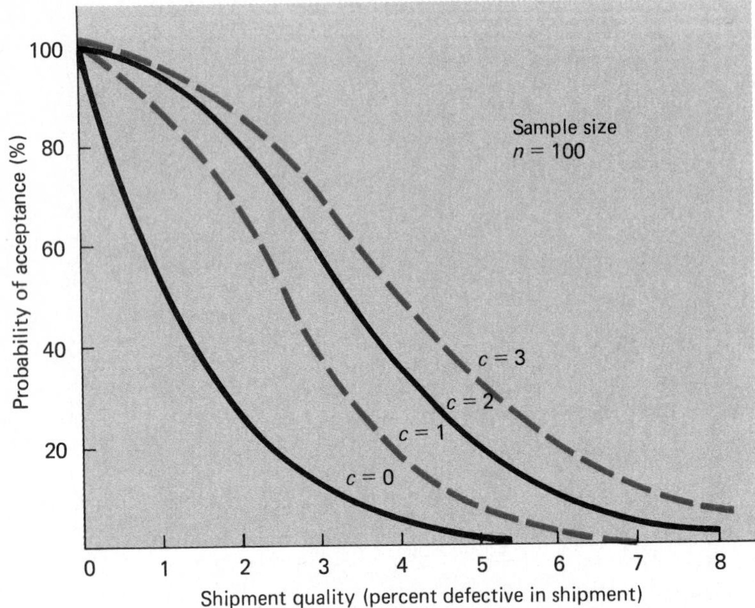

FIGURE 16.11
Effect of variations in c

inspection to have the same sampling plan that the customer's receiving inspection uses. Such a procedure is recommended because it simplifies matters considerably.

Procedure for Constructing OC Curves The sampling plans discussed here are based on the Poisson approximation to the binomial probability distribution. We assume a random sample of size n is taken from a Poisson population that has an average number of defective units, p, in a standard sample size. Then we use tables or graphs to calculate the probability of obtaining c or fewer defectives in the sample or of obtaining more than c defectives. This general approach is adopted here to show how data is obtained for any OC curve.

The chart shown in Figure 16.12 is a convenient substitute for extensive probability computations. Each diagonal curve represents an acceptance number (c) for the sampling plan. Then, for any proposed fraction defective (p) and any sample size (n), the resulting pn is used to find the probability of acceptance (for c or fewer defects) from the left side of the chart. Data points for an OC curve are obtained by using different p values (quality levels) while holding n and c constant.

EXAMPLE We wish to construct the OC curve for a single sampling plan that has an acceptance number $c = 2$ and a sample size $n = 30$. For each of 12 assumed values of shipment fraction defective (p), the probability of acceptance (P_a) is estimated using Figure 16.12, yielding the following data for the OC curve:

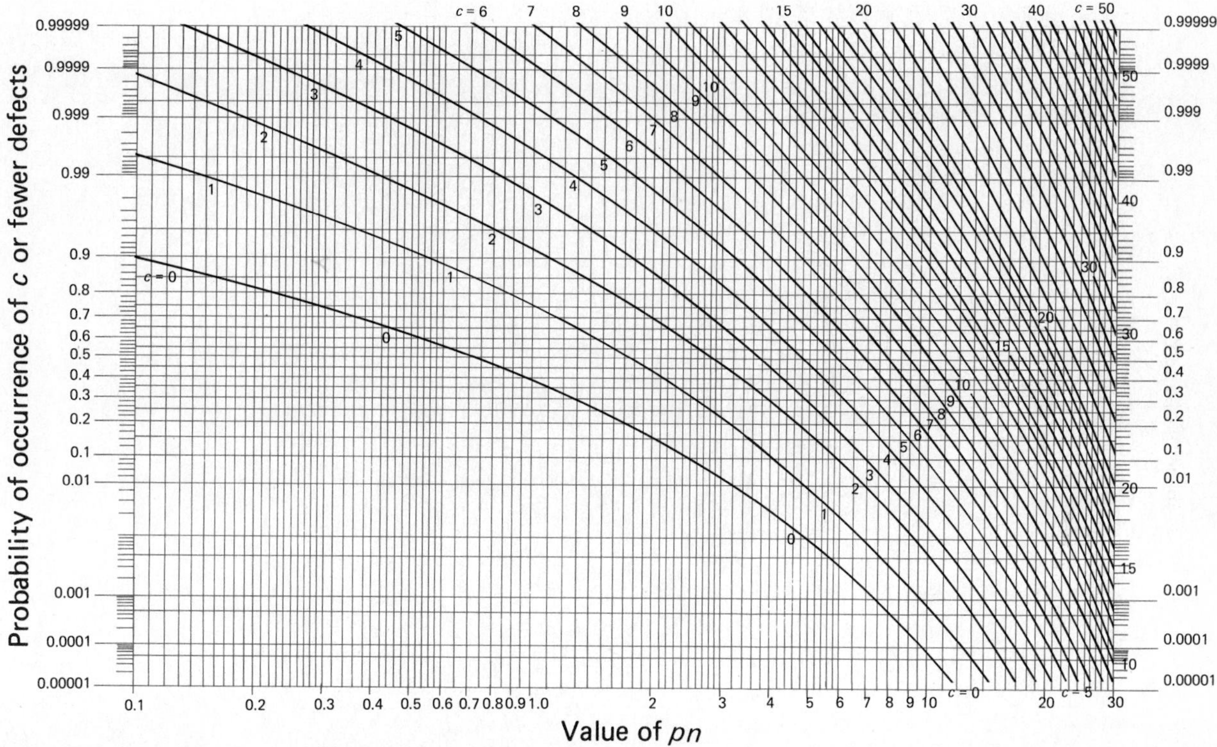

FIGURE 16.12
Probability curves for Poisson distribution

Source: H. F. Dodge and H. G. Romig, *Sampling Inspection Tables* (New York: John Wiley & Sons, Inc., 1959).

p	*n*	*np*	P_a	*p*	*n*	*np*	P_a
.01	30	0.30	.995	.11	30	3.30	.370
.02	30	0.60	.973	.13	30	3.90	.270
.03	30	0.90	.930	.15	30	4.50	.180
.05	30	1.50	.800	.17	30	5.10	.130
.07	30	2.10	.650	.19	30	5.70	.090
.09	30	2.70	.520	.21	30	6.30	.050

The resulting OC curve is shown in Figure 16.13 on page 564.

You may experiment, then, using various combinations of *n* and *c* to obtain an OC curve (and the associated sampling plan) that gives the levels of protection you desire for accepting good quality shipments and rejecting bad quality shipments. More formalized approaches to constructing sampling plans are discussed in the reference books on quality control at the end of this chapter.

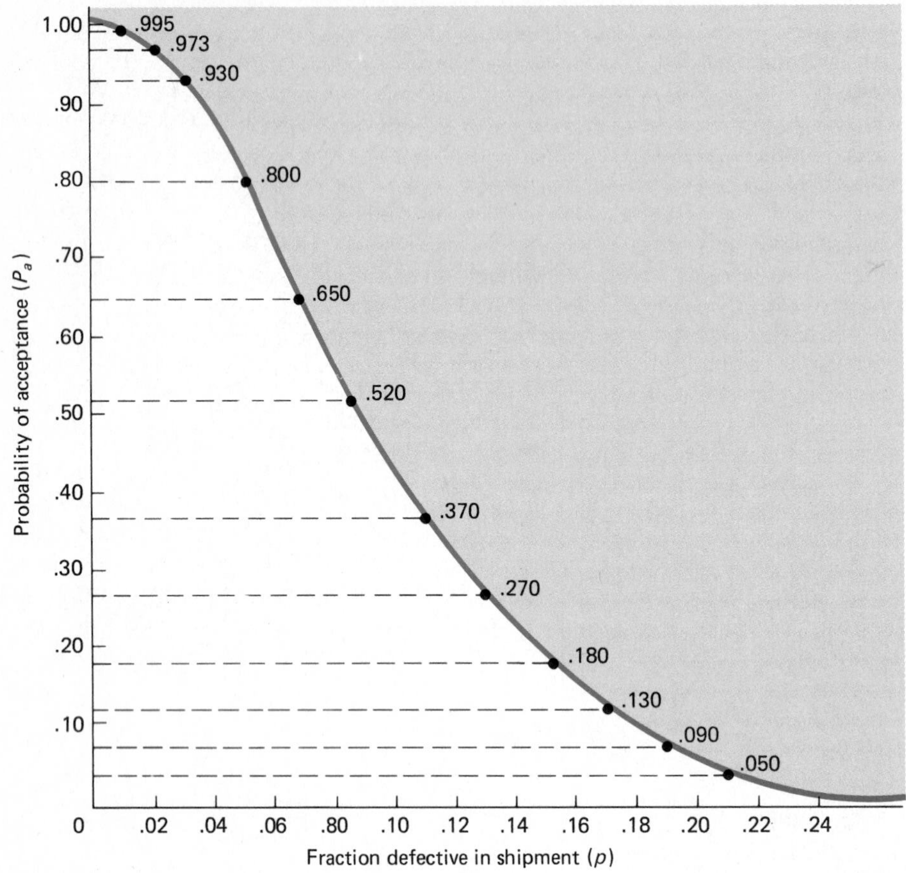

FIGURE 16.13
OC curve for n = 30, c = 2

SUMMARY

The need for quality analysis and control arises from the fact that variation exists in every operating system and it increases the costs of operations. By learning more about it, through process capability studies, we can better understand and control process variation to increase the amount of conforming output from the operating system. The capability study measures process performance under chronic conditions, in the absence of sporadic variations. It provides an estimate of the process's ability to produce output that meets specifications.

Statistical process control (SPC) seeks to detect and eliminate nonrandom (sporadic) variations as they arise while the process is operating. The process is monitored periodically by examining sample units of output. The critical characteristics of the samples are recorded on control charts to determine if they have shifted away from a random pattern. If so, action is initiated to eliminate the causes of the sporadic behavior in the system. Variables control charts, such as $\overline{X}$ and R charts, assist in controlling the average and the variability of measurable characteristics such as length or weight. Attributes charts, such as the p chart for fraction defectives, are used when the sample observations are classified, rather than measured, based on whether they possess a certain characteristic.

Inspection is the set of procedures for observing quality characteristics and for gathering the data for quality analysis and control. It can be done either visually or mechanically to determine the existing characteristics of any inputs and outputs of the conversion system. Inspection is most commonly encountered in materials receiving, work-in-process inspection during conversion, and finished goods after conversion is completed.

Acceptance sampling is a statistical plan for making acceptance/rejection decisions on an existing shipment (or lot) of a product. Rather than inspecting the entire shipment, a random sample of several units is evaluated and is the basis for the decision on the entire lot. The choice of how many to inspect and the limits for nonconformances is determined by the user's tolerance for sampling errors and the desired quality levels. Operating characteristics curves show the risks of each sampling plan, along with its ability to discriminate between good and bad quality lots.

CASE

Hydrolock, Inc.

In 1978 George Thrall founded Hydrolock, Inc., a manufacturing company producing small rubber gaskets used in hydraulic systems. His gaskets were simple in design and relatively easy to produce in large quantities. In 1989, gross sales from servicing customers throughout North America with large quantity shipments reached $8 million. A very autocratic management style exists throughout the company.

Demand for Hydrolock products has increased so rapidly that the manufacturing facility is constantly under pressure to increase output around the clock. Customers and sales personnel in the field often call the home facility to determine estimated lead times for prospective orders and estimated delivery times for existing orders. In response, production foremen have increasingly emphasized to employees the need for increasing output to meet demand.

In late 1989, George Thrall began experiencing a new problem, an increase in customer complaints about the quality of shipments being received. Plant supervision insisted the problem was twofold and that nothing could be done about either: (1) workers were asked to produce at maximum efficiency, so quality suffered; and (2) workers had absolutely no motivation for high quality performance. George decided to add a quality control analyst to the Hydrolock staff in hopes of finding and correcting the sources of customer dissatisfaction.

In his first two weeks the quality analyst uncovered some data that a production foreman had recorded two years previously.

Data for Gasket YB4 (1987)

Sample Number	Sample Size	Number of Defective Gaskets in Sample
1	40	6
2	40	1
3	40	0
4	40	2
5	40	1
6	40	4
7	40	3
8	40	2
9	40	6
10	40	0
11	40	3
12	40	2

The analyst began gathering data on current production of the same gasket. Samples were taken once each day for five consecutive work days with these results.

Data for Gasket YB4 (1989)

Sample Number	Sample Size	Number of Defective Gaskets in Sample
1	40	4
2	40	8
3	40	6
4	40	2
5	40	8

If you were the new analyst, what ideas would you entertain for getting to the bottom of George Thrall's quality problem? Of what value are the data at hand? Does management have a style and outlook toward employees that enhances quality performance? What would you recommend?

REVIEW AND DISCUSSION QUESTIONS

1. Discuss the steps in a process capability study.
2. What are the "natural limits" of a process? How do they relate to product specification limits?
3. Select a convenient operation and identify its sources of variation. Describe how each source can result in output variability.
4. Identify different types of inspection and discuss their roles in the quality assurance and control process.
5. What is the relationship between inspection and acceptance sampling?

6. How does measurement by variables differ from measurement by attributes?
7. What is an acceptance sampling plan? How does it work, what factors must be considered in designing it, and what costs are incurred in using it?
8. What is an OC curve?
9. How do control charts differ from acceptance sampling plans? Under what circumstances is each appropriate?
10. Give examples of control chart patterns that would lead you to conclude that control action may be warranted.

PROBLEMS

Solved Problems

1. An attribute control chart exists (Figure 16.14) for part 223B with average fraction defective .125, upper control limit .200, and lower control limit .050. The chart is based on two months of daily data. Twelve units were sampled each day for the past six days with defectives, 2, 1, 2, 0, 3, and 3.

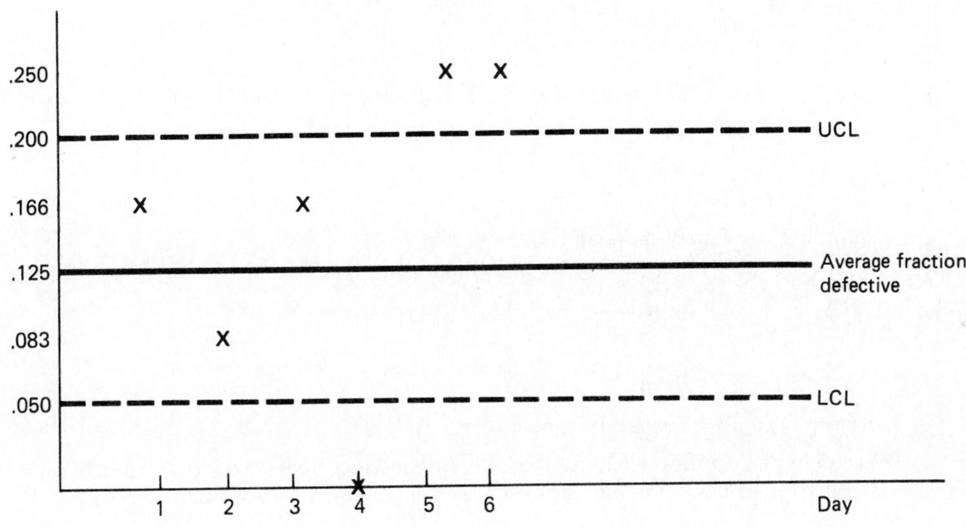

FIGURE 16.14
Example attributes control chart

(a) Construct a control chart for management, carefully labeling the chart, and interpret it for management.
(b) What is the significance of day 4 being below the lower control limit set by the quality control technician?

Solution for Part a: The solution for Part a is shown in Figure 16.14. Fraction defectives for the past six days are:

$$\frac{2}{12} = .166, \ \frac{1}{12} = .083, \ \frac{2}{12} = .166, \ \frac{0}{12} = 0, \ \frac{3}{12} = .250, \ \frac{3}{12} = .250$$

The process is out of control on days 4, 5, and 6.

Solution for Part b: The control limits should be set in such a way that any outcome out of the limits is regarded as a warning signal. The lower control limit for fraction defective is useful because some change in methods, equipment, and so forth has resulted in improved quality. The cause should be found.

2. An electronics manufacturer has a station that always uses a sample size of ten products and has a record for the past 100 samplings as follows:

Number of Defective Products	Total Products Examined
150	1,000

The system is believed to have been under normal operating conditions.
(a) Construct a control chart with control limits such that 95 percent of the products under normal process conditions would fall within the control limits.
(b) Suppose we find the number of defective products over the next five samplings are 3, 4, 2, 0, and 7. What can you tell about the process now? Why?
Solution for Part a:

$$\bar{p} = \frac{150}{1000} = .15$$

$$\sigma_p = \sqrt{\frac{\bar{p}(1-\bar{p})}{n}} = \sqrt{\frac{(.15)(.85)}{10}} = 0.113$$

For 95 percent confidence interval, Z = 1.96

$$UCL = \bar{p} + Z\sigma_{\bar{p}} = .15 + (1.96)(.113) = .371$$
$$LCL = \bar{p} - Z\sigma_{\bar{p}} = .15 - (1.96)(.113) = -.071$$

Solution for Part b:

Sampling	Fraction Defective
1	3/10 = .3
2	4/10 = .4
3	2/10 = .2
4	0/10 = 0
5	7/10 = .7

Two of five samplings fell above the UCL, hence the process is out of control. We are 95 percent sure for any one point that is out of control. (See Figure 16.15.)

Reinforcing Fundamentals

3. Instrumentation, Inc., has been examining a lens during production for scratches. If there are, in the inspector's opinion, too many scratches, the lens is "bad" and rejected. Otherwise the lens is good. Construct a control chart for last month's inspected lenses.

Week	Pieces Inspected	Pieces Rejected
1	60	10
2	60	12
3	60	6
4	60	8
5	60	9

4. An attribute control chart exists for a manufactured part with average fraction defective .250, upper control limit .450, and lower control limit .050. The chart is

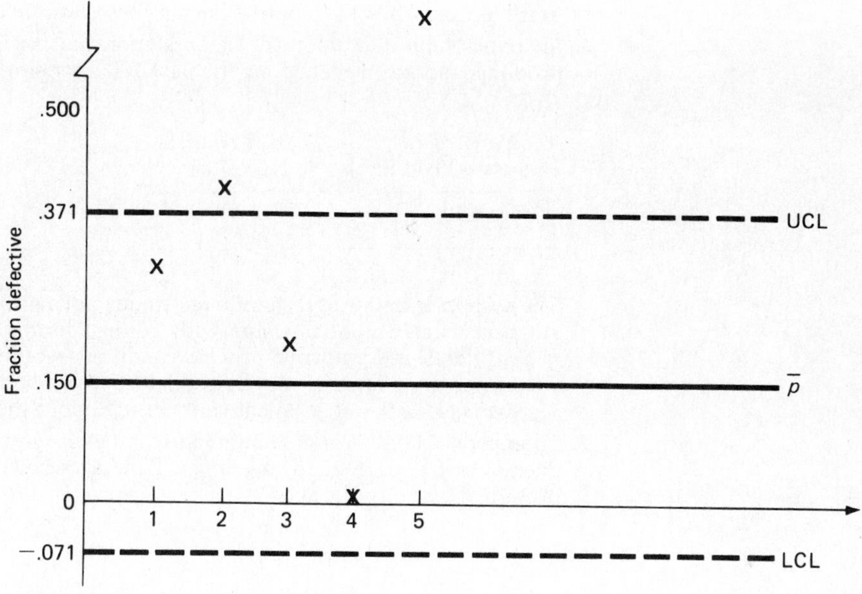

FIGURE 16.15
Electronics attribute control chart

based on two months of daily data. Ten units were sampled each day for the past six days with defectives 2, 4, 2, 0, 3, and 3.

(a) Construct a control chart for management, carefully labeling the chart, and interpret it for management.

(b) A foreman doesn't like the sixth day's results and wants you to resample. What is your response? Why?

5. A relatively new test, a Gravindex Test, has been used by our lab for the past ten weeks. This test indicates pregnancy by determining whether hormones are present in the urine. If hormones are present, the test is positive; in the absence of hormones, the test is negative. We want to establish some means of checking *future* test results to see if the test appears to be staying in control. Each time the test is run, a known positive and known negative test are also run. Data below are for the "known positive" control test, that is, 95 samples were good and 5 samples were bad. Our results to date, using a sample size of 10 tests each week, are:

Negative	Positive	Total Tests
5	95	100

(a) Construct a control chart for this test.

(b) Suppose we collect the following data over the *next* four weeks for our "known positive" Gravindex test.

Week	Negative Results	Positive Results
1	0	10
2	1	9
3	2	8
4	3	7

Is the process (test) in control during these four weeks? If not, what do you do?

6. An optics lens manufacturer has a station that always uses a sample size of 10 products and has a record for the past 100 samplings as follows:

Number of Defective Products	Total Products Examined
150	1,000

The system is believed to have been under normal operating conditions.

(a) Construct a control chart with control limits such that 95 percent of the products under normal process conditions would fall within the control limits.

(b) Suppose we find the number of defective products over the next five samplings are 3, 4, 2, 0, and 7. What can you tell about the process now? Why?

7. Thompson Metal Works manufactures metal screws. The following shows the diameters for part 2735, a standard metal screw, the last time the part was produced two months ago.

Date	Screw Diameters (cm)			
August 5	0.5	0.6	0.4	0.3
6	0.5	0.5	0.4	0.6
7	0.7	0.5	0.5	0.6
8	0.5	0.5	0.5	0.5

(a) Construct a three-sigma control chart for the last production run.

(b) A sample was taken today, the first day of production in two months, on this part. Metal screw diameters were 0.5, 0.9, 0.5, 0.9. Based on the control chart developed above, what can you tell the general foreman about this process?

8. Your reputation as an analyst has gained widespread acclaim in the Allstate University athletic department. The basketball coach asks you to help him with the following problem. Coach Stewart believes that the lack of success of the team in conference play has been because of the way nonconference foes defensed Smith (games 4–8) and the way conference foes defensed him (games 9–13). He gives you the following data concerning the average of Smith's first 11 shots of each game:

Game	Sample Mean of Distance from Basket (feet)	Game	Sample Mean of Distance from Basket (feet)
4	6.0	9	6.0
5	8.0	10	8.0
6	5.0	11	5.0
7	4.0	12	9.0
8	7.0	13	10.0

You are asked to apply what you have learned in quality control, viewing Smith's performance as a process. Inform Coach Stewart whether Smith's conference performance is in control based upon his performance during nonconference games.

9. The results of four samples concerning a shaft diameter were taken three weeks ago when our process was running smoothly ($n = 3$). It is shown here. Since then we have experienced a labor strike, and some business school students are running our production line. Results of two samples taken today are as follows: sample 1—2.30, 2.15, and 1.91; sample 2—1.85, 1.87, 1.78. What can we tell our plant manager about the process today compared with that of our previous base? What should he now do? Support your decision with analysis.

Sample	Diameter (inches)		
1	2.10	2.08	19.6
2	1.97	1.98	2.05
3	1.95	1.91	1.98
4	2.07	2.08	2.03

10. As area coordinator of technical services in a large hospital, you notice the laboratory seems to have problems with a Serum Calcium Test, which is used to indicate a tendency for kidney stones. We are quite proud of the consistency of our tests but are not so sure about this test and would like to track our performance on it. We know our recent test results for five tests each day are:

Test Date	Milligrams/100 cc of Serum				
May 1	9	8	6	8	10
3	8	8	5	7	5
4	7	3	6	12	7
5	10	8	9	8	10
7	9	9	7	9	8

We know that doctors say the expected range is 8.5 to 10.5 milligrams/100 cc of serum for healthy adults. Construct a control chart reflecting historical performance. How might you explain this control chart to laboratory technicians so they can benefit from it in the future (i.e., explain the *interpretative value* of this tool to them)?

11. Construct OC curves for the following sampling plans:
(a) $n = 100, c = 1$
(b) $n = 200, c = 2$
(c) $n = 300, c = 3$

12. Construct OC curves for the following sampling plans:
(a) $n = 100, c = 1$
(b) $n = 100, c = 2$
(c) $n = 100, c = 3$

Challenging Exercises

13. In conjunction with a class assignment, two industrious operations management students decided to study book returns to the campus library by library users. The students collected their data by sitting on the library steps several days and watching books being returned. They observed the following:
Wednesday: 32 people entered the library, 5 of whom were returning books
Thursday: 55 people entered the library, 15 of whom were returning books
Friday: 27 people entered the library, 6 of whom were returning books
These students need your help in constructing a control chart of this "process." After hearing about this, you go over on two successive Mondays and observe:
Monday: 10 people enter the library, 3 of whom are returning books
Monday: 10 people enter the library, 5 of whom are returning books
What inferences can you make concerning your observations based on the data of your fellow students? What, if any, criticism would you make concerning the sampling procedures?

14. A manufacturing facility consists of three workstations for which there are currently no inspection stations. You have estimated the cost of adding inspection stations and gathered some additional information summarized below.

Work Station	Output/ Day (units)	Average Percent Defective	Estimated Inspection Cost/Day	Estimated Cost of Each Undetected Defective
A	1,000	5%	$20	$6
B	1,000	10	30	4
C	1,000	3	25	2

(a) As quality manager your limited budget will allow you to add only one inspection station in your conversion process. Which location would you select from the three possible locations?
(b) What would be your choice if the output rates at A, B, and C were 1,000, 1,500, and 2,000 units/day, respectively?
(c) Develop a heuristic for inspection station selection that considers all of the variables in the problem.

15. Peanuts, Inc., has asked you to check the automatic temperature control of its main baking oven; manufacturing personnel claim the control is broken. Having a business school background (and not an electrical engineering background), you have decided to approach the problem from a statistical quality control standpoint. You have gathered the following data.

Date	Sample Mean of Three Temperature Readings	Date	Sample Mean of Three Temperature Readings
June 1	120°F	July 26	125°F
2	122°F	27	127°F
3	116°F	28	128°F
4	118°F	29	131°F
5	124°F	30	131°F

Specifications:
Manufacturer's guarantee on equipment is for any setting between 100°F–150°F with a variance of ± 7°F from the setting.
Product (peanut) specifications are 120°F ± 5°F.
Specifically, you have been asked to determine as of July 31 if Peanuts, Inc., has a baking oven problem. If so, what do you recommend?

Utilizing the QSOM Computer Software

16. Use the attributes sampling module to find sampling plans for the following specifications: AQL = .02; LTPD = .06; type I error = .05; type II error = .10; shipment size is N = 2,000 units.
(a) Determine the n and c for a single sampling plan.
(b) Determine n_1, n_2/c_1, c_2 for a double sampling plan.
(c) Draw the OC curves for the plans in Parts a and b.
(d) Plot the average outgoing quality (AOQ) curve for the single sampling plan. What does it tell you? Compare it with the AOQ curves of three alternative single sampling plans of your own choosing.

GLOSSARY

Acceptance number One parameter of a single sampling plan; the largest number of defectives allowed in the sample that still permits acceptance of the shipment.

Attributes measurement Type of measurement in which a product characteristic is classified into one of two categories: success or failure, accept or reject, and so on.

Consumer's risk (type II error) Probability of concluding that a poor quality shipment of inputs is of good quality.

Control chart A graphical device, based on sampling results, used to make inferences about the control status of a process.

Control limits Upper and lower bounds of a control chart; used to indicate the control status of the productive process.

Design specifications Detailed requirements of a product specifying its important desired characteristics.

Inspection Observation and measurement of conversion inputs and outputs.

OC curve Operating characteristic curve; the relationship of acceptance probability to level of incoming quality for a specified sampling plan.

Process capability Variation in output that occurs when only random effects are present.

Producer's risk (type I error) Probability of concluding that a good quality shipment of inputs is of poor quality.

Product specification limits Boundaries that define the limits of variation for a product characteristics; any output outside these boundaries is unacceptable.

Receiving inspection Inspection subfunction that focuses on assessing the quality of conversion inputs.

Sampling Process of selecting representative observations from a population.

Sampling plan Specific procedure that incorporates sampling to permit inferences to be made about some population characteristic.

Variables measurement Type of measurement in which a product characteristic is classified according to its degree of conformance on some measurement scale.

SELECTED READINGS

Aubrey, Charles A., II, and Lawrence A. Eldridge, "Banking on High Quality," *Quality Progress* (December 1981), 14–19.

Deming, W. Edwards, "On Some Statistical Aids Toward Economic Production." *Interfaces* 5, no. 5 (August 1975), 1–15.

Dodge, H. F., and H. G. Romig, *Sampling Inspection Tables*. New York: John Wiley, 1959.

Duncan, A. J., (3rd ed.). *Quality Control and Industrial Statistics*. Homewood, Ill.: Richard D. Irwin, 1965.

Grant, E. L., and R. S. Leavenworth, *Statistical Quality Control* (5th ed.). New York: McGraw-Hill, 1980.

Hostage, G. M., "Quality Control in a Service Business," *Harvard Business Review* 53, no. 4 (July –August 1975), 98–106.

Juran, J., *Quality Planning and Analysis*. New York: McGraw-Hill, 1980.

Pfaffenberger, R. C., and J. H. Patterson, *Statistical Methods* (3rd ed.). Homewood, Ill.: Richard D. Irwin, 1987.

Saniga, Erwin M., and Larry E. Shirland, "Quality Control in Practice . . . A Survey," *Quality Progress* 10, no. 5 (May 1977), 30–33.

PART VI DYNAMICS OF OPERATIONS MANAGEMENT

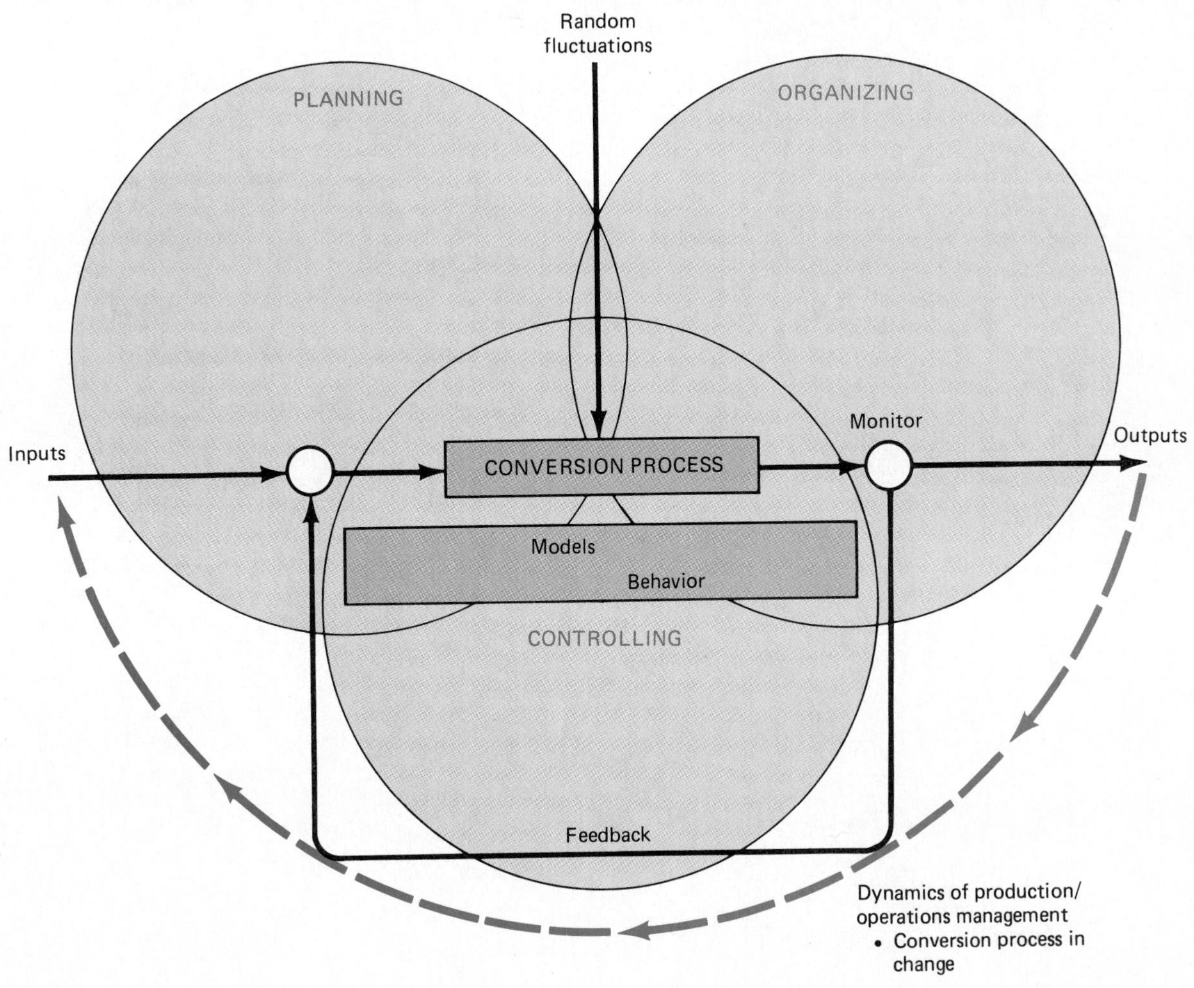

General model for production/operations management

17

The Conversion Process in Change

The United States is engaged in a difficult struggle to retain its industrial leadership in the global marketplace. This is a matter of great concern for the American people, and meeting the challenge is important to the future of the country. The standard of living, economic survival, and national defense are at stake. If industrial leadership declines, it will not be long before the rest of this society goes with it.

The United States has been slow to appreciate that foreign competitors exist for 70 percent of our industrial products. Lack of competitiveness has resulted in a flood of imports and loss of U.S. jobs. The top ten imports from Japan are industrial products such as radios, cars, and videotape machines. It is estimated that for every $1 billion in imports, 25,000 American manufacturing jobs are lost. Over 30 million manufacturing jobs have been lost since 1970, 3 million in *Fortune* 500 companies in one five-year period in the 1980s. Fortunately there is a new American spirit emerging to face this challenge. The rush for the automated factory is creating a revolution in how the United States deals with manufacturing. This will have significant impact on the business organization as a whole.

Since the economic recovery began, there has been increased spending by the private sector for plant and equipment at the rate of 25 percent since late 1982. Sustaining this trend long enough to significantly modernize the industrial base will be the challenge for the future.

There are many exciting changes occurring in the field of manufacturing. While some critics lament the demise of U.S. manufacturing, total industrial production is actually over 30 percent higher today than it was in 1970. It is a myth that the manufacturing base of the United States is shrinking. However, rapid modernization will be necessary to retain a competitive advantage in the global marketplace.

Richard A. Stimson
Director Industrial Productivity
Office of the Under Secretary of Defense
Washington, D.C.

Mr. Stimson's comments reflect a sense of concern and urgency over the future of U.S. industry. How will we respond to the global competitive challenge? Are we so tightly anchored to our past conventional practices that we cannot reorient our operations resources soon enough? In this, our final chapter, we look at change and the future of production and operations management. Whether we agree with Edmund Burke that "You can never plan the future by the past" or with Patrick Henry that "I know of no way of judging the future but by the past," we must at least admit that the past, after all, is all we have. As a basis for prediction, it may be limited, but it is a beginning. Together we'll explore how change comes about in production/operations management, in the hope it will help shape your future role as a production/operations manager or help you understand operations as it changes, even though you might not be actively involved in the discipline.

DYNAMICS OF PRODUCTION AND OPERATIONS MANAGEMENT

Changes in the conversion process do not occur one at a time. Usually, multiple changes of various magnitudes are occurring simultaneously. Further, these changes are not independent of one another; changes in one part result in changes in other parts. Some of these "ripple" effects are predictable; others are not. In short, organizational change can rapidly become a "can of worms" if not approached cautiously. The complexities of change present a management dilemma. Management desires a predictable or stable conversion process that allows the goal of economic efficency to be met; nevertheless, as an open system we must recognize the need for changes in order to remain a viable organization. As a production/operations manager, you must strike a proper balance between stability and adaptability in your organization. If you understand the dynamics of organizational change, you may be able to balance stability and adaptability in a more enlightened way. For these reasons we suggest a somewhat systematic approach to studying the dynamics of the conversion process. The framework we suggest is shown in Figure 17.1, in which the broad dimensions of change flow from left to right. Recognition of the need for change, targets for change, the change process, and the desired results of change are distinct phases usually identifiable in any change situation.

Recognition of Need for Change

Before we can plan and initiate change, we have to recognize that a change is needed, and we have to know why it is needed. Indicators that change is needed can come from sources that are internal or external to the organization. Random fluctuations—unplanned and/or uncontrollable environmental influences that tend to cause actual output to differ from planned output in the conversion process—are necessary in our model

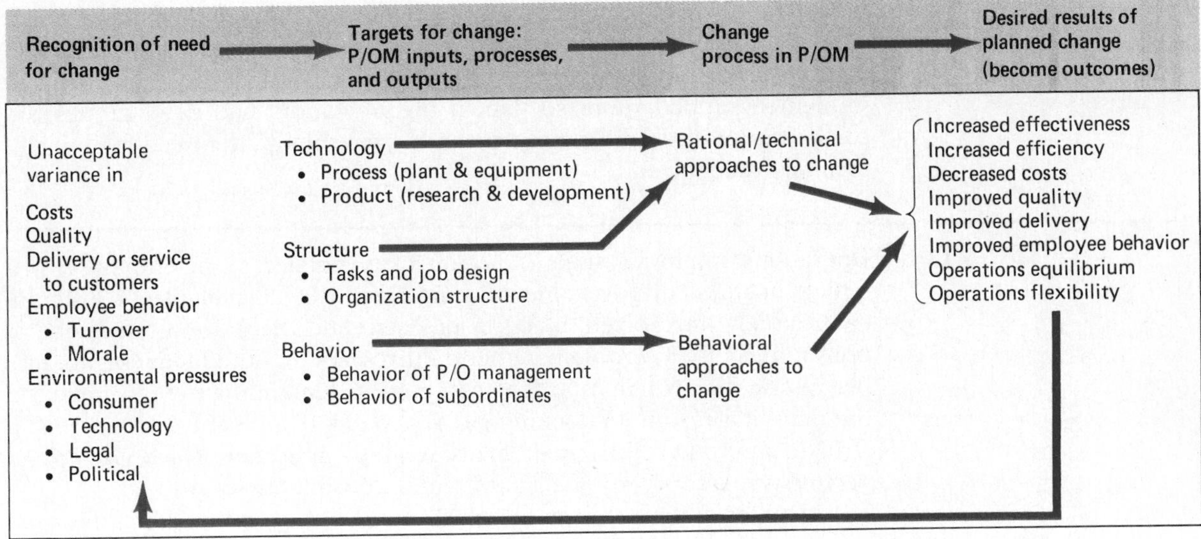

FIGURE 17.1
Dynamics of production/operations management: the conversion process in change

because they happen so often in reality. We may have to make changes to meet existing organizational goals; or it may be necessary to change the goals themselves.

Internal Indicators The conversion process operates to meet predetermined goals and sets performance standards that are consistent with goal attainment. Most commonly, management establishes goals for profitability, product quality, customer service, and commitments to employees. It is not surprising, then, that measures that are closely related to these goals are the primary internal indicators of the need for change. Some of the most commonly used indicators are:

- Costs
- Product quality
- Delivery or service to customers
- Employee behaviors

Some of these indicators are readily quantifiable; others are not. Reports of direct and indirect labor expenses (costs), scrap rates (quality), and employee absences and quitting rates (employee behaviors), for example, are usually reported periodically in standard report forms. These can easily be compared against performance standards, and deviations can be noted and investigated. Some indicators are much more subtle, however. Not all costs are recognized; some aspects of product quality or customer service are not conveniently measurable; and employee dissatisfaction may surface in nonquantifiable form. When the indicators are subtle, formal change may not occur until the underlying problem magnifies itself. By this time, remedial changes may be very costly to implement, much more so than if the indicators had been recognized earlier. Sometimes the change is made even though the need for it is not formally recognized.

EXAMPLE Operations employs a major, if not majority, portion of the employees in a typical business or governmental unit. Employee absenteeism is a significant, largely unresolved, business problem and therefore a major operations management problem. Other cultures, such as the Japanese, are less permissive than North American companies, demanding a commitment to the firm that results in docking pay and quick dismissal for absenteeism. British and other European firms tend to approach North American permissiveness regarding absenteeism and productivity suffers.

Studies estimate absenteeism to equate to a cost of 1.75 times the average daily pay, $150/employee/percent absent/year (1972 dollars), or $66/day/person-day (1977 dollars) of absenteeism. One study traces the impact of absenteeism on added overtime costs, carrying extra employees and inventory quantity, schedule upheavals, and other operating charges.[1] In a representative, but hypothetical, example for a company with $6.5 million in annual sales, 100 employees, a $7/hour wage rate, and a 5 percent absenteeism rate, absenteeism costs totaled $154,385 for the year. These costs totaled 12.5 percent of total direct labor costs, $1,543 per direct employee, $140.35 cost/day/employee, 2.5 times the average daily pay, and 0.64 percent of total production costs.

What is the point of all the absenteeism statistics noted above? Our point is that an internal indicator, like 5 percent absenteeism, can have far-reaching operations cost consequences that are not normally quantified in day-to-day reporting. *A need for change can exist, in this case a behavioral need, and it can gradually increase in significance without management action.* The astute operations manager must pick up on such indicators and express them as costs that upper management can understand, and therefore gain support for the needed change.

External Indicators In general, the conversion process is designed to enable efficient operation shielded from external impingements. The system can never be totally closed, however; as the external environment changes, it imposes changes on internal operations. An obvious example is the change in consumer tastes and desires in a competitive market. If video recorders and players are the rage, organizations with the technological and financial capability will begin producing video units and tapes, or

[1]Ken Kivenko, "Employee Absenteeism—The Deterioration of Productivity," *Production and Inventory Management Review* 4, no. 5 (May 1984), 52–55, 70.

renting the units and taped entertainment, if they wish to establish or improve their market position.

In some instances, external indicators arise in a more direct way. This is particularly true in service industries making products to suit the needs of particular customers. Here a close degree of customer-supplier cooperation results in new product designs. Changes in products or processes are often made on a regular basis.

Besides consumer tastes and technological innovations, there are other significant environmental sources of change. Broad societal changes in values are often reflected in new laws and governmental regulations that require compliance. Today's concern over environmental pollution has a direct impact on the internal operations of most organizations. Scarce energy resources force changes that have been of little concern to operations managers in the past. Legal and political pressures for changes are also evident to the perceptive production/operations manager.

Targets for Change

Once the need for change has been recognized, the manager can identify one or more aspects of the conversion process that must be modified, including the technology, the organization structure, or employee behavior in the conversion process.

Technology The technology consists of the physical or mental processes by which conversion from inputs to outputs is accomplished. The technology for manufacturing refrigerators is dominated by cutting, forming, and assembling of sheet metal, manufacturing electronic and mechanical components, assembly (including the compressors and refrigeration components), painting, and packing. The technology of an automatic carwash includes soap and water sprays, roller brushes, chain drives, and blower-dryers.

In dental clinics, the human components of the technology are more directly visible. Knowledge and skills of dentists and technicians are directly witnessed by the customer (patient). The physical aspects of the dentist's technology range from materials used in treating the patient (drilling equipment, teeth-cleaning preparations, etc.) to elaborate laboratory equipment never seen by the patient.

Changes directed primarily toward the technology often involve redesign of plant and equipment to process existing products as new processes or materials are developed. The development of plastics, for example, resulted in displacement of many refrigerator components formerly made of metals. This necessitated the replacement of metal rolling and forming with plastics extrusion processes. The decision to switch from one processing technology to another can be analyzed in part from an engineering/economic viewpoint. Our product and process design discussion in Chapter 4 were directed at acquainting you with contemporary approaches, including CAD, CAM, robotics, and flexible manufacturing.

Often, the basic product itself must be modified to meet changing consumer needs or to comply with external requirements. The annual model changes and new product introductions practiced by many industries are examples. In fact, one way to compete in some industries is to be effective in quick development, manufacture, and delivery of new products (operations flexibility). The product line, consequently, is very volatile. In the manufacturing equipment industry, it is not unusual for customer-supplier cooperation to produce new designs, features of which will be incorporated in future editions of the supplier's "regular" products. In these cases operating system effectiveness is measured in terms of flexibility, the ability to work with product and customer engineers to develop and manufacture unique products that, in some cases, are later produced in volume. Often, then, new products and processes are necessary from a strategic viewpoint.

Structure Sometimes the organization structure—tasks and jobs within the organization—become the targets for change. When costs, quality, or employee satisfaction indicate that changes are warranted, individual jobs may be redesigned. Job analysis and work methods studies may reveal that some job elements should be eliminated, others simplified, and still others expanded. Task redesign may also be appropriate when new products and processes are developed. Unless the new product is very similar to the old one, old tasks cannot simply be reapplied to new products.

At a broader level, the entire organizational structure may need changing. If goals are not met, new departments and divisions may be formed and old ones dissolved. Perhaps the quality control function may be reassigned from the manager of manufacturing to the vice president of operations to obtain higher level control. Job-shop scheduling and dispatching may be centralized to improve overall shop throughput; or a new customer relations department may be created to improve service to customers.

New products and technological changes may also necessitate structural adjustments. Many manufacturing organizations have created environmental engineering groups to redesign conversion processes and facilities so that environmental contamination is reduced. The computer expertise developed by many organizations has led to computer services departments that serve not only the operations function but the other functional areas of the organization as well.

As companies grow and product markets expand, structures are changed accordingly. Organizations may diversify along product lines to gain greater efficiencies; others may decentralize as a means of developing future managerial skills and experience.

Behavior From the operations manager's viewpoint, behavior is a third target for change. Very often, goal attainment is possible by modifying employee behavior rather than by changing the technology or the structure of the conversion process. Product quality and efficiency goals may be enhanced through on-the-job training of operative employees. These training efforts are designed to modify behavior in favorable directions. Similarly, managerial effectiveness can be improved by development and training programs in such areas as decision making, leadership, and employee/supervisor relationships.

When behavior is the primary target for change, the manager may use several change strategies. How successful the change is depends upon human learning capabilities and the reinforcement/reward procedure that is used. These procedures and the methods by which change is introduced affect how reaily change is accepted or resisted in the organization.

The Change Process in Production/Operations

Obviously, the three targets for change are not independent of one another. Of the three, behavioral change is the most pervasive. It is difficult to conceive of technological and structural changes that do not also result in the need for behavioral change. Consider the computerized checkout systems in many large hardware stores and supermarkets. The technological change from the old system to the new one brought about the need for modified skills and behaviors of employees, particularly as they relate to inventory procedures. Previously, inventory counts of shelf items were periodically updated by hand. In the computer-based system, each transaction is recorded by stock number at the cash register, where inventory levels are updated and reordering may be automatic. Store managers and other employees now focus their skills and efforts on other tasks than counting stock items. Certainly some retraining and reorientation of work behavior are required when such a change is made. Because the behavioral process involved in change has special overall importance, we discuss it here in some detail.

Rational/Technical Change Processes

The Role Of Rationality Managerial intuition, judgment, and experience play major roles in change decisions. Whether these decisions are based on hunch or thoughtful analysis, the full effects of significant change are usually unpredictable to some extent. But managers need not be discouraged by the absence of complete predictability; we can take some careful, systematic steps to increase predictability somewhat and help ourselves cope with change.

One procedure that lends rationality to the change process is the scientific approach to decision problems. Six steps in this approach are:

1. Problem recognition and definition
2. Statement of objectives
3. Formulation of alternative solutions
4. Data collection
5. Evaluation of alternatives
6. Decision or choice

Rationality is emphasized in the final four steps of the scientific approach to change. As managers learn to formulate alternative solutions, collect data, and evaluate alternatives, they become better able to make rational decisions.

By a rational approach, we mean the process of carefully identifying change alternatives, analyzing their effects from a financial, economic, or other logical point of view, comparing the alternatives on this basis, and identifying the best of the alternatives. Typically, this kind of approach involves quantitative analysis. Thereafter, additional nonquantifiable factors can be introduced and considered before the final choice is made. This rational approach to decision making has been stressed throughout this book.

When technology is the target, changes in products, processes, equipment and/or facilities are considered. Ordinarily, formal or rational analysis in these instances is of a financial or engineering nature. When organizational structure or policy is the target, some attempts are made to measure change in financial terms, but to a lesser extent; the impact of these changes can't always be captured in financial terms. Nevertheless, the rational approach is still applicable. We are generally forced to employ nonfinancial measures of system performance, however; changes in crime rate, service to customers, reduction in procurement lead times, and similar patterns often reflect system performance.

The Behavioral Change Process

As shown in Figure 17.1, the behavioral change process includes:

1. Recognition of the need for change
2. Identification of the behavioral targets for change by production/operations managers and/or their subordinates
3. Decision to change in a certain way
4. Strategy for change; the behavioral approach toward change
5. Implementation of the behavioral change; the actual changing of behaviors of participants in the production process

We have already pointed out how to recognize the need for change. Let's examine steps 2–5 of the behavioral change process, concentrating not only on the process itself but on dealing with resistance to it and management's role in changing behavior for the good of the organization. But before we do, let's look at one alternative change model.

Thaw-Move-Refreeze An alternative change model that is perhaps the most widely accepted model of the change process in management involves thawing (or unfreezing) current activities, moving (or changing) to the desired activities and resulting outcomes, and then refreezing activities so the changes are permanent.[2] This model is not inconsistent with the planned change model of Figure 17.1 and the behavioral change process above. Key differences are the need to soften or *thaw* (a way to get the change process ready to take), and the idea of *refreezing*. We'll discuss

---

[2]For a more complete discussion of this change model, see Charles N. Greene, Everett E. Adam, Jr., and Ronald J. Ebert, "Organization Change and Development," *Management for Effective Performance* (Englewood Cliffs, N.J.: Prentice Hall, 1985), Chap. 14.

reinforcement processes directed at this refreezing. The idea that changes must be institutionalized as a regular way of behaving and operating is an excellent concept for operations managers to grasp.

Behavioral Targets for Change

Consistently, experienced P/O managers find that *it is the reblending of behaviors—the behaviors of labor (the operative worker) and management (operations managers at all levels)—that is the most difficult and challenging of all change problems.* Behavioral change involves people, and people have emotions. Furthermore, we often find that in order for managers to change their subordinates, they must change themselves first. Therefore, as a P/O manager, you must think of behavioral change in terms not only of your subordinates but of yourself as well.

Strategies for Behavioral Change

Three distinct strategies have been suggested for changing behavior.[3] As we discuss them, remember that they may help managers change the behaviors of both supervisors and operative workers.

Empirical-rational Strategies Empirical-rational strategies assume that people are rational, that they will act in their own self-interest. If managers wish to advance change, they should show employees that the change is not only desirable for the organization but for the employees' self-interest too. When employees understand that change will benefit them, they will change their behavior.

Normative-reeducative Strategies Normative-reeducative strategies build upon the empirical-rational strategies. Besides assuming that workers are rational, these strategies presume that people act as a result of attitudes and values they have acquired over time. Thus changing behavior involves not only presenting people with facts in their own self-interest but changing their attitudes, skills, and relationships as well.

Power-coercive Strategy This strategy is based on the concept of the application of political, economic, or some other form of power. Power can be legitimate (the proper use of delegated authority), or it can be informal (without formal organization sanction). Often, power is simply the effective use of leadership and position in the organization. In other cases, power may be brought to bear on individuals from peer groups, informal leaders, economic realities, or fear (fear of job loss, for example). Whatever its form, the result is the same; power can be a very effective way to bring about changes in individual and group behavior.

The Learning Process

Employee behaviors evolve in the learning process with the adoption of new skills, attitudes, and experiences. Given a new task, employees will

---

[3]Robert Chin and Kenneth D. Benne, "General Strategies for Effecting Changes in Human Systems," in *The Planning of Change*, 3rd ed., Warren G. Bennis, Kenneth D. Benne, Robert Chin, and Kenneth E. Corey, eds. (New York: Holt, Rinehart, and Winston, Inc., 1976), pp. 22–45. Alternative strategies are identified by Greene, Adam, and Ebert, *Management for Effective Performance*, Chap. 14, Fig. 14.6, that relate the change strategy to change interventions.

learn. The question is whether they will adopt behaviors that are beneficial to the organization or behaviors that are disruptive.

Reinforcement In the learning process, the critical determinants of adopted behaviors are the *environmental consequences of those behaviors.* These consequences are called *reinforcers.*

Positive reinforcers are pleasant, rewarding, and satisfying; they serve to increase the probability that the behavior (response sequence) will occur again. Negative reinforcers are usually unpleasant, undesirable, and even painful. Generally, behaviors with positive consequences tend to be repeated when the situation reoccurs; behaviors with negative consequences tend to be abandoned.

Behavioral Effects of Reinforcement Schedules Not only the reinforcement itself but also its timing are important. One study notes,

> The effectiveness of a given reinforcer will depend upon its magnitude, its quality, the degree to which it has been associated with other reinforcers, and the manner in which it is scheduled. As a matter of fact, the effectiveness will depend as much upon its *scheduling* as upon any of its other features.
>
> A schedule of reinforcement is a more-or-less formal specification of the occurrence of a reinforcer in relation to the behavioral sequence to be conditioned. It is fairly easy, even for individuals with a minimum of training, to follow specified schedules of reinforcement in order to generate predictable behavioral patterns.[4]

Schedules of reinforcement may be either continuous or intermittent. Continuous reinforcement occurs after every response sequence that has been chosen for conditioning. More often, reinforcement is intermittent, occurring occasionally after the response sequence (the behavior). Under continuous reinforcement conditions, although learning takes place more quickly, so does extinction (forgetting the response and reinforcement relationship) once the reinforcement is withdrawn.

Since our interest is changing behavior, we can draw several conclusions from what we've discussed so far. First, new behavior patterns are learned fastest with continuous, or nearly continuous, reinforcement schedules. Second, behavior patterns that have been learned under variable intermittent reinforcement schedules are the most difficult to change. Third, negative reinforcement, when properly administered, can be effective. When punishment (the infliction of pain or discomfort) is administered, however, the consequences can be disastrous. Let's look a little closer at punishment and its consequences in operations.

---

[4]Everett E. Adam, Jr., and W. E. Scott, "The Application of Behavioral Conditioning Procedures to the Problems of Quality Control," *The Academy of Management Journal* 14, no. 2 (June 1971), 175–93.

Punishment There is research to suggest that punishment, under differing circumstances, may increase occurrences of undesirable behavior, cause it to last longer, be a short-lived deterrent, cause people to vary their behavior but be unable to control the direction of the new behavior, and arouse negative feelings. On the other hand, mild punishment may help improve behavior by at least providing negative feedback on performance. Since the effects of punishment are unpredictable and often adverse, we think it might be better to use positive reinforcement instead.

EXAMPLE Two foremen in the same production facility employed different reward systems, each beyond normal organizational rewards. The first foreman seemed always upset and irritated at his subordinates, verbally admonishing them for any small reason, often hours or days after the behavior. His employees tended to ignore his behavior and react neither negatively nor positively over time. The second foreman administered praise and/or candy to his workers intermittently. He was very careful and always praised or offered a piece of candy after outstanding behavior. He was one of the most highly thought of, successful foremen in the facility, and his department was very productive.

Now, of course we aren't recommending that every foreman lay in a supply of candy. The success of the second foreman's reward system resulted not from the magnitude of the reward but from its *systematic administration*. He almost always reinforced acceptable behavior, and often in the presence of others. The real reward was recognition. This is not to say that punishment never brings about beneficial change; but dysfunctional consequences are also a distinct possibility.

Resistance to Change

We suggest that you change behavior by altering positive reinforcers and placing behavior under positive control. The potential for conflict among positive reinforcers suggests that it is important for management to communicate *current* response-reinforcement contingencies clearly.

There are all sorts of reasons why people are reluctant to change. Positive reinforcers for current behavior patterns encourage us to continue acting as we are. Perhaps we're afraid of failing at something new. People like the stability afforded by established patterns of relationships in their personal and professional lives. The security we feel from orderly and familiar ways of doing things can be threatened by change, and so can our status, authority, autonomy, and discretion. Change sometimes makes old skills obsolete and requires us to develop new skills. In general, there are four basic reasons for resisting change:

1. *Economic factors*—a threat to economic security, such as losing a job
2. *Inconvenience*—a threat of making life more difficult, such as having to learn new ways of doing things that were formerly done routinely

3. *Uncertainty*—a threat of not knowing the implications of forthcoming change
4. *Interpersonal relationships*—a threat of disrupting or destroying customary social relationships, group standards, or socially valued skills

If training for change disrupts the current work flow, resistance to change is intensified. Work will be initially disrupted, and higher operating costs can be expected temporarily. The initiator of change must be prepared to accept these added costs. Employee resistance is high at these initial stages; often employees do not clearly perceive the need for change in the first place. All they know is that they are now further behind in their work.

Resistance behaviors may take a variety of forms, including aggression, withdrawal, or regression. These manifest themselves in higher absenteeism, requests for transfer, sabotage, or a series of emotional outbursts.

Overcoming Resistance to Change

As you look over the following suggestions for overcoming resistance to change, remember that each is only a partial solution to the problem. Unfortunately, there is simply no single way to break down all the resistance barriers. You should also keep in mind that resistance to change may appear throughout the organization, from the highest to the lowest levels. Because people occupying high levels within the organization have benefited from the existing system, they may resist changes even more intensely than people at lower levels. Let's examine some factors that are related to resistance to change.

1. *Peer group influences.* Peer groups often encourage group members to meet the job standards that they participate in establishing. Groups significantly influence member behavior, and the effective operations manager attempts to influence the group directly or indirectly through the informal group leaders.
2. *Group discussion.* Participation is most effective if the needs for change are clearly communicated to the group at a level the group members understand, employees want to get involved in the change, and a group meeting is held to encourage discussion and consideration of ideas and suggestions.
3. *Suggestions from employees.* Some employee suggestions should be implemented and the implementation brought to the attention of participants. A superficial "sense of participation" that merely covers an autocratic manager's actions will soon be understood by employees to be no participation; behaviors will adjust accordingly. Toyota, you might recall (Chapter 15), uses employee suggestions effectively to bring about quality improvements.
4. *Manager's job security.* P/O managers can provide a sense of job security for subordinate supervisors. If supervisors feel that their

jobs are secure, they will not perceive employee participation as a threat to their own positions.

5. *Terminology.* Using certain words, such as *change*, for example, can arouse aggressive behaviors unnecessarily from employees whose behavior you want to modify. Also, any reference that infers manipulation of an individual is likely to arouse anxieties and create resistance to change. Once the employee becomes defensive, communication is nearly impossible.

Production/ Operations Changes

Organization Development Organization development (OD) is a broad term used in management to describe organizational change through the application of knowledge from the behavioral sciences, for example, psychology, sociology, and cultural anthropology. A consultant, often a full-time employee, acts as a change agent to facilitate this change process. Our understanding of OD is that it involves the entire planned change process that we've been discussing, but here we focus on interventions specifically applied to production and operations processes. Let's see how the operations manager can actively participate in this change process.

The P/O Manager as Change Agent In behavioral change procedures, it is generally agreed, there are *facilitators* and *learners* of change. In our discussions of the learning process and overcoming resistance to change, we have stressed the production/operations manager's role in initiating change. Essentially, P/O managers are the *facilitators* of change; they are the *change agents.* Production/operations managers continually face the situation of getting changes accomplished through others; operative workers continually face the situation of learning these changes.

Role of Top Management If top management does not support change programs at lower levels, change simply will not occur. Management's support must be strong and consistent. Several studies indicate that unless top management supports new managerial techniques and approaches, even people exposed to training will continue their old behavior. This is the case because top management continues to reinforce old behavior. In fact, under these conditions, training programs can even make matters worse. At one organization, managers were trained to use a human relations approach to dealing with people. At the end of the program, the managers accepted the idea and decided to use it. After a few months, however, those same managers were found to have become even more autocratic than they had been in the first place. Why? Because top management, uninvolved in the program, continued to reinforce autocratic behavior, and subordinate managers, who had learned through the program to emulate top management's style, had actually learned to be more autocratic than they had been before the program.

Actual Changes Processes change and plants and physical facilities wear out—in short, manufacturing and operations facilities go through a life cycle just as products do.[5] Changes brought on by deterioration or by the desire for improvement have been successfully carried out in organizations and documented through company records, reports at professional meetings, and professional publications. Many of you have had work experience in complex organizations. In light of our discussion in this chapter, can you think of a successful or an unsuccessful change that you've observed? What was the need for the change? Who effected the change? Was there resistance to the change? What strategy led to the success or failure of the change? Consider these questions as we examine an example that is concerned with a production scheduling problem, in which the author focused on the change process that led to implementation of a model.[6]

EXAMPLE *A Production Scheduling Change at Baumritter* The Baumritter Corporation is a furniture manufacturer selling primarily under the Ethan Allen brand name. In 1970 sales were approximately $65 million, with manufacturing in 18 factories. The author and several colleagues at the University of Rhode Island have had a five-year research affiliation with Baumritter; the primary orientation is on the process of major system design and implementation. Baumritter has been deeply involved in a system to control materials throughout the organization.

Aggregate Capacity Planning One facet of the research led to the conclusion that a critical need for aggregate capacity planning existed and that Baumritter personnel did not fully comprehend the problem. It was felt that this situation represented a fertile opportunity for the design of an implementation-oriented model. The intent was to plant a seed in the Baumritter system that could be nurtured on a cooperative basis, the research team's relative role decreasing over time. The model was built and demonstrated to the vice president of manufacturing, assistant vice president of manufacturing, plant managers, assistant plant managers, other manufacturing executives, and systems analysis working on the materials flow system.

The reaction of these people was highly positive; their recognition of the seriousness of this problem was improved, and the research team expected that cooperative implementation would take place shortly. However, no amount of prodding on their part caused this to happen.

There is a moral to be learned from this story: the top-down approach of selecting the most critical problem first is conceptually elegant, but the bottom-up approach of finding a problem of present

---

[5]Roger W. Schmenner, "Every Factory Has a Life Cycle," *Harvard Business Review* 61, no. 2 (March–April 1983), 121–129.

[6]Excerpted from Thomas E. Vollman, "A User-Oriented Approach to Production Scheduling" (Paper presented at 3rd Annual American Institute for Decision Sciences Conference, St. Louis, Mo., 1971). This company, Baumritter, is the source of several excellent change examples beyond those described here. See Thomas E. Vollman, William L. Berry, and D. Clay Whybark, *Manufacturing Planning and Control Systems* (Richard D. Irwin, 1984).

concern will usually produce implementable results. The place to be studied was a large factory in Orleans, Vermont.

Production Scheduling The process of scheduling assembly lines at Orleans was somewhat chaotic. All the parts for a complete item were simultaneously started at the cutoff saws, with the expectation that the item would be ready for assembly eight weeks later. As time elapsed, however, the standard eight-week lead time from cutoff saw to the start of final assembly was often missed. Although the stated goal was to assemble an entire manufacturing lot size upon completion, this goal was rarely met. "Hot list" requirements, poorly constituted finished goods inventories, marketing demands, and pool car shipments all led to sizable variation in the quantities being assembled.

Three of the key manufacturing executives at Orleans attempted to design an assembly schedule on the basis of smaller lot sizes than the cutting lot sizes. They attempted to determine what items to make week by week for the next seven or eight weeks on each major assembly line. The effort involved one or two days, or about five labor days per week. The procedure was to arrange pieces of paper on a long table; each piece of paper represented a particular assembly lot of an item. Demand forecasts, standard assembly times, part availabilities, pool car requirements, and dollar output objectives were used.

The actual output from the assembly lines was at considerable variance with what the schedule had predicted. As one week's output was off, corrective actions were taken in subsequent weeks; this made the validity of estimates for future time periods ever more dubious.

At this time the author and his colleagues proposed that the production scheduling process be attacked with a time-shared computer model. The reaction to this suggestion was overwhelmingly negative. Comments included: "The computer is no substitute for manufacturing judgment"; "Go back to your Ivory Tower"; "You are wasting your time, and I will not permit anyone in my organization to waste his time by cooperating with you." No Orleans employee was forbidden to work with us on the project, but no one was encouraged to do so, either.

Implementation The strategy for designing a model that would be implemented in this environment forced consideration of the relative strengths of insiders, or users who understood the goals, criteria, constraints, and data inputs; and outside experts or designers who have model building skills.

The approach to the problem was to send a research assistant to the factory to stay until someone could be convinced. The entree had to be through an individual who could be convinced that the programs could help *him* solve problems with which *he* was personally involved. Finding this kind of individual and getting him on your side is essential.

The individual at Orleans was one of the three men involved in the major assembly scheduling process. His job in the organization was industrial engineer—time study man—assistant to the assistant plant manager. He had had two years of college and no exposure to computers. He didn't see how he could participate in the development of a computer model, nor did he understand why it was necessary for him to be involved. Convincing him of the necessity for his involvement was a key step in the implementation process.

When the inside man or user became convinced that the effort was worth trying, he received a substantial amount of personal harassment from his fellow workers. Some were friendly: "I always knew you was a college professor at heart"; but others were more substantive; he was essentially told that no company time was to be devoted to this project. He did it largely on his own time.

As the model was being developed, people around the plant showed considerable interest. Most of the interest was negative, and when the first run produced results that were clearly wrong, many individuals had a good time saying I told you so. The user, however, expected the first run to be invalid. He also expected the reason for the lack of validity to be apparent; this proved to be correct. His fellow workers only saw the invalid model, not the glaring inconsistencies that could be remedied. The model's requirement for explicitness quickly pointed out major inconsistencies in data inputs, criteria, and the process of scheduling itself. Within a month these inconsistencies were largely removed, and the model was generating valid assembly schedules 18 weeks into the future.

Once the model became operational at Orleans and actual results began to match the schedule, people who had been openly hostile became believers virtually overnight. There was no arguing with success, and the amount of managerial talent freed up to work on other activities was significant. News of the success quickly spread through other Baumritter factories, and the author and his colleagues were besieged with requests for the scheduling model.

The approach to these requests was to promote the original user to the status of expert major assembly scheduling model builder with the job of transplanting the model to other locations. The researchers helped him in the first two or three transplantations, with their role gradually diminishing. He was thereafter able to implement the system in several factories by himself. Interestingly enough, the problems experienced by Orleans were largely universal, and the model did fit in most other applications. In some of these other applications, new problems were uncovered; at least one of these problems was found also to exist at Orleans. The model went through several stages of generalization, but most of this work was accomplished by Baumritter employees.

Benefits The benefits from the production scheduling model are somewhat difficult to tie down explicitly. Companies that implement a good system of production planning and inventory control often achieve a 10 to 20 percent increase in productivity due to better utilization of equipment, reduced expediting, and so forth, and productivity has indeed increased in Baumritter plants since the scheduling system was put in. In addition, major assembly scheduling became so predictable in all factories that order acknowledgement was changed and is now based upon the production schedule. An anticipated problem with filling railway cars did not matter, since improved scheduling allowed for much better planning of railway car needs. Purchasing activities were similarly made easier with a clearer understanding of needs. However, the most fundamental benefit coming from major assembly scheduling model was the clearly perceived need for rationalizing the rest of the production planning and inventory control–materials flow system.

Perhaps most interestingly of all, about a year after major assembly scheduling was working, the vice president of manufacturing became convinced that his most significant problem was aggregate capacity planning; the systems approach had now evolved the problem definition to where the author and his colleagues had seen it two years earlier.

Assessing the Overall Effects of Change

We have discussed some key issues in changing behaviors, technologies, and structures of organizations. At the present time, the change process is more an art than a science. Although managers attempt to be systematic and rational in planning for change, complete rationality is not possible, and no one can accurately predict all the effects of change. At best, we can be aware of some general concepts and procedures to help smooth out the transitions that occur in organizations. In advance of the change, we can make rough estimates of its potential effects by asking some "what if" questions about system behavior and economic consequences. Management used to rely on intuition and experience to assess and prepare for the impacts of change. Now there is a better way. Recently, computer simulations have begun being used to explore the implications of proposed changes in a more explicit manner. Let's briefly examine this approach.

SYSTEM DYNAMICS

The examination of overall system behavior is important for two reasons. First, many individuals make changes in various parts of the organization. The *combined* effects of these changes determine overall system performance. Second, any decision or policy should be judged on how it affects the system over time rather than on its effects at one point in time. While static modeling emphasizes one point in time, dynamic modeling focuses on changes over time. Although we are ultimately interested in the steady-state performance after a change, we are interested in the transient system behavior as well. Since implementing changes takes time, their significant effects are usually not realized immediately. Similarly, the reactions of interrelated system subcomponents may not be visible immediately.

System dynamics is a term for a computer-based simulation methodology that attempts to meet these two needs. Pioneered by Professor Jay W. Forrester at M.I.T., system dynamics is a quantitative methodology for developing and analyzing models of systems and their behavior.[7]

Mathematical relationships are developed to represent physical,

[7]Jay W. Forrester, *Industrial Dynamics* (Cambridge, Mass.: The M.I.T. Press, 1961).

financial, and other flows within production/operations. The boundary spanning activities, or interactions, with other functions within the firm are also modeled. These relationships are programmed for a computer and run on the computer again and again, perhaps for 200 or 300 time periods (e.g., months). Operating data are collected and summarized. After review, management says, "What if we changed capacity, technology, inventory investment, and so forth?" The systems models run again with one or more changes, say for another 200 or 300 periods. Conditions are compared, reflecting the dynamic nature of the situation and allowing system comparisons. This systems dynamics approach is useful but can be quite expensive to implement.

OVERVIEW OF PRODUCTION AND OPERATIONS MANAGEMENT

The purpose of this section is to bring our introductory treatment of production/operations management to an end. Can a book of several hundred pages be summarized in a few pages? Can we accurately select those major trends currently affecting the operations management discipline? Dare we predict the future roles of production/operations managers? The answer to each of these questions is clearly no. Yet, we believe we should end on an integrative note. Therefore, let's take a few pages to briefly address each of these questions.

Production/Operations Management Activities

The general model for managing operations that was logically developed in Chapter 1 is reproduced as Figure 17.2. By presenting operations around the *management* subfunctions of planning, organizing, and control, we strive for an integrative perspective. The focus is on conversion, operations management being the management of conversion where input resources are transformed into useful outputs. Models and behaviors were explained throughout the text in relationship to planning, organizing, and controlling in the various chapters of this book. This general model is dynamic, as we've noticed from the earlier content of this chapter.

Our intent in this book was to introduce you to the situations that a production/operations manager must face—strategic planning, capacity, scheduling, inventory control, and so forth—focusing on the concepts, models, and behaviors that are most useful for goal achievement within operations. Examine Figure 17.2. Glance through the chapters of the book again. Only you can answer whether this intent was realized.

Trends in Production and Operations Management

Although it is difficult to step back and clearly see trends in the production/operations management discipline, a few do seem to emerge. Without the detail already presented, let's highlight a few of the obvious trends.

Operations Strategy Strategic planning in operations involves fitting the operations mission into the corporate strategy, a strategy that should

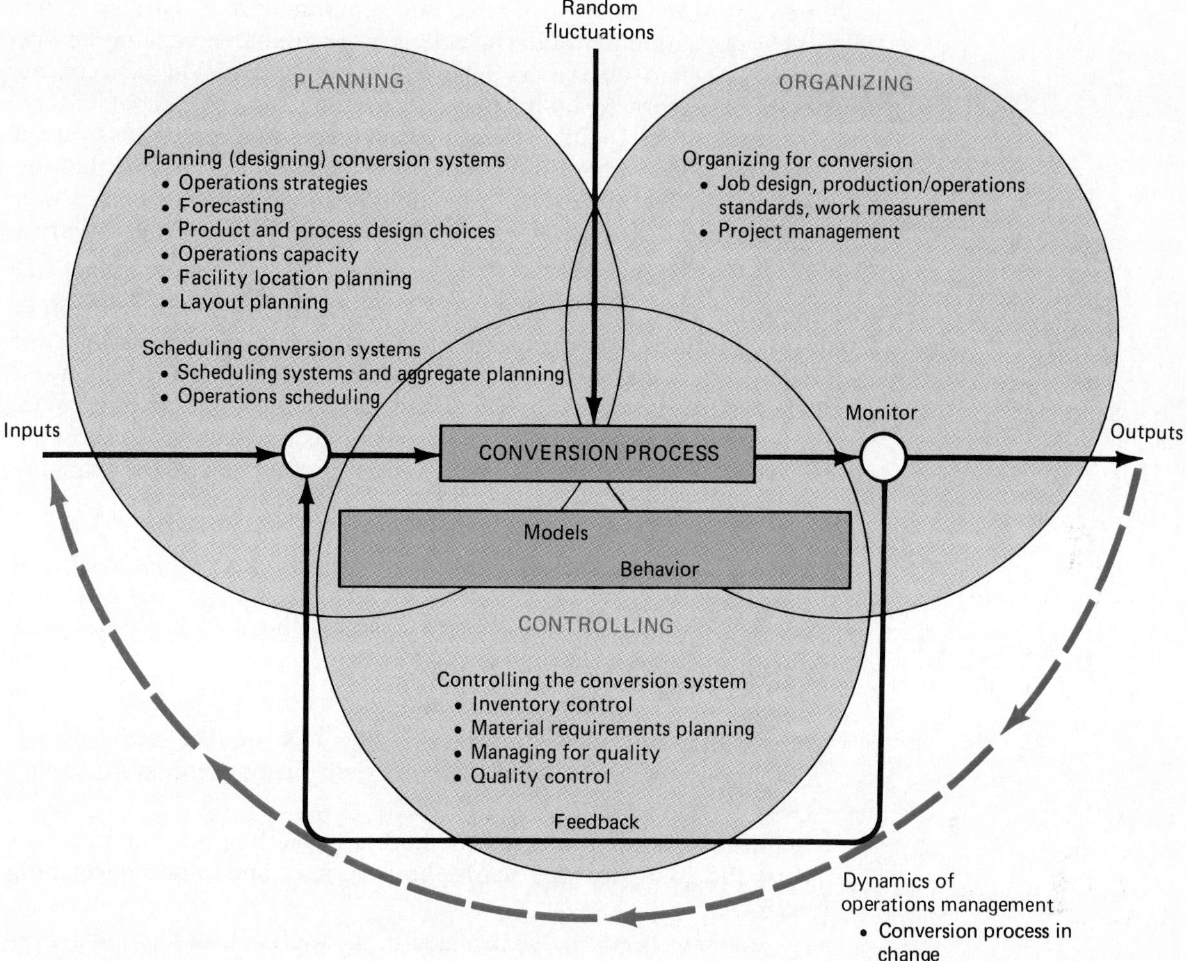

FIGURE 17.2
General model for managing operations

blend the environment and corporate resources into a corporate position statement. Within operations our strategy must reflect the efficiency, dependability, quality, and flexibility to support the direction of the firm. Our belief is that world-class manufacturing and service firms *use operations strategy as an offensive weapon.* These firms either change the operations strategy to maximize the market criteria for success or they choose markets to match their existing operations capability in terms of market criteria for success.

Role of Services Services, as contrasted with manufacturing, involve the conversion of resources into an *intangible* output, a deed, a performance, an effort. Although the manufacturing sector is strong in the United States, Canada, and Europe, service industries typically employ up to 70 percent of the total work force and generate over 50 percent of the domestic gross national product. Challenges are great in managing service operations. We find customers involved in the conversion process, an absence of inventory to buffer demand, staffing for peak capacity, low levels of automation, quality reflecting timeliness and perceptions rather than function over a long time period, and so forth. We suggest that the techniques for effective service operations management are not so well developed as in manufacturing, leaving the service manager with a substantial management task.

International Business and Global Manufacturing Competitiveness As a result of improved transportation, communication, and the transfer of technology, many countries can be viewed as a source of manufactured products. One well-known international manufacturing consulting firm, after interviewing 59 multinational corporation chief executives throughout the world, reported the following major findings regarding changing international business:

- The need to gain access to growing markets is driving international expansion.
- Products and services have to be high in quality and low in price by world standards to set them apart.
- A company's primary focus should be on what it does best.
- Most CEOs interviewed emphasize the U.S. market and pick the developing world, especially Asia, as their primary target for expansion.
- Acquisition is the preferred method of expanding into mature markets; the joint venture works best in Asia and other developing regions.
- A company should be centralized in its approach to global strategy but should still remain sensitive to local market conditions.
- There is universal agreement on the need for people with a truly international perspective.[8]

Although a thorough understanding of international manufacturing is beyond the scope of this introductory book, manufacturing strategies developed in multinational firms require an understanding of such general business conditions. Several of the points, the second and last, for example, directly impact the operations function.

Quality Product and service quality are very important to consumers. Fortunately, corporate leaders are awakening to this fact. We have reflected the growing importance of quality by recognizing this body of knowledge requires two chapters to cover adequately; one on *managing for*

---

[8]Bruce Townsend, "International Manufacturing Consulting Issues," *Proceedings of a Research Symposium on Issues in International Manufacturing* (Fountainbleau, France: INSEAD, September 1987), pp. 1–40.

quality and the second on *quality analysis and control.* This trend has yet to reach its peak since consumers have yet to receive full value for product and service expenditures, in part due to high prices (and costs) but also to low quality.

The Role of Production/Operations Managers

Managerial Behavior and Skills Requirements To what degree should the progressive P/O manager be a technician versus a manager, focus on analysis rather than synthesis, be a specialist or a generalist, deliver standardized products and services with established processes or be creative? Although we cannot answer for every situation, we observe a trend toward managers, synthesis, generalists, and rewards for creativity. Our view is that operations executives are seeking *leaders* who not only have engineering, economic, and analytical skills but who can move beyond these abilities to activate the organization through good managment and people skills.

Careers in Production and Operations Management As you think about a career, your progression from your first position to your retirement depends upon your aspirations, skills, preparation, and luck. Four traditional thoughts are in every manager's career; operations managers are no exception—entry, stepping stones, blockage, and the climb to the top. There are many entry-level jobs in production/operations—line supervisors, staff analysts, staff specialists, and management trainees. Remember, much of the firm's resources are consumed in operations; traditionally many people work there. This provides a great number of opportunities. As for stepping stones, blockages, and the climb to the top, we view operations as a function where each can be experienced, including a route to general management and the top of the organization.

Production and operations management can be fun. If you like people and responsibility, and if you have a propensity for action and a fast pace, operations management might be a good place in which to start your career. Never have the challenges in operations been greater, and never have you had so many tools to utilize as a basis for success.

SUMMARY

Since organizations and their conversion subsystems are dynamic, open systems in constant interaction with their environments, changes of varying magnitude are constantly occurring. Managers must be aware of the process of change and its role in the organization.

Several aspects of change must be understood if change is to be successfully managed. First, one must recognize the need for change as signalled by either internal or external indicators. Next, the targets for change—technology, structure, and behavior—must be identified. Any or all of these are directly involved in the organizational change process.

The behavioral change process involves recognition of the need for change, identification of the behavioral targets for change, decisions to change a certain way, accepting a strategy for change, and implementing the behavioral change.

Strategies for change may be one or a combination of an empirical-rational strategy, a normative-reeducative strategy, or a power-coercive strategy. Regardless of the strategy, the production/operations manager cannot expect a 100 percent behavioral change in subordinate managers and workers.

It is up to the production/operations manager to facilitate learning of behaviors that are supportive of operations goals. Positive rewards should be used intermittently to support (reinforce) worker behaviors that the manager wants continued. The manager must correctly evaluate what reinforcement the worker is currently receiving for undesirable behaviors so that the reinforcements can be withdrawn.

Managers and their subordinates will resist change, some more than others. Worker participation can help reduce the barriers to change. Several other partial solutions exist that can help reduce resistance to change.

Production and operations management was summarized and several trends were identified that could influence operations in the near future.

CASE

Education Copy Services

Before August 1988, two photocopy machines were available for use by the faculty and secretarial staff of the School of Business. This resource provided an easy, quick, and convenient service to faculty in reproducing materials related to personal, teaching, research, and service activities. In an effort to reduce the high copying cost, a new policy was implemented. All copying for small jobs was to be done by the secretarial staff, and automatic devices were installed to monitor and count all copies made. The machine would not operate without one of these devices, preset with a department charge account. Some faculty found that access to copying was considerably less convenient than it had been in the past. It was harder to get last-minute service, and they needed a longer planning horizon for copied material. Secretaries found that they had to make many special trips to the machines, which interrupted their typing and other office responsibilities.

Then it was announced that as of November 26, 1988, the number of machines would be reduced from two to one. Small jobs (fewer than 11 copies) would continue to be run by secretaries on the one machine. Jobs of 11 or more would be transported across campus to Quick Copy Service for reproduction. This change was to be on a trial basis and offered a handsome cost savings to the college. All indications were that copy service to faculty would be at least as good as they had experienced since August.

The management department chairman and secretarial staff thought about the potential implications of the new system. They decided to send a memo to faculty identifying some things that could be done to enhance the service from the new system. The essential points presented to the faculty were:

1. Jobs requiring more than 10 copies will be sent to Quick Copy.
2. Generally, the secretarial staff will mail or deliver jobs to Quick Copy twice daily, once in the morning, once in the afternoon.
3. Quick Copy will deliver the finished jobs back to the departmental office.
4. The secretarial staff will continue to process small jobs on the machine here in the building. This will be done once in the morning and once in the afternoon. This will enable the secretaries to perform their other obligations to faculty more effectively.
5. As a result of these four steps, the faculty is reminded that some lead time will be necessary for getting the jobs done. The necessary lead time is not expected to be any greater, in general, than it was under the old system. If we allow Quick Copy two to three days lead time, they will be able to get us special emergency service on those exceptional occasions when it is needed.

After thinking about the new system and the memo, the chairman wondered about faculty reaction. The new system seemed to have implications for changes in traditional patterns of behavior. What reactions would you expect if you were chairman? What actions should be taken to ensure smooth adaptation to these changes?

REVIEW AND DISCUSSION QUESTIONS

1. Reliable National Bank is considering the installation of automatic teller units at several locations throughout the city. What indicators of the need for change and what desired results led to considering this change?
2. Suppose you are requested to predict the results of Reliable National Bank's contemplated change (see Question 1). Outline your approach for making such a prediction, including a list of the main factors that must be considered.
3. Identify two organizations for which external indicators of the need for change are of minimal importance. List two others for which external indicators are dominant.
4. Identify and discuss the behavioral implications of decisions to change job-shop priority rules, facility layout, and facility location.
5. Give examples showing how changes in the finance and marketing subsystems necessitate changes in the operations subsystem of the organization.
6. Colleges and universities are often bureaucratic in dealing with students. Faculty and staff may be abrupt, inconsiderate, and outright wrong in their behaviors. Think of one experience you've encountered when that was so. Placing yourself in the role of a university operations administrator, use the steps in the behavior change process to show how such an experience could be avoided in the future.
7. State the strategies for behavioral change and briefly explain each. In answering Question 6, which strategy for behavior change were you suggesting?

8. Contrast positive reinforcement, negative reinforcement, and punishment. Which holds the most promise for behavioral change in production/operations management? Why?
9. Contrast the thaw-move-refreeze change model to the planned change model of Figure 17.1.
10. A claims processing clerk is fearful of losing her job when the new computer system is installed. She has been most reluctant to help the system designers understand her current duties. In fact, she has hidden some of the complex tasks from them. Which of the four basic reasons for resisting change is most prevalent here? Why?
11. Explain the role of top management in bringing about change in the organization.
12. Consider the production scheduling change at Baumritter presented in the chapter. Answer these questions, which were posed at the beginning of that section for the Baumritter situation:
    (a) Can you identify successful or unsuccessful changes?
    (b) What was the need for change?
    (c) Who was the change agent?
    (d) Who were the learners?
    (e) Was there resistance to the change?
    (f) What strategy led to the success or failure of the change?
13. Study Figure 17.2, production/operations management activities. Lay the figure aside and try to reproduce it. Which parts of the figure do you think are essential as a framework for practicing as an operations manager? Why?
14. Several discernible trends in production/operations management were presented in this chapter. Select one that you believe should be expanded and expand it. Likely, we overlooked one or more trends. Select a trend in production/operations that you believe should have been summarized and summarize it.

GLOSSARY

Change agent The facilitator of change; the role the production/operations manager takes in bringing about behavioral change in subordinates.

Empirical-rational change strategy Strategy assuming that presented with facts, knowledge, and information, people will act in their own self-interest and rationally change behaviors to that end.

Learning Having a goal, responding to obtain the goal, obtaining feed-back from the response, making additional responses, adjusting the responses or goal until the goal is met.

Normative-reeducative change strategy A strategy assuming that people have attitude and value systems; when presented with facts, knowledge, and information directed at attitudes and values, people will change behaviors as they change their attitudes and values.

Participation Approach to overcoming resistance to change through employee involvement in planning and implementing the change.

Power-coercive change strategy Use of political, economic, or some other form of influence to force change in the behavior of others.

Punishment The infliction of pain or discomfort.

Reinforcement Environmental consequences of behavior.

Reinforcement schedules More or less formal specification of the occurrence of a reinforcer in relation to the behavioral sequence to be conditioned; can be continuous or intermittent.

Synthesis Process of constructing or reconstructing the "whole" by combining various subparts; attempts to understand how the "whole" will behave once it has been created from interrelated subcomponents.

System dynamics A computer-based simulation methodology for developing and analyzing models of systems and their behavior.

SELECTED READINGS

Adam, E. E., and W. E. Scott, "The Application of Behavioral Conditioning Procedures to the Problems of Quality Control," *The Academy of Management Journal* 14, no. 2 (June 1971), 175–93.

Forrester, Jay W., *Industrial Dynamics.* Cambridge, Mass.: M.I.T. Press, 1961.

Greene, Charles N., Everett E. Adam, Jr., and Ronald J. Ebert, *Management for Effective Performance.* Englewood Cliffs, N.J.: Prentice Hall, 1985.

Kivenko, Ken, "Employee Absenteeism—The Deterioration of Productivity," *Production and Inventory Review* 4, no. 5 (May 1984), 52–55; 70.

Schmenner, Roger W., "Every Factory Has a Cycle," *Harvard Business Review* 61, no. 2 (March–April 1983), 121–29.

Slocum, J. W., Jr., and D. Hellriegel, "Using Organizational Designs to Cope With Change," *Business Horizons* 22, no. 6 (December 1979), 65–76.

Student, K. R., "Managing Change: A Psychologist's Perspective," *Business Horizons* 21, no. 6 (December 1978), 28–33.

Sullivan, R. S. "The Service Sector: Challenges and Imperatives for Research in Operations Management," *Journal of Operations Management* 2, no. 4 (August 1982), 211–14.

Townsend, Bruce, "International Manufacturing Consulting Issues," *Proceedings of a Research Symposium on Issues in International Manufacturing.* Fountainbleau, France: INSEAD, September 1987, pp. 1–40.

Vollmann, Thomas E., "A User Oriented Approach to Production Scheduling" (Paper presented at 3rd Annual American Institute for Decision Sciences Conference. St. Louis, Mo., 1971).

Appendix

Appendix Table A Areas of a standard normal distribution*

An entry in the table is the proportion under the entire curve which is between $z = 0$ and a positive value of z. Areas for negative values of z are obtained by symmetry.

z	.00	.01	.02	.03	.04	.05	.06	.07	.08	.09
0.0	.0000	.0040	.0080	.0120	.0160	.0199	.0239	.0279	.0319	.0359
0.1	.0398	.0438	.0478	.0517	.0557	.0596	.0636	.0675	.0714	.0753
0.2	.0793	.0832	.0871	.0910	.0948	.0987	.1026	.1064	.1103	.1141
0.3	.1179	.1217	.1255	.1293	.1331	.1368	.1406	.1443	.1480	.1517
0.4	.1554	.1591	.1628	.1664	.1700	.1736	.1772	.1808	.1844	.1879
0.5	.1915	.1950	.1985	.2019	.2054	.2088	.2123	.2157	.2190	.2224
0.6	.2257	.2291	.2324	.2357	.2389	.2422	.2454	.2486	.2517	.2549
0.7	.2580	.2611	.2642	.2673	.2703	.2734	.2764	.2794	.2823	.2852
0.8	.2881	.2910	.2939	.2967	.2995	.3023	.3051	.3078	.3106	.3133
0.9	.3159	.3186	.3212	.3238	.3264	.3289	.3315	.3340	.3365	.3389
1.0	.3413	.3438	.3461	.3485	.3508	.3531	.3554	.3577	.3599	.3621
1.1	.3643	.3665	.3686	.3708	.3729	.3749	.3770	.3790	.3810	.3830
1.2	.3849	.3869	.3888	.3907	.3925	.3944	.3962	.3980	.3997	.4015
1.3	.4032	.4049	.4066	.4082	.4099	.4115	.4131	.4147	.4162	.4177
1.4	.4192	.4207	.4222	.4236	.4251	.4265	.4279	.4292	.4306	.4319
1.5	.4332	.4345	.4357	.4370	.4382	.4394	.4406	.4418	.4429	.4441
1.6	.4452	.4463	.4474	.4484	.4495	.4505	.4515	.4525	.4535	.4545
1.7	.4554	.4564	.4573	.4582	.4591	.4599	.4608	.4616	.4625	.4633
1.8	.4641	.4649	.4656	.4664	.4671	.4678	.4686	.4693	.4699	.4706
1.9	.4713	.4719	.4726	.4732	.4738	.4744	.4750	.4756	.4761	.4767
2.0	.4772	.4778	.4783	.4788	.4793	.4798	.4803	.4808	.4812	.4817
2.1	.4821	.4826	.4830	.4834	.4838	.4842	.4846	.4850	.4854	.4857
2.2	.4861	.4864	.4868	.4871	.4875	.4878	.4881	.4884	.4887	.4890
2.3	.4893	.4896	.4898	.4901	.4904	.4906	.4909	.4911	.4913	.4916
2.4	.4918	.4920	.4922	.4925	.4927	.4929	.4931	.4932	.4934	.4936
2.5	.4938	.4940	.4941	.4943	.4945	.4946	.4948	.4949	.4951	.4952
2.6	.4953	.4955	.4956	.4957	.4959	.4960	.4961	.4962	.4963	.4964
2.7	.4965	.4966	.4967	.4968	.4969	.4970	.4971	.4972	.4973	.4974
2.8	.4974	.4975	.4976	.4977	.4977	.4978	.4979	.4979	.4980	.4981
2.9	.4981	.4982	.4982	.4983	.4984	.4984	.4985	.4985	.4986	.4986
3.0	.4987	.4987	.4987	.4988	.4988	.4989	.4989	.4989	.4990	.4990

**Source:* Paul G. Hoel, *Elementary Statistics,* 2nd ed. (New York: John Wiley & Sons, Inc., 1966), p. 329.

Appendix Table B 8% Compound interest factors*

	Single Payment		Uniform Series				
	Compound Amount Given P to Find S	Present Worth Factor Given S to Find P	Sinking Fund Factor Given S to Find R	Capital Recovery Factor Given P to Find R	Compound Amount Factor Given R to Find S	Present Worth Factor Given R to Find P	
n	$(1 + i)^n$	$\frac{1}{(1 + i)^n}$	$\frac{i}{(1 + i)^n - 1}$	$\frac{i(1 + i)^n}{(1 + i)^n - 1}$	$\frac{(1 + i)^n - 1}{i}$	$\frac{(1 + i)^n - 1}{i(1 + i)^n}$	n
1	1.0800	0.9259	1.000 00	1.080 00	1.000	0.926	**1**
2	1.1664	0.8573	0.480 77	0.560 77	2.080	1.783	**2**
3	1.2597	0.7938	0.308 03	0.388 03	3.246	2.577	**3**
4	1.3605	0.7350	0.221 92	0.301 92	4.506	3.312	**4**
5	1.4693	0.6806	0.170 46	0.250 46	5.867	3.993	**5**
6	1.5869	0.6302	0.136 32	0.216 32	7.336	4.623	**6**
7	1.7138	0.5835	0.112 07	0.192 07	8.923	5.206	**7**
8	1.8509	0.5403	0.094 01	0.174 01	10.637	5.747	**8**
9	1.9990	0.5002	0.080 08	0.160 08	12.488	6.247	**9**
10	2.1589	0.4632	0.069 03	0.149 03	14.487	6.710	**10**
11	2.3316	0.4289	0.060 08	0.140 08	16.645	7.139	**11**
12	2.5182	0.3971	0.052 70	0.132 70	18.977	7.536	**12**
13	2.7196	0.3677	0.046 52	0.126 52	21.495	7.904	**13**
14	2.9372	0.3405	0.041 30	0.121 30	24.215	8.244	**14**
15	3.1722	0.3152	0.036 83	0.116 83	27.152	8.559	**15**
16	3.4259	0.2919	0.032 98	0.112 98	30.324	8.851	**16**
17	3.7000	0.2703	0.029 63	0.109 63	33.750	9.122	**17**
18	3.9960	0.2502	0.026 70	0.106 70	37.450	9.372	**18**
19	4.3157	0.2317	0.024 13	0.104 13	41.446	9.604	**19**
20	4.6610	0.2145	0.021 85	0.101 85	45.762	9.818	**20**
21	5.0338	0.1987	0.019 83	0.099 83	50.423	10.017	**21**
22	5.4365	0.1839	0.018 03	0.098 03	55.457	10.201	**22**
23	5.8715	0.1703	0.016 42	0.096 42	60.893	10.371	**23**
24	6.3412	0.1577	0.014 98	0.094 98	66.765	10.529	**24**
25	6.8485	0.1460	0.013 68	0.093 68	73.106	10.675	**25**
26	7.3964	0.1352	0.012 51	0.092 51	79.954	10.810	**26**
27	7.9881	0.1252	0.011 45	0.091 45	87.351	10.935	**27**
28	8.6271	0.1159	0.010 49	0.090 49	95.339	11.051	**28**
29	9.3173	0.1073	0.009 62	0.089 62	103.966	11.158	**29**
30	10.0627	0.0994	0.008 83	0.088 83	113.283	11.258	**30**
31	10.8677	0.0920	0.008 11	0.088 11	123.346	11.350	**31**
32	11.7371	0.0852	0.007 45	0.087 45	134.214	11.435	**32**
33	12.6760	0.0789	0.006 85	0.086 85	145.951	11.514	**33**
34	13.6901	0.0730	0.006 30	0.086 30	158.627	11.587	**34**
35	14.7853	0.0676	0.005 80	0.085 80	172.317	11.655	**35**
40	21.7245	0.0460	0.003 86	0.083 86	259.057	11.925	**40**
45	31.9204	0.0313	0.002 59	0.082 59	386.506	12.108	**45**
50	46.9016	0.0213	0.001 74	0.081 74	573.770	12.233	**50**
55	68.9139	0.0145	0.001 18	0.081 18	848.923	12.319	**55**
60	101.2571	0.0099	0.000 80	0.080 80	1 253.213	12.377	**60**
65	148.7798	0.0067	0.000 54	0.080 54	1 847.248	12.416	**65**
70	218.6064	0.0046	0.000 37	0.080 37	2 720.080	12.443	**70**
75	321.2045	0.0031	0.000 25	0.080 25	4 002.557	12.461	**75**
80	471.9548	0.0021	0.000 17	0.080 17	5 886.935	12.474	**80**
85	693.4565	0.0014	0.000 12	0.080 12	8 655.706	12.482	**85**
90	1 018.9151	0.0010	0.000 08	0.080 08	12 723.939	12.488	**90**
95	1 497.1205	0.0007	0.000 05	0.080 05	18 701.507	12.492	**95**
100	2 199.7613	0.0005	0.000 04	0.080 04	27 484.516	12.494	**100**

**Source:* Adapted from Eugene L. Grant, W. Grant Ireson, and Richard S. Leavenworth, *Principles of Engineering Economy*, 6th ed. Copyright © 1976, John Wiley & Sons, Inc., New York.

Appendix Table C 10% Compound interest factors*

	Single Payment		Uniform Series				
n	Compound Amount Given P to Find S $(1+i)^n$	Present Worth Factor Given S to Find P $\frac{1}{(1+i)^n}$	Sinking Fund Factor Given S to Find R $\frac{i}{(1+i)^n-1}$	Capital Recovery Factor Given P to Find R $\frac{i(1+i)^n}{(1+i)^n-1}$	Compound Amount Factor Given R to Find S $\frac{(1+i)^n-1}{i}$	Present Worth Factor Given R to Find P $\frac{(1+i)^n-1}{i(1+i)^n}$	n
1	1.1000	0.9091	1.000 00	1.100 00	1.000	0.909	**1**
2	1.2100	0.8264	0.476 19	0.576 19	2.100	1.736	**2**
3	1.3310	0.7513	0.302 11	0.402 11	3.310	2.487	**3**
4	1.4641	0.6830	0.215 47	0.315 47	4.641	3.170	**4**
5	1.6105	0.6209	0.163 80	0.263 80	6.105	3.791	**5**
6	1.7716	0.5645	0.129 61	0.229 61	7.716	4.355	**6**
7	1.9487	0.5132	0.105 41	0.205 41	9.487	4.868	**7**
8	2.1436	0.4665	0.087 44	0.187 44	11.436	5.335	**8**
9	2.3579	0.4241	0.073 64	0.173 64	13.579	5.759	**9**
10	2.5937	0.3855	0.062 75	0.162 75	15.937	6.144	**10**
11	2.8531	0.3505	0.053 96	0.153 96	18.531	6.495	**11**
12	3.1384	0.3186	0.046 76	0.146 76	21.384	6.814	**12**
13	3.4523	0.2897	0.040.78	0.140.78	24.523	7.103	**13**
14	3.7975	0.2633	0.035 75	0.135 75	27.975	7.367	**14**
15	4.1772	0.2394	0.031 47	0.131 47	31.772	7.606	**15**
16	4.5950	0.2176	0.027 82	0.127 82	35.950	7.824	**16**
17	5.0545	0.1978	0.024 66	0.124 66	40.545	8.022	**17**
18	5.5599	0.1799	0.021 93	0.121 93	45.599	8.201	**18**
19	6.1159	0.1635	0.019 55	0.119 55	51.159	8.365	**19**
20	6.7275	0.1486	0.017 46	0.117 46	57.275	8.514	**20**
21	7.4002	0.1351	0.015 62	0.115 62	64.002	8.649	**21**
22	8.1403	0.1228	0.014 01	0.114 01	71.403	8.772	**22**
23	8.9543	0.1117	0.012 57	0.112 57	79.543	8.883	**23**
24	9.8497	0.1015	0.011 30	0.111 30	88.497	8.985	**24**
25	10.8347	0.0923	0.010 17	0.110 17	98.347	9.077	**25**
26	11.9182	0.0839	0.009 16	0.109 16	109.182	9.161	**26**
27	13.1100	0.0763	0.008 26	0.108 26	121.100	9.237	**27**
28	14.4210	0.0693	0.007 45	0.107 45	134.210	9.307	**28**
29	15.8631	0.0630	0.006 73	0.106 73	148.631	9.370	**29**
30	17.4494	0.0573	0.006 08	0.106 08	164.494	9.427	**30**
31	19.1943	0.0521	0.005 50	0.105 50	181.943	9.479	**31**
32	21.1138	0.0474	0.004 97	0.104 97	201.138	9.526	**32**
33	23.2252	0.0431	0.004 50	0.104.50	222.252	9.569	**33**
34	25.5477	0.0391	0.004 07	0.104 07	245.477	9.609	**34**
35	28.1024	0.0356	0.003 69	0.103 69	271.024	9.644	**35**
40	45.2593	0.0221	0.002 26	0.102 26	442.593	9.779	**40**
45	72.8905	0.0137	0.001 39	0.101 39	718.905	9.863	**45**
50	117.3909	0.0085	0.000 86	0.100 86	1 163.909	9.915	**50**
55	189.0591	0.0053	0.000 53	0.100 53	1 880.591	9.947	**55**
60	304.4816	0.0033	0.000 33	0.100.33	3 034.816	9.967	**60**
65	490.3707	0.0020	0.000 20	0.100 20	4 893.707	9.980	**65**
70	789.7470	0.0013	0.000 13	0.100 13	7 887.470	9.987	**70**
75	1 271.8952	0.0008	0.000 08	0.100 08	12 708.954	9.992	**75**
80	2 048.4002	0.0005	0.000 05	0.100 05	20 474.002	9.995	**80**
85	3 298.9690	0.0003	0.000 03	0.100 03	32 979.690	9.997	**85**
90	5 313.0226	0.0002	0.000 02	0.100.02	53 120.226	9.998	**90**
95	8 556.6760	0.0001	0.000 01	0.100 01	85 556.760	9.999	**95**
100	13 780.6123	0.0001	0.000 01	0.100 01	137 796.123	9.999	**100**

*Source: Adapted from Eugene L. Grant, W. Grant Ireson, and Richard S. Leavenworth, *Principles of Engineering Economy*, 6th ed. Copyright © 1976, John Wiley & Sons, Inc., New York.

Appendix Table D Random digits*

85387	51571	57714	00512	61319	69143	08881	01400	55061	82977
84176	03311	16955	59504	54499	32096	79485	98031	99485	16788
27258	51746	67223	98182	43166	54297	26830	29842	78016	73127
99398	46950	19399	65167	35082	30482	86323	41061	21717	48126
72752	89364	02150	85418	05420	84341	02395	27655	59457	55438
69090	93551	11649	54688	57061	77711	24201	16895	64936	62347
39620	54988	67846	71845	54000	26134	84526	16619	82573	01737
81725	49831	35595	29891	46812	57770	03326	31316	75412	80732
87968	85157	84752	93777	62772	78961	30750	76089	23340	64637
07730	01861	40610	73445	70321	26467	53533	20787	46971	29134
32825	82100	67406	44156	21531	67186	39945	04189	79798	41087
34453	05330	40224	04116	24597	93823	28171	47701	76201	68257
00830	34235	40671	66042	06341	54437	81649	70494	01883	18350
24580	05258	37329	59173	62660	72513	82232	49794	36913	05877
59578	08535	77107	19838	40651	01749	58893	99115	05212	92309
75387	24990	12748	71766	17471	15794	68622	59161	14476	75074
02465	34977	48319	53026	53691	80594	58805	76961	62665	82855
49689	08342	81912	92735	30042	47623	60061	69427	21163	68543
60958	20236	79424	04055	54955	73342	14040	72431	99469	41044
79956	98409	79548	39569	83974	43707	77080	08645	20949	56932
04316	01206	08715	77713	20572	13912	94324	14656	11979	53258
78684	28546	06881	66097	53530	42509	54130	30878	77166	98075
69235	18535	61904	99246	84050	15270	07751	90410	96675	62870
81201	04314	92708	44984	83121	33767	56607	46371	20389	08809
80336	59638	44368	33433	97794	10343	19235	82633	17186	63902
65076	87960	92013	60169	49176	50140	39081	04638	96114	63463
90879	70970	50789	59973	47771	94567	35590	23462	33993	99899
50555	84355	97066	82748	98298	14385	82493	40182	20523	69182
48658	41921	86514	46786	74097	62825	46457	24428	09245	86069
26373	19166	88223	32371	11570	62078	92317	13378	05734	71778
20878	80883	26027	29101	58382	17109	53511	95536	21759	10630
20069	60582	55749	88068	48589	01874	42930	40310	34613	97359
46819	38577	20520	94145	99405	47064	25248	27289	41289	54972
83644	04459	73253	58414	94180	09321	59747	07379	56255	45615
08636	31363	56033	49076	88908	51318	39104	56556	23112	63317
92058	38678	12507	90343	17213	24545	66053	76412	29545	89932
05038	18443	87138	05076	25660	23414	84837	87132	84405	15346
41838	68590	93646	82113	25498	33110	15356	81070	84900	42660
15564	81618	99186	73113	99344	13213	07235	90064	89150	86359
74600	40206	15237	37378	96862	78638	14376	46607	55909	46398
78275	77017	60310	13499	35268	47790	77475	44345	14615	25231
30145	71205	10355	18404	85354	22199	90822	35204	47891	69860
46944	00097	39161	50139	60458	44649	85537	90017	18157	13856
85883	21272	89266	94887	00291	70963	28169	95130	27223	35387
83606	98192	82194	26719	24499	28102	97769	98769	30757	81593
66888	81818	52490	54272	70549	69235	74684	96412	65186	87974
63673	73966	34036	44298	60652	05947	05833	27914	57021	58566
37944	16094	39797	63253	64103	32222	65925	64693	34048	75394
93240	66855	29336	28345	71398	45118	01454	72128	09715	29454
40189	76776	70842	32675	81647	75868	21288	12849	94990	21513

*Source: Reproduced with permission from the Rand Corporation, *A Million Random Digits with 100,000 Normal Deviates.* Copyright, 1955, The Free Press: Glencoe, IL, p. 259.

Index

A

D

G

H

I

J

K

L

M

N

Q

R

S